Autodesk® Revit® 2024 Structure Fundamentals

ASCENT – Center for Technical Knowledge®

SDC Publications
P.O. Box 1334
Mission KS 66222
913-262-2664
www.SDCpublications.com
Publisher: Stephen Schroff

Copyright © 2023 ASCENT – Center for Technical Knowledge®, a division of Rand Worldwide™

All rights reserved. No part of this manual may be reproduced in any form by any photographic, electronic, mechanical or other means, or used in any information storage and retrieval system, without prior written permission of the publisher, SDC Publications.

Examination Copies
Books received as examination copies are for review purposes only and may not be made available for student use. Resale of examination copies is prohibited.

Electronic Files
Any electronic files associated with this book are licensed to the original user only. These files may not be transferred to any other party.

Trademarks
The following are registered trademarks or trademarks of Autodesk, Inc., and/or its subsidiaries and/or affiliates in the USA and other countries: 123D, 3ds Max, Algor, Alias, AliasStudio, ATC, AutoCAD LT, AutoCAD, Autodesk, the Autodesk logo, Autodesk 123D, Autodesk Homestyler, Autodesk Inventor, Autodesk MapGuide, Autodesk Streamline, AutoLISP, AutoSketch, AutoSnap, AutoTrack, Backburner, Backdraft, Beast, BIM 360, Burn, Buzzsaw, CADmep, CAiCE, CAMduct, CFdesign, Civil 3D, Cleaner, Combustion, Communication Specification, Constructware, Content Explorer, Creative Bridge, Dancing Baby (image), DesignCenter, DesignKids, DesignStudio, Discreet, DWF, DWG, DWG (design/logo), DWG Extreme, DWG TrueConvert, DWG TrueView, DWGX, DXF, Ecotect, ESTmep, Evolver, FABmep, Face Robot, FBX, Fempro, Fire, Flame, Flare, Flint, FMDesktop, ForceEffect, FormIt, Freewheel, Fusion 360, Glue, Green Building Studio, Heidi, Homestyler, HumanIK, i-drop, ImageModeler, Incinerator, Inferno, InfraWorks, Instructables, Instructables (stylized robot design/logo), Inventor LT, Inventor, Kynapse, Kynogon, LandXplorer, Lustre, MatchMover, Maya, Maya LT, Mechanical Desktop, MIMI, Mockup 360, Moldflow Plastics Advisers, Moldflow Plastics Insight, Moldflow, Moondust, MotionBuilder, Movimento, MPA (design/logo), MPA, MPI (design/logo), MPX (design/logo), MPX, Mudbox, Navisworks, ObjectARX, ObjectDBX, Opticore, Pipeplus, Pixlr, Pixlr-o-matic, Productstream, RasterDWG, RealDWG, ReCap, Remote, Revit LT, Revit, RiverCAD, Robot, Scaleform, Showcase, ShowMotion, Sim 360, SketchBook, Smoke, Socialcam, Softimage, Sparks, SteeringWheels, Stitcher, Stone, StormNET, TinkerBox, ToolClip, Topobase, Toxik, TrustedDWG, T-Splines, ViewCube, Visual LISP, Visual, VRED, Wire, Wiretap, WiretapCentral, XSI.
All other brand names, product names, or trademarks belong to their respective holders.

ISBN-13: 978-1-63057-596-0
ISBN-10: 1-63057-596-8

Printed and bound in the United States of America.

Contents

Preface xi

In This Guide xiii

Practice Files xv

Introduction to Autodesk Revit and Project Setup

Chapter 1: Introduction to Revit — 1-1

1.1 **BIM and Revit** 1-2
    Workflow and BIM 1-3
    Revit Terms 1-4
    Revit and Construction Documents 1-5

1.2 **Overview of the Interface** 1-6

1.3 **Opening and Saving Projects** 1-27
    Opening Projects 1-28
    Saving Projects 1-29

1.4 **Viewing Commands** 1-31
    Zooming and Panning 1-31
    Viewing in 3D 1-33
    ViewCube 1-38
    Visual Styles 1-40
    Select and Identify Elements in a Project 1-42

Practice 1a: Open and Review a Project 1-43

Chapter Review Questions 1-50

Command Summary 1-52

© 2023, ASCENT - Center for Technical Knowledge®   i

Chapter 2: Starting a Structural Project — 2-1

- 2.1 Selecting a Project Template 2-2
- 2.2 Linking and Importing Files 2-4
  - Linking and Importing Raster Image Files 2-7
  - Linking and Importing PDF Files 2-9
- 2.3 Linking in Revit Models 2-11
- 2.4 Modifying Imported/Linked Files 2-13
  - Managing Links 2-16
  - Modifying the Visibility of Imported/Linked Files 2-17
- Practice 2a: Start a Project and Link Files 2-20
- 2.5 Setting Up Levels 2-25
  - Modifying Levels 2-27
  - Creating Plan Views 2-30
- Practice 2b: Set Up Levels 2-32
- 2.6 Creating Grids 2-39
  - Modifying Grid Lines 2-42
- Practice 2c: Add Grids 2-45
- Chapter Review Questions 2-51
- Command Summary 2-53

Chapter 3: Working with Views — 3-1

- 3.1 Understand the Project Browser 3-2
  - Displaying Views in the Project Browser 3-4
- 3.2 Duplicating Views 3-7
- 3.3 Modify How the View Displays 3-10
  - View Control Bar 3-10
  - View Properties 3-11
  - Hiding and Overriding Graphics 3-14
  - Visibility/Graphic Overrides 3-16
  - View Templates 3-18
- Practice 3a: Duplicate Views and Set the View Display 3-20
- 3.4 Adding Callout Views 3-22
  - Working with Crop Regions 3-24
  - Plan Regions 3-26
- Practice 3b: Add Callout Views 3-29

3.5	Creating Elevations and Sections	3-31
	Elevations	3-32
	Sections	3-34
	Modifying Elevations and Sections	3-35
	3D Section Views	3-38

Practice 3c: Create Elevations and Sections 3-42

Chapter Review Questions 3-49

Command Summary 3-52

Chapter 4: Revit Families — 4-1

4.1	About Revit Families	4-2
	The Different Kinds of Families	4-3
	Working with Component Families	4-5
4.2	Loading Components	4-6
	Placing Components	4-9
	Using Snaps	4-10
	Snap Overrides	4-11
	Snaps Settings	4-12
4.3	Modifying Components	4-13
4.4	Creating Additional Family Types in a Project	4-16
	Structural Elements	4-17

Practice 4a: Load Families 4-18

Chapter Review Questions 4-21

Command Summary 4-22

Chapter 5: Basic Sketching and Modify Tools — 5-1

5.1	Adding General Model Elements	5-2
	Draw Tools	5-3
	Drawing Aids	5-6
	Reference Planes	5-7
	Editing Building Model Elements	5-10
	Selecting Multiple Elements	5-12
	Measuring Tool	5-15
	Filtering Selection of Multiple Elements	5-16

Practice 5a: Sketch and Edit Elements 5-18

5.2	Working with Basic Modify Tools	5-25
	Moving and Copying Elements	5-25
	Rotating Elements	5-27
	Mirroring Elements	5-29
	Creating Linear and Radial Arrays	5-30
	Aligning Elements	5-33

	Practice 5b: Work with Basic Modify Tools	5-35
5.3	**Working with Additional Modify Tools**	**5-42**
	Splitting Linear Elements	5-42
	Trimming and Extending	5-43
	Offsetting Elements	5-45
	Practice 5c: Work with Additional Modify Tools	5-47
	Chapter Review Questions	5-51
	Command Summary	5-55

Design Development

Chapter 6: Adding Columns — 6-1

6.1	**Adding Columns**	**6-2**
	Modifying Columns	6-8
6.2	**Adding Isolated Footings**	**6-11**
	Practice 6a: Place Structural Columns	6-13
6.3	**Copying and Monitoring Elements**	**6-15**
	Practice 6b: Copy and Monitor Elements	6-19
6.4	**Coordinating Linked Models**	**6-25**
	Practice 6c: Coordinate Linked Models	6-29
	Chapter Review Questions	6-32
	Command Summary	6-34

Chapter 7: Foundations — 7-1

7.1	**Modeling Walls**	**7-2**
7.2	**Modifying Walls**	**7-11**
	Wall Joins	7-14
	Editing Wall Profiles	7-15
	Wall Openings	7-16
7.3	**Adding Wall Footings**	**7-19**
	Practice 7a: Model Walls and Wall Footings	7-23
7.4	**Adding Isolated Footings**	**7-27**
	Working with Custom Families	7-29
	Practice 7b: Add Isolated Footings	7-32
	Chapter Review Questions	7-38
	Command Summary	7-42

Chapter 8: Structural Framing — 8-1

8.1 Modeling Structural Framing ... 8-2
- Beam Systems ... 8-4
- Adding Bracing ... 8-8
- Cross Bracing Settings ... 8-9

Practice 8a: Model Structural Framing ... 8-11

8.2 Modifying Structural Framing ... 8-20
- Sloping and Offsetting Beams ... 8-22
- Adding Beam Cantilevers and Cutbacks ... 8-24
- Changing the Cutback ... 8-26
- Changing Justifications ... 8-27
- Attaching a Column to a Beam ... 8-31
- Applying Beam Coping ... 8-32
- Editing Beam Joins ... 8-33

Practice 8b: Modify Structural Framing ... 8-35

8.3 Adding Trusses ... 8-39
- Attaching Trusses to Roofs ... 8-40
- Setting Framing Types in Trusses ... 8-41

Practice 8c: Add Trusses ... 8-43

Chapter Review Questions ... 8-49

Command Summary ... 8-51

Chapter 9: Adding Structural Slabs — 9-1

9.1 Modeling Structural Slabs ... 9-2
- Modifying Slabs ... 9-5
- Slab Edges ... 9-7
- Joining Geometry ... 9-8

Practice 9a: Model Structural Slabs ... 9-9

9.2 Creating Shaft Openings ... 9-17

Practice 9b: Create Shaft Openings ... 9-19

Chapter Review Questions ... 9-22

Command Summary ... 9-24

Chapter 10: Structural Reinforcement — 10-1

- **10.1 Structural Reinforcement** 10-2
  - Setting the Rebar Cover Depth 10-3
  - Reinforcement Settings 10-5
  - Rebar Visibility 10-10
- **10.2 Adding Rebar** 10-12
  - Sketching Rebar Shapes 10-19
  - Multi-planar Rebar 10-20
  - Free-Form Rebar 10-22
- **10.3 Modifying Rebar** 10-24
  - 3D Rebar Shapes 10-30
  - Rebar Coupler 10-33
- **Practice 10a: Add Rebar** 10-35
- **10.4 Reinforcing Walls, Floors, and Slabs** 10-43
  - Area Reinforcement 10-44
  - Path Reinforcement 10-47
  - Fabric Reinforcement 10-49
  - Modifying Area, Path, and Fabric Reinforcement 10-55
- **Practice 10b: Reinforce Structural Elements** 10-58
- **Chapter Review Questions** 10-68
- **Command Summary** 10-71

Construction Documentation

Chapter 11: Creating Construction Documents — 11-1

- **11.1 Setting Up Sheets** 11-2
  - Sheet (Title Block) Properties 11-4
- **11.2 Placing and Modifying Views on Sheets** 11-5
  - Open Sheet 11-8
- **11.3 Swapping Views on a Sheet** 11-10
  - Duplicating Sheets 11-15
- **11.4 Modifying Views and View Titles** 11-17
- **Practice 11a: Set Up Sheets** 11-21
- **11.5 Printing Sheets** 11-29
  - Printing Options 11-29
  - Export Views and Sheets to PDF 11-34
- **Chapter Review Questions** 11-35
- **Command Summary** 11-37

Chapter 12: Working with Annotations — 12-1

12.1 Working with Dimensions — 12-2
- Modifying Dimensions — 12-5
- Setting Constraints — 12-9
- Multi-Rebar Annotation — 12-14

Practice 12a: Work with Dimensions — 12-17

12.2 Working with Text — 12-22
- Editing Text — 12-25
- Spell Checking — 12-29
- Creating Text Types — 12-30

Practice 12b: Work with Text — 12-32

12.3 Adding Detail Lines and Symbols — 12-38
- Using Symbols — 12-39
- Structural Specific Symbols — 12-39

12.4 Creating Legends — 12-42

Practice 12c: Create Legends — 12-45

Chapter Review Questions — 12-51

Command Summary — 12-53

Chapter 13: Adding Tags and Schedules — 13-1

13.1 Adding Tags — 13-2
- Tagging in 3D Views — 13-10
- Beam Annotations — 13-11

Practice 13a: Add Tags and Symbols — 13-15

13.2 Working with Schedules — 13-19
- Building Component Schedules — 13-19
- Schedule View Properties — 13-29
- Filtering Elements from Schedules — 13-31
- Modifying Schedules — 13-32
- Modifying a Schedule on a Sheet — 13-34
- Split a Schedule Across Multiple Sheets — 13-34
- Filter by Sheet — 13-36

Practice 13b: Work with Schedules — 13-38

13.3 Graphical Column Schedules — 13-44
- Modifying Graphical Column Schedules — 13-45

Practice 13c: Create a Graphical Column Schedule — 13-48

Chapter Review Questions — 13-51

Command Summary — 13-52

Chapter 14: Creating Details 14-1

- 14.1 Setting Up Detail Views 14-2
  - Referencing a Drafting View 14-5
  - Saving Drafting Views 14-6
- 14.2 Adding Detail Components 14-9
  - Detail Components 14-9
  - Repeating Details 14-11
- 14.3 Annotating Details 14-13
  - Creating Filled Regions 14-13
  - Adding Detail Tags 14-16
  - Linework 14-17

Practice 14a: Create a Detail Based on a Section Callout 14-18

Practice 14b: Create a Bracing Detail 14-26

Practice 14c: Create Additional Details 14-29

Chapter Review Questions 14-31

Command Summary 14-33

Appendix A: Additional Tools for Design Development A-1

- A.1 Selection Sets A-2
- A.2 Purging Unused Elements A-5
- A.3 Editing Wall Joins A-6
- A.4 Creating Slab Types A-8
- A.5 Creating Rebar Types A-10
- A.6 Introduction to Revit Worksharing A-12
  - Worksharing Definitions A-13
  - Saving a Workshared Project A-16

Command Summary A-19

Appendix B: Additional Tools for Construction Documents B-1

- B.1 Working with Guide Grids on Sheets B-2
- B.2 Revision Tracking B-4
  - Issuing Revisions B-9
- B.3 Annotating Dependent Views B-10
  - Annotating Views B-11
- B.4 Material Takeoff Schedules B-14
- B.5 Importing and Exporting Schedules B-15
- B.6 Creating a Repeating Detail B-17

B.7	**Keynoting and Keynote Legends** **B-19**
	Keynote Legends B-22

Command Summary **B-24**

Appendix C: Project - Concrete Structure — C-1

Practice C1: Start a Structural Project **C-2**

Practice C2: Create Foundation Elements **C-6**

Practice C3: Frame a Concrete Structure **C-9**

Index **Index-1**

Preface

To take full advantage of Building Information Modeling, the *Autodesk® Revit® 2024: Fundamentals for Structure* guide has been designed to teach the concepts and principles of creating 3D parametric models of structural buildings from engineering design through construction documentation.

This guide is intended to introduce you to the user interface and the basic building components of the software that makes Autodesk® Revit® a powerful and flexible structural modeling tool. The goal is to familiarize you with the tools required to create, modify, analyze, and document a parametric model. The examples and practices are designed to take you through the basics of a full structural project, from linking in an architectural model to construction documents.

Topics Covered

- Introduction to the Autodesk Revit software, including navigating the Revit interface
- Starting a structural project based on a linked architectural model and creating levels and grids as datum elements for the model
- Understanding the project browser and working with views
- Understanding Revit families and components
- Working with the basic sketching and modifying tools
- Adding structural columns to a project and copying and monitoring elements from linked models
- Adding foundations and footings
- Creating structural framing, including beams, trusses, and framing systems
- Creating slabs for foundations, structural floors, and roofs
- Creating structural reinforcement, including placing rebar and adding fabric reinforcement
- Setting up sheets and placing and modifying views on sheets
- Working with dimensions, text, annotations, and legends
- Adding tags and working with schedules
- Setting up detail views and adding detail components

Prerequisites

- Access to the 2024.0 version of the software, to ensure compatibility with this guide. Future software updates that are released by Autodesk may include changes that are not reflected in this guide. The practices and files included with this guide might not be compatible with prior versions (e.g., 2023).

- This guide introduces the fundamental skills in learning how to use the Autodesk Revit software, with a focus on the structural tools. It is highly recommended that students have experience and knowledge in structural engineering and its terminology.

Note on Software Setup

This guide assumes a standard installation of the software using the default preferences during installation. This includes the Revit templates and Revit Content (Families) that can be found on the Autodesk website at https://knowledge.autodesk.com/ and searching **How to download Revit Content**. Lectures and practices use the standard software templates and default options.

Note on Learning Guide Content

ASCENT's learning guides are intended to teach the technical aspects of using the software and do not focus on professional design principles and standards. The exercises aim to demonstrate the capabilities and flexibility of the software, rather than following specific design codes or standards, which can vary between regions.

Lead Contributor: Cherisse Biddulph

Cherisse is an Autodesk Certified Professional for Revit as well as an Autodesk Certified Instructor. She brings over 19 years of industry, teaching, and technical support experience to her role as a Learning Content Developer with ASCENT. With a passion for design and architecture, she has worked in the industry assisting firms with their CAD management and software implementation needs as they modernize to a Building Information Modeling (BIM) design environment. Although her main devotion is the Revit design product, she is also proficient in AutoCAD, Autodesk BIM 360, and Autodesk Navisworks. Today, Cherisse continues to expand her knowledge in the ever-evolving AEC industry and the software used to support it.

Cherisse Biddulph has been the Lead Contributor for *Autodesk Revit: Fundamentals for Structure* since 2020.

In This Guide

The following highlights the key features of this guide.

Feature	Description
Practice Files	The Practice Files page includes a link to the practice files and instructions on how to download and install them. The practice files are required to complete the practices in this guide.
Chapters	A chapter consists of the following: Learning Objectives, Instructional Content, Practices, Chapter Review Questions, and Command Summary. • **Learning Objectives** define the skills you can acquire by learning the content provided in the chapter. • **Instructional Content**, which begins right after Learning Objectives, refers to the descriptive and procedural information related to various topics. Each main topic introduces a product feature, discusses various aspects of that feature, and provides step-by-step procedures on how to use that feature. Where relevant, examples, figures, helpful hints, and notes are provided. • **Practice** for a topic follows the instructional content. Practices enable you to use the software to perform a hands-on review of a topic. It is required that you download the practice files (using the link found on the Practice Files page) prior to starting the first practice. • **Chapter Review Questions**, located close to the end of a chapter, enable you to test your knowledge of the key concepts discussed in the chapter. • **Command Summary** concludes a chapter. It contains a list of the software commands that are used throughout the chapter and provides information on where the command can be found in the software.
Appendices	Appendices provide additional information to the main course content. It could be in the form of instructional content, practices, tables, projects, or skills assessment.

Practice Files

To download the practice files for this guide, use the following steps:

1. Type the URL *exactly as shown below* into the address bar of your Internet browser to access the Course File Download page.
   Note: If you are using the ebook, you do not have to type the URL. Instead, you can access the page by clicking the URL below.

   https://www.SDCpublications.com/downloads/978-1-63057-596-0

2. On the Course File Download page, click the **DOWNLOAD NOW** button to download the .ZIP file that contains the practice files.

3. Once the download is complete, unzip the file and extract its contents.
   The recommended practice files folder location is:
   C:\Revit 2024 Fundamentals for Structure Practice Files
   Note: It is recommended that you do not change the location of the practice files folder. Doing so may cause errors when completing the practices.

> **Stay Informed!**
> To receive information about upcoming events, promotional offers, and complimentary webcasts, visit:
> **www.ASCENTed.com/updates**

Introduction to Autodesk Revit and Project Setup

This guide is divided into three sections: Introduction to Autodesk Revit and Project Setup, Design Development, and Construction Documentation.

The first section provides an introduction to the Autodesk® Revit® software, including working with the software interface, setting up a drawing, incorporating datum elements, adding families, and using the basic drawing and modify tools.

This section includes the following chapters:

- Chapter 1: Introduction to Revit
- Chapter 2: Starting a Structural Project
- Chapter 3: Working with Views
- Chapter 4: Revit Families
- Chapter 5: Basic Sketching and Modify Tools

© 2023, ASCENT - Center for Technical Knowledge®

Chapter 1

Introduction to Revit

Building Information Modeling (BIM) and Revit® work hand in hand to help you create smart, 3D models that are useful at all stages in the building process. Understanding the software interface and terminology enhances your ability to create and navigate around in the various views of the model.

Learning Objectives

- Describe the concept of Building Information Modeling in conjunction with applying Revit.
- Navigate the graphic user interface, including the ribbon (where most of the tools are found), Properties (where you make modifications to element information), and the Project Browser (where you can open various views of the model).
- Open existing projects and save projects.
- Use viewing commands to navigate around the model in 2D and 3D views.

1.1 BIM and Revit

Building Information Modeling (BIM) is an approach to the entire building life cycle, including design, construction, and facilities management. The BIM process supports the ability to coordinate, update, and share design data with team members across disciplines.

Revit is a model authoring software. It enables you to create complete 3D building models (as shown on the left in Figure 1–1) that provide considerable information reported through construction documents, and enables you to share these models with other programs for more extensive analysis.

> *Note:* The software includes tools for architectural, mechanical, electrical, plumbing, and structural design.

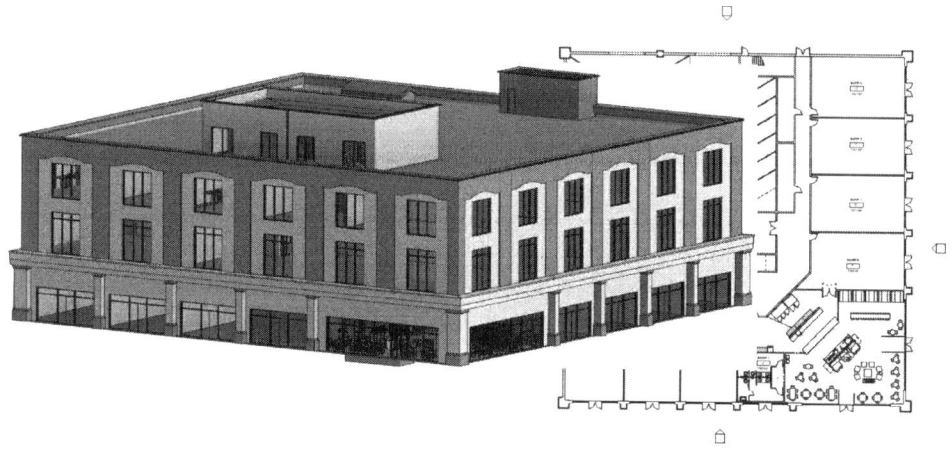

Figure 1–1

Revit is a Parametric Building Modeler software:

- *Parametric:* A relationship is established between building elements: when one element changes, all other related elements and/or geometry is modified as well. For example, when you place a door in a wall, the door removes part of the wall and stays inside that wall if it moves.

- *Building:* The software is designed for working with buildings and the surrounding landscape, as opposed to gears or highways.

- *Modeler:* A project is built in a single file based on the 3D building model, as shown on the left in Figure 1–1. All views, such as plans (as shown on the right in Figure 1–1), elevations, sections, details, construction documents, and reports are generated based on the model.

- It is important that everyone who is collaborating on a project works in the same version and build of the software.

Workflow and BIM

BIM has changed the process of how a building is planned, budgeted, designed, constructed, and (in some cases) operated and maintained.

In the traditional design process, construction documents are created independently, typically including plans, sections, elevations, details, and notes. Sometimes, a separate 3D model is created in addition to these documents. Changes made in one document, such as the addition of a light fixture in a plan, have to be coordinated with the rest of the documents and schedules in the set, as shown in Figure 1-2.

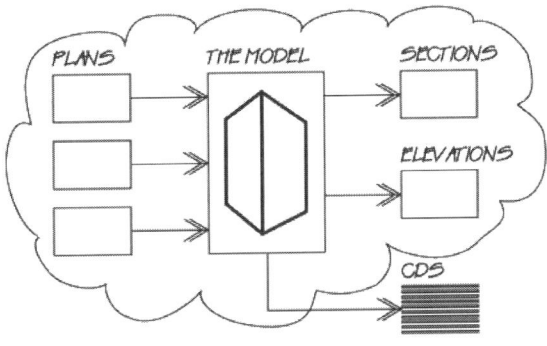

Figure 1-2

In BIM, the design process revolves around the model, as shown in Figure 1-3. Plans, elevations, and sections are simply 2D versions of the 3D model, while schedules are a report of the information stored in the model. Changes made in one view automatically update in all views and related schedules. Even construction documents update automatically with callout tags in sync with the sheet numbers. This is called bidirectional associativity.

By creating complete models and associated views of those models, Revit takes much of the tediousness out of producing a building design.

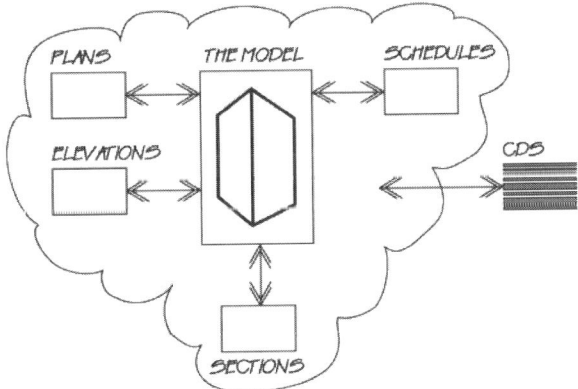

Figure 1-3

Revit Terms

When working in Revit, it is important to know the typical terms used to describe items. Views and reports display information about the elements that form a project. There are three types of elements: model, datum, and view-specific, as shown in Figure 1–4 and described below:

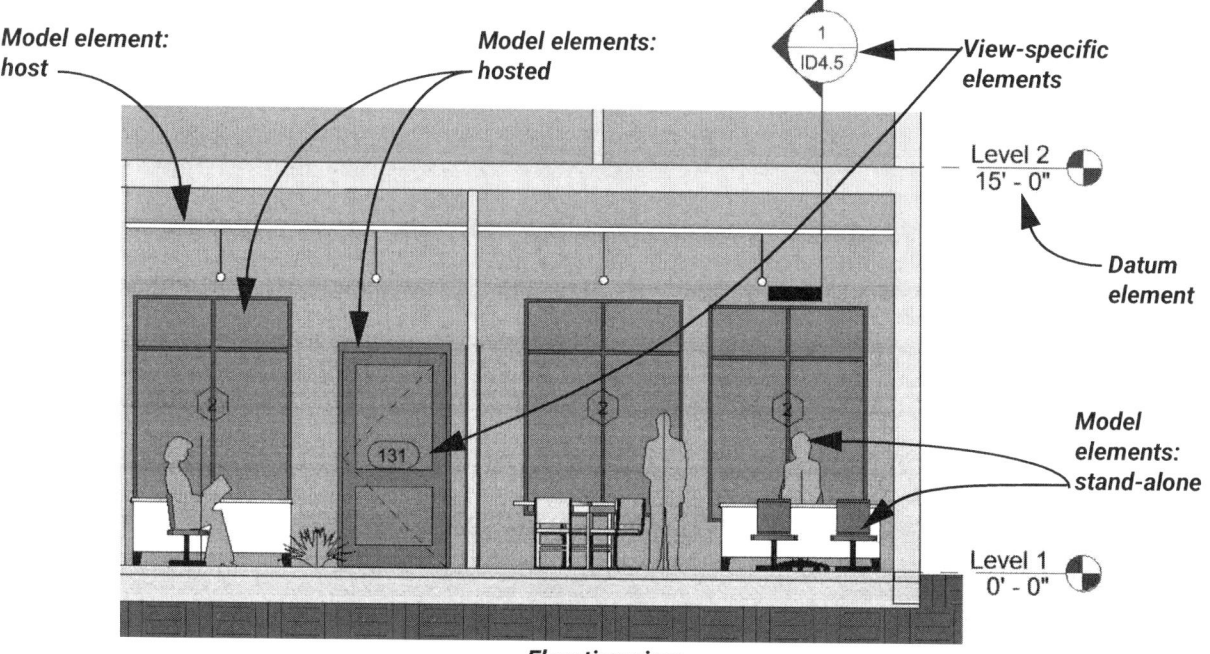

Elevation view

Figure 1–4

Views	Views enable you to display and manipulate the model. For example, you can view and work in floor plans, ceiling plans, elevations, sections, schedules, and 3D views. You can change a design from any view. All views are stored in the project.
Reports	Reports, including schedules, gather information from the building model element that can be presented in the construction documents or used for analysis.
Model Elements	Model elements include all parts of a building, such as walls, floors, ceilings, and roofs.
Component Elements	Component elements are placed from inserted families, such as plumbing fixtures, light fixtures, mechanical equipment, columns, beams, furniture, and plants. • Host elements, such as walls, support other categories of components like doors, windows, and casework. • Hosted elements must be attached to a host element, such as doors must be placed on a (host) wall. • Stand-alone elements do not require hosts.

Datum Elements	Datum elements define the project context, such as the levels for the floors, grids, and reference planes.
View-specific Elements	View-specific elements only display in the view in which they are placed. The view scale controls their size. These include annotation elements such as dimensions, text, tags, and symbols as well as detail elements such as detail lines, filled regions, and 2D detail components.

- Revit elements are "smart": the software recognizes them as walls, columns, plants, ducts, or light fixtures, etc. This means that the information stored in their properties automatically updates in schedules, which ensures that views and reports are coordinated across an entire project, and are generated from a single model.

Revit and Construction Documents

In the traditional workflow, the most time-consuming part of the project is the construction documents. With BIM, the base views of those documents (i.e., plans, elevations, sections, and schedules) are produced automatically and update as the model is updated, saving hours of work. The views are then placed on sheets that form the construction document set.

For example, a floor plan is duplicated. Then, in the new view, all but the required categories of elements are hidden or set to halftone and annotations are added. The plan is then placed on a sheet, as shown in Figure 1–5.

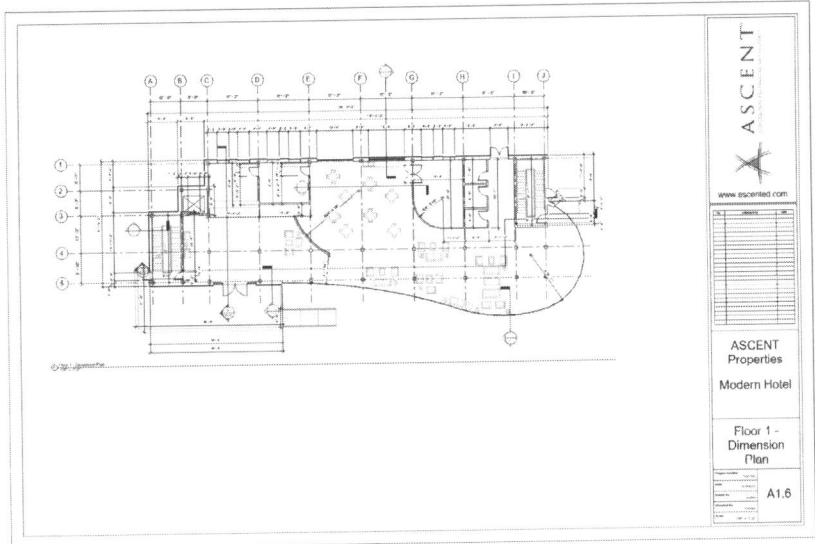

Figure 1–5

- Work can continue on a view and is automatically updated on the sheet.

- Annotating views in the preliminary design phase is often not required. You might be able to wait until you are further along in the project.

1.2 Overview of the Interface

The Revit interface is designed for intuitive and efficient access to commands and views. It includes the ribbon, Quick Access Toolbar, Navigation Bar, and Status Bar, which are common to most of the Autodesk software. It also includes tools that are specific to Revit, including Properties, the Project Browser, and the View Control Bar. Revit includes access to tools for architectural, mechanical, electrical, plumbing, and structural design but can be altered by setting up a customized workspace that is more tailored to your specific discipline. A breakdown of the Revit interface is shown in Figure 1–6.

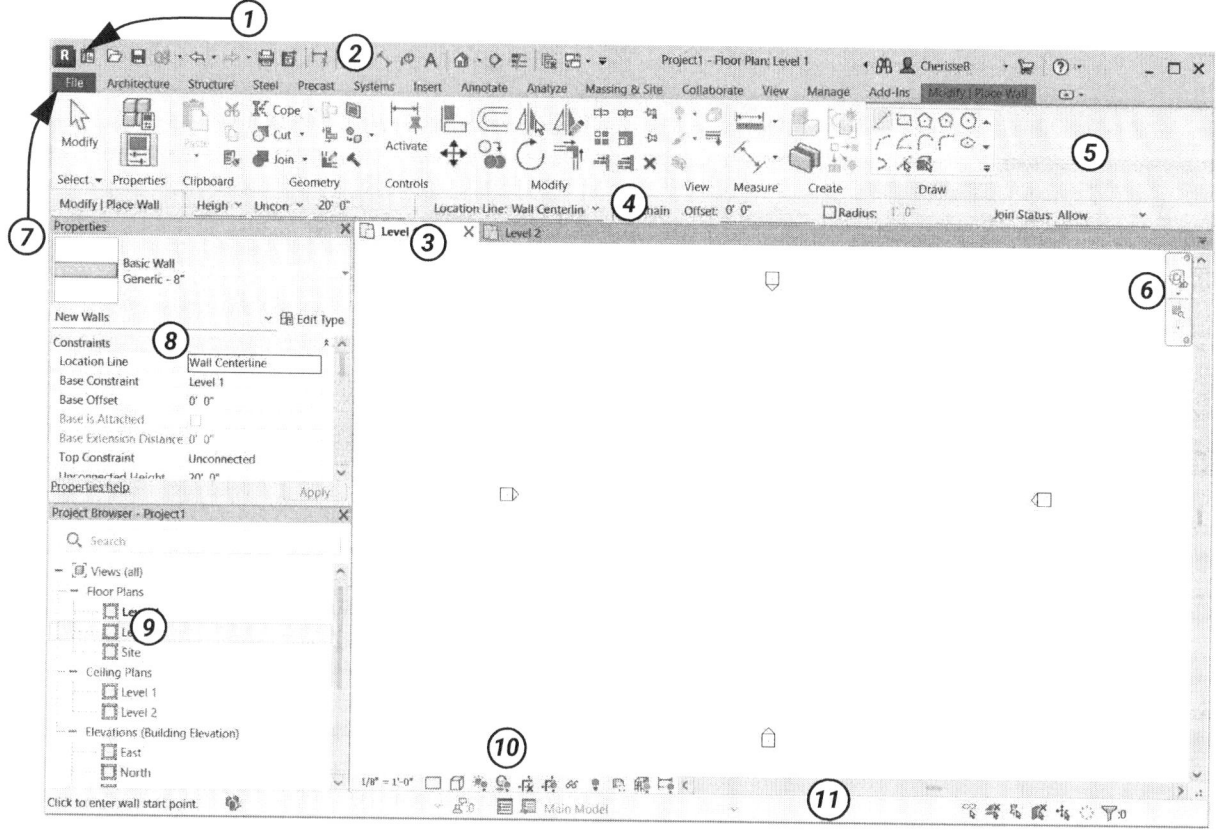

Figure 1–6

1. Home Screen	7. File Tab
2. Quick Access Toolbar	8. Properties
3. View Tabs	9. Project Browser
4. Options Bar	10. View Control Bar
5. Ribbon	11. Status Bar
6. Navigation Bar	

1. The Home Screen

When you first open Revit, the **Home** screen displays with recently used projects and families, as shown in Figure 1-7. Click on a tab along the left side of the interface to open or start a new model or family. There are other feature tabs you can access, like *Autodesk Docs* and *My Insights*, as well as links to **Whats new**, **Online help**, **Community forum**, and **Customer support**.

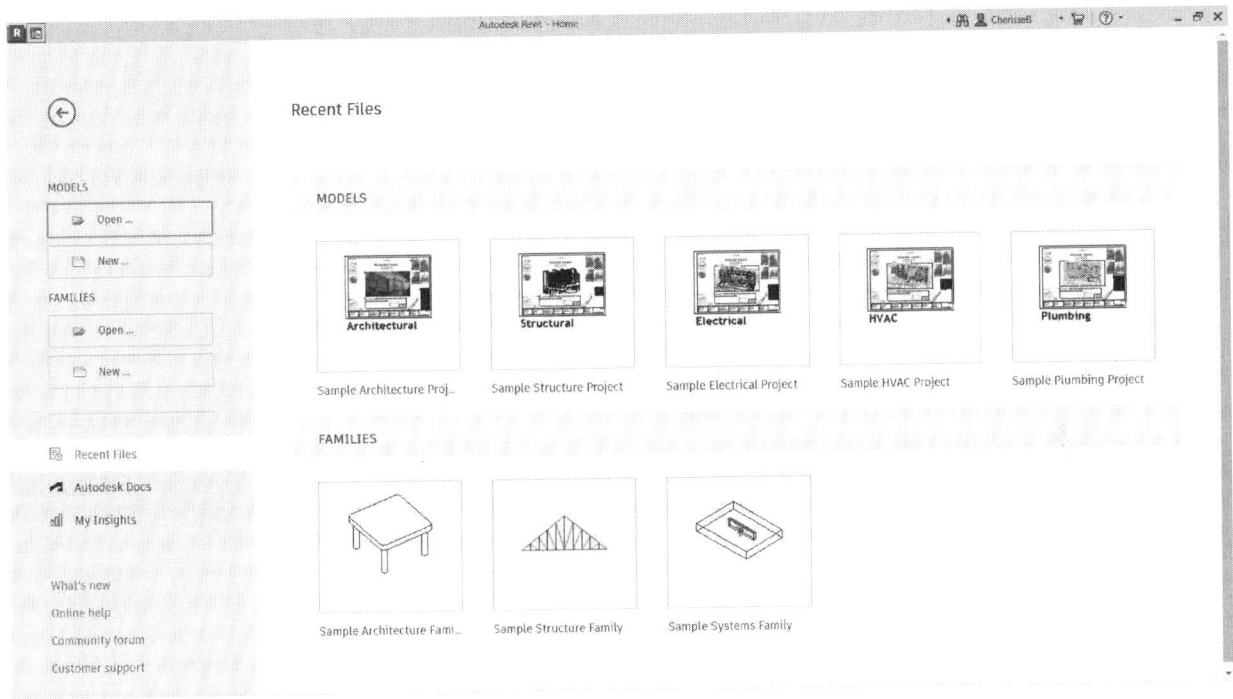

Figure 1-7

- From the Home screen, you can select the image (displaying the file name) of a recently opened project or use one of the options on the left to open or start a new project using the default templates.

- In the Quick Access Toolbar, click (Home) to return to the Home screen.

- On the Home screen, click (Back) to return to the active model.

    - Press <Ctrl>+<D> to toggle between the Home screen and the active model.

    - To view personalized insights based on your usage data, click on the *My Insights* tab from the Home screen. The Insights cards will display topics such as Revit usage details, new commands, and feature recommendations.

2. Quick Access Toolbar

The Quick Access Toolbar (shown in Figure 1–8) includes commonly used commands, such as **Home, Open, Save, Undo, Redo, Print**, and **PDF**. It also includes **Activate Controls and Dimensions** to reduce clutter when selecting multiple elements in a view, and frequently used annotation tools, including Measuring tools, **Aligned Dimension**, **Tag by Category**, and **Text**. Viewing tools, including several different 3D Views and **Sections**, are also easily accessed here.

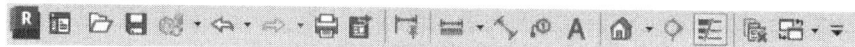

Figure 1–8

The top toolbar also hosts the InfoCenter (as shown in Figure 1–9), which includes the Autodesk sign-in, access to the Autodesk App Store, and Help options.

Figure 1–9

A search field, as shown in Figure 1–10, is also available to find help on the web.

Figure 1–10

Introduction to Revit

> **Hint: Customizing the Quick Access Toolbar**
>
> Right-click on the Quick Access Toolbar, as shown in Figure 1–11, to change the docking location of the toolbar to be above or below the ribbon, or to add, relocate, or remove tools on the toolbar.

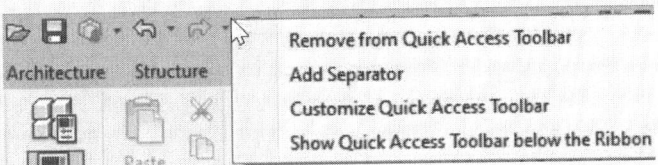

Figure 1–11

You can also right-click on a tool in the ribbon (e.g., the **Move** command) and select **Add to Quick Access Toolbar**, as shown in Figure 1–12.

Figure 1–12

If you have added a lot of icons to the Quick Access Toolbar, ▼ (Expand) will display at the end of the toolbar. Click ▼ to show the additional tool icons you have added, as shown in Figure 1–13.

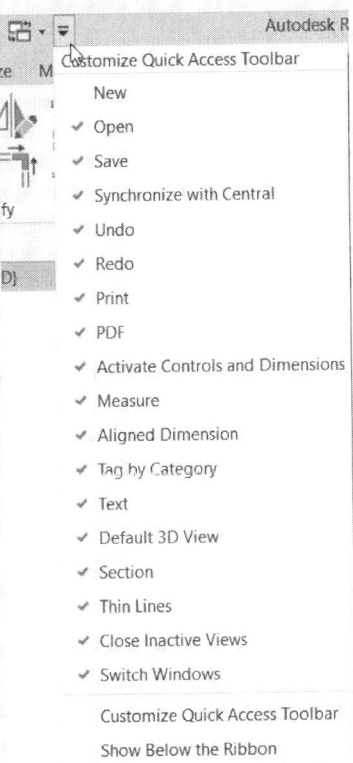

Figure 1–13

3. View Tabs

Each view of a project opens in its own tab and can be pulled out of the application window and moved to another monitor. Each view displays a Navigation Bar (for quick access to viewing tools), the View Control Bar, and elevation markers, as shown in Figure 1–14.

Note: In 3D views, you can also use the ViewCube to orbit the view.

- To close a tab, click the **X** that displays when you hover over the tab or the name in the list, as shown in Figure 1–14.

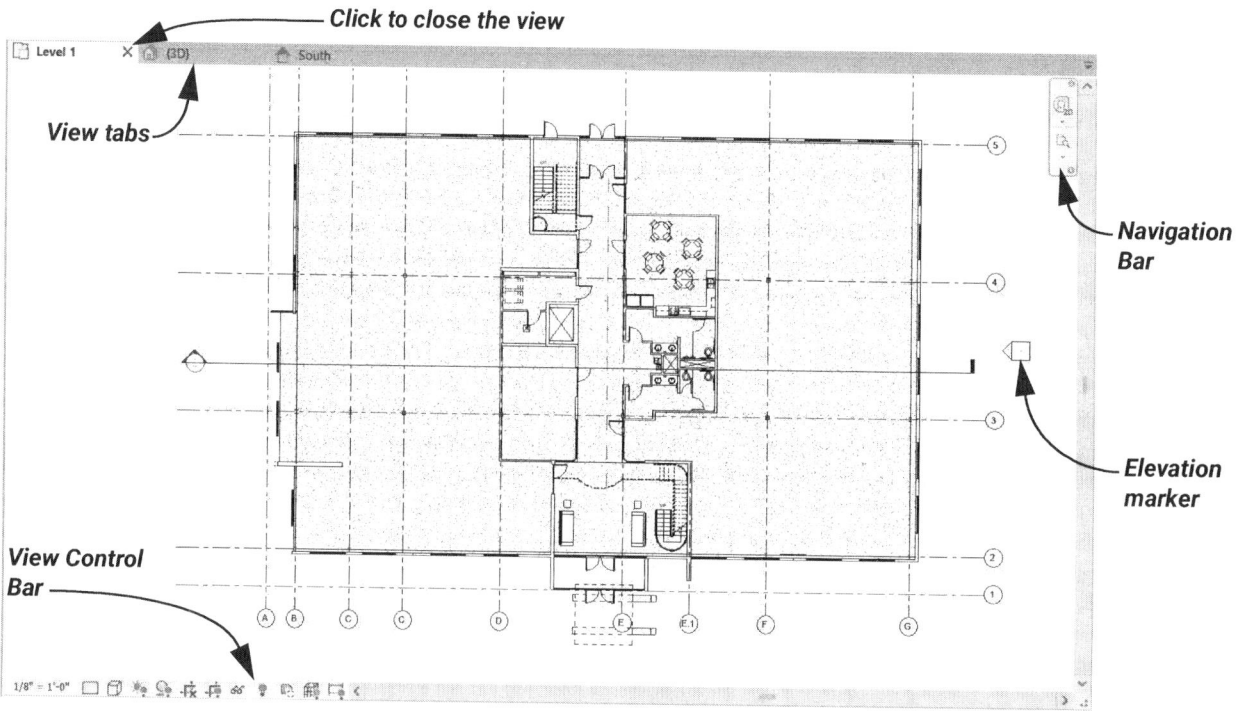

Figure 1–14

Hint: Elevation Markers

You can hover your cursor over a marker's arrowhead to see what the view name is, as shown in Figure 1–15. You can also double-click on the arrowhead to open the view.

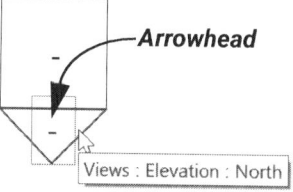

Figure 1–15

Hint: Using Thin Lines

The software automatically applies line weights to views, as shown for a section on the left in Figure 1–16. If a line weight seems heavy or obscures your work on the elements, toggle off the line weights. In the Quick Access Toolbar or in the *View* tab>Graphics panel, click ▦ (Thin Lines), or type **TL**. The lines display with the same weight, as shown on the right in Figure 1–16.

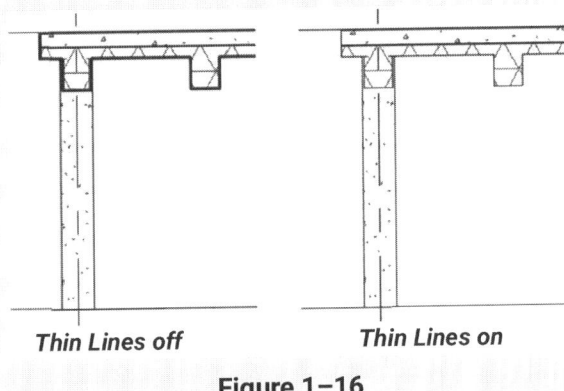

Thin Lines off   Thin Lines on

Figure 1–16

The **Thin Line** setting is remembered until you change it, even if you shut down and restart the software.

- Click on the tab along the top of the drawing area to switch between views. You can also:
  - Press <Ctrl>+<Tab>.
  - Select the view in the Project Browser.
  - In the Quick Access Toolbar (shown on the left in Figure 1–17) or *View* tab>Windows panel (shown on the right in Figure 1–17), expand ▦ (Switch Windows) and select the view from the list.

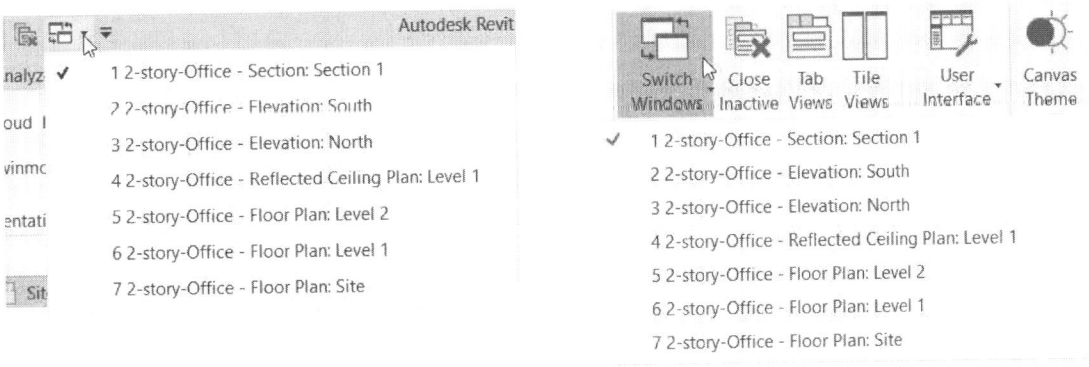

Figure 1–17

- Expand the drop-down list at the far end of the tabs, as shown in Figure 1–18 to select a view from the list.

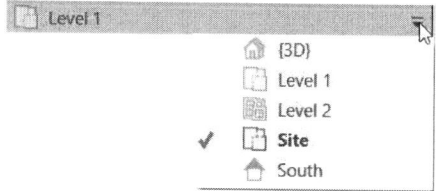

Figure 1–18

- To close all open views except the current view, in the Quick Access Toolbar or *View* tab>Windows panel, click (Close Inactive Views). If you have multiple projects open, one view of each project remains open. If you have dragged a view to another monitor, that view will need to be manually closed by clicking the **X** in the upper-right corner.

- You can switch between tabbed and tiled views from the *View* tab>Windows panel or by typing shortcuts. For tabbed views (as shown on the left in Figure 1–19), click (Tab Views) or type **TW**. For tiled views (as shown on the right in Figure 1–19), click (Tile Views) or type **WT**.

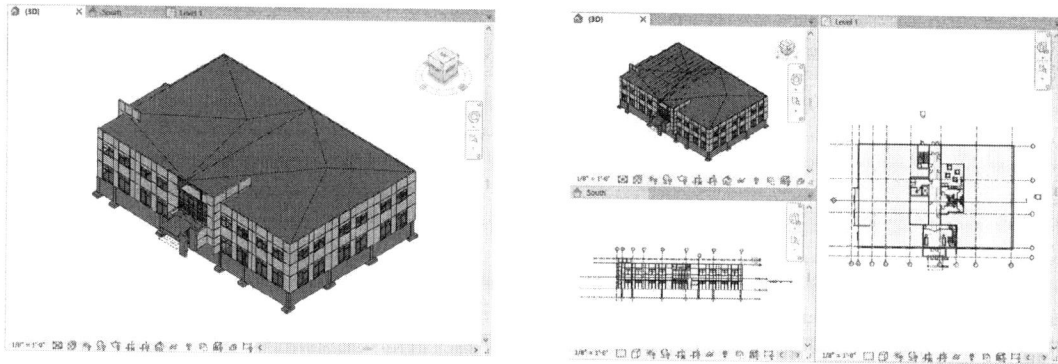

Figure 1–19

- When you are working with tiled views, you can type **ZA** (Zoom All to Fit) to zoom to fit the full model in each of the different views.

- Drag the edge of tiled views to resize them as needed.

4. Options Bar

The Options Bar displays options that are related to the selected command or element. For example, when the **Rotate** command is active it displays options for rotating the selected elements, as shown at the top in Figure 1–20. When the **Place Dimensions** command is active it displays dimension related options, as shown at the bottom in Figure 1–20.

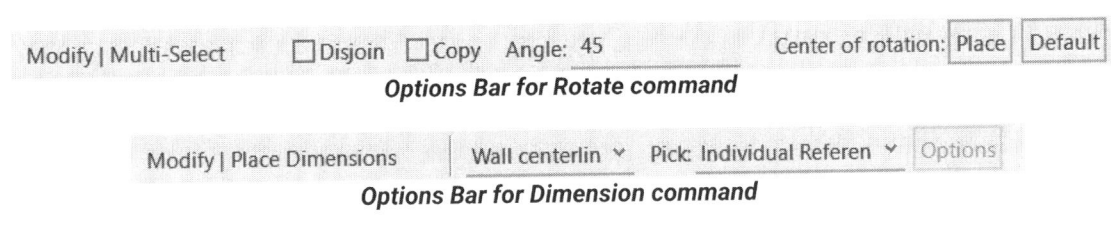

Figure 1–20

5. Ribbon

The ribbon contains tools in a series of tabs and panels, as shown in Figure 1–21. Selecting a tab displays a group of related panels. The panels contain a variety of tools, grouped by task.

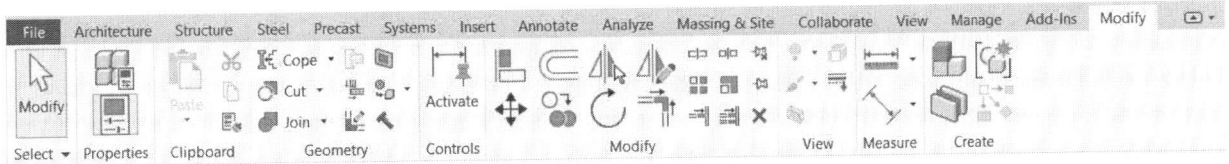

Figure 1–21

When you start a command that creates new elements or you select an element, the ribbon displays the *Modify* contextual tab. This contains general editing commands and command-specific tools, as shown in Figure 1–22.

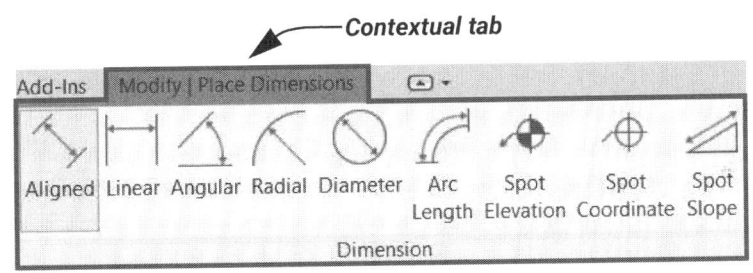

Figure 1–22

- When a command is toggled on, the icon will be highlighted in blue. When it is toggled off, the icon is gray (not highlighted), as shown in Figure 1–23.

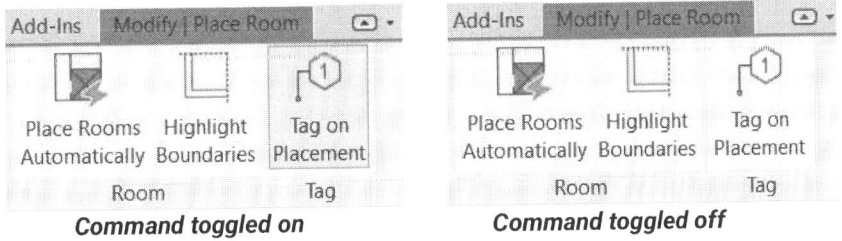

Figure 1–23

- When you hover over a tool on the ribbon, tooltips display the tool's name and a short description. If you continue hovering over the tool, a graphic displays (and sometimes a video), as shown in Figure 1–24.

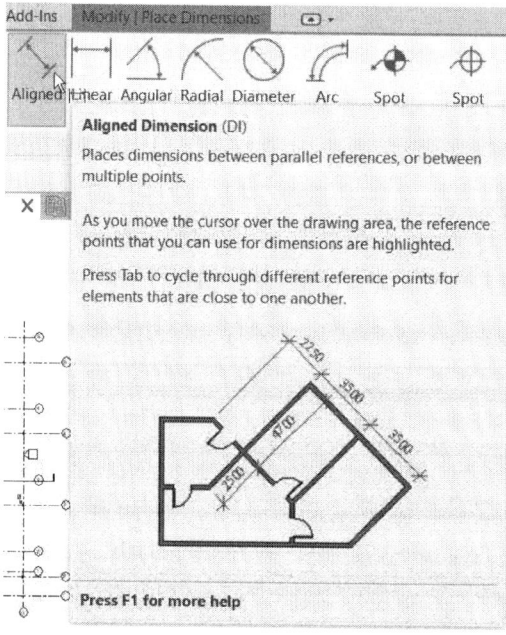

Figure 1–24

- Many commands have shortcut keys. For example, type **AL** for **Align** or **MV** for **Move**. They are listed next to the name of the command in the tooltips. Do not press <Enter> when typing shortcuts. A list of shortcuts can be found in the Autodesk Revit Help, which can be accessed by clicking ⓘ (Help) in the upper-right corner of the interface or pressing <F1>.

    - For convenience, both the RVTKeyboardShortcuts.xlsx and RVTKeyboardShortcuts.pdf files have been downloaded for you and can be found in the practice files *Reference* folder.

- To arrange the order in which the ribbon tabs are displayed, select the tab, hold <Ctrl>, and drag it to a new location. The location is remembered when you restart the software.

- Any panel can be dragged by its title into the view window to become a floating panel. Click the **Return Panels to Ribbon** button (as shown in Figure 1–25) to reposition the panel in the ribbon.

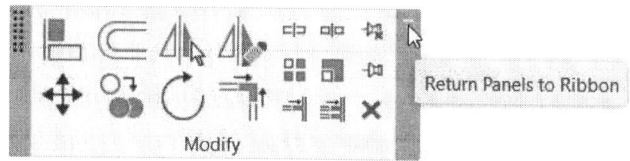

Figure 1–25

Hint: Ending a Command

When you are finished working with a tool, you typically default back to the **Modify** command. To end a command, use one of the following methods:

- In any tab on the ribbon, click (Modify).
- Type the shortcut **MD**.
- Press <Esc> once or twice to revert to **Modify**.
- Right-click and select **Cancel...** once or twice.
- Start another command.

6. Navigation Bar

The Navigation Bar enables you to access the 2D and Full Navigation (3D views) Wheel to navigate the view, as well as the Zoom in Region viewing commands, as shown in Figure 1–26.

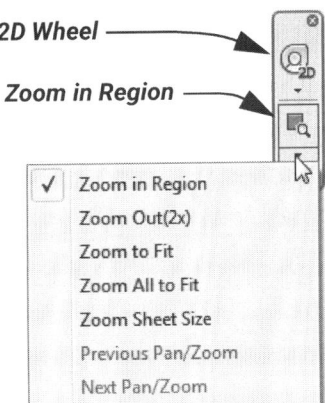

Figure 1–26

7. File Tab

The *File* tab of the ribbon can be expanded and it provides access to file commands, Options settings, and Print, Export, and Save options, as shown in Figure 1–27. Hover the cursor over a command to display a list of additional tools.

Note: If you click the primary icon (e.g., New or Open), rather than the arrow, it starts the default command (except for Save As and Export, which require an option to be selected).

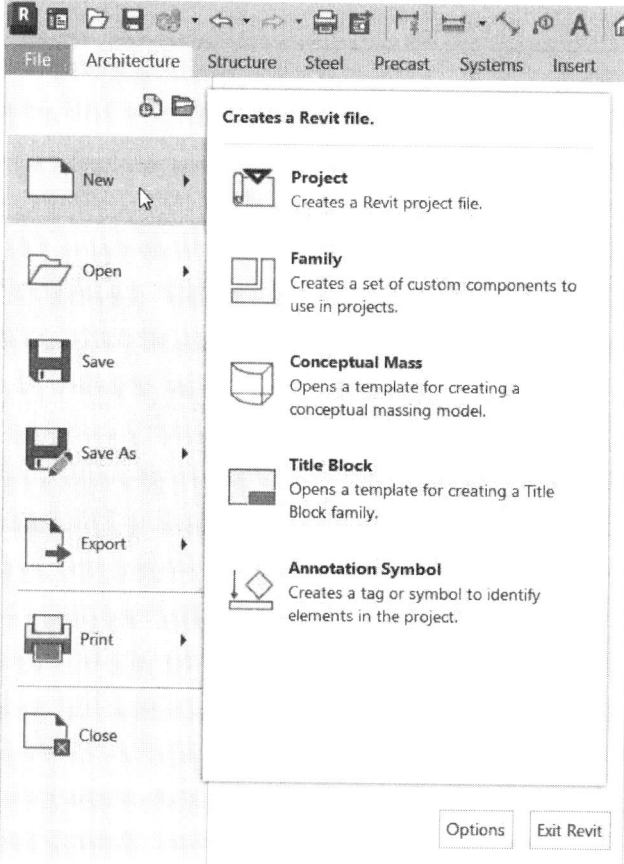

Figure 1–27

- To display a list of recently used documents, click (Recent Documents). The documents can be reordered as shown in Figure 1–28. You can click (Pin) next to a document name to keep it available.

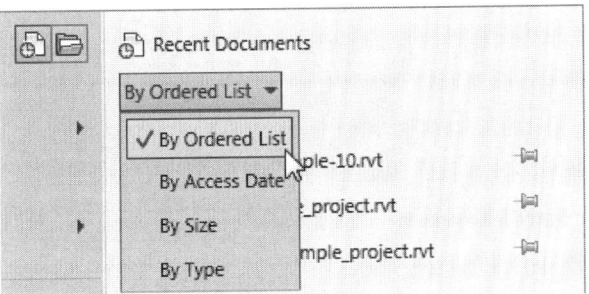

Figure 1–28

- To display a list of open documents and views, click (Open Documents). The list displays the documents and views that are open, as shown in Figure 1–29. You can use the Open Documents list to change between views.

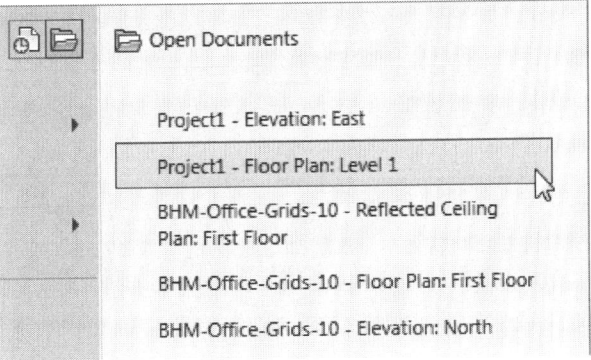

Figure 1–29

- Click (Close) to close the current project.
- At the bottom of the menu, click **Options** to open the Options dialog box or click **Exit Revit** to exit the software.

8. Properties

Properties contains several parts, as shown in Figure 1–30. The Type Selector can be found at the top, which enables you to choose the size or style of the element you are adding or modifying. The options available in Properties enable you to make changes to information (parameters). There are two types of properties:

- **Instance properties** are set for the individual element(s) you are creating or modifying.
- **Type properties** control options for all elements of the same type. If you modify these parameter values, all elements of the selected type change.

Properties is usually kept open while working on a project to easily permit changes at any time.

If it does not display, in the *Modify* tab>Properties panel, click ▣ (Properties), or type **PP**. Alternatively, you can right-click in the view and select **Properties**.

Note: Some parameters are only available when you are editing an element. They are grayed out when unavailable.

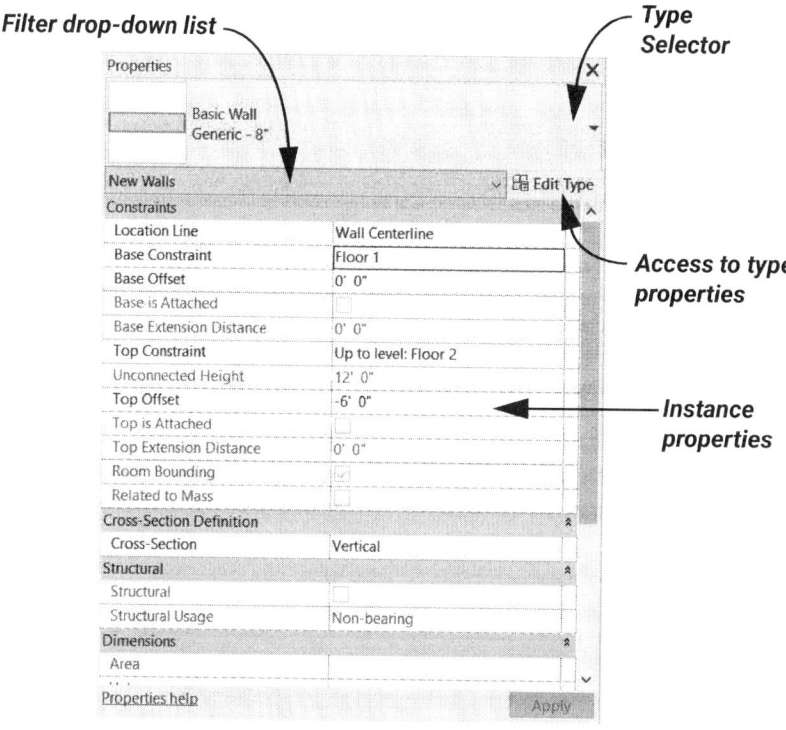

Figure 1–30

- Options for the current view display if the **Modify** command is active, but you have not selected an element.
- If a command or element is selected, the options for the associated element display.
- You can save the changes either by moving the cursor off of Properties, by pressing <Enter>, or by clicking **Apply**.

- When you start a command or select an element, you can set the element type in the Type Selector, as shown in Figure 1–31.

    Note: You can limit what shows in the drop-down list by typing in the search box.

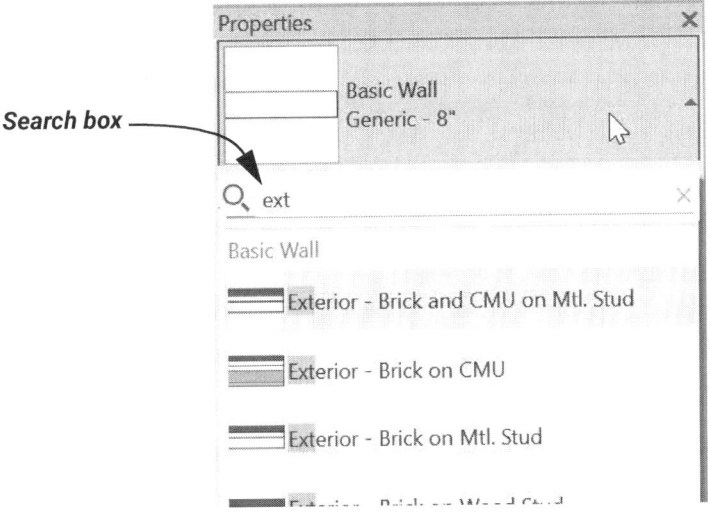

Figure 1–31

- When multiple elements are selected, you can filter the type of elements that display using the drop-down list, as shown in Figure 1–32.

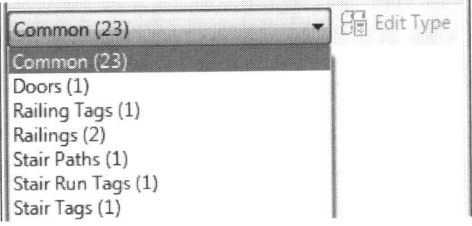

Figure 1–32

- Properties can be placed on a second monitor, or floated, resized, and docked on top of the Project Browser, as shown in Figure 1–33. Click a tab to display its associated information.

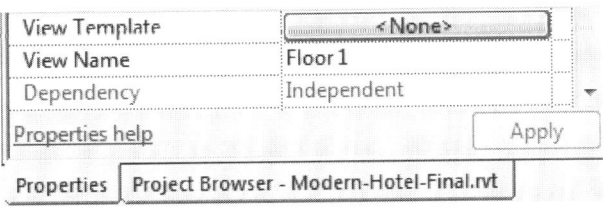

Figure 1–33

9. Project Browser

The Project Browser (shown in Figure 1–34) lists all the views of the model in which you can work and any additional views that you create, such as floor plans, ceiling plans, 3D views, elevations, sections, etc. It also includes schedules, legends, sheets (for plotting), lists of families by category, groups, and Revit links. The name of the active view is bold, and views that are placed on sheets will have a status icon next to the level's name.

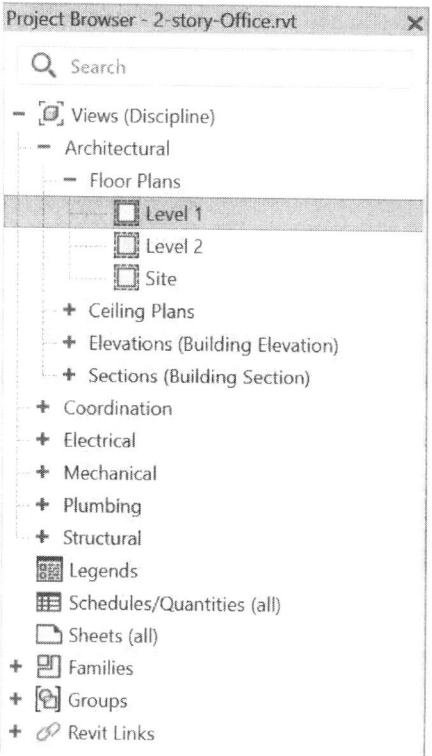

Figure 1–34

- To display the views associated with a view type (e.g., floor plans, ceiling plans, etc.), click ⊞ (Expand) next to the section name. To hide the views in the section, click ⊟ (Collapse). You can also expand and collapse sets using the shortcut menu, as shown in Figure 1–35.

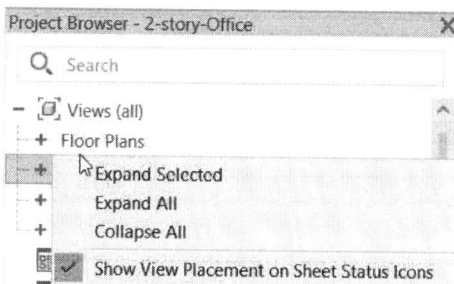

Figure 1–35

- To open a view, double-click on the view name or right-click and select **Open**.

- To open a sheet, right-click on the view in the Project Browser and select **Open Sheet**, as shown in Figure 1–36.

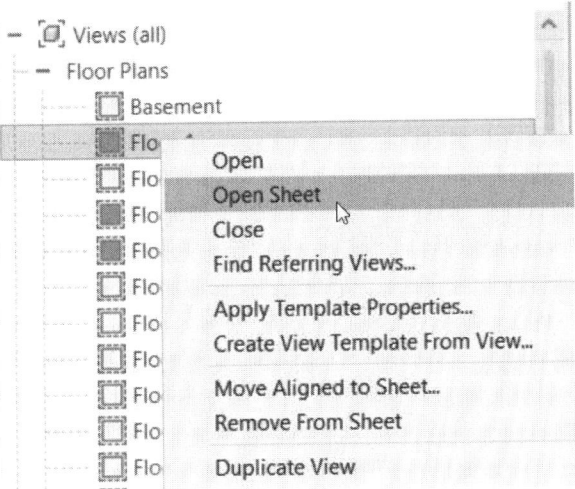

Figure 1–36

- To rename a view, slowly click twice on the view name and the text will highlight so it can be changed. You can also right-click on a view name and select **Rename...**, as shown in Figure 1–37, or press <F2>.

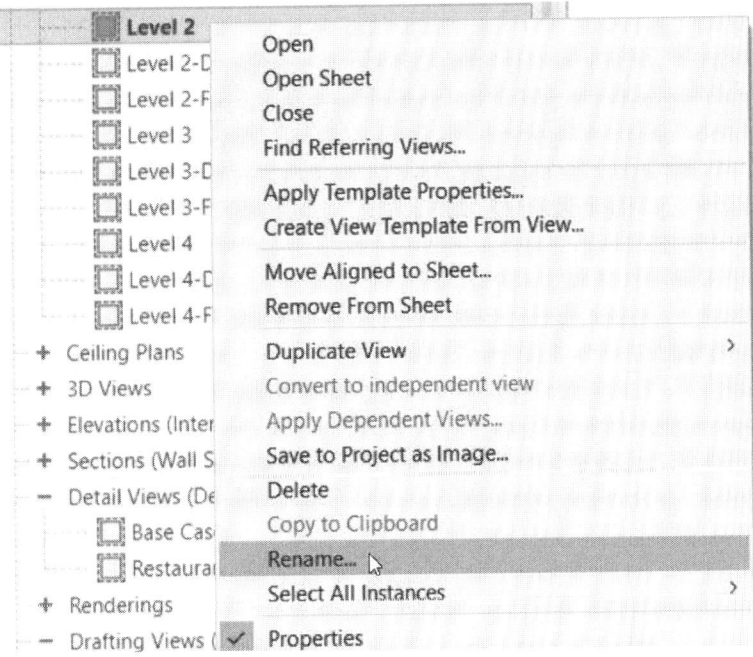

Figure 1–37

Setting the Discipline of a View

You can utilize discipline in a view to display discipline-specific elements and to organize the Project Browser. When you duplicate or create a view, if it is not in the expected grouping in the Project Browser, you would need to set the *Discipline* in Properties. The view properties of *Discipline* (shown in Figure 1–38) control the visibility of some elements and applies grouping in the Project Browser. For example, you can separate the coordination plans from the architectural plans, as shown in Figure 1–39.

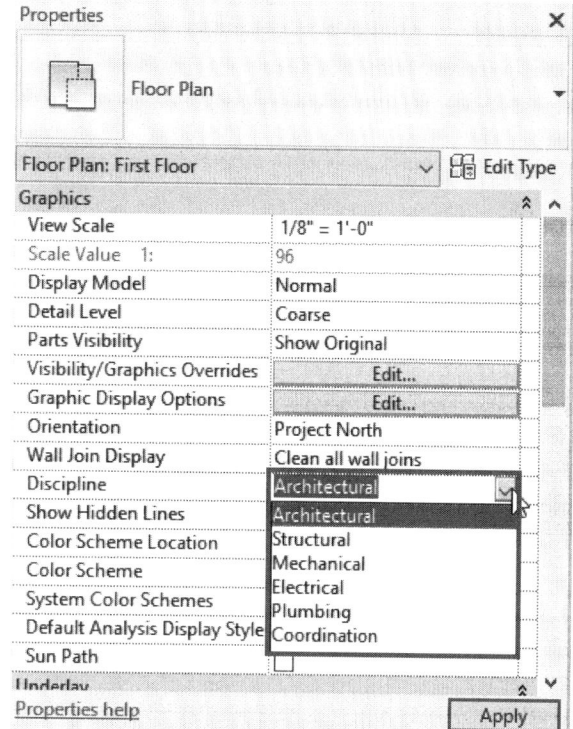

Figure 1–38

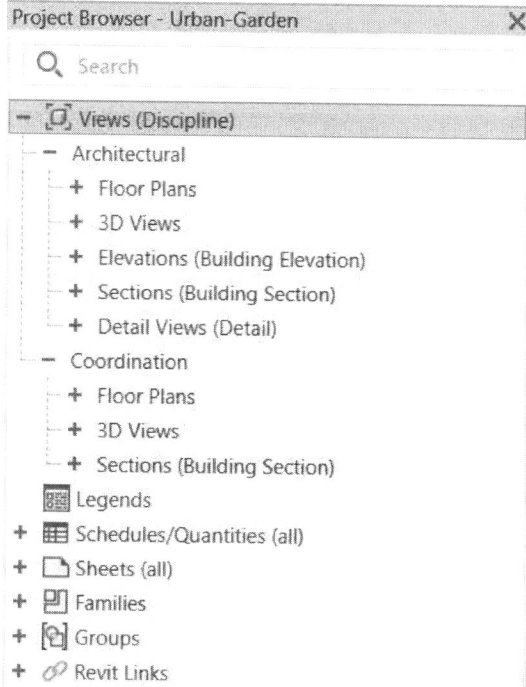

Figure 1–39

10. View Control Bar

The View Control Bar (shown in Figure 1–40) displays at the bottom of each view window. It controls aspects of that view, such as the scale and detail level. It also includes tools that display parts of the view and hide or isolate elements in the view.

Figure 1–40

- The number of options in the View Control Bar change when you are in a 3D view, as shown in Figure 1–41.

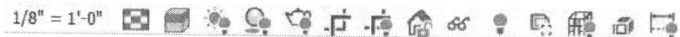

Figure 1–41

Tool	Tooltip	Description
1/8" = 1'-0"	View Scale	Set the scale of individual views.
	Detail Level	Set the detail level of a view.
	Visual Style	Various graphic style representations.
	Sun Path On/Off	Controls the visibility of the sun's path.
	Shadows On/Off	Controls elements' shadow visibility in a view.
	Show/Hide Rendering Dialog	Available in 3D only. Shows or hides the rendering dialog box.
	Crop View	Define the crop boundaries for a view.
	Show/Hide Crop Region	Display the crop region in a view.
	Unlocked/Locked 3D Views	Lock a 3D view's orientation.
	Temporary Hide/Isolate	Temporarily isolate/hide by category or element (view specific).
	Reveal Hidden Elements	View hidden elements or unhide them in the active view.
	Worksharing Display	Available when worksharing is enabled. Controls display settings.
	Temporary View Properties	Enable, apply or restore view properties and display recent templates and apply them.
	Show or Hide the Analytical Model	Only used for Structural and MEP to display the analytical information.
	Highlight Displacement Sets	Also known as exploded views.
	Reveal Constraints	Temporarily view the dimension and alignment constraints in the active view.

11. Status Bar

The left-hand side of the Status Bar provides information about the current process, such as the next step for a command, as shown in Figure 1–42.

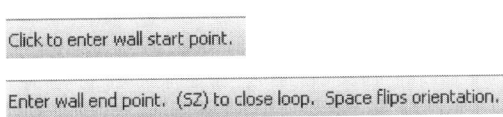

Figure 1–42

The right-hand side of the Status Bar provides selection options that enable you to control how the software selects specific elements in a project by toggling selection options on and off. When a selection option is toggled off, the icon will have a red X on it, as shown in Figure 1–43.

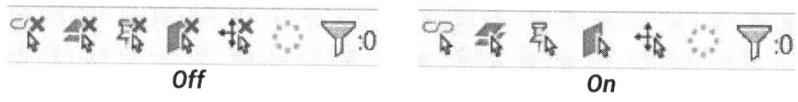

Figure 1–43

- **Select links:** When this option is toggled on, you can select linked CAD drawings or Revit models. When it is toggled off, you cannot select them when using **Modify** or **Move**.

- **Select underlay elements:** When this option is toggled on, you can select underlay elements. When it is toggled off, you cannot select them when using **Modify** or **Move**.

- **Select pinned elements:** When this option is toggled on, you can select pinned elements. When it is toggled off, you cannot select them when using **Modify** or **Move**.

- **Select elements by face:** When this option is toggled on, you can select elements (such as the floors or walls in an elevation) by selecting the interior face or selecting an edge. When it is toggled off, you can only select elements by selecting an edge.

- **Drag elements on selection:** When this option is toggled on, you can hover over an element, select it, and drag it to a new location. When it is toggled off, the Crossing or Box select mode starts when you press and drag, even if you are on top of an element. Once elements have been selected, they can still be dragged to a new location.

You can also set the selection option from the ribbon. Expand the Select panel's title and select the option(s), as shown in Figure 1–44.

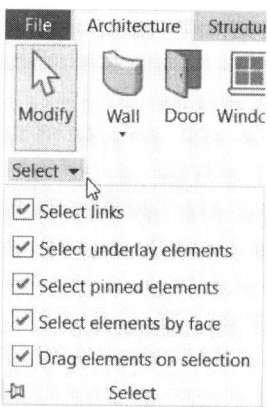

Figure 1–44

Other options in the Status Bar are related to worksets and design options (advanced tools).

Introduction to Revit

💡 Hint: Shortcut Menus

Shortcut menus help you to work smoothly and efficiently by enabling you to quickly access required commands. These menus provide access to basic viewing commands, recently used commands, and the available browsers, as shown in Figure 1–45. Additional options vary depending on the element or command that you are using.

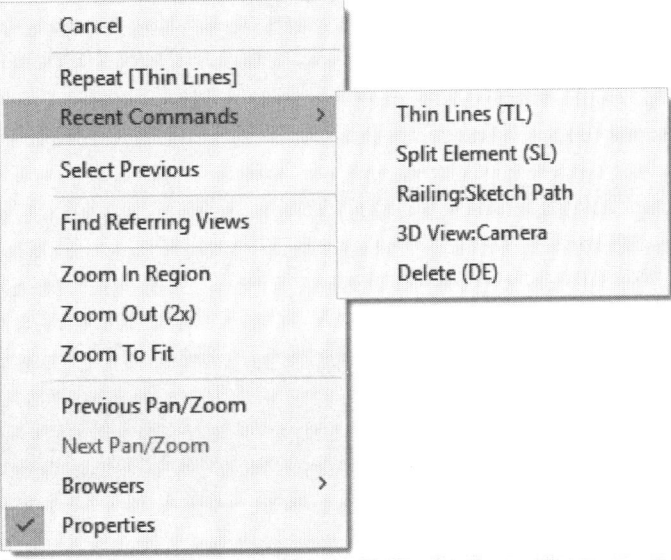

Figure 1–45

Change Interface to Dark Mode

You can change Revit's entire interface to a dark mode or you can change just the drawing area to dark mode. You can also set the interface to dark mode, then click ☀ (Canvas Theme) to change the drawing area back to white.

How To: Change the Entire Interface to Dark Mode

1. From the *File* tab, click **Options**.
2. In the Options dialog box, click on the *Color* tab.
3. Expand *UI active theme* and select **Dark**, as shown in Figure 1–46.

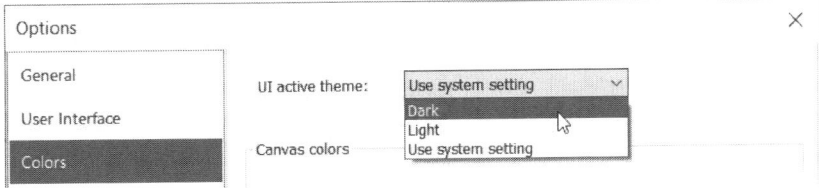

Figure 1–46

4. The entire interface is now in dark mode.

- To return to the interface to the default setting, in the Options dialog box>*Colors* tab, expand the UI active theme drop-down list and select **Use system setting**.

How To: Change the Drawing Area to Dark Mode

1. In the *View* tab>Windows panel, click ☀ (Canvas Theme).
2. Just the drawing area will change to dark mode, as shown in Figure 1–47.
   - If the interface is set to dark mode, you can use this to set the drawing area to display a light background.

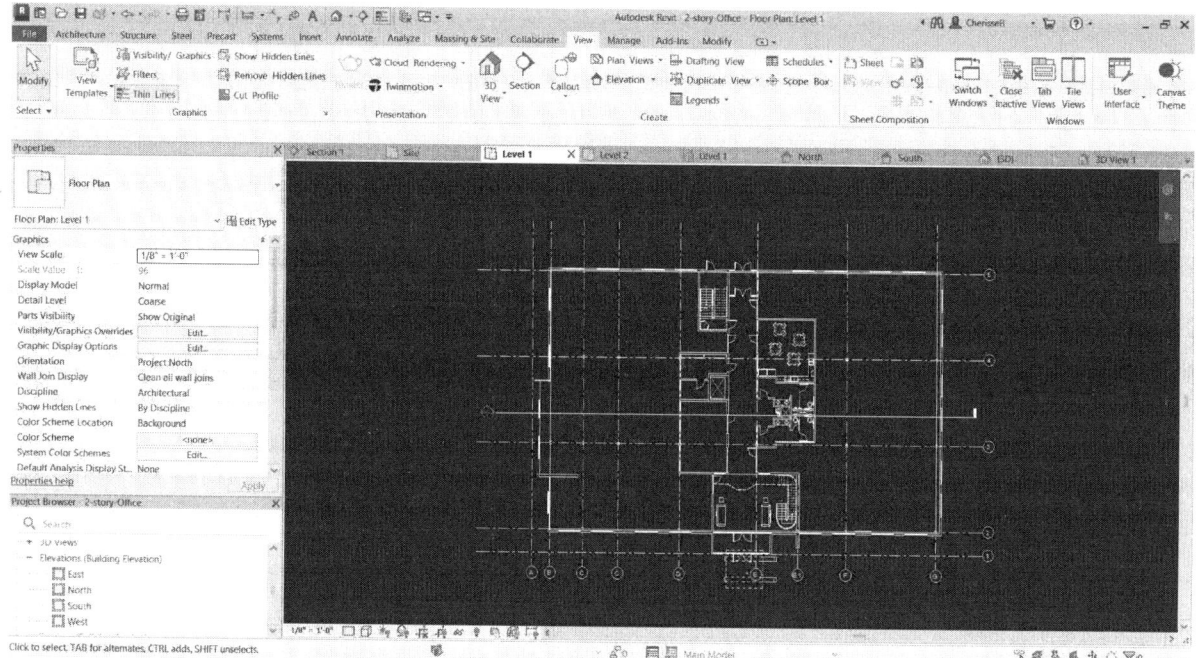

Figure 1–47

1.3 Opening and Saving Projects

File operations to open existing files, create new files from a template, and save files in Revit are found in the *File* tab, as shown in Figure 1–48.

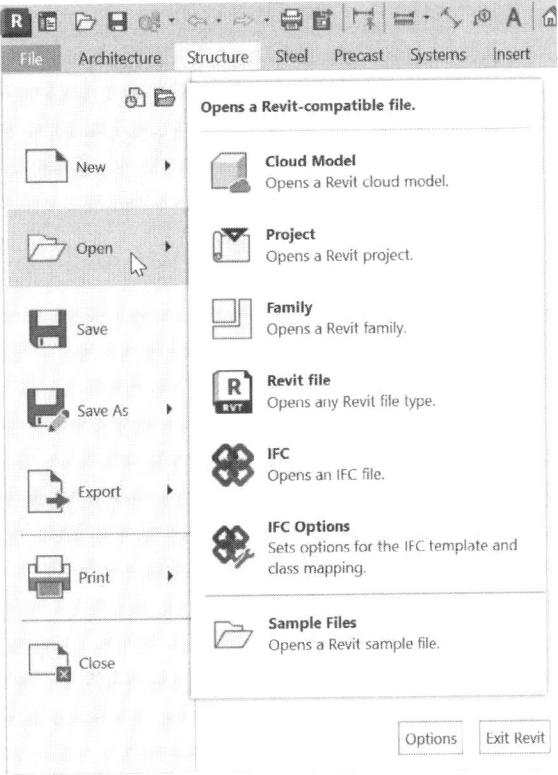

Figure 1–48

There are three main file formats:

- **Project files (.rvt):** These are where you do the majority of your work in the building model by adding elements, creating views, annotating views, and setting up printable sheets. They are initially based on template files.

- **Family files (.rfa):** These are separate components that can be inserted in a project. They include elements that can stand alone (e.g., a table or piece of mechanical equipment) or are items that are hosted in other elements (e.g., a door in a wall or a light fixture in a ceiling). Title block and annotation symbol files are special types of family files.

- **Template files (.rte and .rft):** These are the base files for any new project or family. Project templates (**.rte**) hold standard information and settings for creating new project files. The software includes several templates for various types of projects. You can also create custom templates. Family templates (**.rft**) include base information for creating families. Template files are usually saved as a new file.

Opening Projects

To open an existing project, click **Open** from the Home screen, or in the Quick Access Toolbar or *File* tab, click (Open). You can also press <Ctrl>+<O>. The Open dialog box opens, and you can navigate to the required folder and select a project file. An example of the Open dialog box is shown in Figure 1–49.

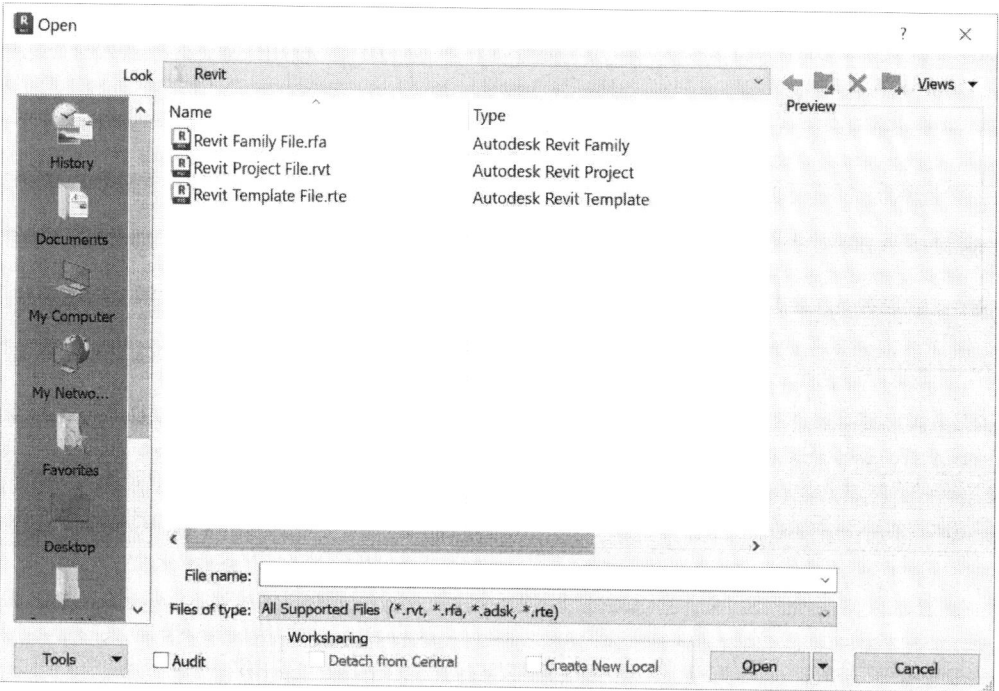

Figure 1–49

- The software release version of the currently selected project displays below the preview. Do not open a drawing that should remain in an earlier version, as you cannot save back to previous versions.

  Note: It is important that everyone working on a project uses the same software version (e.g., 2024) and is on the same updated version (e.g., 2024.1). While your software may be able to open files created in its earlier versions, it will not be able to open files created in versions newer than the one you are using currently as Revit is not backwards compatible. For example, if you are working in Revit 2023, you cannot open a model created in Revit 2024.

- When you open a file created in an earlier version, the Model Upgrade dialog box indicates the release of a file and the release to which it will be upgraded. If needed, you can cancel the upgrade before it completes.

- When you encounter an Unresolved References dialog box upon opening a project, you have two options. You can either click **Ignore and Continue opening the project** to proceed with opening the project, or click **Open Manage Links to correct the problem** to resolve the issue. The details of the Manage Links dialog box will be explained in the next chapter.

Saving Projects

It is important to save your projects frequently. In the Quick Access Toolbar or *File* tab, click (Save), or press <Ctrl>+<S> to save your project. If the project has not yet been saved, the Save As dialog box opens, where you can specify a file location and name.

- To save an existing project with a new name, in the *File* tab, expand (Save As) and click (Project).

- If you have not saved in a certain amount of time, the software will notify you with the Project Not Saved Recently alert box, as shown in Figure 1–50. Select **Save the project**. If you want to set reminder intervals or not save at this time, select one of the other two options shown in Figure 1–50.

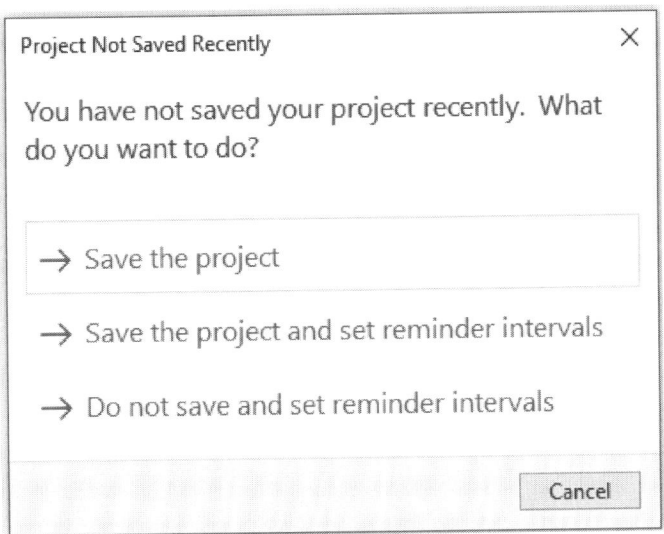

Figure 1–50

- You can set the *Save reminder interval* to **15** or **30 minutes**, **One**, **Two**, or **Four hours**, or to have **No reminders** display. In the *File* tab, click **Options** to open the Options dialog box. Select **General** and set the interval, as shown in Figure 1–51.

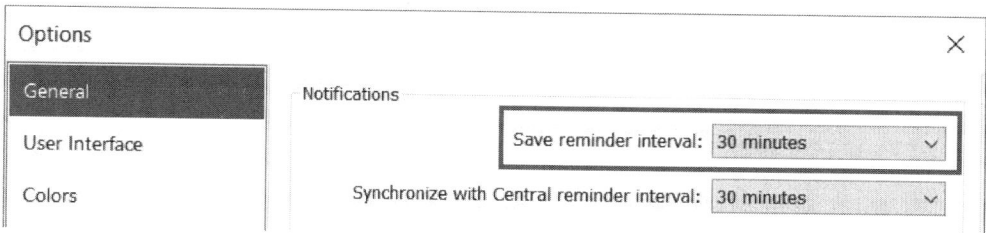

Figure 1–51

Saving Backup Copies

By default, the software saves a backup copy of a project file when you save the project. Backup copies are numbered incrementally (e.g., **My Project.0001.rvt**, **My Project.0002.rvt**, etc.) and are saved in the same folder as the original file. In the Save As dialog box, click **Options…** to control how many backup copies are saved. The default number is three backups. If you exceed this number, the software deletes the oldest backup file.

1.4 Viewing Commands

Viewing commands are crucial to working efficiently in most drawing and modeling programs and Revit is no exception. Once in a view, you can use the Zoom controls to navigate in it. You can zoom in and out and pan in any view. There are also special tools for viewing in 3D.

Zooming and Panning

Use the mouse wheel (shown in Figure 1–52) as the main method of zooming and panning around the models.

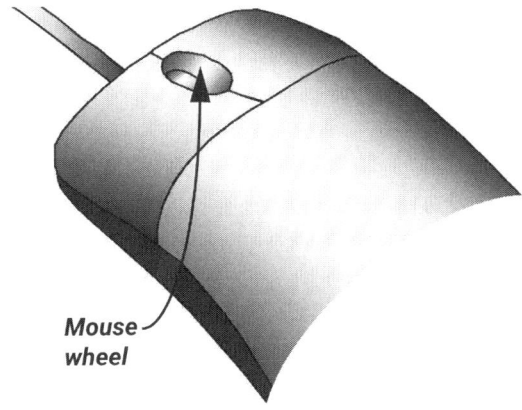

Figure 1–52

- Scroll the wheel on the mouse up to zoom in and down to zoom out.
- Hold the wheel and move the mouse to pan.
- Double-click on the wheel to zoom to the extents of the view.
- In a 3D view, hold <Shift> and the mouse wheel and move the mouse to orbit around the model.

When you save a model and exit the software, the pan and zoom location of each view is remembered. This is especially important for complex models.

Additional Zoom Controls

A number of additional zoom methods enable you to control the screen display. **Zoom** and **Pan** can be performed at any time while using other commands.

- You can access the **Zoom** commands in the Navigation Bar in the upper right corner of the view (as shown in Figure 1–53). You can also access them from most shortcut menus and by typing the shortcut commands.

    Note: (2D Wheel) provides cursor-specific access to **Zoom** and **Pan**.

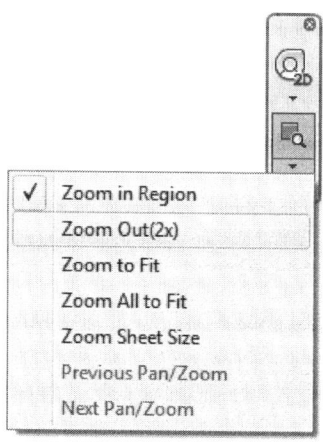

Figure 1–53

Zoom Commands

	Zoom In Region (ZR)	Zooms in to a region that you define. Drag the cursor or select two points to define the rectangular area you want to zoom in to. This is the default command.
	Zoom Out(2x) (ZO)	Zooms out to half the current magnification around the center of the elements.
	Zoom to Fit (ZF or ZE)	Zooms out so that the entire contents of the project only display on the screen in the current view.
	Zoom All to Fit (ZA)	Zooms out so that the entire contents of the project display on the screen in all open views.
	Zoom Sheet Size (ZS)	Zooms in or out in relation to the sheet size.
N/A	**Previous Pan/Zoom (ZP)**	Steps back one **Zoom** command.
N/A	**Next Pan/Zoom**	Steps forward one **Zoom** command if you have done a **Previous Pan/Zoom**.

Viewing in 3D

Even if you started a project entirely in plan views, you can quickly create 3D views of the model, as shown in Figure 1–54. There are two types of 3D views: isometric views created by the **Default 3D View** command, and perspective and orthographic 3D views created by the **Camera** command.

Figure 1–54

Working in 3D views helps you visualize the project and position some of the elements correctly. You can create and modify elements in both isometric and perspective 3D views, just as you can in plan views.

- Once you have created a 3D view, you can save it and easily return to it.

- Perspective 3D views are visual representations of what the model would look like if you were standing in the model.

- Orthographic 3D views can have a scale applied to them so that the entire model's components are at the same size no matter where the camera is positioned or its distance from the model.

How To: Create and Save a 3D Isometric View

1. In the Quick Access Toolbar or *View* tab>Create panel, click (Default 3D View). The default 3D southeast isometric view opens, as shown in Figure 1–55.

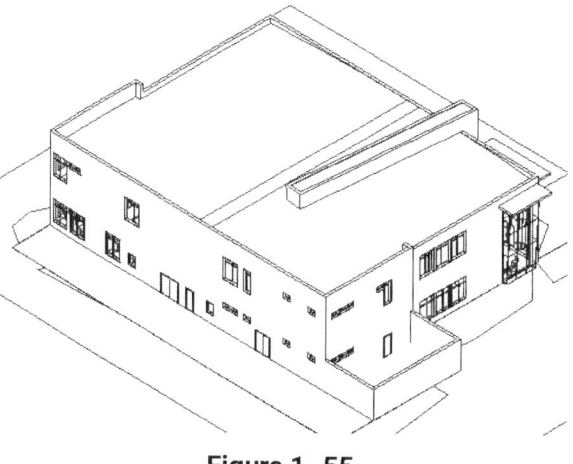

Figure 1–55

Note: You can spin the view to a different angle using the mouse wheel or the middle button of a three-button mouse. Hold <Shift> as you press the wheel or middle button and drag the cursor.

2. Modify the view to display the building from other directions.
3. In the Project Browser, slowly click twice on the {3D} view or right-click on the {3D} view and select **Rename...**. The name is placed in a text box with the original name highlighted, as shown in Figure 1–56.

Figure 1–56

4. Type a new name in the text box, as shown in Figure 1–57.

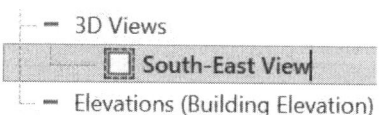

Figure 1–57

Note: All types of views can be renamed.

- When changes to the default 3D view are saved and you start another default 3D view, it displays the southeast isometric view once again. If you modified the default 3D view but did not save it to a new name, the **Default 3D View** command opens the view in the last orientation you specified.

How To: Create a Perspective 3D View

1. Switch to a Floor Plan view.
2. In the Quick Access Toolbar or *View* tab>Create panel, expand (Default 3D View) and click (Camera).
3. In the Options Bar, verify **Perspective** is checked and set the *Scale*, *Offset*, and *From* which level the camera will be placed, as shown in Figure 1–58.

Figure 1–58

4. Place the camera on the view.
5. Point the camera in the direction in which you want it to shoot by placing the target on the view, as shown in Figure 1–59.

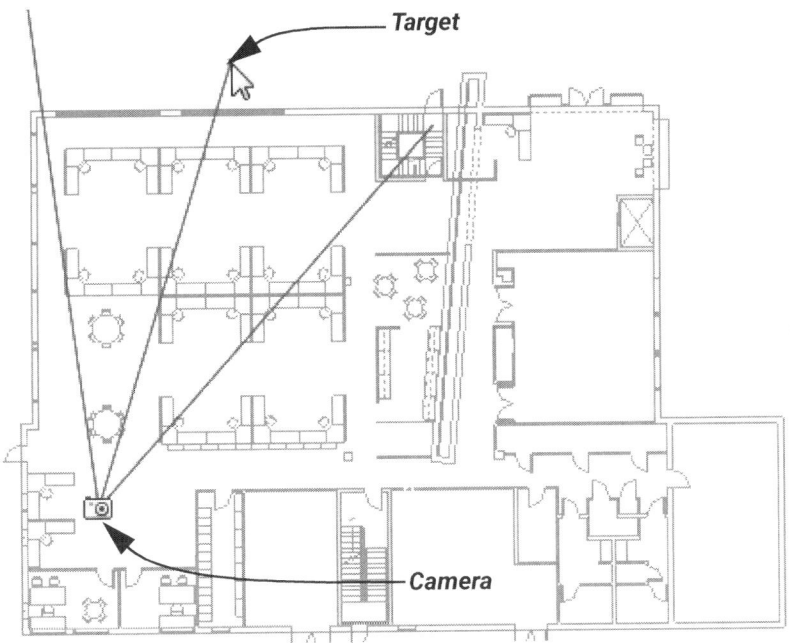

Figure 1–59

A new view is displayed, as shown in Figure 1–60.

Figure 1–60

- You can use the round controls to modify the display size of the view and press <Shift> + the mouse wheel to change the view.

How To: Create an Orthographic 3D View

1. Switch to a floor plan view.
2. In the Quick Access Toolbar or *View* tab>Create panel, expand (Default 3D View) and click (Camera).
3. In the Options Bar, uncheck **Perspective** and set the *Scale*, *Offset*, and *From* which level.
4. Place the camera on the view.

5. Point the camera in the direction in which you want it to shoot by placing the target on the view, as shown in Figure 1–61.

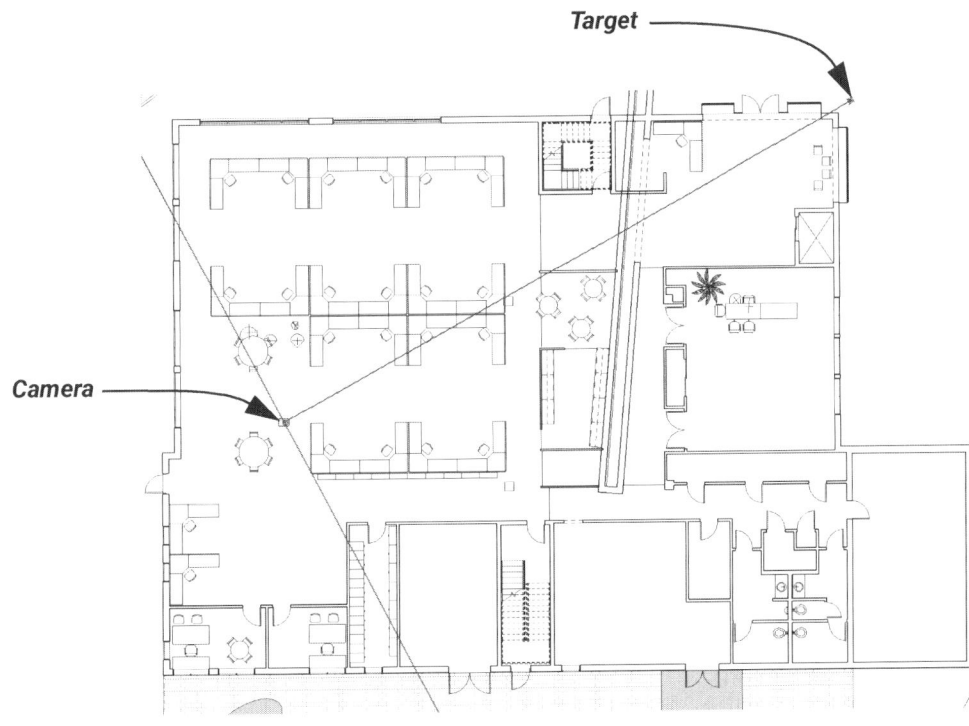

Figure 1–61

- A new view is displayed, as shown in Figure 1–62. If needed, the *Eye Elevation* and *Target Elevation* can be adjusted in Properties.

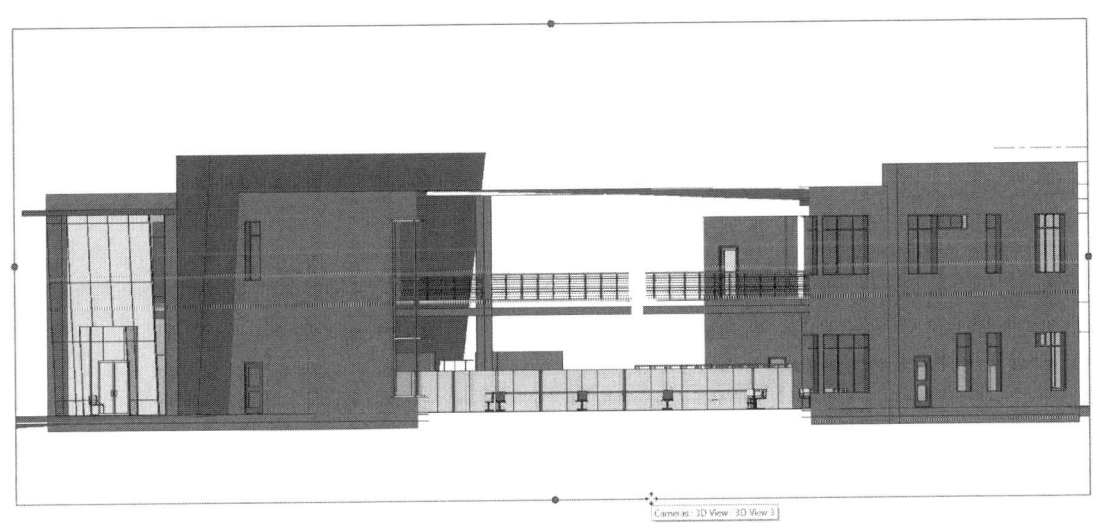

Figure 1–62

6. In Properties, scroll down and adjust the *Eye Elevation* and *Target Elevation* as needed.

How To: Modify Camera 3D Views

1. In a plan view, select the camera or target icon and drag it within the view to reposition the placement.
2. In Properties, scroll down and adjust the *Eye Elevation* and *Target Elevation* as needed.

- To display the camera and camera controls in a plan view, select the camera's crop boundary in the perspective view, then switch back to the plan view.

    - Alternatively, while in a plan view, you can right-click on the perspective 3D view in the Project Browser and select **Show Camera**, as shown in Figure 1–63. The camera and camera crop boundaries will display.

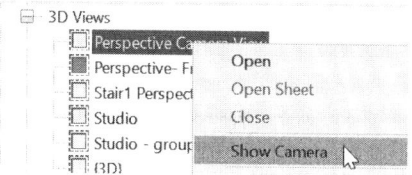

Figure 1–63

- For perspective 3D views, if the view becomes distorted, reset the target so that it is centered in the boundary of the view (called the crop region). In the *Modify | Cameras* tab> Camera panel, click (Reset Target).

ViewCube

The ViewCube provides visual clues as to where you are in a 3D view. It helps you move around the model with quick access to specific views (such as top, front, and right), as well as corner and directional views, as shown in Figure 1–64.

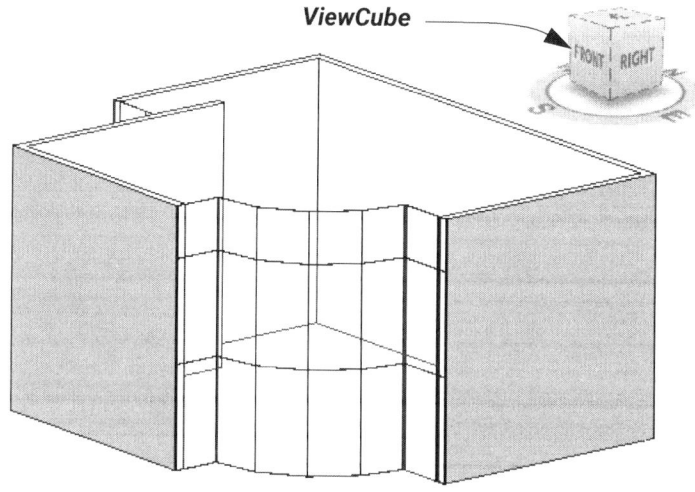

Figure 1–64

Move the cursor over any face of the ViewCube to highlight it. Once a face is highlighted, you can select it to reorient the model. You can also click and drag on the ViewCube to orbit the box, which rotates the model.

- ⌂ (Home) displays when you roll the cursor over the ViewCube. Click it to return to the view defined as **Home**. To change the Home view, set the view as you want it, right-click on the ViewCube, and select **Set Current View as Home**.
- The ViewCube is available in isometric and perspective views.

You can switch between Perspective and Isometric mode by right-clicking on the ViewCube (as shown on the left in Figure 1–65) or clicking on ▽ (ViewCube contextual menu) to the lower right of the ViewCube (as shown on the right in Figure 1–65) and selecting **Perspective** or **Orthographic**.

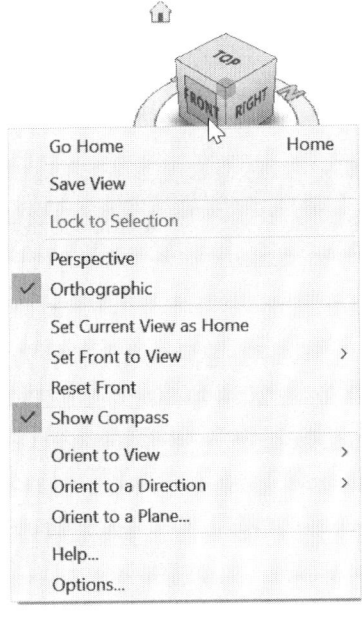   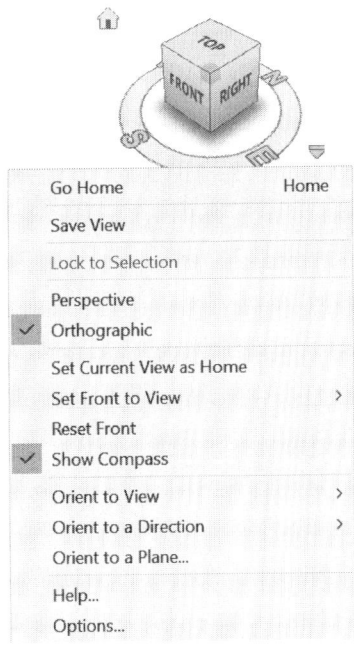

Right-click on ViewCube   *Context menu on ViewCube*

Figure 1–65

You can create 3D views that are oriented to a specific view. For more information, refer to the *Working with Views* chapter.

Visual Styles

Any view can have a visual style applied. The **Visual Style** options found in the View Control Bar (shown in Figure 1–66) specify the shading of the building model. These options apply to plan, elevation, section, and 3D views.

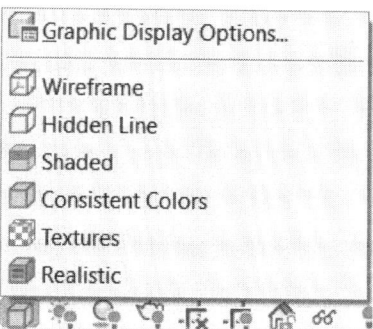

Figure 1–66

- (Wireframe) displays the lines and edges that make up elements, but hides the surfaces. This can be useful when you are dealing with complex intersections.

- (Hidden Line) displays the lines, edges, and surfaces of the elements, but it does not display any colors. This is the most common visual style to use while working on a design.

- (Shaded) and (Consistent Colors) give you a sense of the materials, including transparent glass. An example showing an exterior view using Consistent Colors is shown in Figure 1–67. Landscape components will display as gray outlines of the objects until the Realistic visual style is used.

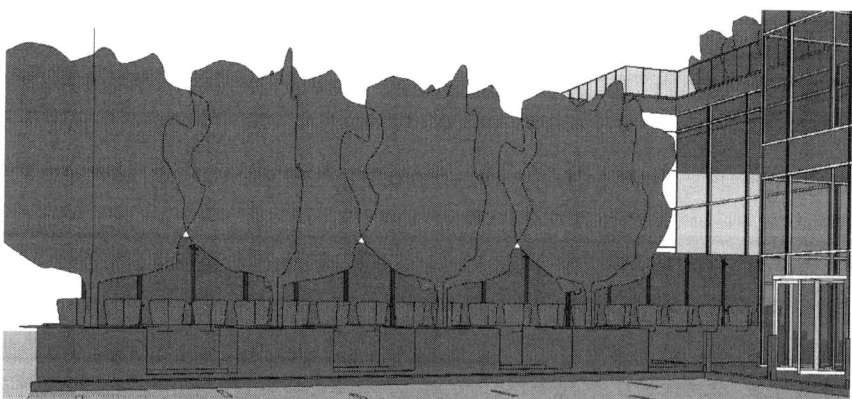

Figure 1–67

- ◩ (Textures) displays the view using Consistent Colors, but if a component has a material applied to it, the Textures visual style displays the material's texture as well. For example, Figure 1–68 appears as if it is using Consistent Colors but it is also showing the texture of the brick material on the planters.

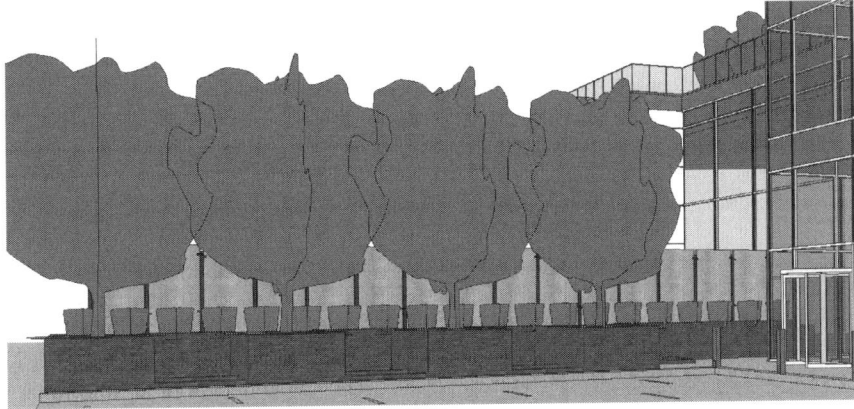

Figure 1–68

- ▣ (Realistic) displays artificial lights in addition to the material's appearance (if material has been applied to a component), as shown in Figure 1–69. It takes a lot of computer power to execute this visual style, so it is better to use the other visual styles most of the time as you are working.

Figure 1–69

Select and Identify Elements in a Project

When selecting an element in the drawing area, the element highlights (as shown on the left in Figure 1–70) and information about the element displays in Properties, helping you further identify the element. When you position the cursor over or near an element in the drawing area (as shown on the right in Figure 1–70), the outline of the element is highlighted with a thicker line weight and a tooltip appears. Additionally, the Status Bar at the bottom of the Revit window displays a description of the element.

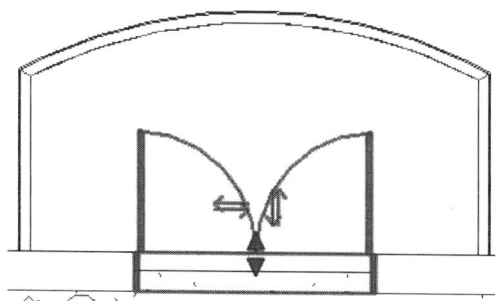 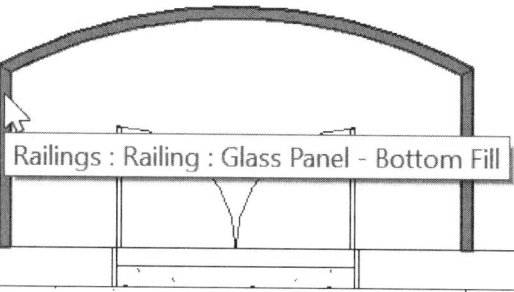

Figure 1–70

To deselect an element, you can do one of the following:

- In any tab on the ribbon, click (Modify).
- Type the shortcut **MD**.
- Click in an empty area in the drawing area to clear the selection.
- Press <Esc> once to revert to **Modify**.
- Right-click and select **Cancel...** once or twice.
- Select another element.

Practice 1a
Open and Review a Project

Practice Objectives

- Navigate the graphic user interface.
- Manipulate 2D and 3D views by zooming and panning.
- Create 3D isometric and perspective views.
- Set the visual style of a view.

In this practice, you will open a project file and view each of the various areas in the interface. You will investigate elements, commands, and their options. You will also open views through the Project Browser and view the model in 3D, as shown in Figure 1–71.

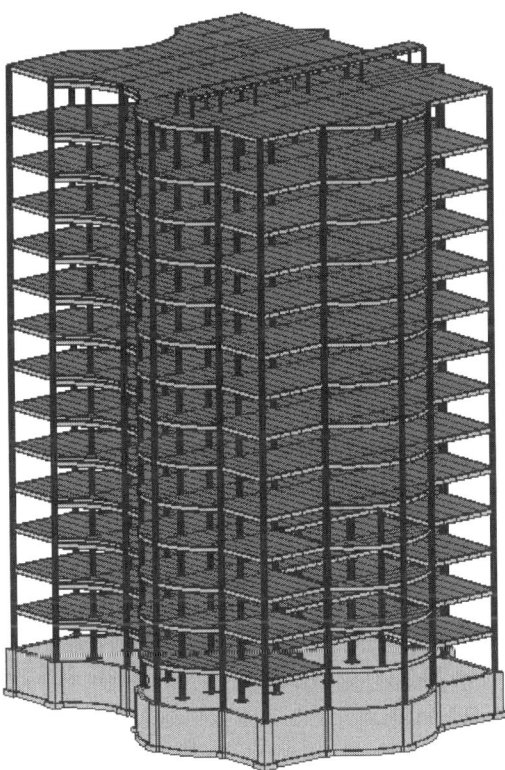

Figure 1–71

- This is a version of the main project you will work on throughout this guide.

Task 1: Explore the interface.

1. In the *File* tab, expand 📂 (Open) and click 📄 (Project).

   - If you are on the Home page, click **Open...** in the *MODELS* area of the sidebar. In the Open dialog box, navigate to the practice files folder and select **Structural-Suite.rvt**.

2. Click **Open**. The 3D view of the building opens in the view window.

   Note: If the Project Browser and Properties palette are docked over each other, use the Project Browser tab at the bottom to display it.

3. In the Project Browser, double-click on the **Structural Plans: 00 GROUND FLOOR** view. It opens a plan with the *Visual Style* set to **Wireframe** so that the footings and foundation walls display, although there is a slab over them.

4. In the View Control Bar, change the *Visual Style* to **Hidden Line**. The lines that are hidden in the view display as dashed lines, as shown in Figure 1-72.

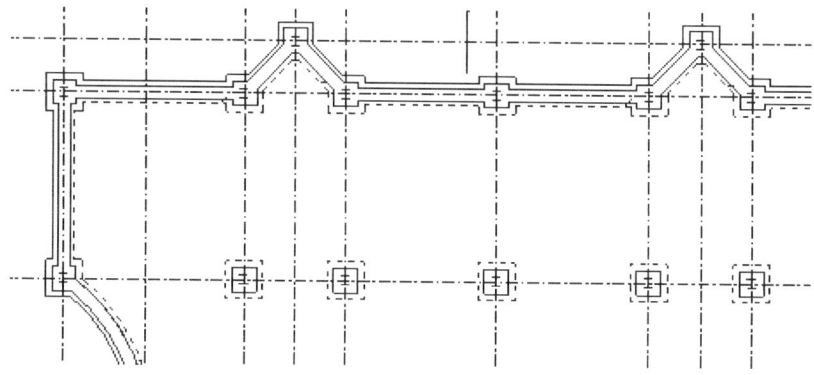

Figure 1-72

5. In the Project Browser, double-click on the **Structural Plans: 00 T.O. FOOTING** view. The strip footings and spread footings display as continuous lines because they are not obscured by a slab, as shown in Figure 1-73.

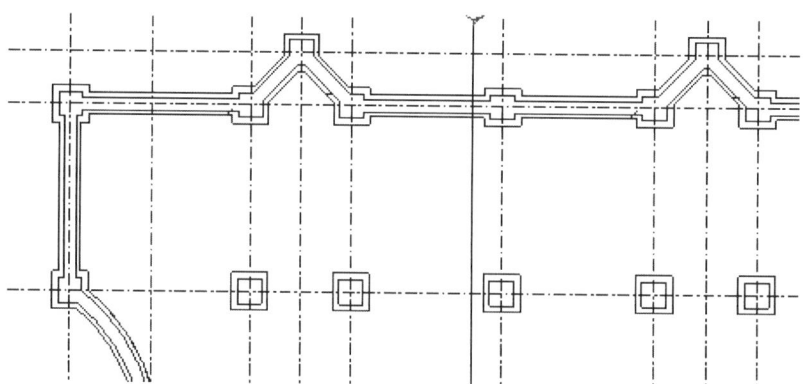

Figure 1-73

6. Zoom in on one corner of the building. The foundation walls are in-filled with the appropriate concrete hatch, as shown in Figure 1–74.

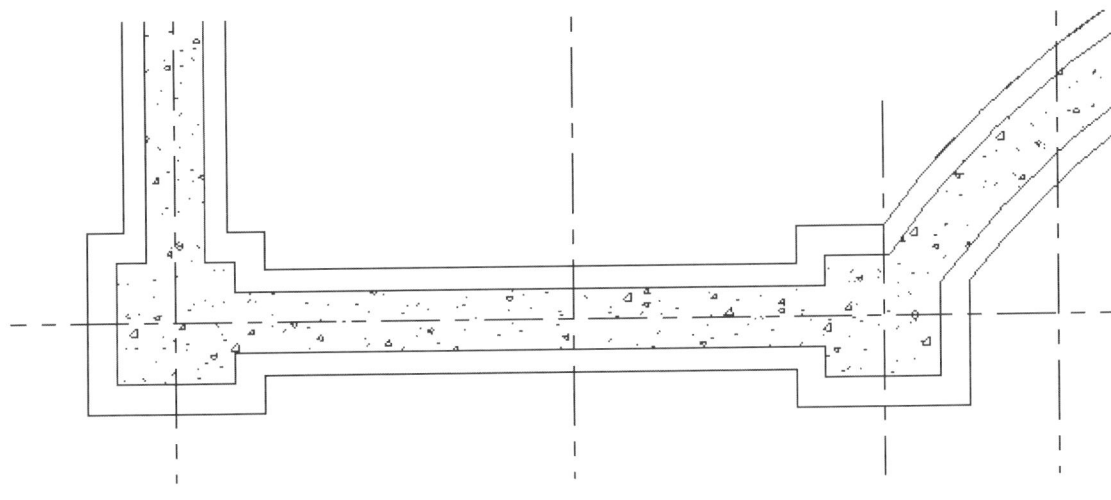

Figure 1–74

7. Double-click the mouse wheel or type **ZE** to zoom to the extents of the view. (**ZA** zooms to the extents of all of the opened view windows.) Find the section marker that extends vertically along the model, as shown in Figure 1–75.

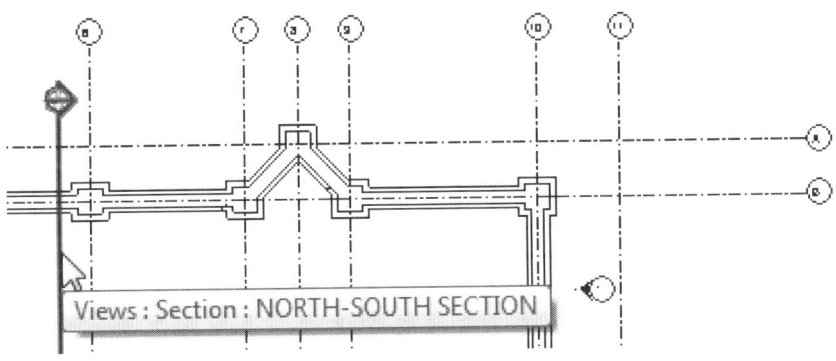

Figure 1–75

8. Double-click on the section head to open the **NORTH-SOUTH SECTION** view.
9. In the Project Browser, navigate to the *Sections (Building Section)* category. The **NORTH-SOUTH SECTION** view name is bold. You can navigate through your model by double-clicking on the element in the Project Browser or by using the graphical view elements in the model.

10. In the section view, zoom in on the area in which the callout has been placed, as shown in Figure 1–76. Double-click on the callout-head to open the **TYPICAL EDGE DETAIL** view.

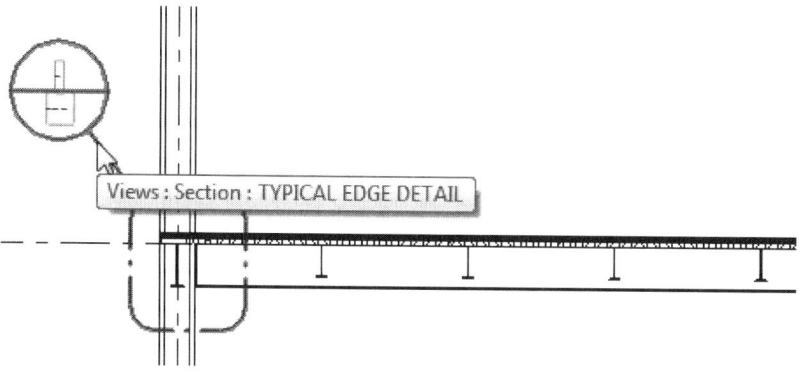

Figure 1–76

11. Toggle on and off (Thin Lines) to see the different line weights.
12. In the **TYPICAL EDGE DETAIL** view, select the floor, as shown in Figure 1–77.

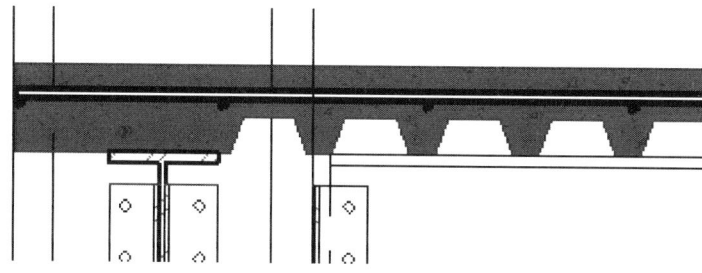

Figure 1–77

13. This is a full 3D floor element. You can edit it using the standard modify tools and the concrete floor-specific tools found in the *Modify | Floors* contextual tab, as shown in Figure 1–78.

Figure 1–78

14. The Properties palette displays the instance parameters for the element, as shown in Figure 1–79.

    Note: Any changes made here are applied to the selected element only.

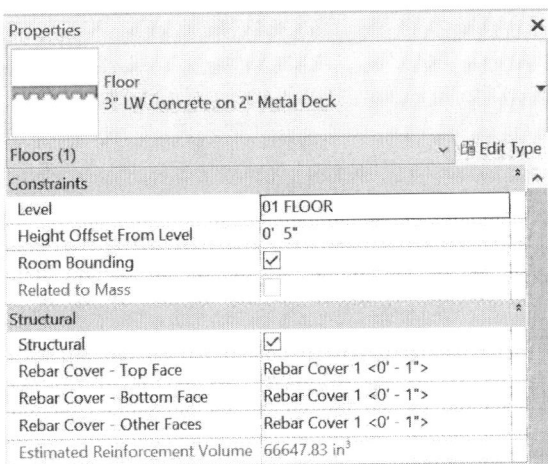

Figure 1–79

15. In Properties, click (Edit Type) to access the *Type Parameters* in the Type Properties dialog box, as shown in Figure 1–80.

    Note: Any changes made to the element here are applied to all of its other instances in the project.

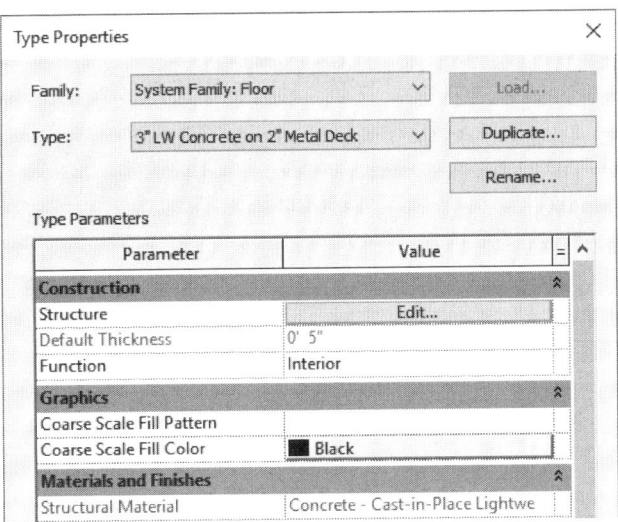

Figure 1–80

16. Click **Cancel** to close the Type Properties dialog box.

17. End the command using one of the following methods:

    - In any tab on the ribbon, click (Modify).
    - Press <Esc> once or twice to revert to **Modify**.
    - Right-click and select **Cancel...** once or twice.
    - Start another command.

18. Select one of the bolted connections. This is a detail component (2D element). The *Modify | Detail Items* contextual tab displays the modifying options specific to this element, as shown in Figure 1–81.

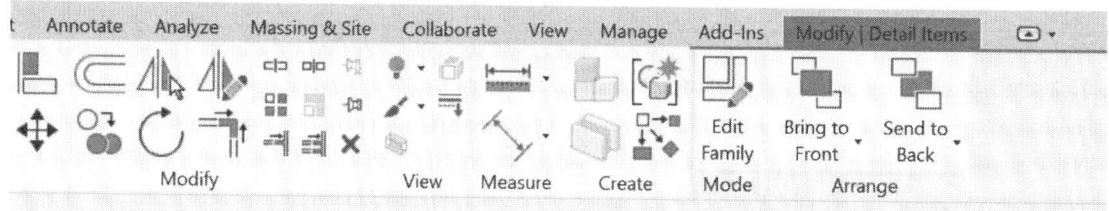

Figure 1–81

19. Click (Modify).

Task 2: Work with multiple views and 3D views.

1. At the top of the view, click each tab to switch between the open views.

2. In the *View* tab>Windows panel, click (Tile Views). All of the open views are tiled. Type **ZA** (for Zoom All) to zoom out to the extents of each view, as shown in Figure 1–82.

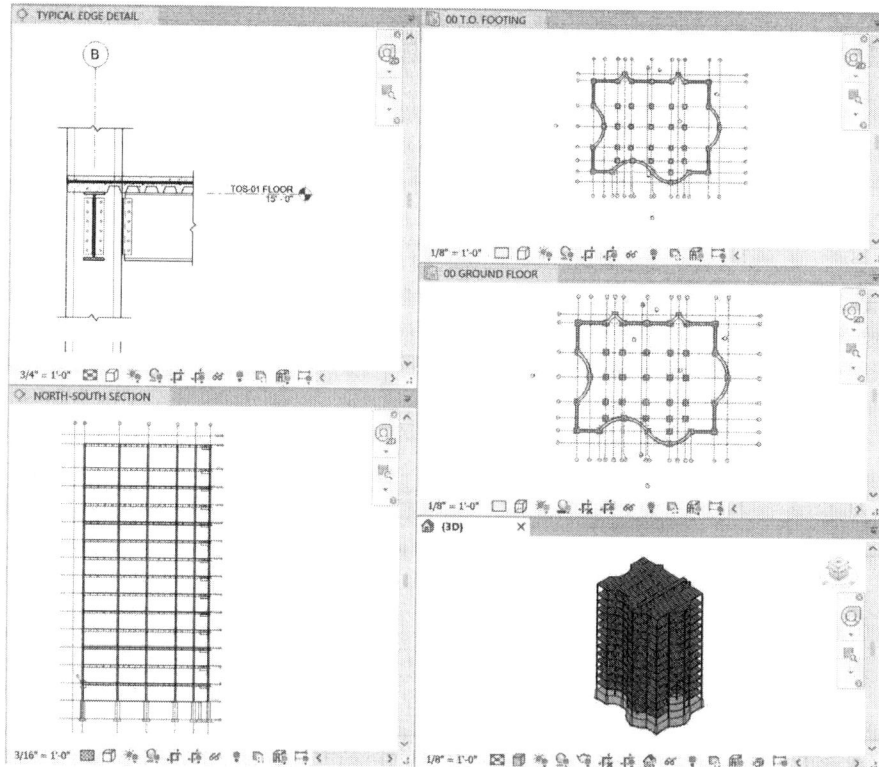

Figure 1–82

3. Click inside the 3D view to make it active.

4. In the *View* tab>Windows panel, click ▦ (Tab Views). The views return to the tabs and the 3D view is first in the group.

5. In the Quick Access Toolbar, click ▦ (Close Inactive Views) so that only the current window remains open.

6. Using the mouse wheel, zoom in on the building.

7. Press and hold <Shift> and then press and hold the wheel on the mouse. Move the mouse to dynamically view the 3D model. You can also navigate in 3D using the ViewCube in the upper-right corner of the view.

8. Expand the *File* tab and click ▦ (Close) to exit the project. Do not save changes.

End of practice

Chapter Review Questions

1. When you create a project in Revit, do you work in 3D or 2D?
   a. You work in 2D in plan views and in 3D in non-plan views.
   b. You work in 3D almost all of the time, even when you are using what looks like a flat view.
   c. You work in 2D or 3D depending on how you toggle the 2D/3D control.
   d. You work in 2D in plan and section views and in 3D in isometric views.

2. What is the purpose of the Project Browser?
   a. It enables you to browse through the building project, similar to a walk through.
   b. It is the interface for managing all of the files that are required to create the complete architectural model of the building.
   c. It manages multiple Revit projects as an alternative to using Windows Explorer.
   d. It is used to access and manage the views of the project.

3. Where do you change the visual style?
   a. Ribbon
   b. View Control Bar
   c. Options Bar
   d. Properties

4. What is the difference between Type Properties and Properties?
   a. Properties stores parameters that apply to the selected individual element(s). Type Properties stores parameters that impact every element of the same type in the project.
   b. Properties stores the location parameters of an element. Type Properties stores the size and identity parameters of an element.
   c. Properties only stores parameters of the view. Type Properties stores parameters of model components.

5. When you start a new project, how do you specify the base information in the new file?
   a. Transfer the base information from an existing project.
   b. Select the right template for the task.
   c. Revit automatically extracts the base information from imported or linked file(s).

6. What is the main difference between a view made using 🏠 (Default 3D View) and a view made using 📷 (Camera)?
   a. Use Default **3D View** for exterior views and **Camera** for interiors.
   b. **Default 3D View** creates a static image and a **Camera** view is live and always updated.
   c. **Default 3D View** is isometric and a **Camera** view is perspective.
   d. **Default 3D View** is used for the overall building and a **Camera** view is used for looking in tight spaces.

Command Summary

Button	Command	Location
General Tools		
	Home	• **Quick Access Toolbar** • **Shortcut:** <Ctrl>+<D>
	Modify	• **Ribbon:** All tabs>Select panel • **Shortcut:** MD
	New	• *File* tab • **Shortcut:** <Ctrl>+<N>
	Open	• **Quick Access Toolbar** • *File* tab • **Shortcut:** <Ctrl>+<O>
	Open Documents	• *File* tab
	Properties	• **Ribbon:** *Modify* tab>Properties panel • **Shortcut:** PP
	Recent Documents	• *File* tab
	Save	• **Quick Access Toolbar** • *File* tab • **Shortcut:** <Ctrl>+<S>
	Type Properties	• **Ribbon:** *Modify* tab>Properties panel • **Properties**>Edit Type
Select Tools		
	Drag elements on selection	• **Ribbon:** All tabs>expanded Select panel • **Status Bar**
	Filter	• **Ribbon:** *Modify	Multi-Select* tab>Filter panel • **Status Bar**
	Select Elements By Face	• **Ribbon:** All tabs>expanded Select panel • **Status Bar**
	Select Links	• **Ribbon:** All tabs>expanded Select panel • **Status Bar**
	Select Pinned Elements	• **Ribbon:** All tabs>expanded Select panel • **Status Bar**

Button	Command	Location
	Select Underlay Elements	• **Ribbon:** All tabs>expanded Select panel • **Status Bar**
Viewing Tools		
	Camera	• **Quick Access Toolbar**, expand Default 3D View • **Ribbon:** *View* tab>Create panel, expand Default 3D View
	Close Inactive Views	• **Quick Access Toolbar** • **Ribbon:** *View* tab>Windows panel
	Default 3D View	• **Quick Access Toolbar** • **Ribbon:** *View* tab>Create panel
N/A	Next Pan/Zoom	• **Navigation Bar** • **Shortcut Menu**
N/A	Previous Pan/Zoom	• **Navigation Bar** • **Shortcut Menu** • **Shortcut:** ZP
	Shadows On/Off	• **View Control Bar**
	Show Rendering Dialog/ Render	• **View Control Bar** • **Ribbon:** *View* tab>Graphics panel • **Shortcut:** RR
	Switch Windows	• **Quick Access Toolbar** • **Ribbon:** *View* tab>Windows panel
	Tab Views	• **Ribbon:** *View* tab>Windows panel • **Shortcut:** TW
	Tile Views	• **Ribbon:** *View* tab>Windows panel • **Shortcut:** WT
	ViewCube Home	• **ViewCube**
	Zoom All to Fit	• **Navigation Bar** • **Shortcut:** ZA
	Zoom in Region	• **Navigation Bar** • **Shortcut Menu** • **Shortcut:** ZR
	Zoom Out (2x)	• **Navigation Bar** • **Shortcut Menu** • **Shortcut:** ZO

Button	Command	Location
	Zoom Sheet Size	• **Navigation Bar** • **Shortcut:** ZS
	Zoom to Fit	• **Navigation Bar** • **Shortcut Menu** • **Shortcut:** ZF, ZE
Visual Styles		
	Consistent Colors	• **View Control Bar**
	Hidden Line	• **View Control Bar** • **Shortcut:** HL
	Realistic	• **View Control Bar**
	Shaded	• **View Control Bar** • **Shortcut:** SD
	Textures	• **View Control Bar**
	Wireframe	• **View Control Bar** • **Shortcut:** WF

Chapter 2

Starting a Structural Project

Starting a structural project in Revit begins by using a template. You can then link in a CAD file or an existing Revit model, if these are available. From there, you can add the framework for a building, including levels to define vertical heights and grids to define the structural layout for architectural and structural columns.

Learning Objectives

- Link and import CAD files to be used as a basis for developing a design.
- Link and import raster image and PDF files.
- Link existing Revit models to develop and coordinate with other disciplines.
- Add and modify levels to define floor-to-floor heights and other vertical references.
- Add and modify grids to provide locations for model elements.

2.1 Selecting a Project Template

New projects are based on a project template file. The template file includes preset levels, views, and some families, such as wall styles and text styles. When using templates, most of the views are set to display only the elements specific to the template, so it is best practice to select a template that reflects your company's discipline.

- Check with your BIM manager about which template you need to use for your projects. Your company might have more than one based on the type of project you are designing.
- Ideally, you should not start your work inside of another discipline or model. Instead, you should start from either the Revit structural template or your company's custom template and link the architectural model into your project.
    - If you link a Revit model into your project, you can use the monitoring and coordinating features to copy/monitor necessary items, such as walls, floors, and grids, from the architect. To learn more about Copy/Monitoring, see *6.3 Copying and Monitoring Elements*.

How To: Start a New Project

1. In the *File* tab, expand ▢ (New) and click ▢ (Project), as shown in Figure 2–1, or press <Ctrl>+<N>.

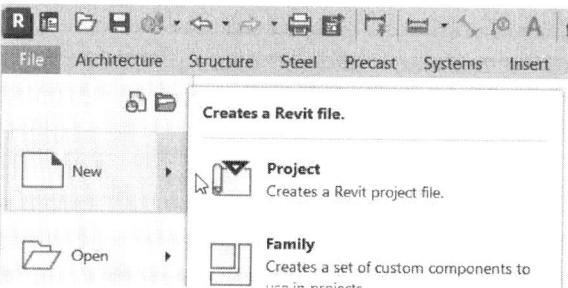

Figure 2–1

2. In the New Project dialog box (shown in Figure 2–2), select the template that you want to use and click **OK**.

    Note: *The list of template files is set in the Options dialog box in the File Locations tab. It might vary depending on the installed product and company standards.*

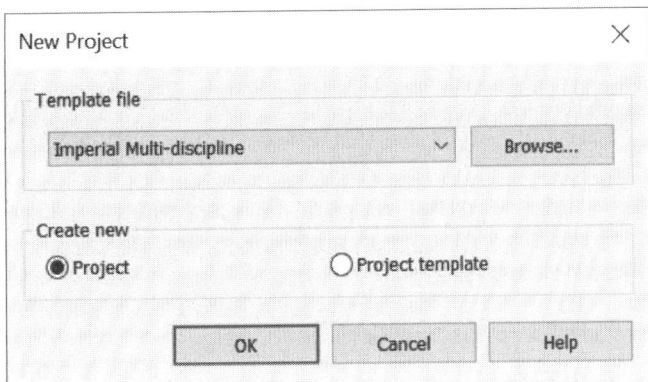

Figure 2–2

> **Hint: Revit Worksharing**
>
> If established by your company that worksharing is needed, you would typically want to start a worksharing project on your local network once a project has been created.
>
> - For more information on worksharing, see *A.6 Introduction to Revit Worksharing*.
> - For more information about establishing and using worksets, refer to the ASCENT guide *Autodesk Revit: Collaboration Tools*.

2.2 Linking and Importing Files

CAD files can be imported or linked into a Revit project. As an example, a designer might lay out a floor plan using the standard 2D AutoCAD software, and you then need to incorporate that information into your structural model. In addition, many renovation projects start with existing 2D drawings. Instead of redrawing from scratch, link or import the CAD file (as shown in Figure 2–3) and trace over it in Revit. You can also print a hybrid drawing that is part Revit project and part imported/linked drawing.

> **Note:** When you hover over an imported or linked CAD file, you can see in the tooltip that it is called an Import Symbol.

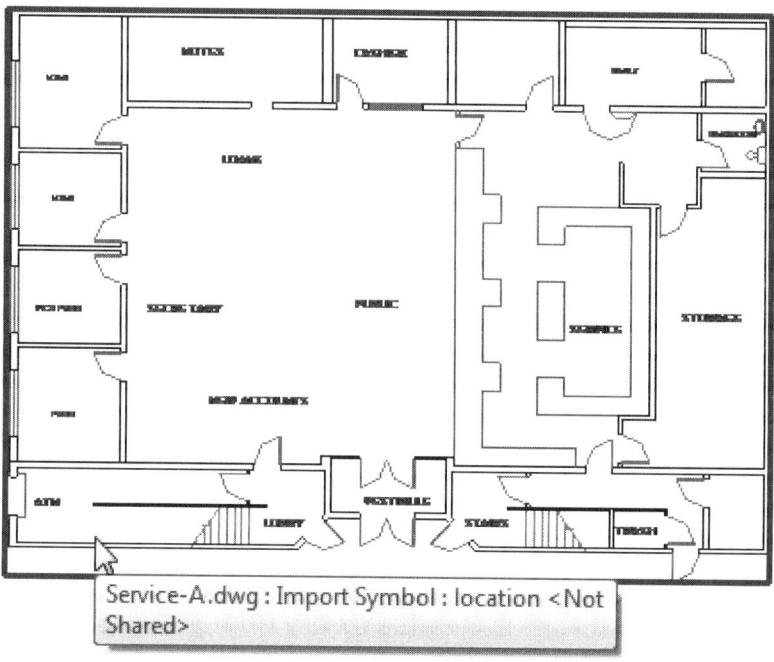

Figure 2–3

- CAD file formats that can be imported or linked include AutoCAD® (DWG and DXF), MicroStation (DGN), 3D ACIS modeling kernel (SAT), Trimble SketchUp (SKP), FormIt (AXM), 3D Shape (OBJ and STL), and Rhino (3dm).

- When linking or importing a CAD file, you can specify a level or a named horizontal reference plane in the project to position the CAD file at.

- You can specify the linking or import units (e.g., feet, meter, or US survey feet).

Linking vs. Importing

- **Link:** A connection is maintained with the original file and the link updates if the original file is updated.
- **Import:** No connection is maintained with the original file. It becomes a separate element in the Revit model.

How To: Link or Import a CAD File

1. Open the view into which you want to link or import the file.
   - For a 2D file, this should be a 2D view. For a 3D file, open a 3D view.
2. In the *Insert* tab>Link panel, click (Link CAD), or in the *Insert* tab>Import panel, click (Import CAD).
3. In the Link CAD Formats (shown in Figure 2–4) or Import CAD Formats dialog box, select the file that you want to import.
   - Select a file format in the **Files of type** drop-down list to limit the files that are displayed.

   Note: The dialog boxes for Link CAD Formats and Import CAD Formats are the same.

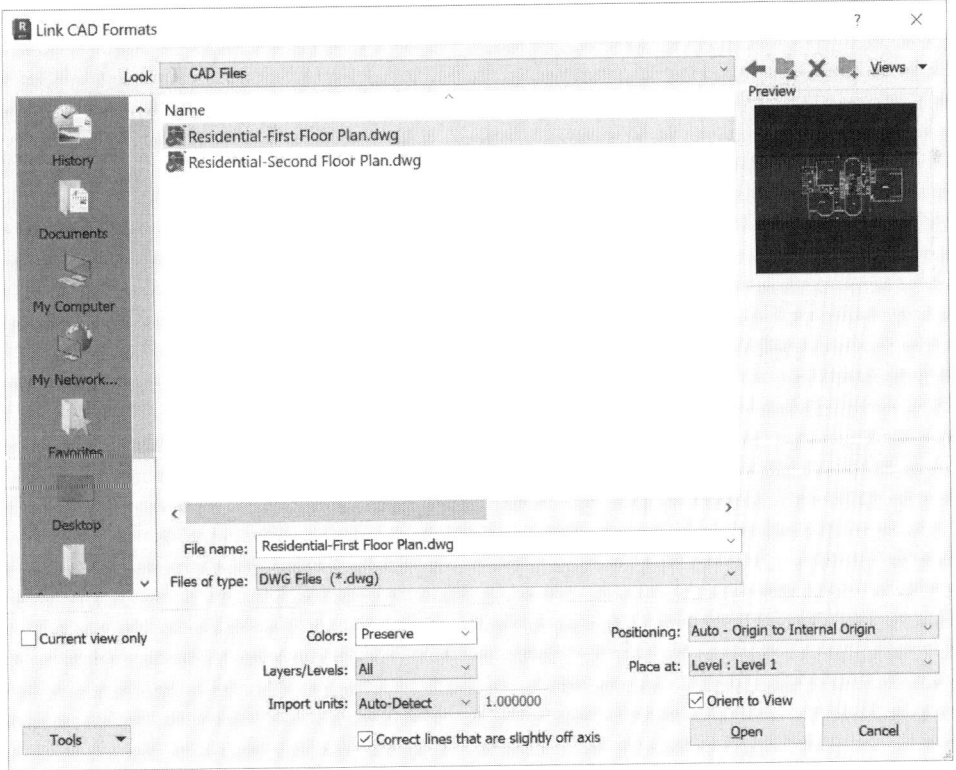

Figure 2–4

4. If **Current view only** is selected, as shown in Figure 2–5, you can set all options except the *Place at* and the *Orient to View* options. The view will only display in the current view.

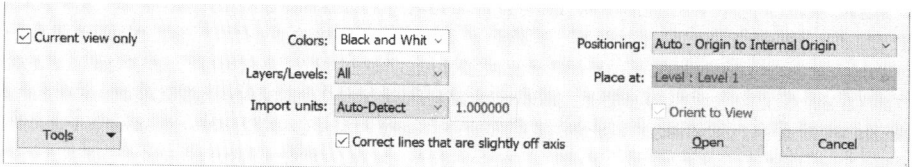

Figure 2–5

5. If you would like to place the CAD file at a level or reference plane, verify **Current view only** is unchecked and set the *Place at* option, as shown in Figure 2–6.

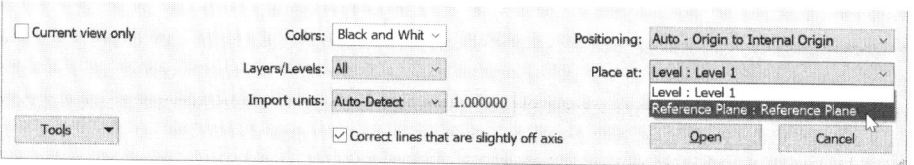

Figure 2–6

6. Click **Open**.

Link and Import Options

Current view only	Determine whether the CAD file is placed in every view, or only in the current view. This is especially useful if you are working with a 2D floor plan that you only need to have in one view.
Colors	Specify the color settings. Typical Revit projects are mainly black and white. However, other software frequently uses color. You can **Invert** the original colors, **Preserve** them, or change everything to **Black and White**.
Layers/Levels	Indicates which CAD layers are going to be brought into the model. Select how you want layers to be imported: **All**, **Visible**, or **Specify…**.
Import units	Select the units of the original file, as required. **Auto-Detect** works in most cases.
Correct lines…	If lines in a CAD file are off axis by less than 0.1 degree, selecting this option straightens them. It is selected by default.
Positioning	Specify how you want the imported file to be positioned in the current project: *Import option*: Auto - Center to Center, Auto - Origin to Internal Origin, Manual - Origin, Manual - Center *Linking option*: Auto - Center to Center, Auto - Origin to Internal Origin, Auto - By Shared Coordinates, Manual - Origin, Manual - Center The default position is **Auto - Origin to Internal Origin**.
Place at	Select a level or named reference plane at which to place the imported file. If you selected **Current view only**, this option is grayed out.
Orient to View	Used to orient the CAD file on import/link.

- When a file is positioned **Auto - Origin to Internal Origin**, it is pinned in place and cannot be moved. To move the file, click on the pin to unpin it, as shown in Figure 2–7.

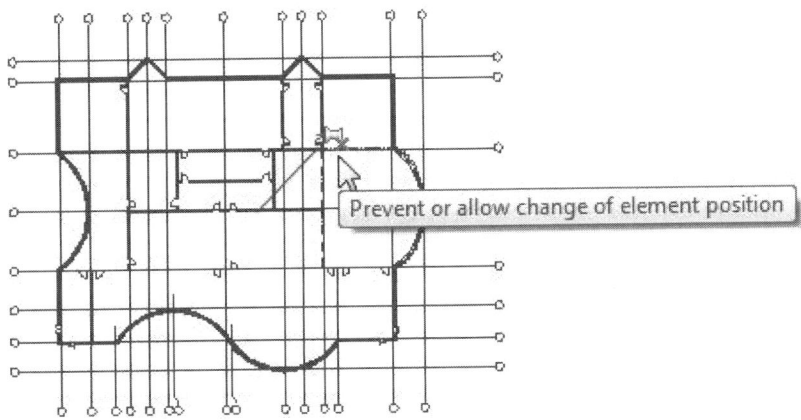

Figure 2–7

Linking and Importing Raster Image Files

Raster images are made up of pixels or dots in a file that create a picture. For example, a raster file is created when you scan a blueprint and then import or link it into Revit to reference or trace. You can add raster images to any 2D view, including sheet views (as shown in Figure 2–8). They can be used as background views or as part of the final drawing. Imported or linked images can be placed behind model objects and annotations.

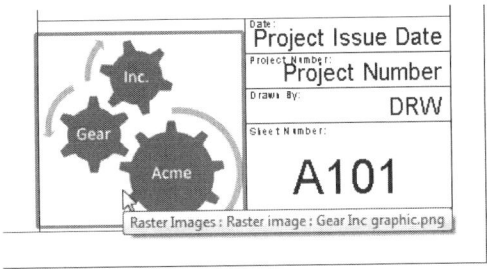

Figure 2–8

- Link a PDF or raster image into a 2D view if you need to reference a file that will be updated throughout the project cycle and to keep the project's file size from increasing when importing files.

- Linked PDFs or raster images can be scaled, rotated, and moved just like an imported PDF or raster image. Any changes made to the PDF or raster image will update in the project it is linked into when you open the project.

- A PDF can be imported into Revit as a raster image. If the PDF contains vector data, you can snap to the elements in the PDF.

How To: Import and Link an Image

To...	Then...
Import an image file	In the *Insert* tab>Import panel, click (Import Image).
Link an image file	In the *Insert* tab>Link panel, click (Link Image).

1. In the Import Image or Link Image dialog box, select the image you want to insert. You can insert .BMP, .JPG, .JPEG, .PNG, and .TIF files.
2. Click **Open**. Four blue dots and an "X" illustrate the default size of the image file, as shown on the left in Figure 2–9. Click on the screen to place the image. It displays with the shape handles still visible, as shown on the right in Figure 2–9.

Figure 2–9

- In Properties, you can adjust the height and width and also set the *Draw Layer* to either **Background** or **Foreground**, as shown in Figure 2–10.

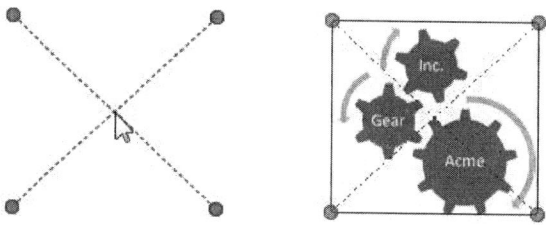

Figure 2–10

- You can select more than one image at a time and move them as a group to the background or foreground.

- In the *Modify | Raster Images* tab (shown in Figure 2–11), you can access the Arrange options and **Manage Links**.

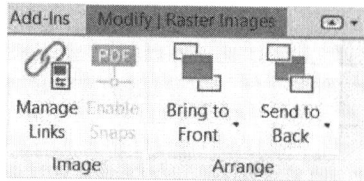

Figure 2–11

Linking and Importing PDF Files

PDF files are often created for sharing information with people that do not have the original program and when you do not want anyone to change the original information. They can also be used as underlays when the original information includes vector data.

How To: Import and Link a PDF File

To...	Then...
Import a PDF file	In the *Insert* tab>Import panel, click (Import PDF).
Link a PDF file	In the *Insert* tab>Link panel, click (Link PDF).

1. In the Import PDF or Link PDF dialog box, navigate to the location where the PDF file is stored, select it, and click **Open**.
2. In the Import PDF or Link PDF dialog box (Figure 2–12 shows the Import PDF dialog box), select the page you want to import/link and click **OK**.

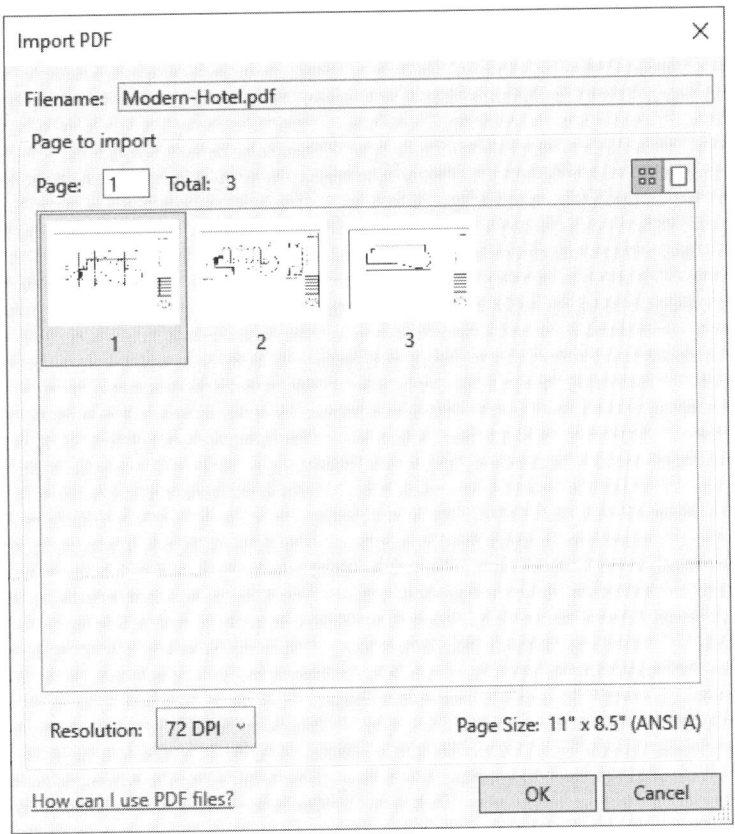

Figure 2–12

- Only one page can be imported/linked at a time, but you can import/link additional pages by repeating the process.

3. In Properties, you can specify the size and scale of the image, as shown in Figure 2–13.
   - If the PDF comes from a vector source, you can also choose to enable snaps and trace over the elements in the PDF.
   - The Foreground/Background status can be set in the Options Bar and in Properties.

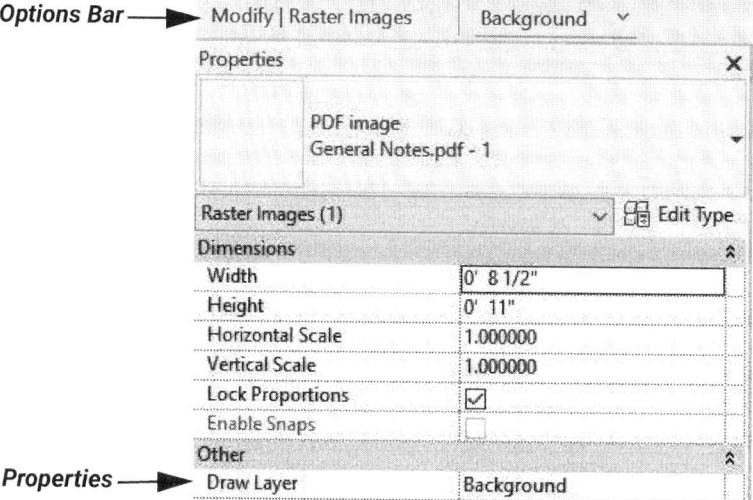

Figure 2–13

2.3 Linking in Revit Models

You can link Revit models directly into a project. These models can be an existing building that you are creating an addition to, as shown in Figure 2–14, or engineering models that you are checking to ensure that they line up with your model. They are also used for campus-like projects where the same building is repeated multiple times. They are full 3D models.

Note: A linked model automatically updates when the original file is changed.

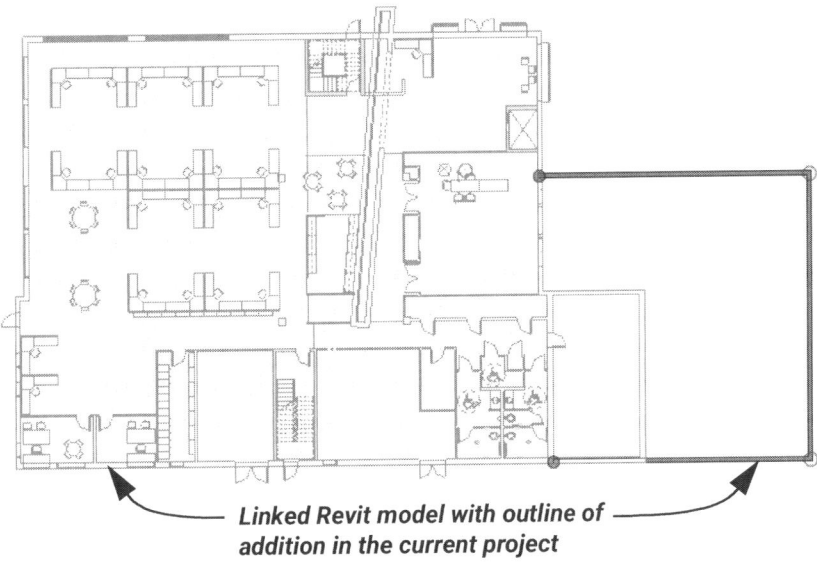

Linked Revit model with outline of addition in the current project

Figure 2–14

- Architectural, structural, and MEP models created in Revit can be linked to each other as long as they are from the same release cycle.
- When you use linked models, clashes between disciplines can be detected and information can be passed between disciplines.
- Revit models are always linked. They cannot be imported.

How To: Add a Linked Model to a Host Project

1. In the *Insert* tab>Link panel, click ▦ (Link Revit).
2. In the Import/Link RVT dialog box, select the file that you want to link. Before opening the file, set the *Positioning*, as shown in Figure 2–15.

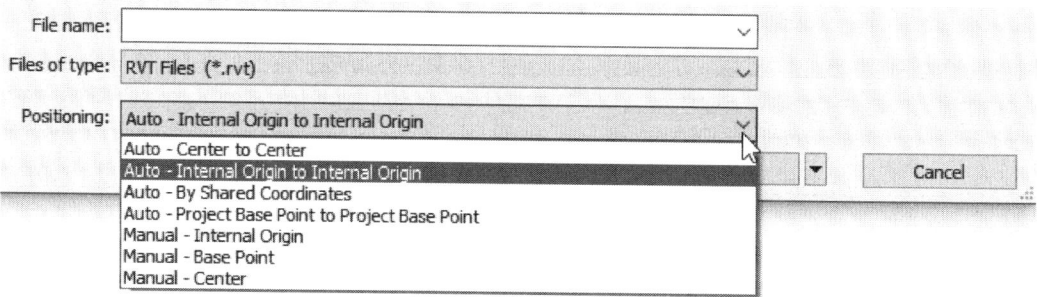

Figure 2–15

3. Click **Open**.
4. Depending on how you decide to position the file, it is automatically placed in the project or you can manually place it with the cursor.

- As the links are loading, do not click on the screen or click any buttons. The more links present in a project, the longer it takes to load.

2.4 Modifying Imported/Linked Files

When you select an imported/linked file, you can modify it by arranging the Foreground/Background status, modifying its Type Properties, querying information about elements in the file, and deleting layers. You can also modify the Visibility/Graphic Overrides of each imported/linked instance.

- An imported/linked file is called an *import symbol* once it is inserted into a project, as shown in Figure 2-16.

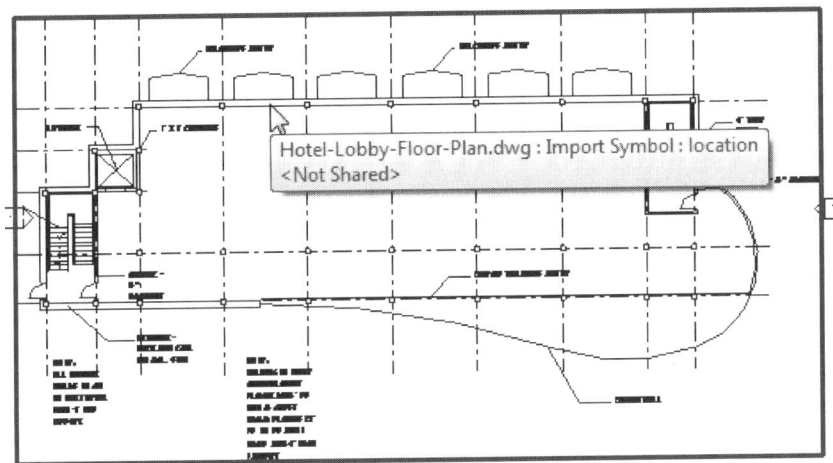

Figure 2-16

Setting an Imported or Linked File to Halftone

To see the difference between the host model elements and the linked or imported file, you can set the linked/imported file to halftone, as shown in Figure 2-17.

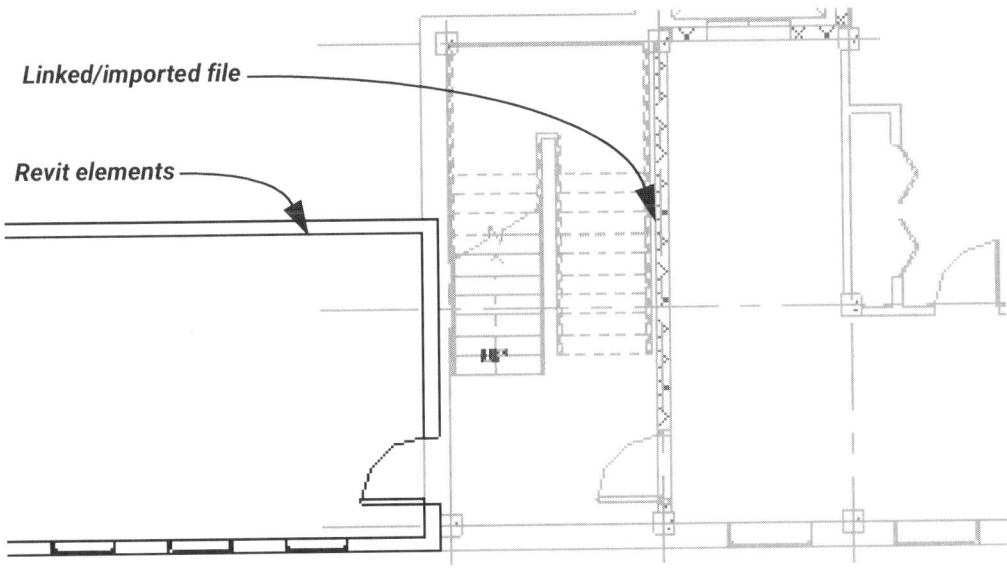

Figure 2-17

How To: Set an Element to Halftone

1. Select the imported file.
2. Right-click and select **Override Graphics in View>By Element...**.
3. In the View Specific Element Graphics dialog box, select **Halftone**, as shown in Figure 2–18.
   - The options shown in the View Specific Element Graphics dialog box will depend on the element selected.

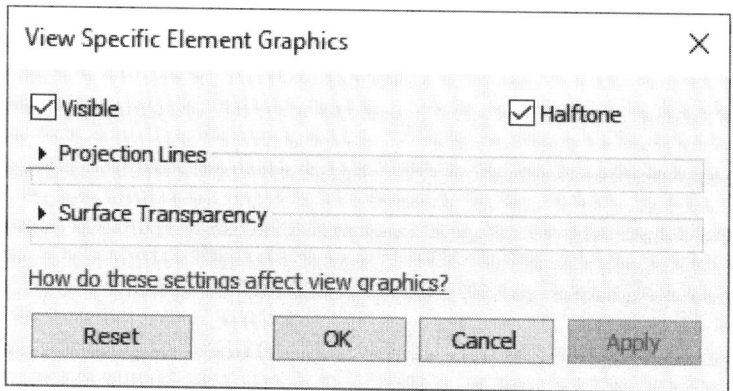

Figure 2–18

4. Click **OK**.

- You can use this method to set any element or category to halftone.

Draw Layer

Linked CAD files are typically in the background of a view. To change this, select the CAD file in the view and in the Options Bar or in Properties, in the *Other* section, change the *Draw Layer* to **Foreground**.

Editing Raster Files

Select an imported/linked image to make changes. Once it is selected, you can resize the image as you did when you first inserted it or specify the *Width* and *Height* values in Properties.

- Select **Lock Proportions** in the Options Bar to ensure that the length and width resize proportionally to each other when you adjust the size of an image.
- Use the standard modification tools to **Move**, **Copy**, **Rotate**, **Mirror**, **Array**, and **Scale** images. Images can also be grouped together into detail groups.

- The Foreground/Background status can also be set in the Options Bar and in Properties, as shown in Figure 2–19.

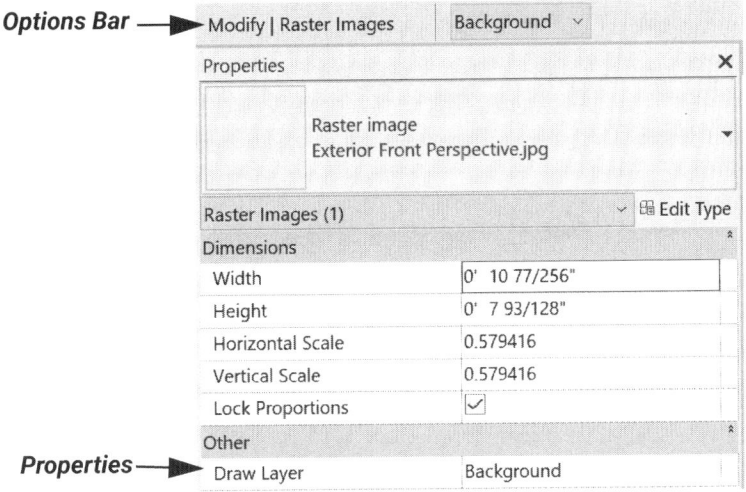

Figure 2–19

- In the *Modify | Raster Images* tab>Arrange panel (shown in Figure 2–20), use the Arrange tools to move images to the front or back of other images or objects.

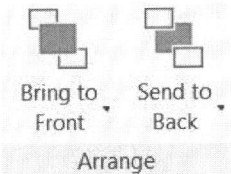

Figure 2–20

- You can snap to edges of images, as shown in Figure 2–21.

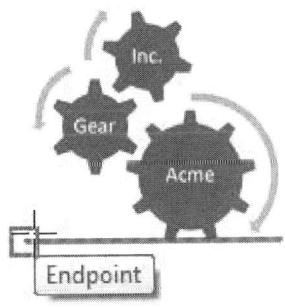

Figure 2–21

Managing Links

The Manage Links dialog box (shown in Figure 2–22) enables you to reload, unload, add, and remove links, and it also provides access for you to set other options. To open the Manage Links dialog box, in the *Insert* tab>Link panel, click (Manage Links). Alternatively, you can go to the *Manage* tab>Manage Projects panel and click (Manage Links).

- You can also select the link and click (Manage Links) in the *Modify | RVT Links* tab>Link panel.

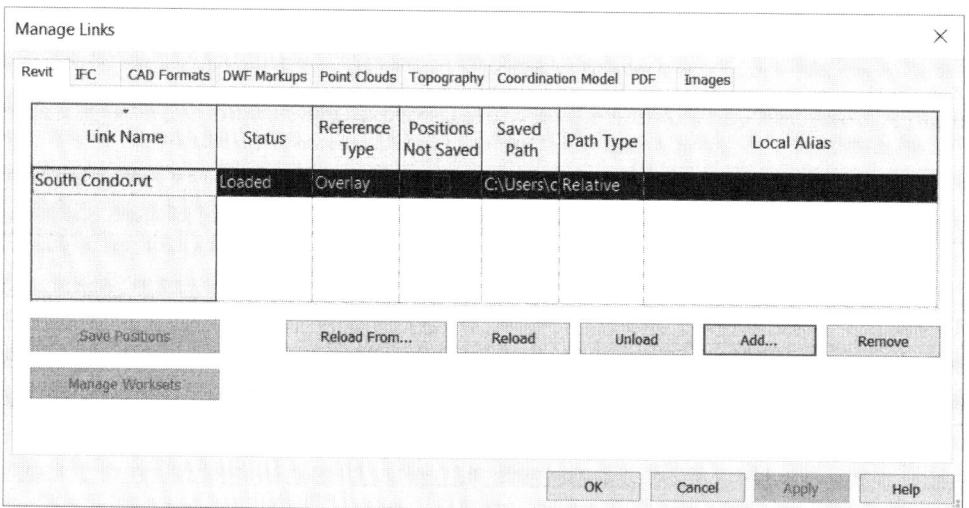

Figure 2–22

- The Manage Links dialog box does not show imported CAD files.
- You can manage both imported and linked images and PDFs.

The following options are available:

- **Reload From:** Opens the Add Link dialog box, which enables you to select the file you want to reload. Use this if the linked file location or name has changed.

- **Reload:** Reloads the file without additional prompts.

- **Unload:** Unloads the file so that the link is kept, but the file is not displayed or calculated in the project. Use **Reload** to restore it.

    *Note: Some of these options are also available in the Project Browser. Expand the Revit Links node, then right-click on the Revit link and select **Reload**, **Unload**, or **Reload From**....*

- **Add:** Opens the Import/Link RVT dialog box, which enables you to link additional models into the host project.

- **Remove:** Deletes the link from the file.

Links can be nested into one another. How a link responds when the host project is linked into another project depends on the option in the *Reference Type* column.

- **Overlay:** The nested linked model is not referenced in the new host project.
- **Attach:** The nested linked model displays in the new host project.

The option in the *Path Type* column controls how the location of the link is remembered.

- **Relative**
  - Searches the root folder of the current project.
  - If the file is moved, the software still searches for it.
- **Absolute**
  - Searches the entire file path where the file was originally saved.
  - If the original file is moved, the software is not able to find it.
- Other options control how the linked file interfaces with worksets and shared positioning.

Modifying the Visibility of Imported/Linked Files

If you have used the imported/linked file as a guideline for tracing, you can toggle off the visibility of the entire image using the Visibility/Graphic Overrides dialog box, without removing it from the project in case you need it later. You can also toggle off individual layers or levels.

How To: Hide Individual Layers

1. In the *View* tab>Graphics panel, click (Visibility/Graphics), or type **VG** or **VV** to open the Visibility/Graphic Overrides dialog box.

2. Switch to the *Imported Categories* tab. It displays a list for each imported instance and their layers/levels, as shown in Figure 2–23.

3. To have the linked/imported file display in halftone, check the box in the *Halftone* column.

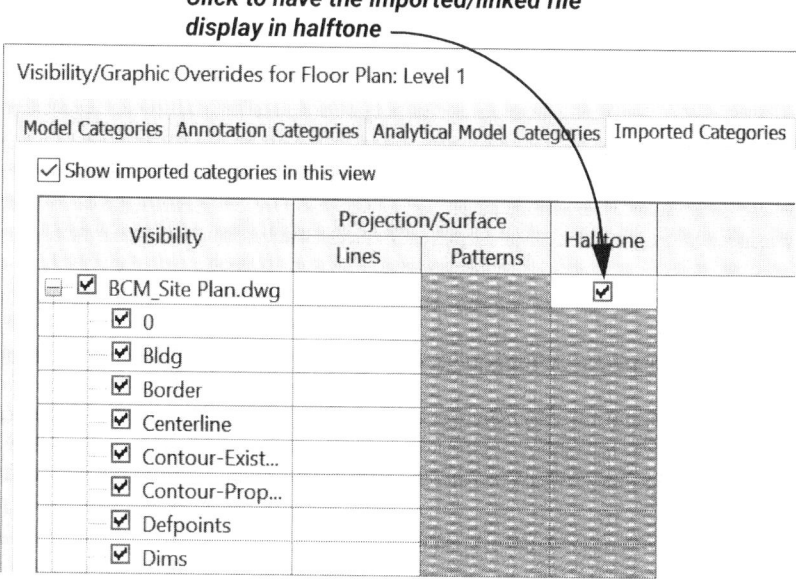

Figure 2–23

4. Click the plus sign beside the file name to expand a list of the layers or levels in that file.

5. Clear the checkmark from the individual layers that you do not want to display.

   - Typically, these layers contain similar information, such as all windows or all notes in a drawing. However, it is not as definite as using Revit elements. An item might have been misplaced on a different layer and, if so, it does not toggle off.

6. Close the dialog box.

- To toggle off the entire file, clear the checkmark next to the file name.

Temporarily Hide/Isolate

You might want to temporarily remove linked or imported files from a view, modify the project, and then restore the elements. Instead of completely toggling the elements off, you can temporarily hide them.

Select the elements you want to hide (make invisible) or isolate (keep displayed while all other elements are hidden) and click 👓 (Temporary Hide/Isolate). Select the method you want to use, as shown in Figure 2–24.

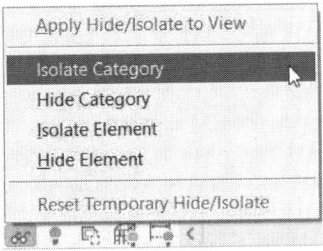

Figure 2–24

- The category or elements are hidden or isolated. A cyan border displays around the view with a note in the upper left corner, as shown in Figure 2–25. It indicates that the view contains temporarily hidden or isolated elements.

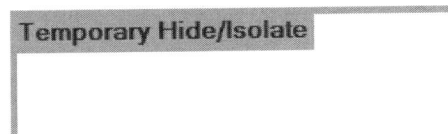

Figure 2–25

- Click 👓 (Temporary Hide/Isolate) again and select **Reset Temporary Hide/Isolate** to restore the elements to the view.
- If you want to permanently hide the elements in the view, select **Apply Hide/Isolate to View**.
- Elements that are temporarily hidden in a view are not hidden when the view is printed.

Hide Linked or Imported Files in a View

When working in views, you can quickly hide linked or imported files. To hide the imported or linked file, select it and right-click to display the shortcut menu, then select **Hide in View** and select either **Elements** or **Category**, as shown in Figure 2–26. Alternatively, select the link in the view and type **VH** to hide the selected file in the view.

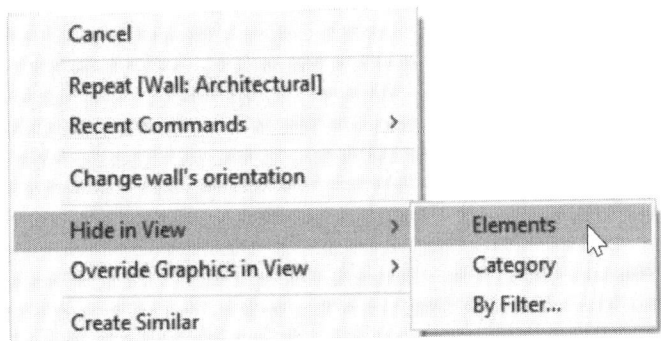

Figure 2–26

Practice 2a
Start a Project and Link Files

Practice Objectives

- Start a Revit project.
- Link a CAD file.
- Link a Revit file.
- Modify the linked files in a view.

In this practice, you will link both an AutoCAD (.DWG) file as well as a Revit model (.RVT). You will then modify the view properties, as shown in Figure 2-27.

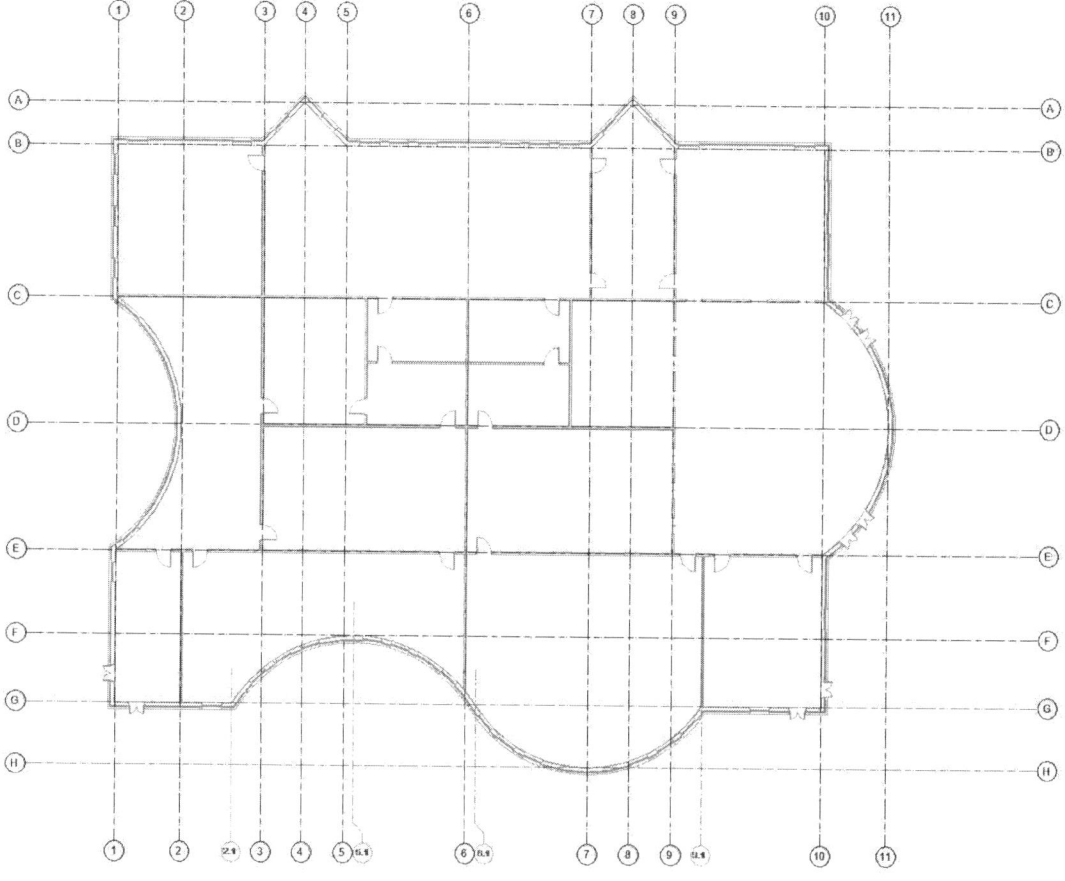

Figure 2-27

Task 1: Start a project.

1. In the *File* tab, expand ☐ (New) and click ☐ (Project).

   - Alternatively, if you are on the Home screen, click the **New** button under the *MODEL* section.

2. In the New Project dialog box, expand the *Template file* list, select the default **Imperial-Structural Template**, and click **OK**. (There are no elements in this file, only datums and basic views.)

   - If you do not have Revit templates installed, open the template from the project files, Template folder.

3. In the Project Browser, open the **Structural Plans: Level 1** view. (The default structural template automatically opens in Level 2. You are importing the **Level 1** floor plan from the AutoCAD file and therefore need to open that view.)

4. Save the project as **Structure-Start.rvt** to the project files folder.

Task 2: Link a CAD file.

1. In the *Insert* tab>Link panel, click ☐ (Link CAD).

2. In the Link CAD Formats dialog box, navigate to the practice files *CAD Files* folder and select the file **First-Floor-Structural-Suites.dwg**, then set the following options:

   - Select **Current view only**
   - *Colors:* **Black and White**
   - *Layers/Levels:* **All**
   - *Import Units:* **Auto-Detect**
   - *Positioning:* **Auto - Origin to Internal Origin**

3. Click **Open**. The linked CAD file is placed in the project on the **Structural Plans: Level 1** view.

4. Select the linked CAD file. In Properties you can see that it is a single imported symbol and in the view you can see a pin at the center of the CAD file because it was imported origin to internal origin.

5. In the Options Bar, change *Background* to **Foreground**.

6. Right-click on the linked file (also called an import symbol) and select **Override Graphics in View>By Element**.

7. In the View-Specific Element Graphics dialog box, select **Halftone**, as shown in Figure 2–28.

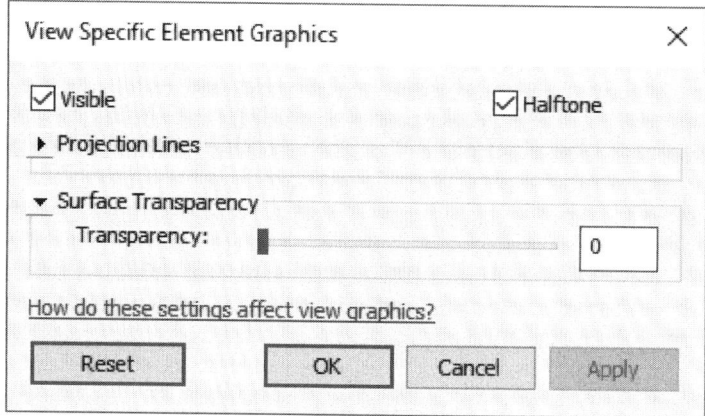

Figure 2–28

8. Click **OK**.
9. Click in an empty space in the view to release the selection.
10. The linked file displays in halftone. Zoom to the extents of the view. (Hint: Type **ZE** or double-click on the mouse wheel.)

    Note: Use a window selection to select both parts of the elevation markers.

11. Move the building elevation markers so that they are on the outside of the imported file, as shown in Figure 2–29. Select both parts of the elevation markers.

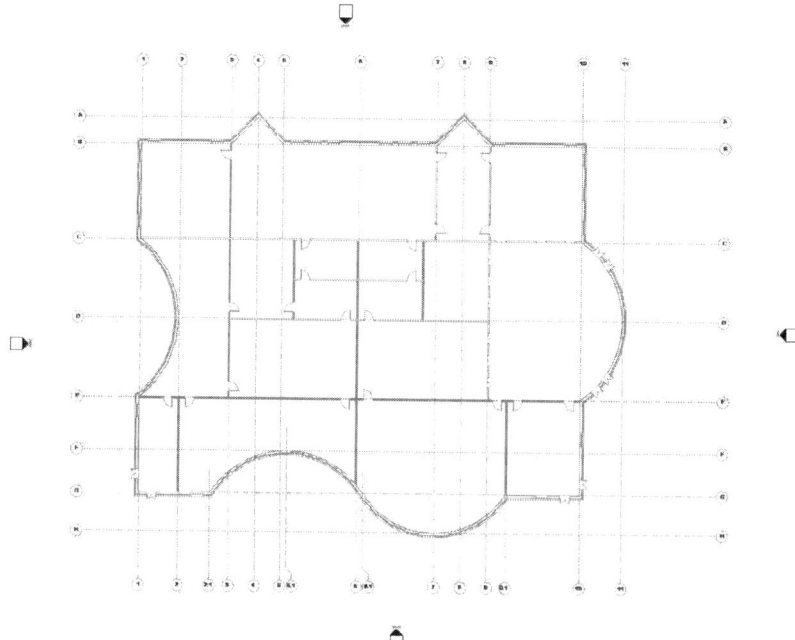

Figure 2–29

12. From the Project Browser, open the **Structural Plans: Level 2** view. The CAD file linked in Level 1 does not display because you specified to link the CAD file with **Current view only** selected.
13. Save the project.

Task 3: Link in a Revit file.

1. In the Quick Access Toolbar, click (Default 3D View), and in the *Insert* tab>Link panel, click (Link Revit).
2. In the Import/Link RVT dialog box, navigate to your practice files *Linked Revit Models* folder and select the file **Arch-Suites.rvt**. Ensure that the *Positioning* is set to **Auto - Internal Origin to Internal Origin** and click **Open**.
3. Select the linked model in the view (only grid lines display) and in the *Modify | RVT Links* tab>Modify panel, click (Pin). This will ensure that the linked model will not be accidentally moved in the view.
4. Click in an empty space in the view and zoom to fit the view. (Hint: Type **ZF**.)
5. In Properties, change the *Discipline* to **Coordination**, as shown in Figure 2–30.

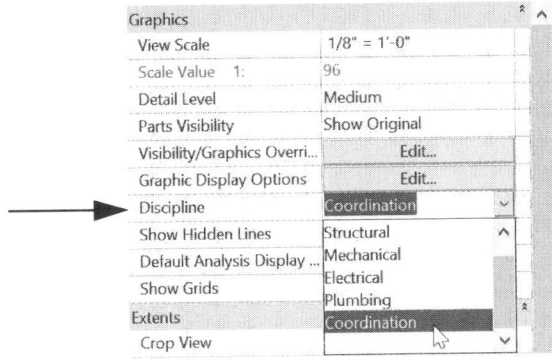

Figure 2–30

6. Click **Apply** or move your cursor into the view to apply changes. The architectural walls now display.

7. From the View Control bar, change the visual style to **Consistent Colors**, as shown in Figure 2–31, to see the walls.

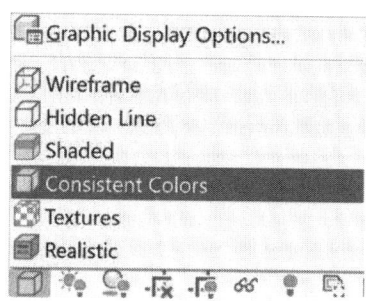

Figure 2–31

8. Save and close the project.

End of practice

2.5 Setting Up Levels

Levels define stories and other vertical heights, such as the parapet and other reference heights shown in Figure 2–32. The default template includes two levels, but you can define as many levels in a project as required. They can go below 0'-0" or in the negative (for basements or 00 T.O. Footing) as well.

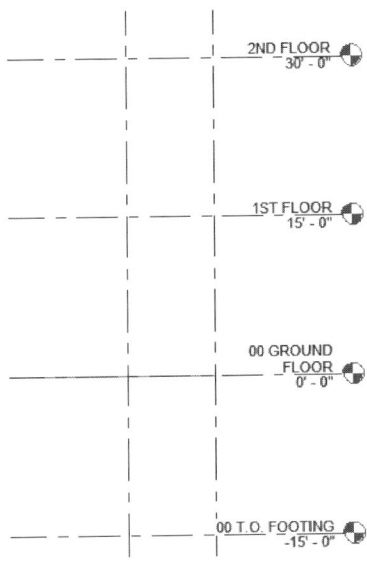

Figure 2–32

- You must be in an elevation or section view to define levels.
- Once you constrain an element to a level, it moves with the level when the level is changed.

How To: Create Levels

1. Open an elevation or section view.
2. In the *Architecture* tab>Datum panel, click (Level), or type **LL**.
3. In the Type Selector, set the level head type, if needed.
4. In the Options Bar, select or clear **Make Plan View** as needed. You can also click **Plan View Types...** to select the types of views to create when you place the level.
5. In the *Modify | Place Level* tab>Draw panel, click either (Pick Lines) to select an element or (Line) to sketch a level.
6. Continue adding levels as needed.

- Level names are automatically incremented as you place them. This automatic numbering is most effective when you use names such as Floor 1, Floor 2, etc. (as opposed to First Floor, Second Floor, etc.). In addition, this makes it easier to find the view in the Project Browser.

- A fast way to create multiple levels is to use the (Pick Lines) option. In the Options Bar, specify an *Offset,* select an existing level, and then pick above or below to place the new level, as shown in Figure 2–33.

    Note: You specify above or below the offset by hovering the cursor on the needed side.

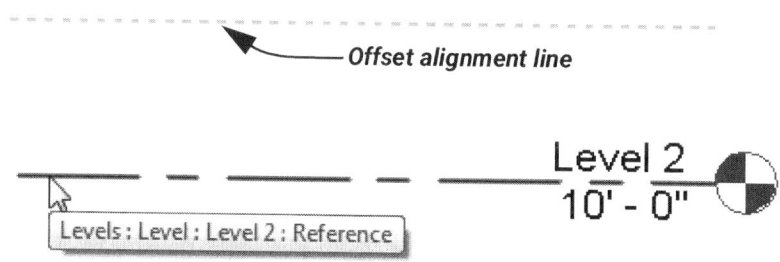

Figure 2–33

- When using the (Line) option, alignments and temporary dimensions help you place the line correctly, as shown in Figure 2–34.

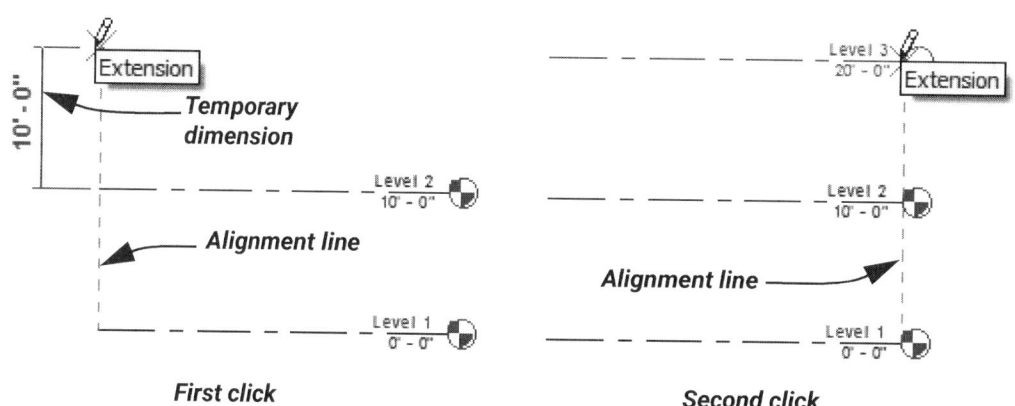

Figure 2–34

- Sketch the level lines from left to right or right to left to keep consistent.

- You can also use (Copy) to duplicate level lines. The level names are incremented but a plan view is not created. These are called **reference levels**.

- Levels display in the default 3D view. They can be modified and copied, but cannot be created in this view.

- Levels can be hidden in any view.

Modifying Levels

You can change levels using standard controls and temporary dimensions, as shown in Figure 2–35 to the levels' appearance. You can also make changes to the name and height of the level by selecting on the individual items in the view as well as change these in Properties. You can change just the name of the level in the Project Browser but not the height.

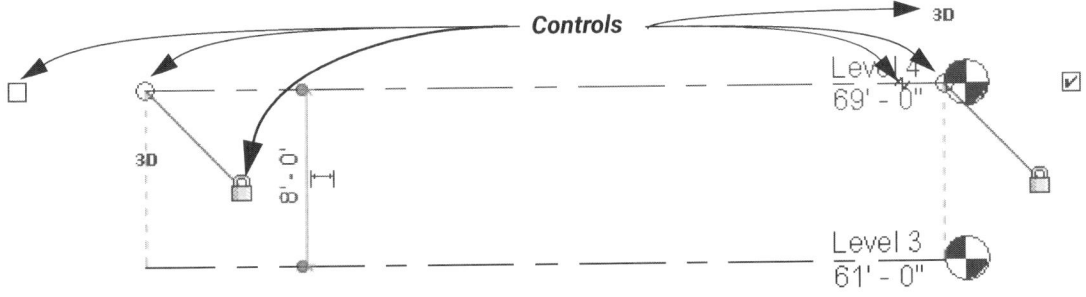

Figure 2–35

- ☑ ☐ (Hide / Show Bubble) displays on either end of the level line and toggles the level head symbol and level information on or off.

- 2D 3D (Switch to 3d / 2d extents) controls whether any movement or adjustment to the level line is reflected in other views (3D) or only affects the current view (2D).

- (Modify the level by dragging its model end) at each end of the line enables you to drag the level head to a new location.

- 🔒 🔓 (Create or remove a length or alignment constraint) controls whether the level is locked in alignment with the other levels. If it is locked and the level line is stretched, all of the other level lines stretch as well. If it is unlocked, the level line stretches independent of the other levels.

- Click ⚡ (Add Elbow) to add a jog to the level line, as shown in Figure 2–36. Drag the shape handles to new locations as needed. This is a view-specific change.

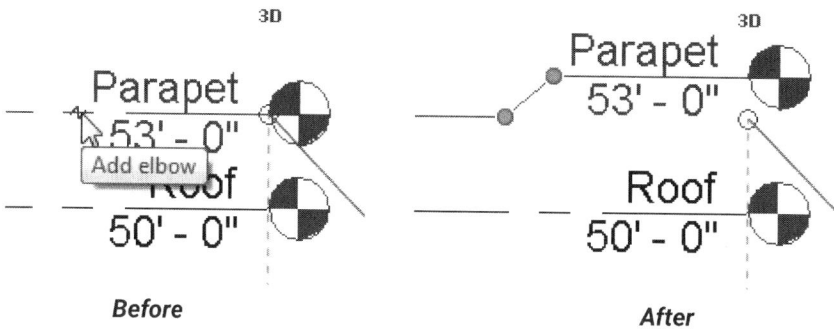

Figure 2–36

- To change the level name or elevation, double-click on the information next to the level head, or select the level and modify the *Name* or *Elevation* fields in Properties, as shown in Figure 2–37.

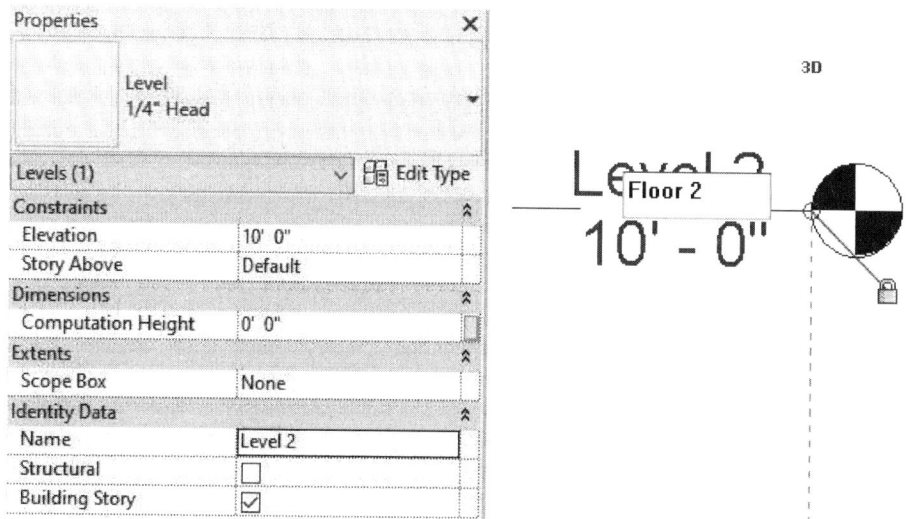

Figure 2–37

- When you rename a level, an alert box opens, prompting you to rename the corresponding views, as shown in Figure 2–38.

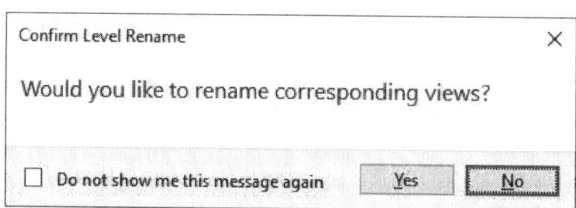

Figure 2–38

- The view is also renamed in the Project Browser.

Starting a Structural Project

> **Hint: Modifying Measurements**

For imperial measurements (feet and inches), the software uses a default of feet. For example, when you type **4** and press <Enter>, it assumes **4'-0"**. For a distance such as 4'-6", you can type any of the following: **4'-6"**, **4'6**, **4-6**, or **4 6** (the numbers separated by a space). To indicate distances less than one foot, type the inch mark (") after the distance, or enter **0**, a space, and then the distance.

- If you delete a level, the views related to that level are also deleted. A warning displays, as shown in Figure 2–39.

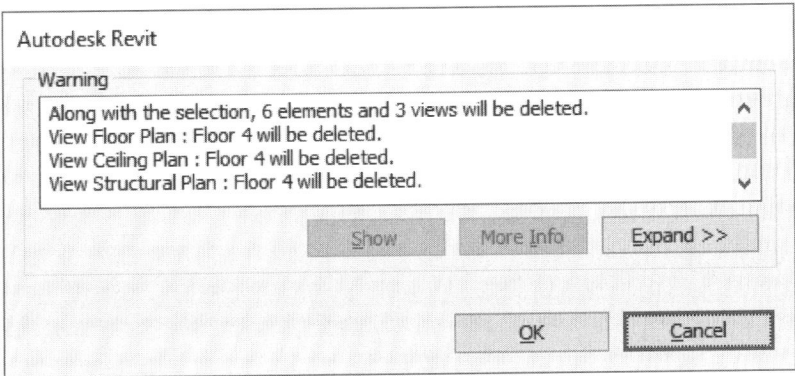

Figure 2–39

> **Hint: Copying Levels and Grids from Other Projects**

Levels and grid lines can be added by drawing over existing levels or grids in an imported or linked CAD file. They can also be copied and monitored from a linked Revit file. Some projects might require both methods.

Creating Plan Views

By default, when you place a level, plan views for that level are automatically created. If **Make Plan View** was toggled off when adding the level, or if the level was copied, you can create plan views to match the levels.

- Level heads with views are blue and level heads without views are black, as shown in Figure 2–40.

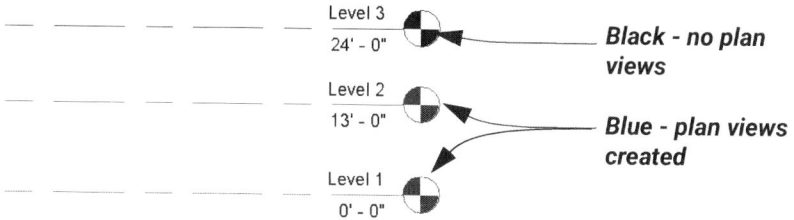

Figure 2–40

Note: Typically, you do not need to create plan views for levels that specify data, such as the top of a storefront window or the top of a parapet.

How To: Create Plan Views

1. In the *View* tab>Create panel, expand (Plan Views) and select the type of plan view you want to create, as shown in Figure 2–41.

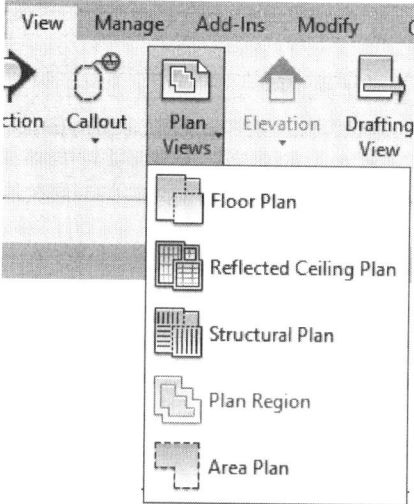

Figure 2–41

2. In the New Plan dialog box (shown in Figure 2–42), select the levels for which you want to create plan views. Hold <Ctrl> to select more than one level.

   - Clear **Do no duplicate existing views** to create a copy of an existing view.

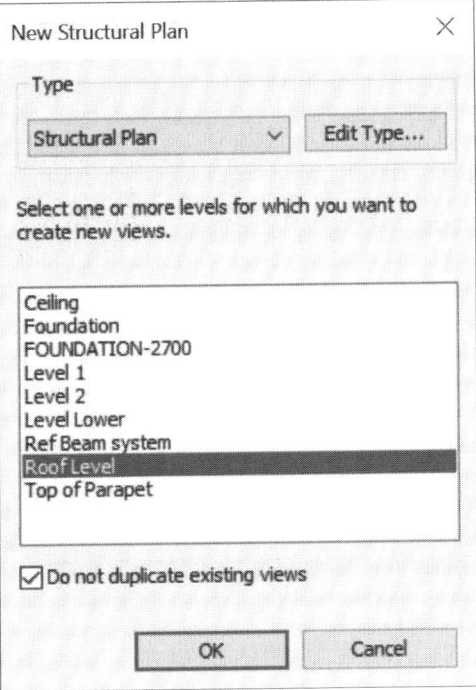

Figure 2–42

3. Click **OK**.

Practice 2b
Set Up Levels

Practice Objective

- Add and modify levels.

In this practice, you will set up the levels required in the project, including the top of the footing, as shown in Figure 2–43. you will then modify the levels names and create plan views.

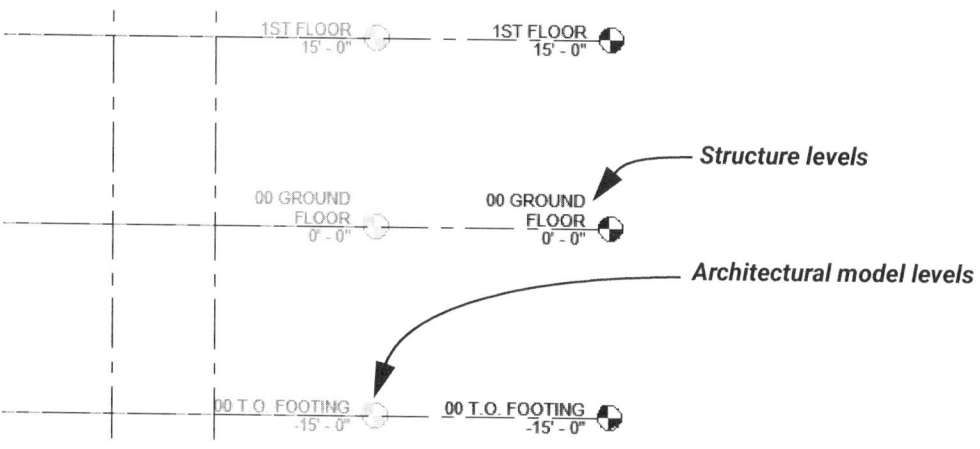

Figure 2–43

The analytical views have been deleted from the project as we will not be using them.

Task 1: Modify existing levels.

1. Open the project **Structural-Levels.rvt** from the practice files folder.
2. In the Project Browser, expand the **Elevations (Building Elevation)** node and open the **South** view. Notice that the architectural walls are not displayed, this is because the views discipline is set to Structural so only structure elements will show.

3. Select the link. There are two existing levels in the current project and a large number of levels in the linked model, as shown in Figure 2–44.

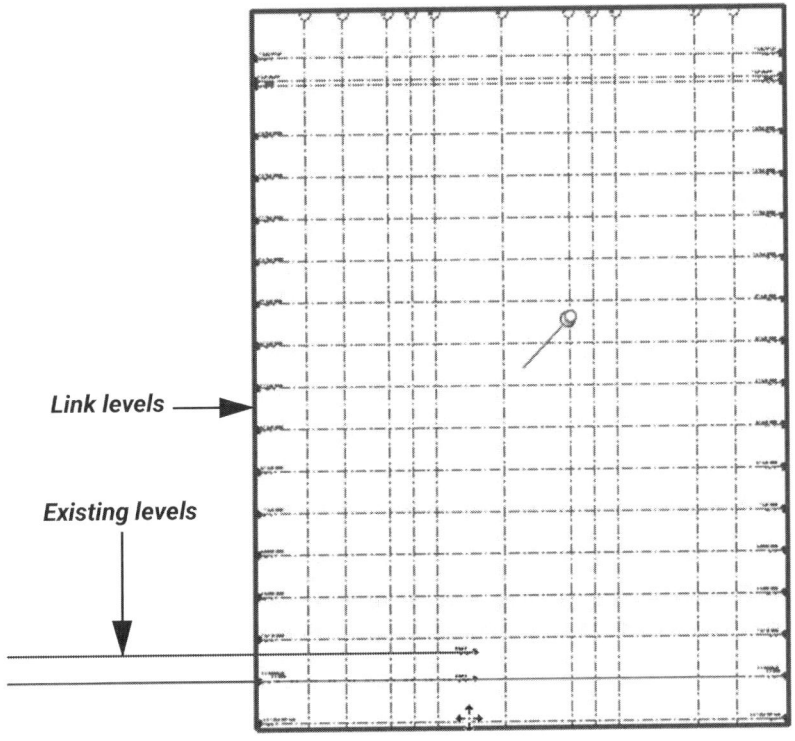

Figure 2–44

4. Right-click on the link and select **Override Graphics in View>By Category**. In the View-Specific Category Graphics dialog box, select **Halftone** and click **OK**.

5. Click (Modify).

6. In the view, select on the project **Level 2** and press <Delete>. A warning dialog box opens, as shown in Figure 2–45. Click **OK** to delete the corresponding view and its elements as they are not required in this project.

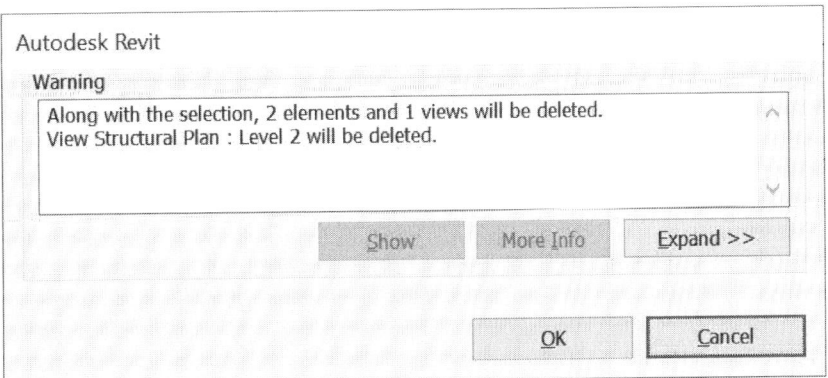

Figure 2–45

7. Double-click on the projects level name *Level 1* and rename it to **00 GROUND FLOOR**, as shown in Figure 2–46. Press <Enter>.

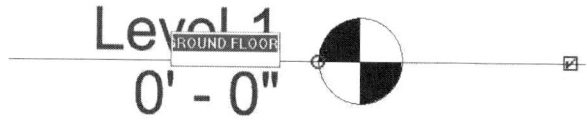

Figure 2–46

8. Click **Yes** or press <Y> when prompted to rename the corresponding views.
9. In the Project Browser, the former **Level 1** view has been renamed **00 GROUND FLOOR**.
10. Select level 00 GROUND FLOOR, click ⊕ (Modify the level by dragging its model end) and drag the level head over to line up with the Revit linked levels, as shown in Figure 2–47. Do not worry about being precise.

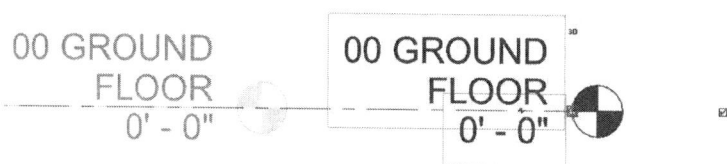

Figure 2–47

11. Save the project.

Task 2: Create new levels.

1. In the *Structure* tab>Datum panel, click (Level).
2. In the *Modify | Place Level* tab>Draw panel, click (Pick Lines).
3. In the Options Bar, verify that **Make Plan View** is selected. Click **Plan View Types...**.

Starting a Structural Project

4. In the Plan View Types dialog box, click **Ceiling Plan** and **Floor Plan** to deselect them (only **Structural Plan** is selected), as shown in Figure 2–48. Click **OK**.

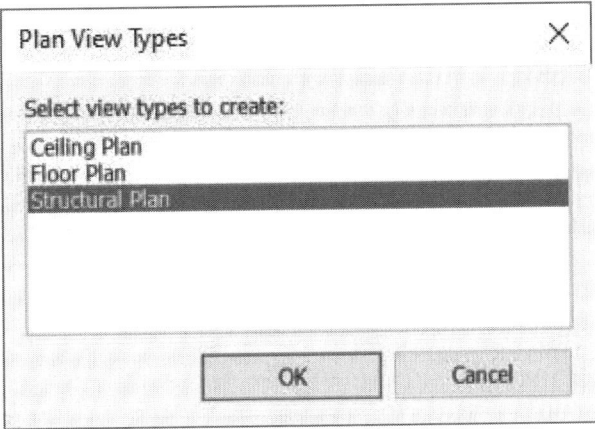

Figure 2–48

5. In the Options Bar, set the *Offset* to **14'-7"**. (This will place a level at the **TOS** height.)
6. Hover the cursor over the project's level line of **00 GROUND FLOOR** and move the cursor slightly upward until you see the dashed alignment line display above the **00 GROUND FLOOR** level, as shown in Figure 2–49. (Alignment line has been enhanced for clarity.)
7. Click to place the level.

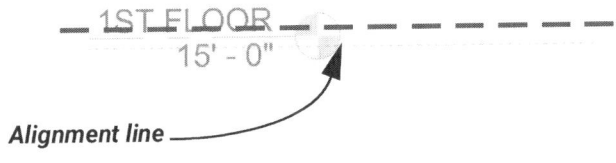

Figure 2–49

8. Click (Modify).
9. Click on the new level and rename it **TOS-1ST FLOOR**.
10. Click **Yes** or press <Y> when prompted to rename the corresponding views.
11. Start the **Level** command again. In the *Modify | Place Level* tab>Draw panel, click (Pick Lines).
12. In the Options Bar, clear the **Make Plan View** option and set the *Offset* to (negative) **-0'-5"**.

13. Hover your cursor over the linked model's **2ND FLOOR**. Make sure the dashed alignment line display below the level and click to place the new level.
14. Click (Modify).
15. Select the level, in Properties, in the *Identity Data* section, change the name to **TOS-2ND FLOOR**, as shown in Figure 2–50 and move the cursor into the view area to apply the changes.

Figure 2–50

16. Notice, in the Project Browser, a plan view was not created.
17. Start the **Level** command again and notice the option to **Make Plan View** is checked again. Verify only structural plan is selected in the *Plan View Types*.
18. Start the **Level** command again. In the *Modify | Place Level* tab>Draw panel, click (Pick Lines).
19. In the Options Bar, verify **Make Plan View** option is checked and set the *Offset* to (negative) **-0'-5"**.
20. Continue adding levels up to level **14 ROOF** making sure the new levels have a prefix of **TOS**.
21. Save the project.

Task 3: Create a structural plan view.

1. In the *View* tab>Create panel, expand (Plan Views) and click (Structural Plan).
2. In the New Structural Plan dialog box, select the level **TOS-2ND FLOOR**, as shown in Figure 2–51, and click **OK**.

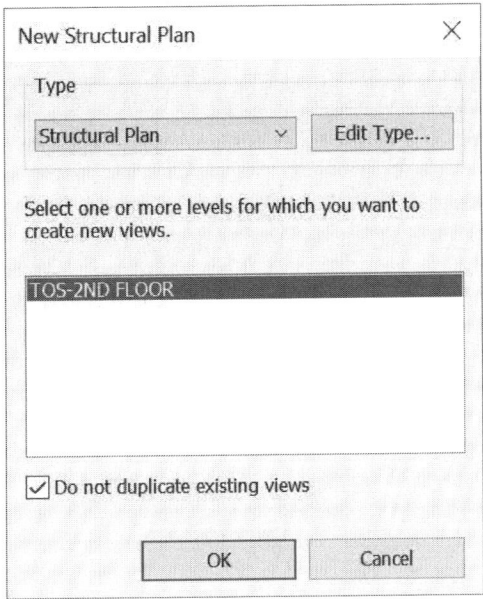

Figure 2–51

- The new view opens and now displays in the Project Browser.

3. Save the project.

Task 4: Create additional levels.

1. Return to the **South** view by clicking on the *Views* tab at the top of the view area.
2. Start the **Level** command, create an additional level above the **TOS-14 ROOF** and rename it to **15 SKYWAY** level. This level does not need an offset.
3. Zoom and pan to the **00 GROUND FLOOR** level and select on it.
4. In the *Modify | Levels* tab>Modify panel, click (Copy).
5. In the Options Bar, deselect **Multiple**.
6. In the view, click 00 GROUND FLOOR'S level line for the copy start point. For the second point, click below 00 GROUND FLOOR (the distance does not matter right now as you will set this in the next few steps).
7. Click (Modify) to end the command.

8. Rename the level to **00 T.O. FOOTING** and set the height to (negative) **-15'-0"**, as shown in Figure 2–52.

    - Notice how the copied level has a black level head while the 00 GROUND FLOOR has blue. This is because when you copy a level, it does not create a plan view.

```
                    00 GROUND
                      FLOOR
                      0' - 0"




                    00 T.O Footing
                      -15' - 0"
```

Figure 2–52

9. Create a structural plan view of the 00 T.O. FOOTING. The view displays in the Project browser and if you return to the South view, you will notice the level head is now blue.

10. Zoom out to display the entire project.

End of practice

2.6 Creating Grids

Grids are annotation elements that display in most views, including plan, ceiling, section, and elevation views. They help organize your design when developing a layout and describe the pattern and location for columns, as shown in Figure 2–53. Grids can be multi-segmented, arcs, or straight lines, and they can be hidden in the view if needed.

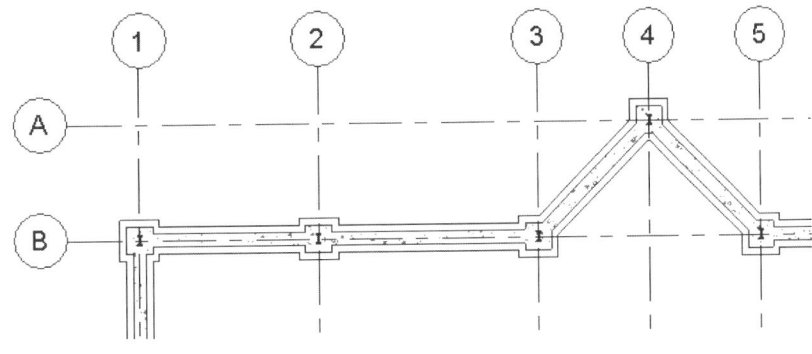

Figure 2–53

Each line or arc in a grid is a separate entity and can be placed, moved, and modified individually.

Grids cannot be drawn in a 3D view but grids can be displayed in a 3D view, perspective view, or in a 3D view with a selection box, and when you click on a grid, the surface contour displays.

Note: *If you are upgrading a model to the 2024 version, you will need to turn on the grids.*

How To: Create a Grid

1. In the *Architecture* tab>Datum panel, click (Grid), or type **GR**.
2. In the Properties Type Selector, select the grid type, which will control the size of the bubble and the linestyle.
3. In the *Modify | Place Grid* tab>Draw panel (shown in Figure 2–54), select the draw method you want to use.

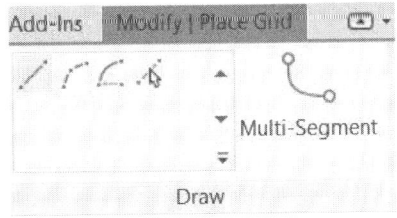

Figure 2–54

4. In the Options Bar, set the *Offset* if needed.
5. Start drawing grid lines.

- Grids can be sketched at any angle, but you should ensure that all parallel grids are sketched in the same direction (e.g., from left to right or from bottom to top).
- When using the Multi-Segment tool (shown in Figure 2–55), sketch the line and click ✔ (Finish Edit Mode) to complete the command.

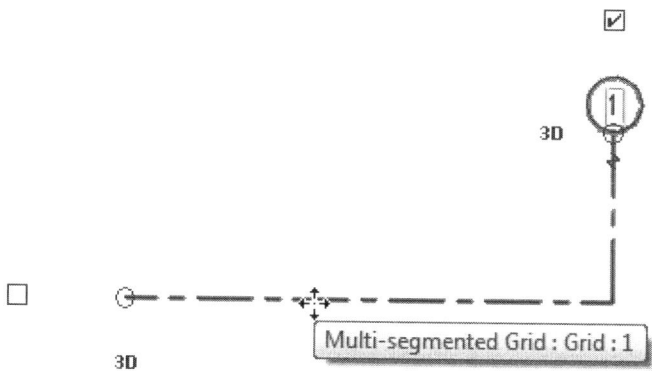

Figure 2–55

How To: Show Grids in 3D

1. Open a 3D or perspective view and press <Esc> twice to verify nothing is selected.
2. In Properties, click **Edit...** next to *Show Grids*, as shown in Figure 2–56.

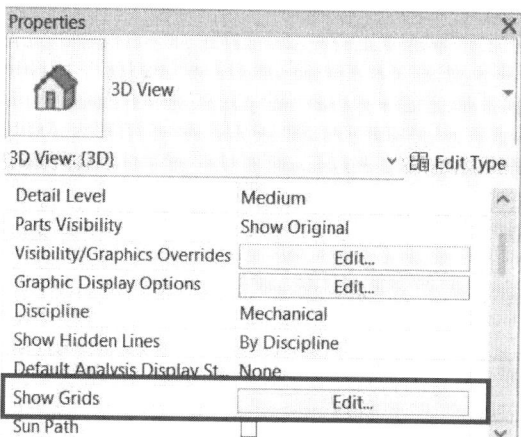

Figure 2–56

3. In the Show Grids dialog box, select the level(s) that you want the grids to display at in the 3D view, as shown in Figure 2–57.

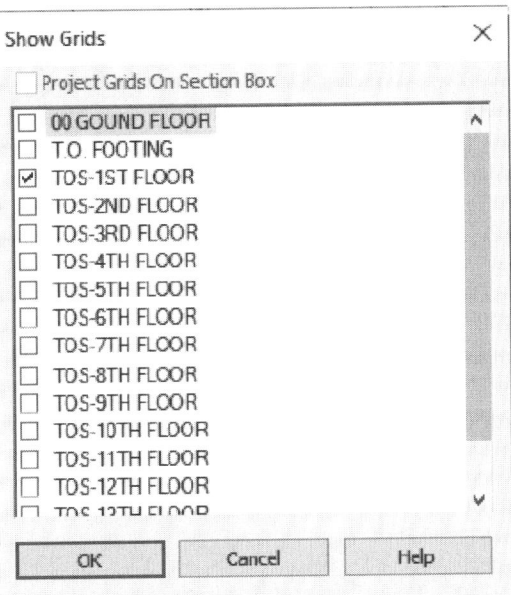

Figure 2–57

4. Click **OK**.
5. (Optional) To display the grids on the bottom of a section box, in Properties, verify that **Section Box** is selected, and click **Edit...** next to *Show Grids*.
6. In the Show Grids dialog box, select only the **Project Grids On Section Box** option, as shown in Figure 2–58, and click **OK**.

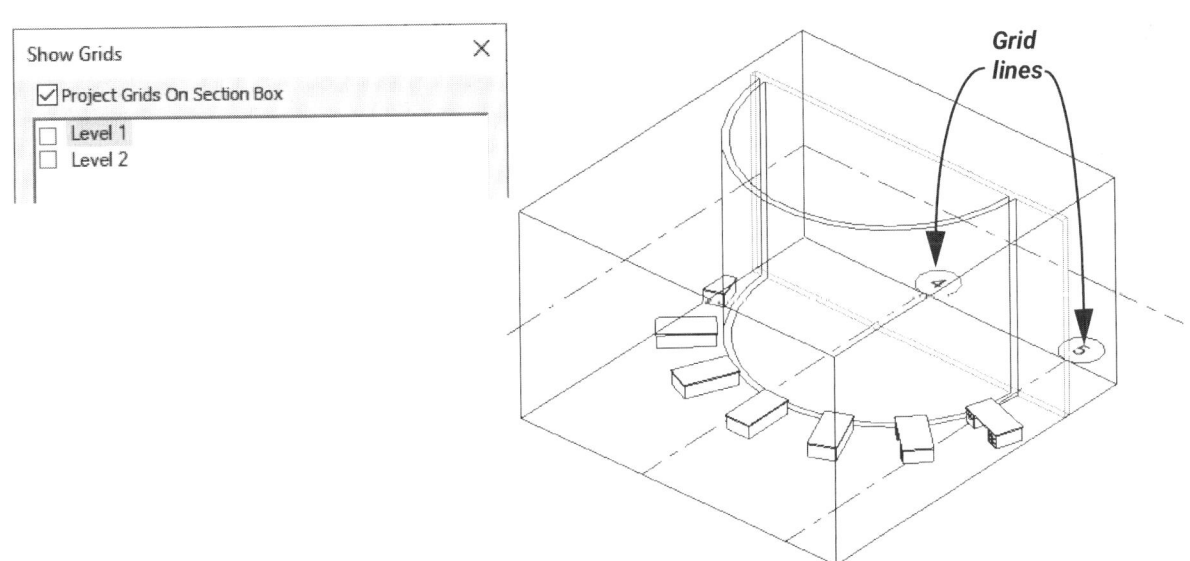

Figure 2–58

Modifying Grid Lines

Grid lines, like levels, are data elements. You can modify grid lines using controls, alignments, and temporary dimensions in the view (as shown in Figure 2–59). You can change the bubble type using the Type Selector.

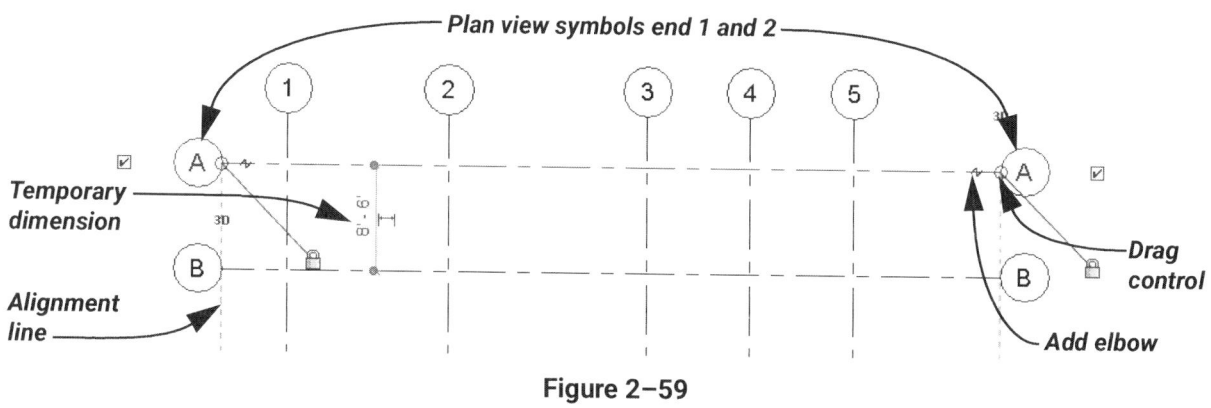

Figure 2–59

- Grid numbers can be numbers, letters, or a combination of the two. To modify a grid number, double-click on the number in the bubble and type the new letter/number. You can also change the grid number by entering a new *Name* in Properties.

- Grid numbers increment automatically.

- In a 3D view, you can modify the grid line name and adjust the grid line and grid distance.

    - Click the (Drag the extents of the grid in the model) control to lengthen the grid line.
    - Modify the temporary dimension (as shown in Figure 2–60) to change the grid line's distance from another grid line.

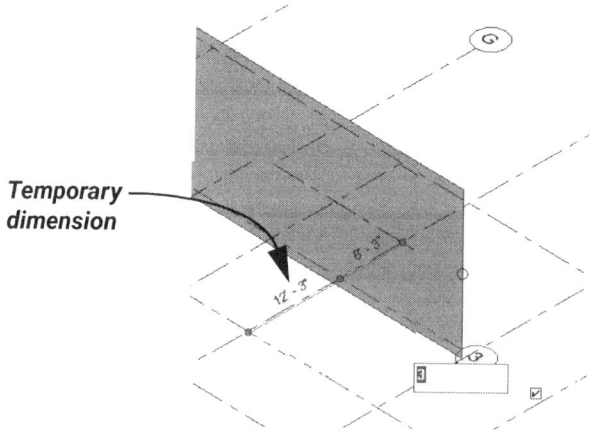

Figure 2–60

- Change the grid line name by selecting the bubble and typing in a new name; alternatively, the name can be changed in Properties.

- In Type Properties, change the way the grid **Plan View Symbols Ends** display, as shown in Figure 2–61. The first pick point is plan view symbol end 1 and the second pick point is plan view symbol end 2.

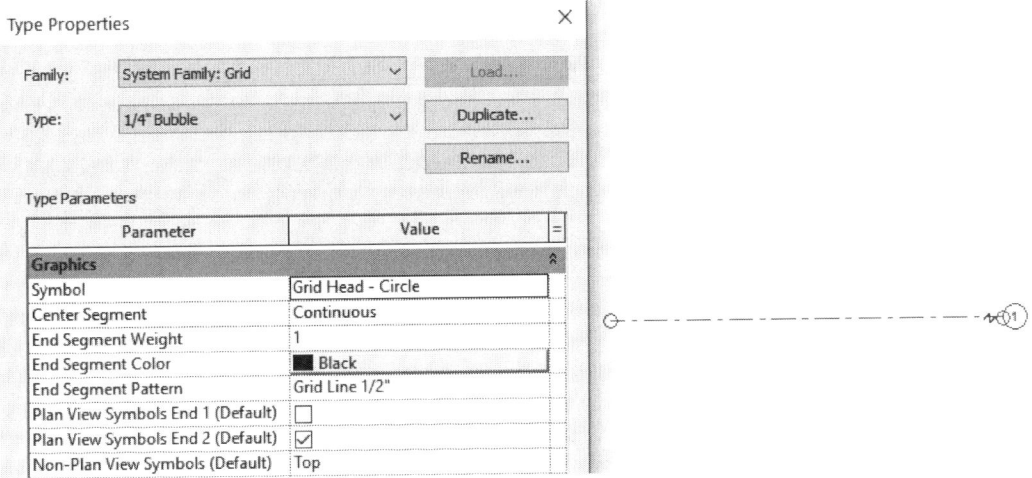

Figure 2–61

Hint: Propagating Datum Extents

If column grids do not display in a view, this might be due to adding a level after the grid lines were added. To display the grid lines in plan views, select the grid lines in a view in which they are displayed. In the *Modify | Grids* tab>Datum panel, click (Propagate Extents). In the Propagate datum extents dialog box (shown in Figure 2–62), select the views to project the grid lines to.

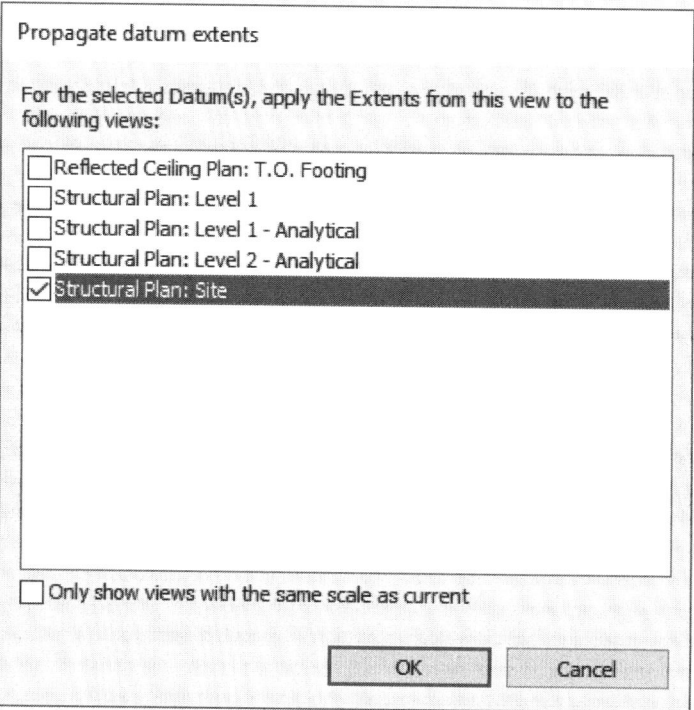

Figure 2–62

- This also works for levels.

- (Propagate Extents) is particularly useful to make grid lines display the same in all views.

Practice 2c
Add Grids

Practice Objective

- Add and modify grid lines.

In this practice, you will place grid lines using the linked Revit and CAD models as a guide. You will then add additional grid lines where curved walls need extra support, as shown in Figure 2–63.

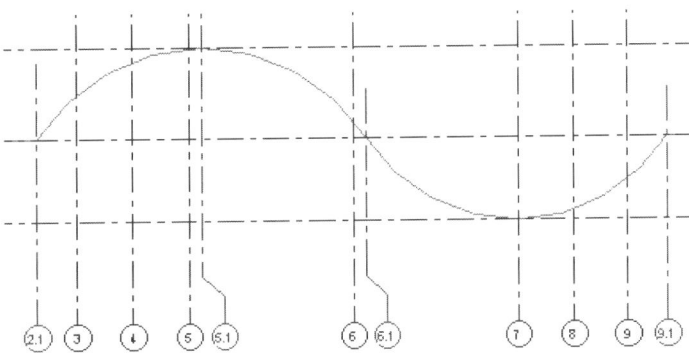

Figure 2–63

Task 1: Add grid lines.

1. Open **Structural-Grids.rvt** from the practice files folder.
2. Open the **Structural Plans: 00 GROUND FLOOR** view.
3. Open the Visibility/Graphics Overrides dialog box by typing **VV**.
4. Click on the *Imported Categories* tab. In the *Visibility* column, clear the checkbox next to the First-Floor-Structural-Suites.dwg as shown in Figure 2–64 to turn off the CAD file in the view.

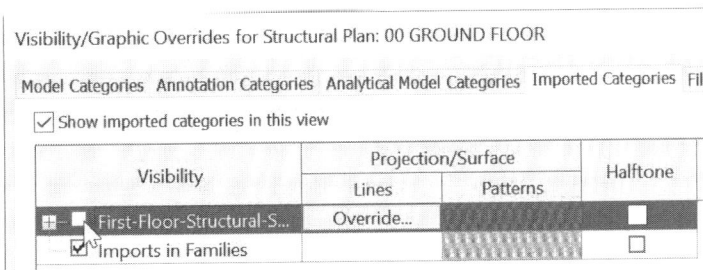

Figure 2–64

5. Click **OK**.

6. In the *Structure* tab>Datum panel, click (Grid).
7. In the *Modify | Place Grid* tab>Draw panel, click (Pick Lines).
8. Select the first horizontal grid line on the linked file. Zoom into the grid head and click inside the bubble, type **A**, and press <Enter>.
9. Continue selecting the vertical grid lines displayed in the imported file. The letters automatically increment.
10. Click the first vertical grid line and change the letter in the bubble to **1**.
11. Continue selecting the horizontal grid lines. The numbers automatically increment.
12. Click (Modify) to end the command.
13. Only the grids should now display, as shown in Figure 2–65. Check the lengths of all grid lines. Modify the length by dragging the ends if needed.

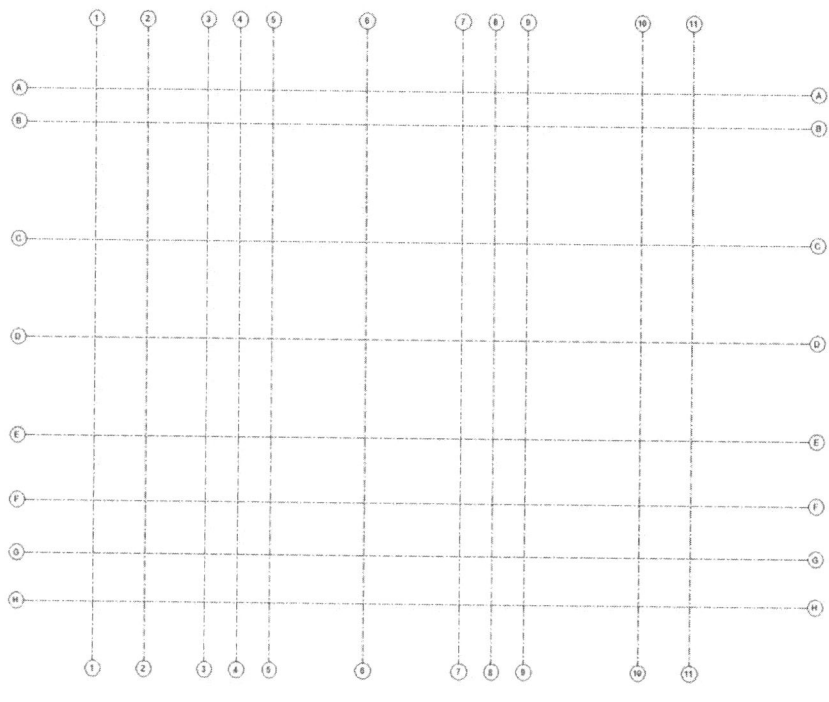

Figure 2–65

14. Open the default 3D.
15. Click (Modify).
16. In Properties, in the *Graphics* section, click **Edit...** next to *Show Grids*.
17. In the Show Grids dialog box, select **00 GROUND FLOOR** and click **OK**.

18. The grids now display as shown in Figure 2–66.

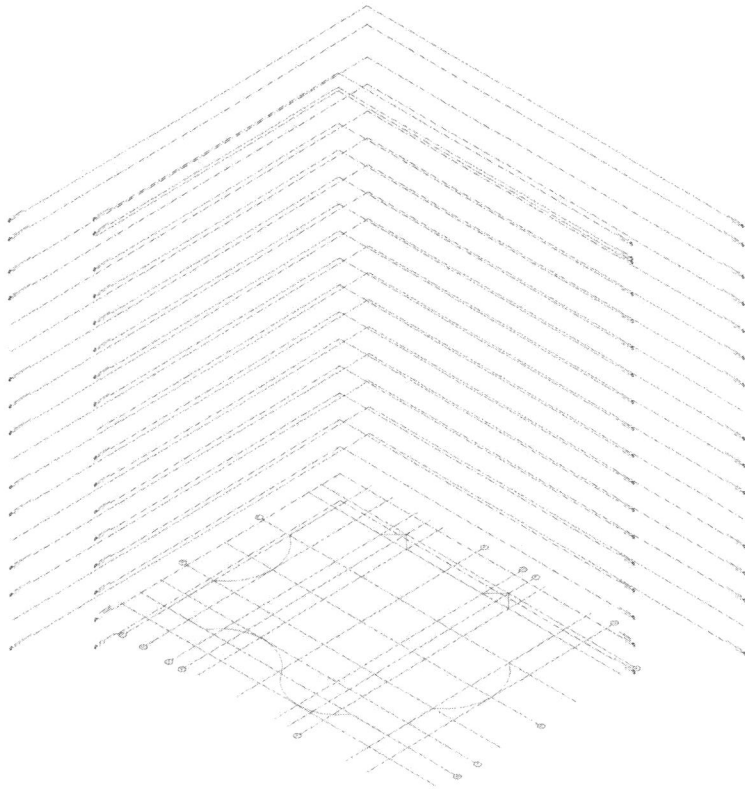

Figure 2–66

19. Save the project.

Task 2: Add grid lines at arc points.

1. In the **Structural Plans: 00 GROUND FLOOR** view, zoom in on the south side of the floor plan, Additional grid lines need to be placed at the midpoints and end points of the arcs to support the curtain wall.
2. Open the Visibility/Graphics Overrides dialog box by typing **VV**.

3. Click on the *Imported Categories* tab. In the Visibility column, check the checkbox next to the **First-Floor-Structural-Suites-M.dwg**, as shown in Figure 2–67 to turn the CAD file back on in the view.

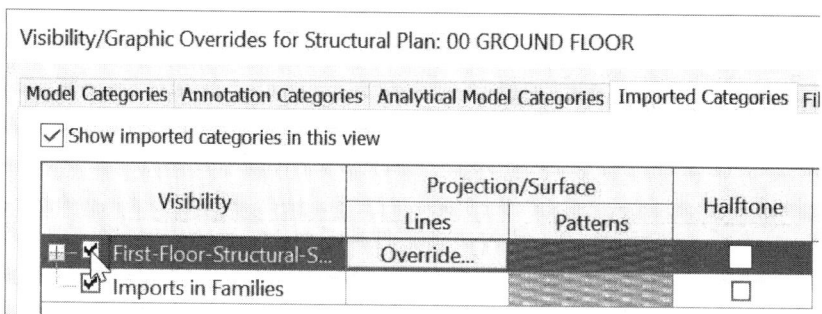

Figure 2–67

4. Click **OK**.
5. Zoom and pan to the south grid heads.
6. In the *Structure* tab>Datum panel, click (Grid). In the *Modify | Place Grid* tab>Draw panel, verify that (Line) is selected.
7. Using the linked DWG as a guide, draw a grid line between grids **2** and **3**, as shown in Figure 2–68.

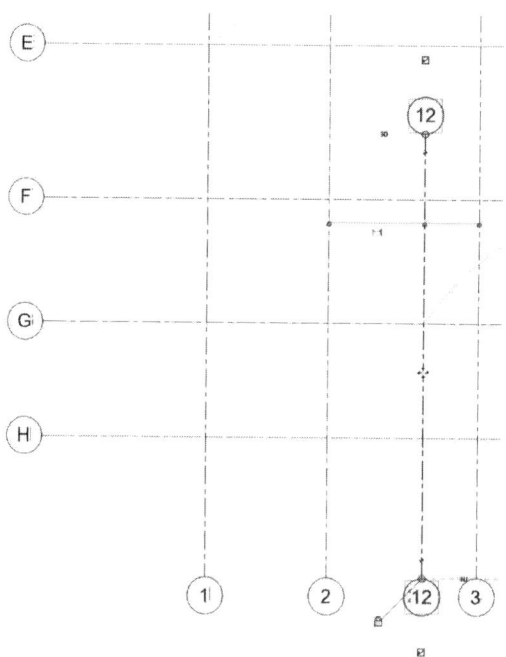

Figure 2–68

8. Once the grid line is in place, rename it to **2.1**.

9. Draw another vertical grid line at the midpoint of the same arc between grid 5 and 6, as shown in Figure 2-69. Align the grid's bubble head with the others.

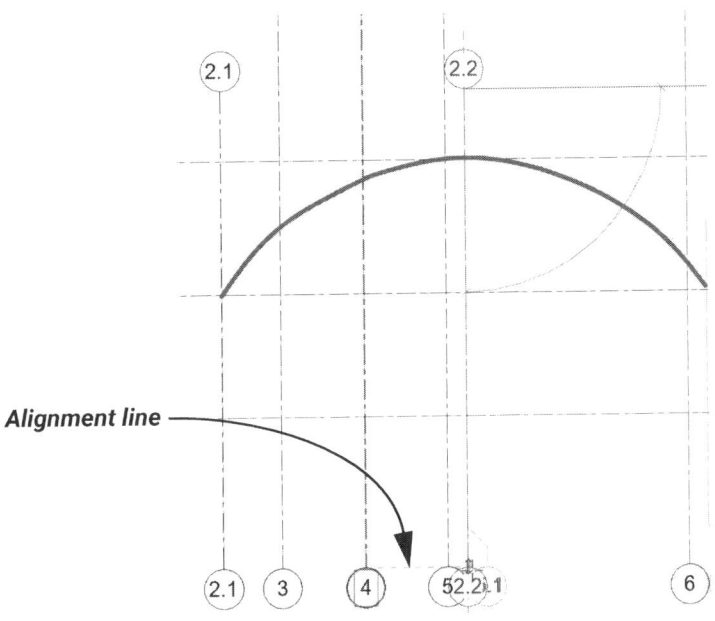

Figure 2-69

10. Click (Modify).
11. Select the new grids, and in Properties, change the *Name* to **5.1**, as shown in Figure 2-70. The grid number changes in the view.

Figure 2-70

12. Close to the grid 5.1 bubble head, click on (Add elbow), as shown in Figure 2-71 to create a jog.

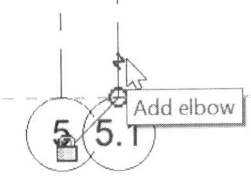

Figure 2-71

13. Click and drag the grip so the grid bubble head is away from grid 5's head, as shown in Figure 2-72.

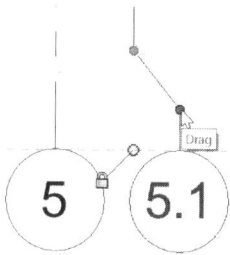

Figure 2-72

14. Add grid lines to the second arc for 6.1 and 9.1, as shown in Figure 2-73. When you are finished, there should be four new grid lines: **2.1**, **5.1**, **6.1**, and **9.1**.

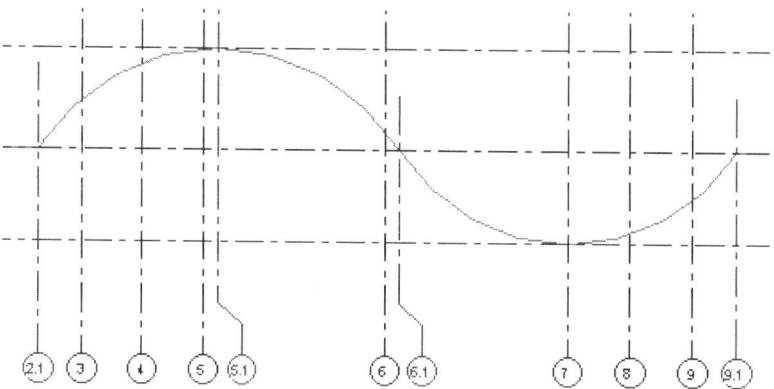

Figure 2-73

15. Click (Modify).
16. Zoom out to see the full layout.
17. Save and close the model.

End of practice

Chapter Review Questions

1. What type of view do you need to be in to add a level to your project?

    a. Any non-plan view.

    b. As this is done using a dialog box, the view does not matter.

    c. Any view except for 3D.

    d. Any section or elevation view.

2. How do you line up grid lines that might be different lengths, as shown in Figure 2–74?

    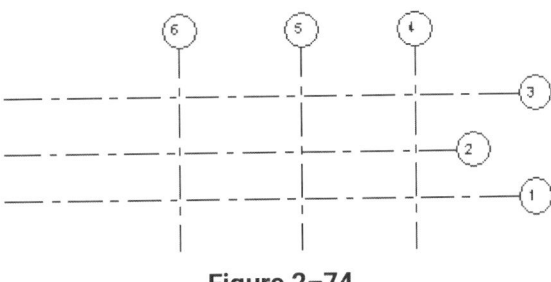

    Figure 2–74

    a. Use ▤ (Trim/Extend Multiple Elements) to line them up with a common reference line.

    b. Select the grid line and use the drag control to line up with the other grid lines.

    c. Select the grid line, right-click and select **Auto-Align**.

    d. In Properties, change the *Length* and then use ✥ (Move) to get them into position.

3. Grids can be displayed in a 3D view.

    a. True

    b. False

4. In order for architectural columns to move with grids, what needs to be selected when placing the column?

    a. In the ribbon, select **At Grids**.

    b. Set the *Top Constraint* to grids.

    c. Columns always move with grids no matter what type.

    d. In Properties, select **Moves With Grids**.

5. Which of the following types of CAD formats can you import into Revit? (Select all that apply.)
    a. .DWG
    b. .XLS
    c. .SAT
    d. .DGN

6. Imported CAD files cannot be reloaded in the Manage Links dialog box.
    a. True
    b. False

7. To modify linked CAD files, you need to open what dialog box?
    a. Type Properties
    b. Link CAD
    c. Manage Links
    d. Insert from File

Command Summary

Button	Command	Location
	Grid	• **Ribbon:** *Architecture* tab>Datum panel • **Shortcut:** GR
	Import CAD	• **Ribbon:** *Insert* tab>Import panel
	Import PDF	• **Ribbon:** *Insert* tab>Import panel
	Level	• **Ribbon:** *Architecture* tab>Datum panel • **Shortcut:** LL
	Link CAD	• **Ribbon:** *Insert* tab>Link panel
	Link PDF	• **Ribbon:** *Insert* tab>Link panel
	Link Revit	• **Ribbon:** *Insert* tab>Link panel
	Multi-Segment (Grid)	• **Ribbon:** *Modify	Place Grid* tab>Draw panel
	Propagate Extents	• **Ribbon:** *Modify	Grids* or *Modify	Levels* tab>Datum panel
	Temporary Hide/Isolate	• **View Control Bar**

Chapter 3

Working with Views

Views are the cornerstone of working with Revit® models as they enable you to see the model in both 2D and 3D. As you are progressing through your project, you can duplicate and change views to display different information based on the same view of the model. Callouts, elevations, and sections are especially important views for construction documents.

Learning Objectives

- Understand the Project Browser.
- Duplicate views so that you can modify the display as you are creating the model and for construction documents.
- Change the way elements display in different views to show required information and set views for construction documents.
- Create callout views of parts of plans, sections, or elevations for detailing.
- Add building and interior elevations that can be used to demonstrate how a building will be built.
- Create building and wall sections to help you create the model and to include in construction documents.
- Create 3D section views using selection boxes and Orient to View.

3.1 Understand the Project Browser

When starting a project using the supplied Revit templates, the Project Browser displays the default organization for the view tabs as **all** (as shown in Figure 3-1). You also see a status icon next to the view that indicates if the view has been added to a sheet: a white box indicates the view is not on a sheet while a colored box indicates the view is on a sheet.

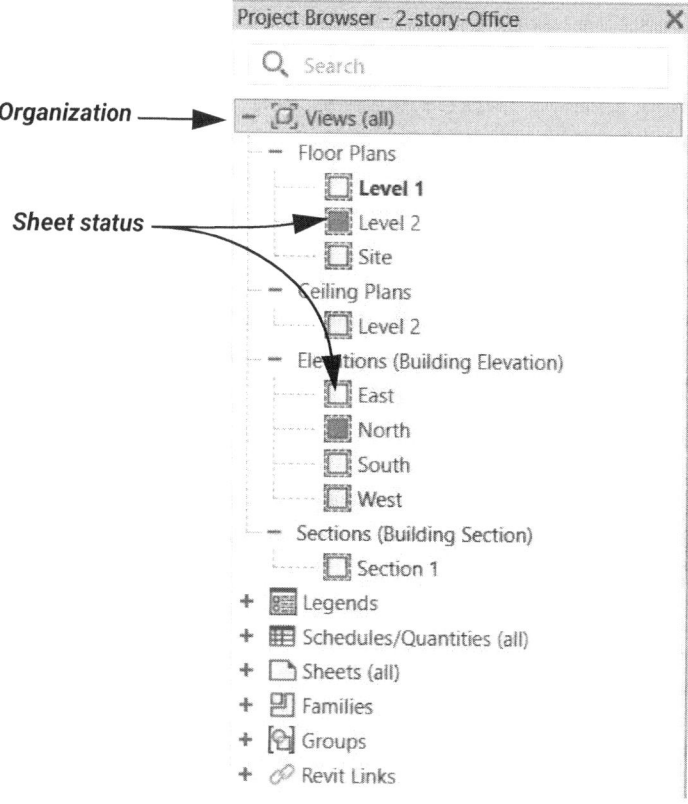

Figure 3-1

- If you no longer require a view, you can delete it. Right-click on its name in the Project Browser and select **Delete**.

    Note: The Project Browser can be floated, resized, or docked on top of Properties. It Project Browser can also be customized by changing the Browser Organization or its location within the application.

How To: Open Multiple Views

1. To open multiple views, press and hold either <Shift> or <Ctrl> and select the views, right-click, and select **Open**, as shown in Figure 3–2.

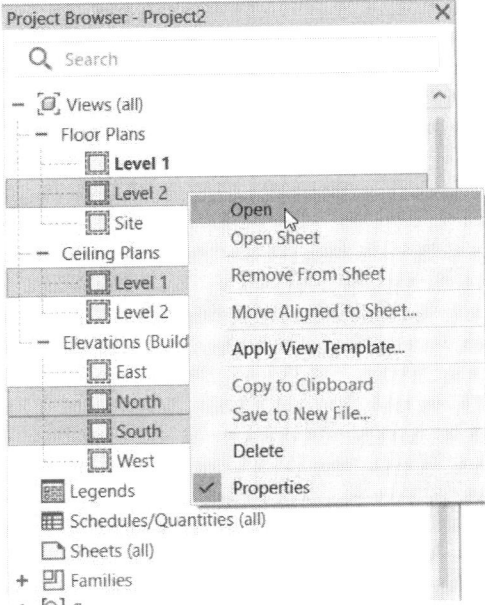

Figure 3–2

2. In the Open View dialog box (shown in Figure 3–3), click **OK**.

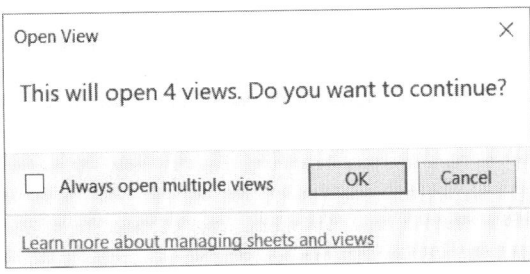

Figure 3–3

- To bypass the Open View dialog box in future, check the **Always open multiple views** checkbox.

View Placement on Sheet Status Icon

The box to the left of the view name indicates if the view has been placed on a sheet.

- A box that's filled in indicates the view is on a sheet.
- A white (empty) box indicates the view is not on a sheet.
- A half-filled box indicates the view is partially placed on a sheet (e.g., in the case where a schedule has multiple views because of the schedule's length).

How To: Turn Off the Sheet Status Icon

1. In the Project Browser, right-click on any of the view names or on the **Views (all)** node at the top.
2. Select **Show View Placement on Sheet Status Icons**, as shown in Figure 3–4.

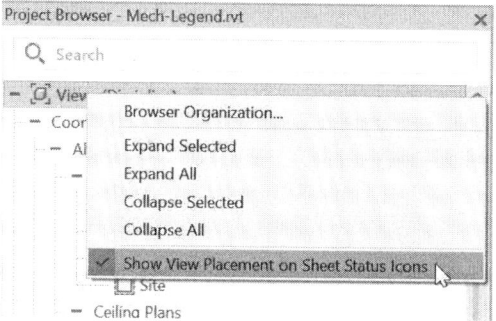

Figure 3–4

Search in Project Browser

At the top of the Project Browser is a search bar so you can quickly find a view. When working in a view, you can locate its location in the Project Browser by right-clicking in an empty area in the view (with nothing selected) and selecting **Find in Project Browser**. The view will highlight in the Project Browser. You can also locate an element in the Project Browser by selecting the element in a view, right-clicking, and selecting **Find in Project Browser**.

Displaying Views in the Project Browser

You can customize how the views are displayed in the Project Browser by changing the Browser Organization for each of the tabs: *Views*, *Sheets* or *Schedules*, as shown in Figure 3–5.

Working with Views

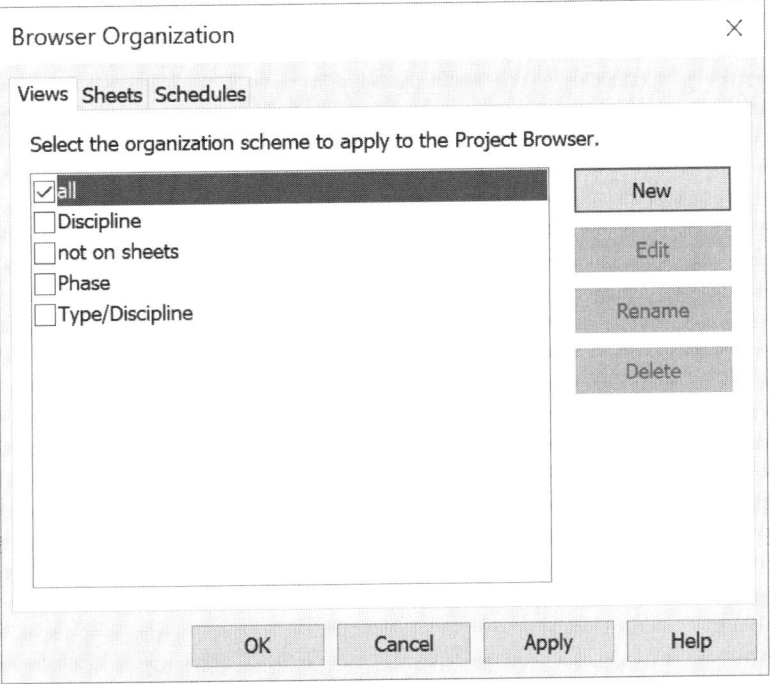

Figure 3–5

How To: Change How the Project Browser Displays Views

1. In the Project Browser, right-click on **Views (all)** and select **Browser Organization...**, as shown in Figure 3–6.

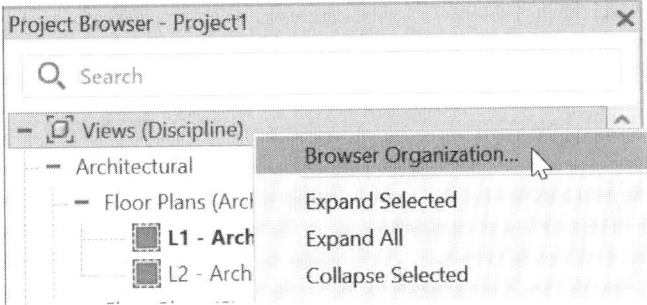

Figure 3–6

2. In the Browser Organization dialog box, select **Type/Discipline**, as shown in Figure 3–7.

Browser Organization
Views
Sheets
Schedules
Select the organization scheme to apply to the Project Browser.
all
Discipline
not on sheets
Phase
Type/Discipline
New
Edit
Rename

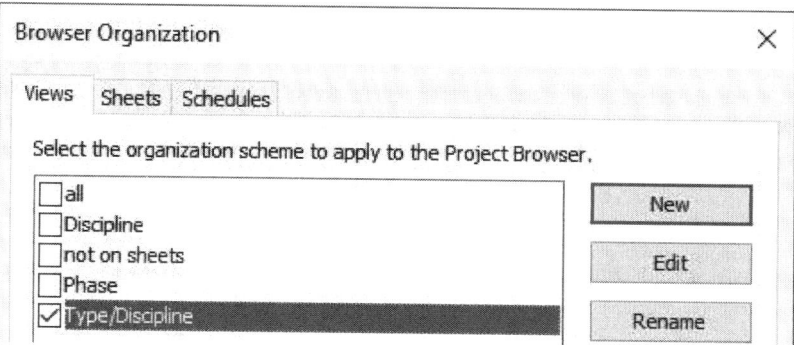

Figure 3–7

3. The Project Browser updates to sort by view type (e.g., Floor Plans, Ceiling Plans, etc.), then by discipline. Figure 3–8 shows the difference between the two browser organization types.

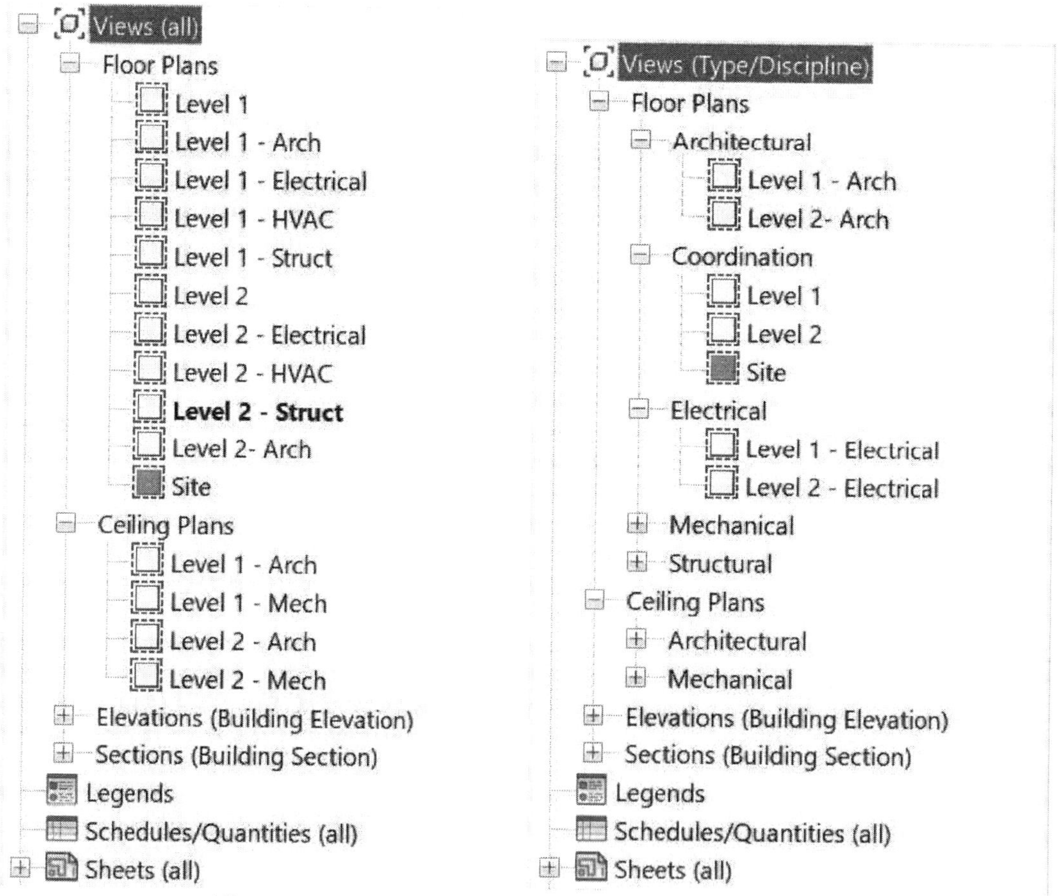

Views (all)
Floor Plans
Level 1
Level 1 - Arch
Level 1 - Electrical
Level 1 - HVAC
Level 1 - Struct
Level 2
Level 2 - Electrical
Level 2 - HVAC
Level 2 - Struct
Level 2- Arch
Site
Ceiling Plans
Level 1 - Arch
Level 1 - Mech
Level 2 - Arch
Level 2 - Mech
Elevations (Building Elevation)
Sections (Building Section)
Legends
Schedules/Quantities (all)
Sheets (all)
Views (Type/Discipline)
Floor Plans
Architectural
Level 1 - Arch
Level 2- Arch
Coordination
Level 1
Level 2
Site
Electrical
Level 1 - Electrical
Level 2 - Electrical
Mechanical
Structural
Ceiling Plans
Architectural
Mechanical
Elevations (Building Elevation)
Sections (Building Section)
Legends
Schedules/Quantities (all)
Sheets (all)

All ***Type/Discipline***

Figure 3–8

3.2 Duplicating Views

Once you have created a model, you do not have to recreate the elements at different scales or copy them so that they can be used on more than one sheet. Instead, you can duplicate the required views and modify the view to suit your needs.

Duplication Types

Duplicate creates a copy of the view that only includes the building elements and view properties, as shown in Figure 3-9. Annotation and detailing are not copied into the new view. Building model elements automatically change in all views, but view-specific changes made to the new view are not reflected in the original view.

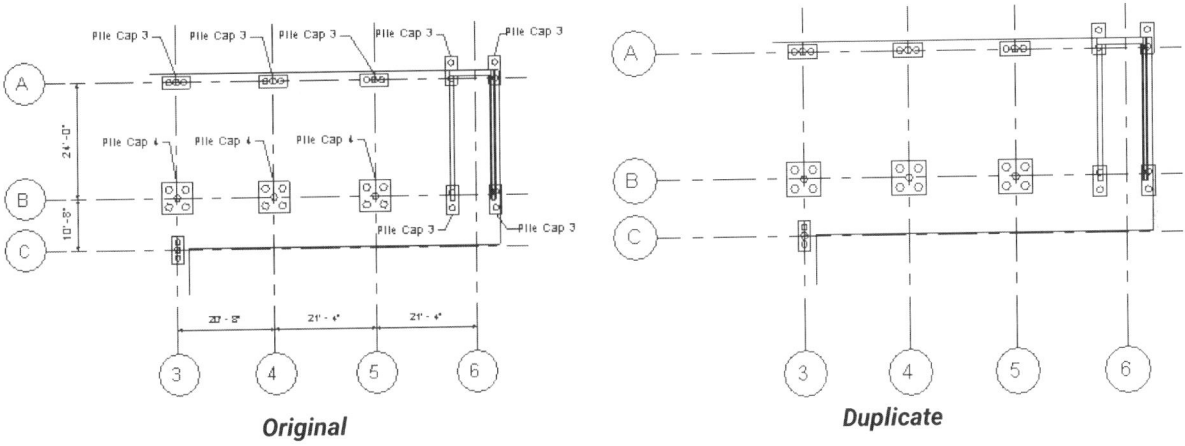

Original   *Duplicate*

Figure 3-9

Duplicate with Detailing creates a copy of the view and includes all annotation and detail elements (such as tags), as shown in Figure 3-10. Any annotation or view-specific elements created in the new view are not reflected in the original view.

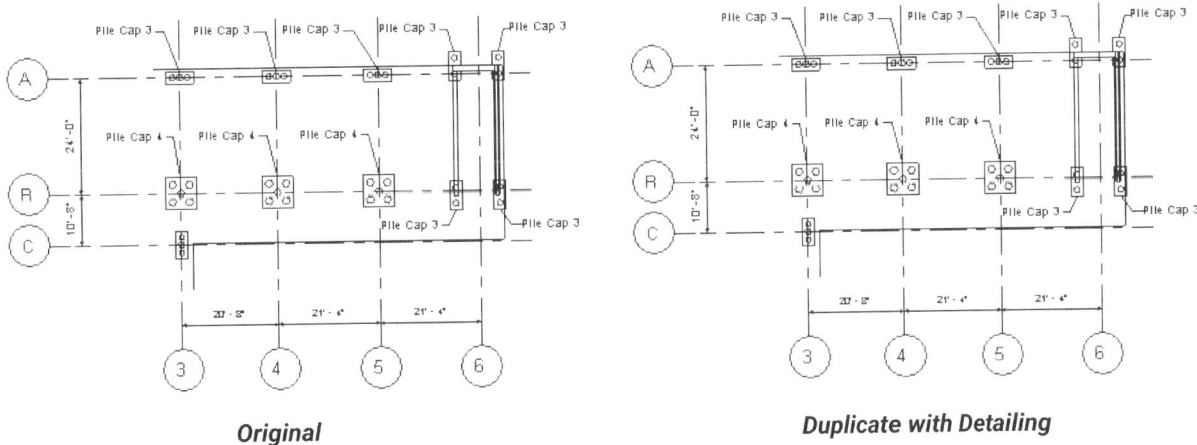

Original   *Duplicate with Detailing*

Figure 3-10

Duplicate as a Dependent creates a copy of the view and links it to the original (parent) view, as shown in the Project Browser in Figure 3–11 (Show View Placement on Sheet Status Icons is turned off). View-specific changes made to the overall view, such as changing the *Scale*, are also reflected in the dependent (child) views and vice-versa.

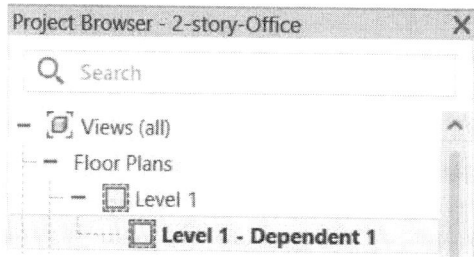

Figure 3–11

- Use dependent views when the building model is so large that you need to split the building onto separate sheets, while ensuring that the views are all at the same scale.

- If you want to separate a dependent view from the original view, right-click on the dependent view and select **Convert to independent view**.

How To: Create Duplicate Views

1. Open the view you want to duplicate.
2. In the *View* tab>Create panel, expand **Duplicate View** and select the type of duplicate view you want to create, as shown in Figure 3–12. Most types of views can be duplicated.

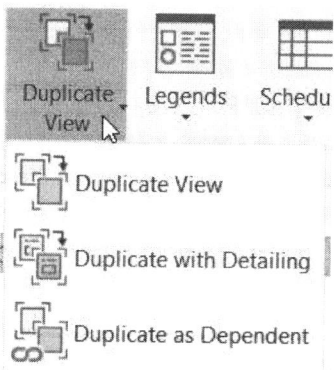

Figure 3–12

- Alternatively, you can right-click on a view in the Project Browser and select the duplicate type you want to use, as shown in Figure 3–13.

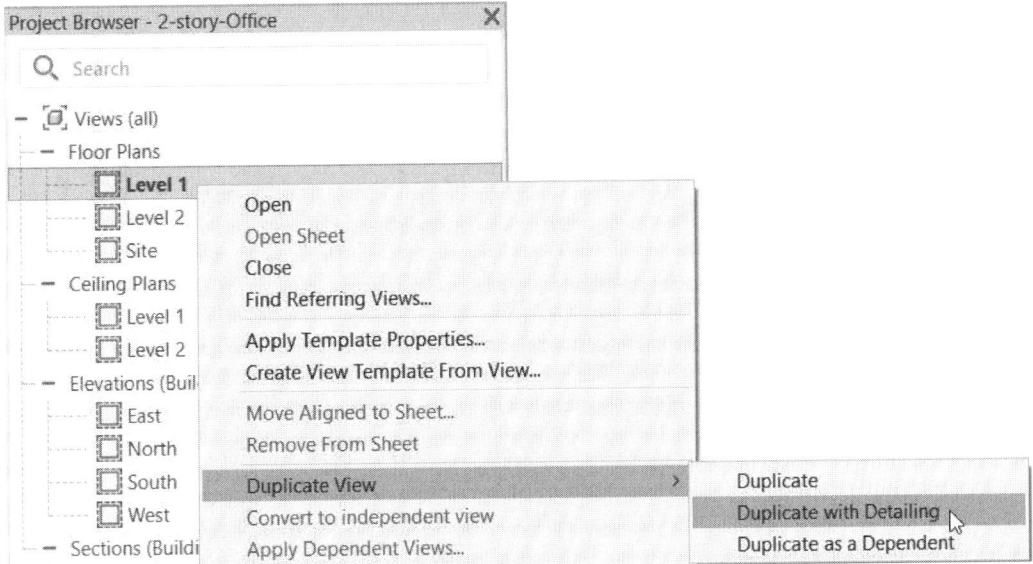

Figure 3–13

3.3 Modify How the View Displays

Views are powerful tools that enable you to create multiple versions of a model without having to recreate building elements. For example, you can have views that are specifically used for working on the model, while other views are annotated and used for construction documents. Different disciplines can have different views that show only the features they require, as shown in Figure 3–14. Properties of one view can be independent of the properties in other views. Once you have modified how a view needs to display, you can create a view template and apply that template to other views.

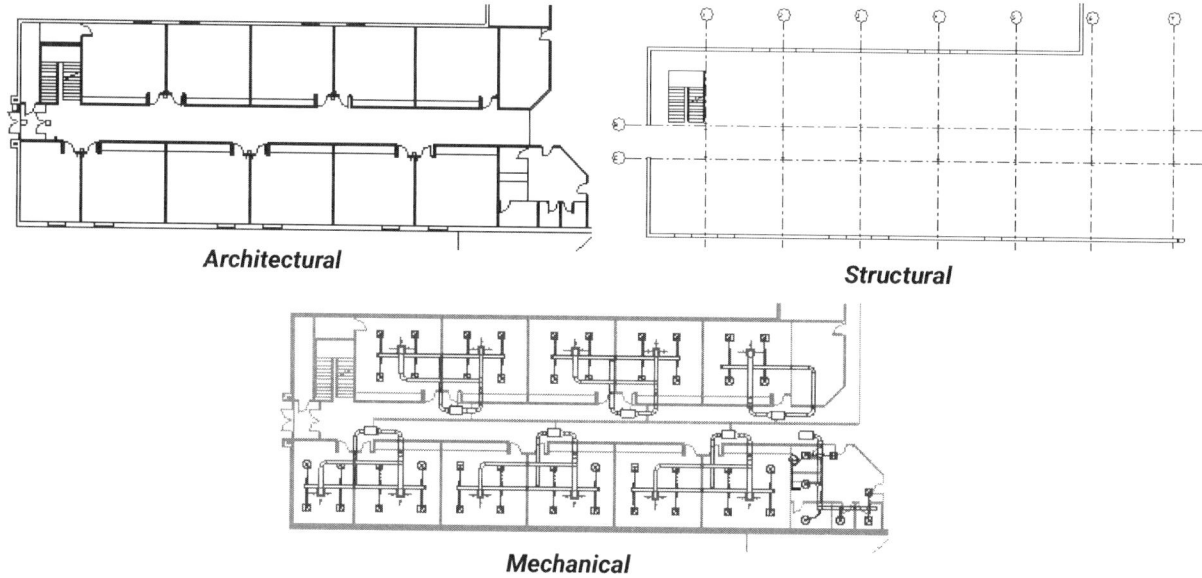

Figure 3–14

The view display can be modified in the following locations:

- View Control Bar
- Properties
- Shortcut menu
- Visibility/Graphic Overrides dialog box

View Control Bar

The most basic properties of a view are accessed using the View Control Bar, shown in Figure 3–15. These include the *Scale*, *Detail Level*, and *Visual Style* options. Additional options include temporary overrides and other advanced settings.

Figure 3–15

- The **Detail Level** controls whether you see compound structure of elements (Coarse Detail) or full scale elements (Medium/Fine Detail), as shown in Figure 3–16.

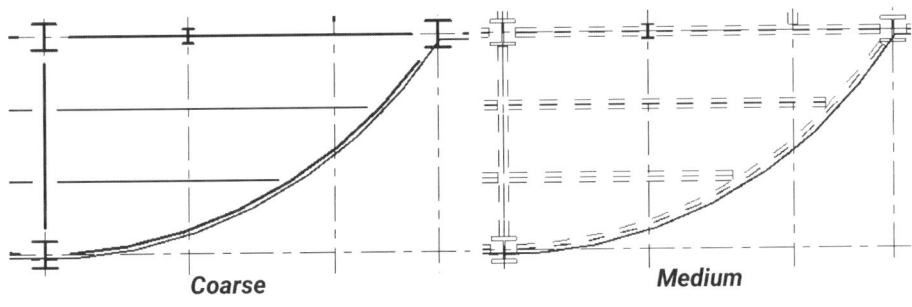

Figure 3–16

View Properties

You can modify how a view displays by modifying the views properties, as shown in Figure 3–17. These properties include *Underlays* and *View Range* as well as many others. The *Discipline* of a view can also be set here.

- The options in Properties vary according to the type of view. A plan view has different properties than a 3D view.

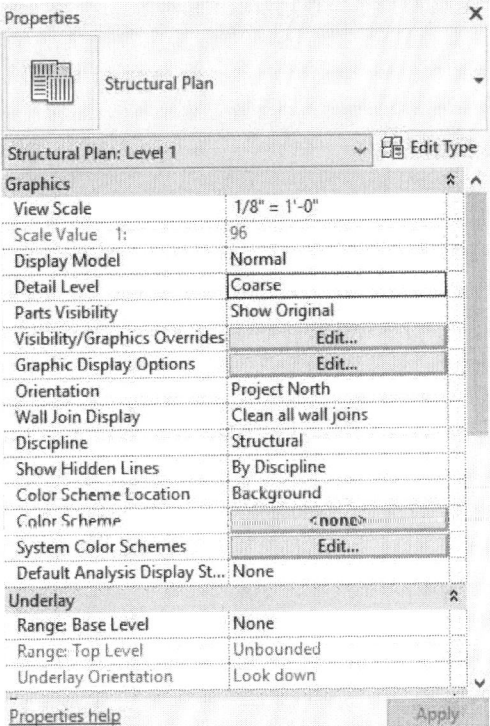

Figure 3–17

Setting an Underlay

Setting an *Underlay* is helpful if you need to display elements on a different level, such as the basement plan shown with an underlay of the first floor plan in Figure 3–18. You can then use the elements to trace over or even copy to the current level of the view.

Note: *Underlays are only available in Floor Plan and Ceiling Plan views.*

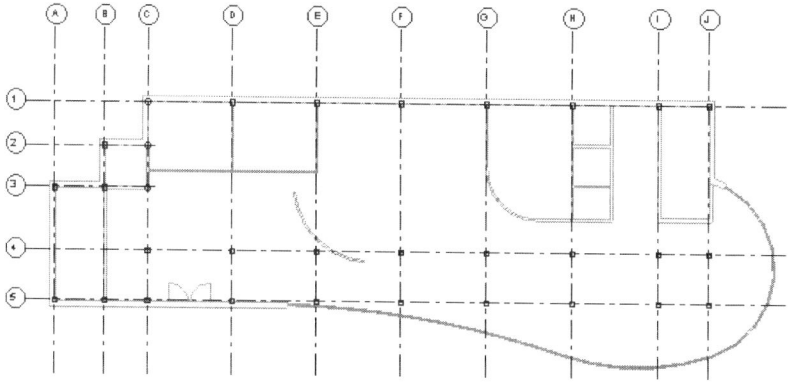

Figure 3–18

In Properties, in the *Underlay* section, specify the *Range: Base Level* and the *Range: Top L*evel. You can also specify the *Underlay Orientation* to **Look down** or **Look up**, as shown in Figure 3–19.

Figure 3–19

- To prevent moving elements in the underlay by mistake, in the Select panel, expand the panel title, and clear **Select underlay elements**. You can also toggle this on/off using (Select Underlay Elements) in the Status Bar.

Setting the View Range

The View Range controls the cut planes that control the visibility of plan views, as shown in the Sample View Range key in Figure 3-20. Elements outside the cut planes do not display unless you include an underlay.

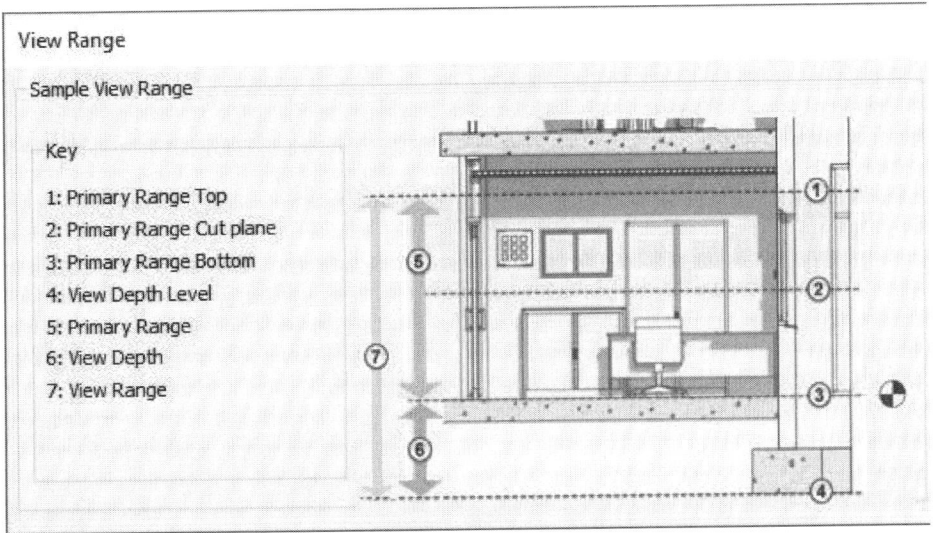

Figure 3-20

How To: Set the View Range

1. In Properties, in the *Extents* section beside *View Range*, select **Edit...**, or type **VR**.
2. In the View Range dialog box, as shown in Figure 3-21, modify the *Levels* and *Offsets* for the *Primary Range* and *View Depth*.
    - Click **<<Show** to display the Sample View Range key.
3. Click **OK**.

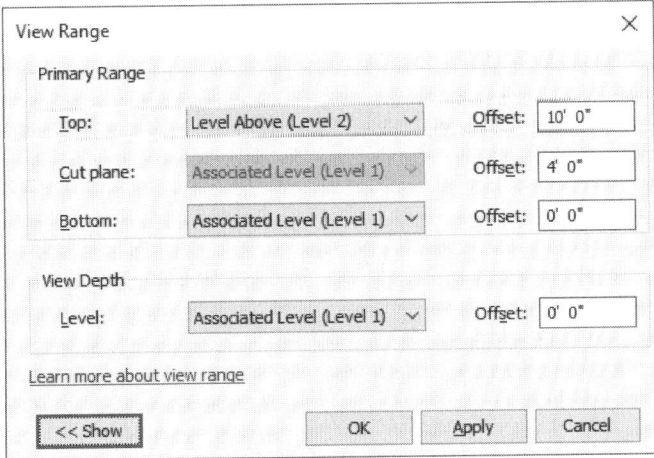

Figure 3-21

- If the settings used cannot be represented graphically, a warning displays, stating the inconsistency.
- A Reflected Ceiling Plan (RCP) is created, as if the ceiling is reflected by a mirror on the floor, so that the ceiling is the same orientation as the floor plan. The cutline is placed just below the ceiling to ensure that any windows and doors below do not display.

Hiding and Overriding Graphics

Two common ways to customize a view are by hiding individual elements or a category in a view and by modifying how elements display graphically in a view by element or category (e.g., altering lineweight, color, or pattern).

An element is an individual object such as one wall or a piece of furniture in a view, while a category includes all instances of a selected element, such as all walls or furniture in a view.

In the example shown in Figure 3–22, a furniture plan has been created by toggling off the structural grids category and then graying out all of the walls and columns.

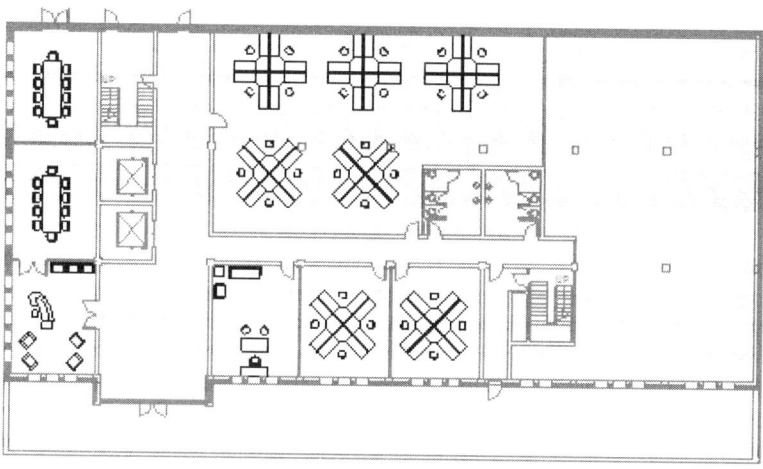

Figure 3–22

How To: Hide Elements or Categories in a View

1. Select the elements or categories you want to hide.
2. Right-click and select **Hide in View>Elements** or **Hide in View>Category**, as shown in Figure 3–23.
   - A quick way to hide entire categories is to select an element(s) and type **VH**.

   Note: The elements or categories are hidden in the current view only.

Working with Views

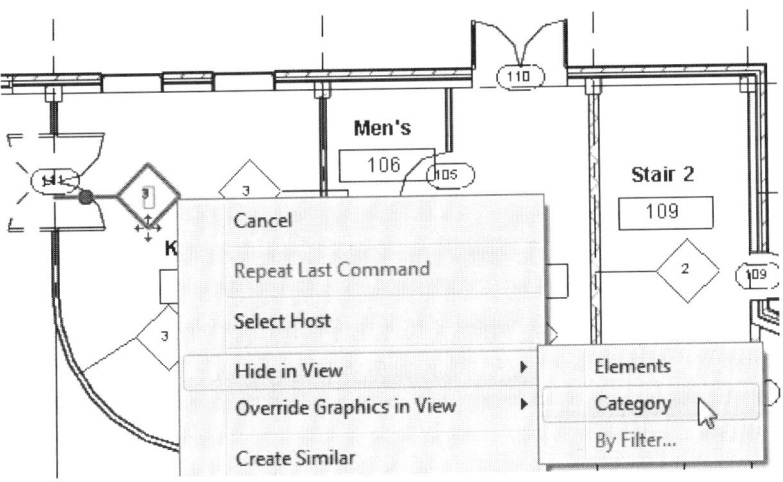

Figure 3–23

How To: Override Graphics of Elements or Categories in a View

1. Select the element(s) you want to modify.
2. Right-click and select **Override Graphics in View>By Element** or **By Category**. The View-Specific Element (or Category) Graphics dialog box opens, as shown in Figure 3–24.

    Note: The exact options in the dialog box vary depending on the type of elements selected.

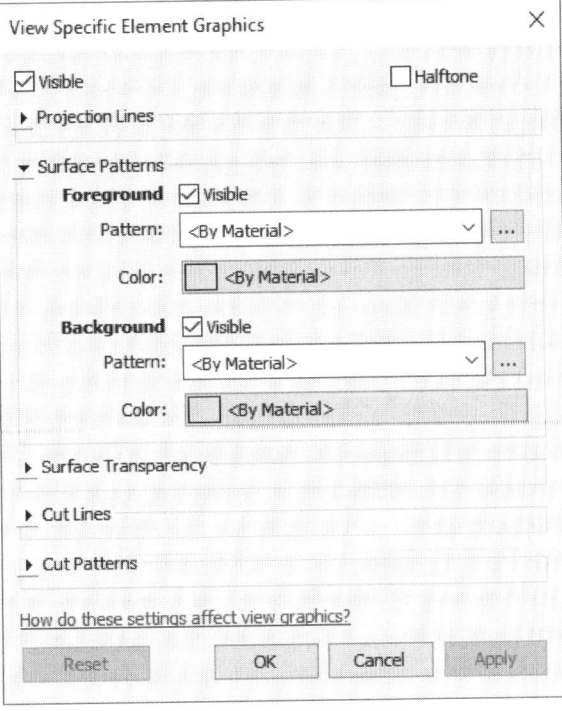

Figure 3–24

3. Select the changes you want to make and click **OK**.

View-Specific Options

- Clearing the **Visible** option is the same as hiding the elements or categories.
- Selecting the **Halftone** option grays out the elements or categories.
- The options for *Projection Lines* and *Cut Lines* include **Weight**, **Color**, and **Pattern**. The options for *Surface Patterns* and *Cut Patterns* include **Visibility**, **Pattern**, and **Color** for the Foreground and Background, as shown previously in Figure 3–24.
- **Surface Transparency** can be set by moving the slider bar, as shown in Figure 3–25.

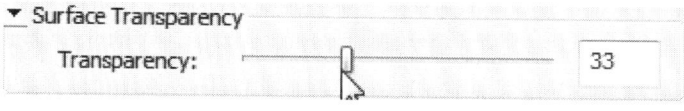

Figure 3–25

- The View-Specific Category Graphics dialog box includes **Open the Visibility Graphics dialog…**, which opens the full dialog box of options.

Visibility/Graphic Overrides

The options in the Visibility/Graphic Overrides dialog box (shown in Figure 3–26) control how every category and sub-category of elements is displayed per view. You can toggle categories on and off, override the *Projection/Surface* and *Cut* information, set categories to *Halftone*, and change the *Detail Level*. To reduce the time it takes to find a category, you can use the *Category name search* to narrow down your search.

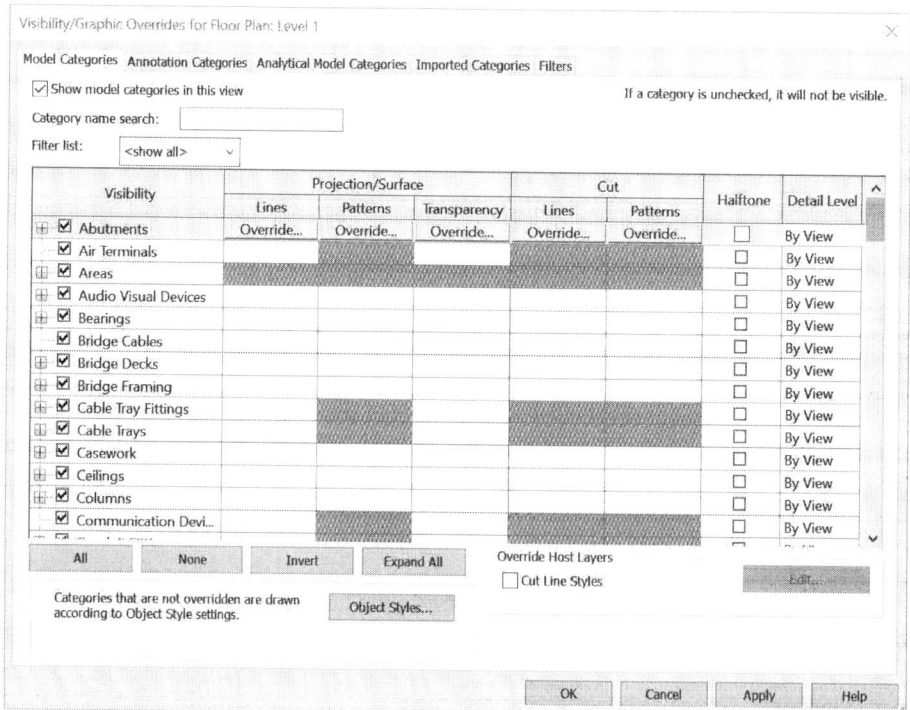

Figure 3–26

To open the Visibility/Graphic Overrides dialog box, type **VV** or **VG**. It is also available in Properties: in the *Graphics* section, beside *Visibility/Graphic Overrides*, click **Edit...**.

- The Visibility/Graphic Overrides are divided into *Model*, *Annotation*, *Analytical Model*, *Imported,* and *Filters* categories.

- Other categories might be available if specific data has been included in the project, including *Design Options*, *Linked Files*, and *Worksets*.

- To limit the number of categories showing in the dialog box, you can type the name of a category in the *Category name search* or select a discipline from the *Filter list*, as shown in Figure 3–27.

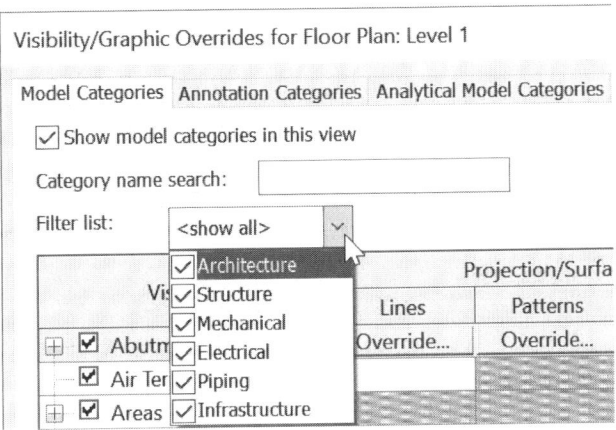

Figure 3–27

- To help you select categories, at the bottom of the Visibility/Graphic Overrides dialog box, use the **All**, **None**, and **Invert** buttons. The **Expand All** button displays all of the sub-categories.

> **Hint: Restoring Hidden Elements or Categories**
>
> If you have hidden categories, you can display them using the Visibility/Graphic Overrides dialog box. To display hidden elements, however, you must temporarily reveal the elements first.
>
> 1. In the View Control Bar, click 💡 (Reveal Hidden Elements). The border and all hidden elements are displayed in magenta, while visible elements in the view are grayed out, as shown in Figure 3–28.
>
>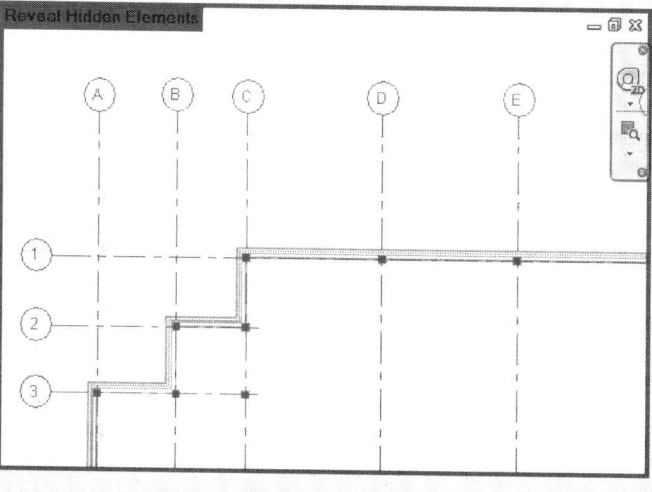
>
> Figure 3–28
>
> 2. Select the hidden elements you want to restore, right-click, and select **Unhide in View>Elements** or **Unhide in View>Category**. Alternatively, in the *Modify* contextual tab> Reveal Hidden Elements panel, click (Unhide Element) or (Unhide Category).
>
> 3. When you are finished, in the View Control Bar, click (Close Reveal Hidden Elements) or, in the *Modify* contextual tab>Reveal Hidden Elements panel, click (Toggle Reveal Hidden Elements Mode).

View Templates

A powerful way to use views effectively is to set up a view and then save it as a view template. You can apply view templates to views individually or through Properties. Setting the view template using Properties helps to ensure that you do not accidentally modify the view while interacting with it.

How To: Create a View Template from a View

1. Set up a view, as needed.

2. In the Project Browser, right-click on the view and select **Create View Template from View**.
3. In the New View Template dialog box, type in a name and click **OK**.
4. The new view template is listed in the View Templates dialog box. Make any modifications needed in the *View properties* section.
5. Click **OK**.

How To: Specify a View Template for a View

1. In the Project Browser, select the view or views to which you want to apply a view template.
2. In Properties, scroll down to the *Identity Data* section and click the button beside *View Template*.
    - Alternatively, in the Project Browser, select a view, right-click, and select **Apply Template Properties...**. If you select more than one view in the Project Browser, right-click and select **Apply View Template...**.
3. In the Apply View Template dialog box, select the view template from the list, as shown in Figure 3–29.

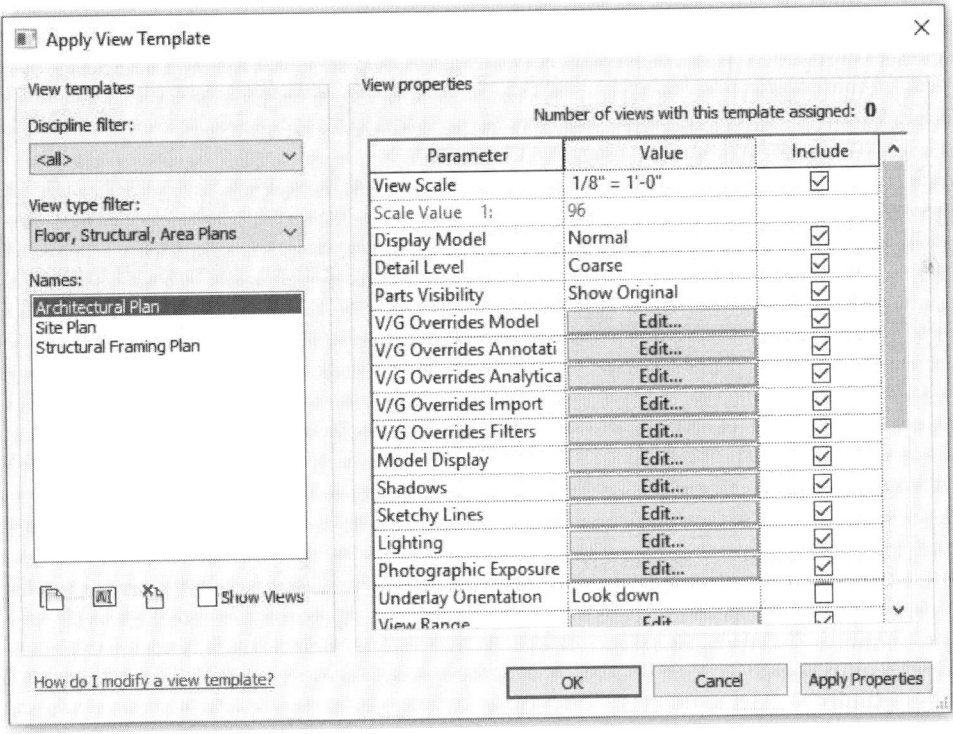

Figure 3–29

4. Click **OK**.

- In the View Control Bar, use (Temporary View Properties) to temporarily apply a view template to a view.

Practice 3a
Duplicate Views and Set the View Display

Practice Objectives

- Duplicate and rename views.
- Hide elements in views.
- Modify the graphic display of elements in views.

In this practice, you will create an analytical view by duplicating a view and then applying an analytical view template that sets the view display shown in Figure 3–30.

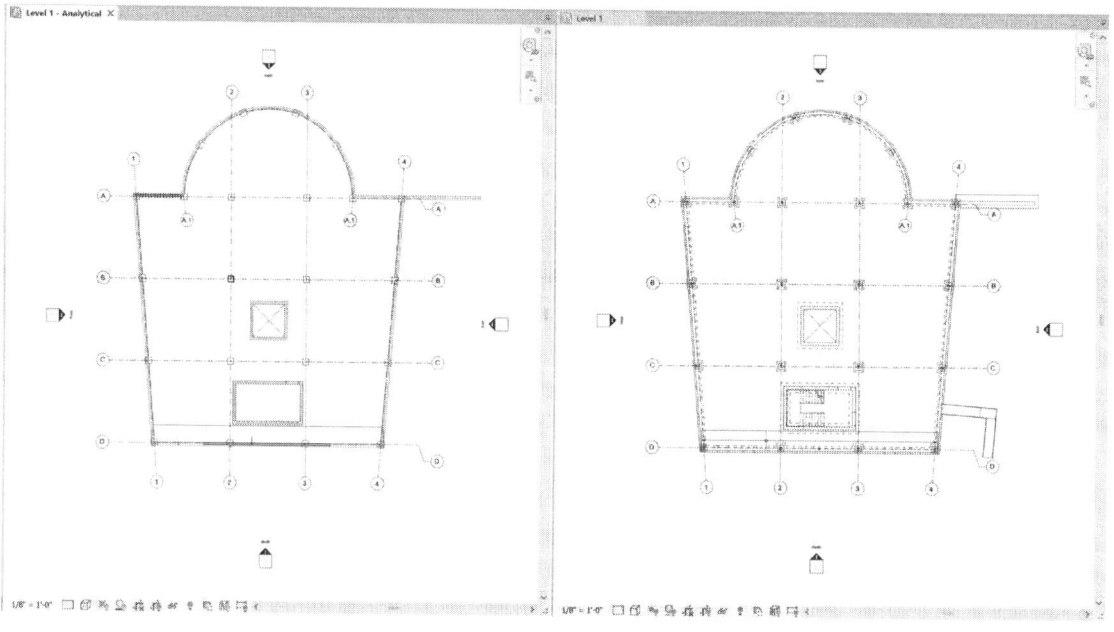

Figure 3–30

1. Open **Structural-Views.rvt** from the practice files folder.
2. From the Project Browser, open the **Structural Plans: Level 2** and **Structural Plans: Level 2 - Analytical** views to see the difference between the two views.
3. Close both of the **Level 2** views.
4. Right-click on **Level 1** and select **Duplicate View> Duplicate**.
5. In the Project Browser, rename the copy as **Level 1 - Analytical**.
6. Verify that only the two **Level 1** views are open and tile them. (Hint: Type **WT**.)
7. Zoom each view so that you can see the entire building. (Hint: Type **ZA**.)

Working with Views

8. Note that both of the views are the same, as shown in Figure 3–31.

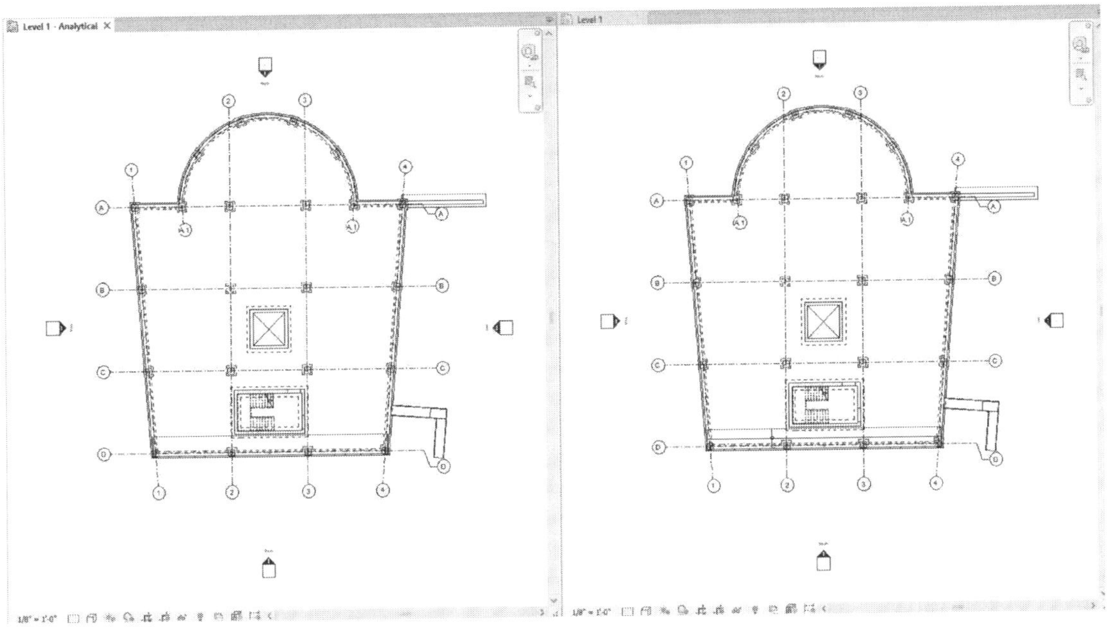

Figure 3–31

9. In the Project Browser, select the new **Level 1 - Analytical** view. Right-click and select **Apply Template Properties...**.

10. In the Apply View Template dialog box, in the *Names* area, select **Structural Analytical Stick** and click **OK**.

11. Zoom in on the view to see the analytical indicators, as shown in Figure 3–32.

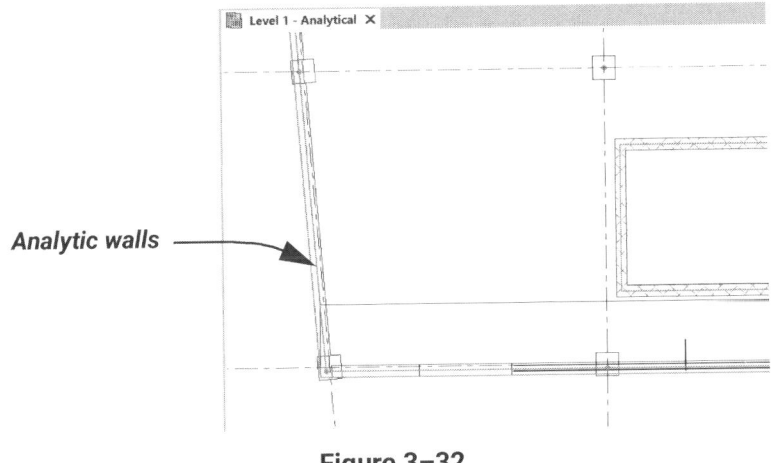

Figure 3–32

12. Close the analytical view.
13. Save and close the project.

End of practice

3.4 Adding Callout Views

Callouts are details of plan, elevation, or section views. When you place a callout in a view, as shown in Figure 3–33, it automatically creates a new view clipped to the boundary of the callout, as shown in Figure 3–34. You can create rectangular or sketched callout boundaries.

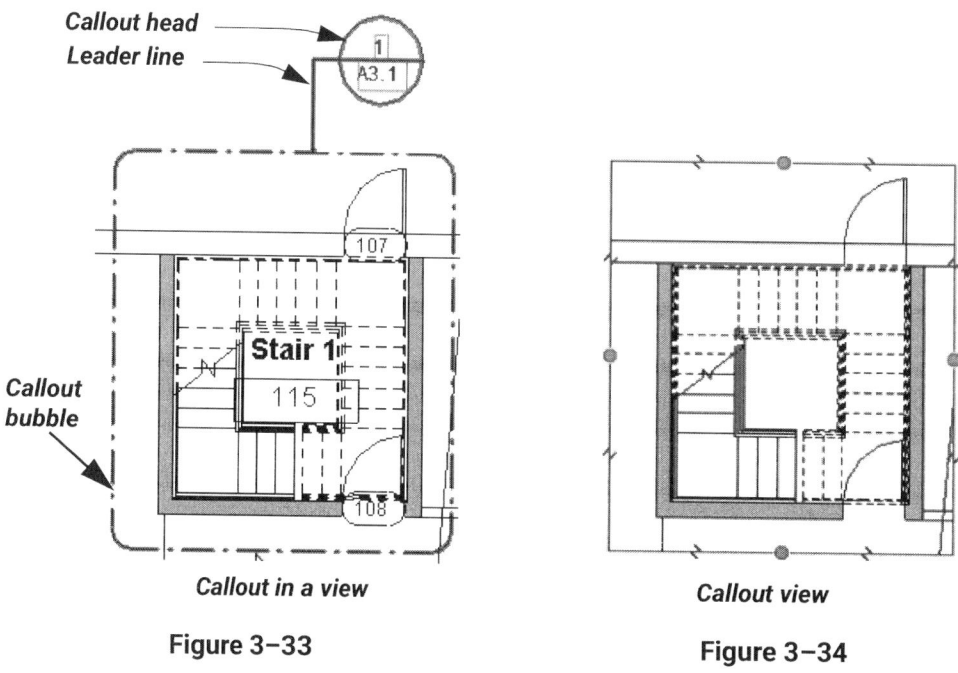

Figure 3–33 Figure 3–34

- Callout views are saved in the same node in the Project Browser as the original view. For example, the callout view of a floor plan is placed within the Floor Plans node.
- To open the callout view, double-click on its name in the Project Browser or on the callout head (verify that the callout bubble is not selected before you double-click on it).

How To: Create a Rectangular Callout

1. In the *View* tab>Create panel, click (Callout).
2. Select points for two opposite corners to define the callout bubble around the area you want to detail.
3. Select the callout bubble and use the shape handles to modify the location of the bubble and any other edges that might need changing.
4. In the Project Browser, you can rename the callout view.

How To: Create a Sketched Callout

1. In the *View* tab>Create panel, expand (Callout) and click (Sketch).

2. Sketch the shape of the callout bubble using the tools in the *Modify | Edit Profile* tab>Draw panel, as shown in Figure 3–35.

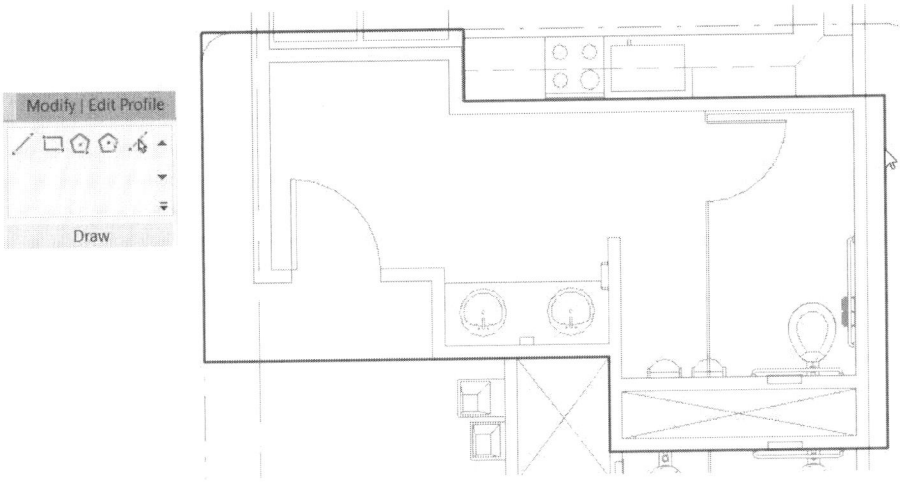

Figure 3–35

3. Click ✔ (Finish) to complete the boundary.
4. Select the callout bubble and use the shape handles to modify the location of the bubble and any other edges that might need to be changed.
5. In the Project Browser, rename the callout.

Modifying Callouts

Callouts are cropped versions of the original view. When you modify them you are changing the crop region of the view.

- You can select the Drag Head grip of the callout bubble (as shown in Figure 3–36) to move the callout head to a different location. You can modify the leader landing by dragging the grip at the landing.

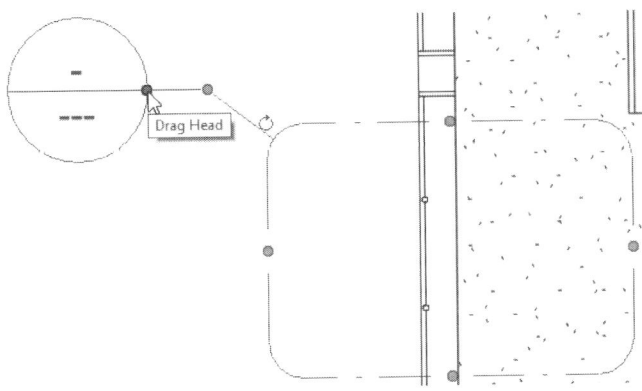

Figure 3–36

- If you change the size of the callout bubble in the original view, it automatically updates the callout view and vice-versa.

- Callouts can be reshaped. Select the callout bubble or crop region and, in the Modify | Floor Plan tab>Mode panel, click (Edit Crop) and use the Draw tools to modify the sketch.
- If you want to return a sketched or modified callout or crop region to a rectangular configuration, click (Reset Crop).

Working with Crop Regions

Plans, sections, elevations, and 3D views can all be modified by changing how much of the model is displayed in a view. One way to do this is to set the Model crop region. If there are dimensions, tags, or text near the crop region, you can also use the Annotation crop region to include these, as shown in Figure 3–37.

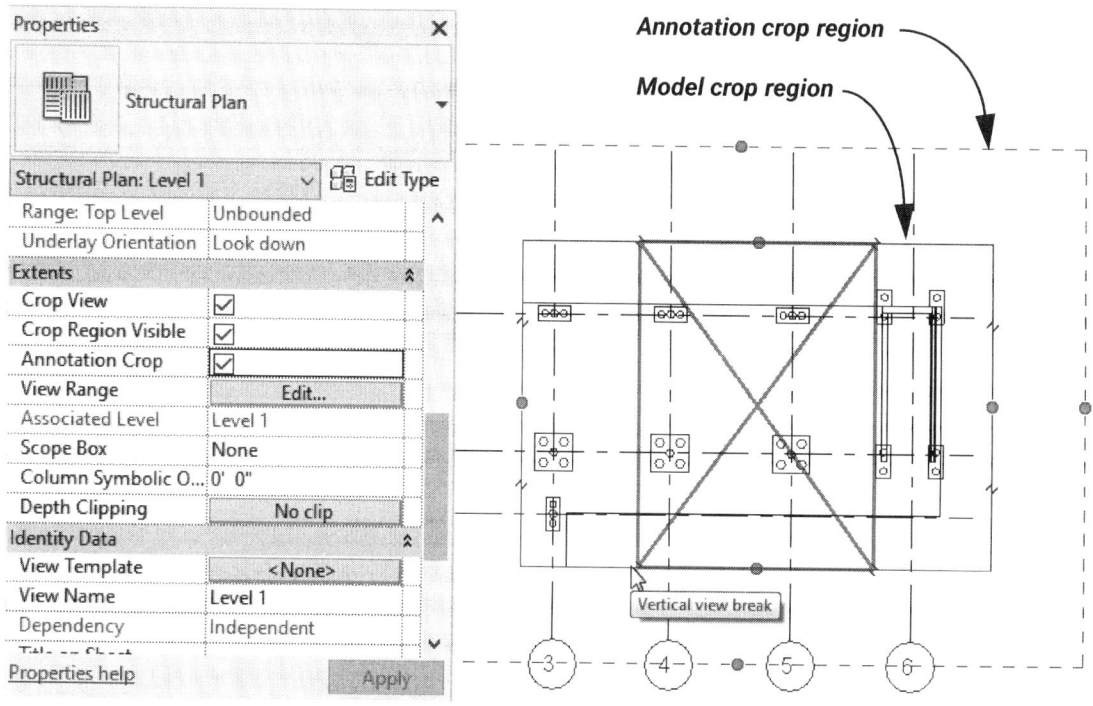

Figure 3–37

- To display the crop region, in the View Control Bar, click (Show Crop Region). Alternatively, in Properties, in the *Extents* section, select **Crop Region Visible**. **Annotation Crop** is also available in this area.

  Note: Zoom out if you do not see the crop region when you set it to be displayed.

- It is best practice to hide a crop region before placing a view on a sheet. In the View Control Bar, click (Hide Crop Region).

- Resize the crop region using the ● control on each side of the region.

- Click ✂ (Break Line) control to split the view into two regions, horizontally or vertically. Each part of the view can then be modified in size to display what is needed and be moved independently.

    Note: Breaking the crop region is typically used with sections or details.

- The annotation crop region crops any annotation outside of the crop region and any annotations that it touches. If the model crop region crops an element that is tagged, the tag or annotation will automatically be cropped as well. You can turn on Annotation Crop and resize the crop region closer to the model crop region using the grip controls or by using the Crop Region Size dialog box, as shown in Figure 3–38. In the *Modify | Floor Plan* tab>Crop panel, click (Size Crop) to open the dialog box.

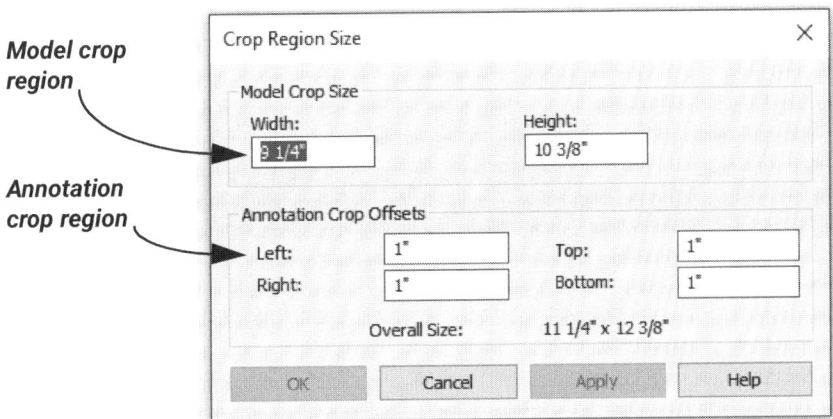

Figure 3–38

Plan Regions

When you have a plan view with multiple levels of floors or ceilings, you can create plan regions that enable you to set a different view range for part of a view (as shown in Figure 3–39) for a set of clerestory windows.

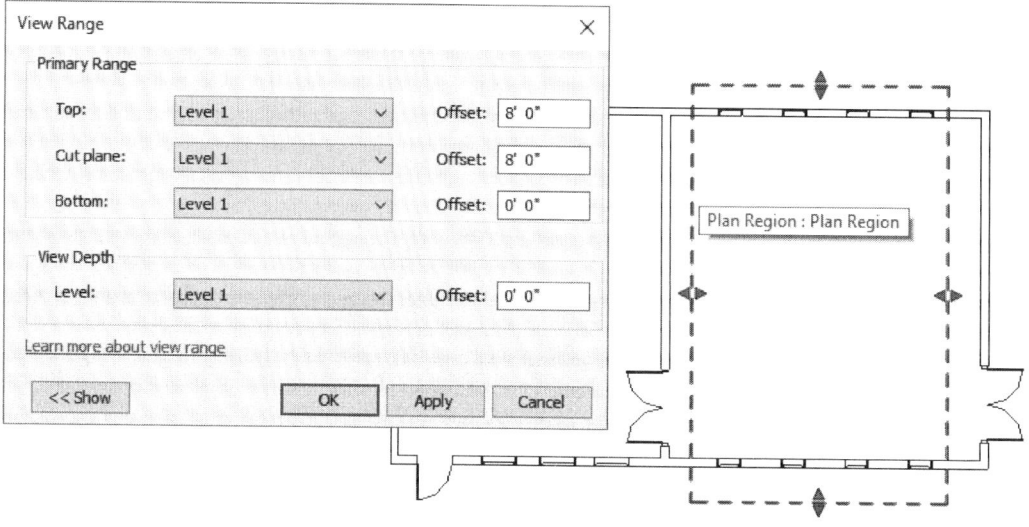

Figure 3–39

How To: Create Plan Regions

1. In a plan view, in the *View* tab>Create panel, expand (Plan Views) and select (Plan Region).

2. In the *Modify | Create Plan Region Boundary* tab>Draw panel, select a draw tool and create the boundary for the plan region.

    - The boundary must be closed and cannot overlap other plan region boundaries, but the boundaries can be side by side.

3. Click (Finish Edit Mode).

4. In the *Modify | Plan Region* tab>Region panel, click (View Range).

5. In the View Range dialog box, specify the offsets for the plan region and click **OK**. The plan region is applied to the selected area.

- Plan regions can be copied to the clipboard and then pasted into other plan views.

- You can use shape handles to resize plan region boundaries without having to edit the boundary.

- If a plan region is above a door, the door swing displays, but the door opening does not display, as shown in Figure 3–40.

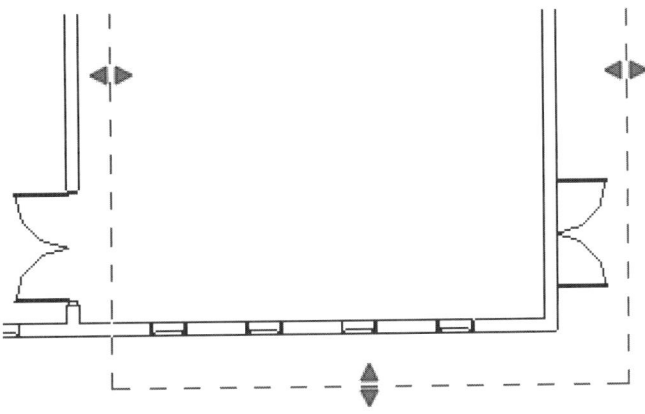

Figure 3–40

- Plan regions can be toggled on and off in the Visibility/Graphic Overrides dialog box on the *Annotation Categories* tab. If they are displayed, the plan regions are not included when printing and exporting.

Hint: Depth Clipping and Far Clipping

Depth Clipping, shown in Figure 3–41, is a viewing option that sets how sloped walls are displayed if the *View Range* of a plan is set to a limited view.

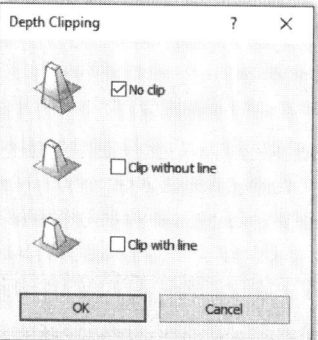

Figure 3–41

Far Clipping (shown in Figure 3–42) is available for section and elevation views.

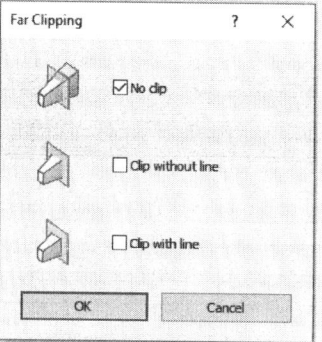

Figure 3–42

- An additional Graphic Display Option enables you to specify *Depth Cueing*, so that items that are in the distance will be made lighter.

Practice 3b
Add Callout Views

Practice Objective

- Create callouts.

In this practice, you will create a callout view of the elevator pit walls, as shown in Figure 3-43.

Figure 3-43

1. Open **Structural-Callouts.rvt** from the practice files folder.
2. Ensure that you are in the **Structural Plans: Level 1** view.
3. In the View Control Bar, check the *Scale* and *Detail Level* of the view, as shown in Figure 3-44.

Figure 3-44

4. In the *View* tab>Create panel, click ⊙ (Callout).

5. Draw a callout around the elevator pit walls, as shown in Figure 3–45. Move the callout head as needed.

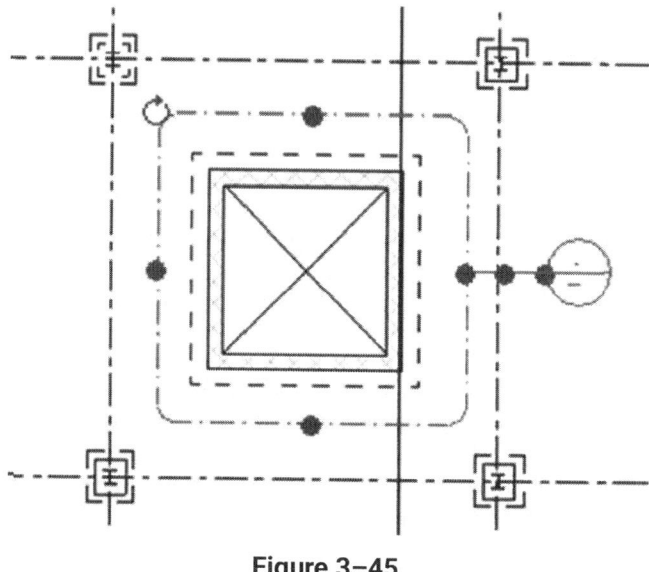

Figure 3–45

6. In the Project Browser, in the *Structural Plans* area, rename *Level 1 - Callout* as **Elevator Pit Enlarged Plan**.

7. Open the view to display the callout.

8. In the View Control Bar, set the *Scale* to **1/4"=1'-0"** and the *Detail Level* to **Fine**.

9. In the View Control Bar, click (Hide Crop Region).

10. Return to the **Level 1** view.

11. Save and close the project.

End of practice

3.5 Creating Elevations and Sections

Elevations and sections are critical elements of construction documents and can assist you as you are working on a model. Any changes made in one of these views (such as the section in Figure 3–46), changes the entire model and any changes made to the project model are also displayed in the elevations and sections.

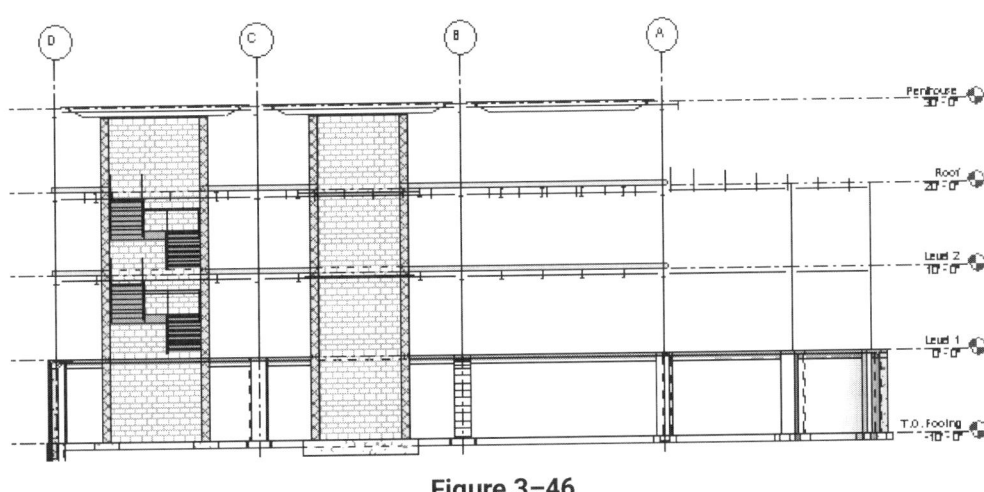

Figure 3–46

- In the Project Browser, elevations are separated by elevation type and sections are separated by section type, as shown in Figure 3–47.

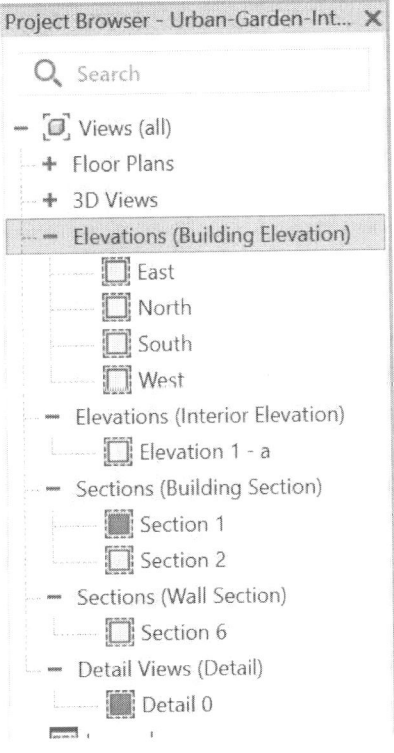

Figure 3–47

- To open an elevation or section view, double-click on the marker arrow or on its name in the Project Browser.
- To give the elevation or section a new name, in the Project Browser, slowly click twice on the name or right-click on it and select **Rename…**.

Elevations

Elevations are *face-on* views of the interiors and exteriors of a building. Four exterior elevation views are defined in the default template: **North**, **South**, **East**, and **West**. You can create additional building elevation views at other angles or interior elevation views, as shown in Figure 3–48.

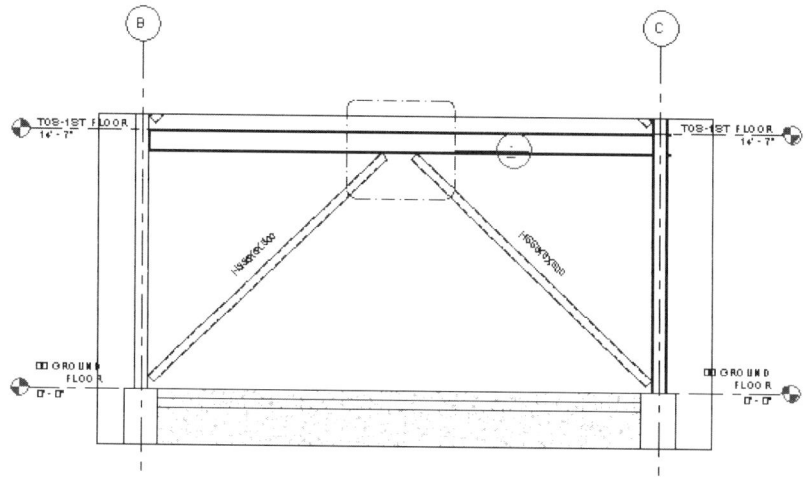

Figure 3–48

- Elevations markers must be placed in plan views.
- A framing elevation is set up to only capture framing elements that are behind other model elements in an elevation of a building.
  - By default, the framing elevation snaps and sets the extents along the grid lines by using **Attach to Grid** in the Options Bar.
- The most common use for a framing elevation is to generate braced frames and shear wall elevations.
- When you add an elevation or section to a sheet, the detail and sheet number are automatically added to the view title and elevation/section marker.

How To: Create Framing Elevations

1. Open a plan view.
2. In the *View* tab>Create panel, expand (Elevation) and click (Framing Elevation).

3. Hover the cursor over a grid line to display an elevation marker, as shown in Figure 3-49. Click to place the marker.

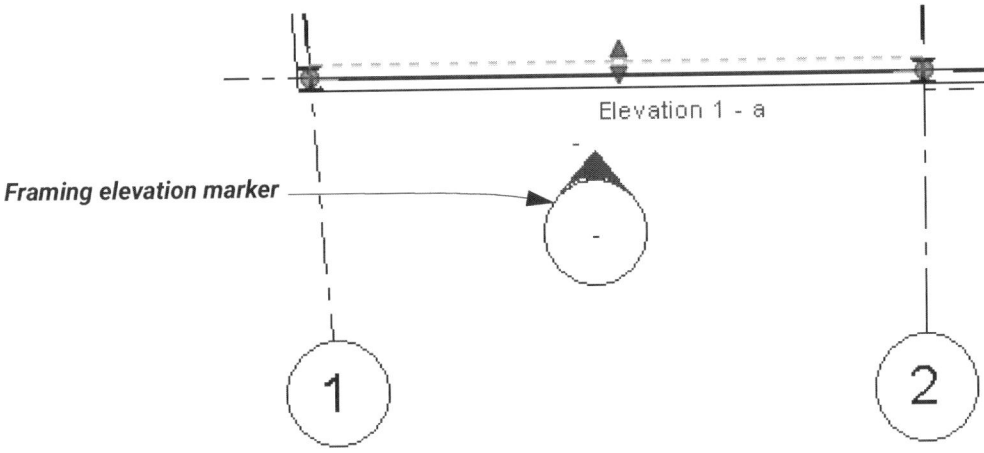

Figure 3-49

4. Click (Modify) and select the marker. The extents focus on the bracing bay only. You can use the round segment handles to expand the length of the elevation, as needed.

How To: Create an Elevation

1. In the *View* tab>Create panel, expand (Elevation) and click (Elevation).

   Note: The software remembers the last elevation type used, so you can click the top button if you want to use the same elevation command.

2. In the Type Selector, select the elevation type. Two types come with the templates: **Building Elevation** and **Interior Elevation**.

3. Move the cursor near one of the walls that defines the elevation. The marker follows the angle of the wall.

4. Click to place the marker.

- The length, width, and height of an elevation are defined by the walls and ceiling/floor at which the elevation marker is pointing.

- When creating interior elevations, ensure that the floor or ceiling above is in place before creating the elevation or you will need to modify the elevation crop region so that the elevation markers do not show on all floors.

Sections

Sections are slices through a model. You can create a section through an entire building or through one wall for a detail. Sections can be created in plan, elevation, and other section views. You can flip, resize, or split a section. Figure 3–50 shows all the components of a section marker.

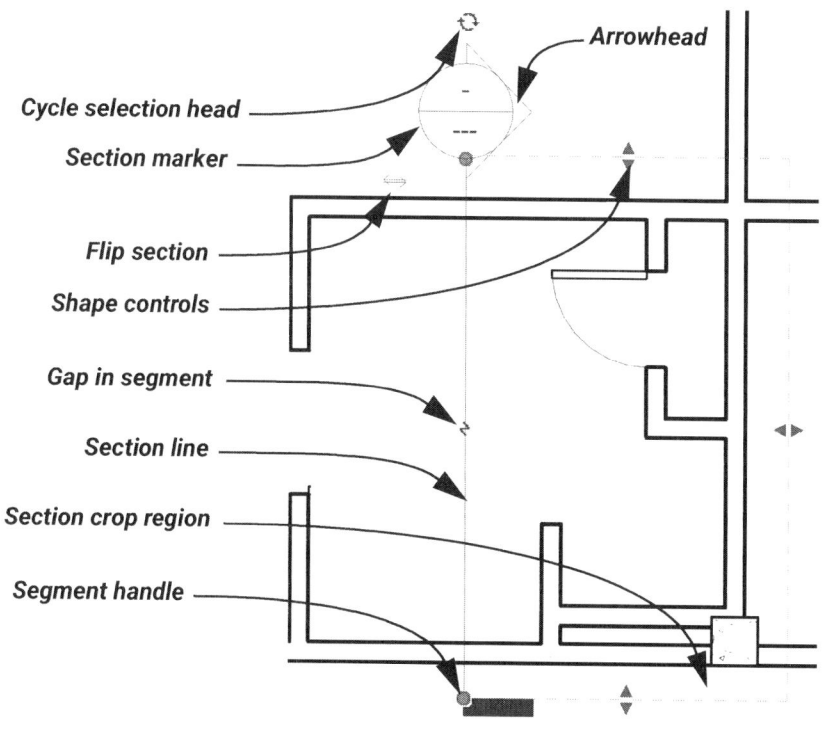

Figure 3–50

How To: Create a Section

1. In the *View* tab>Create panel or in the Quick Access Toolbar, click (Section).
2. In the Type Selector, select **Section: Building Section** or **Section: Wall Section.** If you want a section in a Drafting view select **Detail View: Detail.**
3. In the view, select a point where you want to locate the crop region and section marker.
4. Select the second or end point that defines the section.
5. The shape controls display. You can flip the arrow and change the size of the cutting plane, as well as the location of the bubble and flag.

- When placing a section you can snap to other elements in the model as the start and end points of the section line. You can also use the **Align** command to reorient a section line to an element such as an angled wall.

- Section lines can also be used as an alignment object and can be snapped to when placing other geometry.

Modifying Elevations and Sections

There are two parts to modifying elevations and sections:

- To modify the markers (as shown in Figure 3–51), select the arrowhead (triangle) part of the section marker and use the controls to change the length and depth of elevations and sections. There are other specific type options as well.

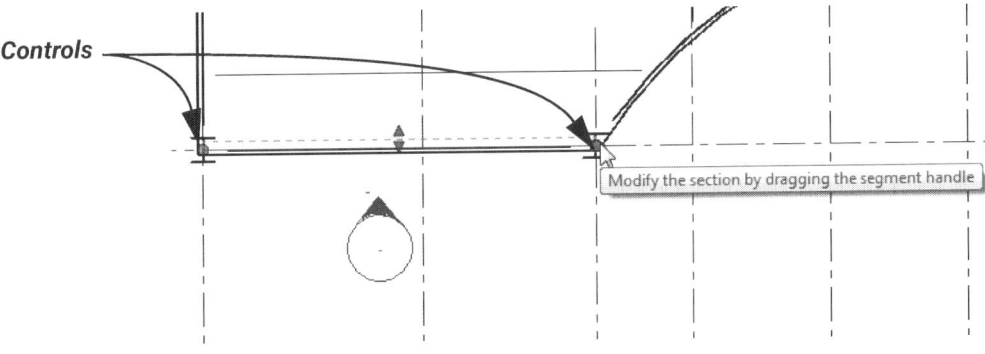

Figure 3–51

- To modify the view (as shown in Figure 3–52), select the crop region and use the controls to modify the size or create view breaks.

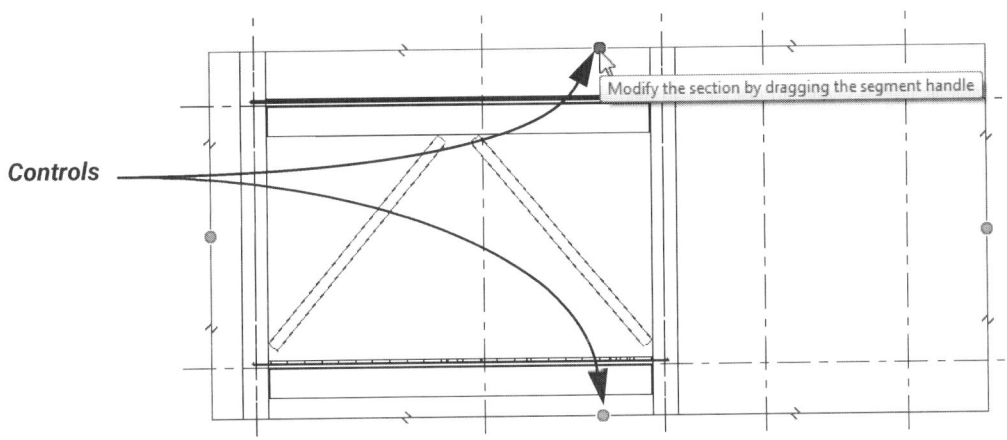

Figure 3–52

Modifying Elevation Markers

When you modify elevation markers, you can specify the length and depth of the clip plane, as shown in Figure 3-53.

- Select the arrowhead of the elevation marker (not the circle portion) to display the clip plane.

- Drag the round shape handles to lengthen or shorten the elevation.

- Adjust the ↕ (Drag) controls to modify the depth of the elevation.

To display additional interior elevations from one marker, select the circle portion (not the arrowhead) and place a checkmark in the Show Arrow box in the directions that you want to display, as shown in Figure 3-53.

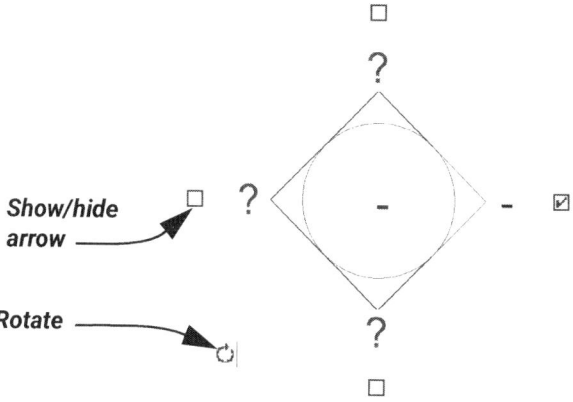

Figure 3-53

- Use the ↻ (Rotate) control to angle the marker (e.g., for a room with angled walls).

Modifying Section Markers

When you modify section markers, various shape handles and controls enable you to modify a section, as shown in Figure 3-54.

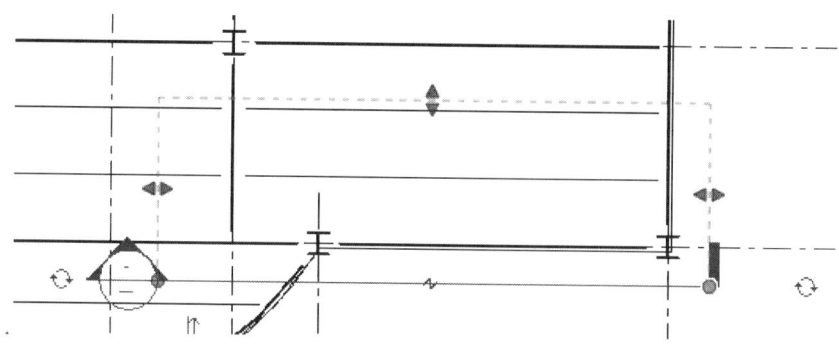

Figure 3-54

- Adjust the (Drag) controls to change the length and depth of the cut plane.
- Drag the segment handle controls at either end of the section line to change the location of the arrow or flag without changing the cut boundary.
- Click (Flip Section) to change the direction of the arrowhead, which also flips the entire section.
- Click (Cycle Section Head/Tail) to switch between an arrowhead, flag, or nothing on each end of the section.
- Click (Gaps in Segments) to create an opening in section lines, as shown in Figure 3–55. Select it again to restore the full section cut.

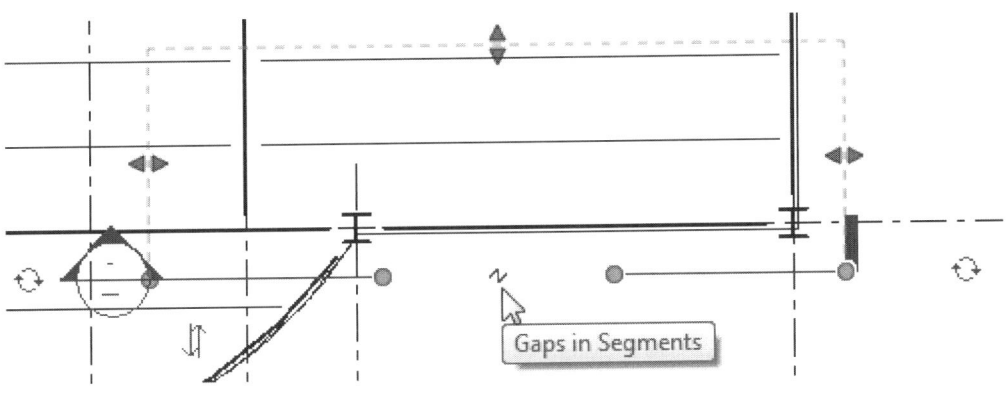

Figure 3–55

How To: Add a Jog to a Section Line

1. Select the section line you want to modify.
2. In the *Modify | Views* tab>Section panel, click (Split Segment).
3. Select the point along the section line where you want to create the split, as shown in Figure 3–56.

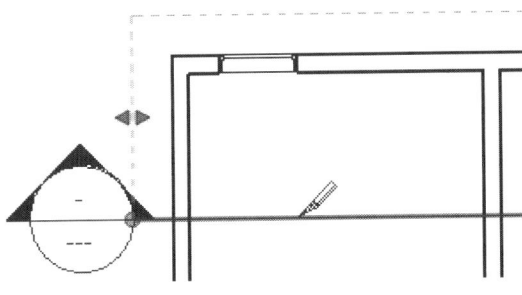

Figure 3–56

4. Specify the location of the split line, as shown in Figure 3–57.

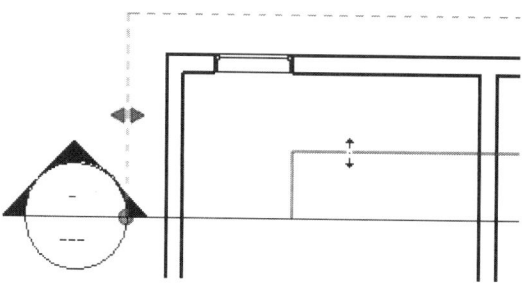

Figure 3–57

- If you need to adjust the location of any segment on the section line, modify it and drag the shape handles along each segment of the line, as shown in Figure 3–58.

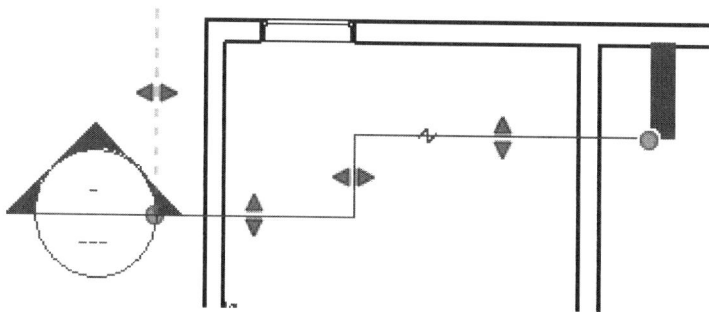

Figure 3–58

- To bring a split section line back into place, use the shape handle to drag the jogged line until it is at the same level with the rest of the line.

3D Section Views

There are two ways you can create section views of your 3D model: creating a selection box, as shown in Figure 3–59, and orienting to a view. Both of these are very helpful as you are working and also can be used in construction documents and presentations.

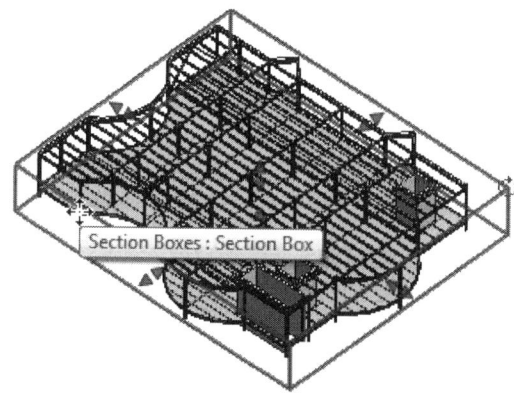

Figure 3–59

How To: Create a Selection Box

1. In a 3D view, select the elements you want to isolate. In the example shown above in Figure 3–59, the front wall was selected.
2. In the *Modify* tab>View panel, click (Selection Box), or type **BX**.
3. The view is limited to a box around the selected item(s).
4. Use the controls of the Section Box to modify the size of the box to show exactly what you want.

- To toggle off a section box and restore the full model, in the view's Properties, in the *Extents* area, clear the check from **Section Box**.

How To: Orient a 3D View to a View

1. Open a 3D view.
2. Right-click on the ViewCube and select **Orient to View>Floor Plans**, **Elevations**, **Sections**, or **3D Views**, as shown in Figure 3–60, and select the view from the list.

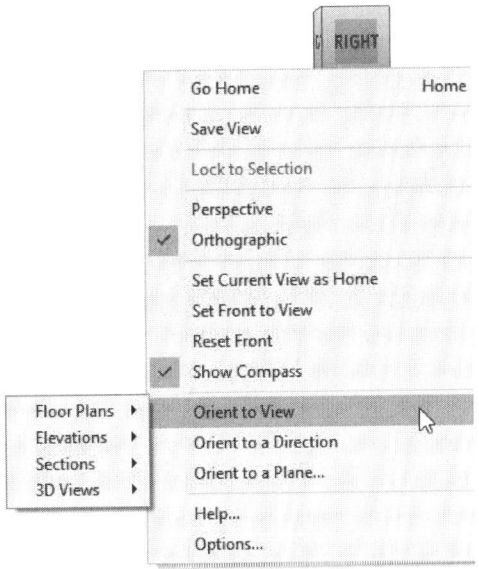

Figure 3–60

3. The view displays as shown, in the partial floor plan view of a stair, in Figure 3-61. Use the 3D view rotation tools to navigate around the 3D model, as shown in Figure 3-62.

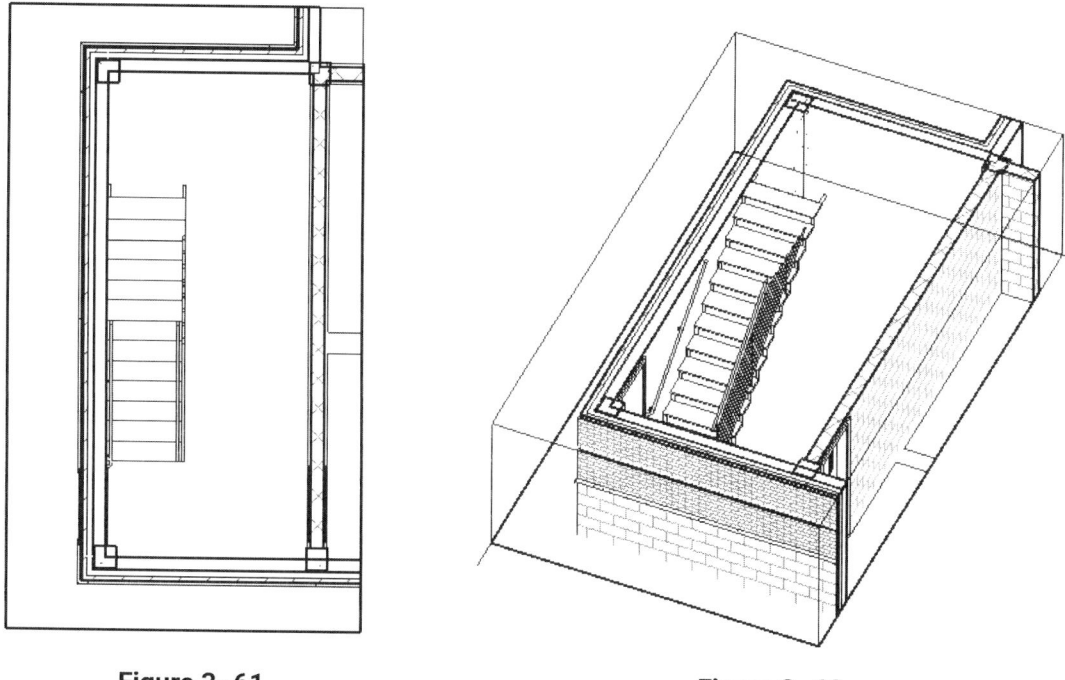

Figure 3-61　　　　　　　　　　Figure 3-62

- **Orient to a Direction** enables you to position the view in a specific direction, as shown in Figure 3-63. This is similar to using the orientation planes of the ViewCube.

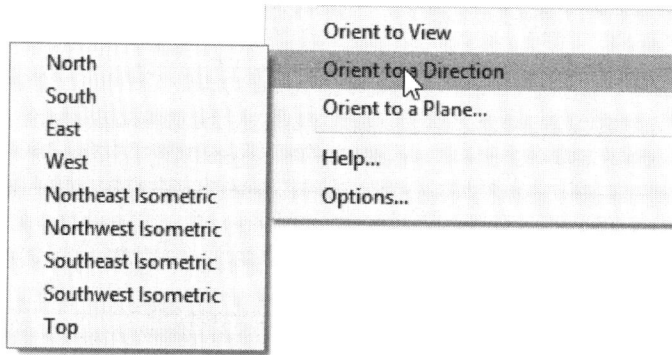

Figure 3-63

- **Orient to a Plane** opens the Select Orientation Plane dialog box and enables you to specify a level, grid, or named reference plane, or pick a plane or a line, as shown in Figure 3–64. The view is not cut at the plane but oriented in that direction.

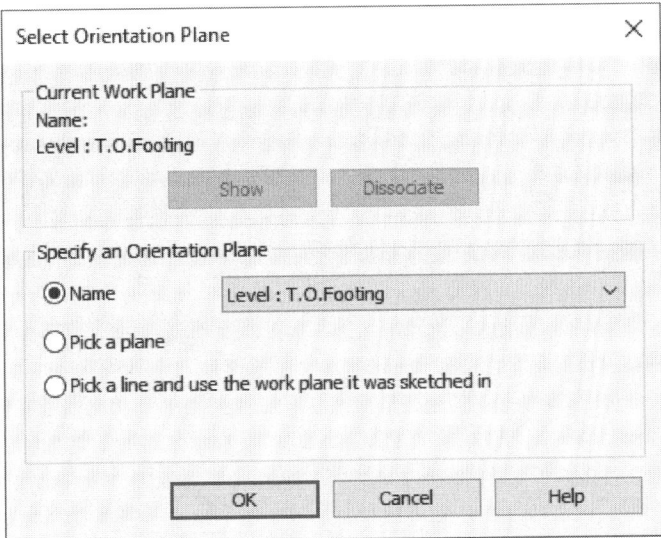

Figure 3–64

Practice 3c
Create Elevations and Sections

Practice Objectives

- Add building sections and wall sections.
- Add a framing elevation.

In this practice, you will add a building section and a wall section to an existing project. You will also add a framing elevation, as shown in Figure 3-65.

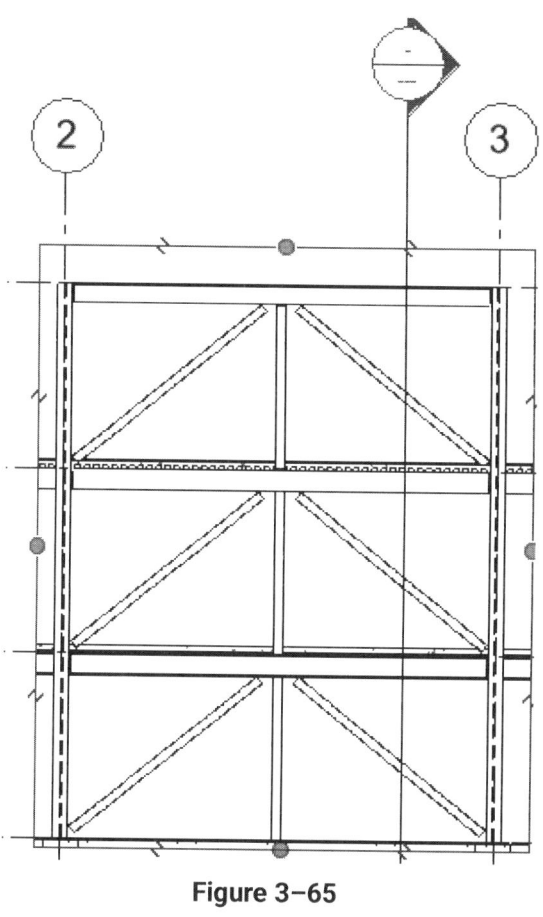

Figure 3-65

Task 1: Create sections.

1. Open **Structural-Sections.rvt** from the practice files folder.
2. In the Project Browser, open the **Structural Plans: Level 1** view.
3. In the *View* tab>Create panel or in the Quick Access Toolbar, click (Section).

4. In Properties, select **Section>Building Section** from the type list.

5. Place a vertical section offset slightly from the middle, between grid lines **2** and **3**. Change the width of the section using the shape controls, as shown in Figure 3-66.

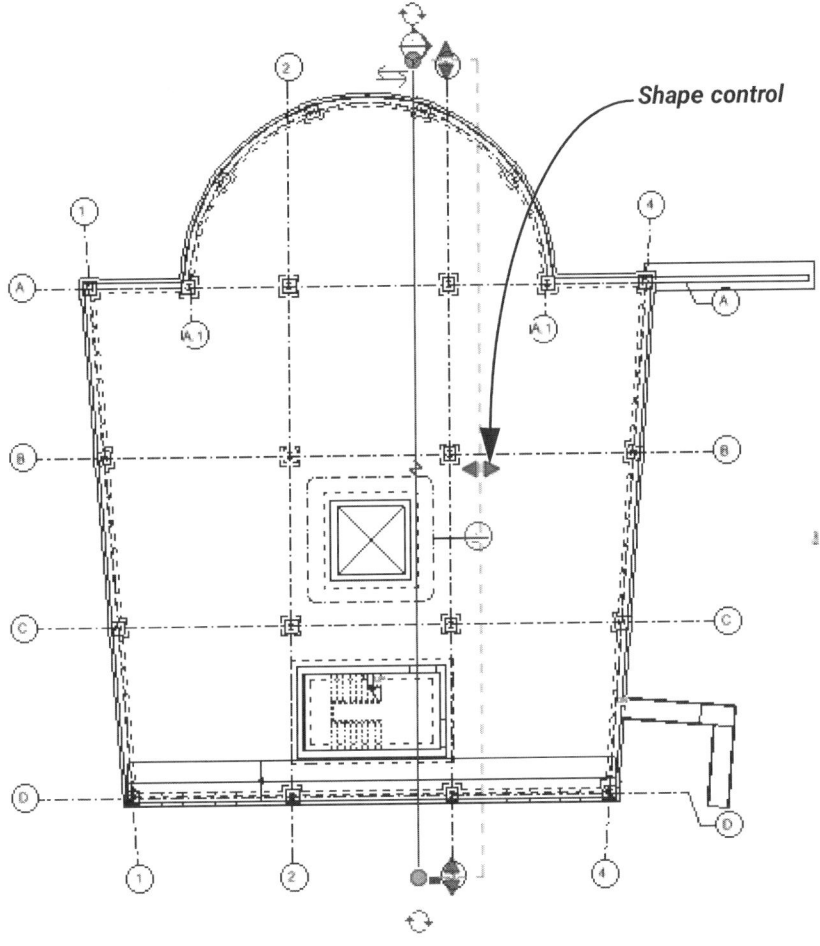

Figure 3-66

6. In the Project Browser, expand *Sections (Building Section)*. Right-click on the new section and rename it **Building Section A**, as shown in Figure 3-67.

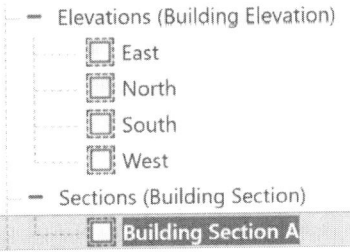

Figure 3-67

7. Open the new section by double-clicking on its name in the Project Browser. The entire building displays, as shown in Figure 3–68. Note that the view varies based on exactly where you placed the section.

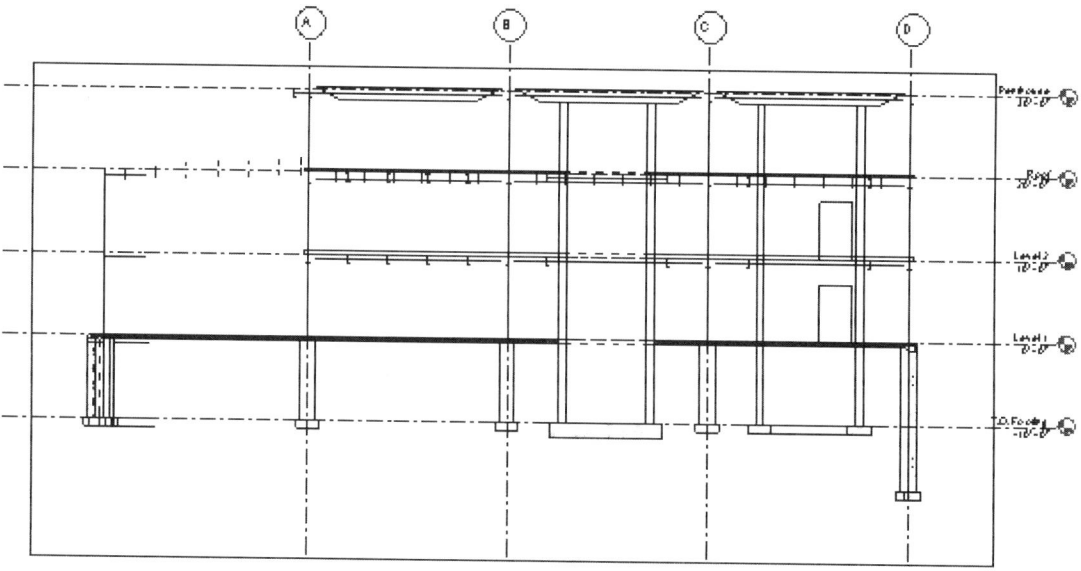

Figure 3–68

8. Select the crop region and use the controls to shorten the section so that the curved walls to the left do not display, shown in Figure 3–69.

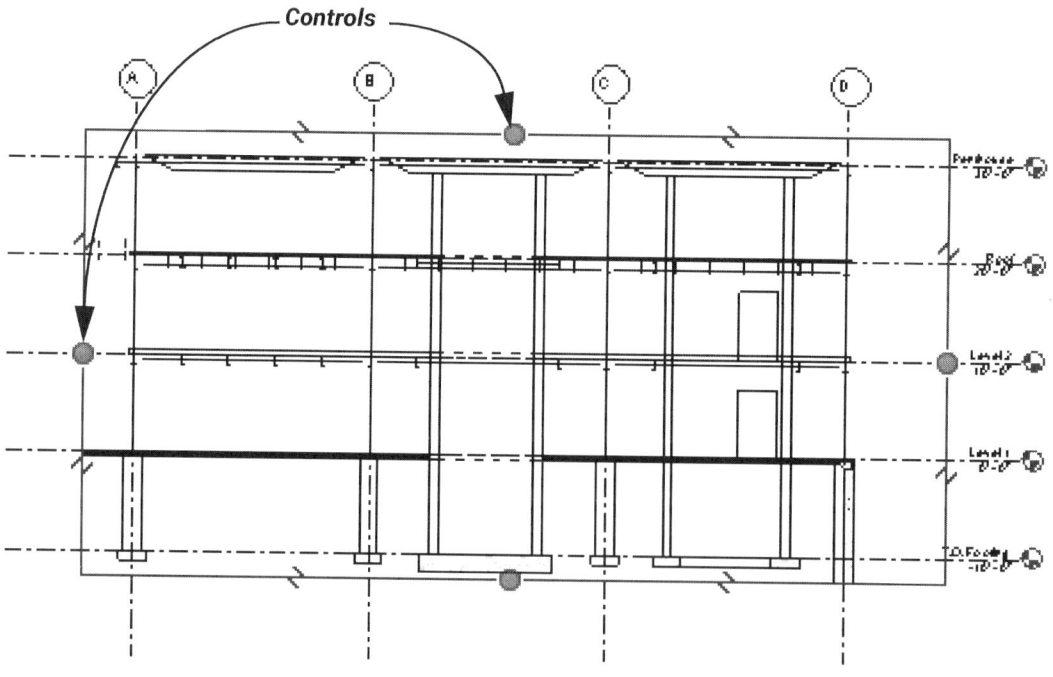

Figure 3–69

9. Return to the Level 1 view. The boundary of the section has changed, as shown on the left in Figure 3–70. Use the segment control to move the section marker's head down, as shown on the right in Figure 3–70.

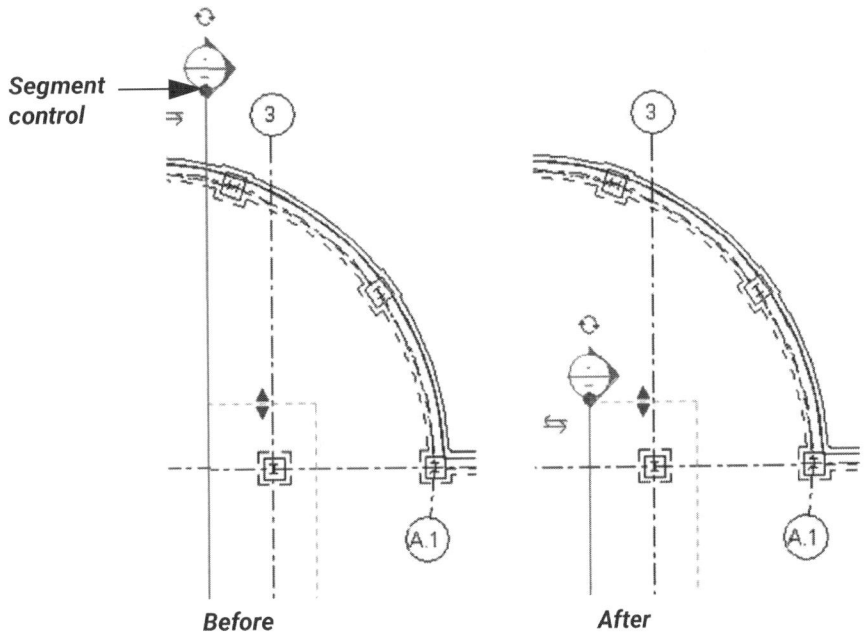

Figure 3–70

10. Start the **Section** command again.
11. In the Type Selector, select **Section: Wall Section**.
12. Draw a short section through the wall shown in Figure 3–71. Modify the section boundary so that it does not touch anything other than the wall.

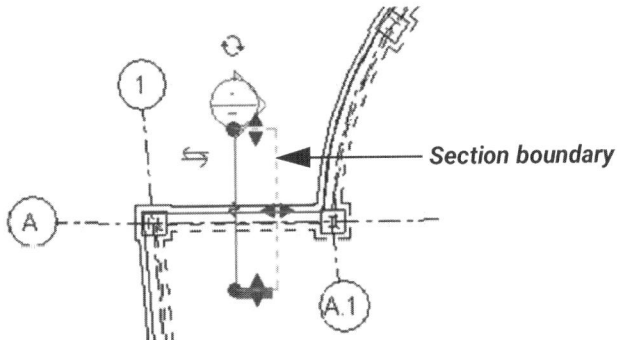

Figure 3–71

13. In the Project Browser, expand *Sections (Wall Section)* and rename the section **Foundation Section**.
14. Open the new section view.
15. In the View Control Bar, change the *Scale* to **1/2"=1'-0"**.

16. By default, the section expands the entire height of the project. Use the controls to resize the section so that only the foundation displays, as shown in Figure 3–72.

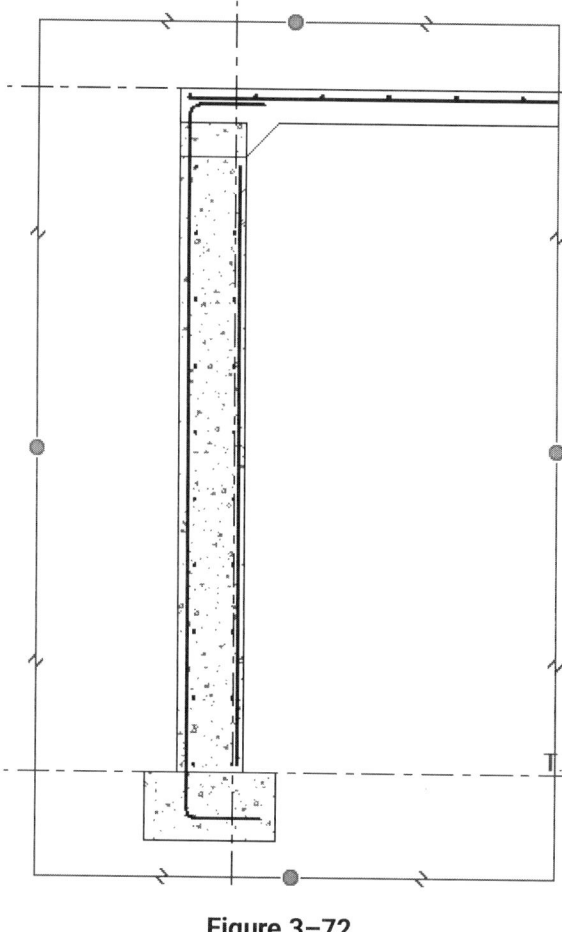

Figure 3–72

17. Save the project.

Task 2: Add a framing elevation.

1. Open the **Structural Plans: Level 1** view.
2. Zoom in on the south wall of the building between grid intersections **D2** and **D3**.
3. In the *View* tab>Create panel, expand (Elevation) and click (Framing Elevation).

4. Hover the cursor over grid line **D**, as shown in Figure 3–73. Pick a point when the framing elevation marker displays on the outside of the building.

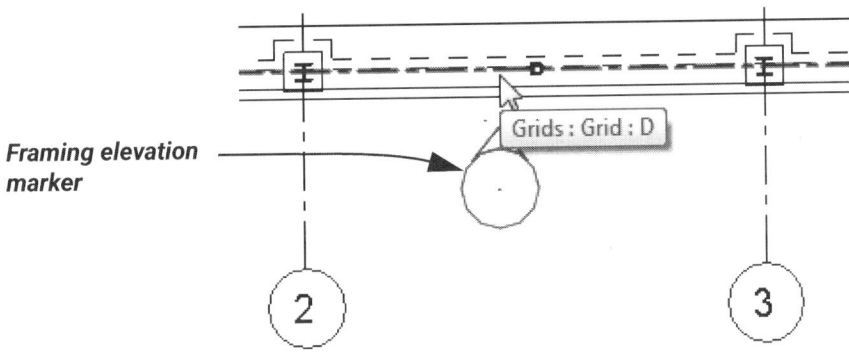

Figure 3–73

5. In the Project Browser, in the *Elevations (Framing Elevation)* area, rename the view as **Typical Bracing**.

6. Click on the arrowhead of the elevation marker to show the boundary. Using the controls, lengthen the elevation boundary so that it is just on each side of the columns, as shown in Figure 3–74.

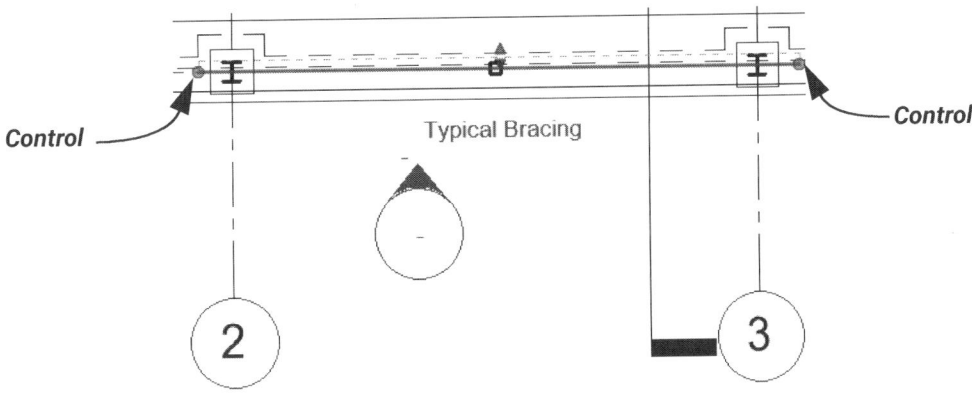

Figure 3–74

7. Open the framing elevation and in the View Control Bar, change the *Detail Level* to ▦ (Fine).

8. Modify the size of the elevation to only display the bracing, as shown in Figure 3–75.

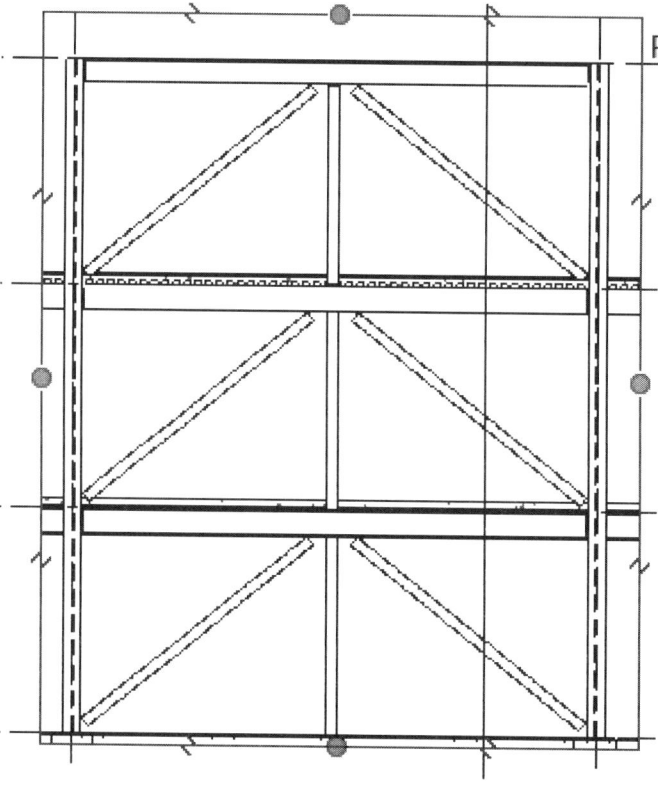

Figure 3–75

9. Return to the **Structural Plans: Level 1** view.
10. Zoom out to display the entire building.
11. In the Quick Access Toolbar, click (Close Inactive Views).
12. Save and close the project.

End of practice

Chapter Review Questions

1. Which of the following commands creates a view that results in an independent view displaying the same model geometry and containing a copy of the annotation?

    a. Duplicate

    b. Duplicate with Detailing

    c. Duplicate as a Dependent

2. Which of the following is true about the Visibility/Graphic Overrides dialog box?

    a. Changes made in the dialog box only affect the current view.

    b. It can only be used to toggle categories on and off.

    c. It can be used to toggle individual elements on and off.

    d. It can be used to change the color of individual elements.

3. If you want to hide just one of the elevation markers in a view, what do you have to do?

    a. Select the elevation marker, then right-click and select **Hide in View>By Filter**.

    b. Select the elevation marker, then right-click and select **Hide in View>Category**.

    c. Select the elevation marker, then right-click and select **Hide in View>Elements**.

    d. In the Visibility/Graphic Overrides dialog box, uncheck **Elevations**.

4. What is the purpose of creating a callout?

    a. To create a boundary around part of the model that needs revising, similar to a revision cloud.

    b. To create a view of part of the model to export to the AutoCAD® software for further detailing.

    c. To create a view of part of the model that is linked to the main view from which it is taken.

    d. To create a 2D view of part of the model.

5. You placed dimensions in a view but only some of them display, as shown on the left in Figure 3–76. You were expecting the view to display as shown on the right in Figure 3–76. What do you need to modify to see the missing dimensions?

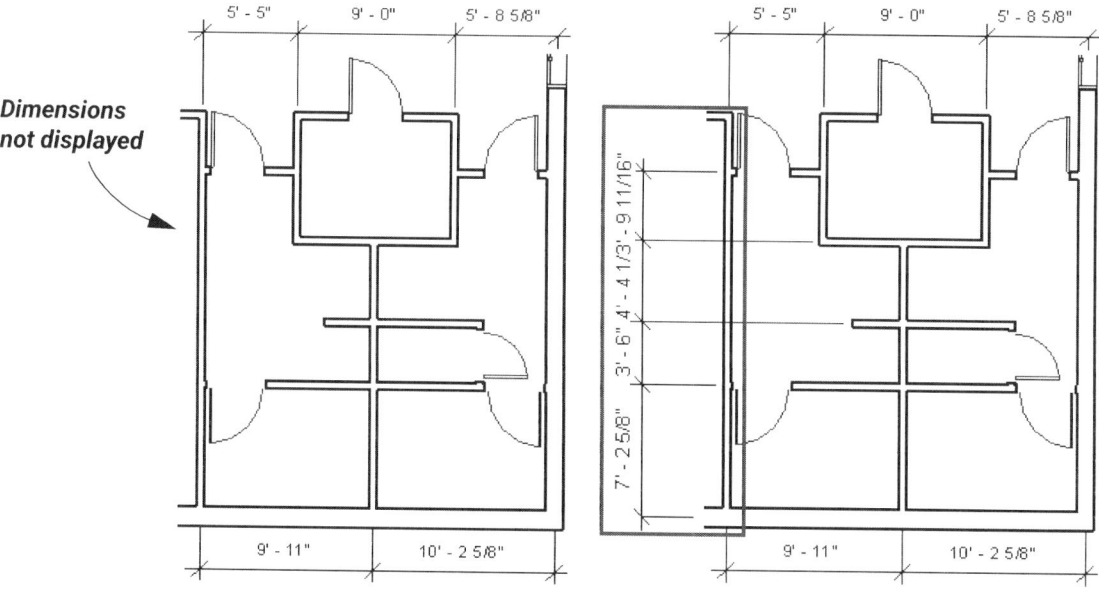

Figure 3–76

   a. Dimension Settings
   b. Dimension Type
   c. Visibility/Graphic Overrides
   d. Annotation Crop Region

6. How do you create multiple interior elevations in one room?

   a. Using the **Interior Elevation** command, place the elevation marker.
   b. Using the **Elevation** command from the Properties Type Selector, change to **Interior Elevation** and place the first marker, select it and select the appropriate Show Arrow boxes.
   c. Using the **Interior Elevation** command, place an elevation marker for each wall of the room you want to display.
   d. Using the **Elevation** command, select a Multiple Elevation marker type, and place the elevation marker.

7. How do you create a jog in a building section, such as that shown in Figure 3-77?

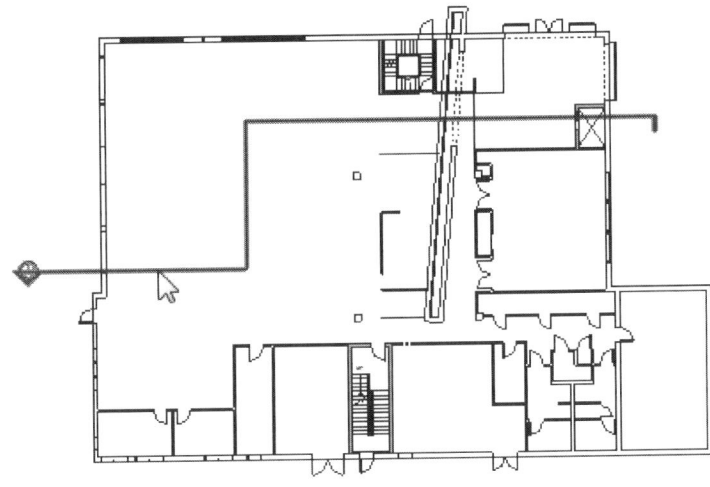

Figure 3-77

a. Use the **Split Element** tool in the *Modify* tab>Modify panel.

b. Select the building section and then click **Split Segment** in the contextual tab.

c. Select the building section and click the blue control in the middle of the section line.

d. Draw two separate sections and use the **Section Jog** tool to combine them into a jogged section.

Command Summary

Button	Command	Location
Views		
	Callout: Rectangle	• **Ribbon:** *View* tab>Create panel, expand Callout
	Callout: Sketch	• **Ribbon:** *View* tab>Create panel, expand Callout
	Duplicate	• **Ribbon:** *View* tab>Create panel, expand Duplicate View • **Right-click:** (*on a view in the Project Browser*) expand Duplicate View
	Duplicate as Dependent	• **Ribbon:** *View* tab>Create panel, expand Duplicate View • **Right-click:** (*on a view in the Project Browser*) expand Duplicate View
	Duplicate with Detailing	• **Ribbon:** *View* tab>Create panel, expand Duplicate View • **Right-click:** (*on a view in the Project Browser*) Duplicate View
	Elevation	• **Ribbon:** *View* tab>Create panel, expand Elevation
	Framing Elevation	• **Ribbon:** *View* tab>Create panel, expand Elevation
	Plan Region	• **Ribbon:** *View* tab>Create panel, expand Plan Views
	Section	• **Ribbon:** *View* tab>Create panel • **Quick Access Toolbar**
	Split Segment	• **Ribbon:** (*when the elevation or section marker is selected*) Modify	*Views* tab>Section panel
Crop Views		
	Crop View	• **View Control Bar** • **View Properties:** Crop View (*check*)
	Do Not Crop View	• **View Control Bar** • **View Properties:** Crop View (*clear*)
	Edit Crop	• **Ribbon:** (*when the crop region of a callout, elevation, or section view is selected*) Modify	*Views* tab>Mode panel
	Hide Crop Region	• **View Control Bar** • **View Properties:** Crop Region Visible (*clear*)

Button	Command	Location
	Reset Crop	• **Ribbon:** *(when the crop region of a callout, elevation or section view is selected)* *Modify	Views* tab>Mode panel
	Show Crop Region	• **View Control Bar** • **View Properties:** Crop Region Visible *(check)*
	Size Crop	• **Ribbon:** *(when the crop region of a callout, elevation or section view is selected)* *Modify	Views* tab>Mode panel

View Display

Button	Command	Location
	Hide in View	• **Ribbon:** *Modify* tab>View Graphics panel>Hide> *Elements or* By Category • **Right-click:** *(when an element is selected)* Hide in View>Elements *or* Category
	Override Graphics in View	• **Ribbon:** *Modify* tab>View Graphics panel>Hide> *Elements or* By Category • **Right-click:** *(when an element is selected)* Override Graphics in View>By Element *or* By Category • **Shortcut:** *(category only)* VV or VG
	Plan Region	• **Ribbon:** *View* tab>Create panel, expand Plan Views
	Selection Box	• **Ribbon:** *Modify* tab>View panel • **Shortcut:** BX
	Reveal Hidden Elements	• **View Control Bar**
	Temporary Hide/Isolate	• **View Control Bar**
	Temporary View Properties	• **View Control Bar**

Chapter 4

Revit Families

To develop your 3D model, you will need to add various Revit® family elements, such as furniture, light fixtures, mechanical equipment, and structural framing elements. These components can be loaded from your company's template, the Revit Library, or a custom library. If the family elements are parametric, you can modify the components to have different sizes to control the visibility of items as needed to relay design intent for various aspects of the project.

Learning Objectives

- Place components in a project to further develop the design.
- Load components from the Revit Library.
- Change component types and locations.

4.1 About Revit Families

All elements added to your projects are created with families. A family contains different elements, materials, and properties (called parameters). Within the family, you can have multiple family types with different parameters. For example, you can have a desk family that contain various family types for different sizes of that desk.

Components are elements that can be loaded externally. These can include freestanding components, such as the structural columns and flanges shown in Figure 4–1. They can also include wall-, ceiling-, floor-, roof-, face-, and line-hosted components. These hosted components must be placed on the referenced element, such as the rebar and footings shown in Figure 4–1.

> **Note:** Family creation is covered in the ASCENT guide Autodesk Revit BIM Management: Template and Family Creation.

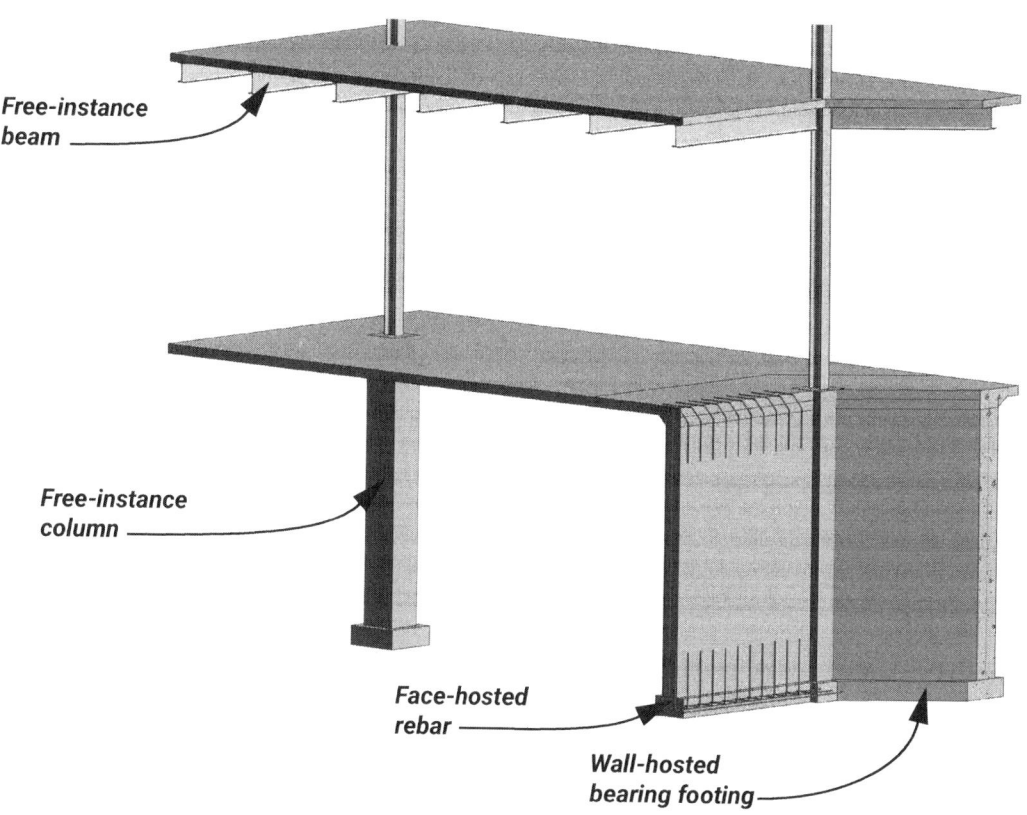

Figure 4–1

Host-based vs. Free-instance Families

Host-based families are dependent on a host. Examples include a pendant light fixture (which requires a ceiling) and a foundation (which requires a wall).

Free-instance families do not need a host.

The Different Kinds of Families

There are three kinds of families: system families, loadable families, and in-place families. Loadable and system families are what are typically used in a project, whereas in-place families are reserved for custom objects that are unique to the project.

System Families

System families are families that are predefined in Revit projects and templates. System families include walls, wall foundations, floors, structural slabs, ceilings, stairs, railings, and roofs, as shown in Figure 4–2. They also include duct, pipe, cable tray, and conduit types, as well as some annotation types, such as text and dimensions.

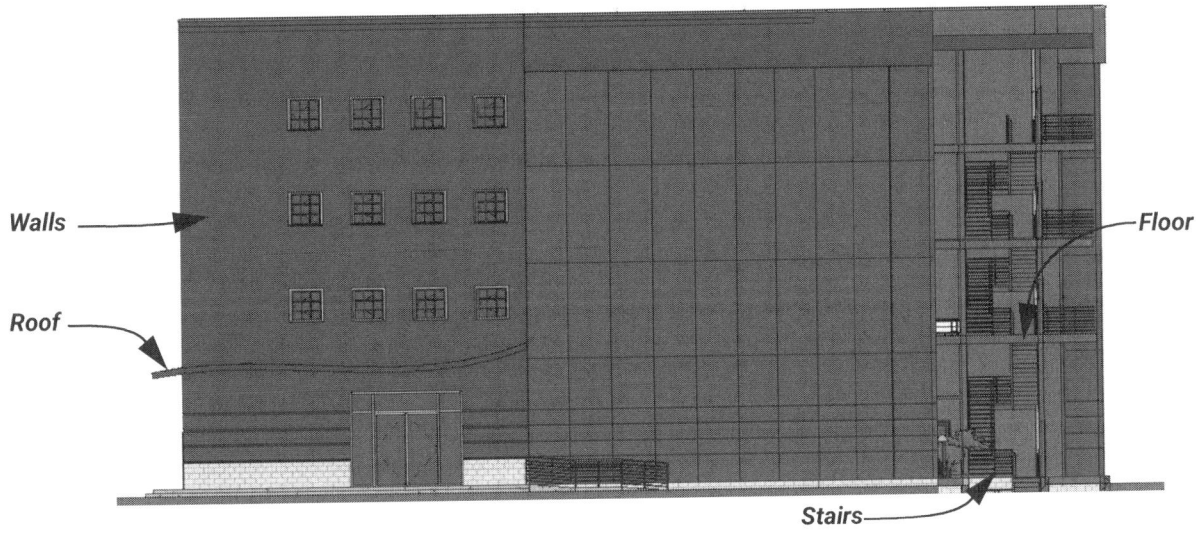

Figure 4–2

- System families are added to the model by starting a specific command from the appropriate tab in the ribbon. These will be further discussed in the *Design Development* section.

- System families cannot be saved out of a project or loaded from a library, but they can be customized by duplicating an existing type and modifying the *Type Parameters*, as shown in Figure 4–3. This can only be done within a project and helps to establish the company standards for the families set up in a template file. System families can be shared by using the **Transfer Project Standards** tool.

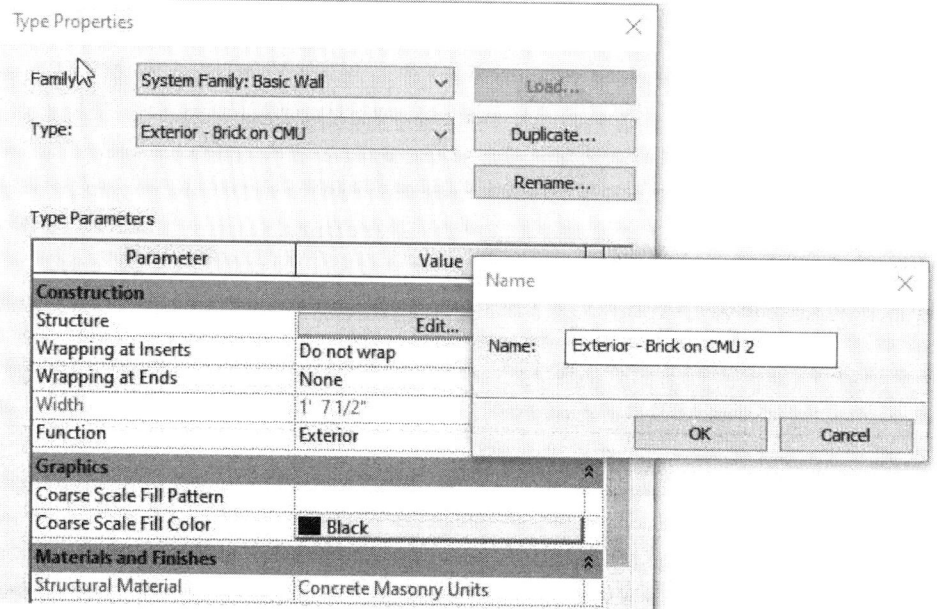

Figure 4–3

Loadable Families

Loadable families are external component families that are created outside of the project. Frequently used components can be saved to a custom library for future use.

- Annotation components are tags (shown in Figure 4–4), symbols, and title blocks. (They will be discussed further in *Adding Tags and Schedules*.)

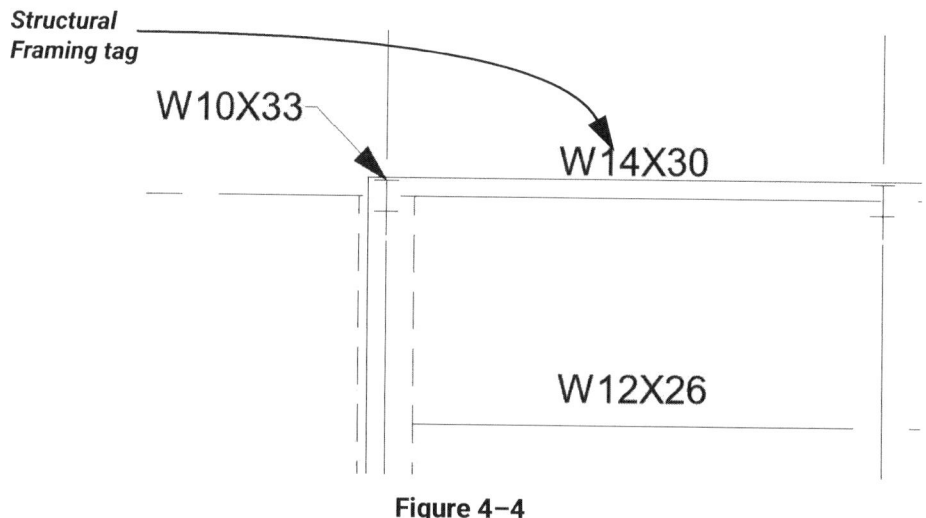

Figure 4–4

In-Place Families

In-place families are families that are created within a project that are unique to the project and will most likely not be used in another, for example a custom built-in shelf system that needs to be built to suit.

Working with Component Families

To optimize project size and improve performance, by default the Revit project templates are not fully loaded with all available Revit families. However, you can load more families with multi-options from the Revit Library or the Autodesk website. You can also load your company's custom component family or families from other manufacturers that you may have available on your local machine. Some Revit component families have a type catalog associated with them that enables you to select specific types of that family to load. This helps with keeping the file size down.

- You can also check which custom component families your company has and find vendor-specific components. More BIM objects can be found at bimobject.com.
- You can copy a component family to the clipboard in one project and paste it into a different project that is open in the same session of Revit.
- You can load as many components into a project as needed or create your own.
- Components are family files with the extension .RFA. For example, a component family named Desk.rfa can contain several types and sizes.

4.2 Loading Components

You can load components from the Revit Library or from a custom library before starting the component command, or you can loading after starting the command. Components (also known as families) are full 3D elements that can be placed at appropriate locations and heights, and which interact with the building elements around them. For example, a light fixture can be designed to be hosted by a face (such as a wall or ceiling), or to stand alone by itself.

- Components are located in family files with the extension .RFA. For example, a component family named **Wall Sconce.rfa** can contain several types and sizes.

How To: Load a Component Family

1. In the *Insert* tab>Load from Library panel, click (Load Family).

   - Note: To use the Load Family method, you must install the **Autodesk Revit 2024 Content** in your desired language. Go to the Autodesk.com website and search *Autodesk Revit 2024 Content*.

2. In the Load Family dialog box, locate the folder that contains the family or families you want to load and select them, as shown in Figure 4–5. To load more than one family at a time, hold <Ctrl> while selecting.

   - If the Load family dialog box does not default to the Revit Library folder, click on **Imperial Library** in the Places panel.

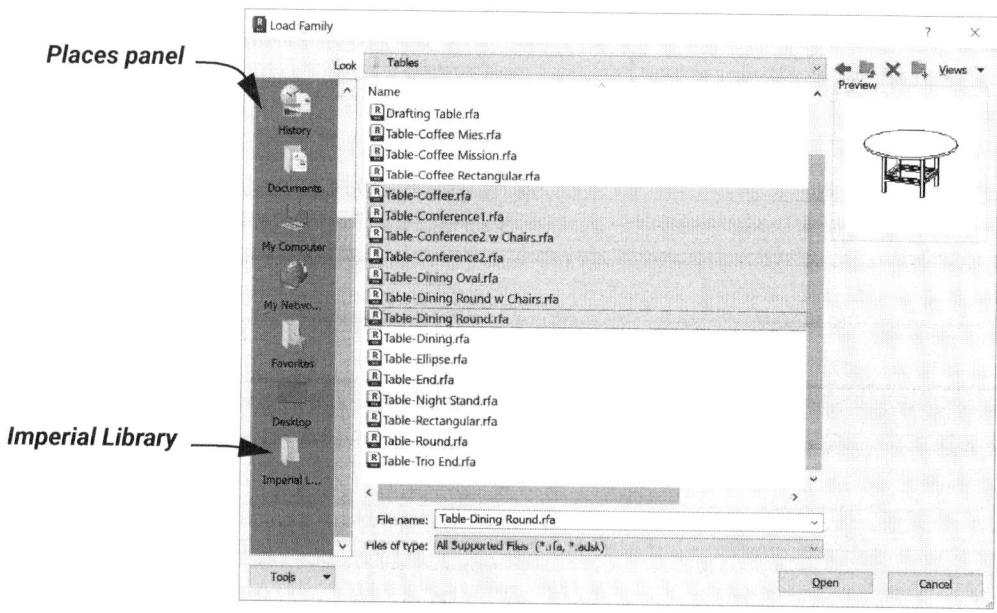

Figure 4–5

- The program remembers the last used folder.

3. Click **Open**.

4. For some families, the Specify Types dialog box displays, as shown for a door in Figure 4–6. Select the types you want to include in your project and click **OK**.

   - To select more than one type, hold <Ctrl> as you select.
   - You can use the drop-down lists under the columns to filter the sizes.
   - When loading several families with extra types, you can choose the element from the *Family* list on the right side and then pick the *Types* on the left side. Repeat for each of the elements listed. Once you are finished, click **OK**.

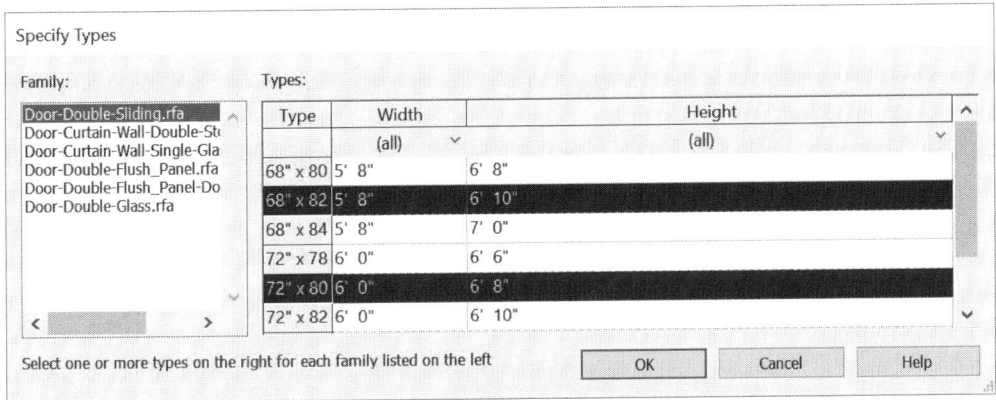

Figure 4–6

5. Once the family (or families) is loaded, in the Type Selector, select the type you want to use, as shown in Figure 4–7.

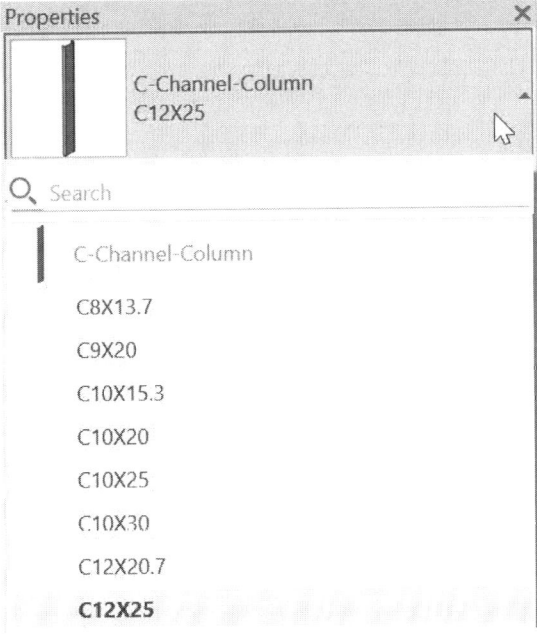

Figure 4–7

> **Hint: Using Families with This Learning Content**
>
> For the practices in this learning content, all families that are used have been provided with the practice files. This was done to ensure that all users can easily locate and use the required files to successfully complete all practices. In general, it is recommended that you use families from the provided Autodesk Revit Content via downloaded content or the cloud, or from your own custom company library.

How To: Use Load Autodesk Family

1. In the *Insert* tab>Load from Library panel, click (Load Autodesk Family).
2. In the Load Autodesk Family dialog box, filter your search by typing in what kind of family you are looking for, or click on a category in the Browse section, as shown in Figure 4–8.

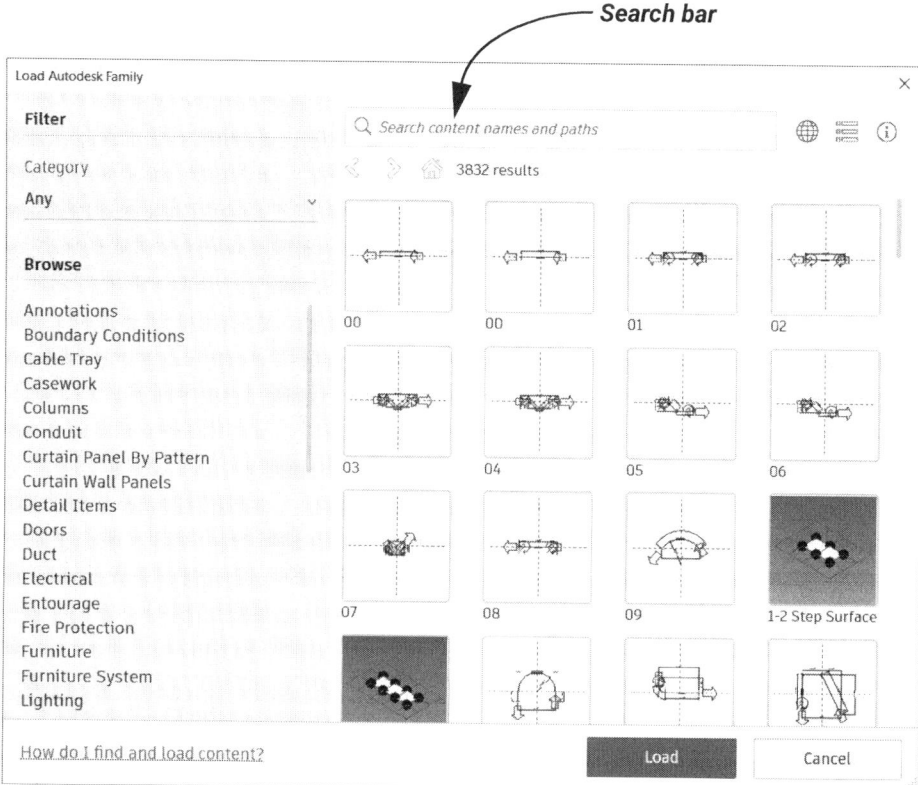

Figure 4–8

3. You can select as many families as needed, then click **Load** to load them into your project.

Placing Components

When placing components, you have several options available to you, including specifying a placement, utilizing snaps, and using snap overrides.

How To: Place a Component

1. In the *Structural* tab>Model panel, click (Place a Component), or type **CM**.
   - If you have not yet loaded your component, in the *Modify | Place Component* tab>Mode panel, click (Load Family) and load your component.
2. In the Type Selector, select the component you want to add to the project.
3. Proceed as follows, based on the type of component used:

If the component is...	Then...
Not hosted	Set the *Level* and *Offset* in Properties, as shown in Figure 4–9.
Wall hosted	Set the *Elevation from Level* in Properties, as shown in Figure 4–10.
Face hosted	Select the appropriate method in the contextual tab>Placement panel, as shown in Figure 4–11. • Vertical Faces include walls and columns. • Faces include ceilings, beams, and roofs. • Work Planes can be set to levels, faces, and named reference planes.

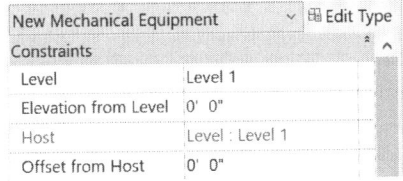
Figure 4–9

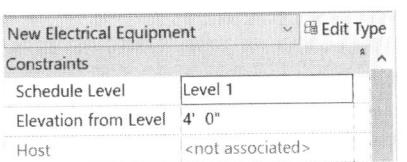
Figure 4–10

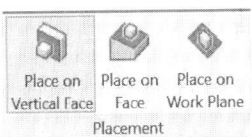
Figure 4–11

4. Place the component in the model.
- Work plane-based families will default to the last work plane option used.
- Many components can be rotated by pressing <Spacebar> when placing them. This will rotate them in 90° increments, unless your cursor is over an angled wall, reference plane, or grid line.

- In the Options Bar, many components will have an option to **Rotate after placement**, as shown in Figure 4–12. This enables you to rotate the element by any degree immediately after placing the family.

Figure 4–12

A fast way to add components that match those already in your project is to select one, right-click on it, and select **Create Similar**, as shown in Figure 4–13. This starts the appropriate command with the same type selected. **Create Similar** works with all elements.

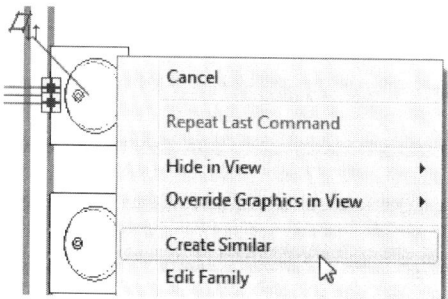

Figure 4–13

Using Snaps

When you move the cursor over an element, the snap symbol displays. Each snap location type displays with a different symbol. Snaps are key points that help you reference existing elements to exact points when modeling, as shown in Figure 4–14.

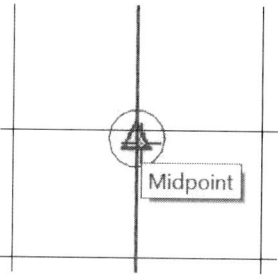

Figure 4–14

Snap Overrides

When placing a component, you can use the **Snap Mid Between 2 Points** temporary snap override by selecting it from the right-click menu (as shown in Figure 4–15) or typing **S2**, then selecting two points in the view.

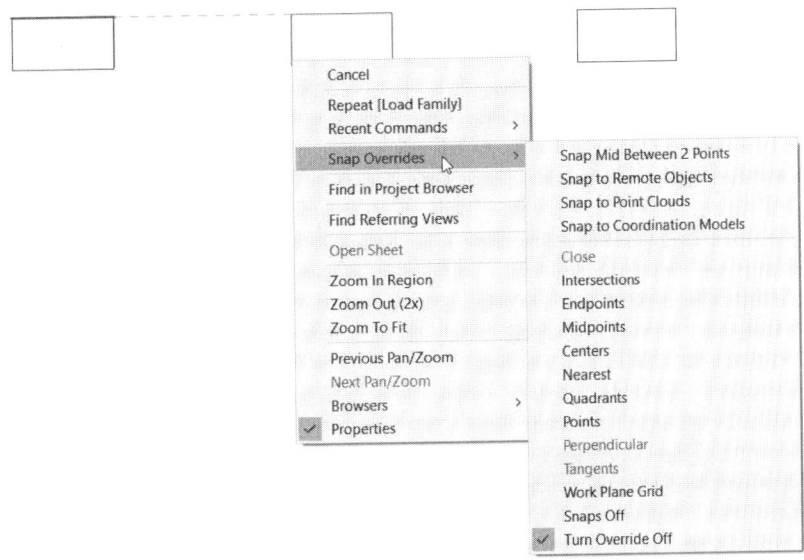

Figure 4–15

- Keyboard shortcuts for each snap can be used to override the automatic snapping. Temporary overrides only affect a single pick, but can be very helpful when there are snaps nearby other than the one you want to use.

- An example of using snap overrides: if you want to place a non-hosted element between two elements, you can type **S2** for *Snap Mid Between 2 Points* then select two points in the view. The new element is placed at the middle of the two selected points, as shown in Figure 4–16.

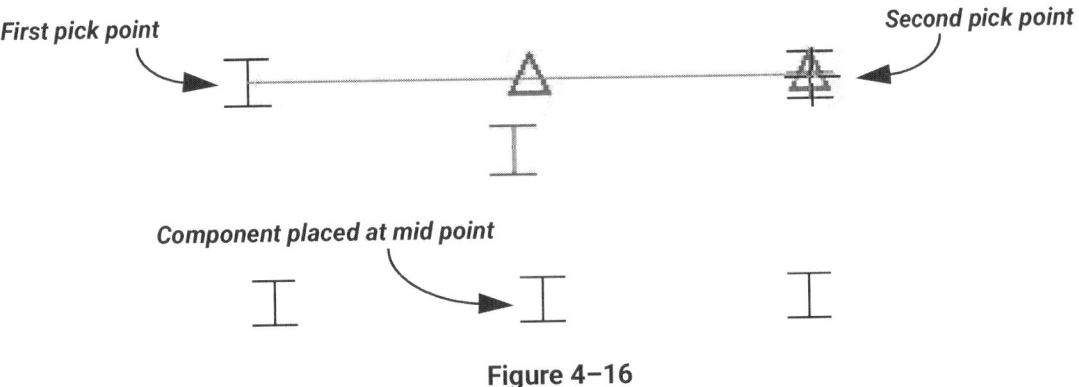

Figure 4–16

Snaps Settings

In the *Manage* tab>Settings panel, click ⬓ (Snaps) to open the Snaps dialog box (shown in Figure 4–17). The Snaps dialog box enables you to set which snap points are active and set the dimension increments displayed for temporary dimensions (both linear and angular).

- The Snaps dialog box shows the keyboard shortcuts for both Object Snaps and Temporary Overrides.

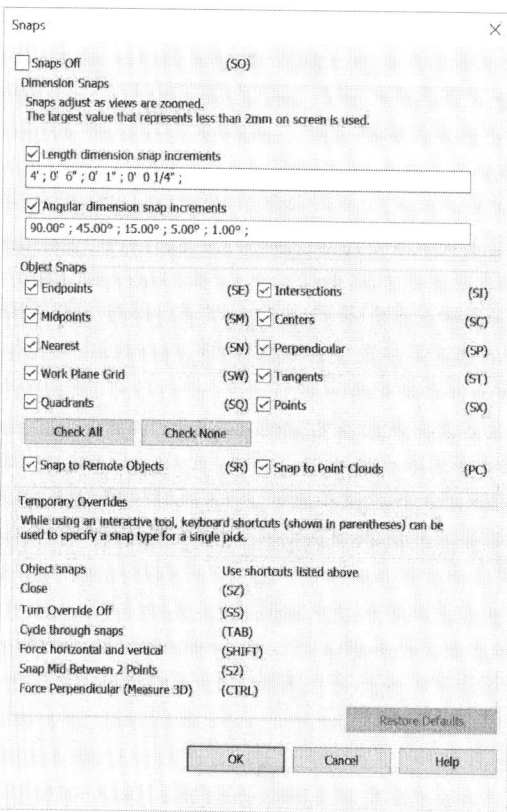

Figure 4–17

4.3 Modifying Components

Components can be modified when they are selected by changing the type in the Type Selector. For example, you might have placed a WWF71x470 column in a project (as shown in Figure 4–18), but now you need to change it to WWF18x337 column. With some types, you can use controls to modify the component. You can also select a new host for a component and move components with nearby elements.

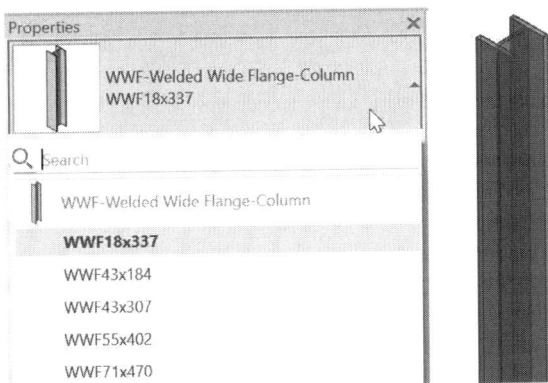

Figure 4–18

How To: Modify a Component

1. Select an element in the model.
2. In the Type Selector, select the family type that you want to change it to.
   - If needed, modify the component's instance or type properties.

Modify Host Elements

If you need to move a component from the level on which it was inserted, you can change its host. For example, one of the light fixtures in Figure 4–19 is floating above the ceiling. It was placed on Floor 1 T.O.P when it was inserted, but it needs to be located on the ceiling that is below the level.

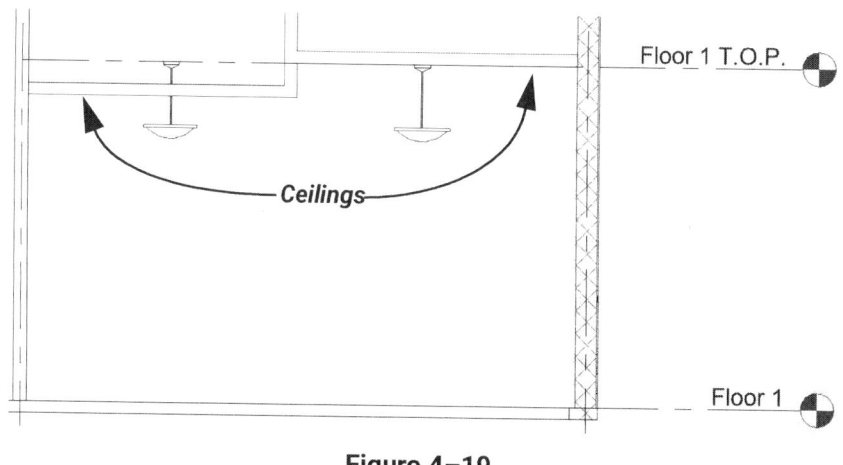

Figure 4–19

How To: Pick a New Host Element

1. Select a component.
2. In the *<component type>* contextual tab>Host panel, click (Pick New Host).
3. Select the new host (e.g., the floor).

- You can select a floor, surface, or level to be the new host for the components depending on the requirements of the component.

Moving with Nearby Host Elements

Components have the capacity to move with nearby host elements (such as walls) when they are moved. Select the component and in the Options Bar, select **Moves With Nearby Elements**. The component is automatically assigned to the closest host elements.

For example, a desk near the corner of two walls is linked to those two walls. If you move either wall, the desk moves as well. However, you can still move the desk independently of the walls.

- You cannot specify which elements the component should be linked to; the software determines this automatically. This option only works with host elements (such as walls), not with other components.

Hint: Copying Elements to Levels

The standard Windows commands ✂ (Cut to Clipboard or <Ctrl>+<X>), 📋 (Copy to Clipboard or <Ctrl>+<C>), and 📋 (Paste from Clipboard or <Ctrl>+<V>) work in Revit just as they do in other Windows-compatible software. They are available in the *Modify* tab>Clipboard panel, but not in the shortcut menu.

In the software, you can also paste elements aligned to various views or levels, as shown in Figure 4–20.

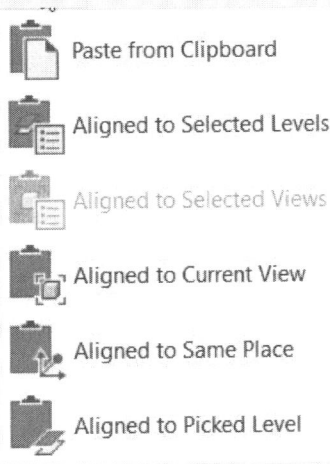

Figure 4–20

- **Aligned to Selected Levels:** Opens a dialog box where you can select the level to which you want to copy. This enables you to copy items on one level and paste them to the same location on another level (e.g., windows in a high-rise building).
- **Aligned to Selected Views:** Copies view-specific elements (such as text or dimensions) into a view that you select in a dialog box. Only the Floor Plan or Reflected Ceiling Plan views are available.
- **Aligned to Current View:** Pastes elements copied in one view to the same location in another view.
- **Aligned to Same Place:** Pastes elements to the same location in the same view.
- **Aligned to Picked Level:** Pastes elements to the level you select in an elevation or section view.

4.4 Creating Additional Family Types in a Project

As you work within your project, you may find that you need different sizes than what is provided. For example, a table family only has one size, but you need several different sizes, as shown on the left in Figure 4–21. You can also duplicate a family type and have the same family but with different materials. Both loadable and system families can be duplicated to modify the parameters within the instance and type properties. Once you duplicate the existing family type, you can choose it in the Type Selector, as shown on the right in Figure 4–21.

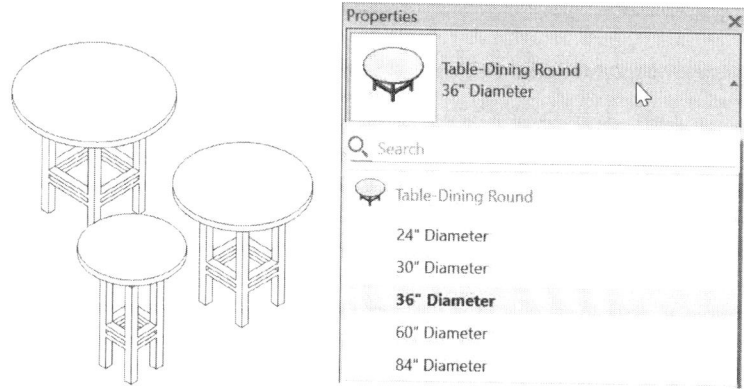

Figure 4–21

- A new family type that is created in a project will only exist in that project.

How To: Create Additional Family Types

1. Start the **Component** command.
2. In the Type Selector, select the type you want to modify. In Properties, click ▣ (Edit Type) or in the *Modify* tab>Properties panel, click ▣ (Type Properties).
3. In the Type Properties dialog box, click **Duplicate**.
4. Type a new name for the element and click **OK**.
5. In the Type Properties dialog box, change the various parameters to the desired values.
6. Click **OK** to close the dialog box. The new type is now available for use.

Structural Elements

Structural framing elements both in the model can be used to generate an analytical model that can be used for structural analysis. The analytical model has all the properties needed for analysis software like analytical nodes, members, panels, openings and links. You can create new or modify existing analytical elements in a project using the analytical automation tool. For more information on how to create an analytical model, click ⓘ (Help) In the upper right corner of the Revit interface to navigate to the online Revit Help and type **The Structural Analytical Model** in the search bar.

Practice 4a
Load Families

Practice Objective

- Load and add components.

In this practice, you will load and create families for up coming practices in this guide. You will load components from the project folders custom library and create a new size. You will then create a new size for a system family. Finally, you will load a symbol from the Load Autodesk Family dialog box.

Task 1: Load families.

1. Open the project **Structural-Compnts.rvt** from the practice files folder.

2. In the *Insert* tab>Load from Library panel, click (Load Family).

3. In the Load Family dialog box, navigate to the practice files *Families* folder and select the following families:

    - **Angled-Footing.rfa**
    - **Concrete-Rectangular-Column.rfa**
    - **K-Series Bar Joist-Rod Web.rfa**

4. Click **Open**.

5. In the Specify Types dialog box, select **K-Series Bar Joist-Rod Web.rfa** from the Family list and then select **16K7** from the *Types* list as shown in Figure 4–22 and click **OK**.

    - The other families do not have any type catalog available to choose sizes from.

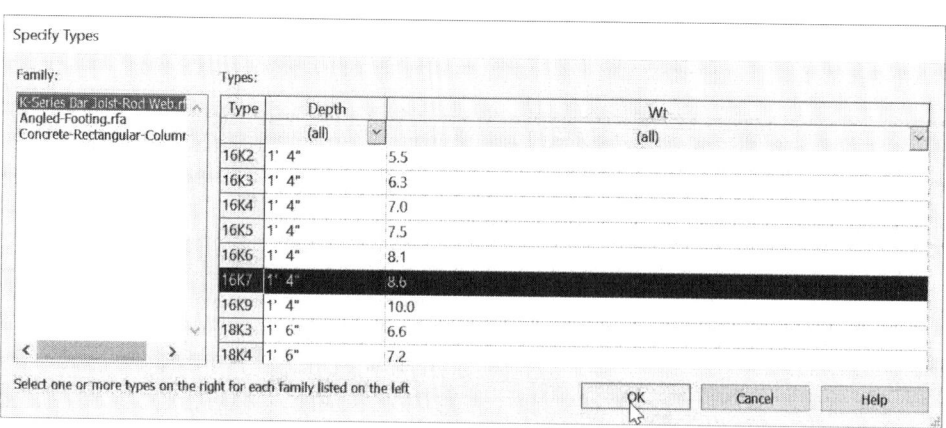

Figure 4–22

6. Save the project.

Task 2: Create a new loadable family size.

1. In the *Structure* tab>Structure panel, click (Structural Column).
2. In the Type Selector, select one of the **Concrete-Rectangular-Column** types.
3. In Properties, click (Edit Type).
4. In the Type Properties dialog box, click **Duplicate**.
5. Rename the column to **24 x 24**. Click **OK**.
6. In the Type Properties dialog box, change the dimensions for both *b* (base) and *h* (height) to **2'-0"**, as shown in Figure 4–23.

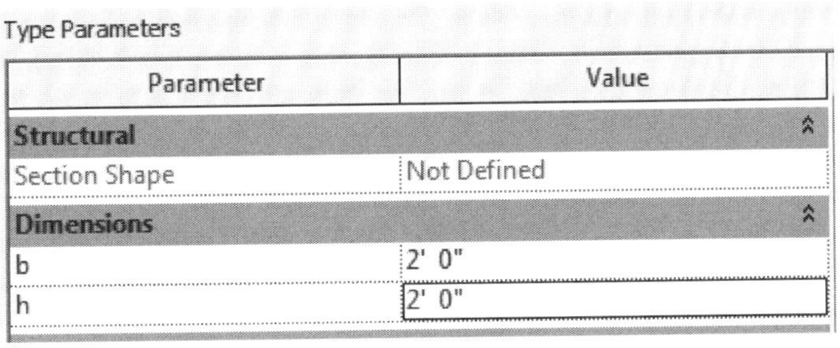

Parameter	Value
Structural	
Section Shape	Not Defined
Dimensions	
b	2' 0"
h	2' 0"

Figure 4–23

7. Click **OK**.
8. Click (Modify).
9. Save the project.

Task 3: Create a new system family type.

1. In the *Structure* tab>Foundation panel, click (Structural Foundation: Wall), or type **FT**.
2. In the Type Selector, select the **Wall Foundation: Bearing Footing - 36" x 12"**.
3. In Properties, click (Edit Type).
4. In the Type Properties dialog box, click **Duplicate...**.
5. In the Name dialog box, type **Bearing Footing - 24" x 12"** and click **OK**.

6. In the Type Properties dialog box, under *Dimensions*, set the *Width* to **2'-0"**, as shown in Figure 4–24.

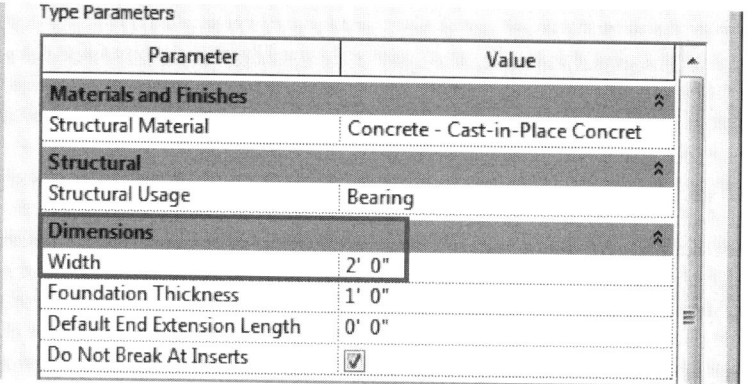

Figure 4–24

7. Click **OK**.

8. Click (Modify).

Task 4: Add a detail family from Load Autodesk Family.

Note: You must have an internet connection to use the Load Autodesk Family method. This family is also provided in the practice files Families>Tables folder.

1. In the *Insert* tab>Load from Library panel, click (Load Autodesk Family).
2. In the Load Autodesk Family dialog box, type **Break line** in the search field. Select the image of the table and chairs (as shown in Figure 4–25) and click **Load**.

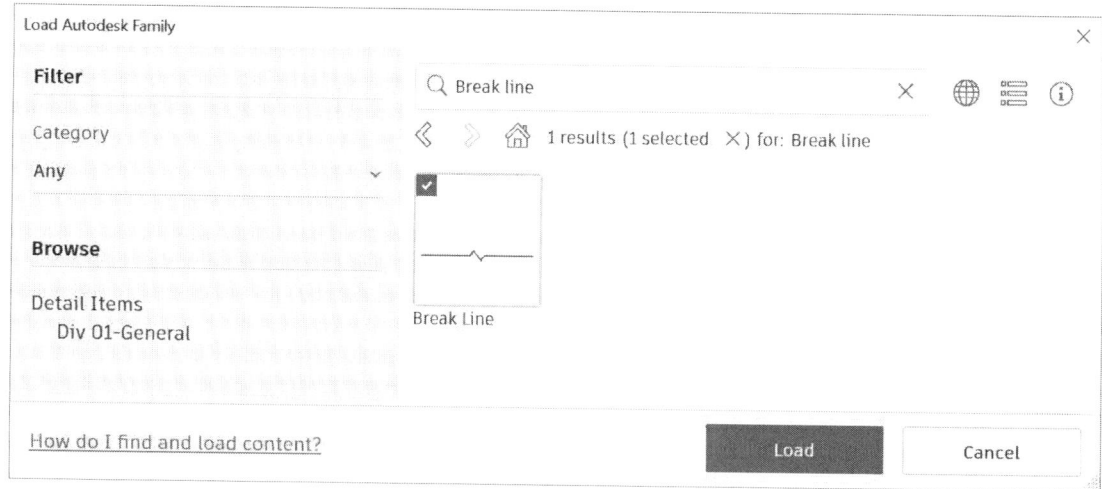

Figure 4–25

3. Save and close the project.

End of practice

Chapter Review Questions

1. How do you change the family type when inserting a component?

    a. Quick Access Toolbar

    b. Type Selector

    c. Options Bar

    d. Properties Palette

2. If the component you want to use is not available in the current project, where do you go to get the component? (Select all that apply.)

    a. In another project, copy the component to the clipboard and paste it into the current project.

    b. In the current project, use (Insert from File) and select the family from the list in the dialog box.

    c. In the current project, use (Load Family) and select the family from the list in the dialog box.

    d. Search a manufacturer's site for a component and download it.

3. When you use the **Moves with Nearby Elements** option, can you control which elements a component moves with?

    a. Yes, select the element with which you want it to move.

    b. No, it moves with the closest host element.

4. How do you create additional column sizes for column types already in the project?

    a. In Properties, duplicate an existing type and change the sizes.

    b. Start a new Revit project and draw it there.

    c. Import additional sizes from another project.

    d. In the Revit Library, load additional sizes from other families.

Command Summary

Button	Command	Location
	Copy to Clipboard	• **Ribbon:** *Modify* tab>Clipboard panel • **Shortcut:** <Ctrl>+<C>
	Cut to the Clipboard	• **Ribbon:** *Modify* tab>Clipboard panel • **Shortcut:** <Ctrl>+<X>
	Paste - Aligned to Current View	• **Ribbon:** *Modify* tab>Clipboard panel, expand Paste
	Paste - Aligned to Same Place	• **Ribbon:** *Modify* tab>Clipboard panel, expand Paste
	Paste - Aligned to Selected Levels	• **Ribbon:** *Modify* tab>Clipboard panel, expand Paste
	Paste - Aligned to Selected Views	• **Ribbon:** *Modify* tab>Clipboard panel, expand Paste
	Paste - Aligned to Picked Level	• **Ribbon:** *Modify* tab>Clipboard panel, expand Paste
	Paste from Clipboard	• **Ribbon:** *Modify* tab>Clipboard panel • **Shortcut:** <Ctrl>+<V>
	Load Autodesk Family	• **Ribbon:** *Modify	Place Component* tab>Load panel or *Insert* tab>Load from Library panel
	Load Family	• **Ribbon:** *Modify	Place Component* tab>Load panel or *Insert* tab>Load from Library panel
	Pick New Host	• **Ribbon:** *Modify	Multi-Select* or *component type* contextual tab>Host panel
	Place Component	• **Ribbon:** *Architecture* tab>Build panel, expand Component • **Shortcut:** CM

Chapter 5

Basic Sketching and Modify Tools

When you start adding general building elements (e.g., structural walls, beams, and slabs) to a project, you will use basic sketching, selecting, and modifying tools. Using these tools with drawing aids helps you to place and modify elements to create accurate building models.

Learning Objectives

- Sketch linear elements such as walls, beams, and pipes.
- Add components.
- Ease the placement of elements by incorporating drawing aids such as alignment lines, temporary dimensions, and snaps.
- Place reference planes as temporary guide lines.
- Use techniques to select and filter groups of elements.
- Modify elements using a contextual tab, Properties, temporary dimensions, and controls.
- Move, copy, rotate, and mirror elements and create array copies in linear and radial patterns.
- Align, trim, and extend elements with the edges of other elements.
- Split linear elements anywhere along their length.
- Offset elements to create duplicates a specific distance away from the original.

5.1 Adding General Model Elements

General building element commands are found on the *Architecture*, *Structure*, and *Systems* tabs (shown in Figure 5–1) and are how you place elements such as walls, slabs, ducts, etc. into your project. You can change the type of these elements using the Type Selector in Properties.

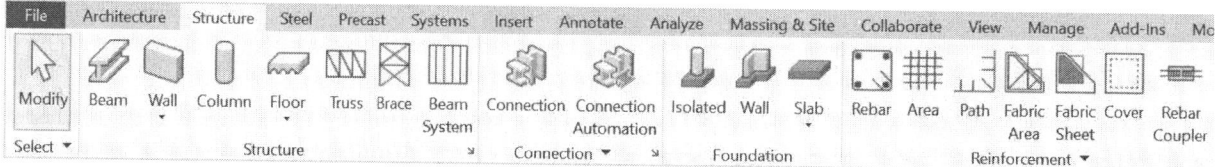

Figure 5–1

When you start a general building element command, the contextual tab on the ribbon, the Options Bar, and Properties (shown in Figure 5–2) enable you to modify element-specific features for the new element you are placing in the project. As you are working, several features called *drawing aids* display, as shown in Figure 5–2. They help you to create designs quickly and accurately. There will be different drawing aid and Options Bar options depending on which building element command is started.

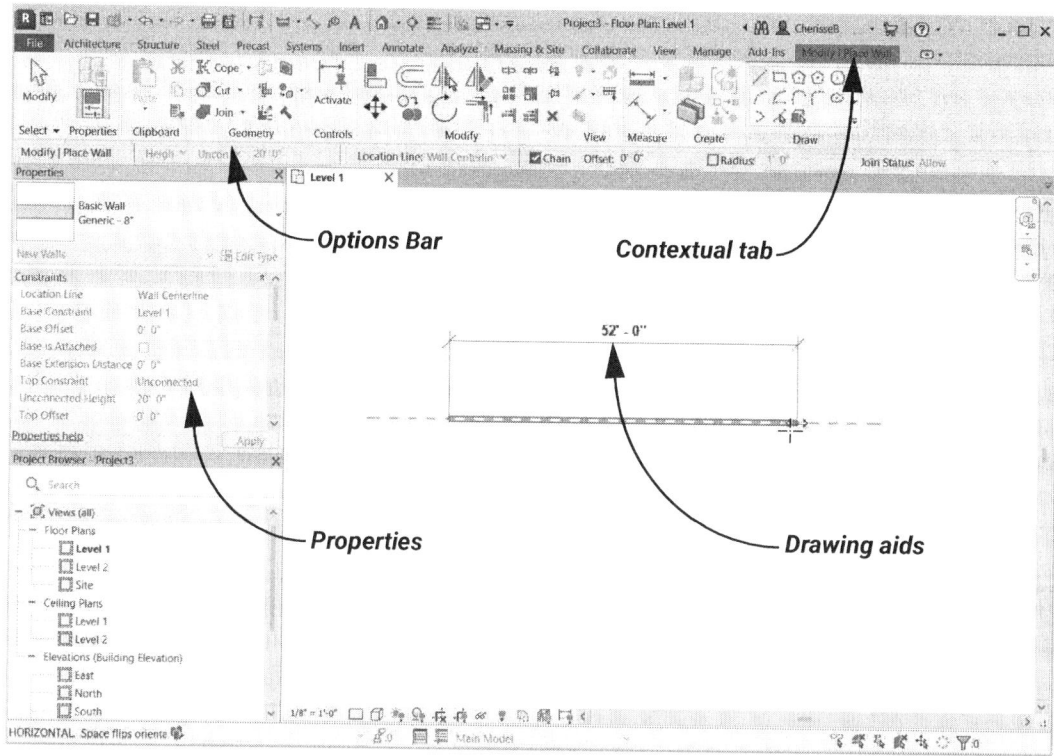

Figure 5–2

- In Revit, you are most frequently creating 3D model elements rather than 2D sketches. These tools work with both 3D and 2D elements in the software.

How To: Start a General Building Element Command

In this How To, a wall has been used as an example, but these steps apply to any general building command in the ribbon.

1. In the *Architecture* tab>Build panel or *Structure* tab>Structure panel, expand ⌑ (Wall) and select ⌑ (Wall: Structural) or ⌑ (Wall: Architectural).
2. In Properties, verify or change the wall type (for example, **Basic Wall: Generic - 8"**) in the Type Selector.
3. Place the wall in the model using the draw tools.

Draw Tools

Many elements (such as walls, beams, ducts, pipes, and conduits) are modeled using the tools on the contextual tab in the *Draw* panel. Other elements (such as floors, ceilings, roofs, and slabs) have boundaries that are sketched using many of the same tools. Draw tools are also used when you create details or schematic drawings.

Note: The exact tools vary according to the element being modeled.

Two methods are available:

- *Draw* the element using a geometric form.
- *Pick* an existing element (such as a line, face, or wall) as the basis for the new element's geometry and position.

How To: Use Draw Tools

1. Start the command you want to use.
2. In the contextual tab>Draw panel (shown in Figure 5–3), select a drawing tool.

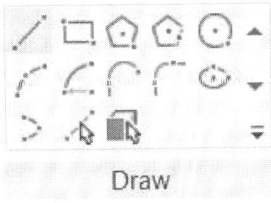

Figure 5–3

Note: You can change from one Draw tool shape to another in the middle of a command.

3. Depending on the draw tool selected, select points to define the elements or watch the Status Bar, in the lower-left corner, for hints on what to do.

4. Finish the command using one of the standard methods:
   - Click (Modify).
   - Press <Esc> twice.
   - Start another command.

Options Bar Draw Options

When you are in drawing mode, several options display in the Options Bar, as shown in Figure 5–4.

Note: Different options display according to the type of element that is selected or the command that is active.

Figure 5–4

- **Chain:** Controls how many segments are created in one process. If this option is not selected, the **Line** and **Arc** tools only create one segment at a time. If it is selected, you can continue adding segments until you press <Esc> or select the command again.
- **Offset:** Enables you to enter values so you can create linear elements at a specified distance from the selected points or element.
- **Radius:** Enables you to enter values when using a radial tool or to add a radius to the corners of linear elements as you sketch them.

Draw Tools

	Line	Draws a straight line defined by the first and last points. If **Chain** is enabled, you can continue selecting end points for multiple segments.
	Rectangle	Draws a rectangle defined by two opposing corner points. You can adjust the dimensions after selecting both points.
	Inscribed Polygon	Draws a polygon inscribed in a hypothetical circle with the number of sides specified in the Options Bar.
	Circumscribed Polygon	Draws a polygon circumscribed around a hypothetical circle with the number of sides specified in the Options Bar.
	Circle	Draws a circle defined by a center point and radius.
	Start-End-Radius Arc	Draws a curve defined by a start, end, and radius of the arc. The outside dimension shown is the included angle of the arc. The inside dimension is the radius.

	Center-ends Arc	Draws a curve defined by a center, radius, and included angle. The selected point of the radius also defines the start point of the arc.
	Tangent End Arc	Draws a curve tangent to another element. Select an end point for the first point, but do not select the intersection of two or more elements. Then, select a second point based on the included angle of the arc.
	Fillet Arc	Draws a curve defined by two other elements and a radius. Because it is difficult to select the correct radius by clicking, this command automatically moves to edit mode. Select the dimension and then modify the radius of the fillet.
	Spline	Draws a spline curve based on selected points. The curve does not actually touch the points (sketches, model lines, and detail lines only).
	Ellipse	Draws an ellipse from a primary and secondary axis (walls, sketches, model lines, and detail lines only).
	Partial Ellipse	Draws only one side of the ellipse, like an arc. A partial ellipse also has a primary and secondary axis (sketches, model lines, and detail lines only).

Pick Tools

	Pick Lines	Use this option to select existing linear elements in the project. This is useful when you start the project from an imported 2D drawing.
	Pick Face	Use this option to select the face of a 3D massing element (walls and 3D views only).
	Pick Walls	Use this option to select an existing wall in the project to be the basis for a new sketch line (floors, ceilings, etc.).

Drawing Aids

As soon as you start sketching or placing elements, the following drawing aids display (as shown in Figure 5–5), depending on which tool you are using:

- Alignment line
- Temporary dimensions
- Snaps

These aids are available with most modeling and many modification commands.

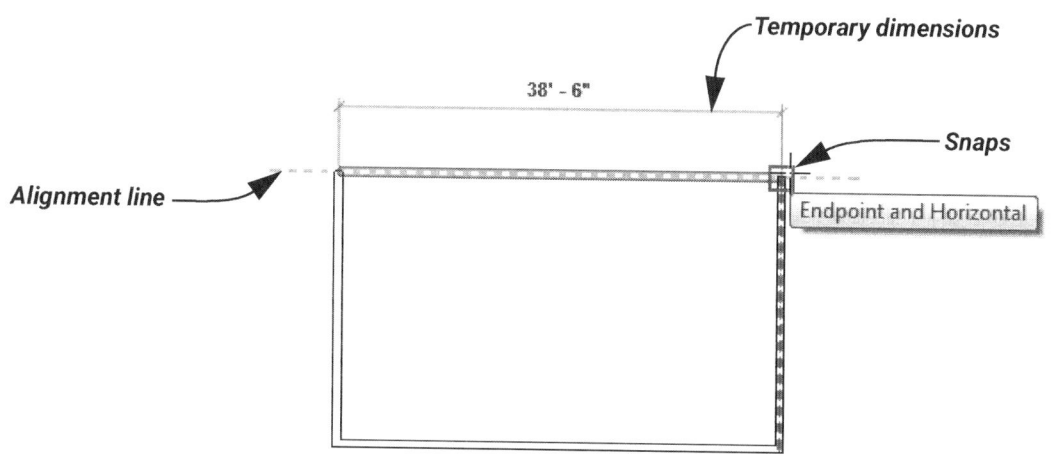

Figure 5–5

Alignment lines display as soon as you select your first point. They help keep lines horizontal, vertical, or at a specified angle. They also line up with the implied intersections of walls and other elements.

- Hold <Shift> to force the alignments to be orthogonal (90° angles only).

Temporary dimensions display to help place elements at the correct length, angle and location.

- You can type in a value, or move the cursor until you see the dimension you want, or you can place the element and then modify the value as needed.

- The length and angle increments shown vary depending on how far in or out the view is zoomed.

- Temporary dimensions disappear as soon as you finish adding elements. If you want to make them permanent, select the dimension symbol (⊢⊣), as shown in Figure 5–6.

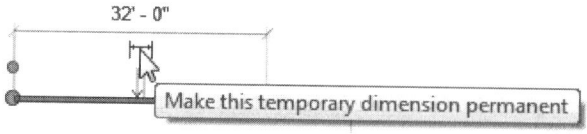

Figure 5–6

Basic Sketching and Modify Tools

Snaps are key points that help you reference existing elements to exact points when modeling, as shown in Figure 5–7.

Figure 5–7

- When you move the cursor over an element, the snap symbol displays. Each snap location type displays with a different symbol.

Reference Planes

As you develop designs in Revit, there are times when you need lines to help you define certain locations. You can sketch *reference planes* (displayed as dashed green lines) and snap to them whenever you need to line up elements. For the example shown in Figure 5–8, the light fixtures in the reflected ceiling plan are placed using reference planes.

- To insert a reference plane, in the *Architecture, Structure*, or *Systems* tab>Work Plane panel, click (Reference Plane), or type **RP**.

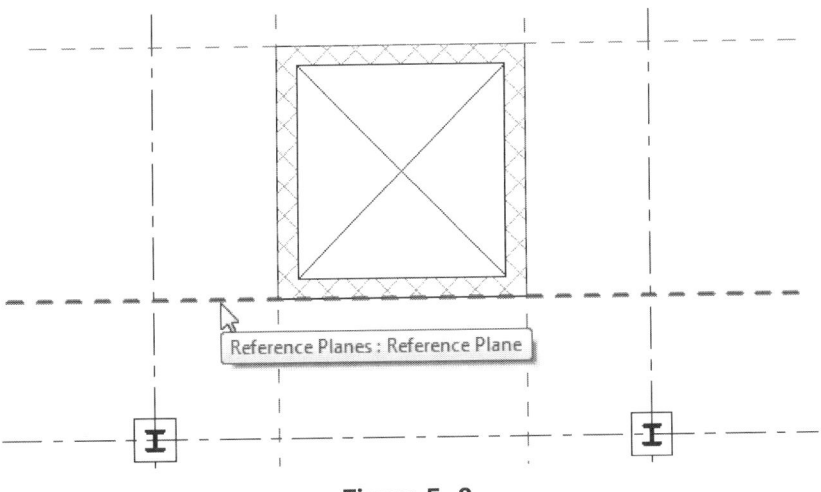

Figure 5–8

- Reference planes display in associated views because they are infinite planes and not just lines.

  Note: *Reference planes do not display in 3D views.*

- You can name reference planes by clicking on **<Click to name>** and typing in the text box, as shown in Figure 5–9.

Figure 5–9

- If you sketch a reference plane in sketch mode (used with floors and similar elements), it does not display once the sketch is finished.

- Reference planes can have different line styles if they have been defined in the project. In Properties, select a style from the *Subcategory* list.

- It is possible to generate additional subcategories for reference planes using different line styles, lineweights, and colors, which can help you distinguish reference planes used for different functions. Moreover, you can manage the visibility of reference plane subcategories separately.

Hint: Model Line vs. Detail Line

While most of the elements that you create are representations of actual building elements, there are times you may need to add lines to clarify the design intent. These can be either detail lines, as shown in Figure 5–10, or model lines. Detail lines are also useful as references because they are only reflected in the view in which you sketch them.

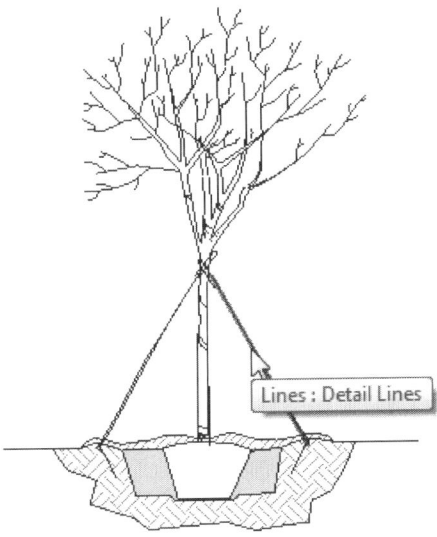

Figure 5–10

- A model line (*Architecture* or *Structure* tab>Model panel> (Model Line)) functions as a 3D element and displays in all views.

- A detail line (*Annotate* tab>Detail panel> (Detail Line)) is strictly a 2D element that only displays in the view in which it is drawn.

- In the *Modify* contextual tab, select a *Line Style* and then the Draw tool that you want to use to draw the model or detail line.

Editing Building Model Elements

Building design projects typically involve extensive changes to the model. Revit was designed to make such changes quickly and efficiently. You can change an element using the following methods, as shown in Figure 5–11:

- The Type Selector enables you to specify a different type. This is frequently used to change the size and/or style of the elements.

- Properties enables you to modify the information (parameters) associated just with the selected elements. These are referred to as **instance properties**.

- **Type properties** are accessed through Properties by clicking **Edit Type**. They enable you to modify parameters for all of the same element type in the model.

- The contextual tab in the ribbon contains the Modify commands and element-specific tools.

- Temporary dimensions enable you to change the element's dimensions or position.

- Controls enable you to drag, flip, lock, and rotate the element.

- Shape handles enable you to drag elements to modify their height or length.

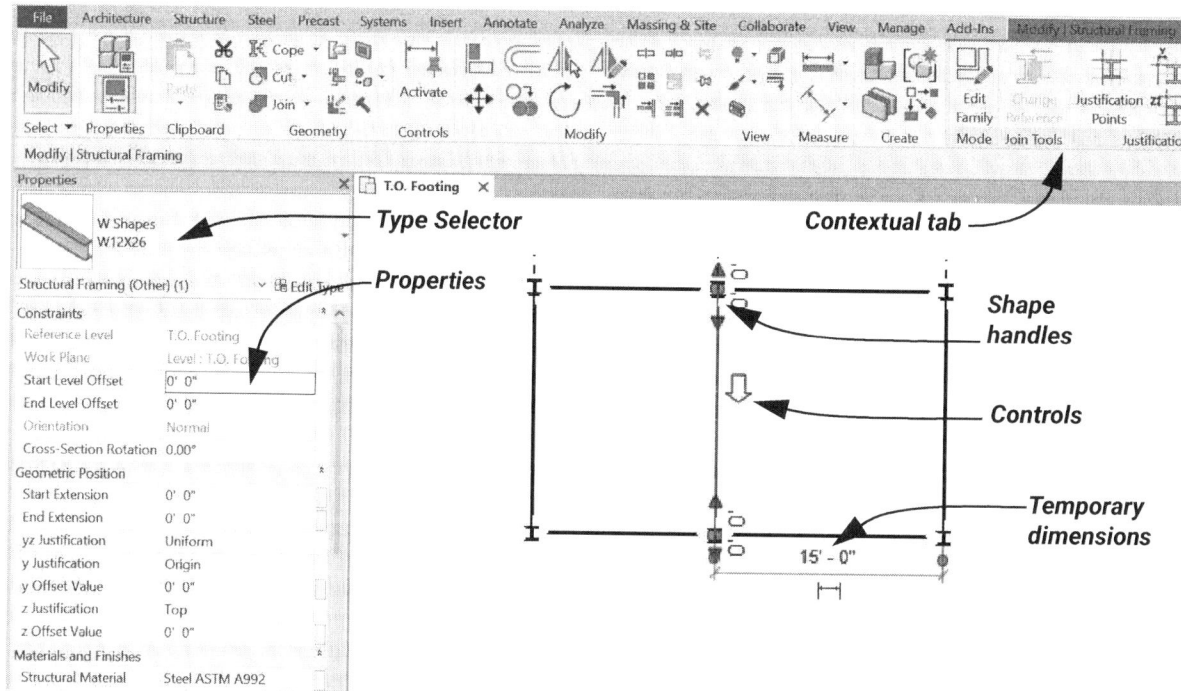

Figure 5–11

- To delete an element, select it and press <Delete>, right-click and select **Delete**, or in the Modify panel, click ✖ (Delete).

Working with Controls and Shape Handles

When you select an element, various controls and shape handles display depending on the element and view. For example, in plan view you can use controls to drag the ends of an element and change its orientation. You can also use the controls to drag the ends in a 3D view, as shown in Figure 5–12.

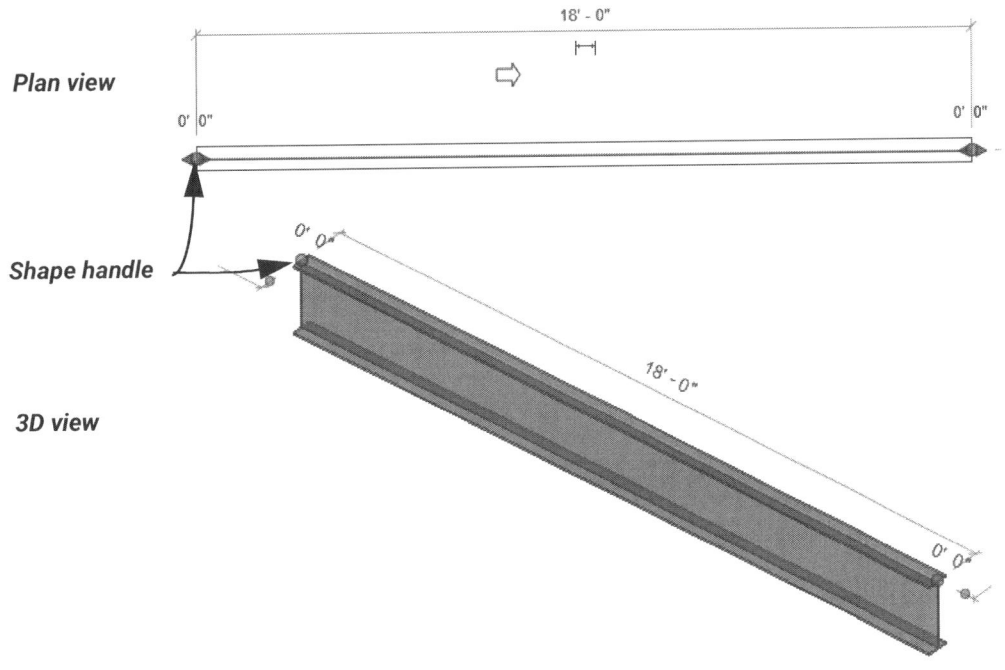

Figure 5–12

- If you hover the cursor over the control or shape handle, a tooltip displays showing its function.

Editing Temporary Dimensions

Temporary dimensions automatically link to the closest wall. To change this, drag the *Witness Line* control, as shown in Figure 5–13, to connect to a new reference. You can also click on the control to toggle between justifications in the wall.

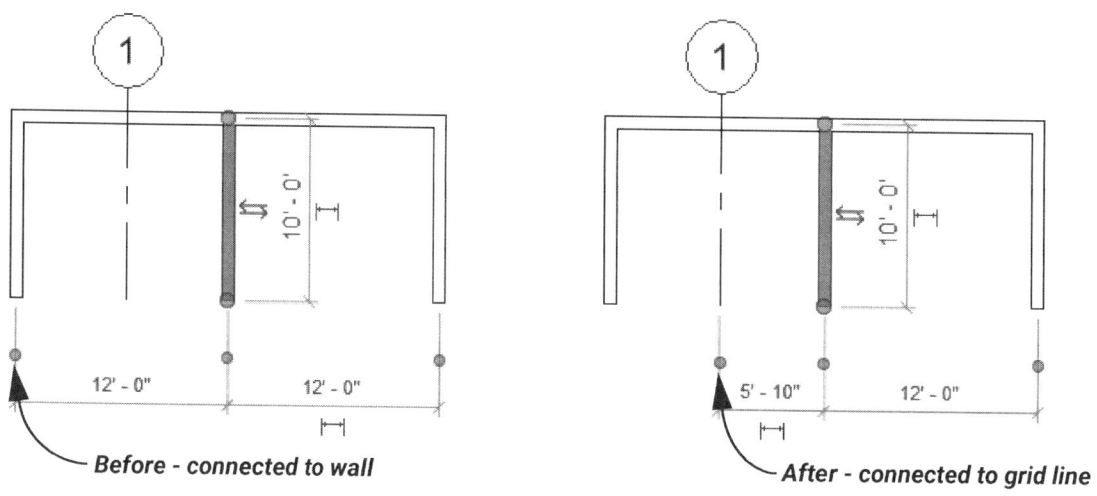

Figure 5–13

- The new location of a temporary dimension for an element is remembered as long as you are in the same session of the software.

Selecting Multiple Elements

You can select more than one element at a time using the various methods described below, as well as remove elements from a group of selected elements by filtering out specific categories. When selecting more than one element in a model, you may also see controls like temporary dimensions and pin controls, as shown in Figure 5–14. You have the ability to hide these controls and temporary dimensions if they make viewing the selected elements difficult using the **Activate Controls and Dimensions** option.

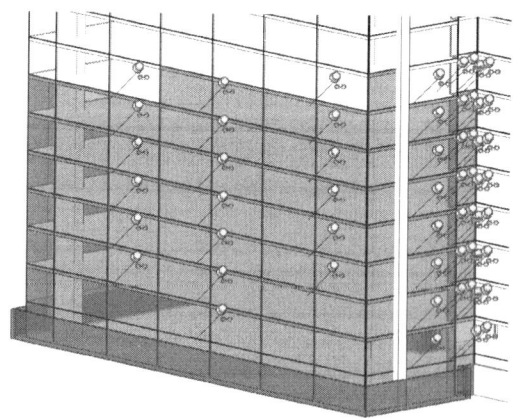

Figure 5–14

Note: You can save selections and use them again. For more information, see A.1 Selection Sets.

How To: Manually Select Multiple Elements

1. Once you have selected at least one element, hold <Ctrl> and select another item to add it to your selection.
2. To remove an element from a group of selected elements, hold <Shift> and select the element you want removed.
   - If several elements are on or near each other, hover your cursor over an edge and press <Tab> to cycle through them before you click.
   - If there are elements that might be linked to each other, such as walls that are connected, pressing <Tab> selects the chain of elements.

How To: Select Multiple Elements with a Window Selection

1. Click and drag the cursor to *window* around elements using one of two selection options:
   - **Selection window (or containing window):** Click and drag your cursor from left to right (as shown in Figure 5–15). With this option, you only select the elements completely inside the window.
   - **Crossing window:** Click and drag your cursor from right to left (as shown in Figure 5–15). With this option, you select elements that are both inside and crossing the window.

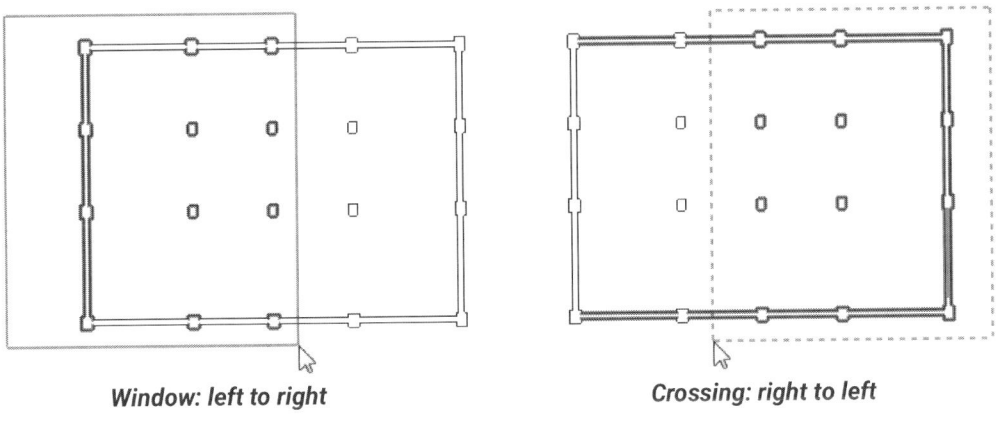

Window: left to right *Crossing: right to left*

Figure 5–15

- If you are accidentally clicking on elements and dragging them out of place when trying to window around elements, you can turn off (Drag Elements on Selection) in the lower-right corner of the Status Bar. When off, the icon will display with a red X.

How To: Quickly Select a Previous Group of Selected Elements

1. Press <Ctrl>+<Left Arrow> to reselect the previous group of element selection.
   - Alternatively, right-click in the view window with nothing selected and select **Select Previous**.

How To: Quickly Select All of the Same Element

1. To select all elements of a specific type, right-click on an element.
2. In the menu, select **Select All Instances>Visible in View**, **In Entire Project**, or **In Entire Project Including Legends**, as shown in Figure 5–16. For example, if you select a column of a specific size and use this command, only the columns of the same size are selected.

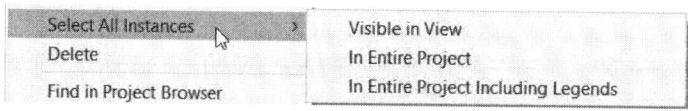

Figure 5–16

- Alternatively, select the element in the view and type **SA**. This selects all elements of the same type in the view.

How To: Use Activate Controls and Dimensions

1. With multiple elements selected in the model, in the *Modify* contextual tab>Controls panel, click (Activate Controls and Dimensions).
   - Alternatively, in the Quick Access Toolbar, click (Activate Controls and Dimensions), or type **AC**.
2. When this option is toggled on, the controls and temporary dimensions are hidden in the view, as shown on the left in Figure 5–17. Toggle (Activate Controls and Dimensions) off to display the controls and dimensions again, as shown on the right.

Basic Sketching and Modify Tools

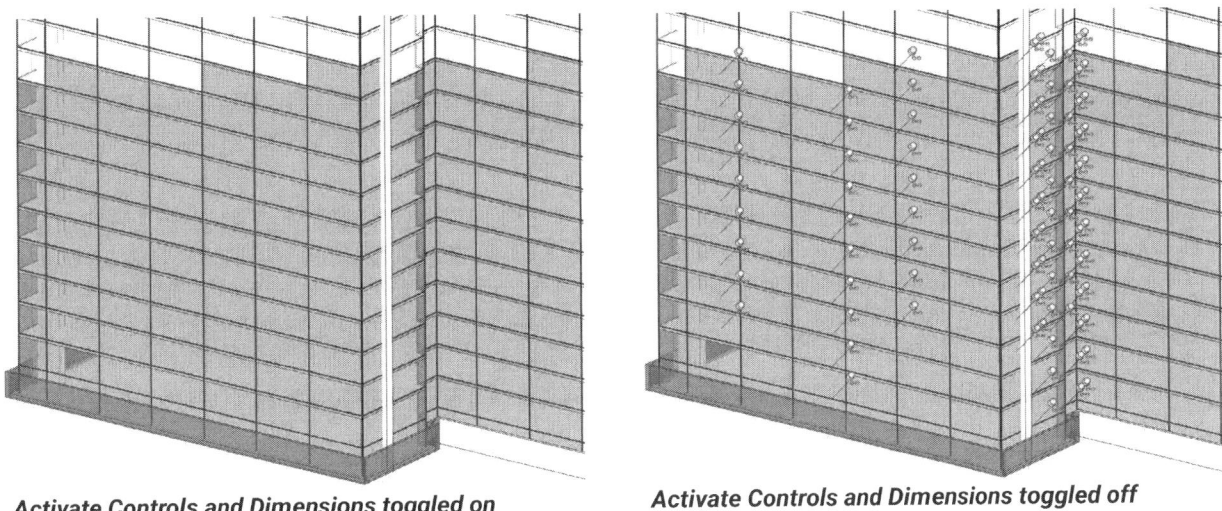

Activate Controls and Dimensions toggled on   *Activate Controls and Dimensions toggled off*

Figure 5–17

Measuring Tool

When modifying a model, it is useful to know the distance between elements. This can be done with temporary dimensions or, more frequently, by using the measuring tools found in the Quick Access Toolbar or in the *Modify* tab>Measure panel, as shown in Figure 5–18.

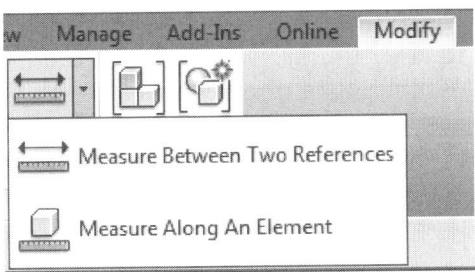

Figure 5–18

- (Measure Between Two References): Select two elements and the measurement displays. This can be done in both 2D and 3D views.
    - If you select **Chain** in the Options Bar (as shown in Figure 5–19), you can get the total length of multiple measurements.

Figure 5–19

- 📄 (Measure Along An Element): Select the edge of a linear element and the total length displays. Use <Tab> to highlight other elements and then click to measure along all of them, as shown in Figure 5–20. This can be done in 2D views only.

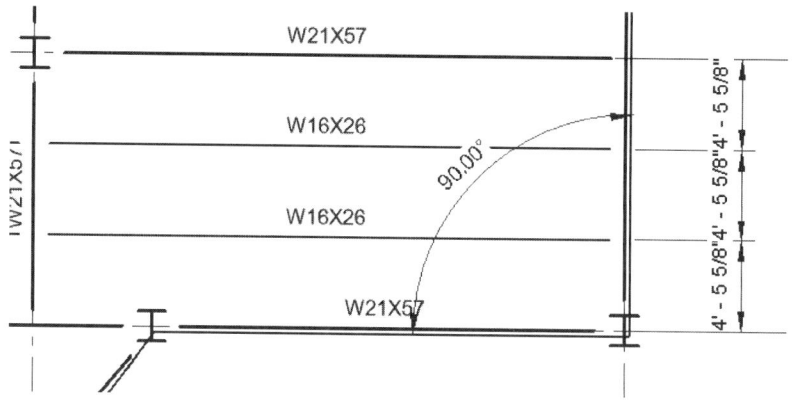

Figure 5–20

- References include any snap point, wall lines, or other parts of elements (such as door center lines).

Filtering Selection of Multiple Elements

When multiple element categories are selected, the *Multi-Select* contextual tab opens in the ribbon. This gives you access to all of the Modify tools and the **Filter** command. The **Filter** command enables you to specify the types of elements to select. For example, you might only want to select columns, as shown in Figure 5–21.

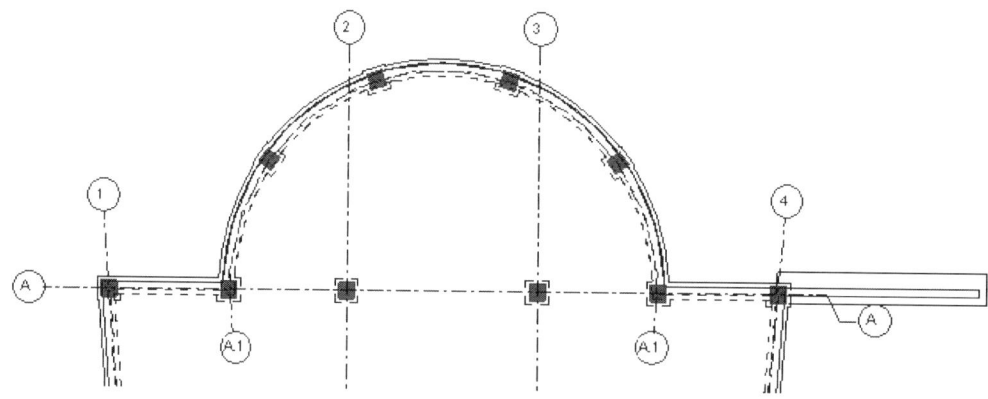

Figure 5–21

Basic Sketching and Modify Tools

How To: Filter a Selection of Multiple Elements

1. Select everything in the area using either a crossing window or window selection that includes the elements you want to work with.

2. In the *Modify | Multi-Select* tab>Selection panel or in the Status Bar, click (Filter). The Filter dialog box opens, as shown in Figure 5–22.

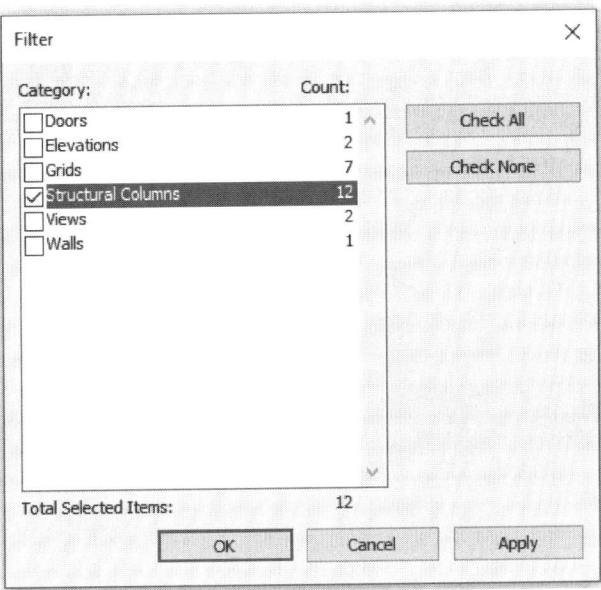

Figure 5–22

3. The Filter dialog box displays all types of elements in the original selection. Click **Check None** to clear all of the options or **Check All** to select all of the options. You can also select or clear individual categories as needed.

4. Click **OK**. The selection is now limited to the elements you specified.

- The number of elements selected displays on the right end of the Status Bar and in Properties.

Practice 5a
Sketch and Edit Elements

Practice Objective

- Use modify tools and drawing aids.

In this practice, you will use a variety of ways to select elements, use the Filter dialog box to only select one type of element, select only elements of one type in the view, and use the Type Selector to change the type. You will then modify element locations using temporary dimensions, as shown in Figure 5–23.

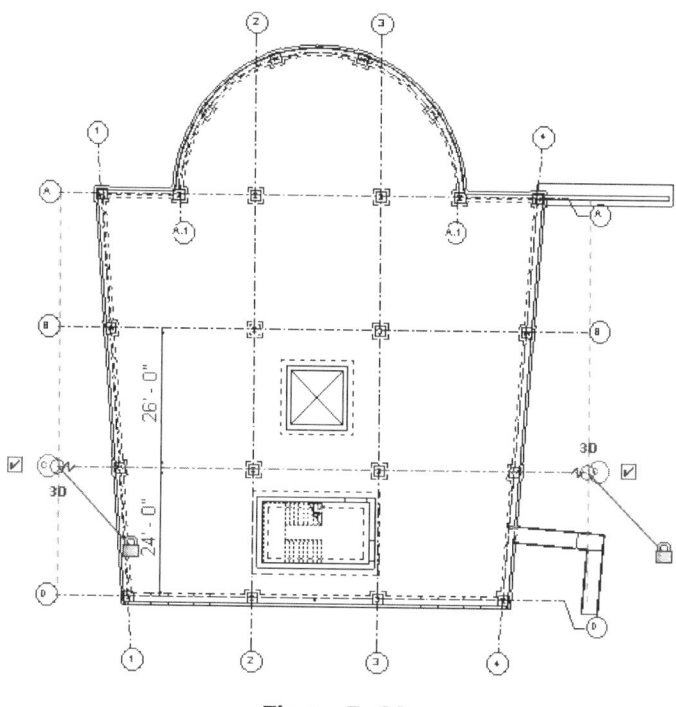

Figure 5–23

Task 1: Select elements.

1. Open **Structural-Select.rvt** from the practice files folder.
2. The file should automatically open to the **Structural Plans: Level 1** view.
3. Create a selection window around the building by selecting a point just outside the upper-left corner of the building and, while continuing to hold the left mouse button, drag the mouse toward the lower-right corner and click to select the second point, as shown in Figure 5–24.

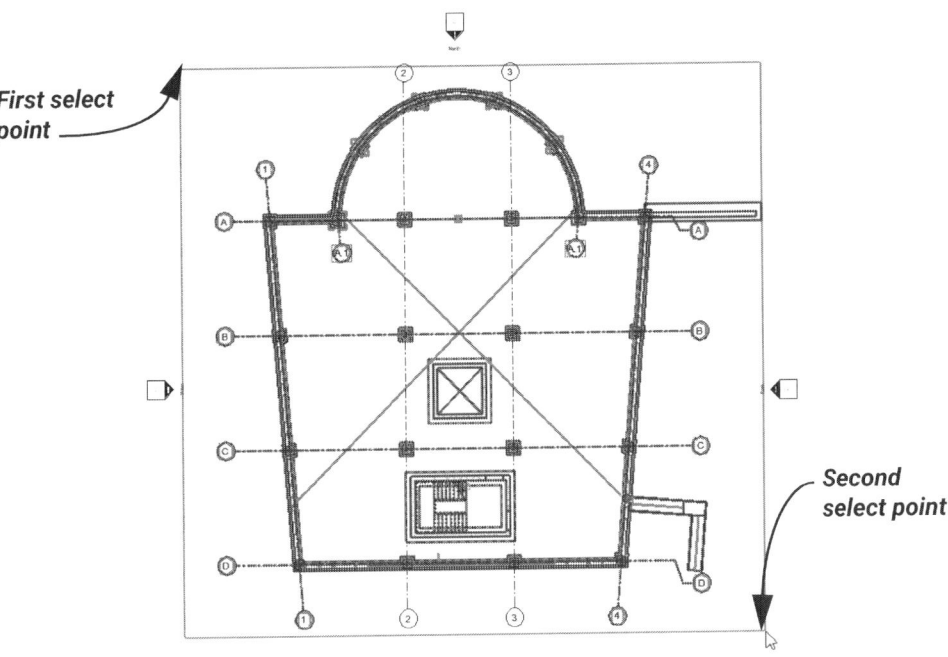

Figure 5–24

4. All of the elements inside the window are selected and those outside the window are not selected. Press <Esc>.

5. Select the building again, but this time use a crossing window by selecting a point just outside the upper-right corner of the building and, while continuing to hold the left mouse button, drag the mouse toward the lower-left corner, as shown in Figure 5–25. All of the elements inside and touching the window are selected.

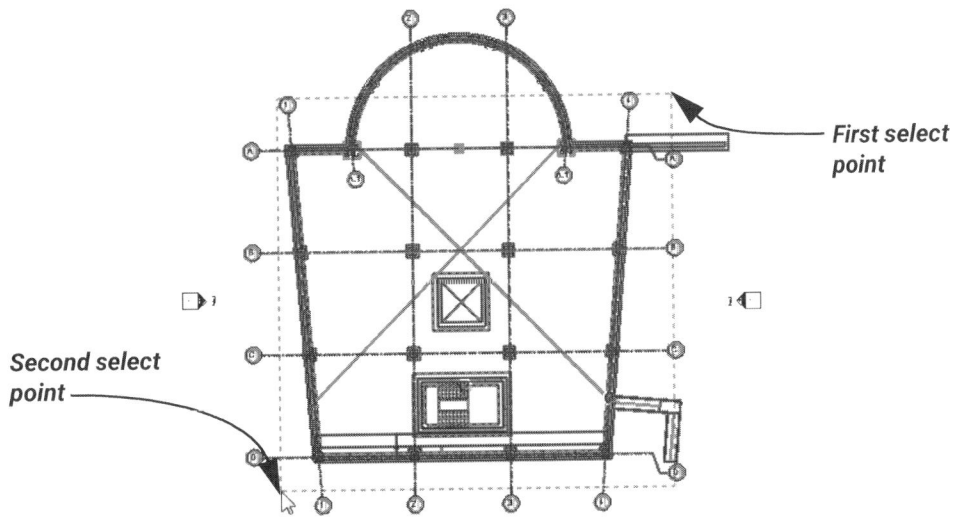

Figure 5–25

6. In the Status Bar, click (Filter).
7. In the Filter dialog box, shown in Figure 5–26, review the selected element categories.

   Note: The numbers here and in the next steps might be slightly different depending on your selection.

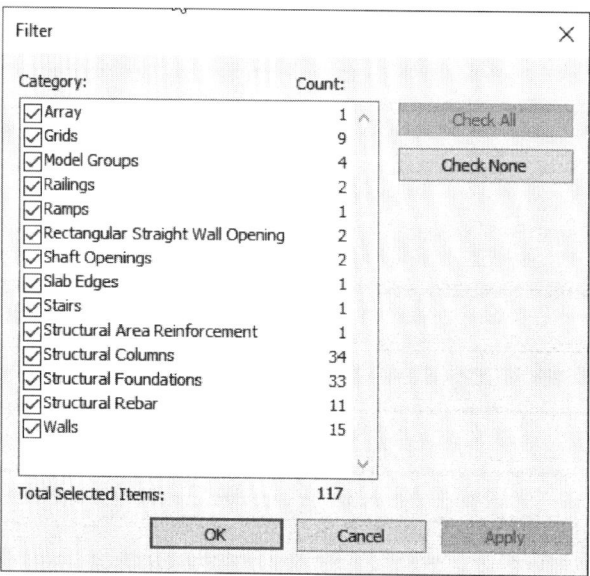

Figure 5–26

8. Click **Check None**.
9. Select only the **Structural Columns** category and click **OK**.
10. The total number of structural columns in the selection set displays in the Status Bar, as shown in Figure 5–27.

Figure 5–27

11. In Properties, the display indicates that multiple families are selected.
12. Click in an empty space in the view to clear the selection.

13. Zoom in on the lower-left corner of the building and select one structural column, as shown in Figure 5-28.

Figure 5-28

14. In the Type Selector, the column name and type are displayed, as shown in Figure 5-29.

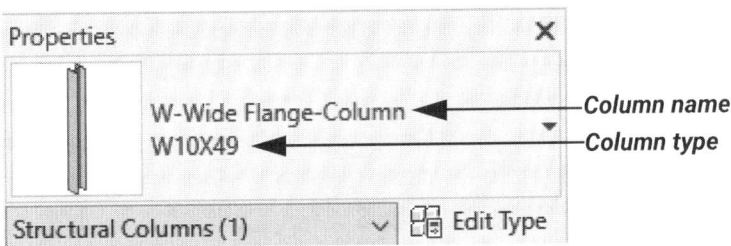

Figure 5-29

15. In the view, right-click, expand **Select All Instances**, and select **Visible in View**, as shown in Figure 5-30.

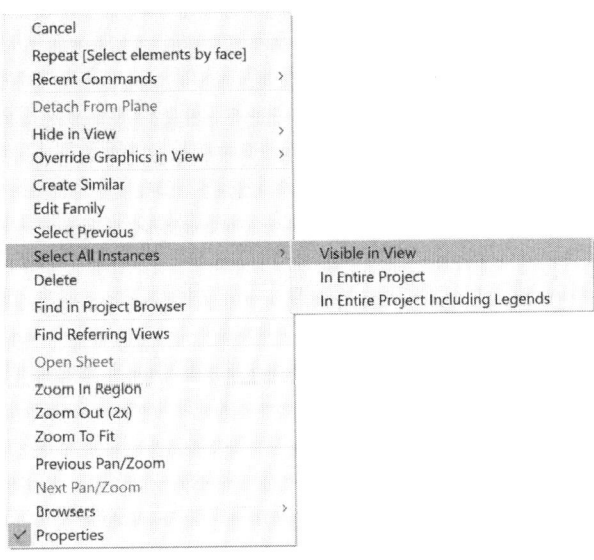

Figure 5-30

16. The total number of this type of column displays in the Status Bar beside the Filter and in Properties.

17. Expand the Type Selector, as shown in Figure 5–31, and select **W-Wide Flange-Column: W12x40**.

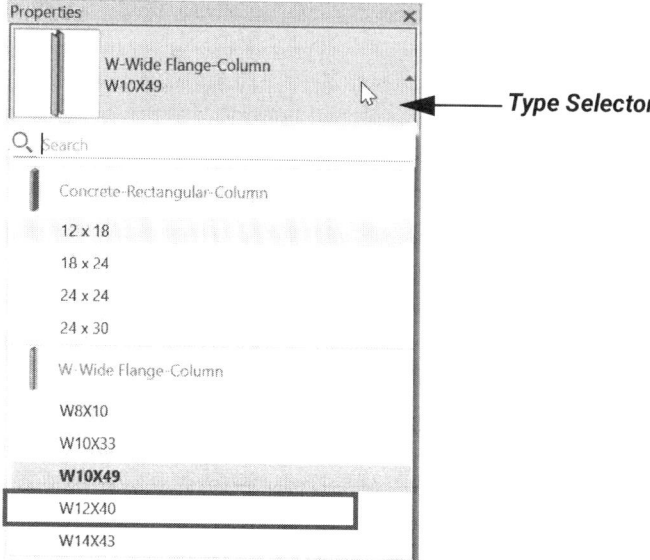

Figure 5–31

18. The view regenerates and the selected columns are updated to the new type. Press <Esc> to release the selection set.

Task 2: Use temporary dimensions.

1. Zoom out to see the entire building.
2. Select **grid line C**.
3. If the temporary dimensions are not displayed, in the Options Bar, click **Activate Dimensions**.
4. The temporary dimensions are automatically connected to the closest structural elements.
5. Use the **Move Witness Line** controls on the temporary dimensions and move them to the nearest grid lines, as shown in Figure 5–32.

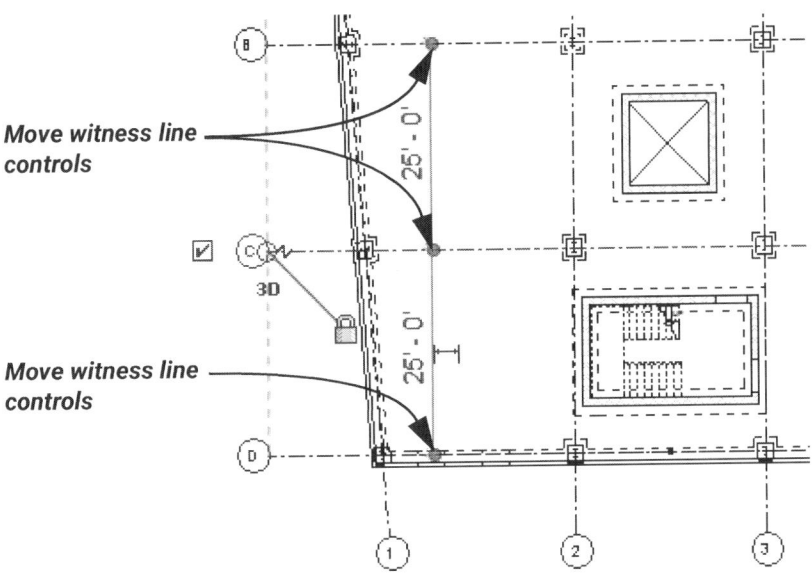

Figure 5–32

6. Click (Make this temporary dimension line permanent).
7. Click in an empty space in the view to release the selection. The new dimensions are now part of the view.
8. Select **grid line C** again.
9. Click **Activate Dimensions,** if needed.
10. Select the lower dimension text and change it to **24'-0"**, as shown in Figure 5–33. Press <Enter>.

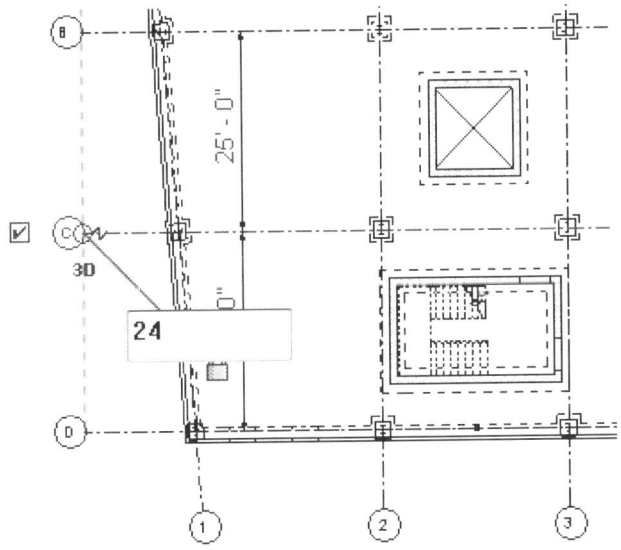

Figure 5–33

- The model regenerates and the percentage of completion is displayed in the Status Bar, as shown in Figure 5–34. This change is being made to the grid line and throughout the model, wherever elements touch the grid line.

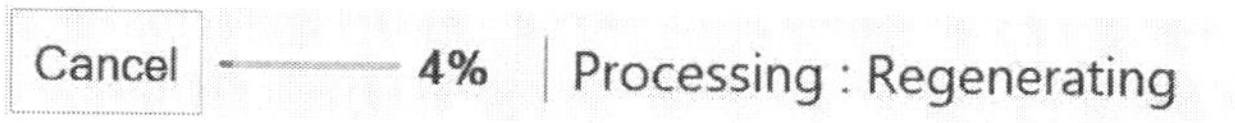

Figure 5–34

11. Save and close the project.

End of practice

5.2 Working with Basic Modify Tools

The basic modifying tools, **Move**, **Copy**, **Rotate**, **Mirror**, **Align**, and **Array**, can be used with individual elements or any selection of elements. They are found in the Modify panel (shown in Figure 5–35), in the *Modify* tab, and in contextual tabs.

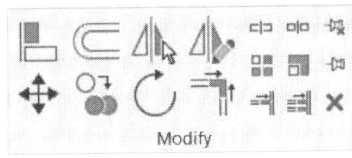

Figure 5–35

- For these modify commands, you can either select the elements and start the command, or start the command, select the elements, and press <Enter> to finish the selection and move to the next step in the command.

Moving and Copying Elements

The **Move** and **Copy** commands enable you to select the element(s) and move or copy them from one place to another. You can use alignment lines, temporary dimensions, and snaps to help place a second column, as shown in Figure 5–36.

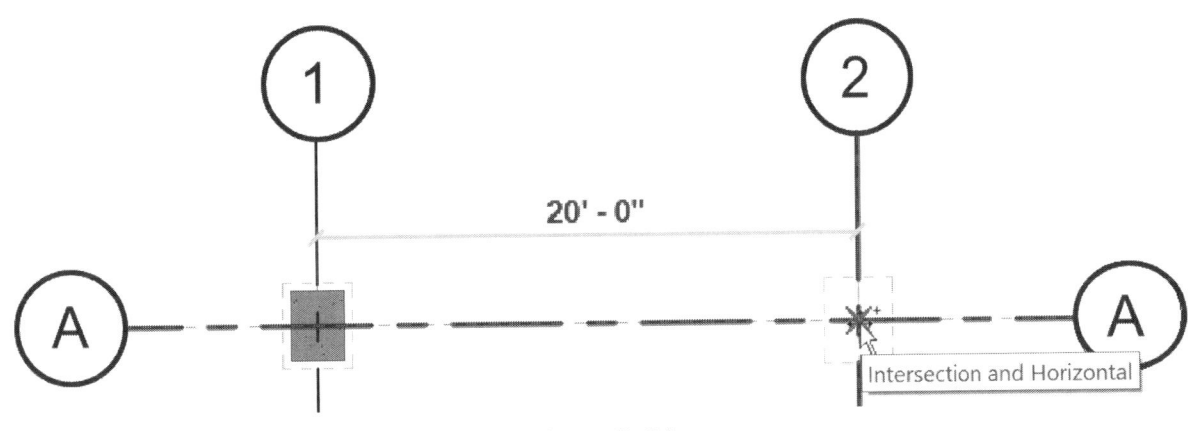

Figure 5–36

How To: Move or Copy Elements

1. Select the elements you want to move or copy.

2. In the Modify panel, click ✢ (Move) or ⟲ (Copy). Alternatively, you can type **MV** for **Move** and **CO** for **Copy**. A boundary box displays around the selected elements.

3. Select a start point on or near the element.

4. Select a second point. Use alignment lines and temporary dimensions to help place the elements.

5. When you are finished, you can start another modify command using the elements that remain selected, or select ▷ (Modify) to end the command.

- You can drag elements to new locations without starting the **Move** command. Holding <Ctrl> and dragging copies the element. This is quick but not very precise.

Move/Copy Elements Options

The **Move** and **Copy** commands have several options that display in the Options Bar, as shown in Figure 5-37.

☐ Constrain ☐ Disjoin ☑ Multiple

Figure 5-37

Constrain	Restricts the movement of the cursor to horizontal or vertical, or along the axis of an item that is at an angle. This keeps you from selecting a point at an angle by mistake. **Constrain** is off by default.
Disjoin (Move only)	Breaks any connections between the elements being moved and other elements. If **Disjoin** is on, the elements move separately. If it is off, the connected elements also move or stretch. **Disjoin** is off by default.
Multiple (Copy only)	Enables you to make multiple copies of one selection.

- These commands only work in the current view, not between views or projects. To copy between views or projects, in the *Modify* tab>Clipboard panel, use 📋 (Copy to Clipboard), ✂ (Cut to the Clipboard), and 📋 (Paste from Clipboard).

Basic Sketching and Modify Tools

> **Hint: Pinning Elements**
>
> If you do not want elements to be moved, you can pin them in place, as shown in Figure 5–38. Select the elements and in the *Modify* tab, in the Modify panel, click (Pin) or type **PN**. Pinned elements can be copied, but not moved. If you try to delete a pinned element, a warning dialog displays reminding you that you must unpin the element before the command can be started.

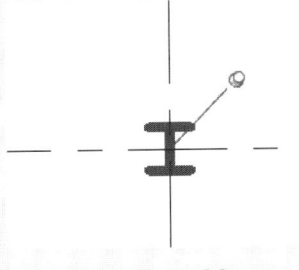

Figure 5–38

Select the element and click (Unpin) or type **UP** to unpin the element.

Rotating Elements

The **Rotate** command enables you to rotate selected elements around a center point or origin, as shown in Figure 5–39. You can use alignment lines, temporary dimensions, and snaps to help specify the center of rotation and the angle. You can also create copies of the element as it is being rotated.

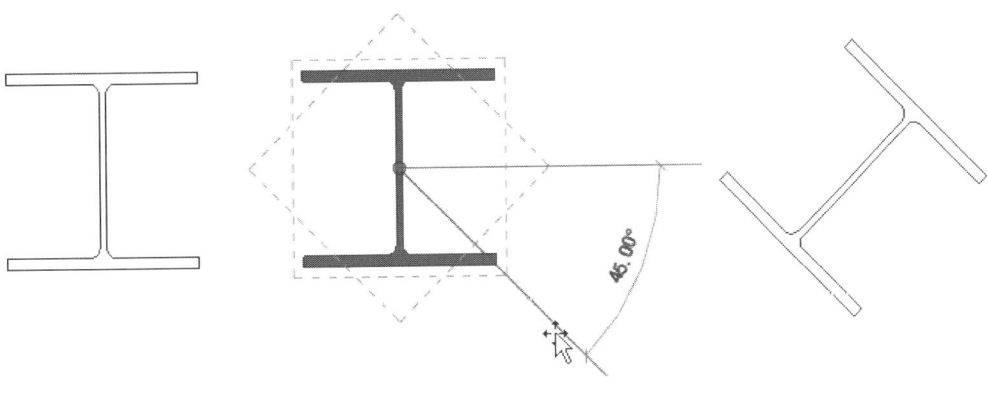

Figure 5–39

How To: Rotate Elements

1. Select the element(s) you want to rotate.

2. In the Modify panel, click (Rotate), or type **RO**.

3. The center of rotation is automatically set to the center of the element or group of elements, as shown on the left in Figure 5–40. To change the center of rotation, as shown on the right in Figure 5–40, use the following:

- Drag the ↻ (Center of Rotation) control to a new point.
- In the Options Bar, next to **Center of rotation**, click **Place** and use snaps to move it to a new location.
- Press <Spacebar> to select the center of rotation and click to move it to a new location.

*Note: To start the **Rotate** command with a prompt to select the center of rotation, select the elements first and type **R3**.*

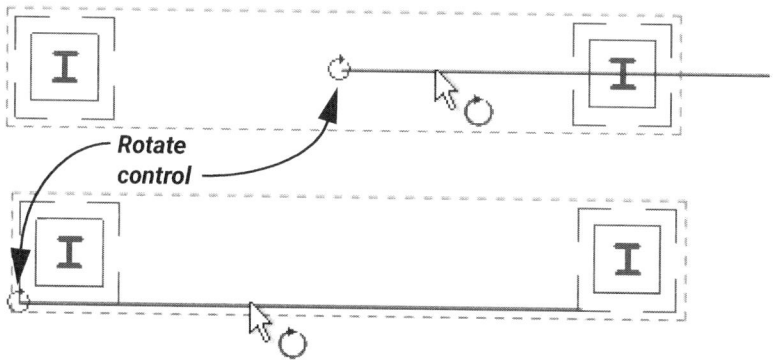

Figure 5–40

4. In the Options Bar (shown in Figure 5–41), specify if you want to make a copy (select **Copy**), type an angle in the *Angle* field, and press <Enter>. You can also specify the angle on screen using temporary dimensions.

Figure 5–41

5. The rotated element(s) remain highlighted, enabling you to start another command using the same selection, or click ▷ (Modify) to finish.

- The **Disjoin** option breaks any connections between the elements being rotated and other elements. If **Disjoin** is on (selected), the elements rotate separately. If it is off (cleared), the connected elements also move or stretch, as shown in Figure 5–42. **Disjoin** is toggled off by default.

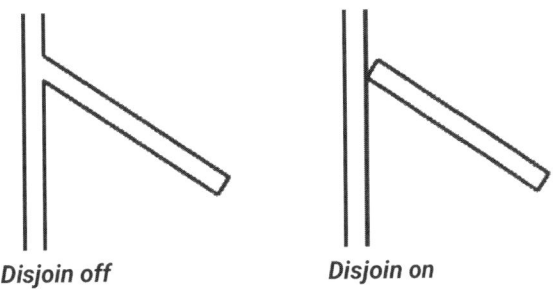

Disjoin off *Disjoin on*

Figure 5–42

Mirroring Elements

The **Mirror** command enables you to mirror elements about an axis defined by a selected element, as shown in Figure 5–43, or by selected points.

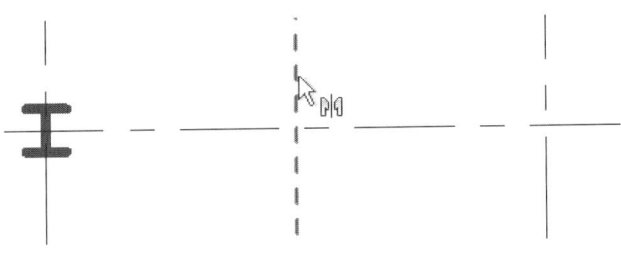

Figure 5–43

How To: Mirror Elements

1. Select the element(s) to mirror.
2. In the Modify panel, select the method you want to use:

    - Click (Mirror - Pick Axis) or type **MM**. This prompts you to select an element as the **Axis of Reflection** (mirror line).

    - Click (Mirror - Draw Axis) or type **DM**. This prompts you to select two points to define the axis about which the elements mirror.

3. The new mirrored element(s) remain highlighted, enabling you to start another command, or return to **Modify** to finish.

- By default, the original elements that were mirrored remain. To delete the original elements, clear the **Copy** option in the Options Bar.

> **Hint: Scale**
>
> Revit is designed with full-size elements. Therefore, not much should be scaled. For example, scaling a wall increases its length but does not impact the width, which is set by the wall type. However, you can use ⛶ (Scale) in reference planes, images, and imported files from other programs.

Creating Linear and Radial Arrays

The **Array** command creates multiple copies of selected elements in a linear or radial pattern, as shown in Figure 5–44. For example, you can array a row of columns to create a row of evenly spaced columns on a grid, or array a row of parking spaces. The arrayed elements can be grouped or placed as separate elements.

> *Note: A linear array creates a straight line pattern of elements, while a radial array creates a circular pattern around a center point.*

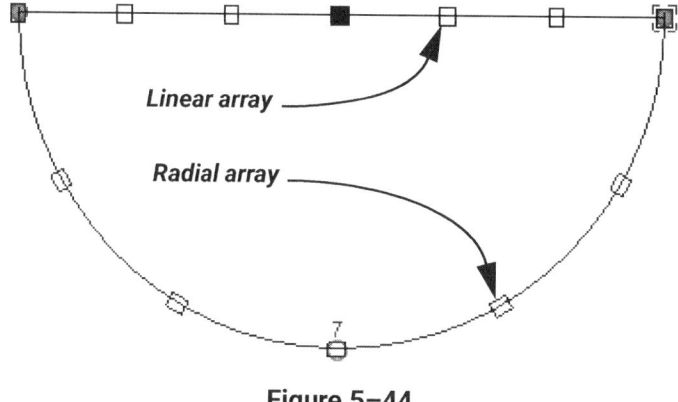

Figure 5–44

How To: Create a Linear Array

1. Select the element(s) to array.
2. In the Modify panel, click ▦ (Array), or type **AR**.
3. In the Options Bar, click 🔲 (Linear).
4. Specify the other options as needed.
5. Select a start point and an end point to set the spacing and direction of the array. The array is displayed.

6. If **Group and Associate** is selected, you are prompted again for the number of items, as shown in Figure 5–45. Type a new number or click on the screen to finish the command.

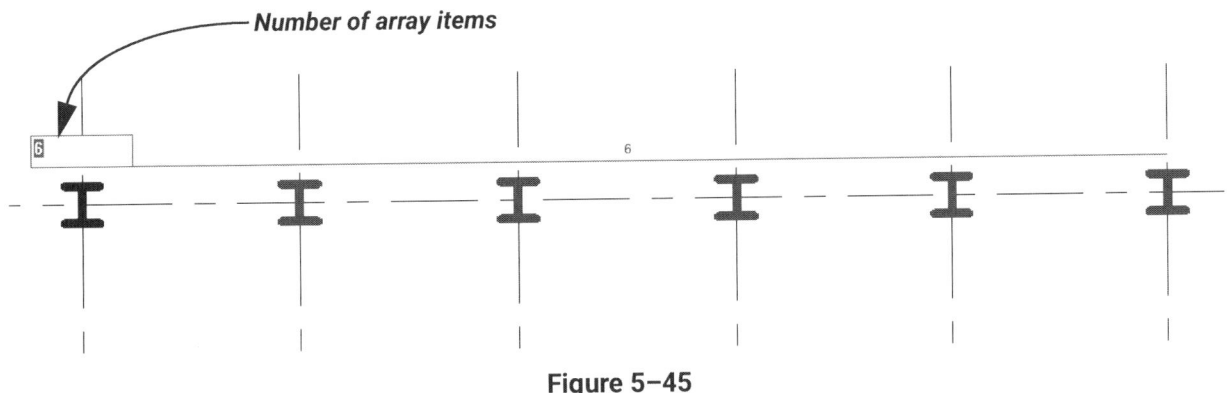

Figure 5–45

- To make a linear array in two directions, you need to array one direction first, select the arrayed elements, and then array them again in the other direction.

Array Options

In the Options Bar, set up the **Array** options for **Linear Array** (top of Figure 5–46) or **Radial Array** (bottom of Figure 5–46).

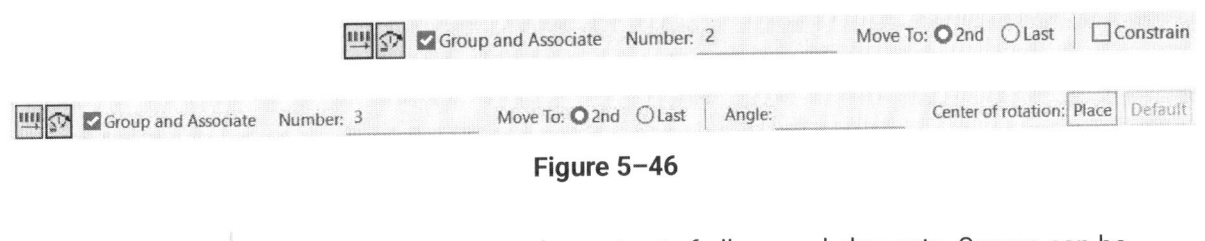

Figure 5–46

Group and Associate	Creates an array group element out of all arrayed elements. Groups can be selected by selecting any elements in the group.
Number	Specifies how many instances you want in the array.
Move To:	**2nd** specifies the distance or angle between the center points of the two elements. **Last** specifies the overall distance or angle of the entire array.
Constrain	Restricts the direction of the array to only vertical or horizontal (Linear only).
Angle	Specifies the angle (Radial only).
Center of rotation	Specifies a location for the origin about which the elements rotate (Radial only).

How To: Create a Radial Array

1. Select the element(s) to array.

2. In the Modify panel, click ☷ (Array).

3. In the Options Bar, click 🗘 (Radial).

4. Drag ⟳ (Center of Rotation) or use **Place** to the move the center of rotation to the appropriate location, as shown in Figure 5–47.

   Note: *Remember to set the **Center of Rotation** control first, before specifying the angle.*

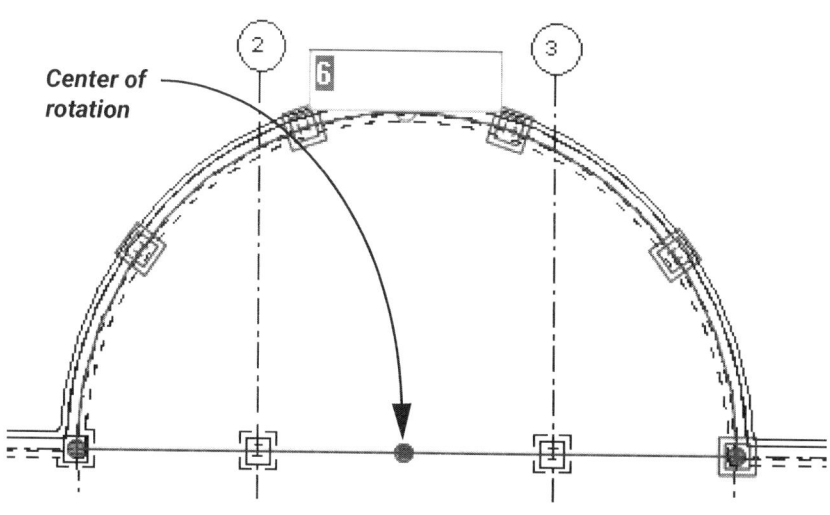

Figure 5–47

5. In the Options Bar, type an angle and press <Enter>, or specify the rotation angle by selecting points on the screen.

6. Specify the other options as needed.

Modifying Array Groups

When you select an element in an array that has been grouped, you can change the number of instances in the array, as shown in Figure 5–48. For radial arrays, you can also modify the distance to the center.

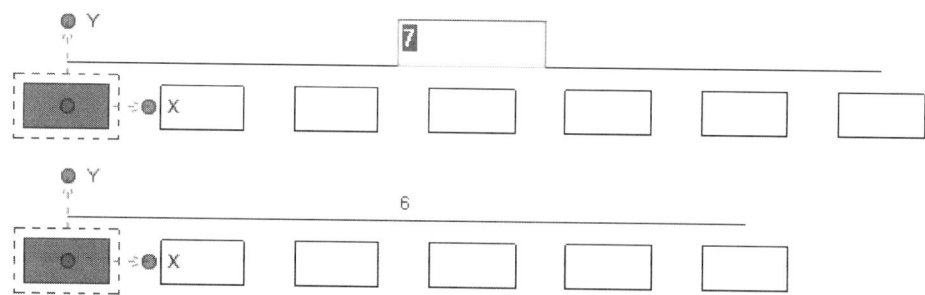

Figure 5–48

- Dashed lines surround the element(s) in a group, and the XY control lets you move the origin point of the group.

If you move one of the elements in the array group, the other elements move in response based on the distance and/or angle, as shown in Figure 5–49.

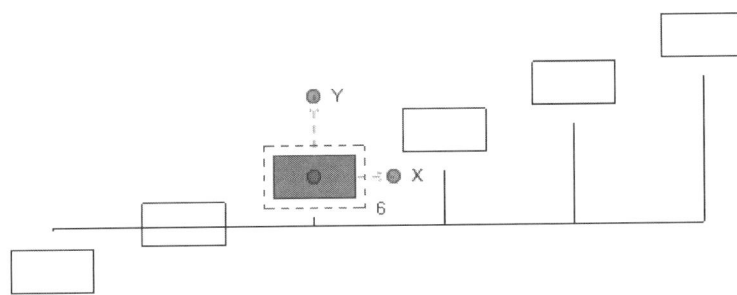

Figure 5–49

- To remove the array constraint on the group, select all of the elements in the array group and, in the *Modify* contextual tab>Group panel, click (Ungroup).

- If you select an individual element in an array and click (Ungroup), the element you selected is removed from the array, while the rest of the elements remain in the array group.

- You can use (Filter) to ensure that you are selecting only **Model Groups**.

Aligning Elements

The **Align** command enables you to line up one element with another, as shown in Figure 5–50. Most Revit elements can be aligned. For example, you can line up the tops of windows with the top of a door, or line up furniture with a wall.

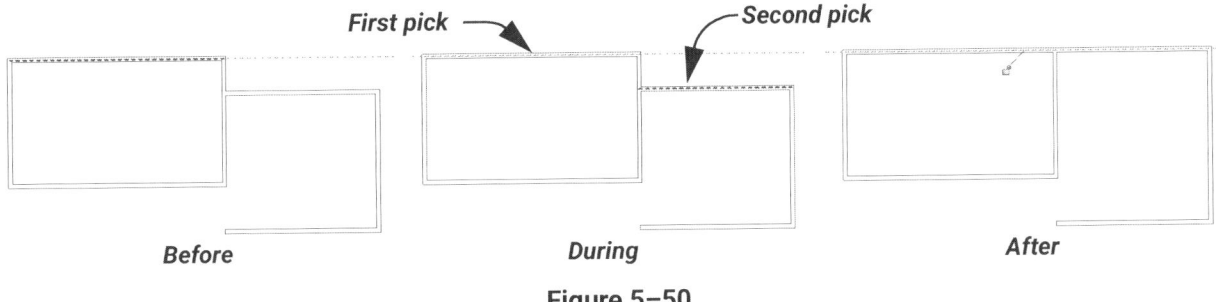

Figure 5–50

- The **Align** command works in all model views, including parallel and perspective 3D views.

How To: Align Elements

1. In the *Modify* tab>Modify panel, click (Align), or type **AL**.

2. Select a line or point on the element that is going to remain stationary.

   Note: *For elements that are close together, press <Tab> to select the correct element.*

3. Select a line or point on the element to be aligned. The second element moves into alignment with the first one.

- You can manually lock alignments so that the elements move together if either one is moved.

- Once you have created the alignment, a padlock is displayed. Click on the padlock to lock it, as shown in Figure 5–51.

   Note: *Locking elements enlarges the size of the project file, so use this option carefully.*

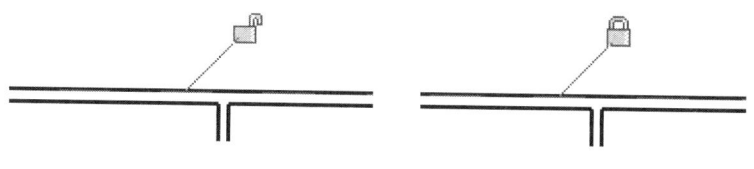

Figure 5–51

Align Contextual Tab Options

- If you need to align multiple elements, in the *Modify | Align* tab>Align panel, select **Multiple Alignment** to select multiple elements to align with the first element. You can also hold <Ctrl> to select multiple elements to align.

- If you want to lock your alignments as you go, in the *Modify | Align* tab>Align panel, you can check the checkbox for **Lock** to lock any alignments made so you do not need to go back and lock them manually.

- For walls, you can specify if you want the command to prefer **Wall centerlines**, **Wall faces**, **Center of core**, or **Faces of core**, as shown in Figure 5–52. The core refers to the structural members of a wall as opposed to facing materials, such as sheet rock.

- For *Pattern*, you can choose how surface patterns are aligned by selecting either the **Entire Surface** or **Selected Face** option. If you select **Entire Surface**, the pattern will be aligned across the entire surface, creating a seamless and consistent appearance. On the other hand, if you choose **Selected Face**, each face of the element can have its own pattern alignment, allowing for greater flexibility and customization. Ultimately, the choice between these options depends on your specific design needs and preferences.

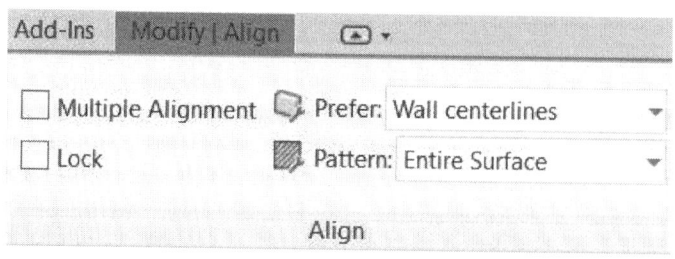

Figure 5–52

Practice 5b
Work with Basic Modify Tools

Practice Objective

- Use basic modify tools, such as Move, Copy, Rotate, and Array.

In this practice, you will use **Move** and **Copy** to create grid lines with columns using existing elements in a project. You will then rotate one of the grid lines and the columns along that grid line and mirror the new grid lines to create the opposite part of the building. Finally, you will array a set of columns around an arc and create a grid line of the array, as shown in Figure 5-53.

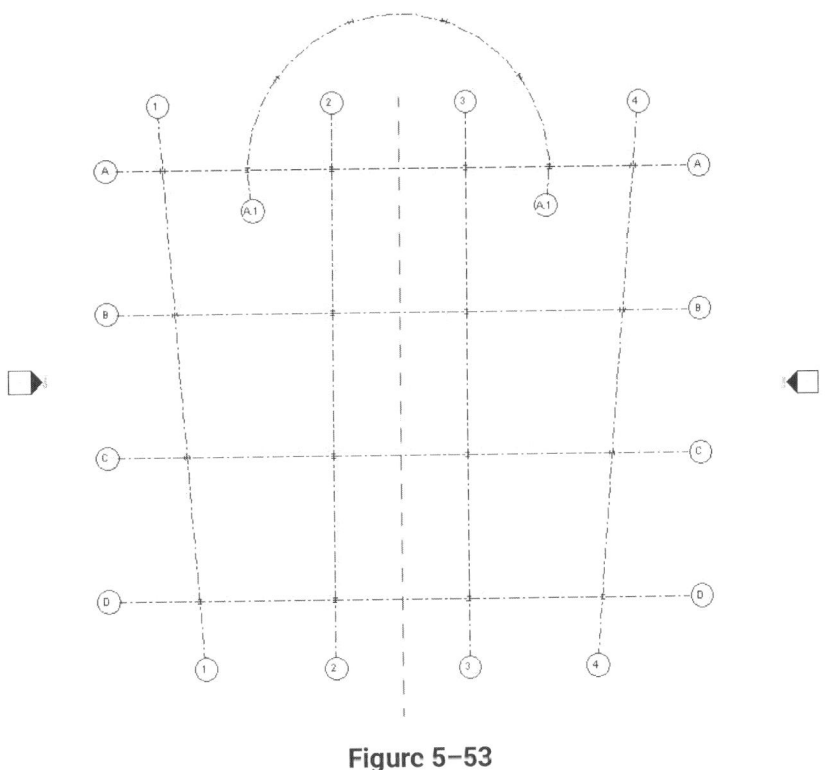

Figure 5-53

Task 1: Move and copy elements.

1. Open **Structural-Editing.rvt** from the practice files folder.
2. The file should automatically open to the **Structural Plans: Level 2** view.
3. Select **grid line A** and the structural column that is at the intersection. (**Hint:** Hold <Ctrl> to select more than one element.)
4. In the *Modify | Multi-Select* tab>Modify panel, click (Copy).

5. In the Options Bar, select **Multiple**, as shown in Figure 5–54.

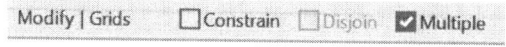

Figure 5–54

6. Pick a point anywhere along grid line **A** for the start point.
7. Move the cursor down below grid line **A** and type **24**. Create two more copies that are **24'-0"** apart for a total of four horizontal grid lines.
8. Click (Modify) to end the **Copy** command.
9. Select grid line **1** and the four columns along grid line **1**. Copy the elements to the right at a distance of **24'-0"** until you have a total of four vertical grid lines with the associated columns. Click (Modify) to end the command.
10. Click twice inside each grid bubble and renumber the grid lines as shown in Figure 5–55.

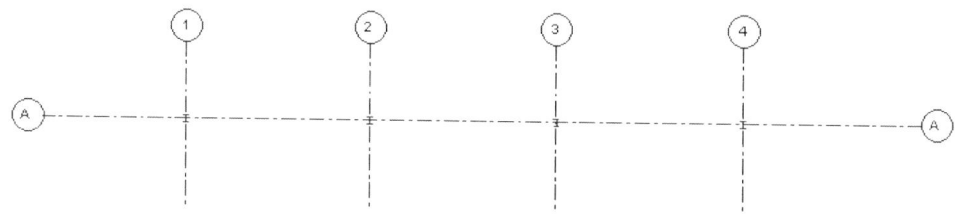

Figure 5–55

11. Zoom in on the column at grid intersection **A1**.
12. Select the column (but not the grid line). In the *Modify* tab> Modify panel, click (Move) and move the column **6'-0"** to the left, as shown in Figure 5–56.

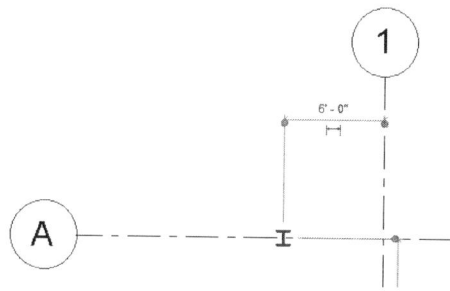

Figure 5–56

13. Click (Modify).
14. Save the project.

Task 2: Rotate elements.

1. Select **grid line 1**.
2. In the *Modify | Grids* tab>Modify panel, click ⟲ (Rotate).
3. Move the center of rotation by going to the Options Bar and clicking **Place**. Select the midpoint of column **D1** as the center of rotation.
4. Specify the first ray of rotation by clicking on the **A1** grid intersection.
5. Specify the second ray of rotation to finish the rotation by selecting the midpoint of the column you moved **6'** to the left of grid line **1** earlier, as shown in Figure 5–57.

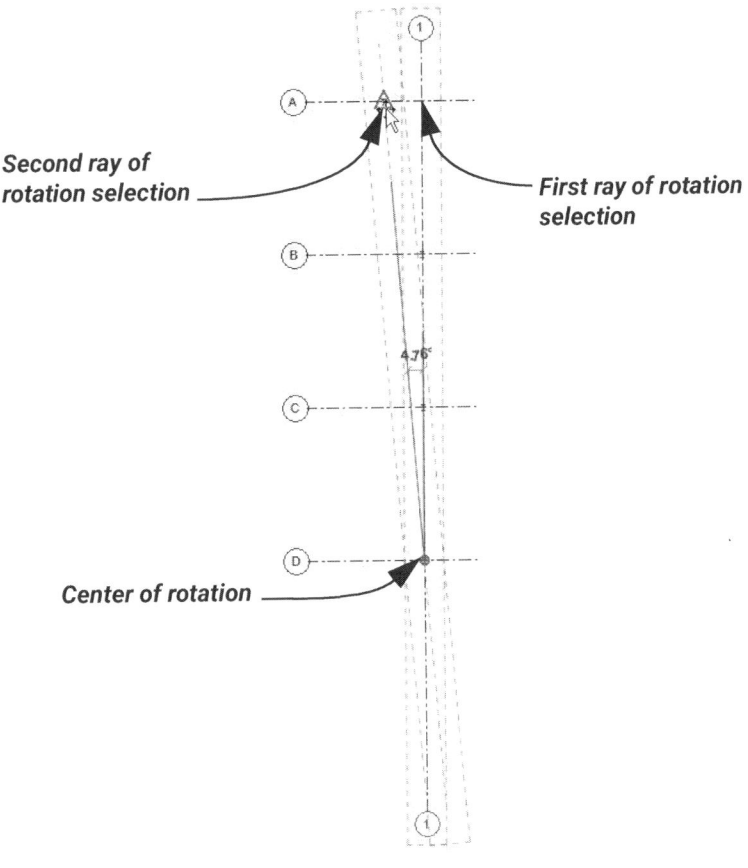

Figure 5–57

Task 3: Rotate columns to match grid line.

1. Zoom in on the **A1** grid intersection. Select the column at the **A1** intersection.
2. Click ⟲ (Rotate). Keep the center point in the current location, which is the center of the column.

3. For the first ray of rotation, select a point to the right along grid line **A**, as shown in Figure 5–58.

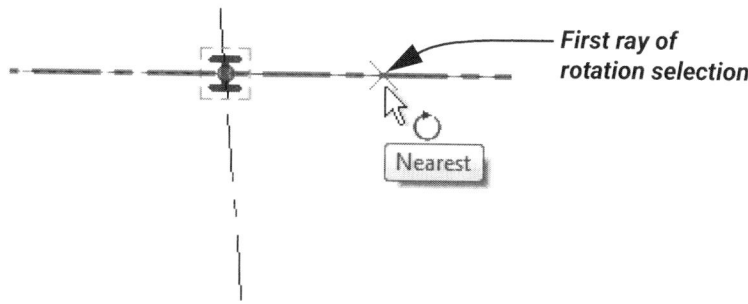

Figure 5–58

4. For the second ray of rotation, select a point along grid line **1**, as shown on the left in Figure 5–59. The column is now rotated perpendicular to the angle of grid line **1**, as shown on the right in Figure 5–59.

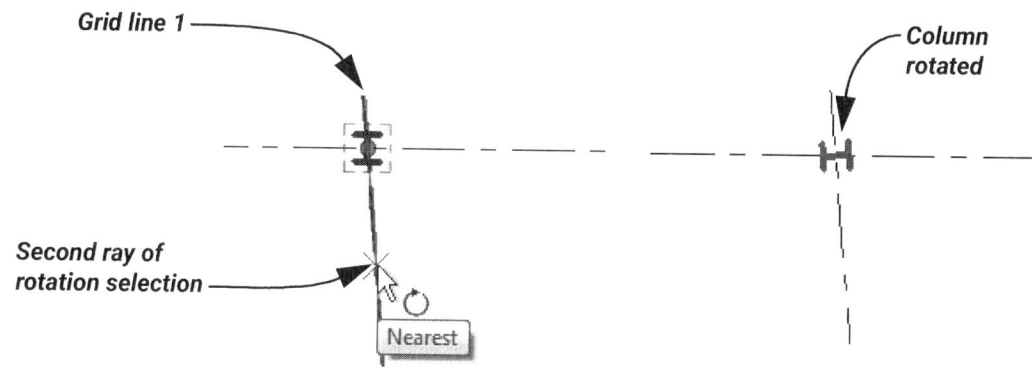

Figure 5–59

5. Repeat the process for the rest of the columns along grid line **1**.

6. Click (Modify).

7. Save the project.

Task 4: Mirror elements.

1. Delete grid line **4** and its columns. You are going to mirror grid line **1** and its columns to this location.

2. In the *Structure* tab>Work Plane panel, click (Ref Plane).

3. In the *Modify | Place Reference Plane* tab>Draw panel, click (Line).

4. Draw a vertical line between **grid line 2** and **grid line 3** and use temporary dimensions to set the distances from each grid line to **12'-0"**, as shown in Figure 5–60. When finished, click (Modify) to end the command.

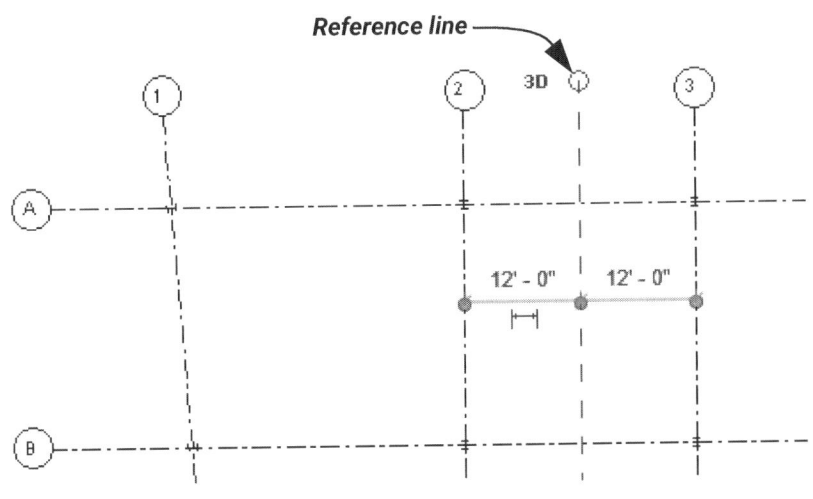

Figure 5–60

5. Select **grid line 1** and all of the columns on the grid line. (To select multiple elements, draw a window around the group or hold <Ctrl> as you select.)

6. In the *Modify | Multi-Select* tab>Modify panel, click ▵ (Pick Mirror Axis).

7. Select the vertical reference plane that you created earlier, as shown in Figure 5–61. Grid line **1** and all of its columns are mirrored about the selected reference plane. If the new grid line is not automatically renumbered, select the bubble and rename it to **4**.

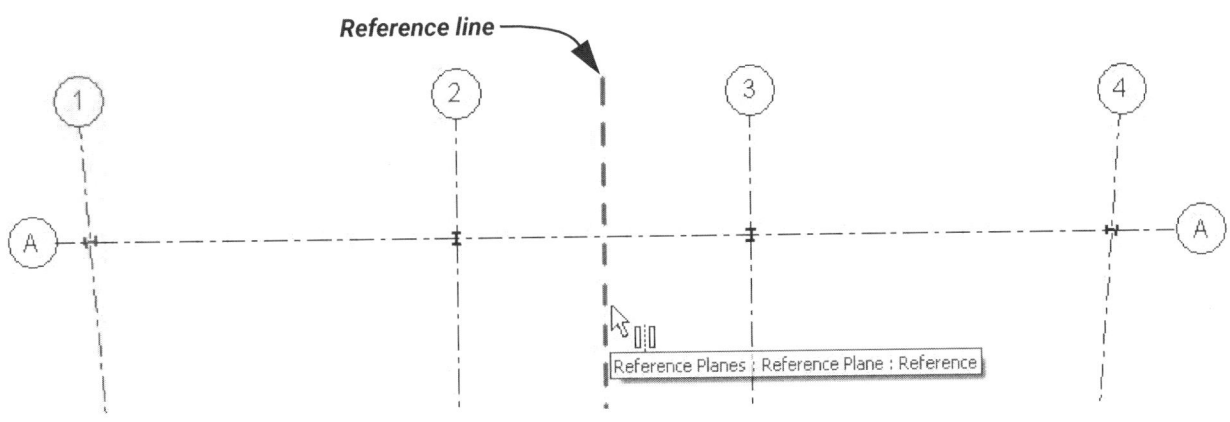

Figure 5–61

8. Click ▸ (Modify).
9. Save the project.

Task 5: Array elements.

1. Select the column at grid intersection **A3**. Click (Copy) and copy this *column* to the right by **15'-0"**. The new copied column is now the current selected column.

2. In the *Modify | Structural Columns* tab>Modify panel, click (Array).

3. A warning dialog box opens. This issue will be corrected in later steps. Click **OK**.

4. In the Options Bar, click (Radial). Select **Group And Associate**, set the *Number* to **8**, and set *Move to:* to **Last**.

5. Relocate the center of the array by dragging to the intersection of the vertical reference plane, as shown in Figure 5–62. Alternatively, in the Options Bar, click **Place** next to *Center of rotation*. In the drawing, click to place the center of rotation.

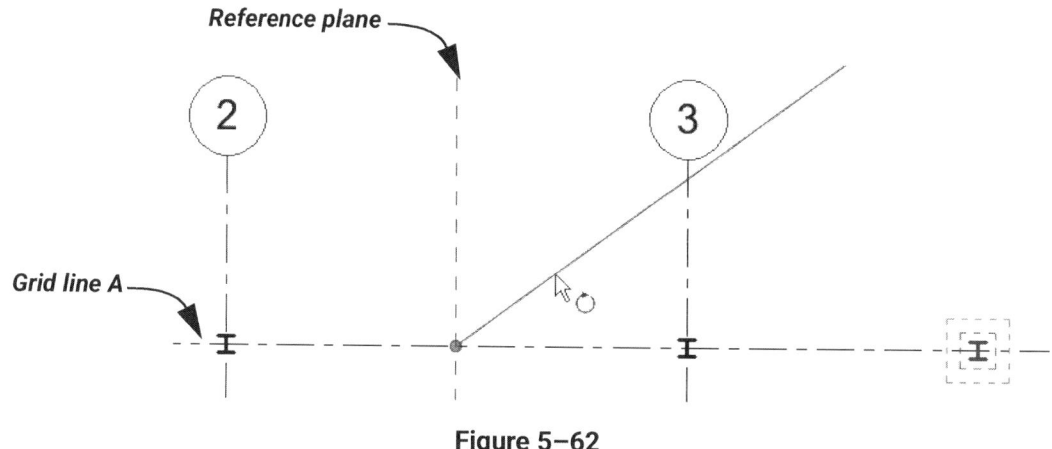

Figure 5–62

6. In the Options Bar, set the *Angle* to **180** and press <Enter>. The new columns display along the arc. The number of array is displayed at the top of the arc, allowing for further modifications to the number of arrayed items, as shown in Figure 5–63.

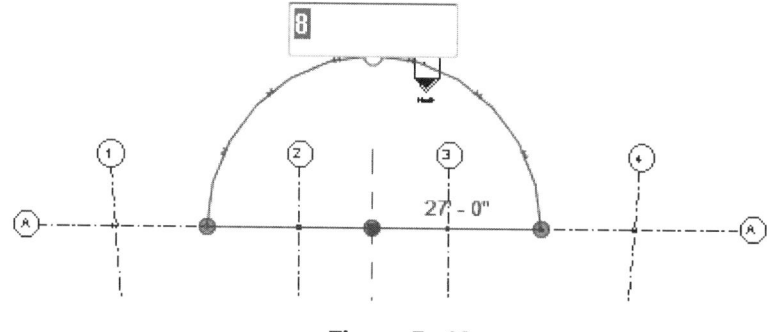

Figure 5–63

7. Change the number to **6** and the array updates.

8. Click in an empty space in the view to release the selection and end the Array command.
9. Draw a grid line for the new array of columns by going to the *Structure* tab>Datum panel and clicking (Grid).
10. In the Draw panel, click (Pick Lines).
11. Move the cursor over the area of the array. When your cursor is over the arc, it will highlight, as shown in Figure 5–64. Select it to create the grid line.

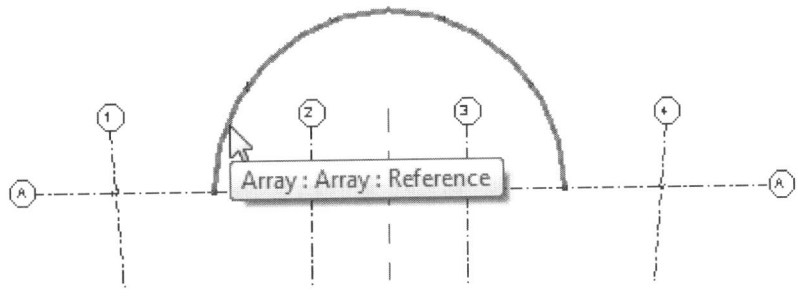

Figure 5–64

12. Click (Modify).
13. The new grid bubbles are on top of the columns. Drag the grid bubbles down past the columns and rename the new grid line **A.1**, as shown in Figure 5–65.

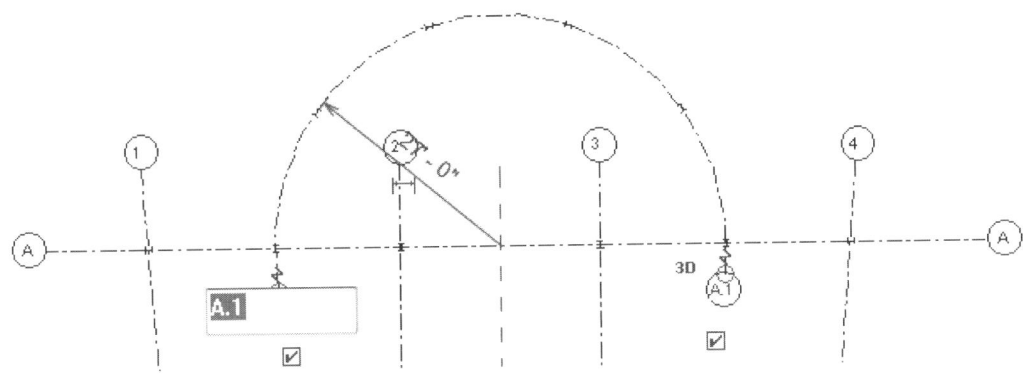

Figure 5–65

14. Save and close the project.

End of practice

5.3 Working with Additional Modify Tools

As you work on a project, some additional tools found on the *Modify* tab>Modify panel, as shown in Figure 5–66, can help you with placing, modifying, and constraining elements. **Align** can be used with a variety of elements, while **Split Element**, **Trim/Extend**, and **Offset** can only be used with linear elements.

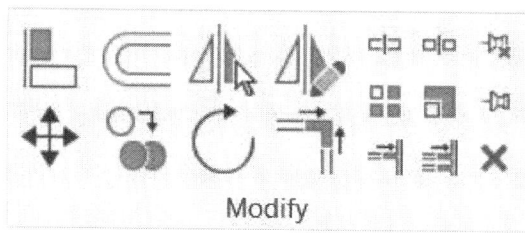

Figure 5–66

Splitting Linear Elements

The **Split Element** command enables you to break a linear element at a specific point. You can use alignment lines, snaps, and temporary dimensions to help place the split point. After you have split the linear element, you can use other editing commands to modify the two parts, or change the type of one part, as shown with walls in Figure 5–67. You can split walls in plan, elevation, or 3D views.

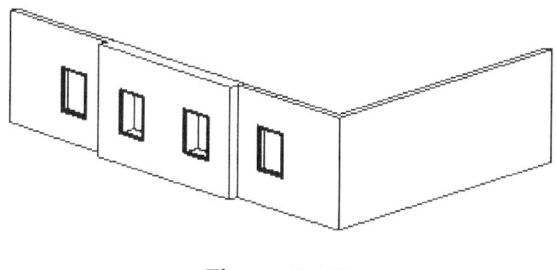

Figure 5–67

How To: Split Linear Elements

1. In the *Modify* tab>Modify panel, click ⊏⊐ (Split Element), or type **SL**.
2. In the Options Bar, select or clear the **Delete Inner Segment** option.
3. Move the cursor to the point you want to split and select the point.
4. Repeat for any additional split locations.
5. Modify the elements that were split, as needed.

- The **Delete Inner Segment** option is used when you select two split points along a linear element. When the option is selected, the segment between the two split points is automatically removed.
- An additional option, ◫ (Split with Gap), splits the linear element at the point you select, as shown in Figure 5–68, but also creates a *Joint Gap* specified in the Options Bar.

    Note: This command is typically used with structural precast walls.

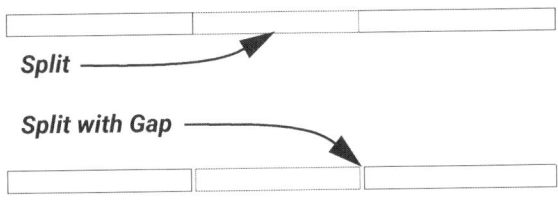

Figure 5–68

Trimming and Extending

There are three trim/extend methods that you can use with linear elements: **Trim/Extend to Corner**, **Trim/Extend Single Element**, and **Trim/Extend Multiple Elements**.

- When selecting elements to trim, click the part of the element that you want to keep. The opposite part of the line is then trimmed.

How To: Trim/Extend to Corner

1. In the *Modify* tab>Modify panel, click ⌐ (Trim/Extend to Corner), or type **TR**.
2. Select the first linear element on the side you want to keep.
3. Select the second linear element on the side you want to keep, as shown in Figure 5–69.

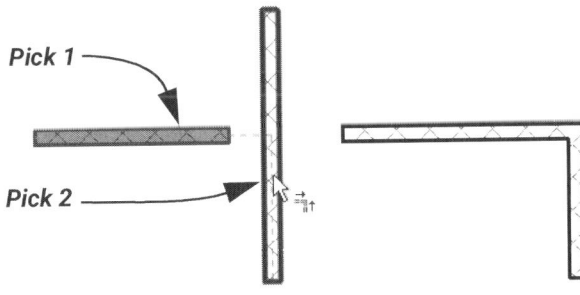

Figure 5–69

How To: Trim/Extend a Single Element

1. In the *Modify* tab>Modify panel, click (Trim/Extend Single Element).
2. Select the cutting or boundary edge.
3. Select the linear element to be trimmed or extended, as shown in Figure 5–70.

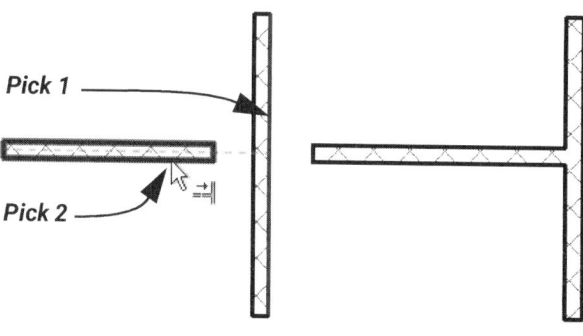

Figure 5–70

How To: Trim/Extend Multiple Elements

1. In the *Modify* tab>Modify panel, click (Trim/Extend Multiple Elements).
2. Select the cutting or boundary edge.
3. Select the linear elements that you want to trim or extend by selecting one at a time, or by using a crossing window, as shown in Figure 5–71. For trimming, select the side you want to keep.

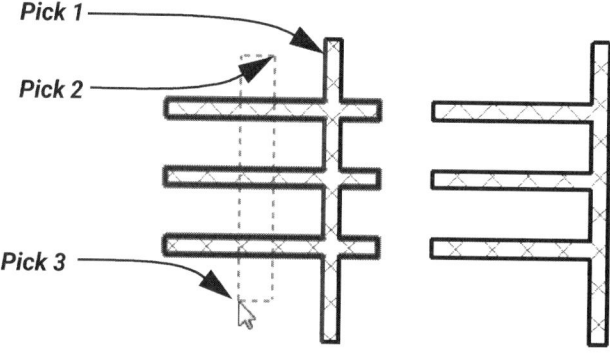

Figure 5–71

- You can click in an empty space in the view to clear the selection and select another cutting edge or boundary.

Offsetting Elements

The **Offset** command is an easy way of creating parallel copies of linear elements at a specified distance, as shown in Figure 5–72. Walls, beams, braces, and lines are among the elements that can be offset.

Figure 5–72

- If you offset a wall that has a door or window embedded in it, the elements are copied with the offset wall.

The offset distance can be set by typing the distance (**Numerical** method, as shown in Figure 5–73) or by selecting points on the screen (**Graphical** method).

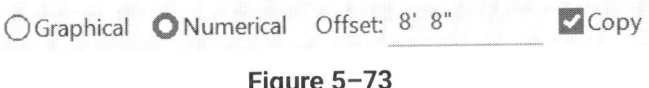

Figure 5–73

How To: Offset Using the Numerical Method

1. In the *Modify* tab>Modify panel, click ⊂ (Offset), or type **OF**.
2. In the Options Bar, select the **Numerical** option.
3. In the Options Bar, type the required distance in the *Offset* field.
    - From the Options Bar, the **Copy** option (which is on by default) makes a copy of the element being offset. If this option is not selected, the **Offset** command moves the element the set offset distance.
4. Move the cursor over the element you want to offset. A dashed line previews the offset location. Move the cursor to flip the sides, as needed.
5. Click to create the offset.
6. Repeat Steps 4 and 5 to offset other elements by the same distance, or to change the distance for another offset.

- With the **Numerical** option, you can select multiple connected linear elements for offsetting. Hover the cursor over an element and press <Tab> until the other related elements are highlighted. Select the element to offset all of the elements at the same time.

How To: Offset Using the Graphical Method

1. In the *Modify* tab>Modify panel, click ⊆ (Offset), or type **OF**.
2. In the Options Bar, select **Graphical**.
3. Select the linear element to offset.
4. Select two points that define the distance of the offset and which side to apply it. You can type an override in the temporary dimension for the second point.

- Most linear elements connected at a corner automatically trim or extend to meet at the offset distance, as shown in Figure 5–74.

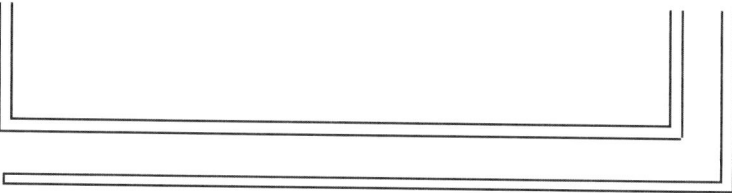

Figure 5–74

Practice 5c
Work with Additional Modify Tools

Practice Objective

- Align, Split, Trim/Extend, and Offset elements.

In this practice, you will use **Split** and **Trim** to clean up existing walls in a project. You will then offset the entire foundation from the centerline, Figure 5–75, where it can support an architectural brick facade.

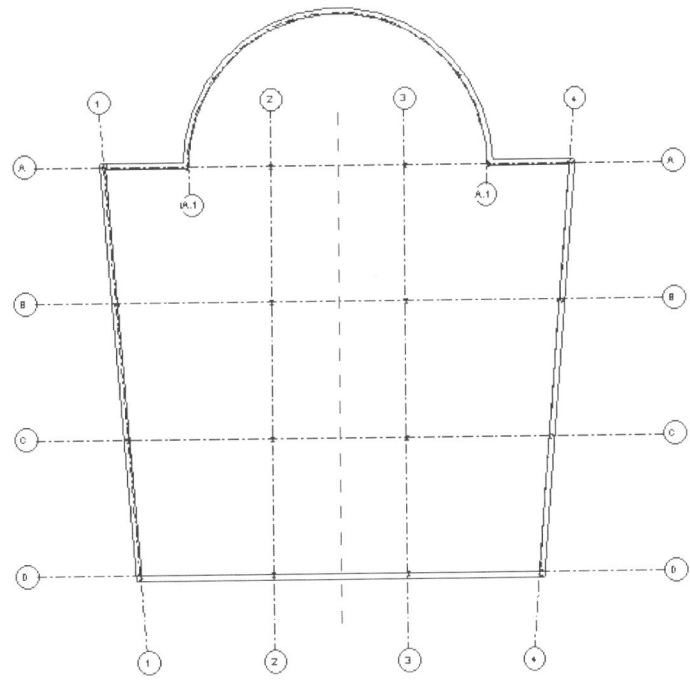

Figure 5–75

Task 1: Split and trim elements.

1. Open **Structural-Modify.rvt** from the practice files folder.
2. The file should automatically open to the **Structural Plans: Level 2** view.
3. Select the foundation wall on grid line **A**. In the *Modify | Walls* tab>Modify panel, click ⇥⇤ (Split Element).

4. Select the intersection of the reference plane and grid line **A**, between grid lines **2** and **3**, as shown in Figure 5–76.

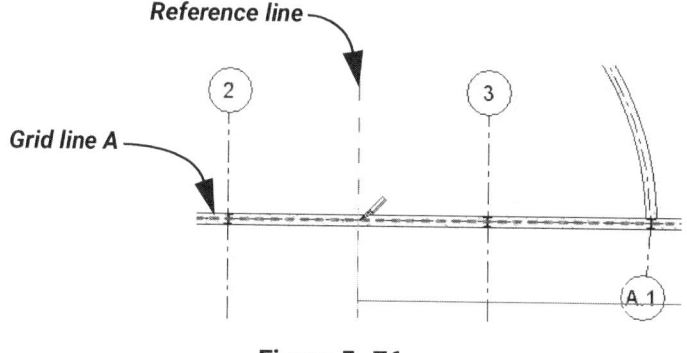

Figure 5–76

5. Click (Modify) to end the command.
6. Connect the arc foundation wall on grid line **A.1** with the foundation wall on grid line **A** by going to the *Modify* tab> Modify panel and clicking (Trim/Extend to Corner).
7. Select the horizontal wall along grid line **A** on the left side of the arc, as shown in Figure 5–77.

    • Remember to select the side of the wall that you want to keep.

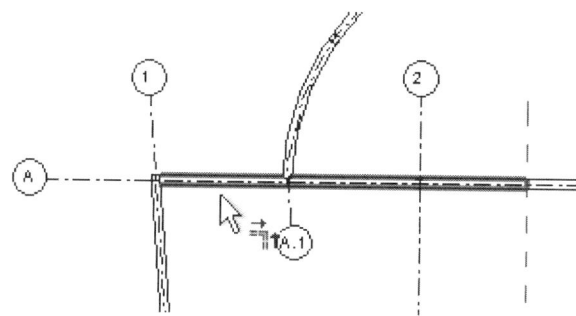

Figure 5–77

8. Select the arc wall. The walls are trimmed and joined together and the excess wall is deleted (the before and after are shown in Figure 5–78).

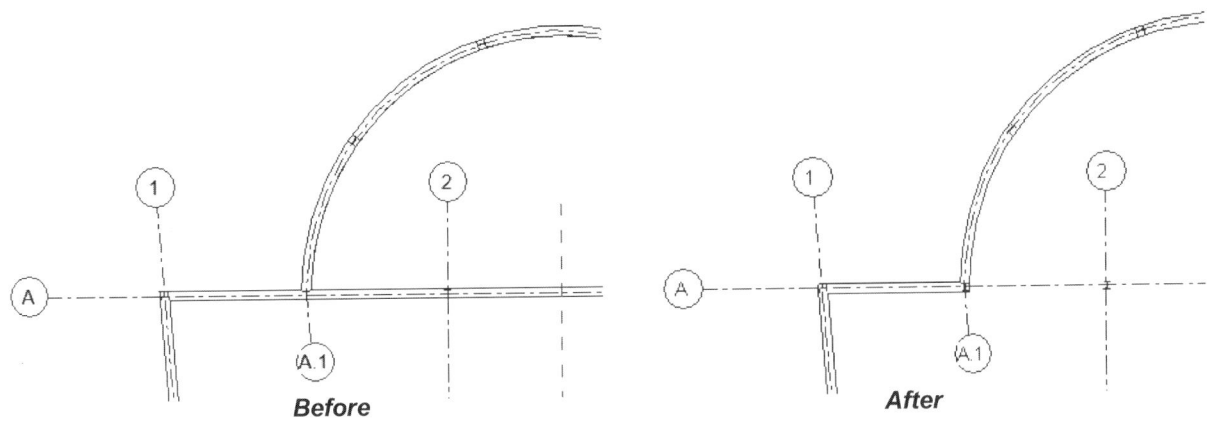

Figure 5–78

9. Repeat the process on the other side.
10. Save the project.

Task 2: Offset foundation walls.

1. Offset all of the foundation walls by going to the *Modify* tab>Edit panel and clicking ⊂ (Offset).
2. In the Options Bar, select **Numerical**, set the *Offset* to **4"**, and clear the **Copy** option, as shown in Figure 5–79.

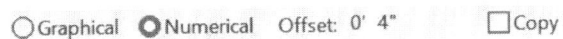

Figure 5–79

3. Hover the cursor over one of the foundation walls but do not select the wall. The blue alignment line should display on the inside of the wall and above the grid line, as shown in Figure 5–80.

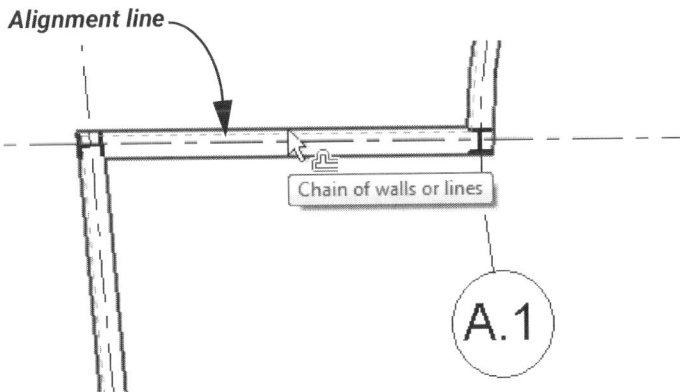

Figure 5–80

4. Press <Tab> until all of the foundation walls are highlighted, meaning they are all selected, and click to offset the walls 4", as shown in Figure 5–81.

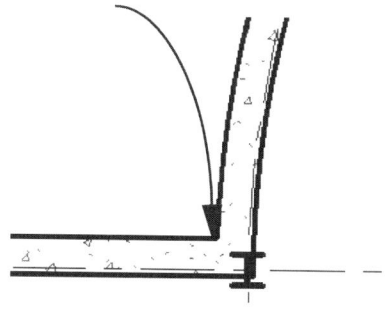

Figure 5–81

5. Click (Modify).
6. Save and close the model.

End of practice

Chapter Review Questions

1. What is the purpose of an alignment line?

    a. Displays when the new element you are placing or modeling is aligned with the grid system.

    b. Indicates that the new element you are placing or modeling is aligned with an existing element.

    c. Displays when the new element you are placing or modeling is aligned with a selected tracking point.

    d. Indicates that the new element is aligned with true north rather than project north.

2. Temporary dimensions snap to the nearest perpendicular element.

    a. True

    b. False

3. When you are modeling (not editing) a linear element, how do you edit the temporary dimension?

    a. Select the temporary dimension and enter a new value.

    b. Type a new value and press <Enter>.

    c. Type a new value in the Distance/Length box in the Options Bar and press <Enter>.

4. How do you select all the doors of various sizes, but no other elements in a view?

    a. In the Project Browser, select the *Door* category.

    b. Select one door, right-click and select **Select All Instances>Visible in View**.

    c. Select all of the elements in the view and use (Filter) to clear the other categories.

    d. Select one door, and click (Select Multiple) in the ribbon.

5. What are the two methods for starting commands such as **Move**, **Copy**, **Rotate**, **Mirror**, and **Array**?

   a. Start the command from the *Modify* tab and select the elements, then start the command.

   b. Start the command from the *Modify* tab and select the elements, then select the command from the Status Bar.

   c. Start the command from the *Modify* tab and select the elements, then right-click and select the command from the list.

6. Where do you change the wall type for a selected wall, as shown in Figure 5–82?

Figure 5–82

   a. In the *Modify | Walls* tab>Properties panel, click  (Type Properties) and select a new wall type in the dialog box.

   b. In the Options Bar, click **Change Element Type**.

   c. Select the dynamic control next to the selected wall and select a new type in the drop-down list.

   d. In Properties, select a new type in the Type Selector drop-down list.

7. Both ⟳ (Rotate) and ▦ (Array) with ⌖ (Radial) have a center of rotation that defaults to the center of the element or group of elements you have selected. How do you move the center of rotation to another point, as shown in Figure 5–83? (Select all that apply.)

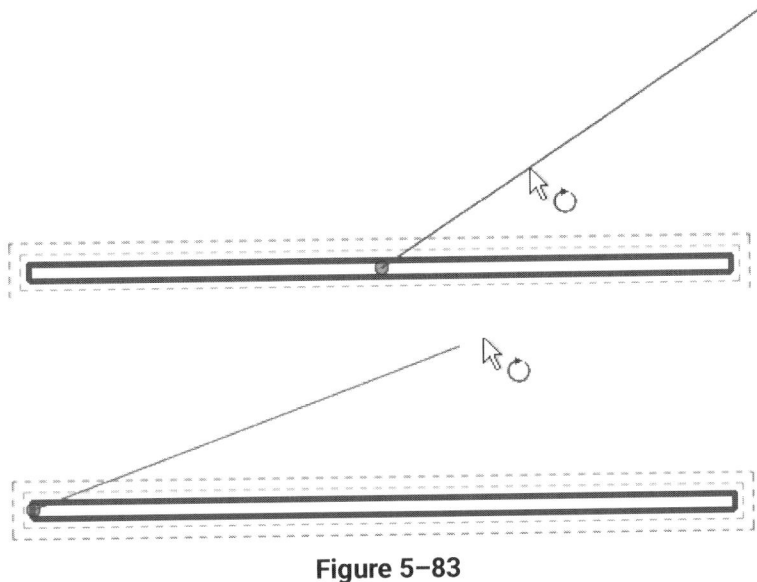

Figure 5–83

   a. Select the center of rotation and drag it to a new location.
   b. In the Options Bar, click **Place** and select the new point.
   c. In the *Modify* tab>Placement panel, click ⊘ (Center) and select the new point.
   d. Right-click and select **Snap Overrides>Centers** and select the new point.

8. Which command would you use to remove a part or a segment of a wall?
   a. ⊢⊣ (Split Element)
   b. ⌐ (Wall Joins)
   c. ⌑ (Cut Geometry)
   d. 🔨 (Demolish)

9. Which of the following are ways in which you can create additional parallel walls, as shown in Figure 5–84? (Select all that apply.)

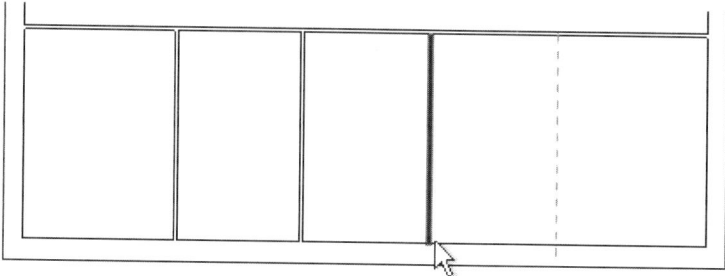

Figure 5–84

a. Use the **Trim/Extend Multiple Elements** tool.
b. Use the **Offset** tool in the *Modify* tab.
c. Select an existing wall, hold <Ctrl> and drag the wall to a new location.
d. Use the **Align** command with an offset.

10. Which command do you use if you want two walls that are not touching to come together, as shown in Figure 5–85?

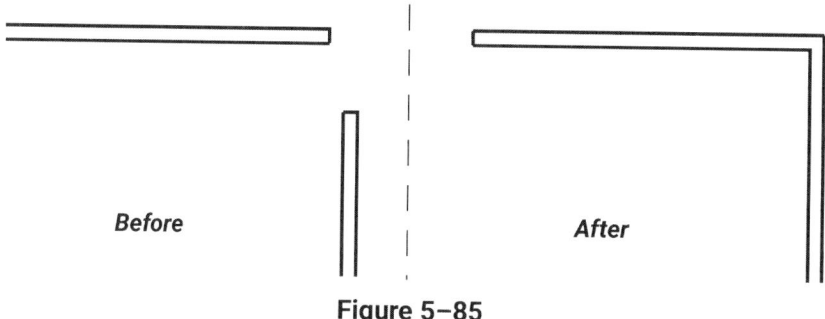

Figure 5–85

a. (Edit Wall Joins)

b. (Trim/Extend to Corner)

c. (Join Geometry)

d. (Edit Profile)

Command Summary

Button	Command	Location
Draw Tools		
	Center-ends Arc	• **Ribbon:** *Modify	(various linear elements)* tab>Draw panel
	Circle	• **Ribbon:** *Modify	(various linear elements)* tab>Draw panel
	Circumscribed Polygon	• **Ribbon:** *Modify	(various linear elements)* tab>Draw panel
	Ellipse	• **Ribbon:** *Modify	(various linear elements)* tab>Draw panel
	Ellipse Arc	• **Ribbon:** *Modify	(various linear elements)* tab>Draw panel
	Fillet Arc	• **Ribbon:** *Modify	(various linear elements)* tab>Draw panel
	Inscribed Polygon	• **Ribbon:** *Modify	(various linear elements)* tab>Draw panel
	Line	• **Ribbon:** *Modify	(various linear elements)* tab>Draw panel
	Pick Faces	• **Ribbon:** *Modify	Place Wall*>Draw panel
	Pick Lines	• **Ribbon:** *Modify	(various linear elements)* tab>Draw panel
	Pick Walls	• **Ribbon:** *Modify	(various boundary sketches)*>Draw panel
	Rectangle	• **Ribbon:** *Modify	(various linear elements)* tab>Draw panel
	Spline	• **Ribbon:** *Modify	Place Lines, Place Detail Lines, and various boundary sketches*>Draw panel
	Start-End-Radius Arc	• **Ribbon:** *Modify	(various linear elements)* tab>Draw panel
	Tangent End Arc	• **Ribbon:** *Modify	(various linear elements)* tab>Draw panel

Button	Command	Location
Modify Tools		
	Align	• **Ribbon:** *Modify* tab>Modify panel • **Shortcut:** AL
	Array	• **Ribbon:** *Modify* tab>Modify panel • **Shortcut:** AR
	Copy	• **Ribbon:** *Modify* tab>Modify panel • **Shortcut:** CO
	Copy to Clipboard	• **Ribbon:** *Modify* tab>Clipboard panel • **Shortcut:** <Ctrl>+<C>
	Delete	• **Ribbon:** *Modify* tab>Modify panel • **Shortcut:** DE
	Mirror - Draw Axis	• **Ribbon:** *Modify* tab>Modify panel • **Shortcut:** DM
	Mirror - Pick Axis	• **Ribbon:** *Modify* tab>Modify panel • **Shortcut:** MM
	Move	• **Ribbon:** *Modify* tab>Modify panel • **Shortcut:** MV
	Offset	• **Ribbon:** *Modify* tab>Modify panel • **Shortcut:** OF
	Paste	• **Ribbon:** *Modify* tab>Clipboard panel • **Shortcut:** <Ctrl>+<V>
	Pin	• **Ribbon:** *Modify* tab>Modify panel • **Shortcut:** PN
	Rotate	• **Ribbon:** *Modify* tab>Modify panel • **Shortcut:** RO, R3
	Scale	• **Ribbon:** *Modify* tab>Modify panel • **Shortcut:** RE
	Split Element	• **Ribbon:** *Modify* tab>Modify panel • **Shortcut:** SL
	Split with Gap	• **Ribbon:** *Modify* tab>Modify panel
	Trim/Extend Multiple Elements	• **Ribbon:** *Modify* tab>Modify panel
	Trim/Extend Single Element	• **Ribbon:** *Modify* tab>Modify panel

Button	Command	Location
	Trim/Extend to Corner	• **Ribbon:** *Modify* tab>Modify panel • **Shortcut:** TR
	Unpin	• **Ribbon:** *Modify* tab>Modify panel • **Shortcut:** UP

Additional Tools

Button	Command	Location
	Aligned Dimension	• **Ribbon:** *Modify* tab>Measure panel • **Quick Access Toolbar**
	Component	• **Ribbon:** *Architecture/Structure/Systems* tab • **Shortcut:** CM
	Detail Line	• **Ribbon:** *Annotate* tab>Detail panel • **Shortcut:** DL
	Filter	• **Ribbon:** *Modify	Multi-Select* tab>Filter panel • **Status Bar**
	Model Line	• **Ribbon:** *Architectural* tab>Model panel • **Shortcut:** LI
	Reference Plane	• **Ribbon:** *Architecture/Structure/Systems* tab>Work Plane panel

Design Development

The second section of this guide focuses on teaching you how to use the tools available in Revit® to create the structural building model.

This section includes the following chapters:

- Chapter 6: Adding Columns
- Chapter 7: Foundations
- Chapter 8: Structural Framing
- Chapter 9: Adding Structural Slabs
- Chapter 10: Structural Reinforcement

Chapter 6

Adding Columns

Revit includes two types of columns: architectural and structural. Architectural columns are placeholders or decorative elements, while structural columns include more precise information relative to strength and load-bearing parameters.

Learning Objectives

- Add structural columns to the project as the first design consideration.
- Copy and monitor elements from linked Revit models so that you know when changes have been made.

6.1 Adding Columns

Structural columns can be vertical or slanted, placed at grids or at columns, and tagged upon placement. Additionally, you can modify structural column settings in the Options Bar and Properties. Structural columns (shown on the right in Figure 6–1) are typically placed from the level you are on down to a specific depth.

Architectural columns (shown on the left in Figure 6–1) are typically placed from the level that you are on up to a specific height. Architectural columns can only be placed vertically with settings that can be modified in the Options Bar and Properties. They cannot be placed at grid lines or slanted.

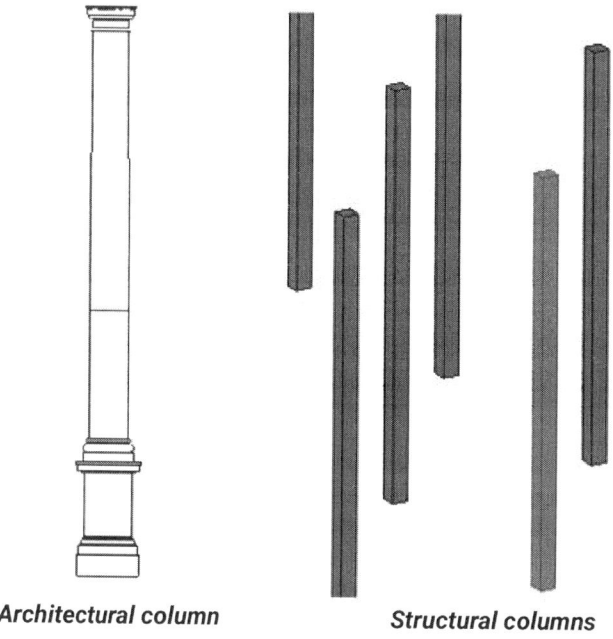

Architectural column   Structural columns

Figure 6–1

How To: Add Columns

1. In the *Structure* tab>Structure panel, click (Structural Column).
2. In the Type Selector, select the column you want to use.
3. In the Options Bar, set the *Height* (or *Depth*) for the column. For the Level/Unconnected drop-down list, you can either select a level (as shown in Figure 6–2) or select **Unconnected** to specify a height.

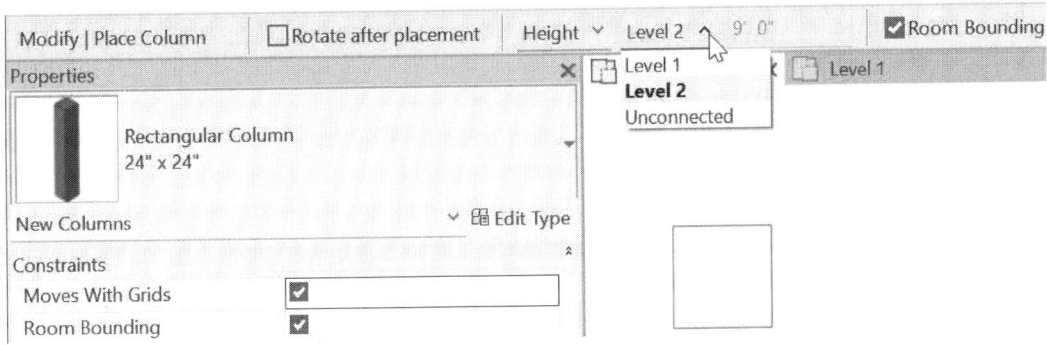

Figure 6–2

4. Place the column as required. It snaps to grid lines and walls.

   - Columns can be placed as a free instance unconnected to any grid lines.
   - If you select **Rotate after placement**, you are prompted for a rotation angle after you select the insertion point for the column.

5. Continue placing columns as needed.

- If you are working with structural columns, you have two additional options for placing columns in the *Modify | Place Structural Column* tab>Multiple panel:

   - To place columns at the intersection of grid lines, click (At Grids) and select the grid lines. Columns will only be placed at the intersections of the selected grid lines.
   - To place structural columns wherever you have an architectural column, in the *Modify | Place Structural Column* tab>Multiple panel, click (At Columns) and select the architectural columns. The structural columns are placed at the center of the architectural columns, as shown in Figure 6–3.

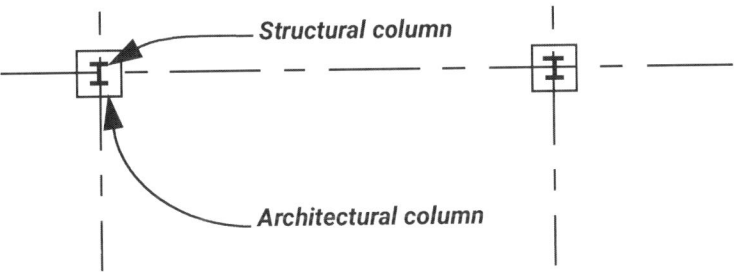

Figure 6–3

- An architectural column placed in a wall is automatically cleaned up if the material of the column and wall match. Structural columns remain separate even if they are the same material as the surrounding walls, as shown in Figure 6–4.

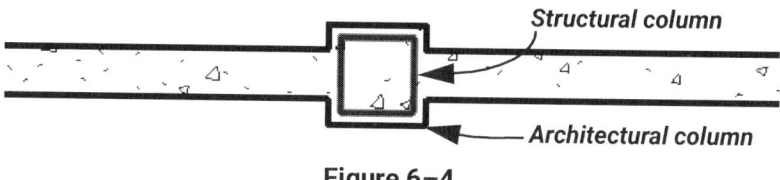

Figure 6–4

- You can select additional column types from the *Columns* (for architectural) or *Structural Columns* folders in the Revit Library, as shown in Figure 6–5.

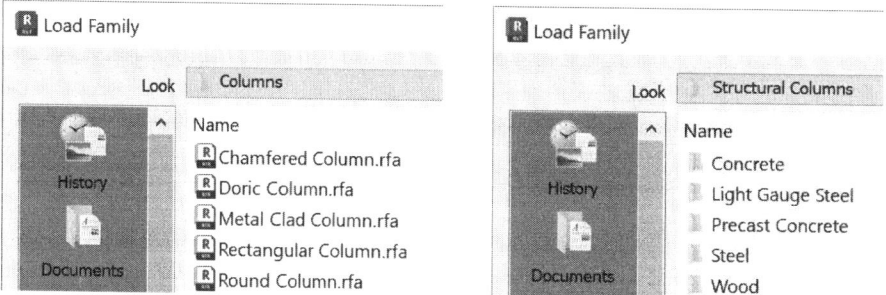

Figure 6–5

- When you open a structural column family, you are prompted to choose from a list of types, as shown in Figure 6–6. Hold <Ctrl> or <Shift> to select more than one and click **OK** to load them.

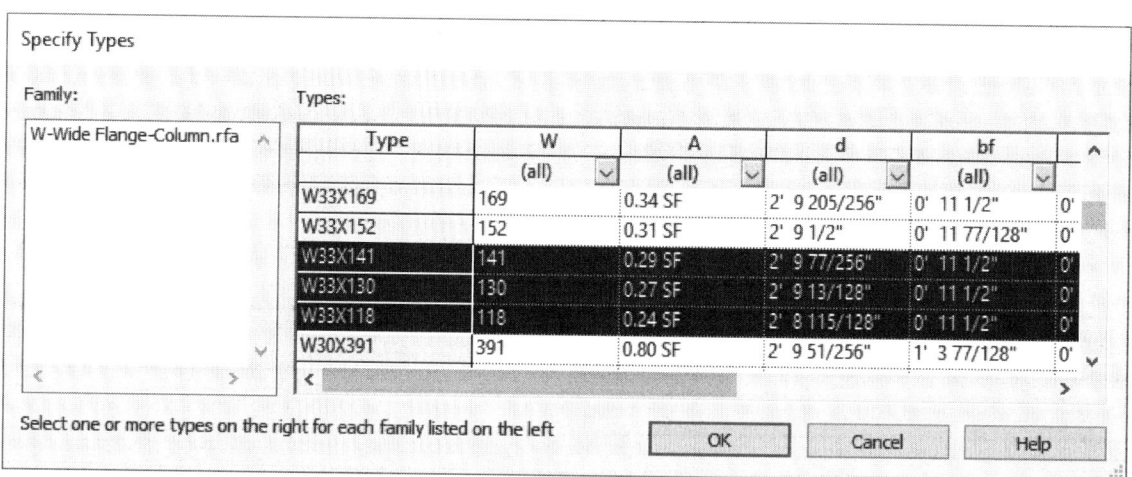

Figure 6–6

Placing Slanted Structural Columns

In today's building designs, it is not uncommon to come across slanted (tilted) structural columns, as shown in Figure 6–7. Slanted structural columns can be placed in plan views, elevations, sections, or 3D views.

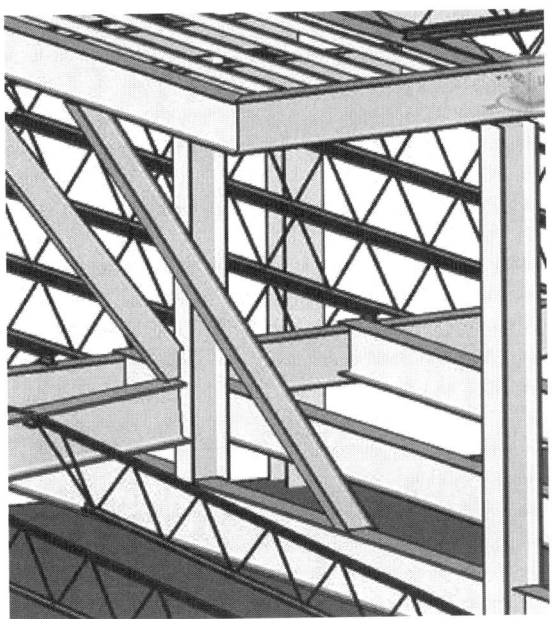

Figure 6–7

- Slanted columns are not included in graphical column schedules, but can be included in building component schedules based on structural columns.

How To: Place Slanted Structural Columns in Plan Views

1. In the *Structure* tab>Structure panel, click (Column).
2. In the Type Selector, select the required column type.
3. In the *Modify | Place Structural Column* tab>Placement panel, click (Slanted Column).
4. In the Options Bar, set the elevation for the *1st Click* and *2nd Click*, as shown in Figure 6–8. You can also set the offsets from the elevation.

Figure 6–8

5. Select a point for the *1st Click*.
6. For the *2nd Click* location (with the elevation set in the Options Bar), select a point on any required element or anywhere in the drawing area.

Working in 3D Views

The simplest way to place a slanted column in a 3D view is to set the **3D Snapping** option and then select two points anywhere along a structural element or on an endpoint, as shown on the left in Figure 6–9.

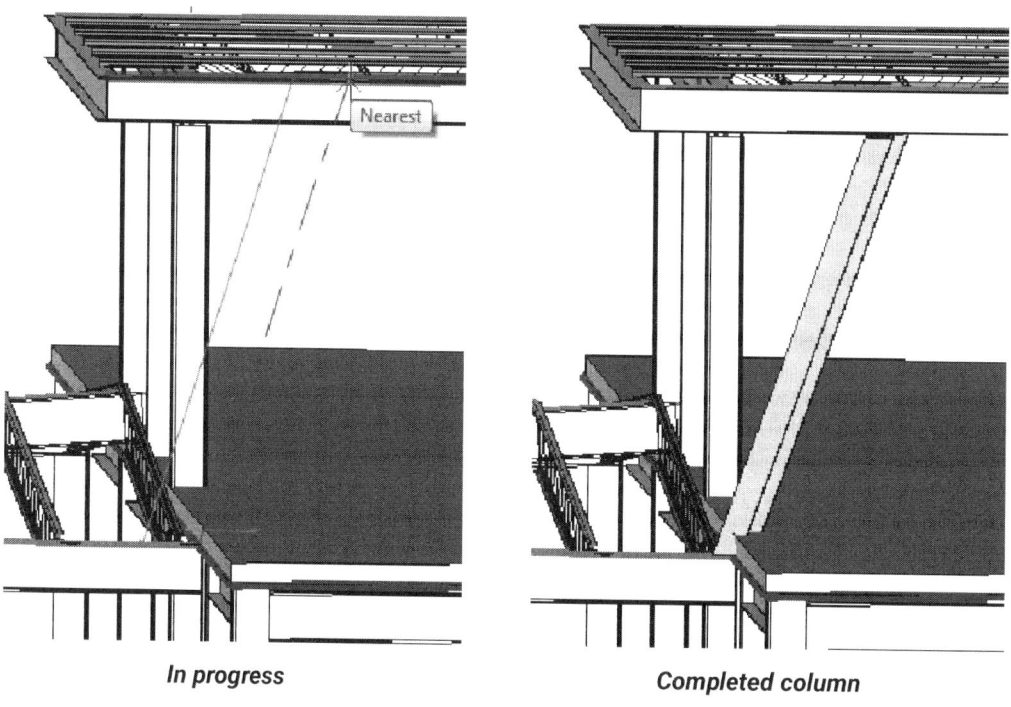

In progress   *Completed column*

Figure 6–9

- The selection of structural elements defaults to the structural analysis line. This ensures that the slanted structural column is joined correctly for support and analysis.

Working in Elevations or Sections

While placing a slanted structural column in an elevation or a section view, you want to set the work plane along a grid line or named reference plane. This can be done before or during the **Structural Column** command.

- In the Work Plane dialog box, select a work plane from the **Name** drop-down list, as shown in Figure 6–10. Click **OK**.

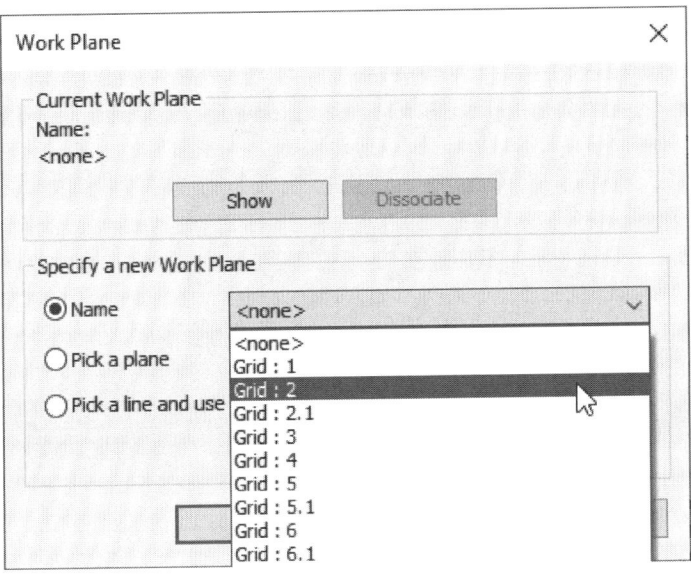

Figure 6–10

Modifying Slanted Structural Columns

Several tools enable you to modify slanted structural columns:

- A slanted column can be adjusted along an attached beam and be able to cut the slanted column to an attached structural floor or slab.
- A slanted column can be cut horizontally, vertically, or perpendicularly, even when it is not attached to an element.

Beam joins automatically adjust when resizing an existing slanted column.

Piers and Pilasters

Revit does not have specific categories for piers and pilasters. If you need to create these elements, the best method is to use concrete columns, as shown in Figure 6–11. You can then analyze them as part of the foundation system and independently schedule them from the main column schedule. A concrete column also automatically embeds itself into a concrete wall.

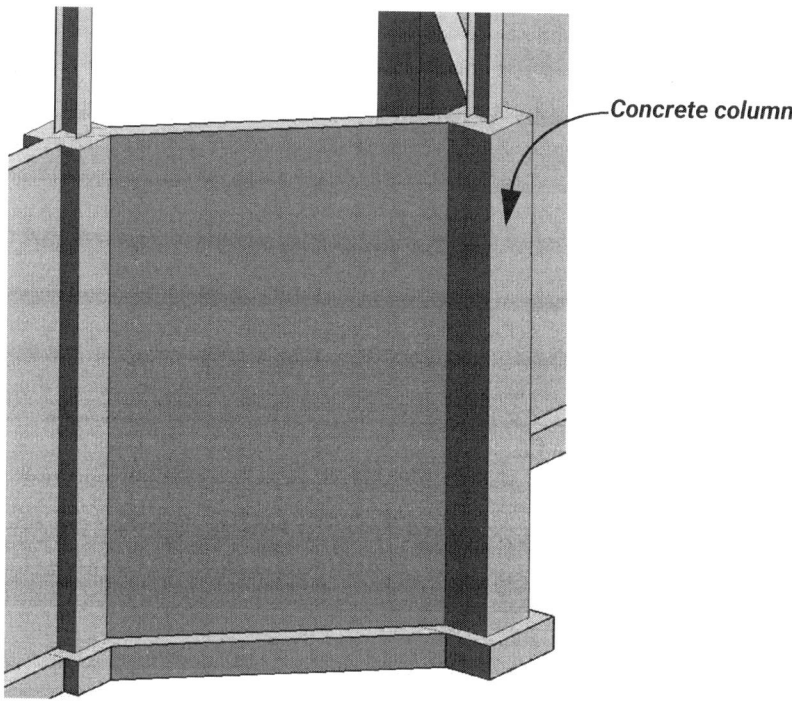

Figure 6–11

Modifying Columns

When selecting a column, you can modify the constraints within Properties and change the *Base Level* and *Top Level*, as well as the offsets from these levels and several other options, as shown in Figure 6–12. You can also attach columns to other elements so that they move with those elements.

Note: Structural columns have additional parameters.

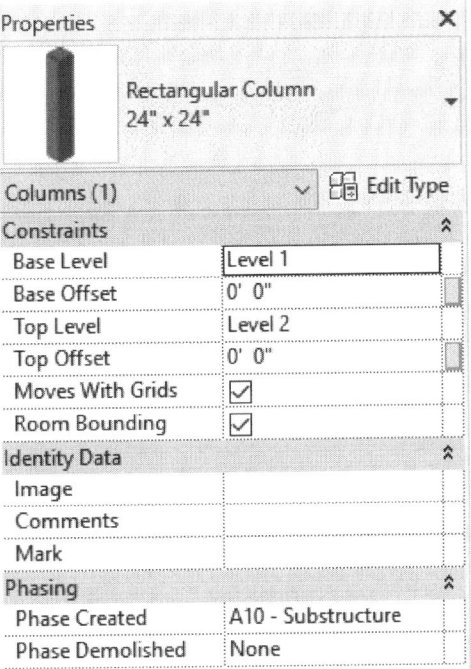

Figure 6–12

- When changing the top and base levels and offsets, you should make these changes in a logical order, as having a zero or negative height column results in an error message.

- Deleting a grid line or wall does not delete the columns placed on them.

- By default, columns placed at grid intersections will move with the grids, although you can still move the columns independently of the grid. Select the column(s) and, in the Options Bar or Properties, select or clear **Move With Grids** to change the method. This toggle is normally on by default, but it is good practice to check its status.

- In the *Modify | Column* tab>Modify Column panel, shown in Figure 6–13, you can attach or detach a column's top and base to floors, ceilings, roofs, reference planes, and structural framing.

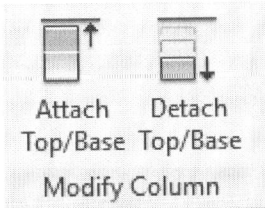

Figure 6–13

How To: Attach Columns to Other Elements

1. Select a column or group of columns.

2. In the *Modify | Structural Columns* tab>Modify Column panel, click (Attach Top/Base).

3. In the Options Bar, set *Attach Column* to **Top** or **Base** and set the *Attachment Style* (as shown in Figure 6–14), *Attachment Justification*, and *Offset From Attachment*.

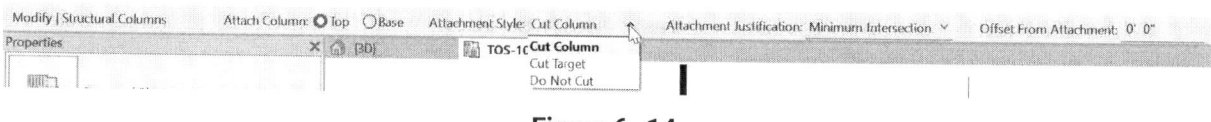

Figure 6–14

4. Select the floor, roof, footing, beam, reference plane, or level to which you want the column(s) attached.

- Attaching columns to other objects associates or constrains certain parameters, such as the height.

- If you want to detach a column that has been attached, select the column and click (Detach Top/Base).

- You can use the **Attach Top/Base** command to attach structural columns to isolated foundations and footings. If the foundation height changes, the length of the column changes with it.

6.2 Adding Isolated Footings

Footings for columns (shown in Figure 6–15) are placed using the **Structural Foundation: Isolated** command. When you select a column, the footing automatically attaches to the bottom of the column. This is true even when the bottom of the column is on a lower level than the view you are working in.

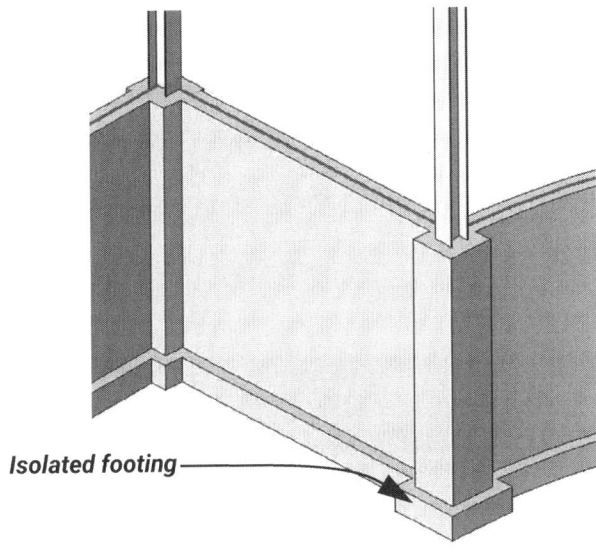

Figure 6–15

- Isolated footings can be placed in a plan or 3D view.

How To: Place an Isolated Footing

1. In the *Structure* tab>Foundation panel, click (Isolated) to start the **Structural Foundation: Isolated** command.
2. In the Type Selector, select a footing type.
3. In the view, click to place the individual footing, as shown in Figure 6–16.
   - If needed, press <Spacebar> to rotate the isolated footings after they are placed.

   *Note: When hovering your cursor over a column, type **SM** to snap to the midpoint.*

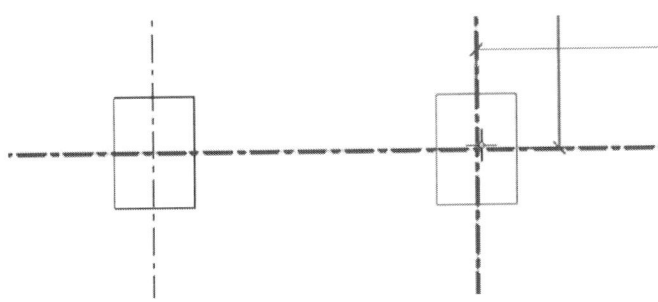

Figure 6–16

- To add more than one footing at a time, in the *Modify | Place Isolated Foundation* tab> Multiple panel, select (At Grids) or (At Columns) and select the grids or columns.
  - If needed, press <Spacebar> to rotate the isolated footings after they are placed.
- If the material of the wall footing and the material of the isolated footing are the same, they automatically join, as shown in Figure 6–17.

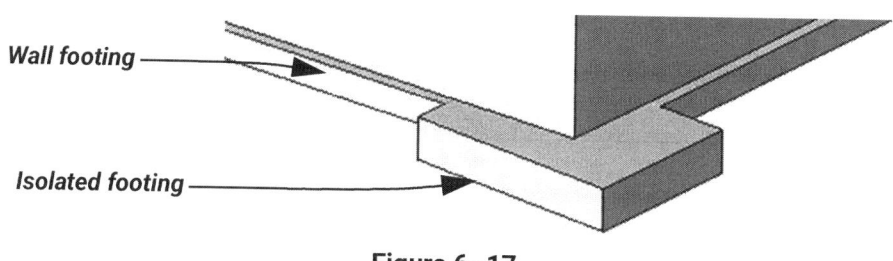

Figure 6–17

Hint: Foundation Element Properties

Some of the element properties are automatically generated from the location and size of the element in the model and are grayed out, for example *Host*, *Elevation at Top*, and *Elevation at Bottom*, as shown in Figure 6–18. These can be used in tags and schedules.

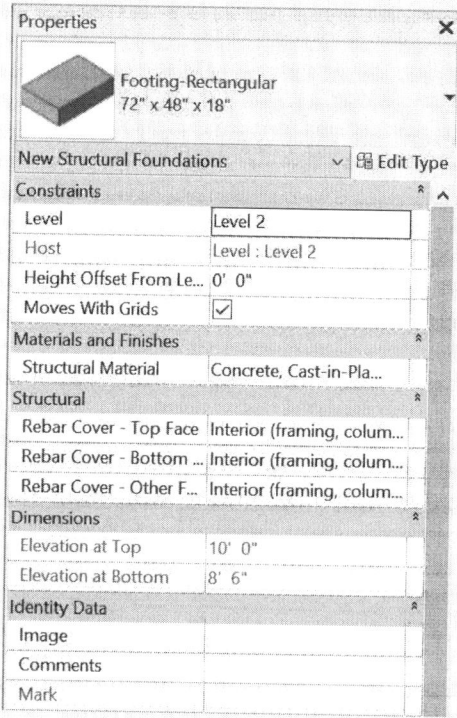

Figure 6–18

Practice 6a
Place Structural Columns

Practice Objective

- Place columns on grids.

In this practice, you will place columns at the grid intersections. The completed practice is shown in 3D in Figure 6–19.

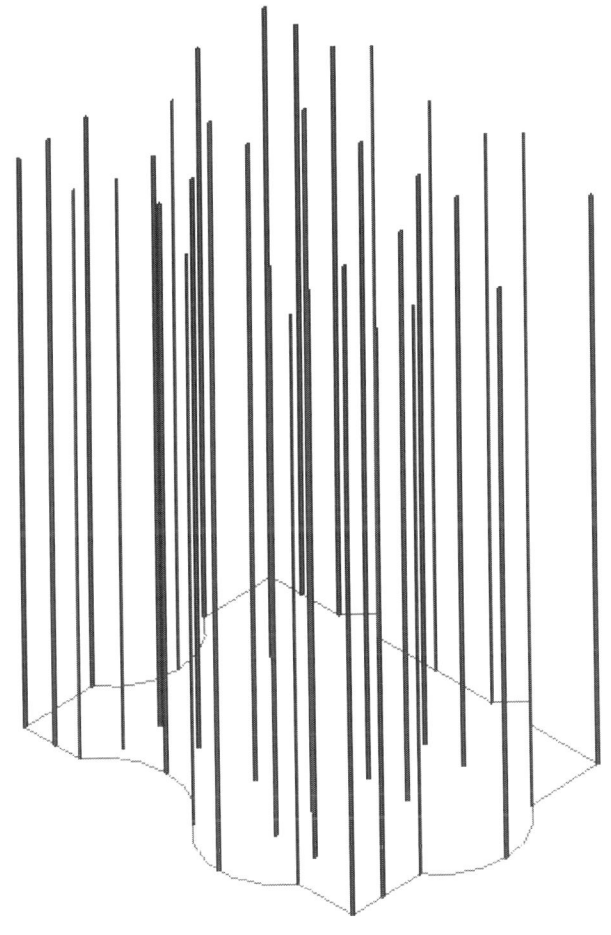

Figure 6–19

1. Open **Structural-Columns.rvt** from the practice files folder.
2. Ensure that you are in the **Structural Plans: 00 GROUND FLOOR** view.
3. In the *Structure* tab>Structure panel, click (Structural Column).
4. In the Type Selector, select **W-Wide flange-Column: W10x33**.

5. In the Options Bar, change *Depth* to **Height** and set the *Height* to **Level TOS-14 Roof**.
6. Place columns at the locations shown in Figure 6–20. (In some cases, it might be faster to place columns at the grid intersections and then delete any extra columns.)

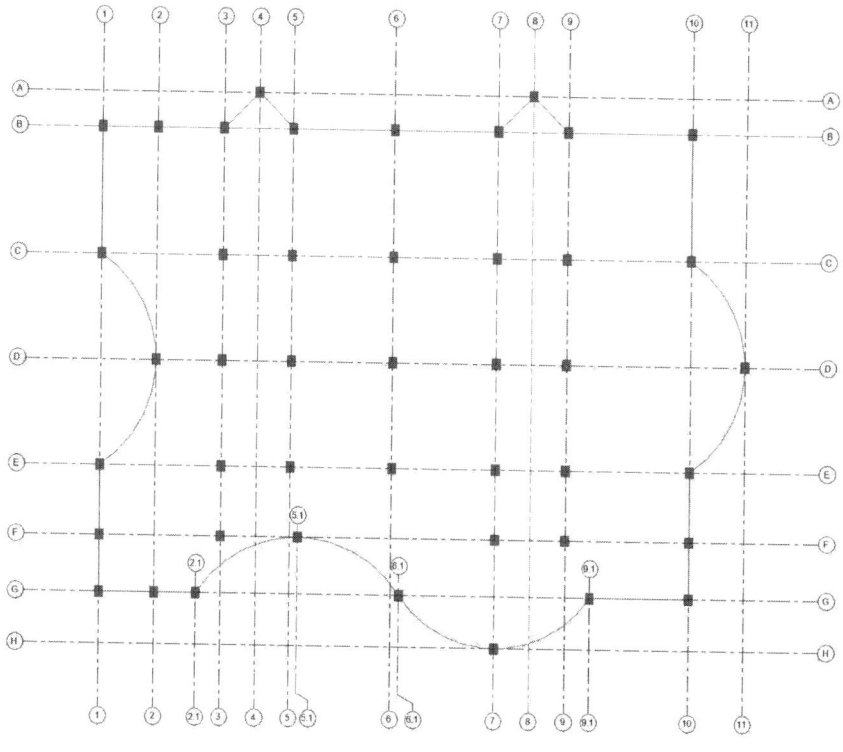

Figure 6–20

7. Open the **Default 3D** view to display the full height of the columns.
8. Save and close the project.

End of practice

6.3 Copying and Monitoring Elements

Once a linked architectural model is in place, the next step is to copy and/or monitor elements that you need from the linked file into the structural project. These elements most often include grid lines, levels, columns, walls, and floors. You cannot copy monitor beams or braces. A monitoring system keeps track of the copied elements and prompts for updates if something is changed. In the example shown in Figure 6–21, grid lines have been linked from an architectural model, and the (Monitor) icon indicates the elements are being monitored.

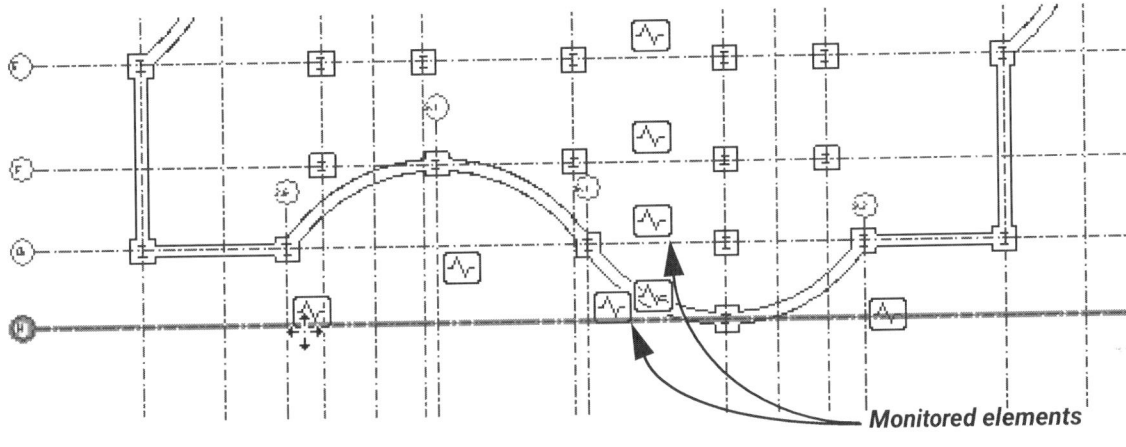

Figure 6–21

Before you start the Copy/Monitor command, you can specify options for levels, grid lines, columns, walls, and floors. You can choose to copy or monitor from the current project or from a linked Revit model. Use **Select Link** to monitor a linked file's elements if they could potentially be moved and affect your system.

- **Copy** copies the selected element from the linked model to the current model or host model, then monitors the element for any changes that may happen in the linked model.

- **Monitor** compares two elements of the same type against each other, either from a linked model to the current project (as shown in Figure 6–22) or within the current project.

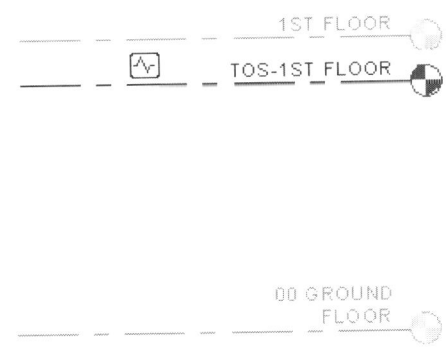

Figure 6–22

Copy/Monitor Settings

You can specify copy/monitor options for the specific element types before starting the copy/monitor process. These options only apply to elements selected after the options have been modified.

In the *Copy/Monitor* tab>Tools panel, click (Options). In the Copy/Monitor Options dialog box, select the tab for the type of element that you want to copy: *Levels*, *Grids*, *Columns*, *Walls*, or *Floors*, as shown in Figure 6–23. Tabs display for the categories that exist in the linked project.

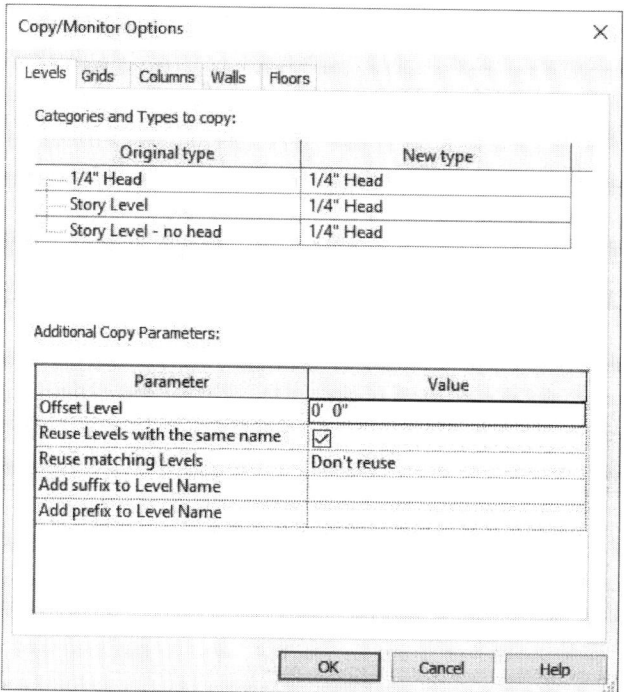

Figure 6–23

Additional Copy Parameters

Offset Level	Specify a level offset for a copied level.
Reuse Levels with the same name	If the current model has a level with the same name as a level in the linked model, you can select this option so a new level is not created. If the linked model's level is at a different height, then the level in the current model will change to match it.

Reuse matching Levels	**Don't reuse:** When selected, if the current model has a level at the same elevation as the linked model, it will still copy the level from the linked model. **Reuse if Elements Match Exactly:** When selected, if the current model and linked model have a level at the same elevation, the level in the linked model is not copied. **Reuse if within offset:** When selected, if the current model has a level within the offset level parameter's elevation, the linked model's level is not copied.
Add suffix to Level Name	Specify a suffix to add to the name of a copied level.
Add prefix to Level Name	Specify a prefix to add to the name of a copied level.
Split Columns by Levels	If copying columns from a linked model extends through multiple levels, selecting this option will break the continuous column into individual columns that stop and start at level lines.
Location line to align	Specify the copied wall's location line to match that of the structural walls.
Copy windows/doors/openings	When selected, the openings of windows and doors are copied over from the linked model.
Copy openings/inserts	When selected, if any floors copied from linked models have openings or hosted inserts, the openings/inserts will also copy over as well.

How To: Copy and Monitor Elements from a Linked File

1. In the *Collaborate* tab>Coordinate panel, expand (Copy/Monitor) and click (Select Link).
2. Select the link.
3. In the *Copy/Monitor* tab>Tools panel, click (Copy) or (Monitor).
4. If copying from the linked file, select each element that you want to copy. Alternatively, use the **Multiple** option:

    - In the Options Bar, select **Multiple**, as shown in Figure 6–24.

    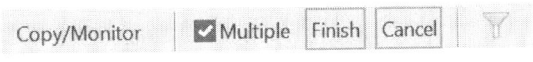

    Figure 6–24

    - Hold <Ctrl> and select the elements that you want to copy into your model individually, or use a pick and drag window around multiple elements.

    Note: *Warnings about duplicated or renamed types might display.*

- In the Options Bar, click **Finish**.

If monitoring elements in the current project with elements in the linked model, first select the element in the current project and then select the element in the linked model.

5. Click ✔ (Finish) to end the session of Copy/Monitor.

How To: Copy and Monitor Elements in the Current Project

1. In the *Collaborate* tab>Coordinate panel, expand (Copy/Monitor) and click (Use Current Project).
2. In the *Copy/Monitor* tab>Tools panel, click (Copy) or (Monitor).
3. Select the two elements you want to monitor.
4. Repeat the process for any additional elements.
5. Click ✔ (Finish) to end the command.

- The elements do not have to be at the same elevation or location for the software to monitor them.

Practice 6b
Copy and Monitor Elements

Practice Objectives

- Monitor architectural linked model's grids.
- Copy and monitor columns from the linked model into the current project.

In this practice, you will monitor the linked architectural model's grids so that any updated models notify you of changes. Then you will copy/monitor columns from a linked architectural model into the current structural project, as shown in Figure 6–25 to be used to place footings in another practice.

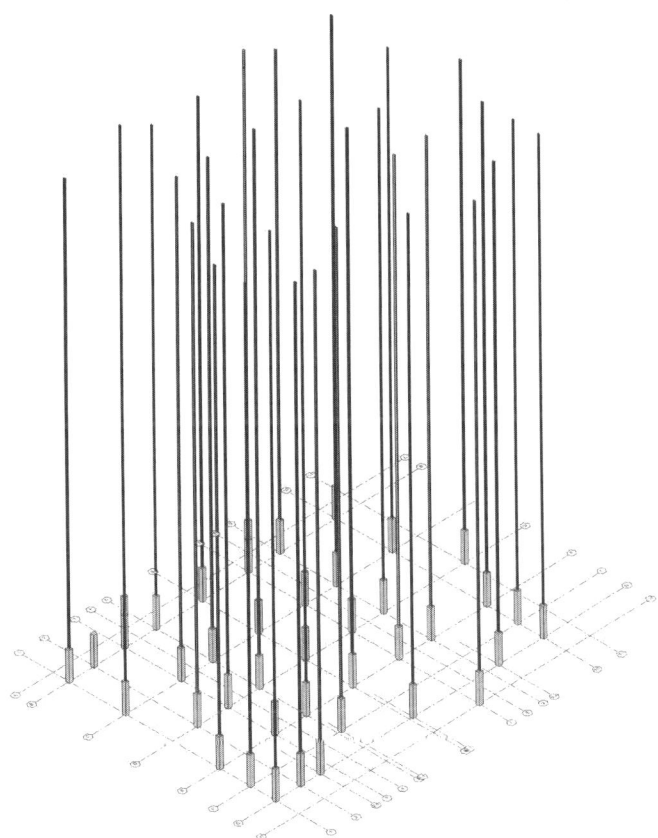

Figure 6–25

Additional columns have been added to the architectural linked model for copy/monitor purposes only. Changes to this practice are solely for the purpose of learning the Copy/Monitor tools.

Task 1: Prepare to copy/monitor linked model columns.

1. Open **Structural-Monitor.rvt** from the practice files folder. (This model is using a linked Revit model called **Arch-Col-Montr.rvt** for copy/monitor lesson only.)

2. The project opens in a 3D view. There are concrete columns below the steel columns, as shown in Figure 6–26.

   Note: Grids were manually added in Practice 2c: Add Grids.

3. Select one of the concrete columns they all highlight because they are a part of the linked Revit model, as shown in Figure 6–26.

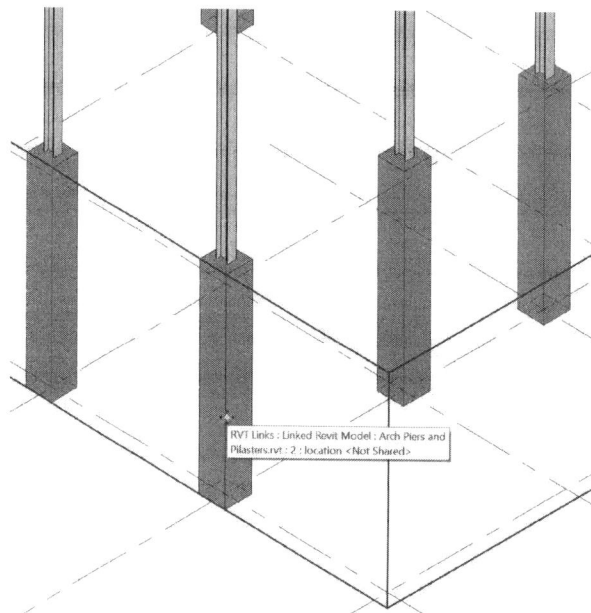

Figure 6–26

4. In the Project Browser, open the **Structural Plans - 00 T.O.FOOTING** view. You should only see the linked model's concrete columns and not the steel columns.

5. Hover over the concrete column and press <Tab> until the Revit linked model highlights and click to select it.

   - Look at the Status Bar in the lower left or the tooltip to see what can potentially be selected.

6. Right-click on the link and select **Override Graphics in View>By Category**. In the View-Specific Category Graphics dialog box, select **Halftone** and click **OK**.

7. Click (Modify).

Task 2: Monitor architectural grids.

In this task, you will monitor the architectural linked model's grids. If they get moved for any reason, you will be notified once the structural model is opened.

1. While remaining in the **00 T.O. FOOTING** view, zoom and pan to the grid lines **A1** in the upper left corner so you can see a few grid lines.
2. In the *Collaborate* tab>Coordinate panel, expand (Copy/Monitor) and click (Select Link).
3. Select the architectural linked model. Press <Tab> if you need to select the linked model.
4. In the *Copy/Monitor* tab>Tools panel, click (Monitor).
5. Notice the Status Bar in the lower left of the interface displays *Pick an element to monitor*.
6. Hover your cursor over grid line **A** and the tooltip displays **Grids: Grid: A** (shown in Figure 6–27) indicating you are hovering over grid **A** in your structural model.
7. Click to select grid **A**.

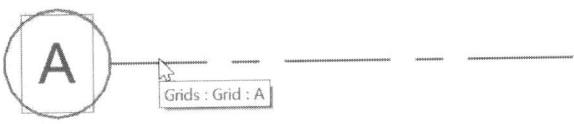

Figure 6–27

Note: When only monitoring elements in a linked model you can only set the monitoring one element at a time.

8. Notice the Status Bar in the lower left of the interface displays *Pick corresponding element to monitor*.
9. Hover your cursor over grid line **A** again, notice the tooltip now displays RVT Links and the architectural linked model's name, as shown in Figure 6–28.
10. Click to select grid **A** in the RVT linked model.

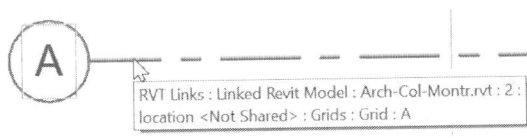

Figure 6–28

- The (Monitor) will display along grid A. (You may need to zoom out to see it.)

11. Repeat steps 5 through 10, and monitor the rest of the grids in the project to the linked Revit models grids.

    - Make sure you see the tooltip before each click and watch the Status Bar so you know what your cursor is hovering over and what step you are on.
    - If you accidentally select a grid line that you have already done, a warning will display that the elements are already monitored, as shown in Figure 6–29. Ignore the warning and continue monitoring the next grid line.

Figure 6–29

12. In the *Copy/Monitor* tab>Copy/Monitor panel, click ✔ (Finish).
13. Save the project.

Task 3: Copy/Monitor linked model columns

1. While remaining in the **00 T.O. FOOTING** view, from the *Collaborate* tab>Coordinate panel, expand (Copy/Monitor) and click (Select Link).
2. Select the architectural linked model.
3. In the *Copy/Monitor* tab>Tools panel, click (Options).
4. Click the *Columns* tab.

    - The Original type column shows columns in Revit linked model, New type is the column you want copied into your project.

5. In the New type column, expand the column type and select **Don't Copy this Type** for all columns except the Concrete-Rectangular-Column 24 x 24, as shown in Figure 6–30.
6. Set Concrete-Rectangular-Column 24x 24 to **Copy original type** as shown in Figure 6–30 and click **OK**.

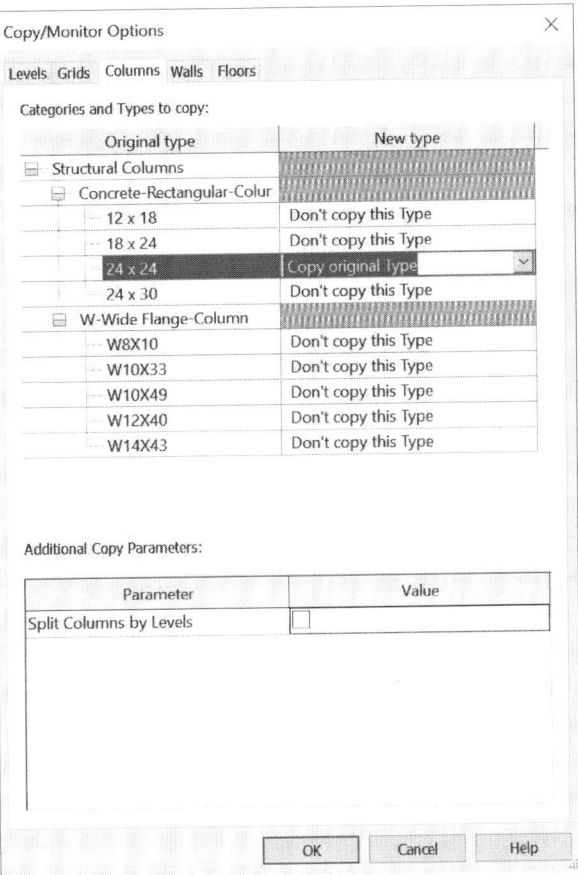

Figure 6–30

7. In the *Copy/Monitor* tab>Tools panel, click (Copy).
8. In the Options Bar, check the checkbox next to Multiple, as shown in Figure 6–31.

Figure 6–31

9. In the view, draw a selection window around all the columns to select all of them.
10. In the Options Bar, click (Filter).

11. In the Filter dialog box, verify you only selected the Structural columns. If any other elements were selected, uncheck them (as shown in Figure 6–32) and click **OK**.

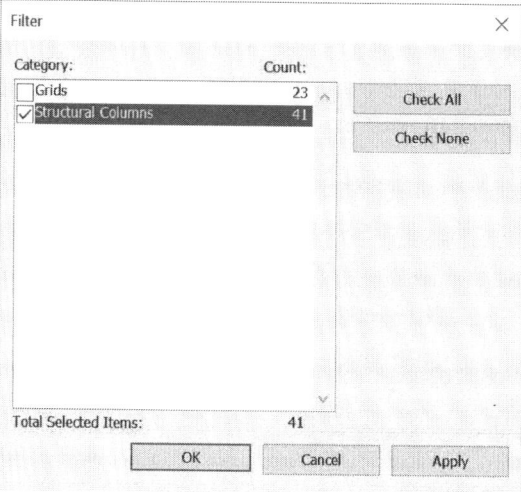

Figure 6–32

12. In the Options Bar, click **Finish**.
13. All the columns in the view will display (Monitor) next to them as shown in Figure 6–33.

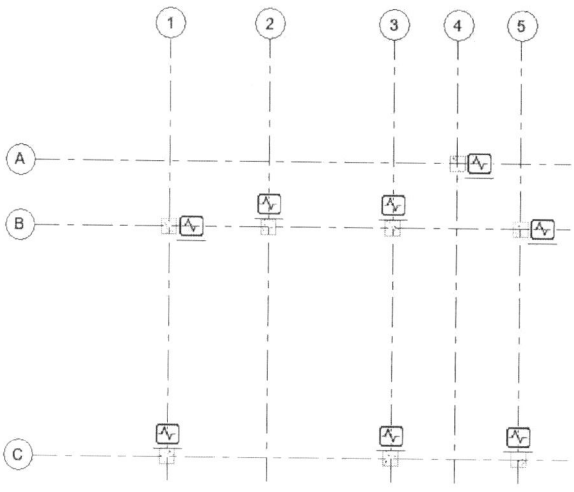

Figure 6–33

14. In the *Copy/Monitor* tab>Copy/Monitor panel, click (Finish).
15. The concrete columns have been copied into the structural model.
16. Zoom in to a column and select on it. You will see (Monitor) next to it and on the *Modify | Structural Column* tab>Monitor panel, (Stop Monitoring) will display.
17. Save and close the project.

End of practice

6.4 Coordinating Linked Models

Monitoring elements identifies changes in the data as well as changes in placement. For example, if you move a grid line, a Coordination Monitor alert displays, as shown in Figure 6–34. You can run a Coordination Review to correct or accept these changes.

Figure 6–34

- If you open a project with a linked file that contains elements that have been modified and monitored, the warning shown in Figure 6–35 displays.

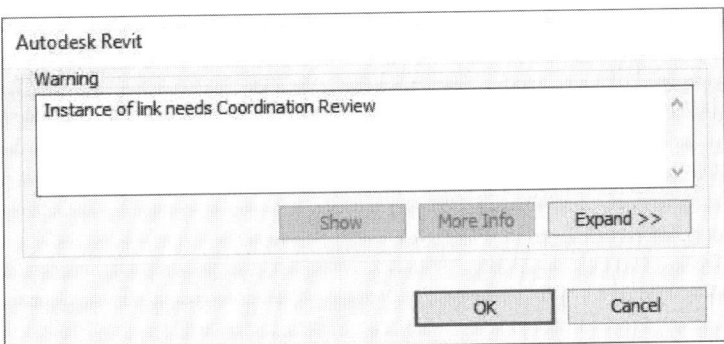

Figure 6–35

- Warnings do not prevent you from making a change, but alert you that the element is monitored and needs further coordination.

- If you no longer want an element to be monitored, select it and in the associated *Modify* tab>Monitor panel, click (Stop Monitoring).

How To: Run a Coordination Review

1. In the *Collaborate* tab>Coordinate panel, expand (Coordination Review) and click (Use Current Project) or (Select Link). The Coordination Review dialog box lists any conflicts detected, as shown in Figure 6–36.

    - If there are no conflicts, the *Message* area is empty.

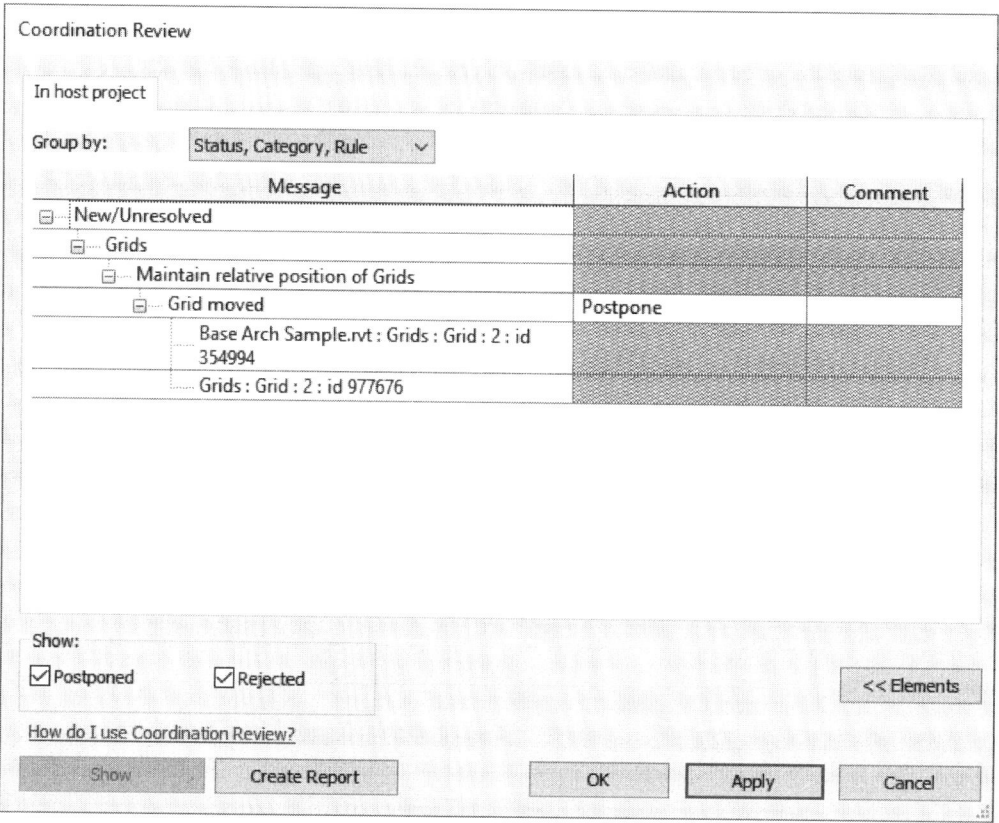

Figure 6–36

2. Use the Group by: drop-down list to group the information by **Status**, **Category**, and **Rule** in a variety of different ways. This is important if you have many elements to review.

3. Select an *Action* for each conflict related to the elements involved, as shown in Figure 6–37.

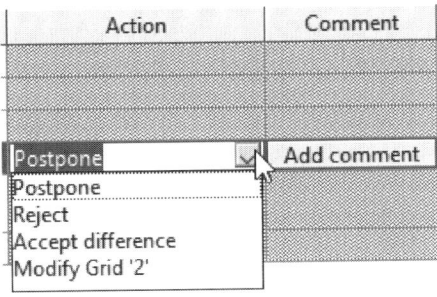

Figure 6–37

- **Postpone:** Do nothing, but leave it to be handled later.
- **Reject:** Do not accept the change. The change needs to be made in the other model.
- **Accept difference:** Make no change to the monitored element in the current project, but accept the change (such as a distance between the elements) in the monitor status.
- **Rename/Modify/Move:** Apply the change to the monitored element.
- Other options display when special cases occur. See the Autodesk Revit help documentation for more information.

4. To add a comment, click **Add comment** in the column to the right. This enables you to make a note about the change, such as the date of the modification

5. Select the element names or click **Show** to display any items in conflict. Clicking **Show** changes the view to center the elements in your screen. Selecting the name does not change the view.

6. Click **Create Report** to create an HTML report that you can share with other users, as shown in Figure 6–38.

Revit Coordination Report

In host project

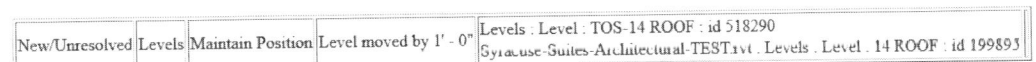

Figure 6–38

💡 Hint: Troubleshooting

When working with various elements, warnings (such as the one shown in Figure 6–39) display when something is wrong, but you can keep on working. In many cases, you can close the dialog box and fix the issue or wait and do it later.

Figure 6–39

Sometimes Errors display where you must take action. These force you to stop and fix the situation.

When you select an element for which there has been a warning, ⚠ (Show Related Warnings) displays in the ribbon. It opens a dialog box in which you can review the warning(s) related to the selected element. You can also display a list of all of the warnings in the project by clicking 🔍 (Review Warnings) in the *Manage* tab>Inquiry panel.

Practice 6c
Coordinate Linked Models

Practice Objective

- Run a Coordination Review and modify the structural project against the architectural model.

You will need to run a Coordination Review and update and reject the structural project to the change in the architectural model.

Note: Columns and grids in the architectural linked model have been modified for coordination purposes only. Changes to this practice are solely for the purpose of learning the Coordination Tool.

Task 1: Coordinate the architectural and structural models.

1. Open **Structural-Coordination.rvt** from the practice files folder. (This model is using a linked Revit model called **Arch-Col-Coord.rvt**.)
2. A warning dialog box displays with a warning that the linked file needs a Coordination Review, as shown in Figure 6–40.

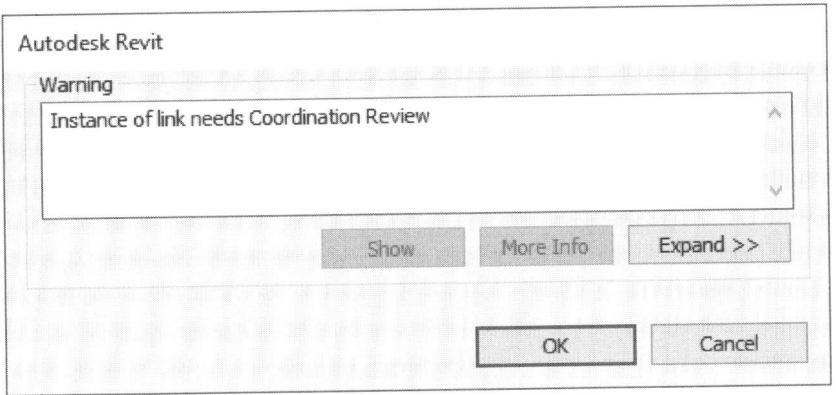

Figure 6–40

3. Click **OK**.
4. Select the linked model and in the *Modify RVT Links* tab>Monitor panel, click (Coordination Review).

5. In the Coordination Review dialog box>Message column, expand the **Maintain relative position of Grids**>*Grid Moved* nodes. Select the top **Grid Moved** to see the grid highlight in the model.

    - Move the dialog box so you can see the element that is highlighted in the view.
    - While the Coordination Review dialog box is open, you can zoom and pan around the view.

6. In the *Action* column, expand the drop-down list (as shown in Figure 6–41) and select **Modify Grid '6.1'** and click **Apply** to see your grid move to match the architectural grid.

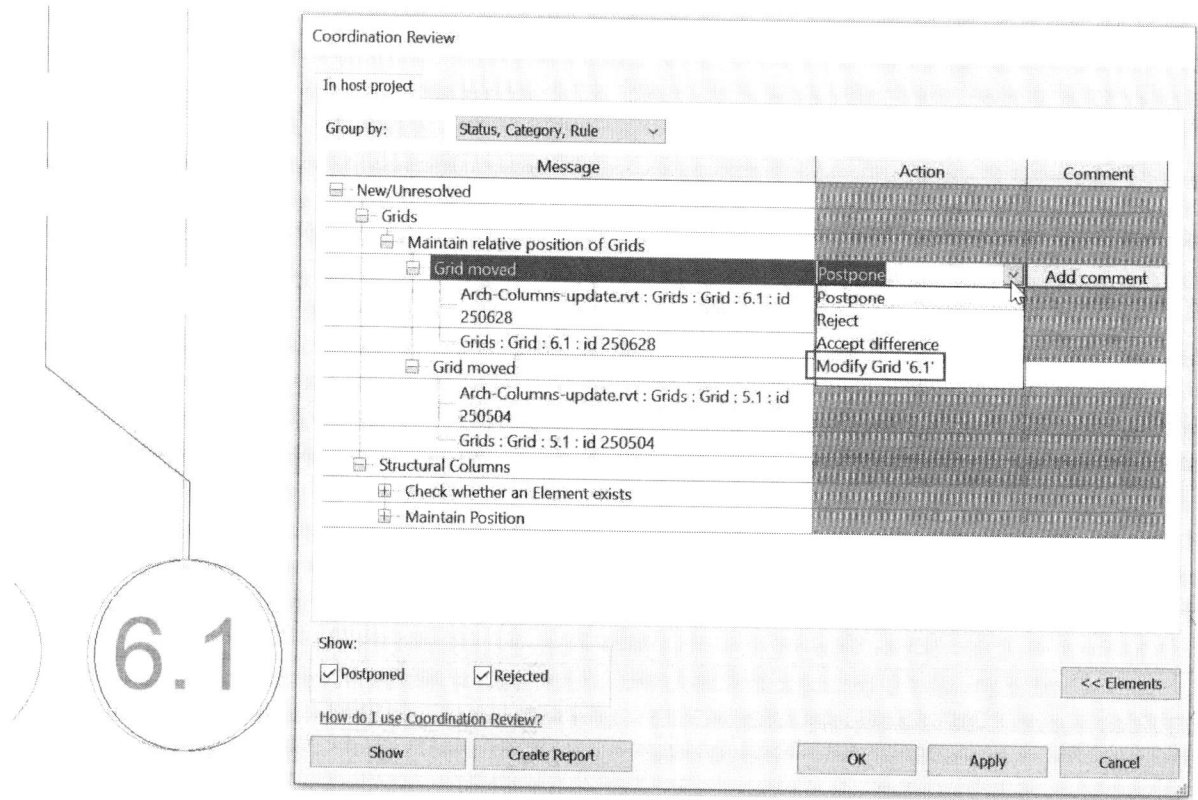

Figure 6–41

- Notice that the message is no longer in the message column.

7. Repeat modifying the next Grid moved message for Grid 5.1 and select **Modify Grid '5.1'** from the *Action* column and click **Apply**.

8. Keep the dialog box open and under the **Structural columns** node, expand **Check whether an Element exists** and select **Element deleted**.

9. The column that was deleted in the linked architectural model highlights. If needed, move the dialog box, and zoom and pan on the model to see the highlighted column.

10. In the *Action* column, expand the drop-down list (as shown in Figure 6–42) and select **Reject** and click **Apply** to keep the column.

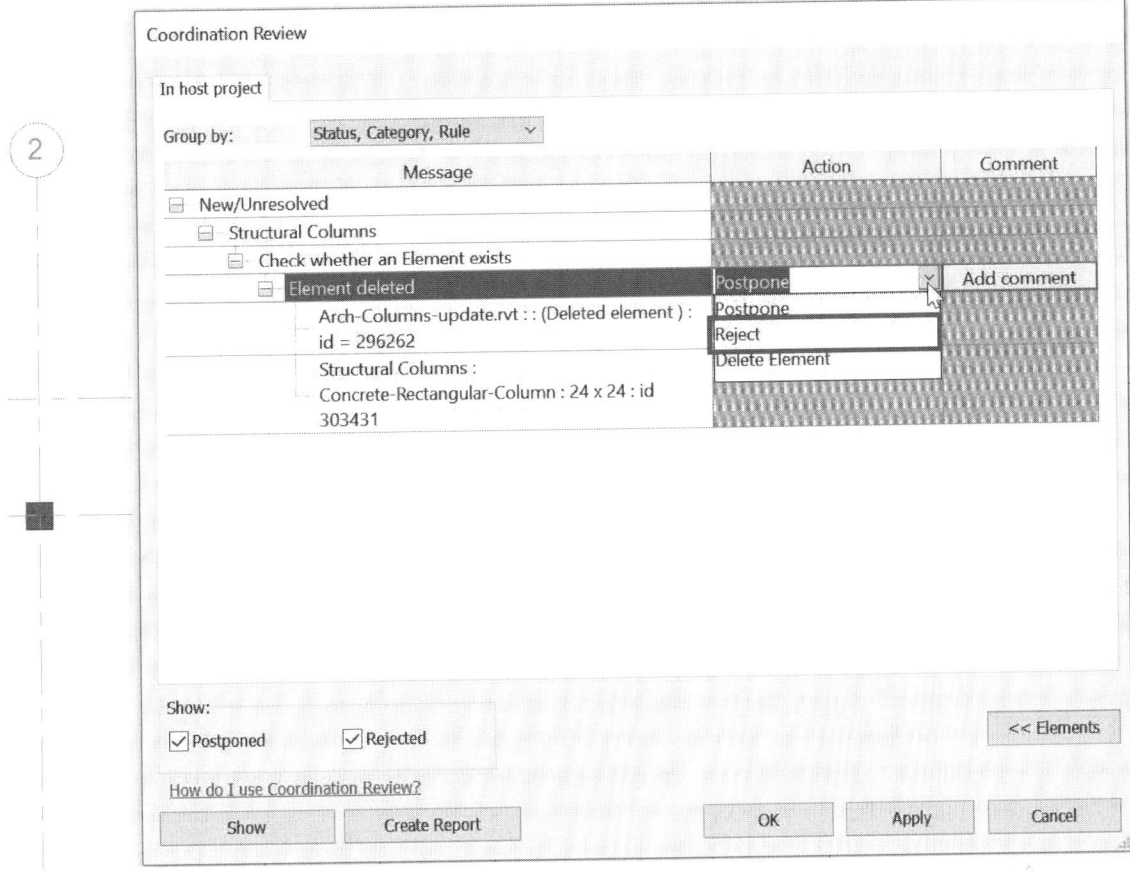

Figure 6–42

11. Click **OK** to close the dialog box.
12. Save and close the project.

End of practice

Chapter Review Questions

1. Where can columns be placed?

    a. Columns can only be placed on grids.

    b. Architectural columns can be placed anywhere, but structural columns can only be placed on grids.

    c. Both types of columns can be placed wherever you want.

    d. Grid-based column types must be placed on the grid, but free-standing column types can be placed anywhere.

2. Structural columns can only be placed on grids.

    a. True

    b. False

3. How do you add additional column families to use in a project?

    a. Import them.

    b. Copy and paste them from another file.

    c. Draw them in the project.

    d. Load them from the Revit Library.

4. In order for structural columns to move with grids, what needs to be selected when placing the column?

    a. In the ribbon, select **At Grids**.

    b. Set the *Top Constraint* to grids.

    c. Columns always move with grids no matter what type.

    d. In Properties, select **Moves With Grids**.

5. Which of the following elements can be copied and monitored? (Select all that apply.)

    a. Grid lines

    b. Levels

    c. Beams

    d. Braces

6. On which of the following element types can a coordination review with the host project be performed?

    a. CAD link
    b. CAD import
    c. Revit link
    d. Revit import

Command Summary

Button	Command	Location
	At Columns	• **Ribbon:** *Modify	Place Structural Column* tab>Multiple panel
	At Grids	• **Ribbon:** *Modify	Place Structural Column* tab>Multiple panel
	Column	• **Ribbon:** *Architecture* tab>Build panel
	Column>Column: Architectural	• **Ribbon:** *Architecture* tab>Build panel, expand Column
	Column>Structural Column	• **Ribbon:** *Architecture* tab>Build panel, expand Column
	Coordination Review	• **Ribbon:** *Collaborate* tab>Coordinate panel
	Copy (from linked file)	• **Ribbon:** *Copy/Monitor* tab>Tools panel
	Copy/Monitor>Select Link	• **Ribbon:** *Collaborate* tab>Coordinate panel, expand Copy/Monitor
	Copy/Monitor>Use Current Project	• **Ribbon:** *Collaborate* tab>Coordinate panel, expand Copy/Monitor
	Monitor	• **Ribbon:** *Copy/Monitor* tab>Tools panel
	Options (Copy/Monitor)	• **Ribbon:** *Copy/Monitor* tab>Tools panel

Chapter 7

Foundations

Structural foundations are created using concrete walls, columns, and footings. Revit® includes standard tools for creating walls and columns in several different materials, as well as specific tools for adding footings.

Learning Objectives

- Create walls that can be used in foundations.
- Add bearing and retaining wall footings under the walls.
- Create column types to be used as piers and pilasters.
- Place isolated footings under the columns.

7.1 Modeling Walls

Walls in Revit are more than just two lines on a plan. They are full 3D elements that store detailed information, including height, thickness, and materials. This means they are useful in 2D and 3D views. Structural walls (as shown in Figure 7–1) are bearing walls that can act as exterior, foundation, retaining, and shaft walls.

- Walls also impact material takeoff schedules.
- Walls are a system family that is predefined in the Revit template file and cannot be loaded in from an external location or saved out to a external location.
- Walls can be customized to suit your company needs, if necessary.

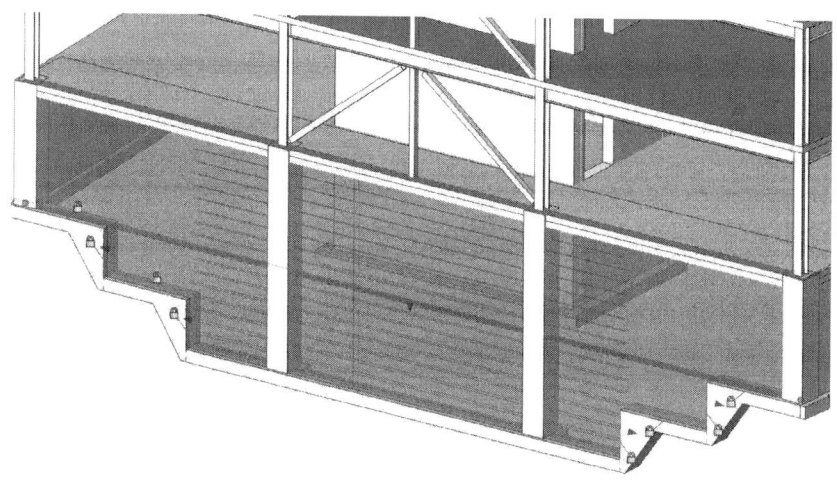

Figure 7–1

There are three broad categories of walls:

- *Basic walls:* Compound walls that contain one or more layers (e.g., blocks, air space, bricks, etc.).
- *Curtain walls:* Walls that are divided horizontally and vertically into a grid system.
- *Stacked walls:* Consist of two or more basic walls stacked vertically, such as a brick wall over a concrete wall.

Wall Cross-Section

The *Cross-Section* for the basic wall category can be modified to be **Vertical**, **Slanted**, or **Tapered**, as shown in Figure 7–2.

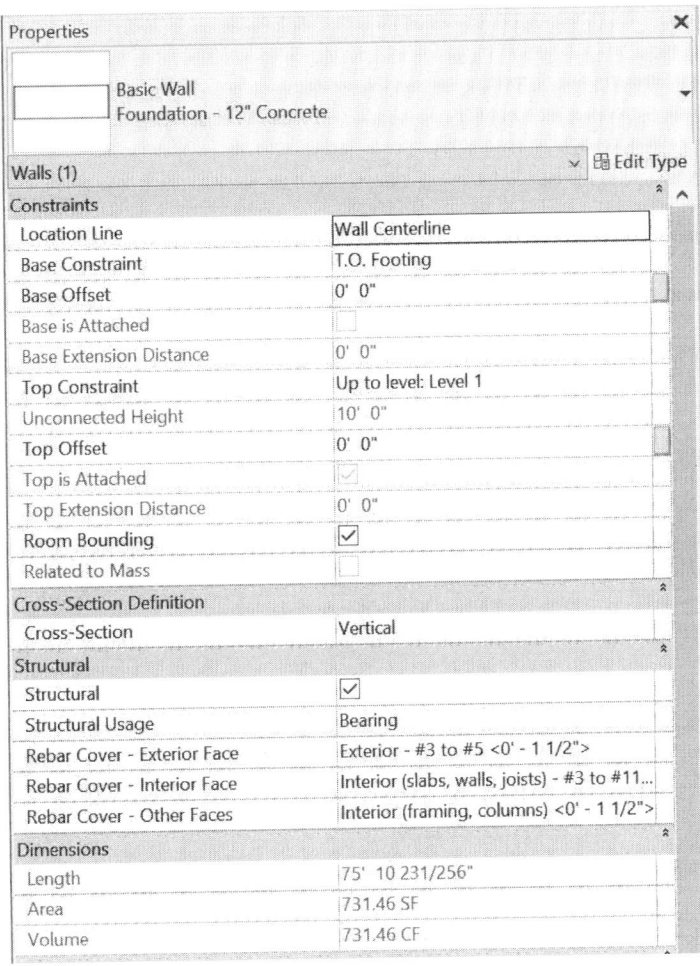

Figure 7–2

Vertical Wall

All walls are drawn by default as a vertical wall and are at a 0° vertical when comparing it to a slanted wall type.

Note: If you change a wall's cross-section to **Tapered** and adjust the settings for the tapered wall, then you will see only the Tapered wall types displayed in the Type Selector. If you need to draw a vertical or slanted wall after the tapered wall is drawn, you will need to set the cross-section back to **Vertical** or **Slanted** so that you can see all the wall types in the Type Selector.

Slanted Wall

You can draw a slanted wall type and specify the **Angle From Vertical** degree value in Properties. The slant degree needs to be within -90° to 90°. You can also change a vertically drawn wall to a slanted wall type. If there are any doors, door openings or window added to the wall, you will need to select those objects and, in Properties, specify their *Orientation*. The direction to which the wall has been drawn (right to left or left to right) will determine the direction the angle will go. Figure 7–3 shows that when drawing from left to right the wall slant will go in the negative direction, and drawing from right to left the slant wall goes in the positive direction.

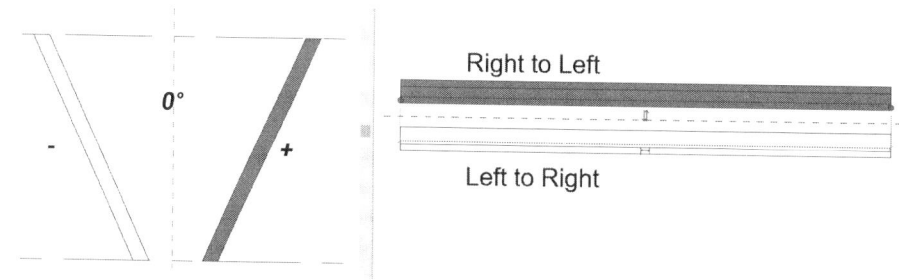

Figure 7–3

- Slanted walls can be modified in a plan, 3D, section, and perspective views.
- You can create a slanted wall with curved, circle, arc, polygon, or elliptical paths.
- If the angle is not going in the correct direction, + or -, you can add a (negative) - symbol in front of the degree value in Properties.

Tapered Wall

You can create a tapered wall from any wall type except walls with sweeps and reveals. You must first edit the structure of the wall to set the variable thickness for the available wall layers. If not, you are prompted to set this before drawing the wall, as shown in Figure 7–4.

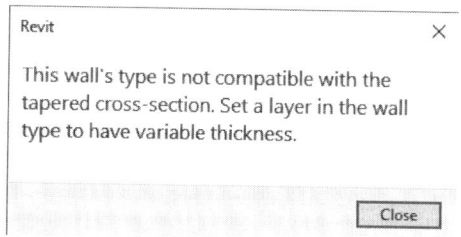

Figure 7–4

- To set the default angles of the tapered wall, in Type Properties, you can set the *Default Exterior* and *Interior Angle*.

- If you have multiple instances of the same tapered wall type, you can select a tapered wall, and in Properties, override the angles by selecting the **Override Type Properties** option and also setting the *Exterior Angle* and *Interior Angle*, as shown in Figure 7–5.

Cross-Section	Tapered
Override Type Properties	✓
Exterior Angle	5.00°
Interior Angle	0.00°

Figure 7–5

- Curtain walls and stacked wall types cannot be tapered.
- If doors, door openings, or windows are placed in a tapered wall, you can specify the orientation of the door and wall.

Wall Display per View

You can alter the way a wall is displayed in the active view by setting the *Detail Level*, as shown in Figure 7–6. You can also override the visibility settings of all walls in a view by opening the Visibility/Graphic Overrides dialog box and modifying the wall category. To change the way selected walls display in the active view, you would override the setting for graphics in view by element.

- To display the hatching in all walls in the active view where a wall is being cut through, in the View Control Bar, set the *Detail Level* to **Coarse**, **Medium** or **Fine**, as shown in Figure 7–6.

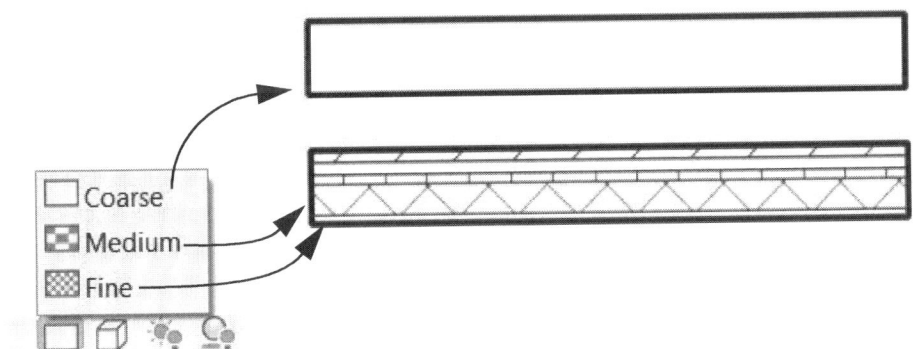

Figure 7–6

- To access the Visibility/Graphic Overrides dialog box to change all walls in a view, go to the *View* tab>Graphics panel and click (Visibility/Graphics), or type **VG** or **VV**. You can uncheck **Non-Core Layers** (as shown in Figure 7–7) to only view the core layer in the view. This overrides all walls in the view.

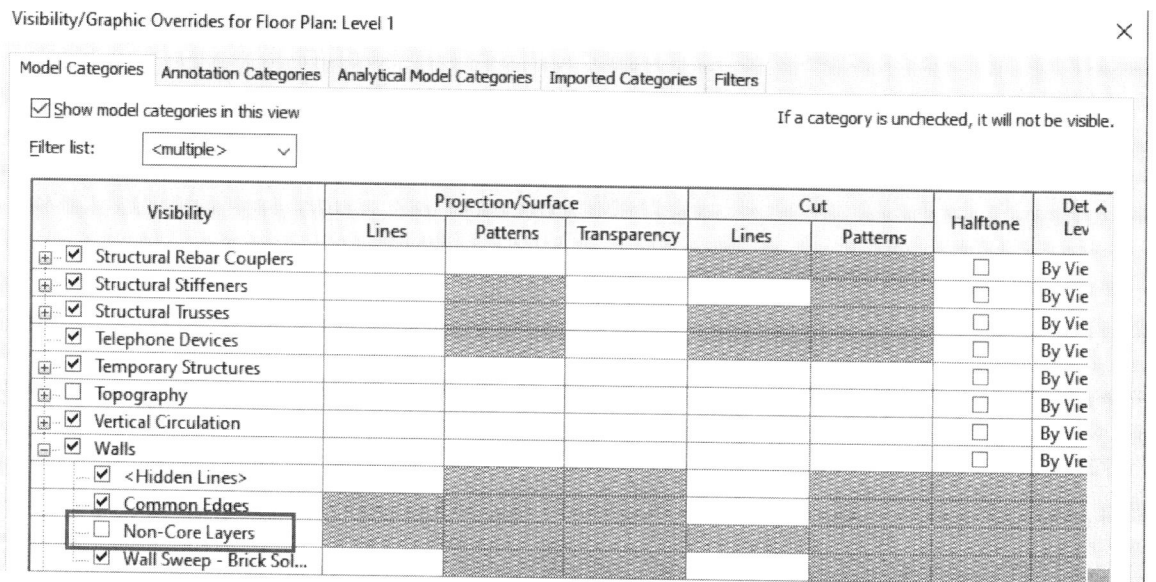

Figure 7–7

- To modify a single or a select few walls in the view, select the walls, right-click, and select **Override Graphics in View>By Element**, as shown in Figure 7–8.

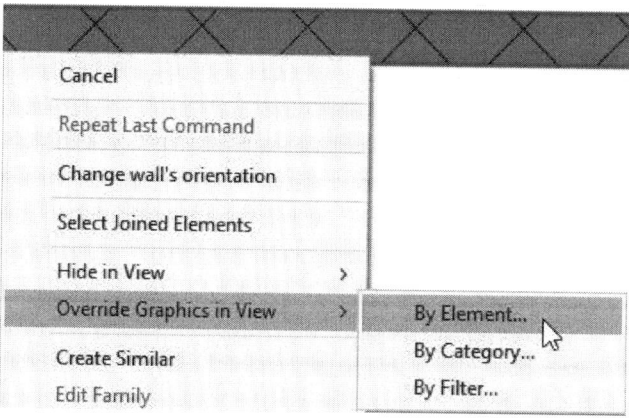

Figure 7–8

How To: Model a Wall

1. In the *Structure* tab>Structure panel, click (Wall: Structural), or type **WA**.
   - Architectural walls (which are created with the **Wall: Architectural** command) are typically non-bearing walls, such as curtain walls and partitions. They do not display when the view *Discipline* is set to **Structural**.
2. In the Type Selector, select a wall type, as shown in Figure 7–9. You can use the search box to quickly find specific types of walls.

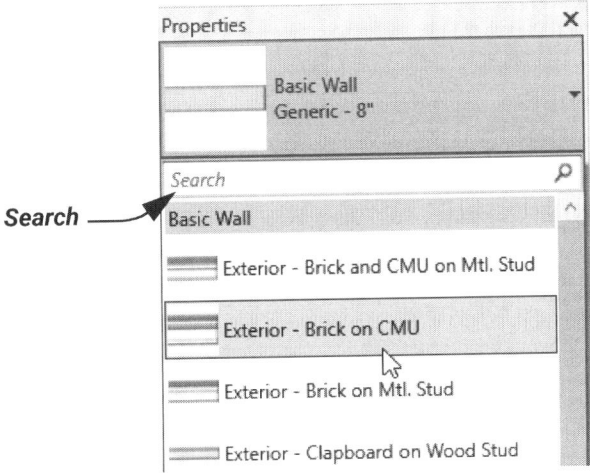

Figure 7–9

3. In Properties, set the *Cross-Section* to **Vertical**, **Slanted**, or **Tapered**, depending on the wall you need to create, as shown in Figure 7–10. Specify the Properties and Type Properties as needed. If this is not set at the beginning of drawing a wall, the last cross-section used will be the default.

   - If you set the *Cross-Section* to **Slanted**, you are able to set the *Angle From Vertical* degree, as shown in Figure 7–10.

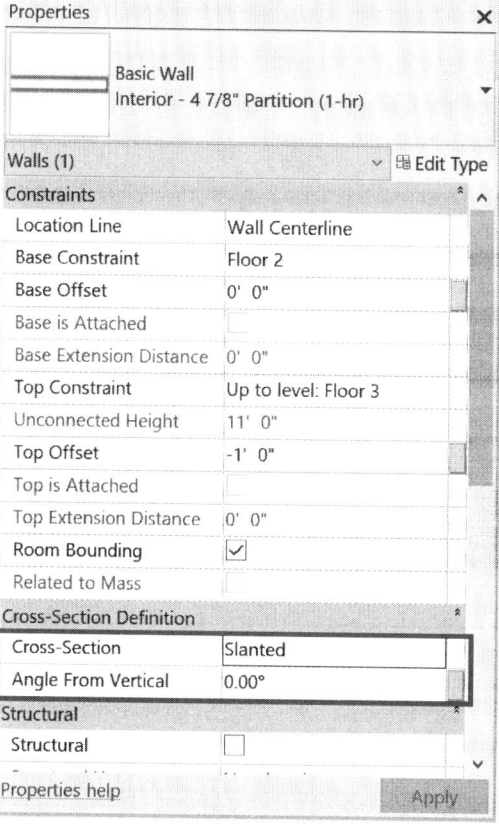

Figure 7–10

- If you set the *Cross-Section* to **Tapered**, you will get a warning about the wall type. You must first edit the structure of the wall before setting the *Cross-Section* to **Tapered**.

   a. With the wall type selected, click **Edit Type** in Properties.

   b. Click **Edit...** next to *Structure*.

c. In the Edit Assembly dialog box, select the option in the *Variable* column (as shown in Figure 7–11) for the layer that you want tapered.

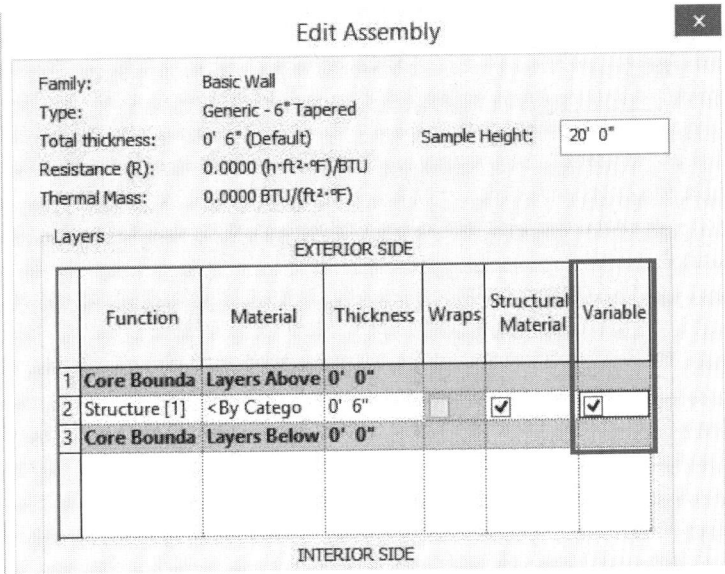

Figure 7–11

d. Click **OK**.
e. In the Type Properties dialog box, you will now have the ability to set the *Cross Section Properties*, as shown in Figure 7–12.

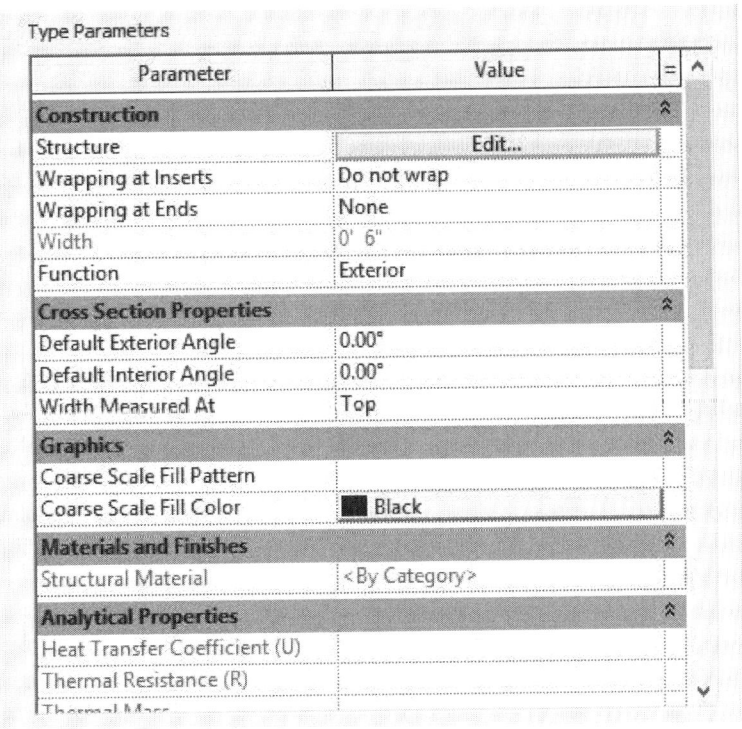

Figure 7–12

4. In the Options Bar (shown in Figure 7–13), specify the following information about the wall before you start modeling:

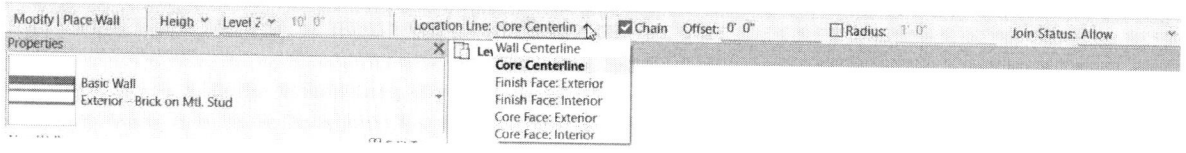

Figure 7–13

- **Height:** Set the height of a wall to either **Unconnected** (with a specified height) or to a level.
- **Location Line:** Set the justification of the wall using the options shown above in Figure 7–13.
- **Chain:** Enables you to model multiple connected walls.
- **Offset:** Enables you to enter the distance at which a new wall is created from an existing element.
- **Radius:** Adds a curve of a specified radius to connected walls as you model.
- **Join Status: Allow** or **Disallow** automatic wall joins.

5. In the *Modify | Place Wall* tab>Draw panel (shown in Figure 7–14), select one of the options to create the wall.

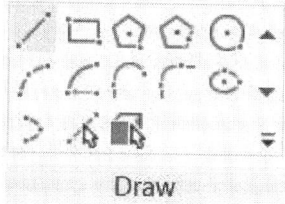

Figure 7–14

- Use alignment lines, temporary dimensions, and snaps to place the walls.
- As you are sketching, you can press <Spacebar> to flip the orientation of compound walls.
- When using the *Chain* option, press <Esc> once to finish the string of walls and remain in the **Wall** command or press <Esc> twice to get out of the wall command completely. Hint: <Esc> works similarly on other commands.

7.2 Modifying Walls

There are several methods of modifying walls. You can change the type of wall using the Type Selector, modify the Properties, use controls and shape handles to modify the length and wall orientation, and use temporary and permanent dimensions to change the location or length of a wall in 2D and 3D views, as shown in Figure 7–15. Additional tools enable you to modify wall joins, edit the profile of a wall, and add wall openings.

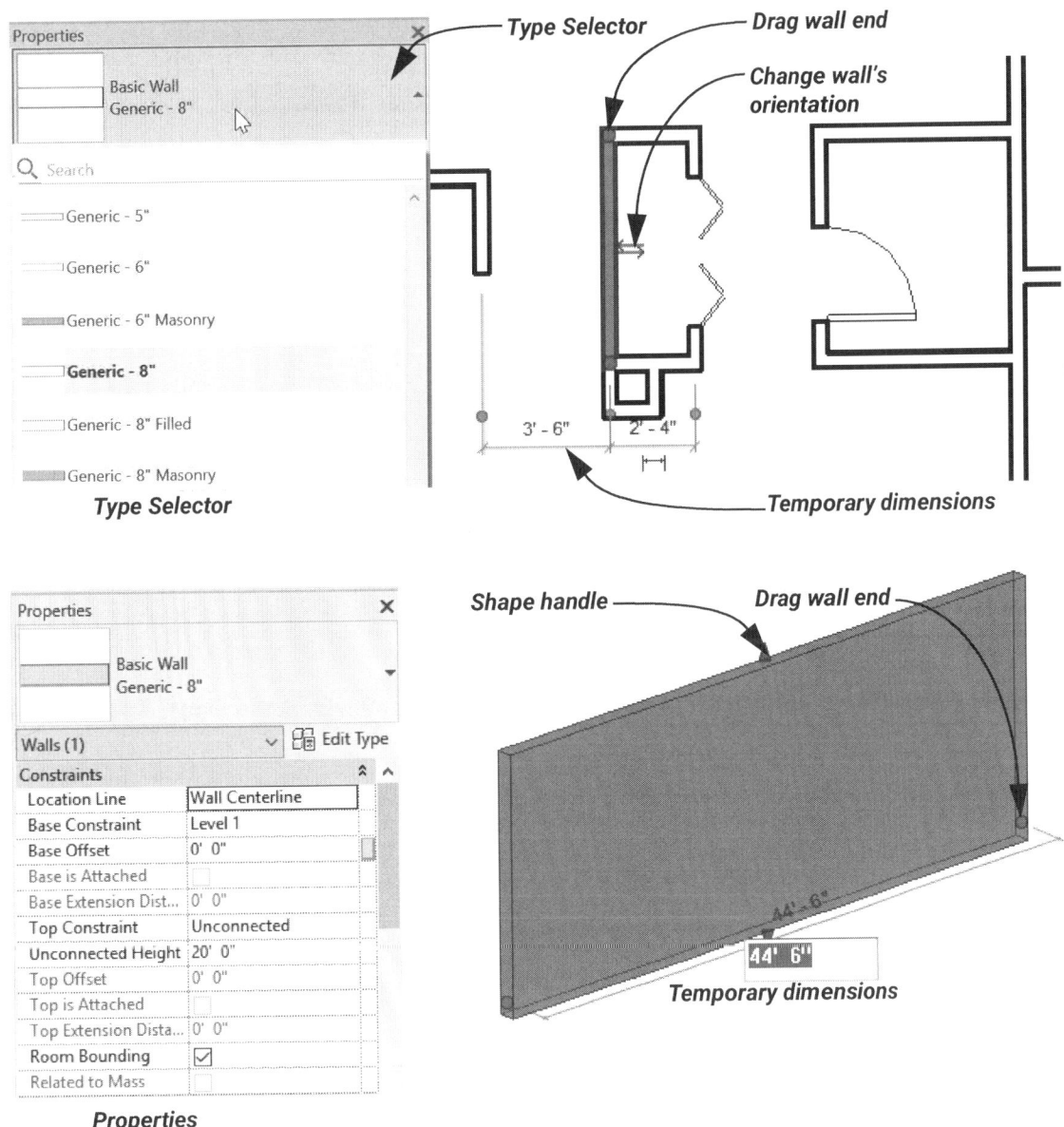

Figure 7–15

Modifying Slanted and Tapered Walls

Modifying a slanted or tapered wall is similar to modifying a vertical wall type with the exception of modifying the angle.

* When modifying a slanted wall type, you have the ability to modify the Drag Wall Slant grip or modify the temporary dimension in a 3D, section, elevation, or isometric view, as shown in Figure 7–16.

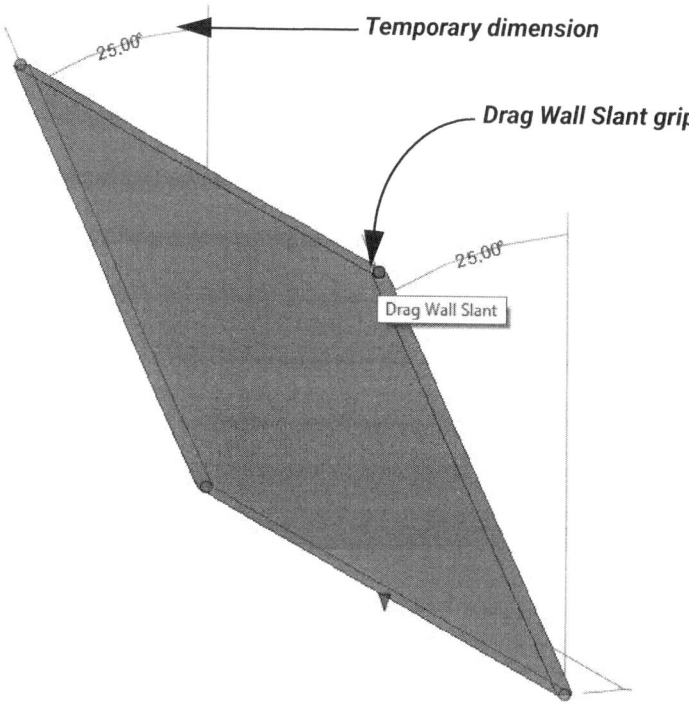

Figure 7–16

- When modifying a tapered wall, you have the ability to modify the Drag Wall Exterior Face Slant and Drag Wall Interior Face Slant grips or modify the temporary dimension in a 3D, section, elevation, or isometric view, as shown in Figure 7–17.

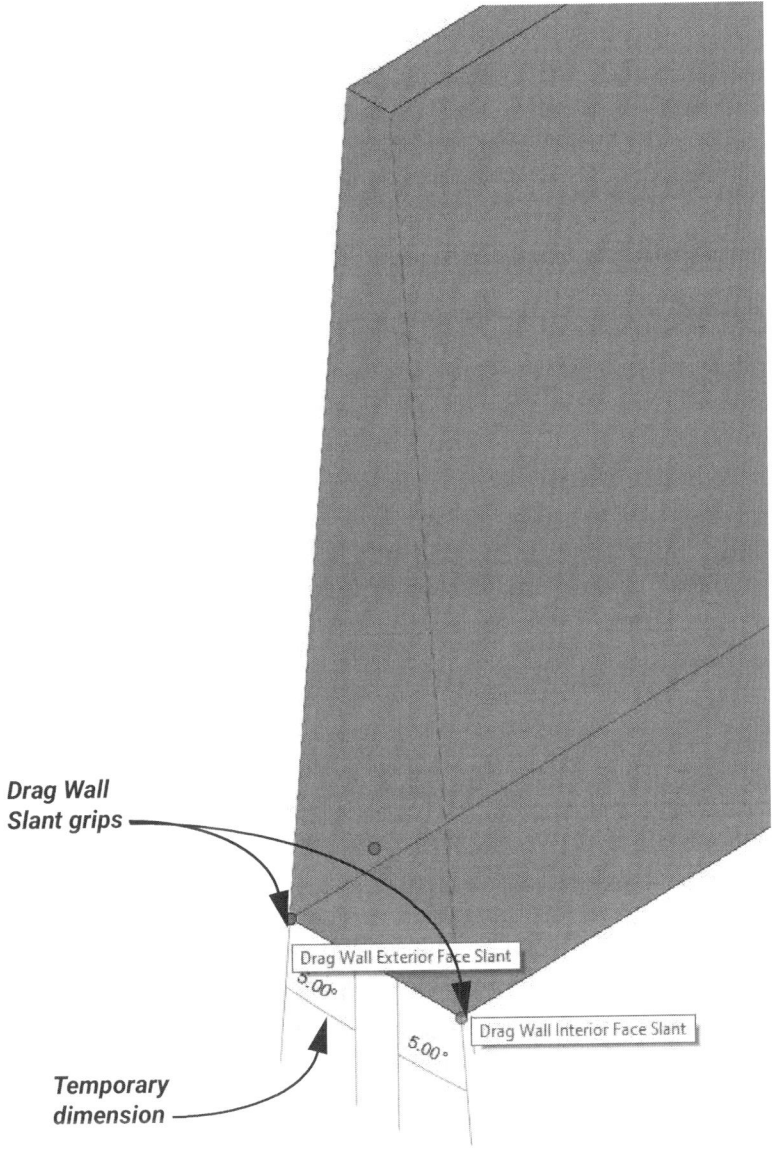

Figure 7–17

- You can set the wall's structural properties as **Non-bearing**, **Bearing**, **Shear**, or **Structural Combined**, as shown in Figure 7–18.

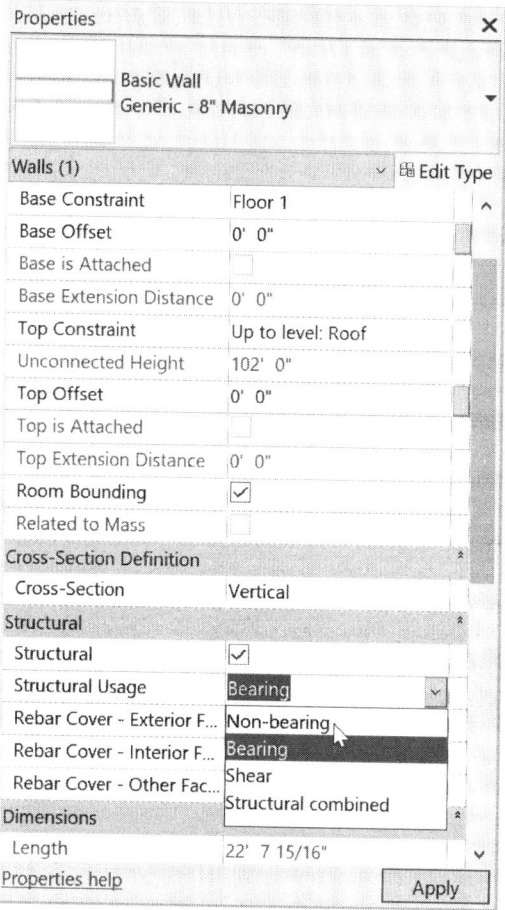

Figure 7–18

Wall Joins

The software automatically joins walls with common materials when they come together at an intersection, as shown on the left in Figure 7–19. However, there are times when you do not want the walls to clean up, such as when one fire-rated wall butts into another, or when a wall touches a column surround, as shown on the right in Figure 7–19.

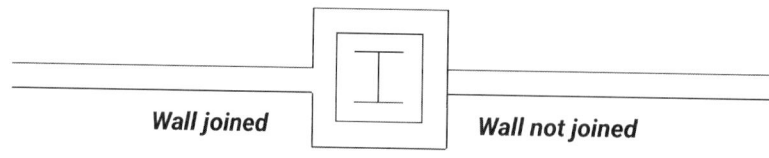

Figure 7–19

- While you are creating walls, change the *Join Status* to **Disallow** in the Options Bar.

- If a wall is already placed, select the wall and right-click on the Drag Wall End control at the end of the wall and select **Disallow Join**, as shown on the left in Figure 7–20. Once the end is not joined, you can drag it to the appropriate location, as shown on the right in Figure 7–20.

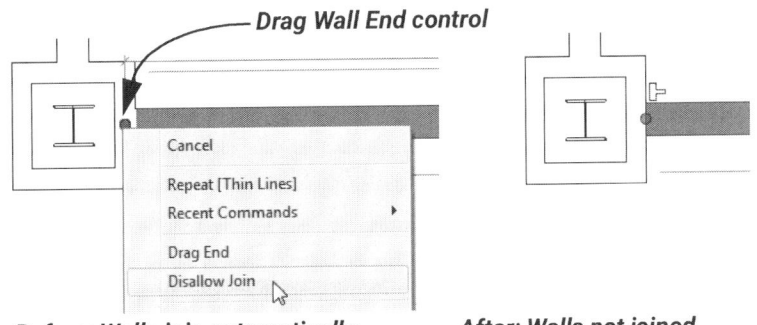

Before: Walls join automatically   *After: Walls not joined*

Figure 7–20

- To rejoin the walls, click ⌐ (Allow Join) or right-click on the end control and select **Allow Join**. Manually drag the wall back to where you want it to touch the target wall.

Editing Wall Profiles

Walls often follow the contours of a site or an angle, such as following a line of stairs, as shown in Figure 7–21. If needed, you can edit the profile of a wall.

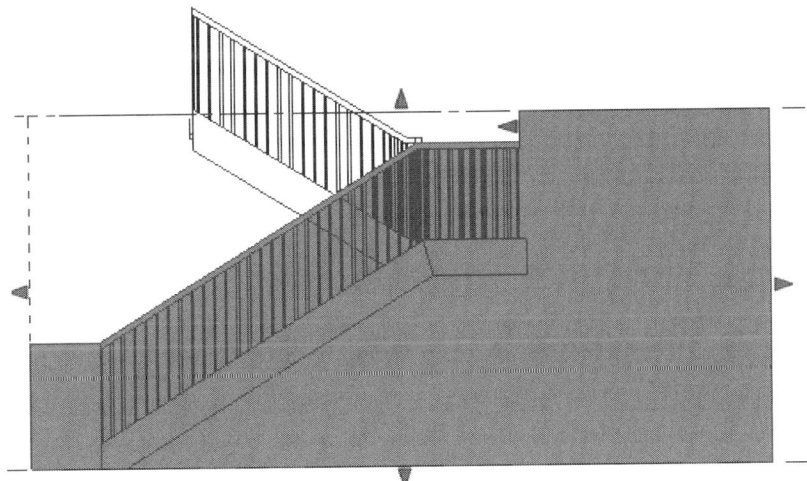

Figure 7–21

How To: Edit the Profile of a Wall

1. Open an elevation or section view in which you can see the face of the wall that you want to edit.
2. Select the wall (by highlighting the wall boundary). You can also double-click on a wall to edit the profile.
   - You cannot edit the profile of a tapered wall.
3. In the *Modify | Walls* tab>Model panel, click (Edit Profile). The wall is outlined in magenta, indicating the profile of the wall.
4. In the *Modify | Walls>Edit Profile* tab>Draw panel, use the tools to modify the profile sketch of the wall, as shown on the top in Figure 7–22.

   Note: *The sketch must form a continuous loop. Verify that the lines are clean without any gaps or overlaps. Use any of the tools in the Modify panel to clean up the sketch.*

5. Once the profile is complete, click (Finish Edit Mode). The wall now follows the new profile, as shown on the bottom in Figure 7–22.

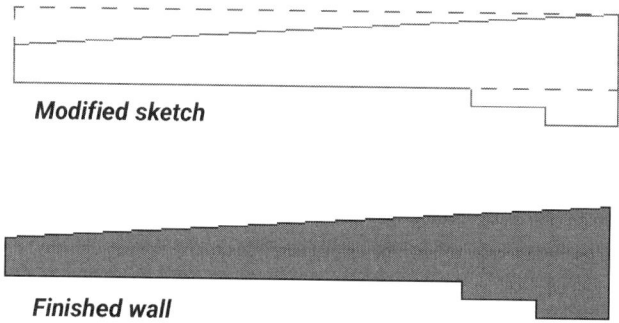

Figure 7–22

- After you adjust the sketch, you can add isolated footings to create the appropriate shape.
- For more information about editing walls and wall joins, see *A.3 Editing Wall Joins*.

Wall Openings

You can add openings in walls that are not windows or doors by using the **Wall Opening** tool. This creates rectangular openings for both straight and curved walls, as shown in Figure 7–23.

Foundations

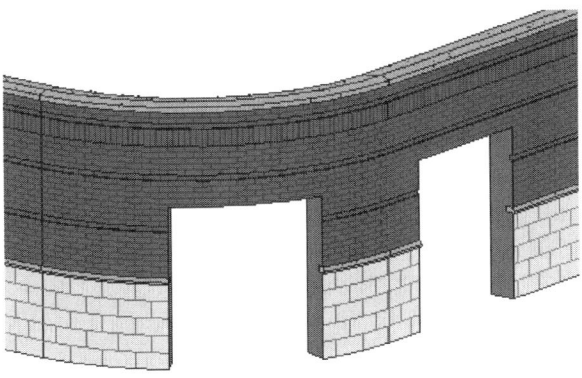

Figure 7–23

How To: Add Wall Openings

1. Open a plan, elevation, section, or 3D view.
2. In the *Architecture* tab>Openings panel, click (Wall Opening).
3. Select the wall.
4. Pick two points on the diagonal to determine the opening size, if in elevation, section, or 3D view. If you are in plan, you need to pick the start and stop points for the wall opening.

- You can use temporary dimensions to size the opening while in the command and both temporary dimensions and shape handles to modify the opening when it is selected, as shown in Figure 7–24.

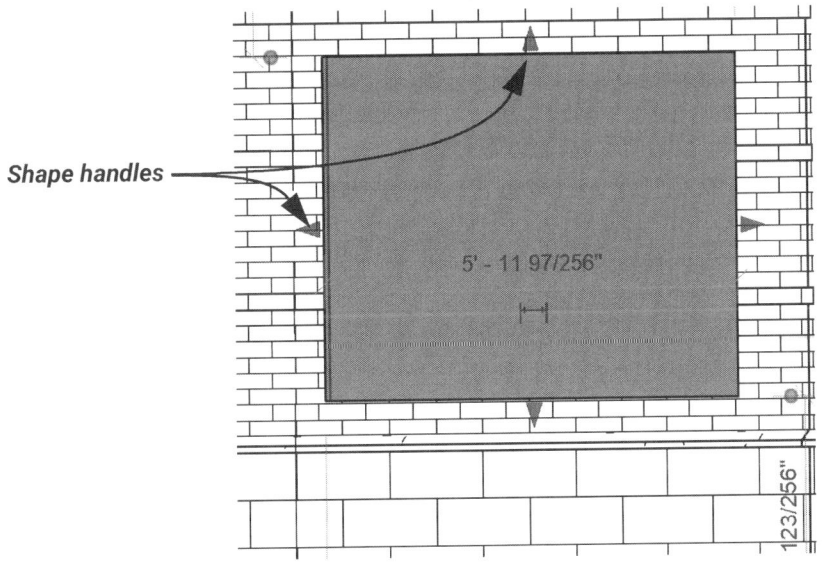

Figure 7–24

> **Hint: Matching Properties**
>
> You can select an existing wall and use it to assign the wall type and instance properties to other walls by using the **Match Type** command. This command also works with all elements that have types.
>
> 1. In the *Modify* tab>Clipboard panel, click ▣ (Match Type), or type **MA**. The cursor changes to an arrow with a clean paintbrush.
> 2. Select the source element that you want all of the others to match. The paintbrush changes to look as if it has been dipped in black paint, as shown in Figure 7–25.
>
>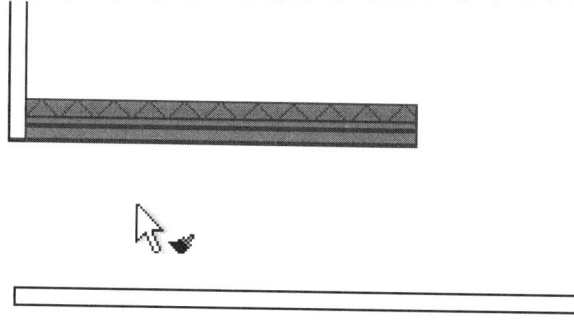
>
> Figure 7–25
>
> 3. To select more than one element, in the *Modify | Match Type* tab>Multiple panel, click ▣ (Select Multiple). You can then use windows, crossings, <Ctrl>, and <Shift> to create a selection set of elements to change.
> 4. Click ✓ (Finish) to apply the type to the selection.
> - Click in an empty space in the view to empty the brush so that you can repeat the command with a different element.
> - Elements to be matched must be of the same type (e.g., all walls, all doors, etc.).
> 5. Click ▷ (Modify) to end the command.

7.3 Adding Wall Footings

Footings are appended to the bottom of a wall, which means that any change to the base of the host wall influences the footing. This occurs for lateral movement and horizontal movement. For the example shown in Figure 7–26, when the wall profile changes based on a sloped site (as shown on the left), the footing breaks and follows the modified profile (as shown on the right). This is accomplished by editing the profile of the foundation wall.

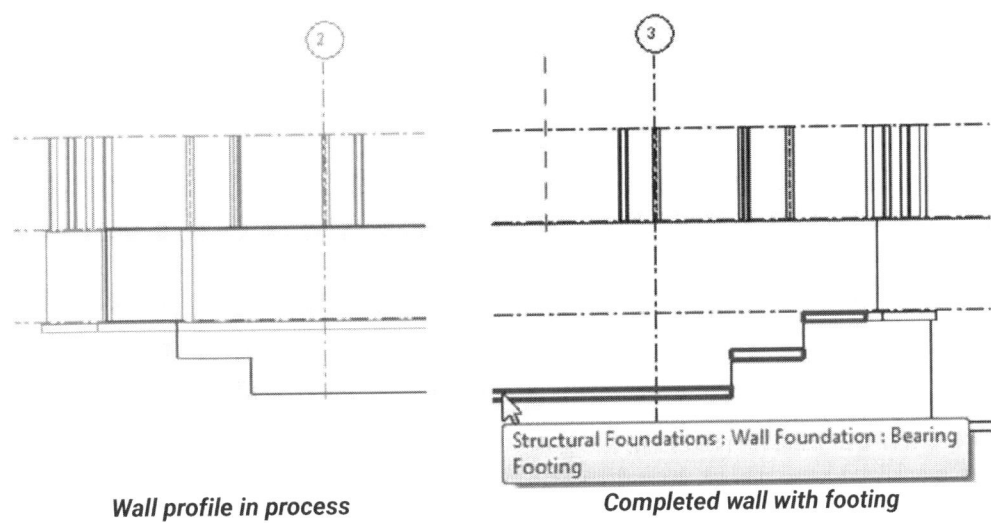

Figure 7–26

- Once a footing is in place, you can add reinforcement in a section view, as shown in Figure 7–27. With the advantages of having a true foundation in place, you can accurately tag and schedule the footings.

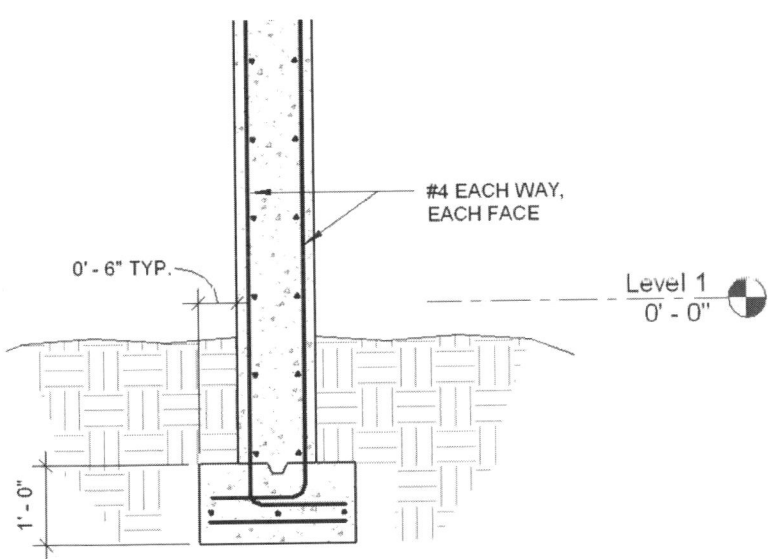

Figure 7–27

- You can edit a footing's profile the same way you would edit a wall profile.
- You can apply two types of continuous footing systems, as shown in Figure 7–28. You must have walls in your model to add a footing system.
    - **Retaining footings:** A footing with one side offset to accommodate additional lateral loads and reinforcement.
    - **Bearing footings:** A footing with an equal distance on either side of the bearing wall.

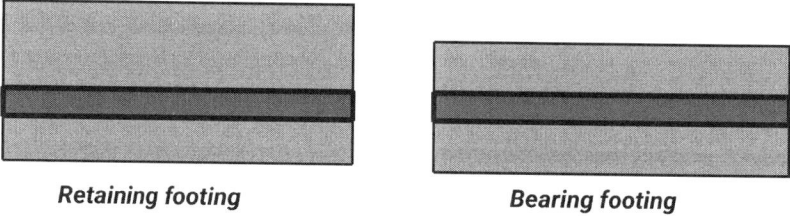

Retaining footing   *Bearing footing*

Figure 7–28

How To: Place a Bearing or Retaining Footing

1. Create or use existing walls in a 3D, section, or elevation view.
    - A wall must be in place to add a bearing or retaining footing.
2. Open a foundation plan and set it up so that the walls are displayed and you can select them.
3. In the *Structure* tab>Foundation panel, click (Structural Foundation: Wall) to start the **Structural Foundations: Wall** command, or type **FT**.
4. In the Type Selector, select a type, as shown in Figure 7–29.

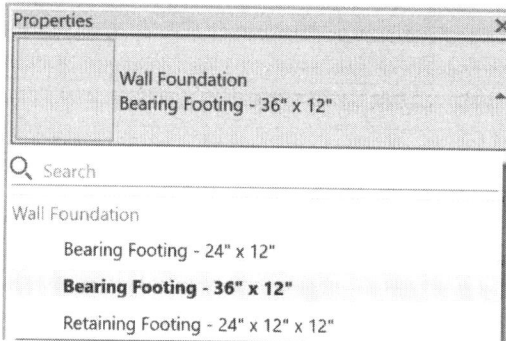

Figure 7–29

5. Select a wall. The footing is placed beneath the wall, as shown in Figure 7-30.

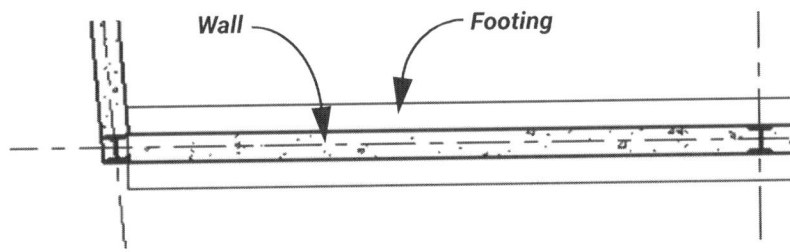

Figure 7-30

- To select multiple walls, hover over one wall and then press <Tab> to select all connected walls. Alternatively, in the *Modify | Place Wall Foundation* tab>Multiple panel, click (Select Multiple). Select the walls using any selection method and click (Finish) to place the footings.

- You can flip retaining footings using the Flip control, as shown in Figure 7-31.

Figure 7-31

> **Hint: Materials**
>
> When you are creating some types, such a wall footings, one option is to set the *Structural Material*. In Type Properties, in the *Materials and Finishes* section, click in the *Value* column and then click ⋯ (Browse), as shown in Figure 7–32.

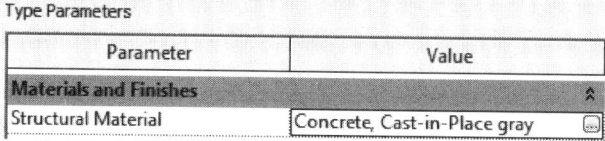

Figure 7–32

In the Material Browser (shown in Figure 7–33), specify the material you want to use and click **OK**.

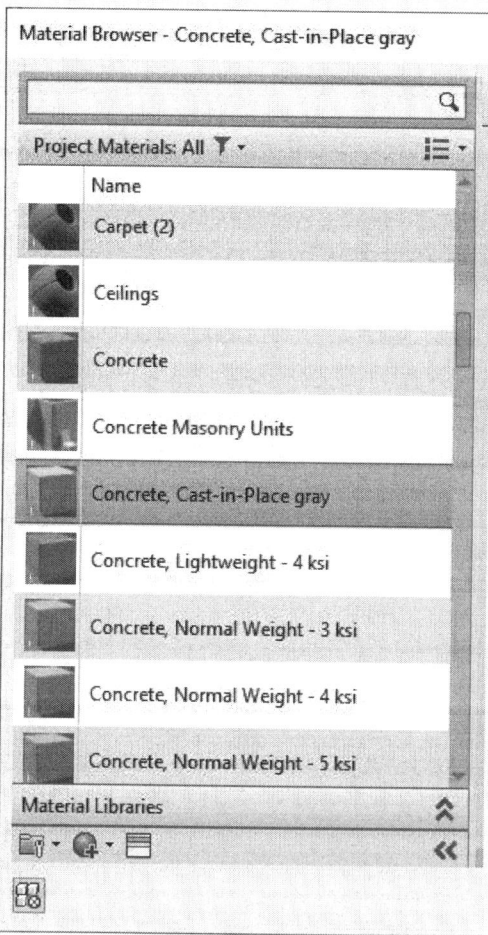

Figure 7–33

Practice 7a
Model Walls and Wall Footings

Practice Objectives

- Place structural walls.
- Create and apply wall footings.

In this practice, you will model the perimeter foundation walls, as shown in Figure 7–34. (Grids have been turned off in the image for clarity.)

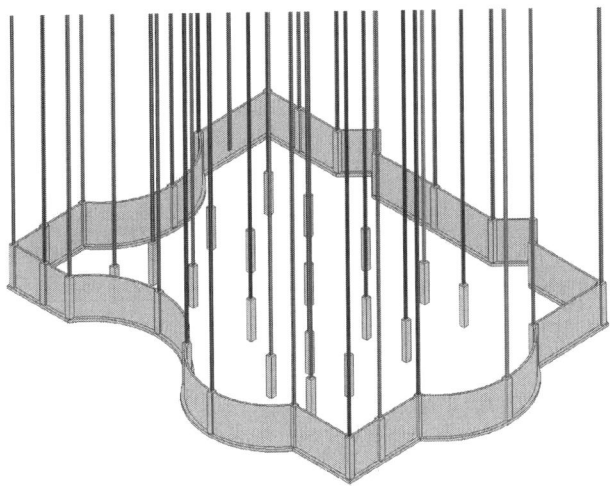

Figure 7–34

Task 1: Add walls.

1. Open **Structural-Walls.rvt** from the practice files folder.
2. Open the **Structural Plan: 00 GROUND FLOOR** view. (The green lines are the outline of the building.)
3. In the *Structure* tab>Structure panel, click (Wall: Structural).
4. In the Type Selector, select **Basic Wall: Exterior - 8" Concrete**.
5. In the Options Bar, set the *Depth* to **00 T.O. FOOTING** and ensure that the *Location Line* is set to **Wall Centerline** and that **Chain** is selected.
6. In the *Modify | Place Structural Wall* tab>Draw panel, click (Line).

7. Select the start point by snapping to the **G1** grid intersection, as shown in Figure 7–35.

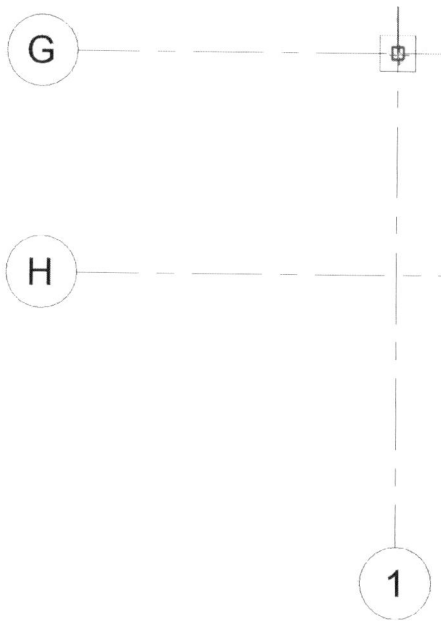

Figure 7–35

8. Draw the wall up to the **E1** grid intersection.

9. In the Draw panel, click (Start-End-Radius Arc). Select the second point at the **C1** grid intersection and then the third point anywhere along the green arc to specify the radius of the arc, as shown in Figure 7–36.

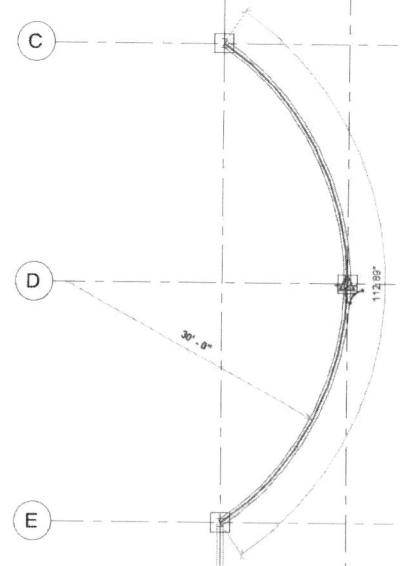

Figure 7–36

Foundations

10. Click ∕ (Line) again and select the **B1** grid intersection.
11. Following the green outline, continue drawing walls all the way around the perimeter, as shown in Figure 7–37.

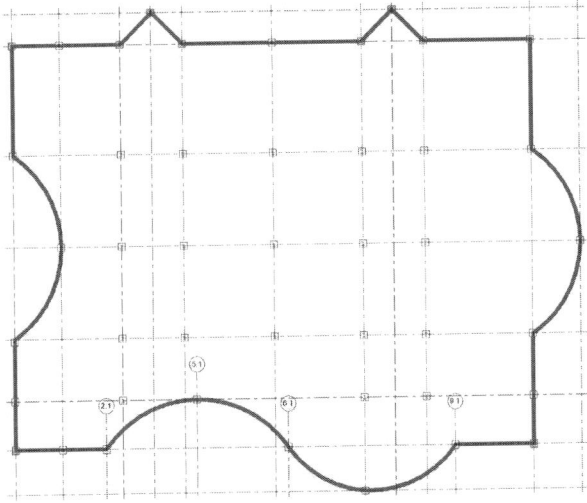

Figure 7–37

12. Click ▷ (Modify).
13. Save the project.

Task 2: Apply wall footings.

1. Open the **Structural Plans: 000 FOUNDATION PLAN** view.
2. In the *Structure* tab>Foundation panel, click 🖉 (Structural Foundation: Wall), or type **FT**.
3. In the Type Selector, select the **Wall Foundation: Bearing Footing - 36" x 12"**, as shown in Figure 7–38.

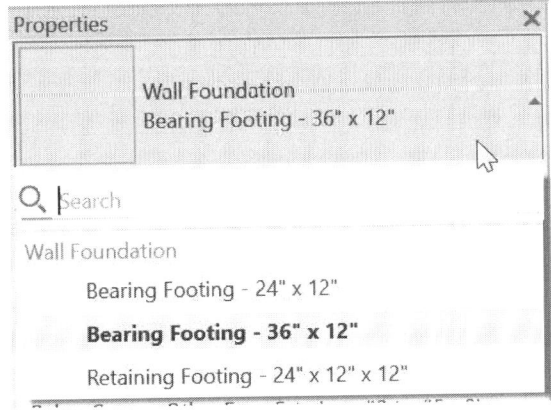

Figure 7–38

4. Hover the cursor over one of the existing walls and press <Tab> to highlight the entire wall system. Click to select the walls. The footing is placed under the entire structure.

5. If you do not see the new wall foundation elements, you might be in an area of the view where they are not visible. Open the **Structural Plans: 000 FOUNDATION PLAN** view.

6. Click (Modify).

7. In the Quick Access Toolbar, click (Default 3D View) to go to a 3D view. Verify that the footing is placed correctly, as shown in part in Figure 7–39. Change the visual style as needed.

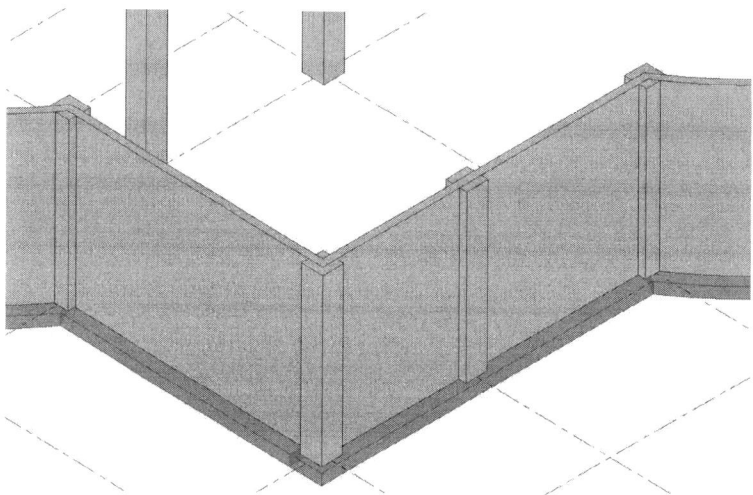

Figure 7–39

8. Save and close the project.

End of practice

7.4 Adding Isolated Footings

Footings for columns (shown in Figure 7–40) are placed using the **Structural Foundation: Isolated** command. When you select a column, the footing automatically attaches to the bottom of the column. This is true even when the bottom of the column is on a lower level than the view you are working in.

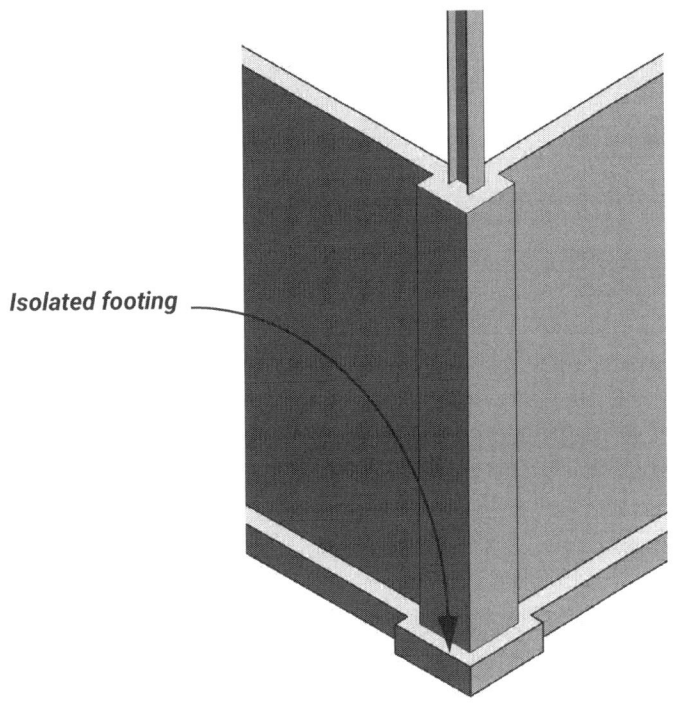

Figure 7–40

How To: Place an Isolated Footing

1. Open a plan view, such as a top of footing structural floor plan.

2. In the *Structure* tab>Foundation panel, click (Isolated) to start the **Structural Foundation: Isolated** command.

3. In the Type Selector, select a footing type.

4. In the view, click to place the individual footing, as shown in Figure 7–41.
   - If needed, press <Spacebar> to rotate the isolated footings after they are placed

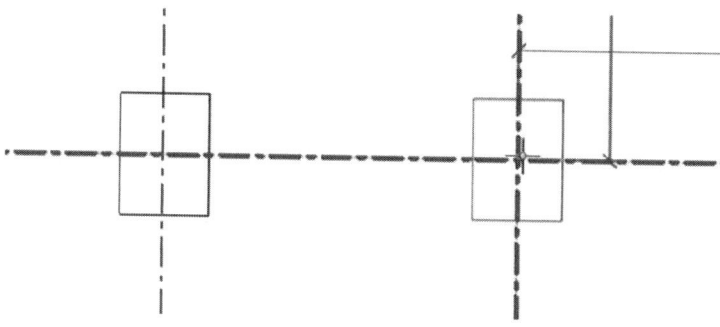

Figure 7–41

- To add more than one footing at a time, in the *Modify | Place Isolated Foundation* tab>Multiple panel, select (At Grids) or (At Columns) and select the grids or columns.
  - If needed, press <Spacebar> to rotate the isolated footings after they are placed.
- If the material of the wall footing and the material of the isolated footing are the same, they automatically join, as shown in Figure 7–42.

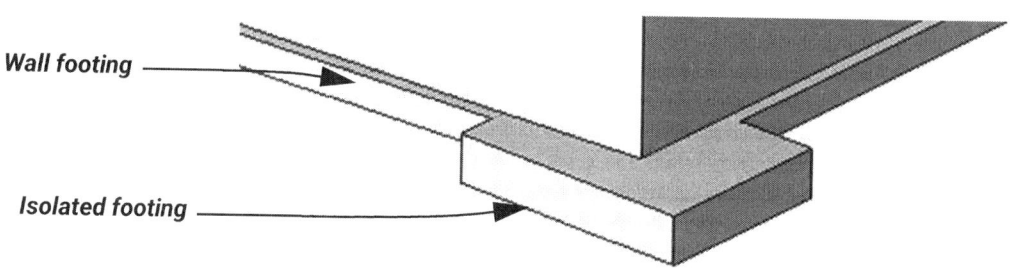

Figure 7–42

Foundations

> **Hint: Foundation Element Properties**
>
> Some of the element properties are automatically generated from the location and size of the element in the model and are grayed out, for example *Host*, *Elevation at Top*, and *Elevation at Bottom* as shown in Figure 7–43. These can be used in tags and schedules.

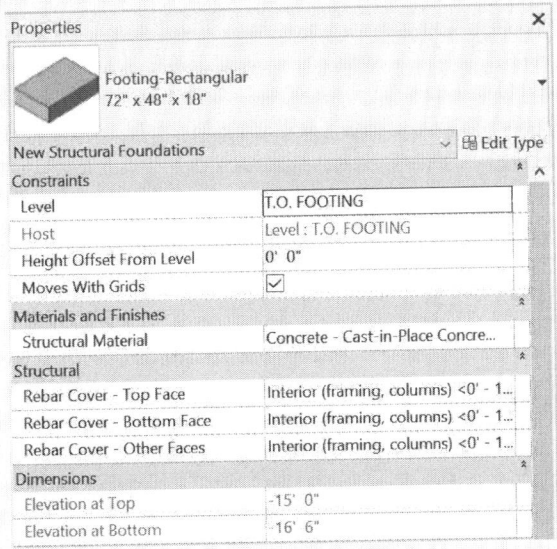

Figure 7–43

Working with Custom Families

Sometimes you need to work with a custom family that has parameters that you can manipulate to fit a specific situation. For example, to add the step footings shown in Figure 7–44, you need to insert an angled isolated footing and modify it to fit the exact size and location.

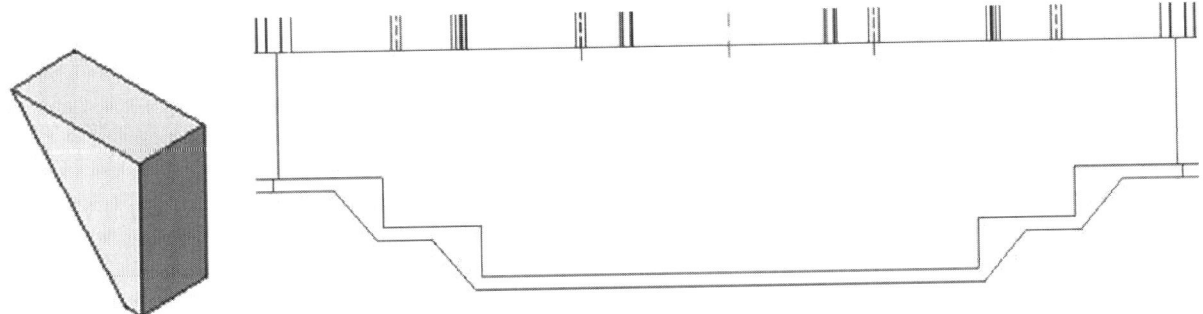

Figure 7–44

How To: Load, Insert, and Modify a Custom Footing

1. Open a plan view.
2. In the *Structure* tab>Foundation panel, click (Isolated).
3. In the *Modify | Place Isolated Foundation* tab>Mode panel, click (Load Family).
4. In the Load Family dialog box, find the structural foundation family that you want to use and click **Open**.
5. Place the footing in the plan view. It might not be in the right place, but you can modify it in a section or elevation view.
6. Open an elevation or section view.
7. Move the footing to the correct location. As long as it is in line with another footing, it automatically cleans up, as shown in Figure 7–45.

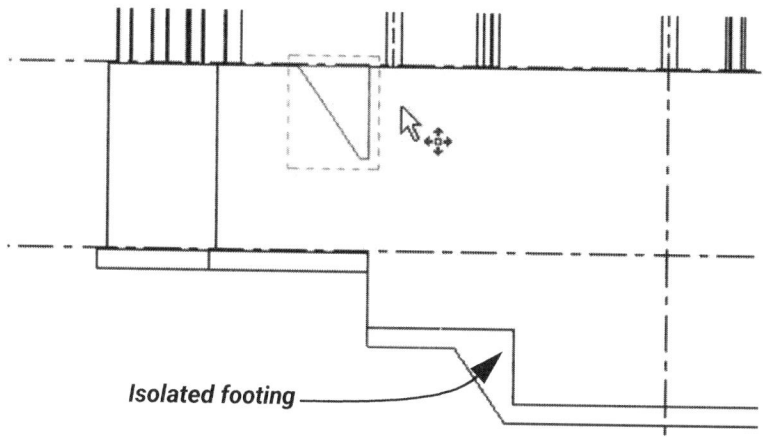

Figure 7–45

- Use (Align) to align the isolated footing with the footing already in the model. When it is aligned, select the lock, as shown in Figure 7–46. This ensures that if the elevation of the footing wall changes, the step footing will also adjust appropriately.

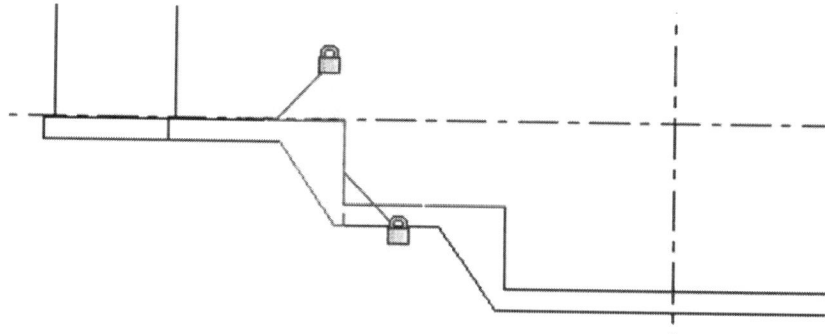

Figure 7–46

- Some custom families have sizing options in either Properties (per instance) or in the Type Properties (as shown in Figure 7–47) so that you can create additional types in various sizes as needed in the project.

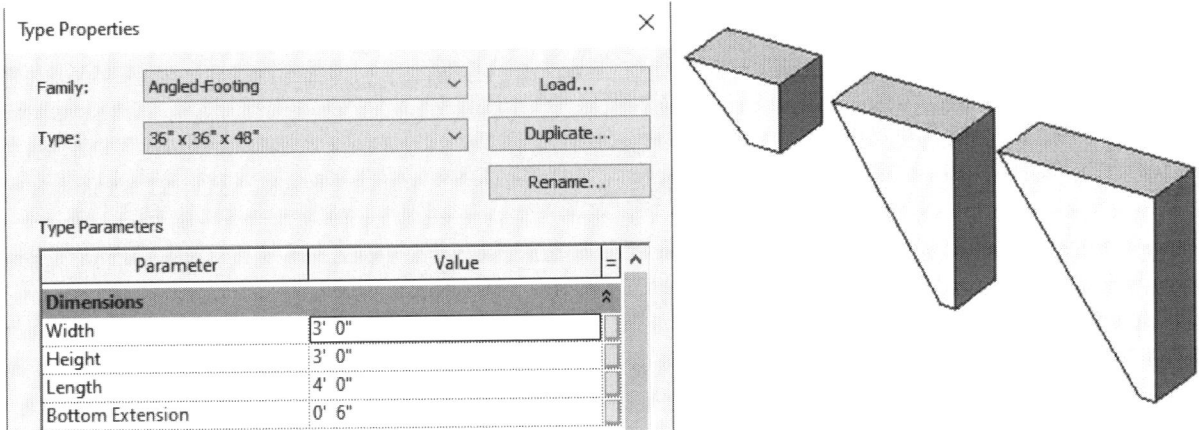

Figure 7–47

Practice 7b
Add Isolated Footings

Practice Objectives

- Place isolated footings.
- Modify a wall profile and add stepped footings.

In this practice, you will place isolated footings, as shown in Figure 7–48. You will also create a series of stepped footings by modifying a wall profile and adding custom footings.

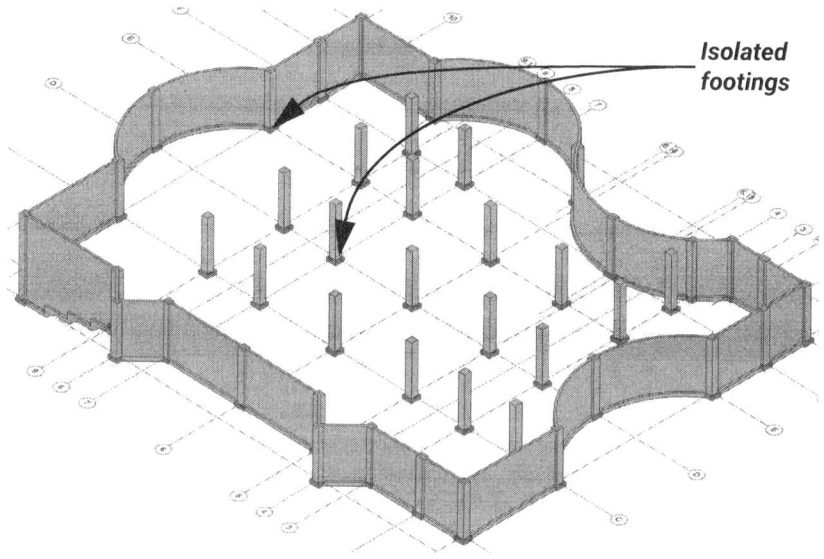

Figure 7–48

Task 1: Place isolated footings.

1. Open **Structural-Footings.rvt** from the practice files folder.
2. Open the **Structural Plans: 00 T.O. FOOTING** view.
3. In the *Structure* tab>Foundation panel, click (Isolated).
4. In Properties, click (Edit Type).
5. In the Type Properties dialog box, click **Duplicate...** and name it **36"x36"x12"**.

6. Set the following values for each of the parameters below, as shown in Figure 7–49:
   - *Width*: **3'-0"**
   - *Length*: **3'-0"**
   - *Thickness*: **1'-0"**

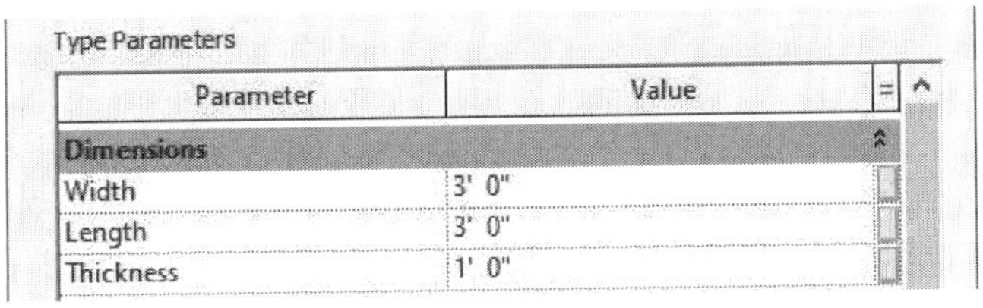

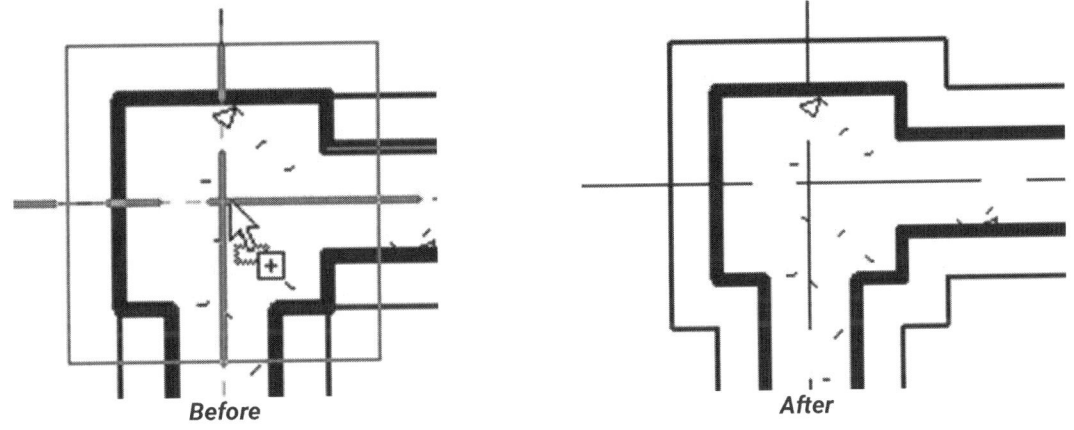

Figure 7–49

7. Click **OK**.
8. Zoom in to the column at the **B1** grid intersection and place the isolated footing. The isolated footing and wall footing automatically join together, as shown in Figure 7–50.

Figure 7–50

9. In the *Modify | Place Isolated Foundation* tab>Multiple panel, click (At Columns). Use a pick window to select all of the columns and click (Finish).
10. Reopen the default 3D view.

11. There should be an isolated footing under each pier and pilaster, as shown in Figure 7–51.

    Note: The steel columns were hidden in this figure for clarity.

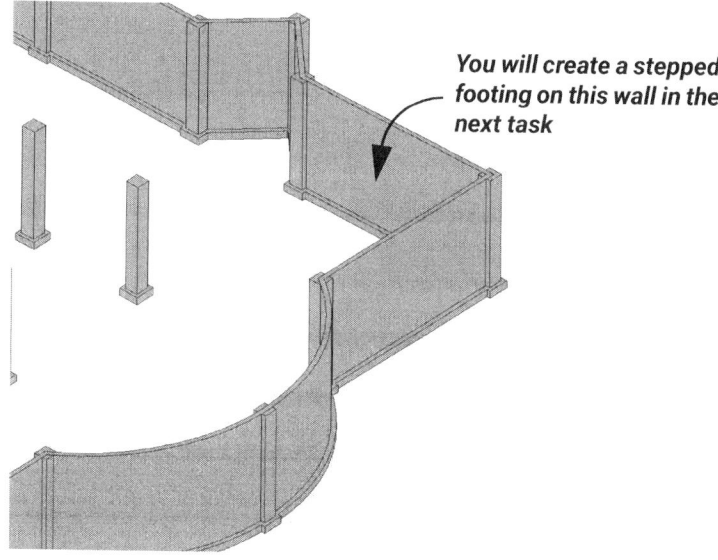

Figure 7–51

12. Save the project.

Task 2: Modify the profile of a wall and add stepped footings.

1. Open the **Elevations (Building Elevation): North** view.
2. Zoom in on the left end of the foundation wall and select the wall located between grid lines **10** and **9**, as shown in Figure 7–52.

    Hint: You can turn on (Crop View) and (Show Crop Region) to show less in this view and make it easier to see the grid lines.

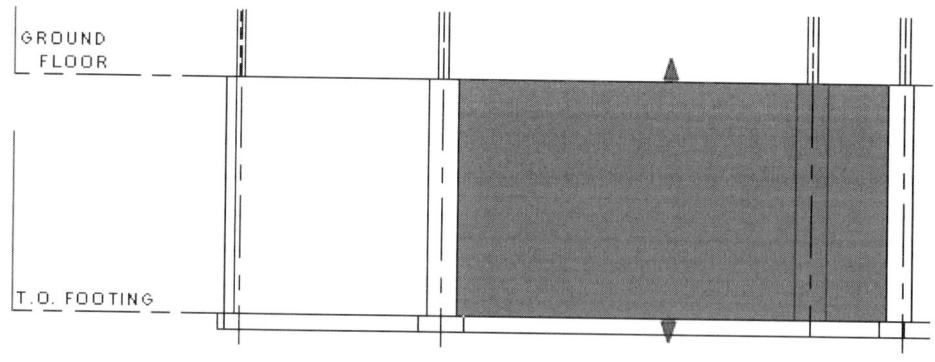

Figure 7–52

3. In the *Modify | Walls* tab>Mode panel, click (Edit Profile).

4. Select the wall. Click on the lock at the bottom of the wall.
5. Using the dimensions shown in Figure 7–54, use the Draw and Modify tools to add the stepped profile shown in Figure 7–54. The dimensions are for information only.

   Make sure to remove the bottom of the wall's constraint by clicking on the lock or by moving the line and clicking **Remove Constraints** in the Error - cannot be ignored dialog box that displays as shown in Figure 7–53.

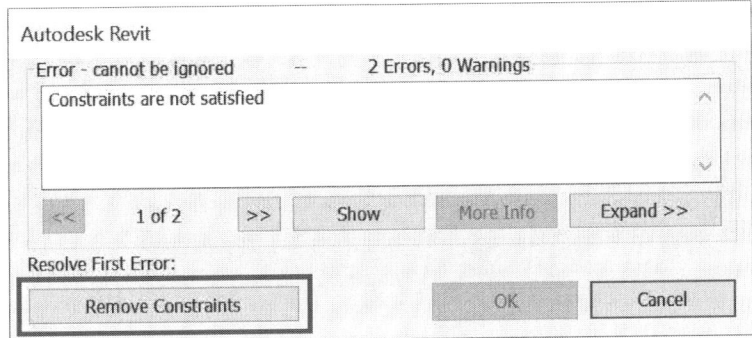

Figure 7–53

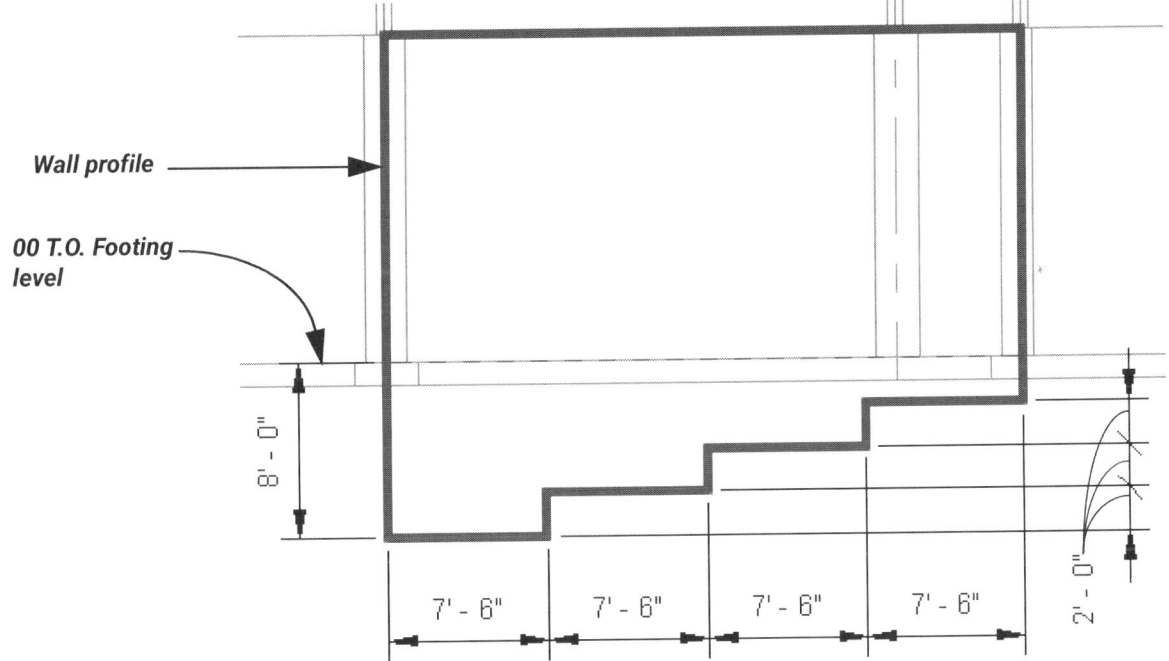

Figure 7–54

6. Click ✓ (Finish Edit Mode). The wall profile is modified along with the footings, as shown in Figure 7–55.

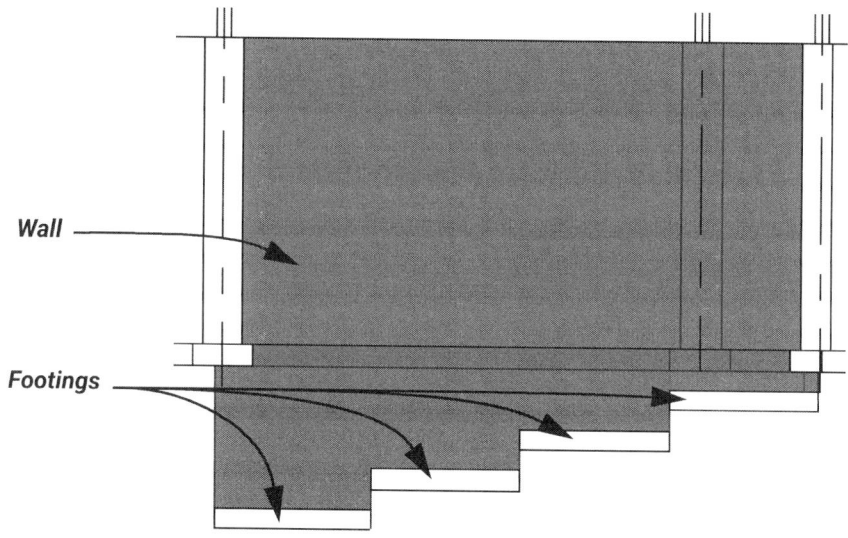

Figure 7–55

7. Open the **Structural Plans: 00 T.O. Footing** view and zoom in on the upper right corner of the **B10** grid intersection. You should be able to see lines that show the steps of the footing below.

8. In the *Structure* tab>Model panel, click (Place a Component), or type **CM**.

9. In the Type Selector, select **Angled-Footing: 24" x 24" x 36"**.

10. Place three footings along the wall, similar to those shown in Figure 7–56.

    Note: The exact location does not matter at this time.

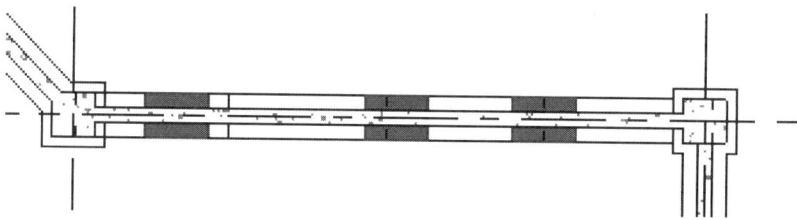

Figure 7–56

11. Return to the **North** elevation view. The three footings are still on the level where they were placed, as shown in Figure 7–57.

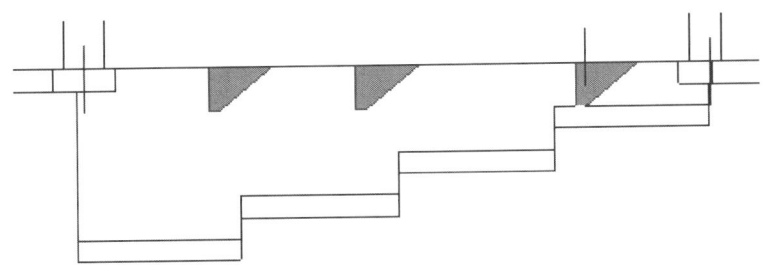

Figure 7–57

12. In the *Modify* tab>Modify panel, click (Align), or type **AL**.
13. Align each angled footing to the wall footings, as shown in Figure 7–58.

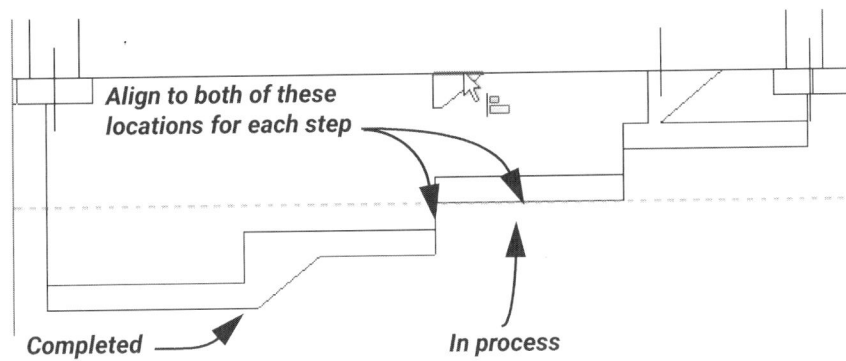

Figure 7–58

14. View the new footings in 3D, as shown in Figure 7–59.

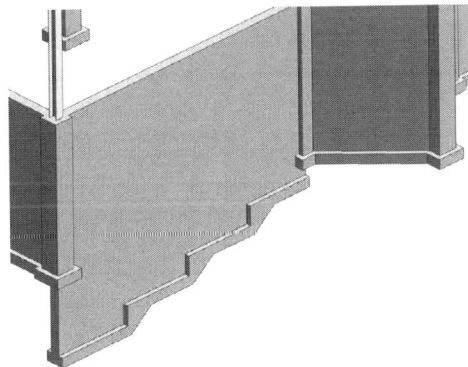

Figure 7–59

15. (Optional) Modify the nearby wall, columns, and footings to match up with the new stepped footings.
16. Save and close the project.

End of practice

Chapter Review Questions

1. Which of the following are ways that you can create walls in a project? (Select all that apply.)

   a. Draw Lines

   b. Pick Lines

   c. Insert Lines

   d. Pick Face

2. Which command do you use to insert a pier or a pilaster such as those shown in Figure 7–60?

   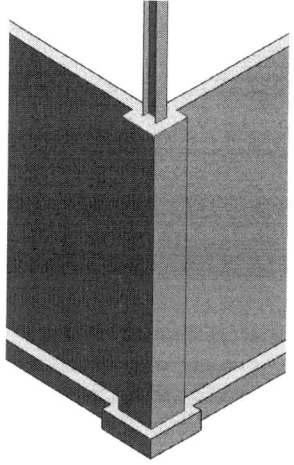

   Figure 7–60

   a. Structural Foundation

   b. Isolated Foundation

   c. Structural Column

   d. Isolated Column

3. The 🔲 (Structural Foundation: Wall) command requires a host wall to already be in place.

   a. True

   b. False

4. Some walls are made from multiple layers of materials, such as brick, block, and drywall, as shown on the bottom in Figure 7–61. If the hatching for these materials is not displayed (as shown at the top in Figure 7–61), how do you change this?

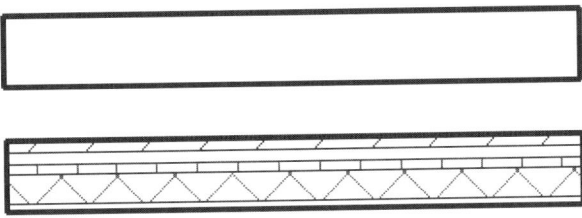

Figure 7–61

   a. Set the *Visual Style* to **Realistic**.
   b. Set the *Detail Level* to **Medium**.
   c. Set the *View Scale* to be higher.
   d. Set the *Phase* to **New**.

5. Which command do you use to add a custom footing type under a wall such as the ones shown in Figure 7–62?

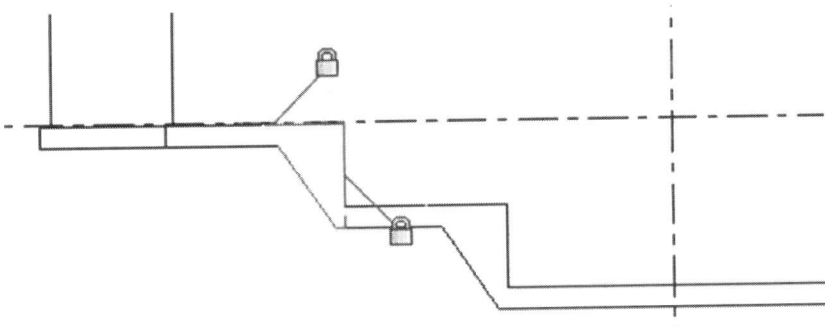

Figure 7–62

   a. Component
   b. Structural Foundation: Isolated
   c. Structural Foundation: Wall
   d. Component: Structural Foundation

6. Which command do you use to add a custom footing type under a wall such as the ones shown in Figure 7–63?

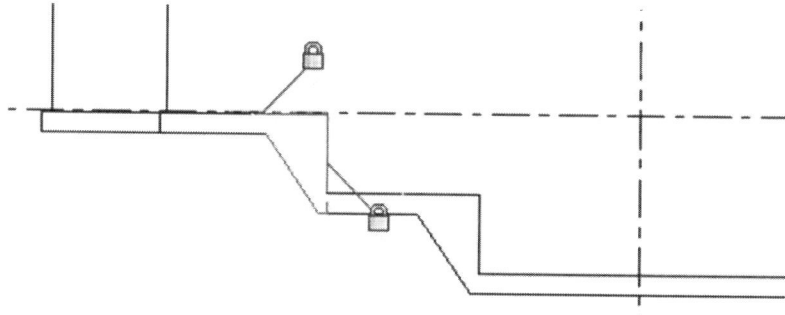

Figure 7–63

   a. Component
   b. Structural Foundation: Isolated
   c. Structural Foundation: Wall
   d. Component: Structural Foundation

7. Which of the following are potential differences between the column surround wall and the associated walls, as shown in Figure 7–64? (Select all that apply.)

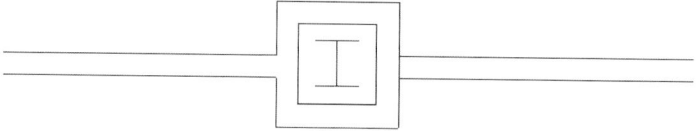

Figure 7–64

   a. The column surround and wall on the left are made with the same wall type, while the wall type on the right is a different wall type.
   b. The wall on the left has been joined together with the column surround, while the wall on the right was set to **Disallow Join**.
   c. The wall on the left was trimmed against the column surround.
   d. The wall on the right was extended to the column surround.

8. Which of the following would be true if you changed the top constraint of one wall from an unconnected height to a level?

    a. All walls of that type would also change height.

    b. Only that wall would change height.

    c. You cannot change just one walls height.

Command Summary

Button	Command	Location
	Detail Level: Coarse	• View Control Bar
	Detail Level: Fine	• View Control Bar
	Detail Level: Medium	• View Control Bar
	Edit Profile	• **Ribbon:** (when a wall is selected) *Modify	Walls* tab>Mode panel
	Isolated	• **Ribbon:** *Structure* tab>Foundation panel
	Match Type	• **Ribbon:** *Modify* tab>Clipboard panel • **Shortcut:** MA
	Properties	• **Ribbon:** *Modify* tab>Properties panel • **Shortcut:** PP
	Structural Foundation: Wall	• **Ribbon:** *Structure* tab>Foundation panel
N/A	Type Selector	• **Properties palette** • **Ribbon:** *Modify* tab (*Optional*) • **Quick Access Toolbar** (*Optional*)
	Wall	• **Ribbon:** *Architecture* tab>Build panel
	Wall Opening	• **Ribbon:** *Architecture* tab>Opening panel
	Wall: Structural	• **Ribbon:** *Structure* tab>Structure panel

Chapter 8

Structural Framing

The skeleton of a building is its structural framing. Together, elements such as columns, beams, bracing, and trusses give buildings the stability they need. While the basic process of adding these elements to the project is simple, you also need to complete more complex tasks, such as manipulating connections (by setting bearing offsets, cantilevers, cut backs, and justifications), applying beam coping, and editing beam joins.

Learning Objectives

- Sketch individual beams for girders connecting columns and structural walls.
- Create beam systems of multiple similar sized beams spaced at equal intervals to speed up adding joists.
- Add bracing to support the integrity of other framing members.
- Make changes to framing members so that the connections fit the exact situation.
- Add trusses to support long spans of open space.

8.1 Modeling Structural Framing

Revit enables you to frame a building with wood, concrete, and steel framing and bracing, such as the steel example shown in Figure 8–1. You can add individual beams, as well as beam systems and bracing elements.

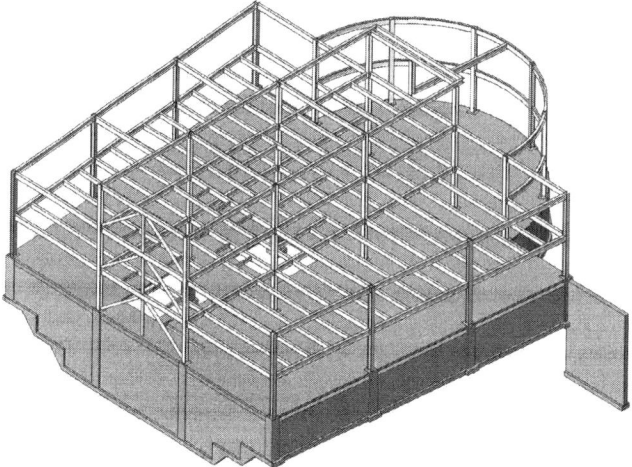

Figure 8–1

- Framing types include **Concrete**, **Light Gauge Steel**, **Precast Concrete**, **Steel**, and **Wood**.
- In views set to a **Coarse** detail level, the software assigns a line weight to the structural members based on their structural usage. For example, a girder displays in a heavier line weight than a joist, while a purlin displays with a dashed line, as shown in Figure 8–2.

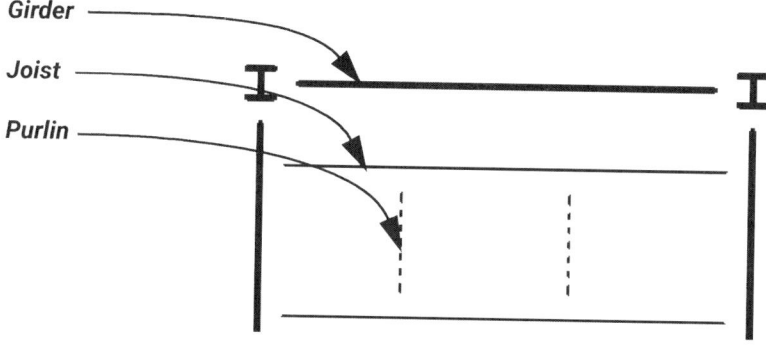

Figure 8–2

How To: Add Beams

1. In the *Structure* tab>Structure panel, click (Beam).
2. In the Type Selector, select a beam type.
3. In the Options Bar, specify the options, as shown in Figure 8–3 and described below.

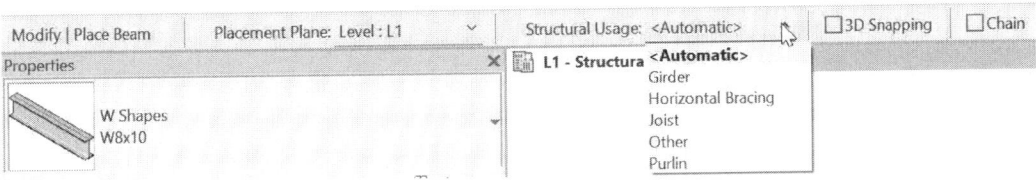

Figure 8–3

- *Placement Plane:* Defaults to the current level if you are in a plan view but can be modified to other levels.
- *Structural Usage:* Select a type (as shown in Figure 8–3), or accept the default of **<Automatic>**.
- *3D Snapping:* Select this if you want to draw a beam from one point to another at different heights.
- *Chain:* Select this if you want to draw a series of beams in a row.
    - To stay in the command and start another chain, press <Esc> once.

4. For automatic tagging, in the *Modify | Place Beam* tab>Tag panel, click (Tag on Placement).
5. In the *Modify | Place Beam* tab>Draw panel, use the Draw tools to draw the beams.
    - If needed, use (Split Element) to break beam into two beams.

How To: Add Multiple Beams on Grid Lines

1. Start the **Beam** command and specify the type and other options, as outlined above.
2. In the *Modify | Place Beam* tab>Multiple panel, click (On Grids).

3. Select the grid lines where you want to place the beams. A beam is placed between each grid intersection, as shown in Figure 8–4. Hold <Ctrl> to select more than one grid line, or use a selection window to select multiple grid lines at one time. Columns must be in place in order to add multiple beams at the same time.

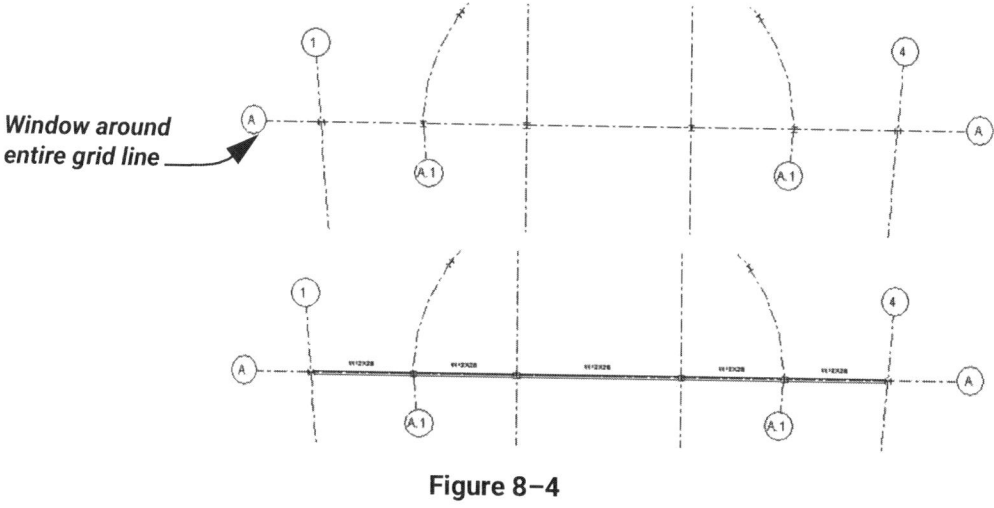

Figure 8–4

4. In the *Modify | Place Beam>On Grid Line* tab>Multiple panel, click ✓ (Finish).

- Sometimes this can be the quickest way to add beams. If you need to use various sizes of beams, when you are finished, select those beams and make any changes in the Type Selector.
    - If needed, use (Split Element) to break beam into two beams.

Beam Systems

Beam systems are layouts of parallel beams within a structural quadrant giving the structure added support, as shown in Figure 8–5. Typically used in joist layouts, beam systems can be set up to use either a fixed distance or number of beams.

- Beam systems can be created automatically with sufficient bounding elements (other beams). You can also sketch the boundary for a beam system.
- To use the automatic beam system, you need to have framing in the model already.

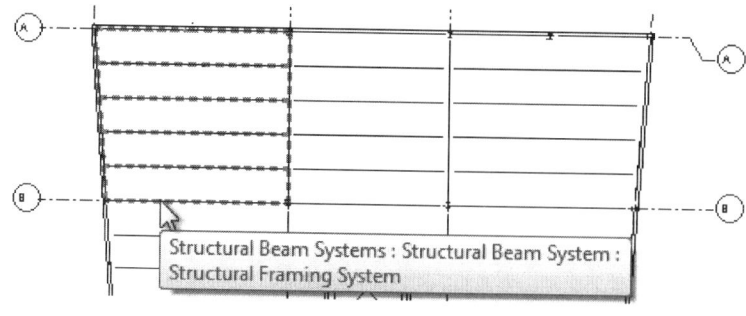

Figure 8–5

How To: Add Automatic Beam Systems

1. In the *Structure* tab>Structure panel, click (Beam System), or type **BS**.

2. In the *Modify | Place Structural Beam System* tab>Beam System panel, click (Automatic Beam System).

   - If you do not have framing in the level, you are directed to the *Modify | Create Beam System Boundary* tab, where you will need to create your bay boundary.

3. When (Tag on Placement) is selected, in the Options Bar, set the *Tag Style* (as shown in Figure 8-6).

   - **Framing:** Tags each individual member.
   - **System:** Places one tag for the entire framing system.

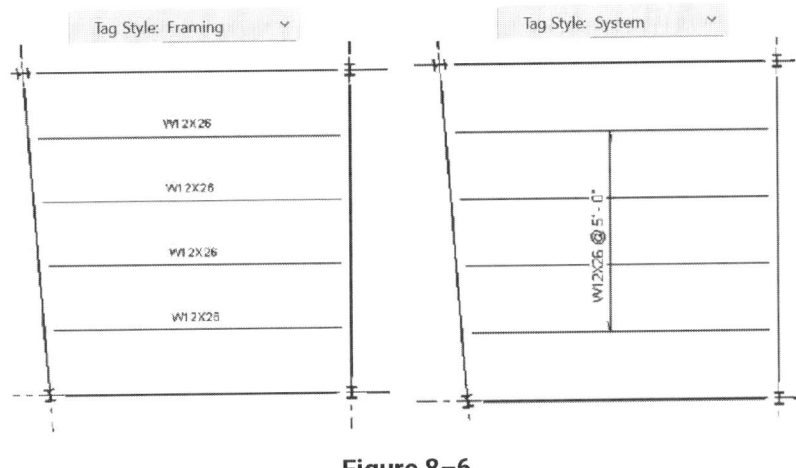

Figure 8-6

4. In the Options Bar (shown in Figure 8-7), set the *Beam Type*, *Justification*, and *Layout Rule*.

Figure 8-7

- The *Layout Rule* options include **Clear Spacing**, **Fixed Distance**, **Fixed Number**, and **Maximum Spacing**. Set the required distance or number.
- Make changes in Properties or in the Options Bar as needed to establish the required beam system.

5. Move the cursor over an existing beam until the guide lines display in the correct area and direction, as shown vertically and horizontally in Figure 8–8. This can also identify angled lines.

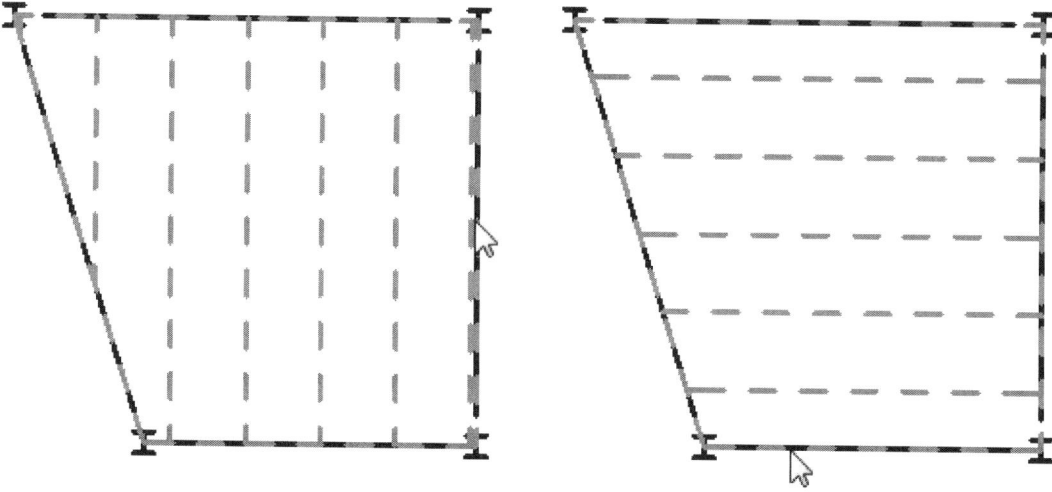

Figure 8–8

6. Select the existing beam to place the system.
7. Repeat this step in other bays, as needed.

- The beam system is one uniform group. You can change the beam type and spacing in the Options Bar or in Properties.

- If a grid line is moved, the beams automatically space themselves. If the bay increases beyond the minimum spacing, a beam is added. If the bay shrinks below the allowable spacing, a beam is removed.

- If you need to change the system to individual beams, in the *Modify | Structural Beam Systems* tab>Beam System panel, click (Remove Beam System). The individual beams remain but are no longer grouped together.

How To: Sketch a Beam System

1. In the *Structure* tab>Structure panel, click ▦ (Beam System).

2. In the *Modify | Place Structural Beam System* tab>Beam System panel, click ▦ (Sketch Beam System).

3. In the *Modify | Create Beam System Boundary* tab>Draw panel, click ▧ (Pick Supports) or use one of the other drawing tools. The first beam that you select will be the beam direction.

4. To modify the beam direction, from the Draw panel, click ▥ (Beam Direction) and select one of the sketch lines that you want the system to run parallel to, as shown on the top horizontal beam in Figure 8–9.

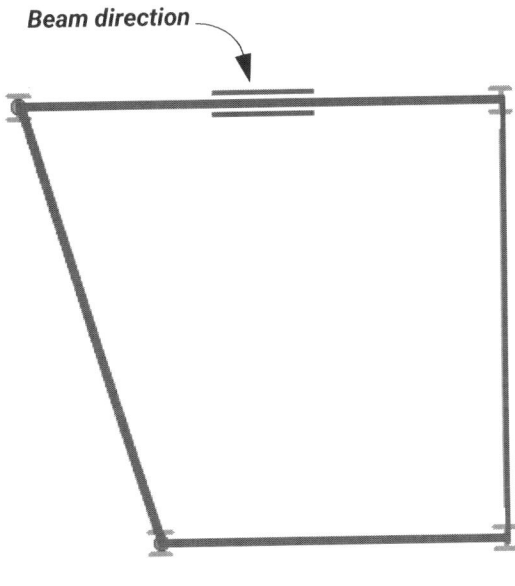

Figure 8–9

5. Clean up all of the corners so that there are no overlaps or gaps.

6. In the *Modify | Create Beam System Boundary* tab>Mode panel, click ✓ (Finish Edit Mode).

7. Make changes in Properties or in the Options Bar as needed to establish the required beam system.

- To include an opening in a beam system, select the beam system and in the *Modify | Structural Beam Systems* tab> Mode panel, click ▱ (Edit Boundary). In the Draw panel, select ▨ (Boundary Line) and draw another opening inside the original sketched boundary.

Adding Bracing

Braces automatically attach to other structural elements, such as beams, columns, and walls. They recognize typical snap points, such as the end point of a column and the middle of a beam, as shown in Figure 8–10.

Figure 8–10

- Bracing can be added in plan view or, more typically, in a framing elevation view.

How To: Add Bracing

1. Create and open a framing elevation.
2. In the *Structure* tab>Structure panel, click ⊠ (Brace).
3. In the Type Selector, select a brace type.
4. Pick two points for the end points of the brace.

Cross Bracing Settings

In plan view, cross bracing needs to be displayed graphically, usually by hidden lines. The software has a separate setting that controls cross bracing as viewed in a plan. This setting enables you to display bracing above, below, or both. You can set the bracing to be displayed as parallel lines or as a line at an angle, as shown in Figure 8–11.

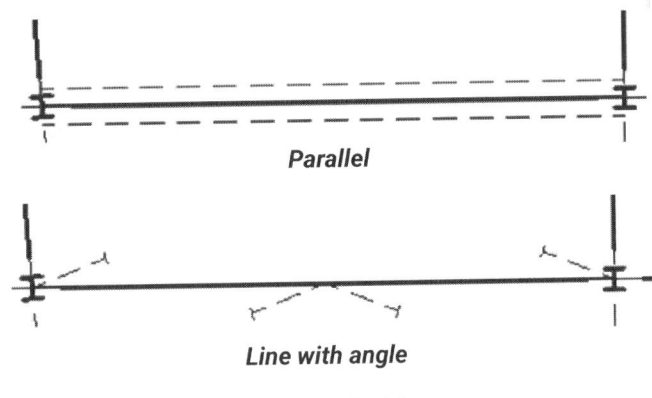

Figure 8–11

- In the *Manage* tab>Settings panel, expand (Structural Settings) and click (Structural Settings). In the Structural Settings dialog box, in the *Symbolic Representation Settings* tab, select the **Brace Symbols** options, as shown in Figure 8–12.

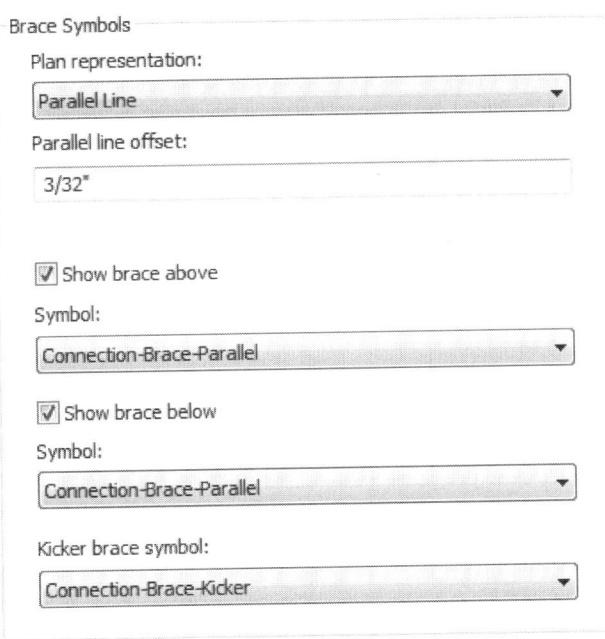

Figure 8–12

Hint: Copying Elements to Multiple Levels

Instead of drawing the same elements on each level, you can copy them to the clipboard and then paste them aligned to the other levels.

1. Select the required elements.

2. In the *Modify* contextual tab>Clipboard panel, click (Copy to Clipboard).

3. In the *Modify* tab>Clipboard panel, expand (Paste) and click (Aligned to Selected Levels).

4. In the Select Levels dialog box (shown in Figure 8–13), select the levels to which you want to copy the elements.

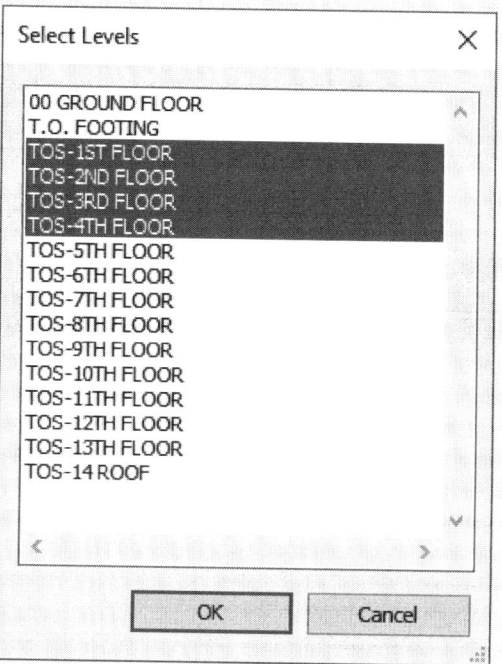

Figure 8–13

5. Click **OK**.

- This command is for copying model elements only. If you want to include tags or other annotations, use **Paste>Aligned to Selected Views**.

Practice 8a
Model Structural Framing

Practice Objectives

- Place beams and beam systems.
- Copy framing to additional levels.
- Create a framing elevation.
- Add bracing.

In this practice, you will add framing for one floor of a building (as shown in Figure 8–14), and then copy and paste the framing to the levels above. You will then add bracing to one part of the structure.

   Note: This graphic is modified for clarity.

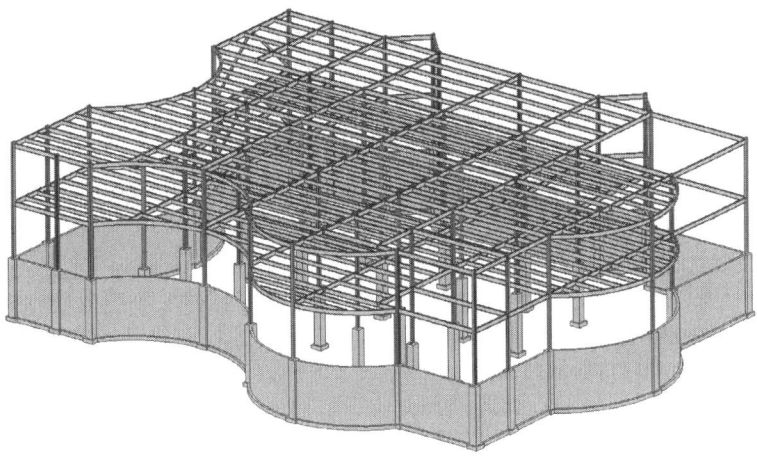

Figure 8–14

Task 1: Place perimeter beams.

In this task, you will add framing between each column (and in some cases, between beams), as shown in Figure 8–15.

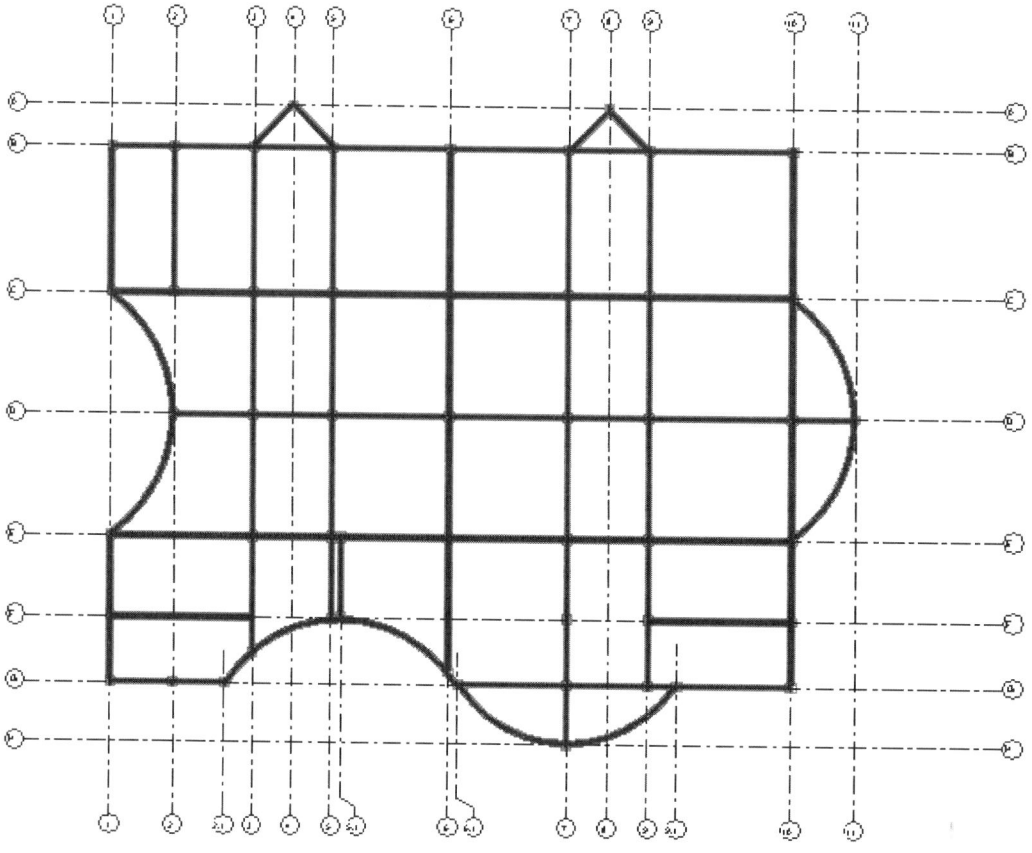

Figure 8–15

1. Open **Structural-Beams.rvt** from the practice files folder.
2. Open the **Structural Plans: TOS-1ST FLOOR** view.
3. In Properties, in the *Underlay* section, set the *Range: Base Level* to **00 T.O. FOOTING** so that you can see the outline of the building.
4. In the View Control Bar, set the *Detail Level* to (Medium).
5. In the *Structure* tab>Structure panel, click (Beam).
6. In the Type Selector, select **W Shapes: W14x30**.

7. Use the following techniques to place the beams:

- If you use ⛓ (On Grids), ensure that you select the correct grid lines. Delete beams that are not used. Click ✓ (Finish). You can continue drawing beams or click **Modify** to finish.
- If you want to sketch the beams, use one of the draw tools from the *Modify | Place Beam* tab, Draw panel.
- To place the curved beams, use either ⛓ (Pick Lines) or the ⌒ (Start-End-Radius Arc) tool.
    - If you are sketching the beams, in the Options Bar, select **Chain** to keep the sketching active between picks. Press <Esc> once to end the chain but remain in the command.
    - Press <Tab> to cycle through selection options near the cursor. When the desired placement highlights, click to place the beam.

8. Select the curved beams and in Properties, in the *Structural* section, change the *Structural Usage* to **Girder**.
9. Click ⛓ (Modify).
10. Save the project.

Task 2: Create beam systems.

1. In the *Structure* tab>Structure panel, click ▥ (Beam System).
2. In the *Modify | Place Structural Beam System* tab, verify that ▥ (Automatic Beam System) is selected.
3. In the Tag panel, click ⛓ (Tag on Placement) to toggle it off.
4. In the Options Bar, set the following:
    - *Beam Type:* **W12x26**
    - *Layout Rule:* **Maximum Spacing** of **6'-0"**

5. Click inside each bay, ensuring that the beams are running in a west-east direction. Exclude the bays on the corners of the east end shown in Figure 8–16.

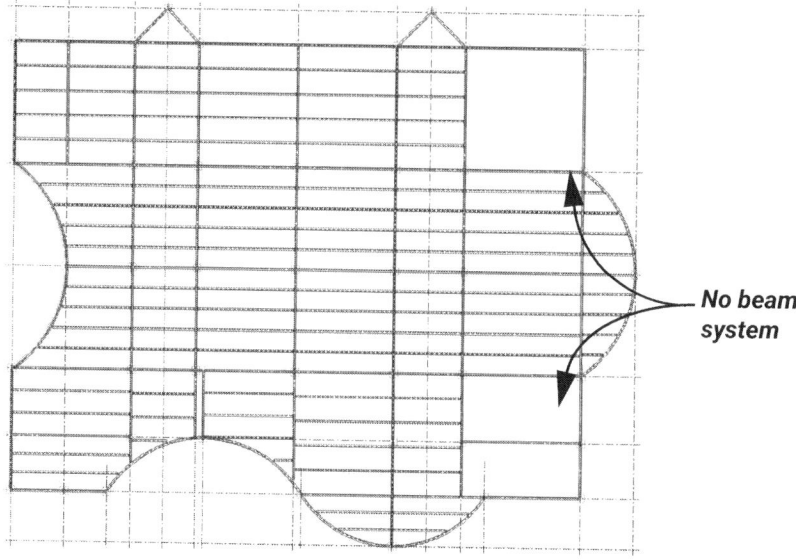

Figure 8–16

6. Use ▥ (Sketch Beam System) for any bays that cannot be applied automatically.
    - In Properties, in the *Identity Data* section, set *Tag new members in view* to **None**.
7. Once all of the framing is in place, end the command.
8. Save the project.

Task 3: Copy the framing to the other levels.

1. Select everything on the first floor except the grid lines.
2. In the Status Bar, click ▽ (Filter).
3. In the Filter dialog box, clear the **Structural Columns** category, as shown in Figure 8–17. If elements other than framing are displayed, clear those categories as well.

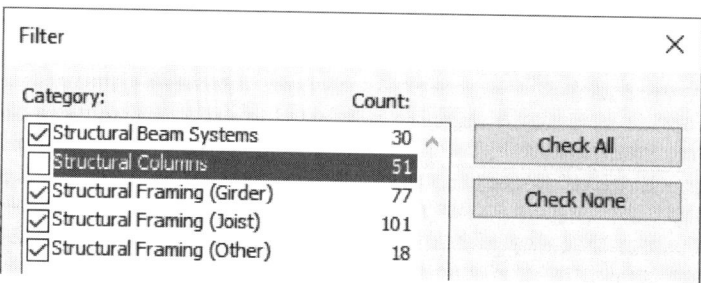

Figure 8–17

4. Click **OK**.

5. In the *Modify | Multi-Select* tab>Clipboard panel, click (Copy to Clipboard).

6. In the Clipboard panel, expand (Paste) and click (Aligned to Selected Levels).

7. In the Select Levels dialog box, select **TOS-2ND FLOOR** to **TOS-13TH FLOOR**, as shown in Figure 8–18. (Hint: Hold <Ctrl> or <Shift> to select multiple levels.)

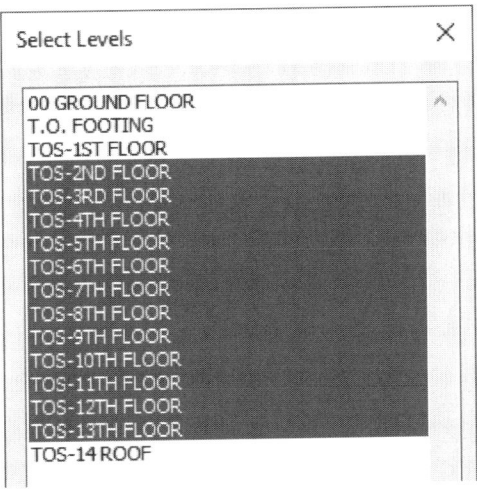

Figure 8–18

8. Click **OK**. This will take some time to process.

9. Open the **Structural Plans: TOS-13TH FLOOR** view.

10. Only the girder beams of each bay are required on the roof level. With a crossing window, select everything and filter out everything but **Structural Framing (Girder)**.

11. Press <Ctrl>+<C> (the **Copy to Clipboard** shortcut).

12. In the Clipboard panel, expand (Paste) and click (Aligned to Selected Levels).

13. In the Select Levels dialog box, select **TOS-14 ROOF** and click **OK**.

14. Open the **TOS-14 Roof** view and set the *Detail Level* to **Medium** so you can see the girder placement.

15. Open a 3D view to see the full model, as shown in Figure 8–19.

Figure 8–19

16. Save the project.

Task 4: Create a framing elevation.

1. Open the **TOS-1st FLOOR** structural plan view.

2. In the *View* tab>Create panel, expand ⌂ (Elevation) and click ⌔ (Framing Elevation).

3. Select the beam between grid intersections **B1** and **C1**, as shown in Figure 8–20.

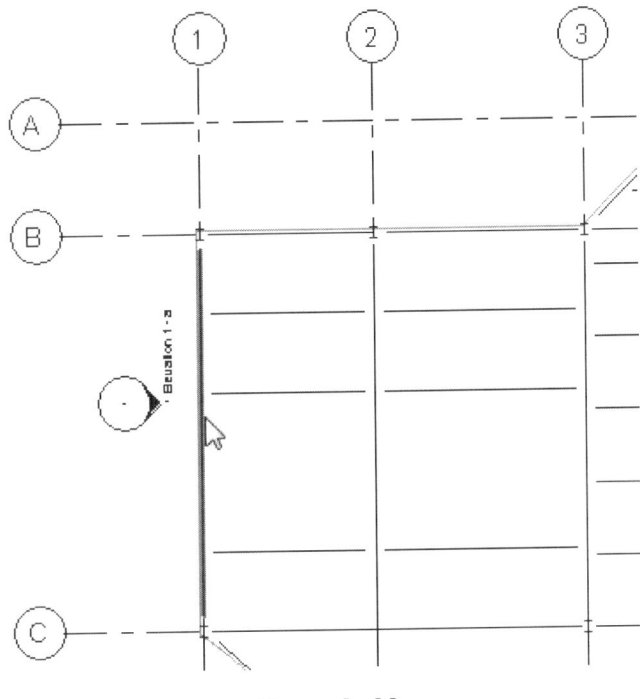

Figure 8–20

4. Click (Modify).
5. In the Project Browser, expand *Elevations (Framing Elevation)* and rename Elevation 1 – a as **West Bracing**.
6. Open the framing elevation.
7. Modify the crop region to display the columns.
8. In the View Control Bar, set the *Detail Level* to (Fine).
9. Zoom in to display the **00 GROUND FLOOR** and **TOS-1ST FLOOR** level heads. If needed, drag the level heads out so you can see the column clearly.
10. Save the project.

Task 5: Add bracing.

1. In the *Structure* tab>Structure panel, click (Brace).
2. In the Type Selector, select **HSS Square: HSS6X6X1/2**.

3. Draw from the centerline of the base of the column on the left to the midpoint **SM** of the beam located on **TOS-1ST FLOOR**, as shown in Figure 8–21. Repeat this step on the other side.

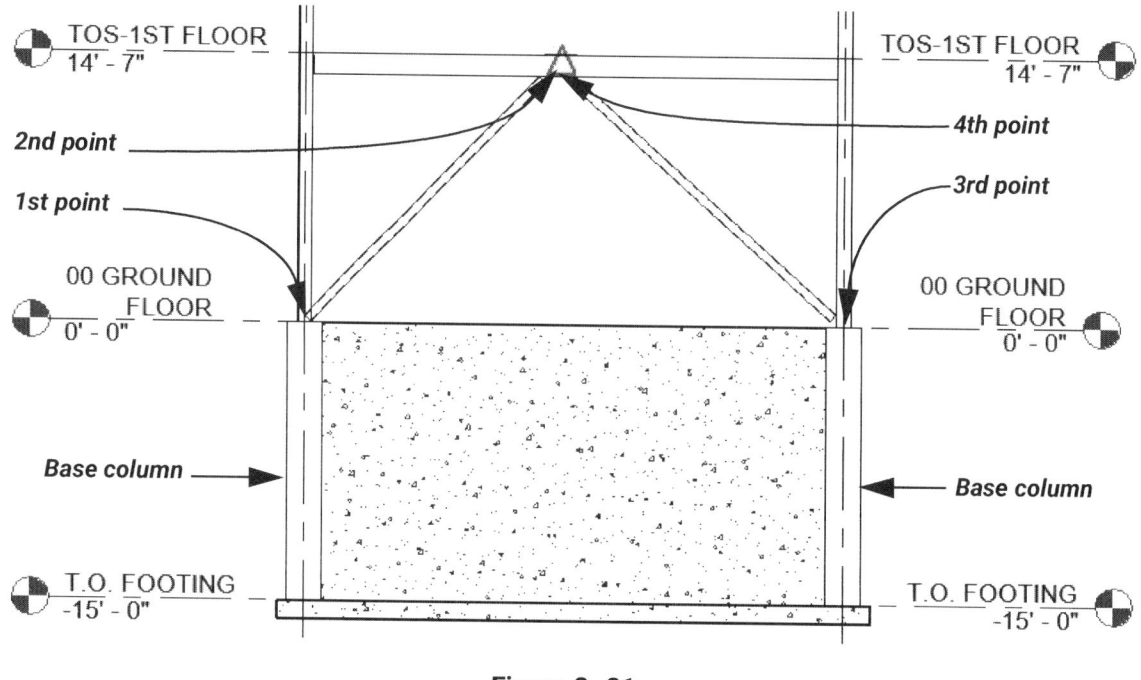

Figure 8–21

4. Click ▸ (Modify) and select the two new braces.

   Note: *Note that the entrance level is listed as **Ground Floor**. This is typical in some Canadian and British naming schemes.*

5. Copy the braces to the clipboard and use **Paste>Aligned to Selected Levels** to place them on each of the levels from **TOS-1ST FLOOR** to **TOS-13TH FLOOR**. Exclude the **00 GROUND FLOOR**, **T.O.FOOTING**, and **TOS-14 ROOF** levels.

6. In the West Bracing elevation, pan up to the top level.

7. Select the top two braces and drag the circular control to the midpoint of the beam above it, as shown in Figure 8–22.

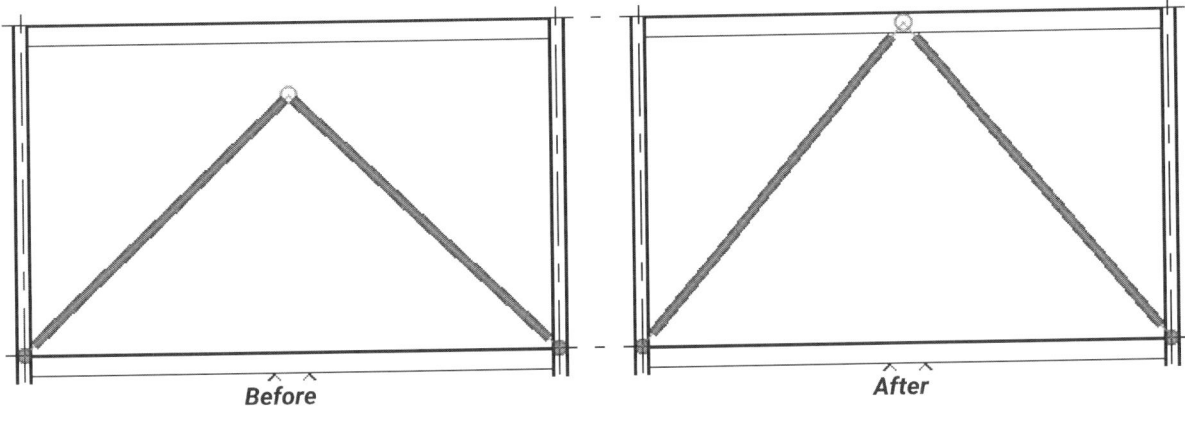

Figure 8–22

8. Click ▷ (Modify).
9. Zoom out to see the entire framing elevation.
10. Save and close the project.

End of practice

8.2 Modifying Structural Framing

The default connections of columns, beams, and braces might need to be modified to suit specific situations, such as when the beams are offset from their associated level or cantilevered beyond a framing member. Modifications can be made by using graphical controls and shape handles, the Properties palette, or special tools found on the *Modify | Structural Framing* tab, as shown in Figure 8–23.

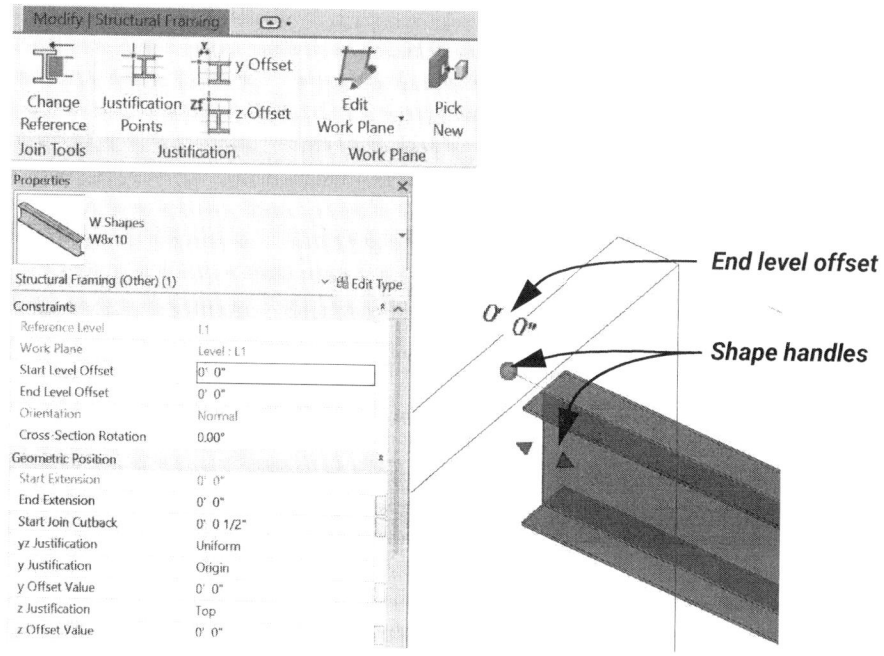

Figure 8–23

- The *Detail Level* of a view impacts the way in which framing members display, as shown in Figure 8–24. Some editing tools only work in a Medium or Fine detail view.

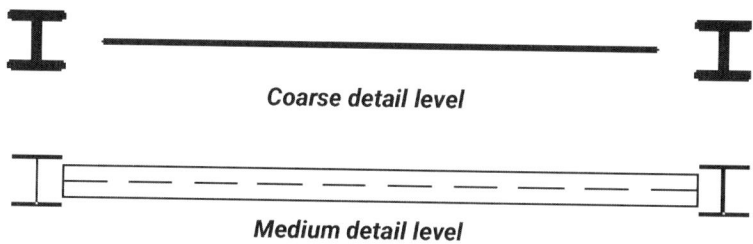

Figure 8–24

- For a visual reference, you can use either location lines (shown in Figure 8–25).
  - To show location lines, in the Visibility/Graphic Overrides dialog box>*Model Categories* tab, expand **Structural Framing** and then select **Location Line**.

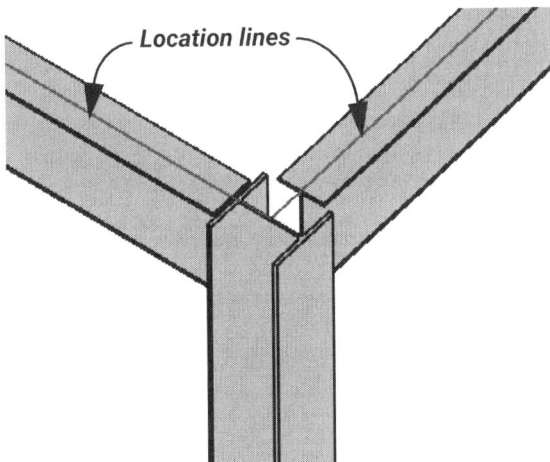

Figure 8–25

- When you draw framing members, the start/end orientation is based on the first and second points picked. In some modification instances, it is important to know the start point versus the end point. To flip the start and end points:
  - In a plan view, click the **Flip Structure Framing ends** icon, as shown in Figure 8–26.
  - In a 3D view, right-click on the member and select **Flip Structural Framing ends**.

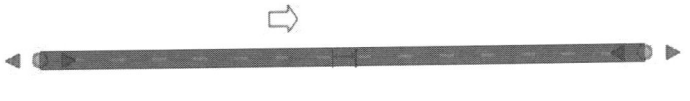

Figure 8–26

Sloping and Offsetting Beams

Beams can be modified to slope or offset from the level where they are placed. This can be done by first unpinning the beam, selecting it, and clicking the ⚲ (Prevent or allow change of element position) icon in the view, and then using the *Start/End Level Offset* control (as shown in Figure 8–27) or modifying the *Start Level Offset* and *End Level Offset* in Properties (as shown in Figure 8–28).

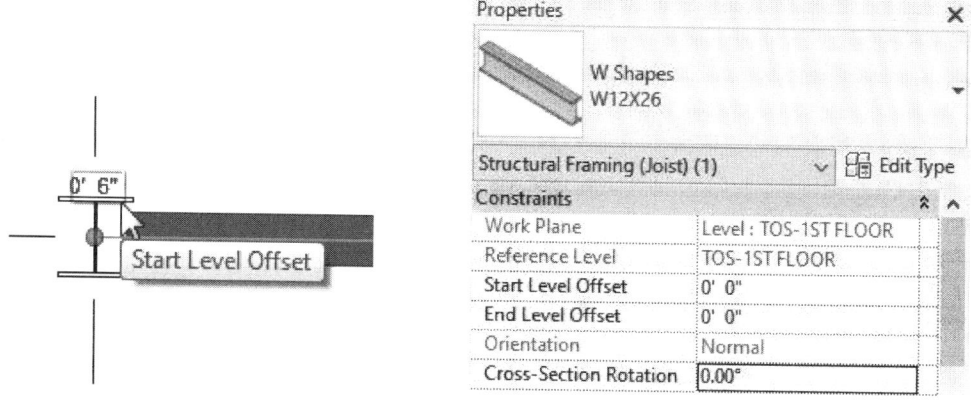

Figure 8–27   Figure 8–28

- Setting the offset at only one end slopes the beam, as shown in Figure 8–29.

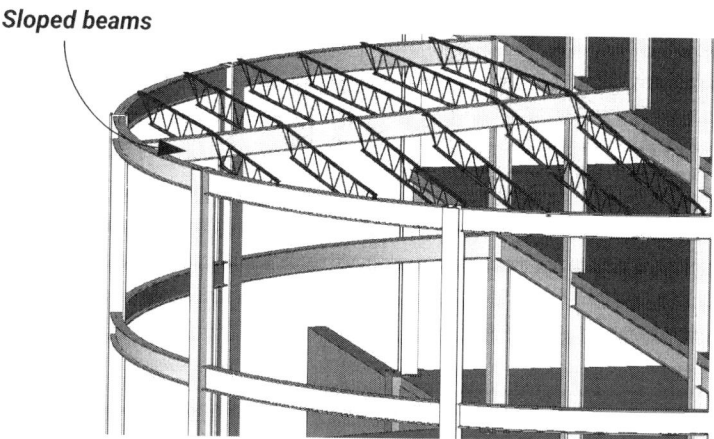

Figure 8–29

- The *Cross-Section Rotation* option in Properties rotates the beam along its axis at the angle specified.

- Setting the *Start Level Offset* and *End Level Offset* the same at each end raises or lowers the entire beam. For example, when wide flange beams are supporting open web steel joists (as shown in Figure 8–30), you need to offset that increment based on the specific joist's seat.

Structural Framing

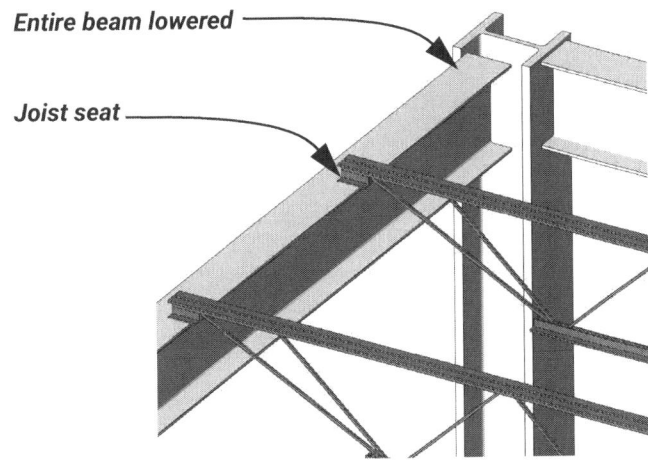

Figure 8–30

> **Hint: Using 3D Snapping**
>
> When you draw beams, you can toggle on **3D Snapping** from the Options Bar. This allows you to snap to other beams or structural walls of different heights.
>
> You can also use 3D Snapping when placing beam systems using the Automatic Beam System tool. When you toggle on 3D Snapping, you have an additional option, which is **Walls Define Slope**. When selected, this option allows you to use walls to define the slop of your beam system.
>
> On the left in Figure 8–31, the **3D Snapping** and **Walls Define Slope** options are selected, while on the right they are not.

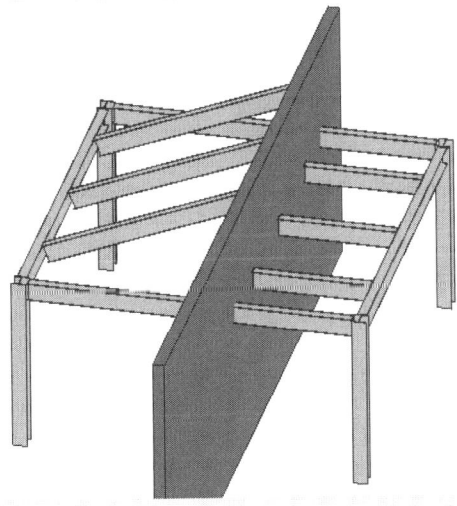

Figure 8–31

Adding Beam Cantilevers and Cutbacks

It is common to need a joist extension that cantilevers a bearing member. In the example shown in Figure 8–32, the joist seat needs to extend past the beam it bears on to frame into a cantilevered ridge beam. By modifying the individual joists, you can extend either end to meet the requirements.

Note: Use this method to extend joists for a fascia system or in any situation in which a roof or slab extends past the main structure.

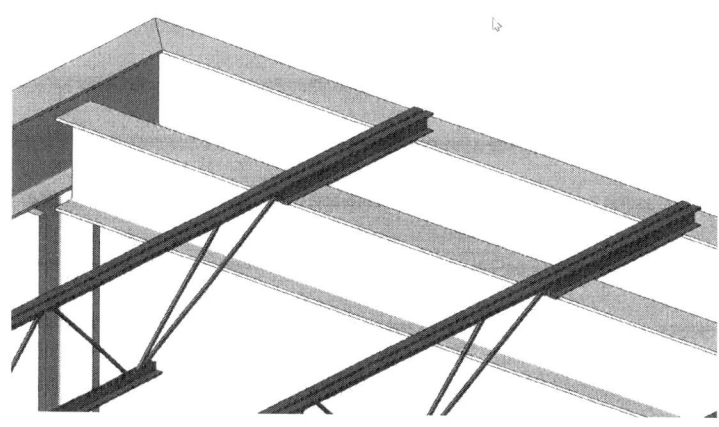

Figure 8–32

To cantilever or cutback a beam that is joined to other structural elements, use the shape handles to drag it to a new location, or set the *Start* or *End Join Cutback* in Properties, as shown in Figure 8–33.

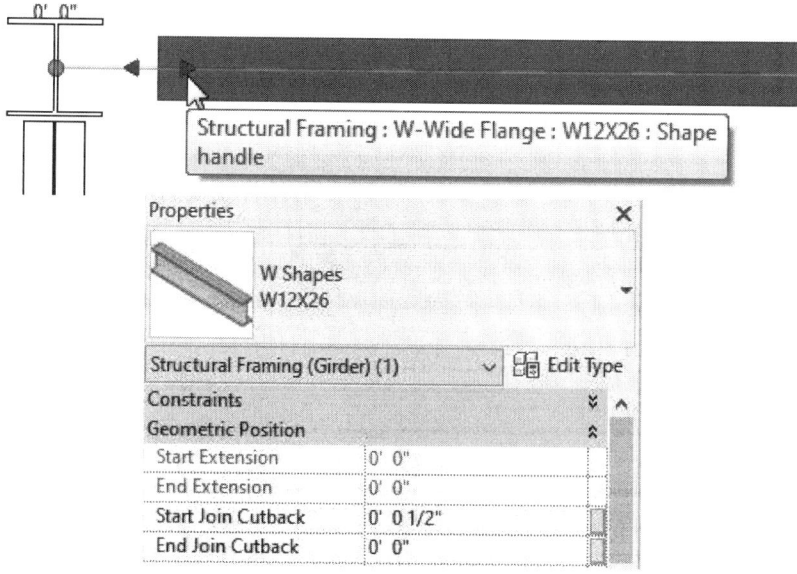

Figure 8–33

To cantilever a beam when the beam is not joined to other elements, you can use the **Drag Structural Framing Component End** shape handle (as shown in Figure 8–34), or set the *Start* or *End Extension* in Properties.

Figure 8–34

- When modifying beams, you first need to unpin the individual beam you want to work with. Select it and click the (Prevent or allow change of element position) icon.

> **Hint: Structural Connections and Fabrication**
>
> Over 150 standard structural connections can be added to framing joins to share in-depth information about the join with the contractor and fabricator. You can also add fabrication elements, such as plates, bolts, and welds, and modify plates and other steel elements using copes and other cuts. These tools, which are beyond the scope of this learning guide, are found on the *Steel* tab (shown in Figure 8–35).

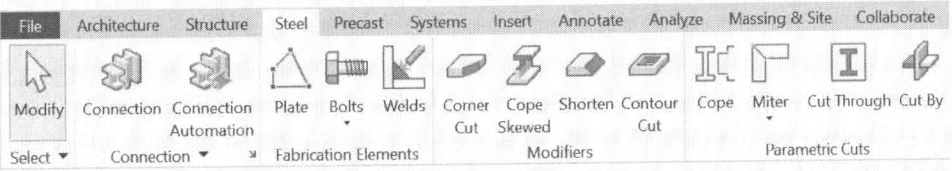

Figure 8–35

Changing the Cutback

Modifying the join connection of structural framing can be done by changing the cutback from the connected element. For example, the default cutback of the column shown in Figure 8–36 is the bounding box of the column, not the vertical support. You can change the reference to a more appropriate part of the framing.

Note: You can select more than one element to adjust as long as they are connected to the same reference.

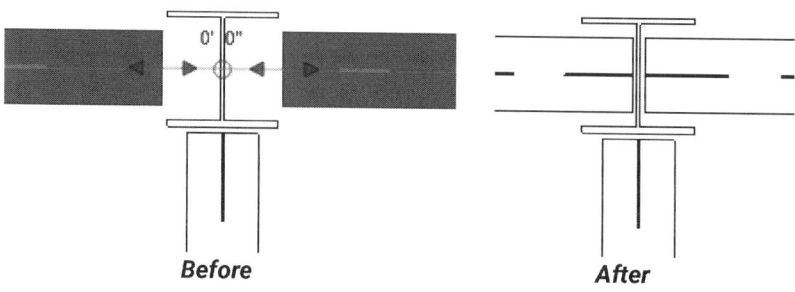

Before   *After*

Figure 8–36

- You can change the reference in plan and 3D views if the *Display Level* is set to **Medium** or **Fine**.

Hint: Bounding Boxes

An element bounding box is an invisible rectangular box around the element that defines a single element and how it reacts to other elements. Figure 8–37 shows the bounding box for a column in dashed lines.

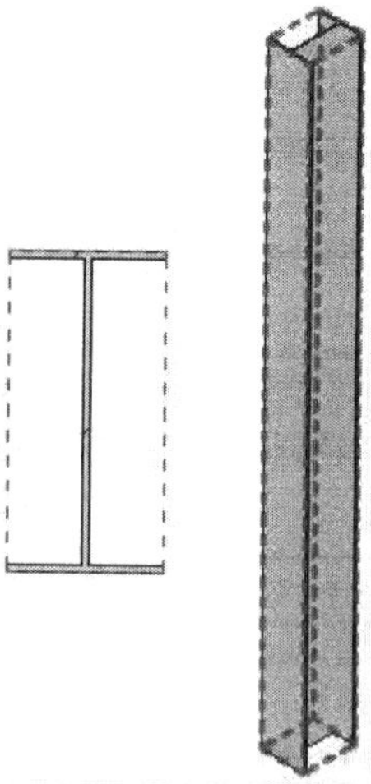

Figure 8–37

Structural Framing

How To: Adjust the Cutback of Structural Framing

1. Select the structural framing member you want to modify.
2. In the *Modify | Structural Framing* tab>Join Tools panel, click (Change Reference).
3. Select the reference point for alignment, as shown on the left in Figure 8–38. This can be another beam, a structural column, or a structural wall.

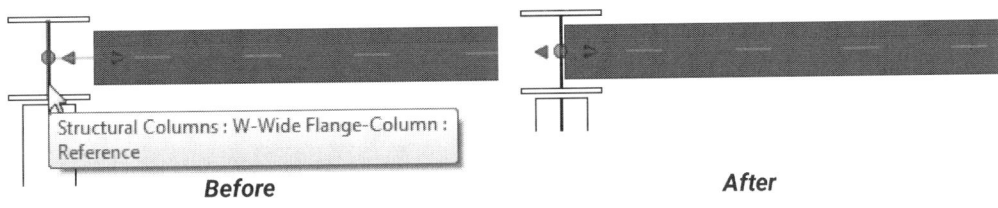

Figure 8–38

- The end of the member lengthens to the new reference location (it does not move the beam), as shown on the right in Figure 8–38.

4. In Properties, modify the *Start Join Cutback* or *End Join Cutback* distance, as needed.

- To return the beam end to its default setback position, click (Change Reference) again and select the bounding box (dashed lines) of the other element.

Changing Justifications

Modifying the location of a framing element can be done by modifying the justification. You can set the horizontal (y) and vertical (z) justification points to one of nine different points, such as **Origin Left** (as shown in Figure 8–39). The location line remains in place, with the framing element moved to the new justification. You can also change the offset from the justification point in either the **y** (left to right) or **z** (top to bottom) directions. Both of these options can be modified either graphically or in Properties.

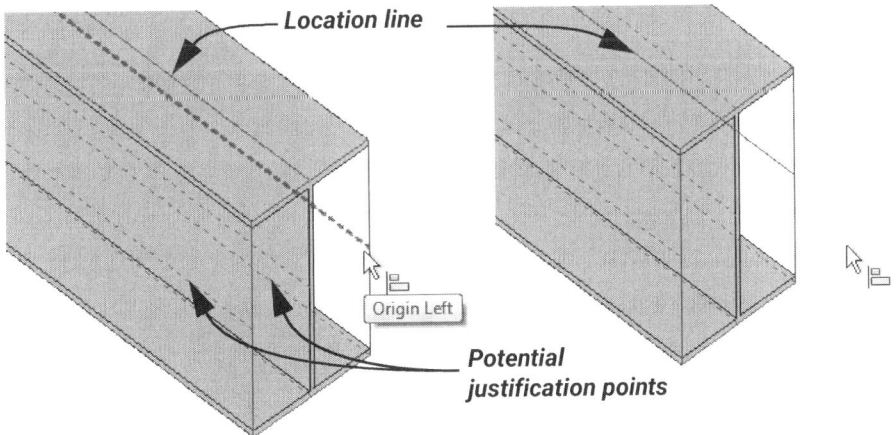

Figure 8–39

How To: Set the Justification of Framing Elements Graphically

1. Select the beam you want to modify.
2. In the *Modify | Structural Framing* tab>Justification panel, click (Justification Points), or type **JP**.
3. Select the justification points you want to use, as shown in Figure 8–40.

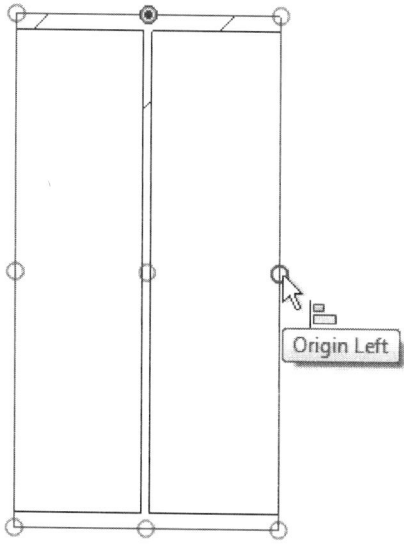

Figure 8–40

- The location line does not change, but the framing element repositions to the selected justification point.

- You can also modify the justification points using the *y Justification* and *z Justification* parameters in Properties, as shown in Figure 8–41.

Structural Framing

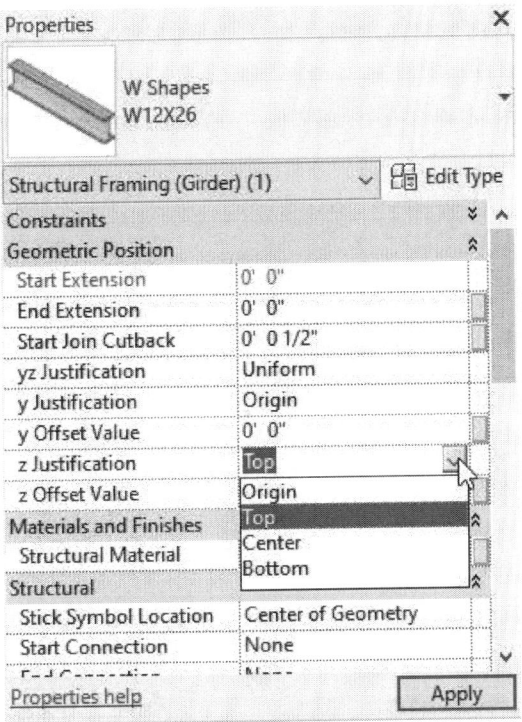

Figure 8–41

How To: Change the Justification Offset Graphically

1. Select the structural framing element.
2. In the *Modify | Structural Framing* tab>Justification panel:

    - Modify the horizontal offset and distance by clicking (y Offset), or type **JY**.

    - Modify the vertical offset and distance by clicking (z Offset), or type **JZ**.

3. Select the offset start point and then the offset end point.

- You can also modify the offset values in Properties by using the *y Offset Value* and *z Offset Value* parameters.

- You can set the *yz Justification* (shown in Figure 8–42) to the following:
  - **Uniform:** The same justification offset is applied to both ends.
  - **Independent:** The justification offset can be different for each end.

  When the *yz Justification* is selected, you can set the *Start y* (or *Start z*) *Offset Value* and the *End y* (or *End z*) *Offset Value* in Properties.

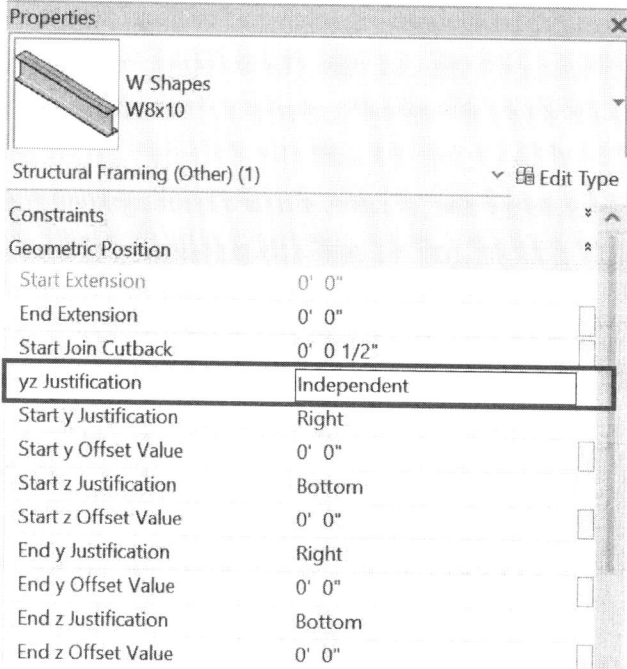

Figure 8–42

Structural Framing

> **Hint: Viewing Justifications**
>
> At the Coarse detail level, when you select the beam, the justification line is displayed, as shown in Figure 8–43.

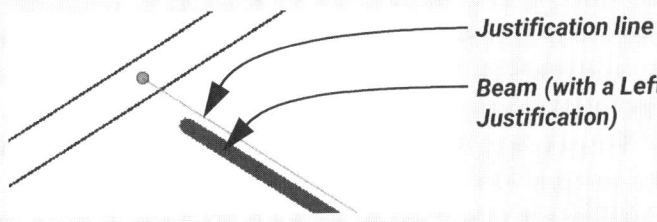

Figure 8–43

When working in the Medium (or Fine) detail level, you can toggle on or off the location line in Visibility/Graphic Overrides, as shown in Figure 8–44. (Justification line has been exaggerated for emphasis.)

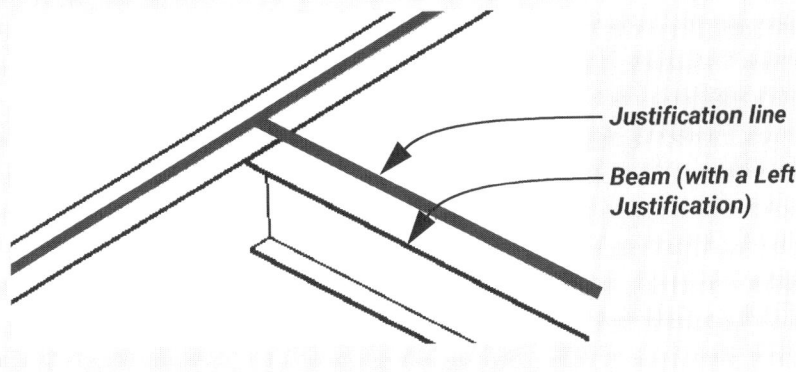

Figure 8–44

Attaching a Column to a Beam

The columns that support the cantilever can be attached to the bottom of the framing member, as shown in Figure 8–45. This removes the need to estimate the actual bearing depth of the framing member and ensures that the column always remains connected to the beam.

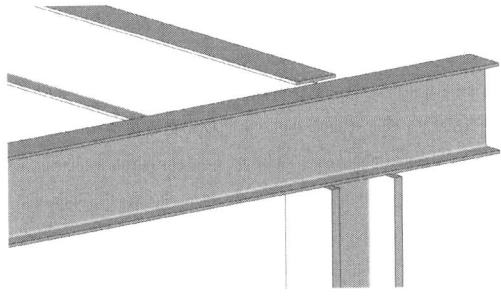

Figure 8–45

How To: Attach a Column to the Bottom of a Beam

1. Select a column.
2. In the *Modify | Structural Columns* tab>Modify Column panel, click (Attach Top/Base).
3. In the Options Bar, set the options as needed. If you need to add a bearing plate, set the *Offset from Attachment* value.
4. Select the beam that the column will attach to.

- You can also use this command to attach the base of a beam to structural footings. When the footing moves in height, the length of the column resizes to match.

Applying Beam Coping

When one beam connects with another beam, you might need to modify the connection. In the example shown in Figure 8–46, the lower joist-bearing beam runs into the perimeter beam. This is a coping situation.

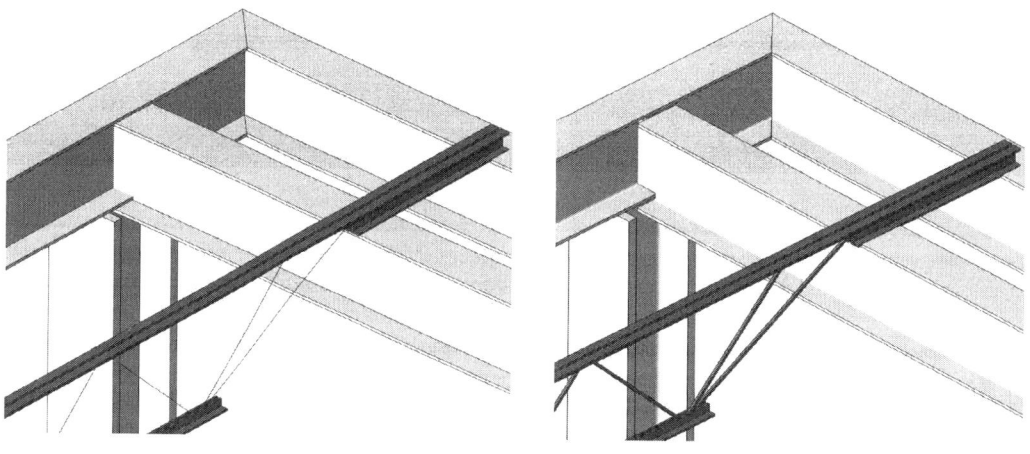

Figure 8–46

How To: Cope Beams

1. Open a 3D, section, or detail view.
2. Zoom in to a beam-to-beam (or beam-to-column) connection.
3. In the *Modify* tab>Geometry panel, expand (Cope) and select (Apply Coping).
4. Select the beam to be coped first, followed by the column/beam from which to cut. The cope is then completed.

   - You can change the coping distance by selecting the beam and changing the *Coping Distance* value in Properties.

Editing Beam Joins

When you add beams to a project, there is a default layout to the beam joins. However, you might need to override the joins. You can do this by adjusting how the beams frame into each other, as shown in Figure 8–47.

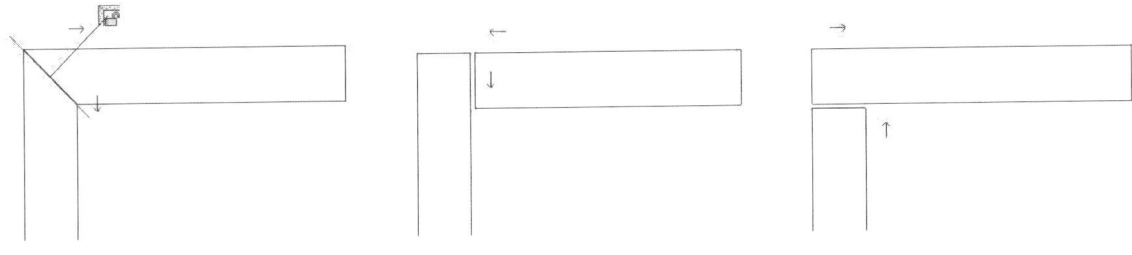

Figure 8–47

How To: Edit Beam Joins

1. In the *Modify* tab>Geometry panel, click (Beam/Column Joins). The work area switches to sketch mode.

    - Only the beams and/or columns that can be changed are highlighted.
    - You cannot use this tool on beams that are attached to vertical columns.

2. In the Options Bar, specify the types of beams that you want to work with, as shown in Figure 8–48.

    Figure 8–48

3. Click the **Change Beam Status** control to toggle the join, as shown in Figure 8–49.

    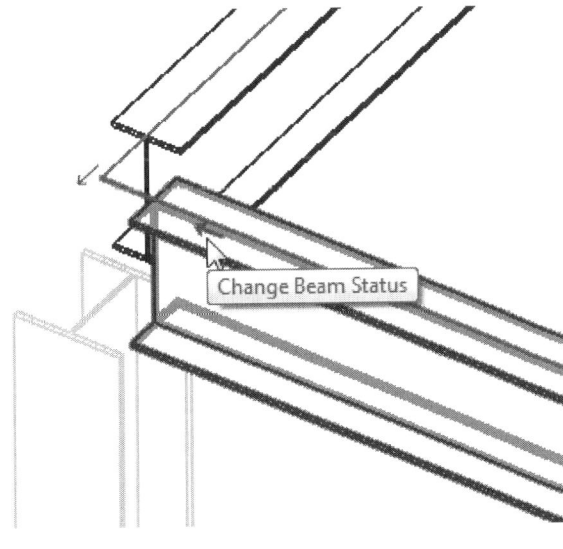

    Figure 8–49

4. Click (Beam/Column Joins) again or click (Modify) to end the command.

- If you are mitering a corner, you can lock the miter, as shown in Figure 8–50.

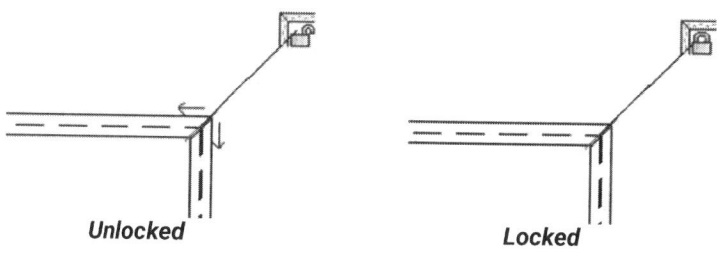

Figure 8–50

> **Hint: Join Status**
>
> You can modify the *Join Status* of structural frames to position framing that butts against a wall or other beams. Right-click on the join control (the circle), select **Disallow Join** (as shown on the left in Figure 8–51), and make the required modifications. Click **Allow Join** to rejoin the elements.

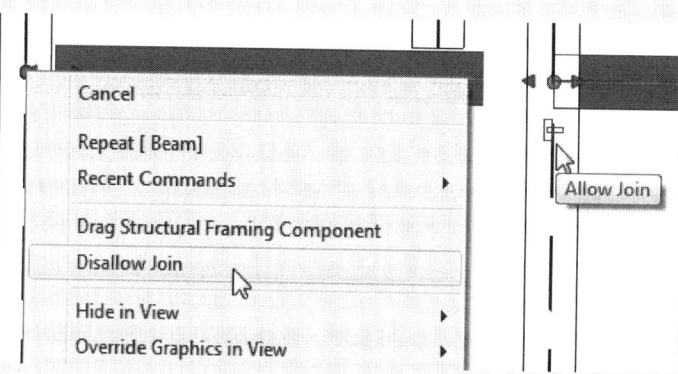

Figure 8–51

- *Join Status* is a field that can be used in schedules. You can modify the join status in the schedule and it will update in the model.

Practice 8b
Modify Structural Framing

Practice Objectives

- Modify beam level offsets.
- Add beam systems.

In this practice, you will modify beam level offsets for correct joist bearing and add beam systems using the automatic method where you can. Then, you will sketch beam systems in areas where they cannot be automatically placed, as shown in Figure 8–52.

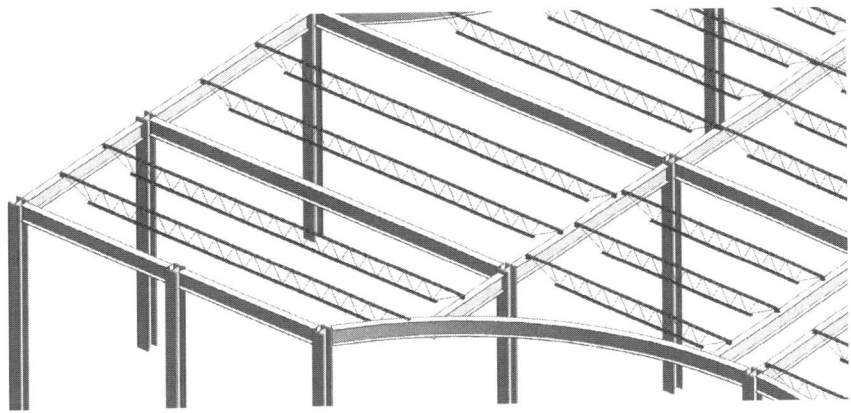

Figure 8–52

Task 1: Modify beam level offsets.

1. Open **Structural-Framing.rvt** from the practice files folder.
2. Open the **Structural Plans: TOS-14 ROOF** view.
3. Hide the grid lines.

4. For this level, you need to lower the beams of each bay. Select all of the beams running in the north-south direction for the joist bearing, including the arc beams, as shown in Figure 8–53.

   Note: If you selected bracing elements, you need to filter them out.

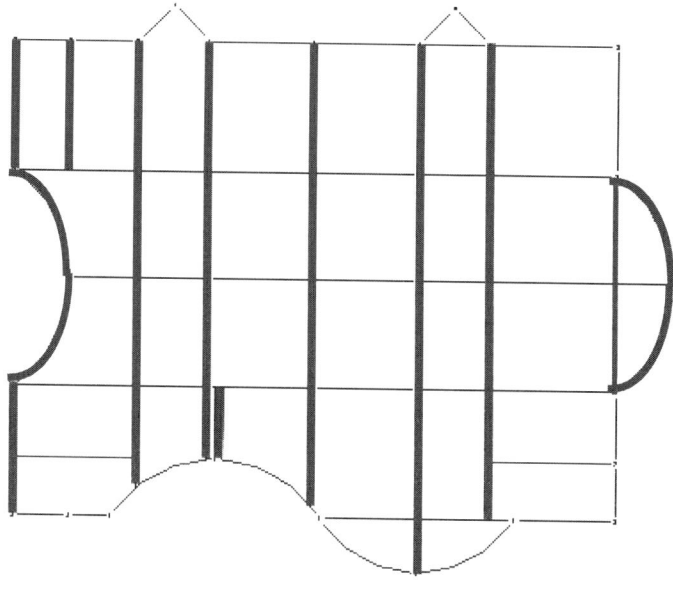

Figure 8–53

5. In Properties, change both the *Start Level Offset* and *End Level Offset* to (negative) **-2 1/2"**.
6. Click **Apply** or move your cursor into the view area.
7. Open a 3D view and zoom in on one of the top floor intersections. The north-south girders should be displayed below the east-west girders, as shown in Figure 8–54. Look at the ViewCube in the upper right corner of the view to see in which direction the beams are running.

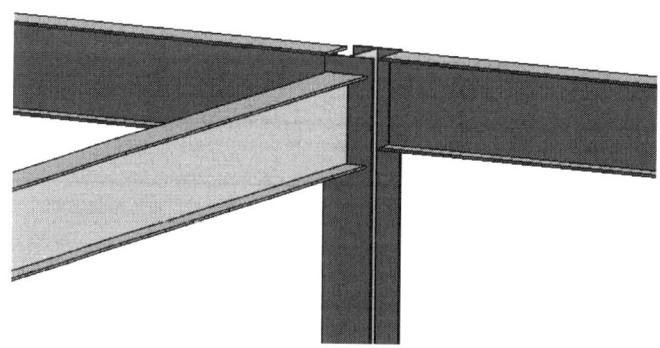

Figure 8–54

8. Save the project.

Task 2: Add beam systems.

1. Switch to the **Structural Plans: TOS-14 ROOF** view.

2. In the *Structure* tab>Structure panel, click ▦ (Beam System). In the Options Bar, set the following parameters:

    - *Beam Type:* **16K7**
    - *Layout Rule:* **Maximum Spacing**
    - *Maximum Spacing:* **6'-0"**

3. Use ▦ (Automatic Beam System) to fill in as many bays as possible, as shown in Figure 8–55.

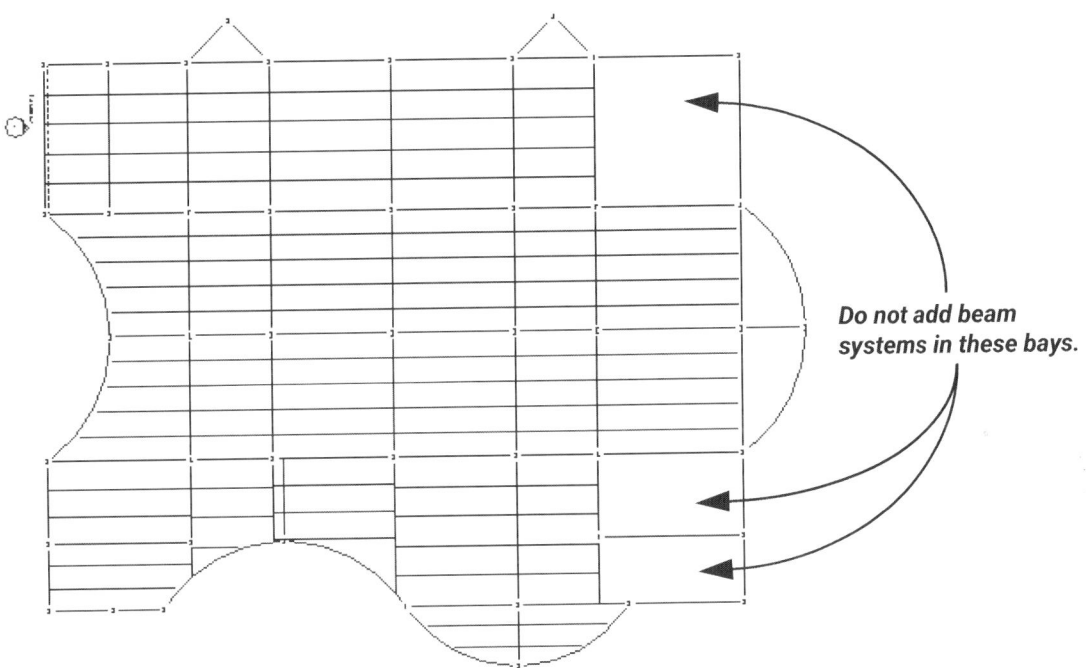

Figure 8–55

4. If you end up with areas where the automatic method does not work (such as the example shown in Figure 8–56), switch to (Sketch Beam System). Then, in Properties, in the *Identity Data* section, change *Tag new members in view* to **None**.

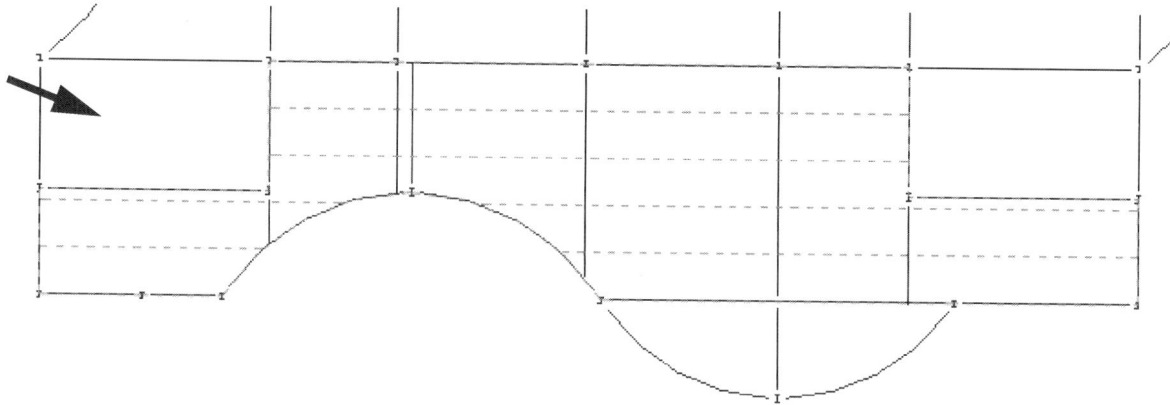

Figure 8–56

5. If the error shown in Figure 8–57 opens, the space for the joist might be too small to be created by the **Beam System** command. Click **Delete Type**. You can add a beam separately, as needed.

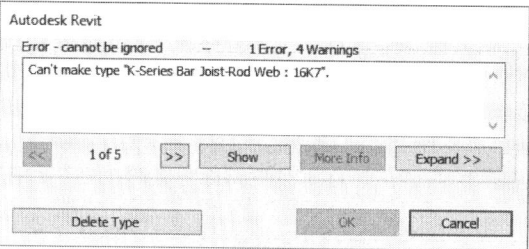

Figure 8–57

6. Click (Modify).
7. Switch to the 3D view to see the newly placed joists.
8. Save and close the project.

End of practice

8.3 Adding Trusses

A truss can be added to a project using the same basic method as placing a beam. Trusses are typically composed of one or more triangular sections, as shown in Figure 8–58. These sections are constructed with structural members whose ends are connected at joints, which are referred to as nodes. As various forces act on these nodes, the triangular shape provides structural stability to prevent bending.

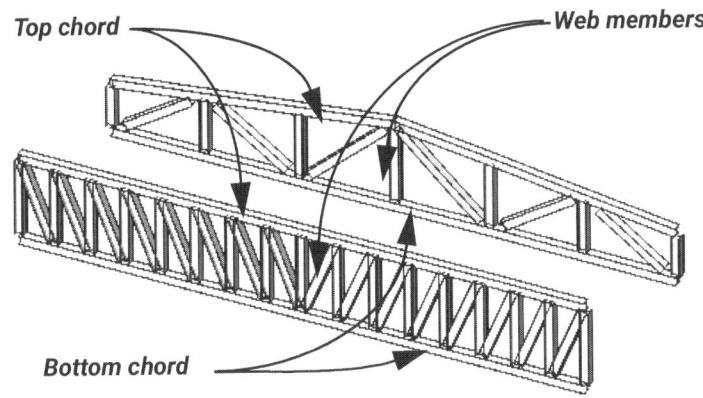

Figure 8–58

The elements of a truss are:

- the lower horizontal member, called the **bottom chord**;
- the upper horizontal member, called the **top chord**; and
- the series of structural framing elements that stabilize the truss, called the **web**.

The top and bottom chords fulfill the same function as a beam's top and bottom flanges. The web takes the place of the beam's continuous plate.

How To: Add Trusses

1. In the *Structure* tab>Structure panel, click (Structural Trusses).
2. In the Type Selector, select the type of truss you want to use.
   - Click (Load Family) and navigate to the *Structural Trusses* folder in the Revit Library to add families to the project.
3. In the *Modify | Place Truss* tab>Draw panel, click (Line) or (Pick Lines) and add the trusses to the project.

Attaching Trusses to Roofs

Trusses can be attached to roofs or floor slabs. They can also follow the slope of the roof and automatically extend to fit, as shown in Figure 8–59.

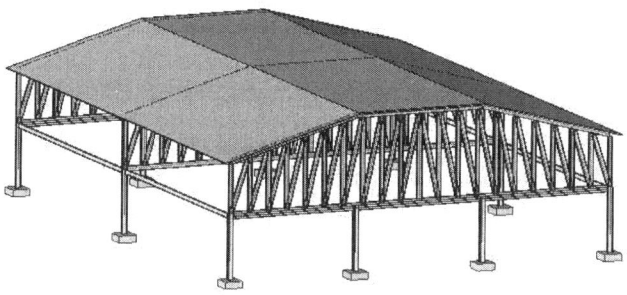

Figure 8–59

How To: Attach Trusses to Roofs

1. In the *Modify | Structural Trusses* tab>Modify Truss panel, click (Attach Top/Bottom).
2. In the Options Bar, set *Attach Trusses* to **Top** or **Bottom**.
3. Select the roof or floor element. The truss attaches to the element and follows the angle or slope, as shown in Figure 8–60.

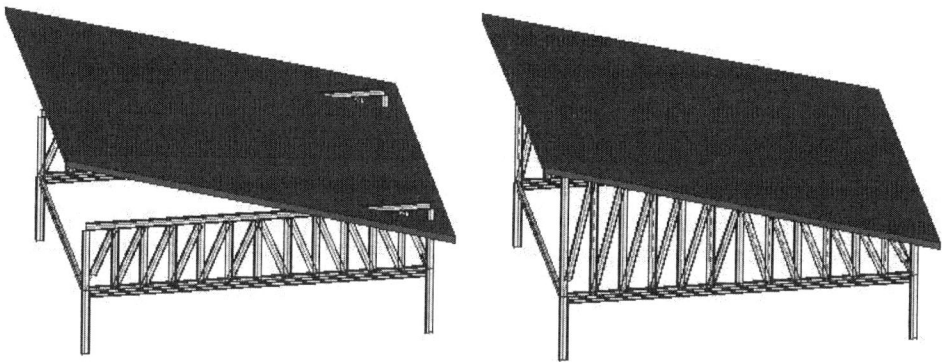

Figure 8–60

- The top chord must be one continuous line in the family. If it is broken into segments, attaching it might not work properly.
- Verify that the bottom chord is specified as the bearing chord in the element properties of the truss. This ensures that the roof loads are carried throughout the truss appropriately.
- If the roof/floor slab does not cover the length of the truss, an error message opens and you might have to detach the truss.

Setting Framing Types in Trusses

When truss families are created, they can include structural framing members for the chords and webs. However, they often just use default members. Therefore, you need to specify the precise framing types you want to use in the project.

In the Type Properties dialog box, select the *Structural Framing Type* from a list of families loaded into the project, as shown in Figure 8–61. This should be set for the **Top Chords**, **Vertical Webs**, **Diagonal Webs**, and **Bottom Chords**.

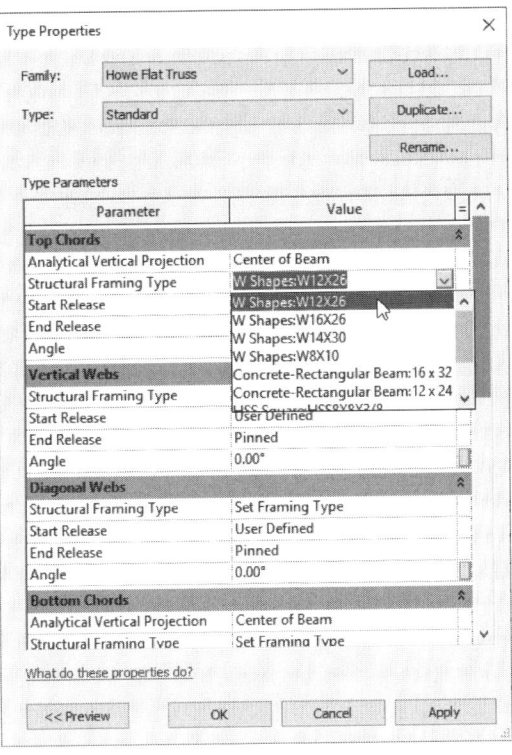

Figure 8–61

- To select an entire truss, ensure that the dashed lines are displayed, as shown on the left in Figure 8–62. To select one element of the truss, press <Tab> until the element that you want to select is highlighted, as shown on the right in Figure 8–62.

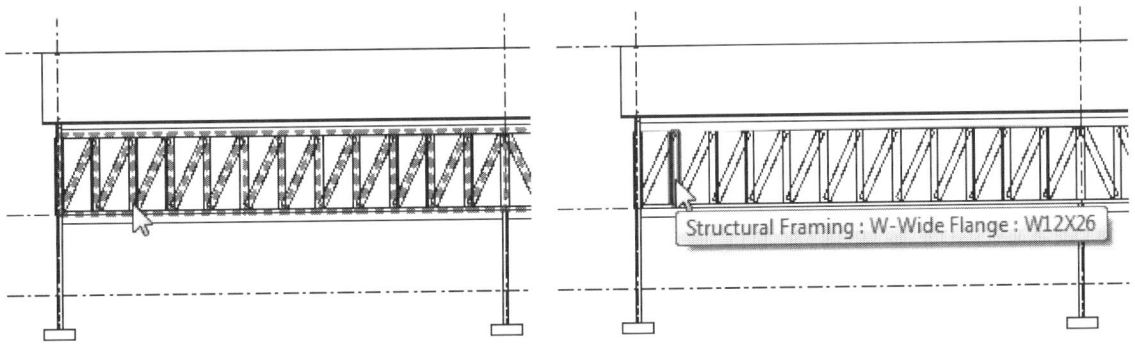

Figure 8–62

- Individual truss members are pinned to the truss framework. If you want to modify one of these, you need to click (Prevent or allow change of element position) to unpin only that member.

- You can rotate trusses and specify if the chords rotate with the truss. In Properties, type in a *Rotation Angle* and select or clear *Rotate Chords With Truss*, as shown in Figure 8–63.

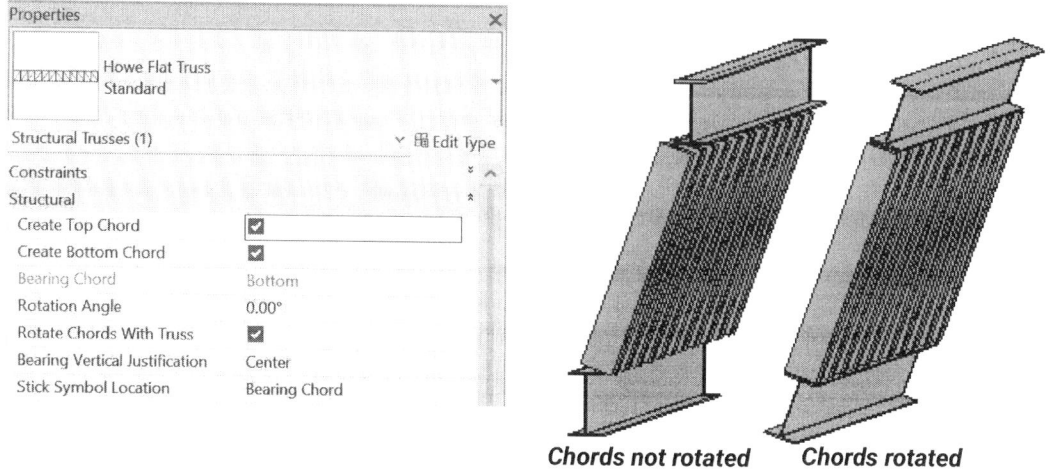

Figure 8–63

Practice 8c
Add Trusses

Practice Objectives

- Set up a truss type.
- Add trusses to a project.
- Attach trusses to a roof.

In this practice, you will set up a truss using specific structural framing types for the chords and webs. You will then draw a truss and array it across an open span. Finally, you will attach the trusses to an existing roof element, as shown in Figure 8–64.

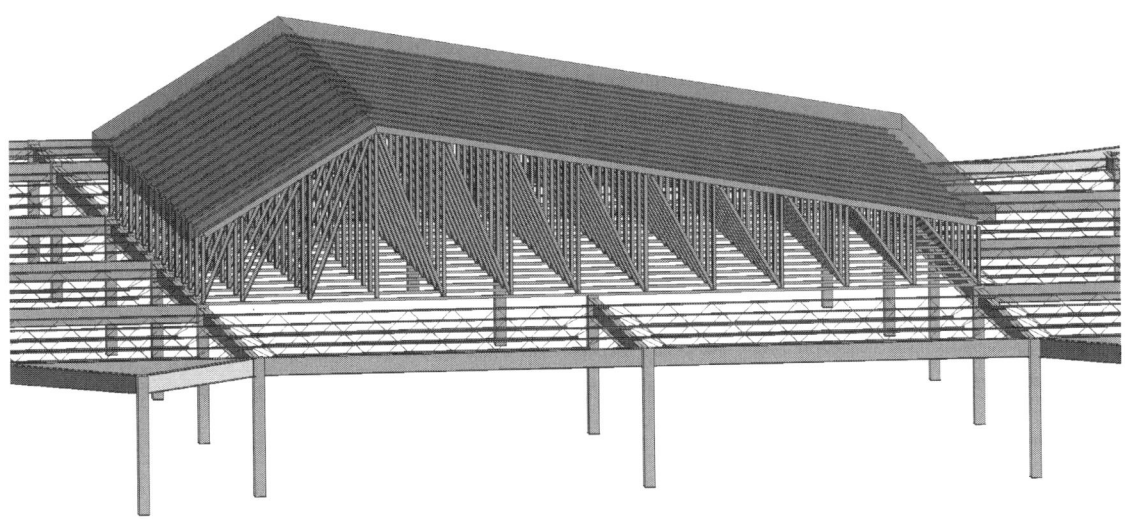

Figure 8–64

Task 1: Set up a truss type.

1. Open **Structural-Trusses.rvt** from the practice files folder.
2. In the *Structure* tab>Structure panel, click (Truss).
3. In the Type Selector, select **Howe Flat Truss: Standard**. In Properties, click (Edit Type).
4. In the Type Properties dialog box, click **Duplicate**.
5. In the Name dialog box, type **Skylight** and click **OK**.

6. In the Type Properties dialog box, set the following properties, as shown in Figure 8–65:

   - **Top Cords** and **Bottom Chords:**
     Set the *Structural Framing Type* to **LL-Double Angle:2L6X4X5/8LLBB**.

   - **Vertical Webs** and **Diagonal Webs:**
     Set the *Structural Framing Type* to **LL-Double Angle:2L3X2-1/2X1/2LLBB**.

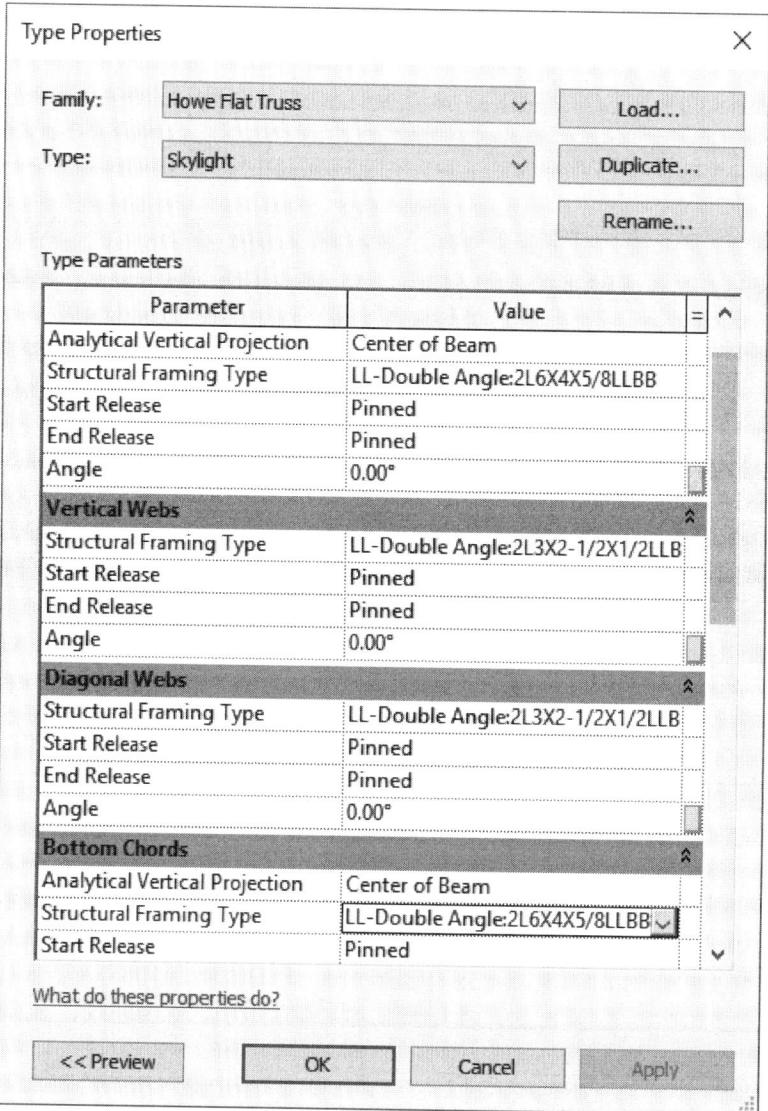

Figure 8–65

7. Click **OK**.
8. Save the project.

Task 2: Add trusses.

1. Open the **Structural Plans: TOS-14 ROOF** view. Some of the structural framing has been removed in this plan to make way for a large skylight, as shown in Figure 8–66.

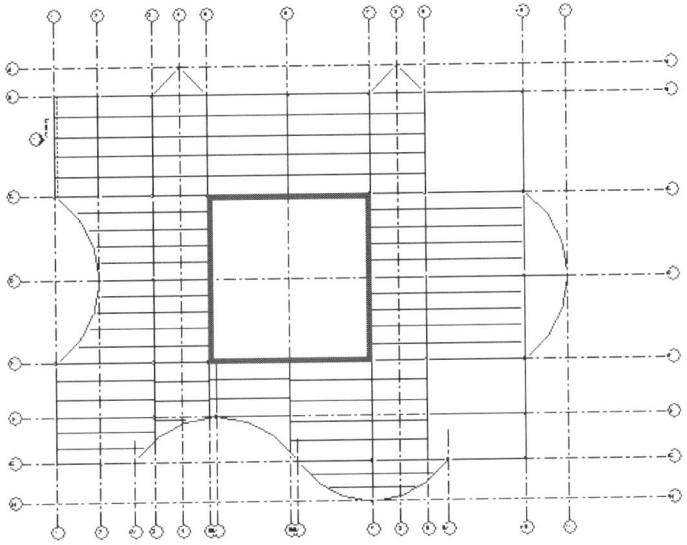

Figure 8–66

2. Start the (Truss) command.
3. In the Type Selector, verify that the **Howe Flat Truss: Skylight** is selected.
4. In Properties, set the *Bearing Chord* to **Bottom** and the *Truss Height* to **4'-0"**.

5. Draw the first truss between grid intersections **C5** and **C7**, as shown in Figure 8–67. (The image has been cropped for clarity.)

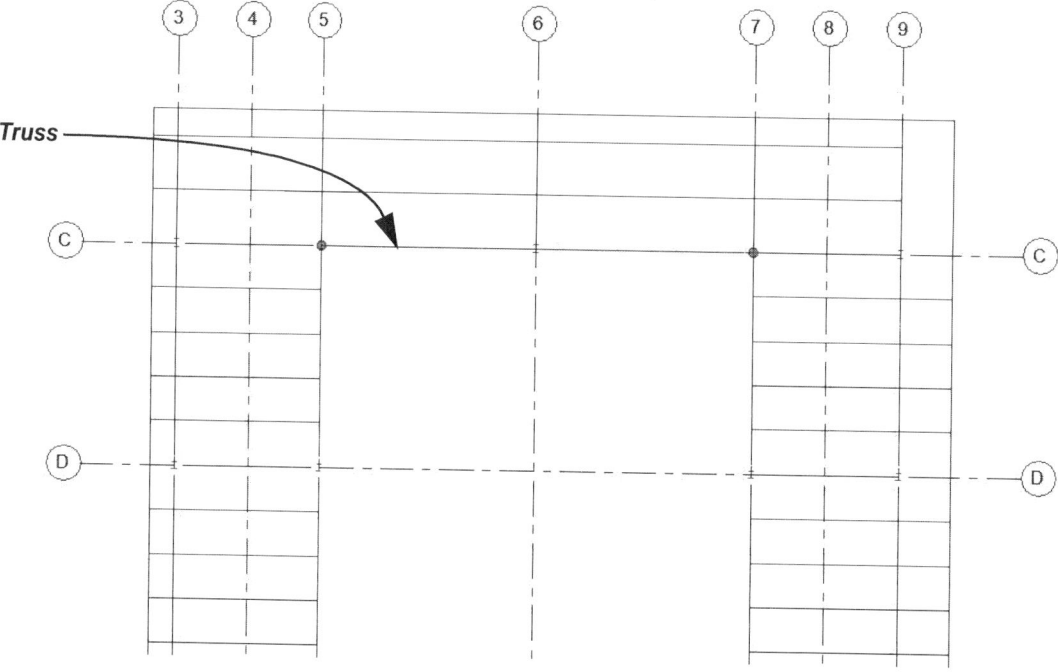

Figure 8–67

6. Click (Modify) and select the new truss.
7. In the *Modify | Structural Trusses* tab>Modify panel, click (Array).
8. In the Options Bar:

    - Select (Linear).
    - Uncheck **Group And Associate**.
    - Set *Number* to **15**.
    - Set *Move To:* to **Last**.
    - Check **Constrain**.

9. To specify the length of the array, click on grid line **C** and then on grid line **E**.
10. Click (Modify).

11. Open the **3D Views: Roof and Skylight** view and rotate the view to display the trusses, as shown in Figure 8–68.

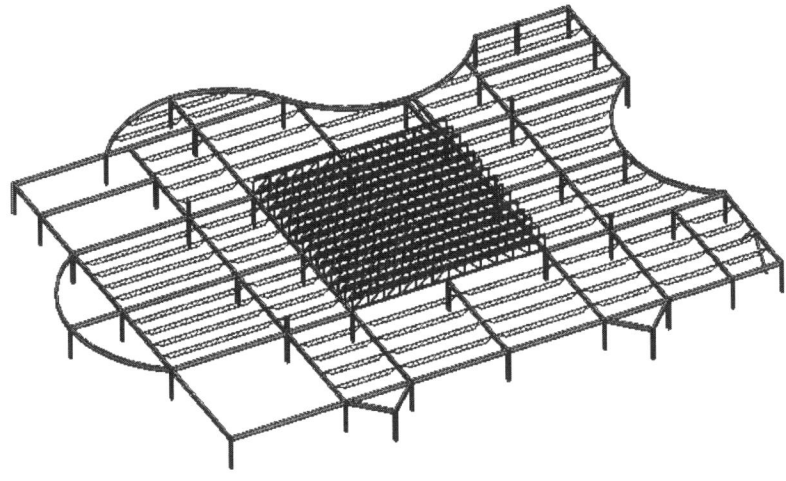

Figure 8–68

12. Save the project.

Task 3: Attach the trusses to a roof.

1. Open the Visibility/Graphic Overrides dialog box and toggle on **Roofs**. An existing roof (referencing the location of the skylight) displays.

2. In the Quick Access Toolbar, click (Close Inactive Views) so that only the 3D view displays.

3. Open the **Elevations (Building Elevations): East** and **South** views.

4. Type **WT** to tile the three views and **ZA** so that they are all zoomed out fully.

5. Zoom in on the skylight roof in the two elevation views, similar to that shown in Figure 8-69.

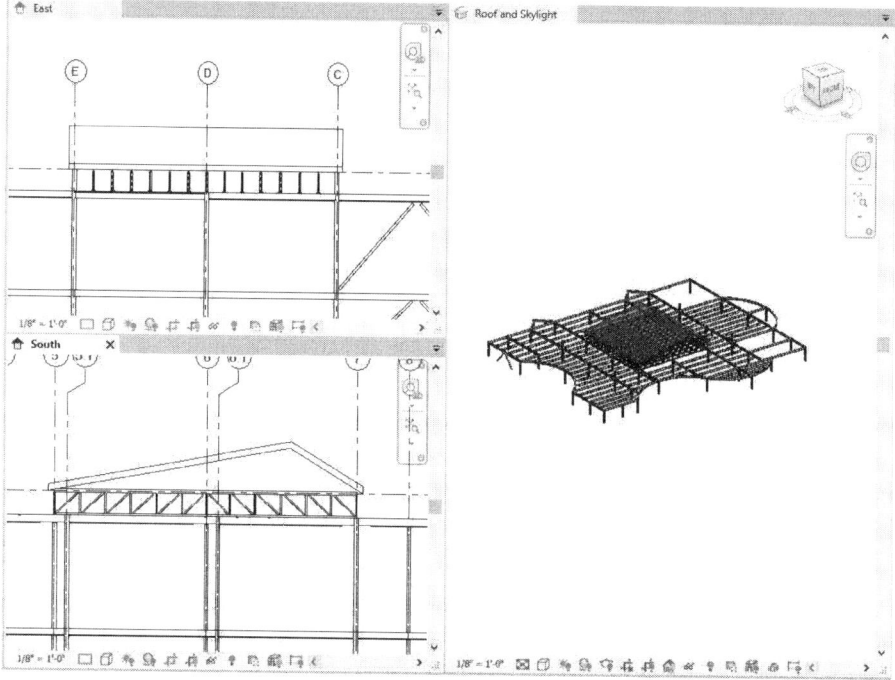

Figure 8-69

6. In the **Elevation: East** view, select one truss, then right-click and select **Select all Instances> In Entire Project**.

7. In the *Modify |Structural Trusses* tab>Modify Truss panel, click (Attach Top/Bottom) and verify in the Options Bar that *Attach Trusses* is set to **Top**.

8. Select the roof. Allow time for it all to process until the trusses expand to touch the roof, as shown in Figure 8-70.

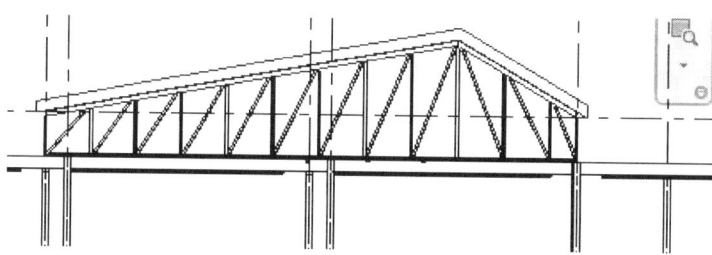

Figure 8-70

9. Make the **3D View: Roof and Skylight** view active and type **TW** to return to the tabbed view.
10. Save and close the project.

End of practice

Chapter Review Questions

1. When placing a beam from the Options Bar, which of the following is NOT an option?

    a. Structural Usage

    b. Placement Plane

    c. 3D Snapping

    d. At Columns

2. Which of the following describes a beam system?

    a. Parallel beams grouped together after they are placed.

    b. Parallel beams placed at the same time.

    c. All beams in a bay grouped together after they are placed.

    d. All beams in a bay placed at the same time.

3. In a plan view, which of the following changes the display to show the stick symbol for beams, as shown in Figure 8–71?

    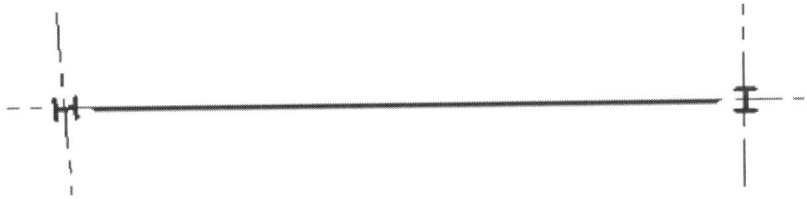

    Figure 8–71

    a. Detail Level: Coarse

    b. Detail Level: Medium

    c. Visual Style: Wireframe

    d. Visual Style: Hidden

4. How do you create sloped beams such as those shown in Figure 8–72?

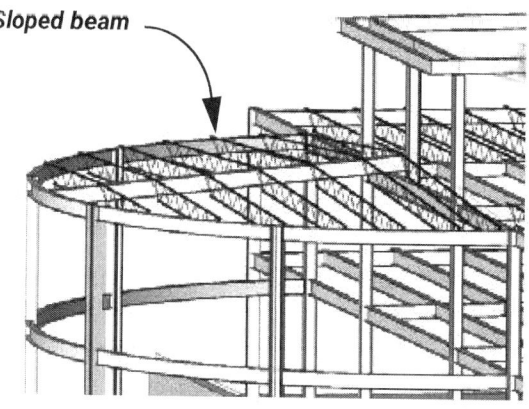

Figure 8–72

   a. Specify the *Slope* before you start drawing the beam.
   b. Specify the *Start/End Level Offset* before you start drawing the beam.
   c. Change the *Slope* after you have drawn the beam.
   d. Change the *Start/End Level Offset* after you have drawn the beam.

5. Where do you assign the structural member types and sizes for the components of a truss? (Select all that apply.)

   a. In Family Types
   b. In Properties
   c. In Type Properties
   d. In the Options Bar

Command Summary

Button	Command	Location
Clipboard		
	Copy to Clipboard	• **Ribbon:** *Modify* tab>Clipboard panel • **Shortcut:** <Ctrl>+C
	Paste	• **Ribbon:** *Modify* tab>Clipboard panel • **Shortcut:** <Ctrl>+<V>
	(Paste) Aligned to Selected Levels	• **Ribbon:** *Modify* tab>Clipboard panel
	(Paste) Aligned to Selected View	• **Ribbon:** *Modify* tab>Clipboard panel
Structural Framing Elements		
	Beam	• **Ribbon:** *Structure* tab>Structure panel
	Beam System	• **Ribbon:** *Structure* tab>Structure panel
	Brace	• **Ribbon:** *Structure* tab>Structure panel • **Shortcut:** BR
	Structural Trusses	• **Ribbon:** *Structure* tab>Structure panel
Structural Framing Modification		
	Apply Coping	• **Ribbon:** *Modify* tab>Geometry panel, expand Cope
	Attach Top/Base	• **Ribbon:** *Modify	Structural Columns* tab>Modify Column panel
	Attach Top/Bottom	• **Ribbon:** *Modify	Structural Trusses* tab>Modify Truss panel
	Beam/Column Joins	• **Ribbon:** *Modify* tab>Geometry panel
	Change Reference	• **Ribbon:** *Modify	Structural Framing* tab>Join Tools panel
	Connection	• **Ribbon:** *Structure* tab>Connection panel

Button	Command	Location
	Detach Top/Base	• **Ribbon:** *Modify	Structural Columns* tab>Modify Column panel
	Detach Top/Bottom	• **Ribbon:** *Modify	Structural Trusses* tab>Modify Truss panel
	Justification Points	• **Ribbon:** *Modify	Structural Framing* tab>Justification panel • **Shortcut:** JP
	Offset	• **Ribbon:** *Modify	Structural Framing* tab>Justification panel
	y Offset	• **Ribbon:** *Modify	Structural Framing* tab>Justification panel • **Shortcut:** JY
	z Offset	• **Ribbon:** *Modify	Structural Framing* tab>Justification panel • **Shortcut:** JZ

Chapter 9

Adding Structural Slabs

Structural slabs can be used for foundation slabs (slab on grade), floors, and roofs. Slab edges can be added to foundation slabs and floors to provide additional stability. For multi-story buildings, you can cut holes in the slabs, either individually or by creating a shaft that passes through several slabs.

Learning Objectives

- Create slabs for foundations, structural floors, and roofs.
- Add slab edges for stability along each side of the slab.
- Create shaft openings that pass through multiple levels for elevators and stairwells.

9.1 Modeling Structural Slabs

Floors, some roofs, and foundation slabs (shown in Figure 9–1) are created by sketching a boundary and then applying options such as span direction and slope. After you create a structural slab, you can add and modify the slab thickness and edges.

Note: The term slab in this topic applies to structural foundation slabs, floors, and roofs.

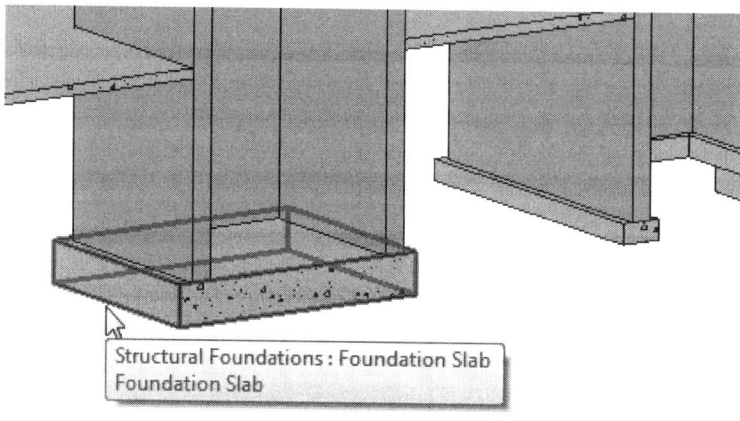

Figure 9–1

How To: Place a Structural Slab for Foundations or Floors

1. In the *Structure* tab>Foundation panel, click (Slab), or in the *Structure* tab>Structure panel, click (Floor: Structural), or type **SB**.
2. In the Type Selector, select the slab or floor type you want to use.
3. In Properties, you can adjust *Constraints* and *Structural* values.
4. In the Options Bar, you can set an offset that places the sketched line at a distance offset from a selected wall or another sketched line.
5. The **Extend into wall (to core)** option is also available in the Options Bar. Use this if you want the slab to cut into the wall. For example, the slab would cut through the gypsum wall board and the air space but would stop at a core layer, such as CMU.
6. In the *Modify | Create Floor Boundary* tab>Draw panel, use one of the following options to create a closed boundary:
   - Use the Draw tools, such as (Line) or (Pick Lines) when the slab is not defined by walls or other structural elements.
   - Use (Pick Walls) when walls define the perimeter.
   - Use (Pick Supports) and select structural walls or beams if support beams have already been placed in the project.

7. Click (Span Direction) to modify the direction for floor spans. The first pick or line drawn is automatically the boundary line and is displayed with the span direction symbol, as shown in Figure 9–2.

8. (Flip) switches the inside/outside status of the boundary location if you have a wall selected, as shown in Figure 9–2.

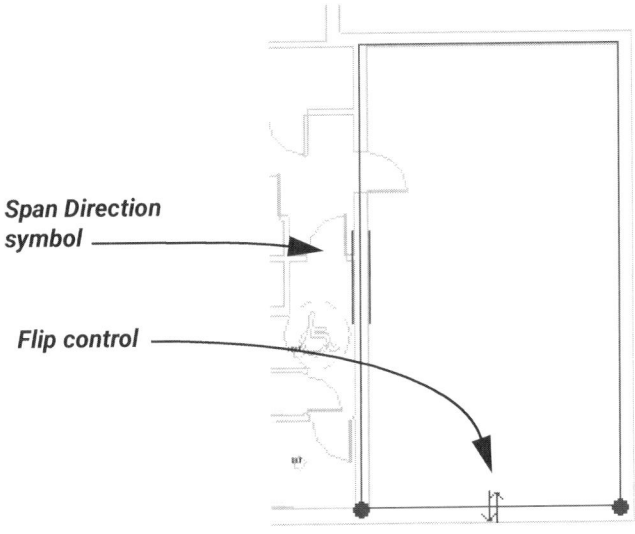

Figure 9–2

- If you select one of the boundary sketches, you can also set *Cantilevers* for *Concrete* or *Steel*, as shown in Figure 9–3.

Figure 9–3

- Each line that defines the perimeter of the slab has its own set of properties. This is because different sides of the building can have different slab edge conditions. Setting a cantilever can control the detail, as shown in Figure 9–4.

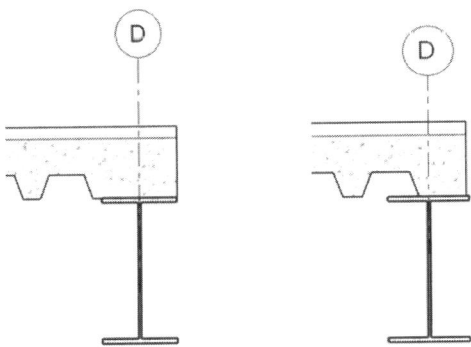

Figure 9–4

- If you specify a cantilever, such as the example shown in Figure 9–5, both the magenta line for the sketch and the black line for the actual slab edge display. This affects how the decking is terminated.

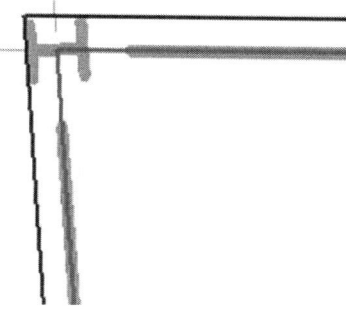

Figure 9–5

- This does not add a pour stop or edge angle. You can do so after you finish the sketch.
- To create an opening inside the sketch, create a separate closed loop inside the first sketch, as shown in Figure 9–6.

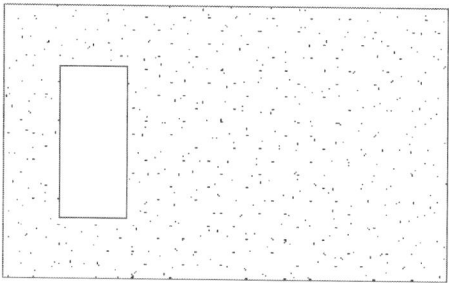

Figure 9–6

9. In the *Modify | Create Floor Boundary* tab>Mode panel, click ✓ (Finish Edit Mode).

- If you create a floor on an upper level, an alert box displays asking if you want the walls below to be attached to the underside of the floor and its level. If you have a variety of wall heights, it is better to click **No** and attach the walls separately.
- Another alert box might open referencing joining geometry between the floor/roof and walls. You can automatically join the geometry now or later.
- If the *Visual Style* is set to (Hidden Line), the slab hides any lines that are underneath it, usually displaying as a dashed line, as shown in Figure 9–7.

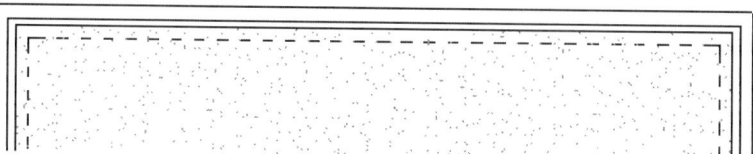

Figure 9–7

Adding Structural Slabs

How To: Place a Roof Slab

Note: Structural floor elements are occasionally used in place of roof elements.

1. In the *Architecture* tab>Build panel, expand (Roof) and click (Roof by Footprint)
2. In the Type Selector, select the roof type you want to use.
3. In the *Modify | Create Roof Footprint* tab>Draw panel, use the Draw tools to create a closed boundary, such as (Line), (Pick Lines), or (Pick Walls) when walls define the perimeter.
4. In the Options Bar, set the slope and overhang options. For a flat roof, clear the **Defines slope** option and set *Overhang* to **0**, as shown in Figure 9–8.

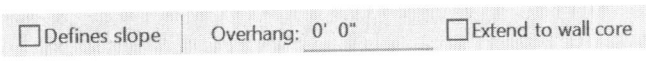

Figure 9–8

5. Click (Finish Edit Mode).

Modifying Slabs

You can change a slab to a different type in the Type Selector. In Properties, you can modify parameters including the *Height Offset From Level*, as shown for a structural floor in Figure 9–9. When you have a slab selected, you can also edit the boundaries.

Note: The slab type controls the thickness of a slab. For information on slab types, see A.4 Creating Slab Types.

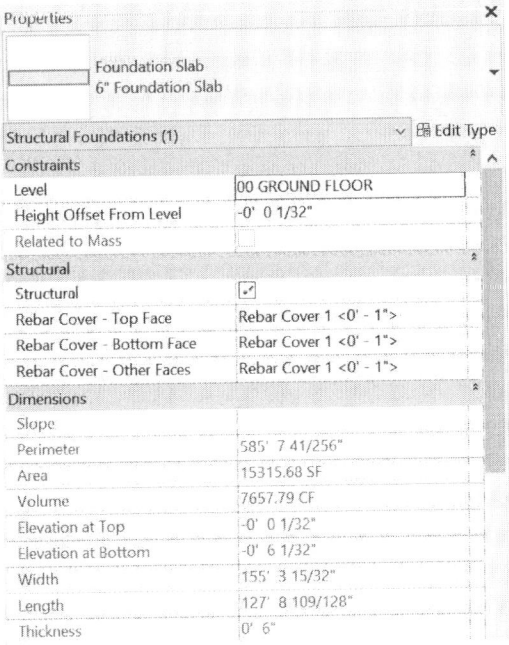

Figure 9–9

How To: Modify the Slab Boundaries

1. Select a slab. You might need to hover your cursor over an element near the slab and press <Tab> until the type displays in the Status Bar or in a tooltip, as shown in Figure 9–10.

Figure 9–10

> **Hint: Selecting Slab Faces**
>
> If it is difficult to select the slab edges, toggle on (Select elements by face). This enables you to select the slab face in addition to the edges. This is also helpful to use when selecting walls in elevation or section views.

2. In the *Modify* contextual tab>Mode panel, click (Edit Sketch). You are placed in sketch mode.

3. Modify the sketch lines by using the Draw tools, controls, and other modify tools.
   - Double-click on a slab to move directly to editing the boundary.
   - When modifying a slab, you can add an opening by drawing a closed loop within the slab boundaries.
   - Sketches can be edited in plan and 3D views, but not in elevations. If you try to edit a sketch in an elevation view, you are prompted to select another view for editing.

4. Click (Finish Edit Mode).
   - You can modify the Foundation Span Direction symbol (shown in Figure 9–11) after a slab has been placed by selecting it, clicking (Align Perpendicular) in the *Modify | Foundation Span Direction Symbol* tab, and selecting the slab edge, grid line, or beam edge to realign the span direction. This is useful if you are placing metal decking.

Adding Structural Slabs

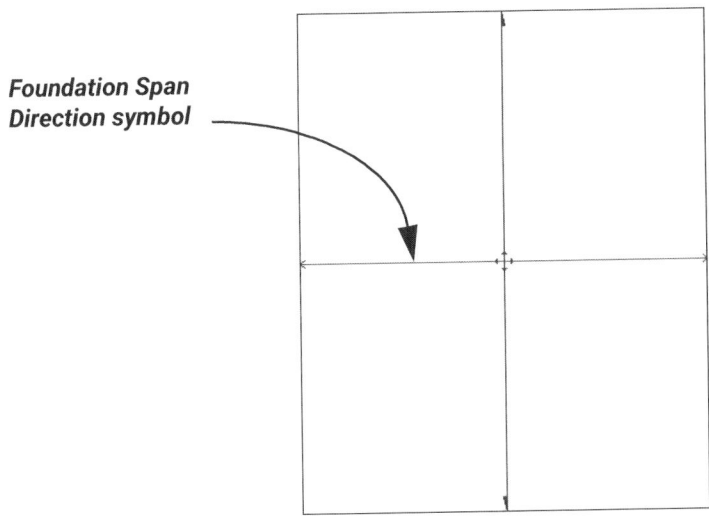

Figure 9–11

Slab Edges

You can add elements to a foundation slab or structural floor for a haunched or thickened slab edge, as shown in Figure 9–12. Once the slab edge is in place, it needs to be joined to the slab or structural floor.

Note: Cutting a section through the objects you want to join helps to display them more clearly.

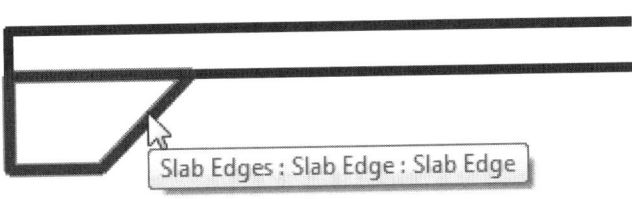

Figure 9–12

- Slab edges cannot be applied to roof elements.

How To: Place a Slab Edge

1. Open a 3D view showing the slab.
2. In the *Structure* tab>Foundation panel, expand (Slab), or in the *Structure* tab>Structure panel, expand (Floor) and click (Floor: Slab Edge).
3. In the Type Selector, select the slab edge type.

4. Select the edges of the slab or floor where you want to apply the slab edge, as shown in Figure 9–13. You can press <Tab> to highlight and select all sides of the slab.

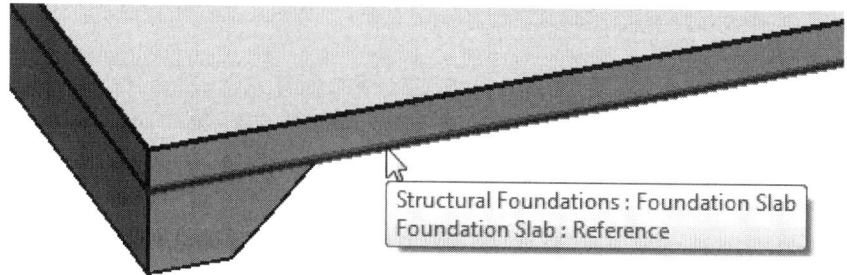

Figure 9–13

Joining Geometry

Join Geometry is a versatile command used to clean up intersections. The elements remain separate, but the intersections are cleaned up. It can be used with many types of elements, including slabs, floors, walls, and roofs. A typical use is to connect slab edges with the slab, as shown in the section views in Figure 9–14.

Note: If the material is not exactly the same, a thin line still separates the elements.

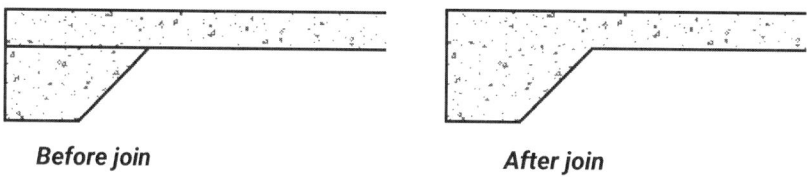

Before join | After join

Figure 9–14

- Joining geometry makes two separate elements display as one, but they can still be modified individually after being joined.

How To: Join Geometry

1. In the *Modify* tab>Geometry panel, expand (Join) and click (Join Geometry).
2. For the first pick, you will select the element you want to join to another. For the second pick, you will select the element to be joined to.

- If you toggle on the **Multiple Join** option in the Options Bar, you can select several elements to join to the first selection.

- To remove the join, expand (Join), click (Unjoin Geometry), and select the elements to unjoin.

Practice 9a
Model Structural Slabs

Practice Objectives

- Add a slab with an edge.
- Add structural floors.

In this practice, you will create slab foundations at the base of elevator shafts and add a slab edge to them. You will also create a floor slab and then copy and modify the type to create the rest of the floors and roof deck, as shown in Figure 9–15.

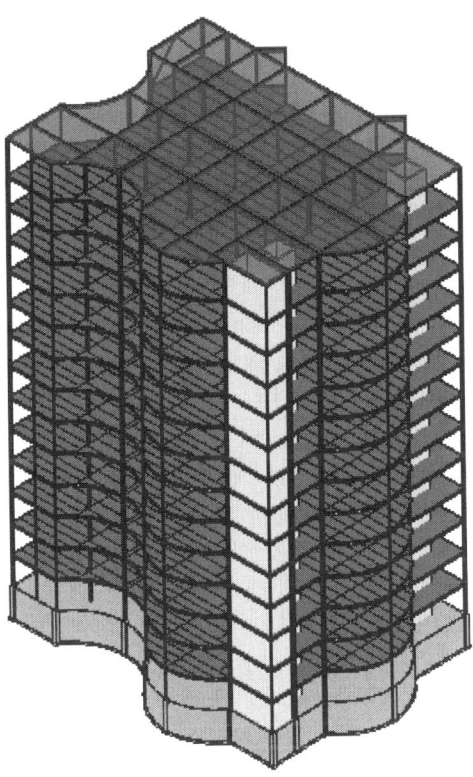

Figure 9–15

- This practice file contains additional wall elements.

Task 1: Add slab foundations for elevator shafts.

1. Open **Structure-Slab.rvt** from the practice files folder.
2. Open the **Structural Plans: 00 T.O. FOOTING** view.

3. Zoom in to the lower-right corner of the building to the elevator shaft between grid intersections **E9** and **F10**, where the section marker is.
4. In the *Structure* tab>Foundation panel, click (Slab).
5. In the Type Selector, select **Foundation Slab: 12" Foundation Slab.**
6. In the *Modify | Create Floor Boundary* tab>Draw panel, click (Pick Walls).
7. In the Options Bar, set the *Offset* to **2'-0"**,
8. Click on each wall to create a boundary line, as shown in Figure 9–16, that goes around the four walls.

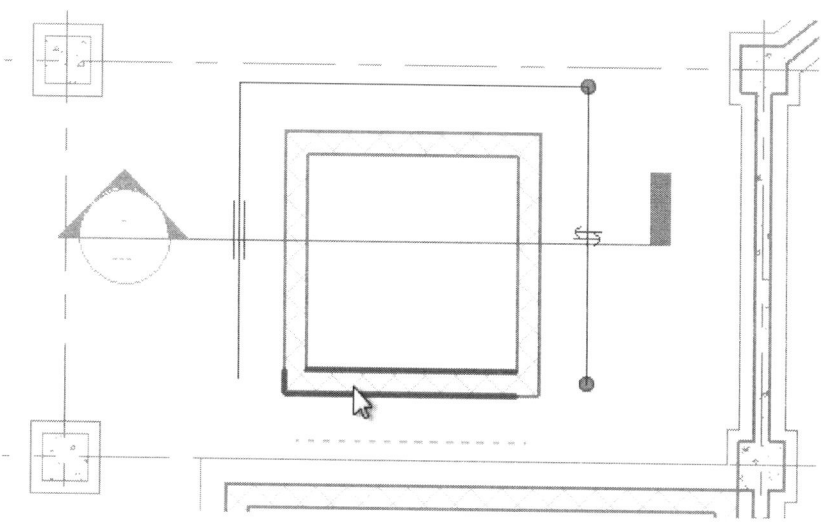

Figure 9–16

9. Click (Finish Edit Mode).

10. Click (Modify) and select the **Foundation Span Direction** symbol, which is automatically added when you finish the sketch. Open the Visibility/Graphic Overrides dialog box (type **VG** or **VV**) and on the *Annotation Categories* tab, turn off **Span Direction Symbol**. Alternatively, you can delete the symbol in this view (it can be added again in a working document view).

11. Save the project.

Task 2: Add a slab edge to the slab.

1. Open the default 3D view.
2. Select at least one beam, beam system, column, and wall. in the View Control Bar, expand (Temporary Hide/Isolate) and select **Hide Category**. Hide any other elements that might be in the way of seeing just the slabs, such as rebar.

3. Use the ViewCube to rotate the model so you are viewing the bottom of the slab, as shown in Figure 9–17. (Hint: In the ViewCube, click the corner at the intersection of the **FRONT**, **RIGHT**, and **BOTTOM** planes.)

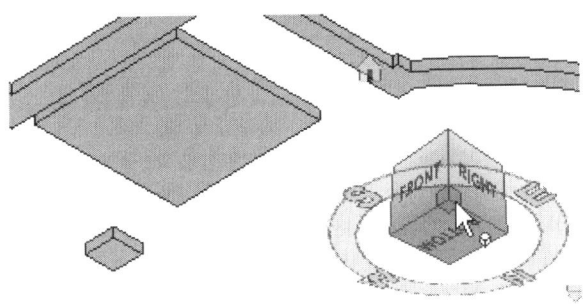

Figure 9–17

4. Zoom in on the slab.
5. In the *Structure* tab>Foundation panel, expand (Slab) and click (Floor: Slab Edge).
6. Select the four bottom edges of the slab, as shown in Figure 9–18. Rotate the view as required to see each edge.

   Note: If you add a slab edge in a plan view, the software selects the top edge of the slab rather than the bottom.

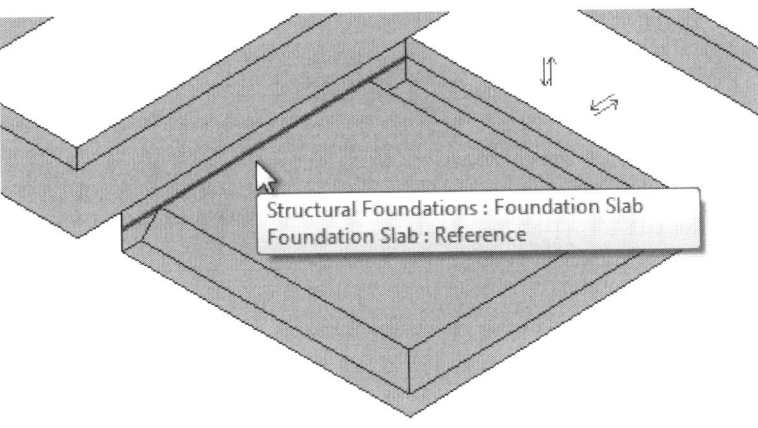

Figure 9–18

7. Click (Modify).
8. Reorient the view and select **Reset Temporary Hide/Isolate**.

9. Switch back to the **Structural Plans: 00 T.O. FOOTING** view and double-click on the section heads arrow to open the section of the slab. The geometry should look similar to that shown in Figure 9–19.

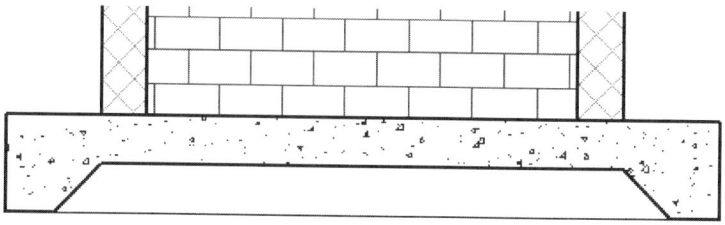

Figure 9–19

10. In the *Modify* tab>Geometry panel, click (Join). Select the foundation and then the thickened slab edge. You only need to select one segment of the edge as it is one element.
11. Return to the **Structural Plans: 00 T.O. FOOTING** view.
12. Select the slab and copy it to the elevator shaft located between grid intersections **B9** and **C10**, as shown in Figure 9–20. (Note: The image has been cropped for clarity.)

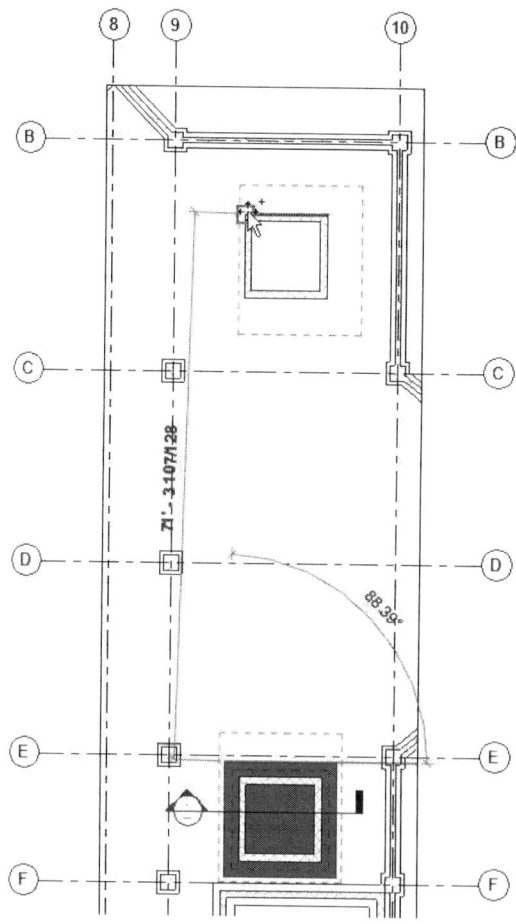

Figure 9–20

13. Click in an empty area in the view to clear the selection.
14. Save the project.

Task 3: Add a structural floor to the ground floor level.

1. Open the **Structural Plans: 00 GROUND FLOOR** view.
2. In the *Structure* tab>Structure panel, click (Floor: Structural).
3. In the Type Selector, select **Floor: 6" Concrete**.
4. In the Options Bar, set the *Offset* to **0** and clear the checkmark from **Extend into wall (to core)**.
5. In Properties, set the *Height Offset From Level* to **0'-0"** and verify in the *Structural* section that **Structural** is checked.
6. In the *Modify | Create Floor Boundary* tab>Draw panel, click (Pick Walls).
7. Hover over one of the perimeter walls and press <Tab> until all walls are highlighted, and then, click to select all of the walls, as shown in Figure 9–21. Ensure that the cursor is on the outside of the wall. Click to accept the selection.

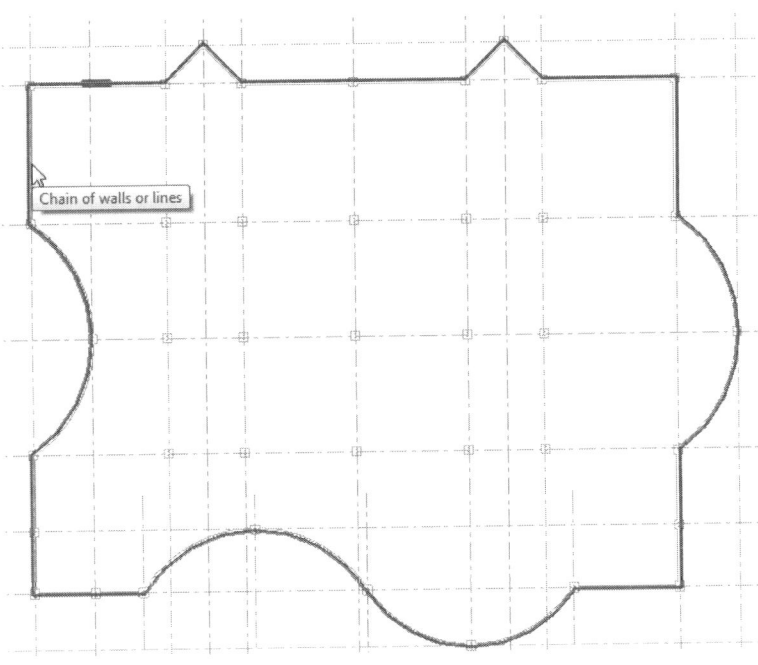

Figure 9–21

- If you selected the inside of the walls, use the Flip control to relocate the sketch lines to the outside of the walls.

8. In the Mode panel, click (Finish Edit Mode).

9. Click **Attach** in the Attaching to floor dialog box to attach walls that go up to this floor's level to its bottom.
10. Click in an empty area in the view to clear the selection.
11. Zoom out and save the project.

Task 4: Add floor slabs to the rest of the floors.

1. Open the default 3D view and select the slab.

   Note: *If it is difficult to select the slab, toggle on* (Select elements by face).

2. In the *Modify | Floors* tab>Clipboard panel, click (Copy to Clipboard).
3. In the same panel, expand (Paste) and click (Aligned to Selected Levels).
4. In the Select Levels dialog box, select **TOS-1ST FLOOR** and click **OK**.
5. The new slab is highlighted on level **TOS-1ST FLOOR**, as shown in Figure 9–22. In the Type Selector, change the floor type to **Floor: 3" LW Concrete on 2" Metal Deck**.

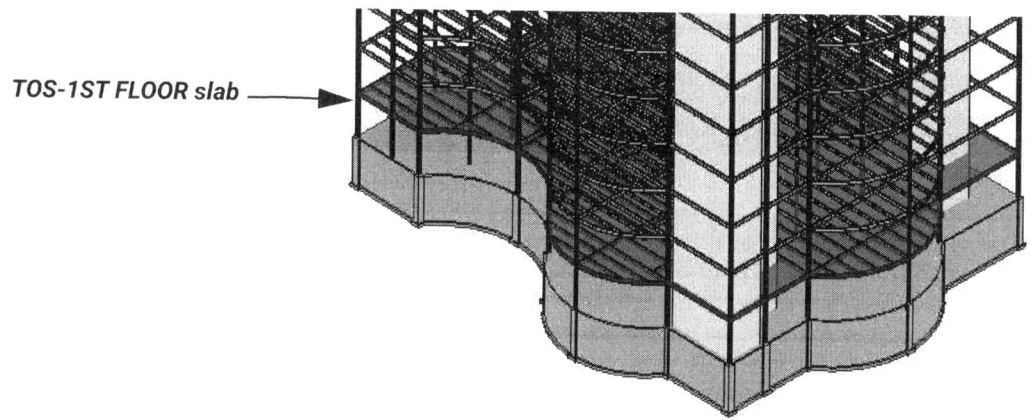

Figure 9–22

6. In Properties, under *Constraints*, change the *Height Offset From Level* to **5"** to leave room for the steel structure below the slab. Click **Apply**.
7. Using **Copy to the Clipboard** and **Paste Aligned to Selected Levels**, copy the metal deck floor to the rest of the floors, from **TOS-2ND FLOOR** up to **TOS-14 ROOF**.

8. Zoom out to see the entire building. The top slab is still selected, as shown on the right in Figure 9–23. In the Type Selector, change the type to **Floor: 1 1/2" Metal Roof Deck**, and in Properties, change the *Height Offset From Level* to **0'-1 1/2"**, as shown on the left in Figure 9–23.

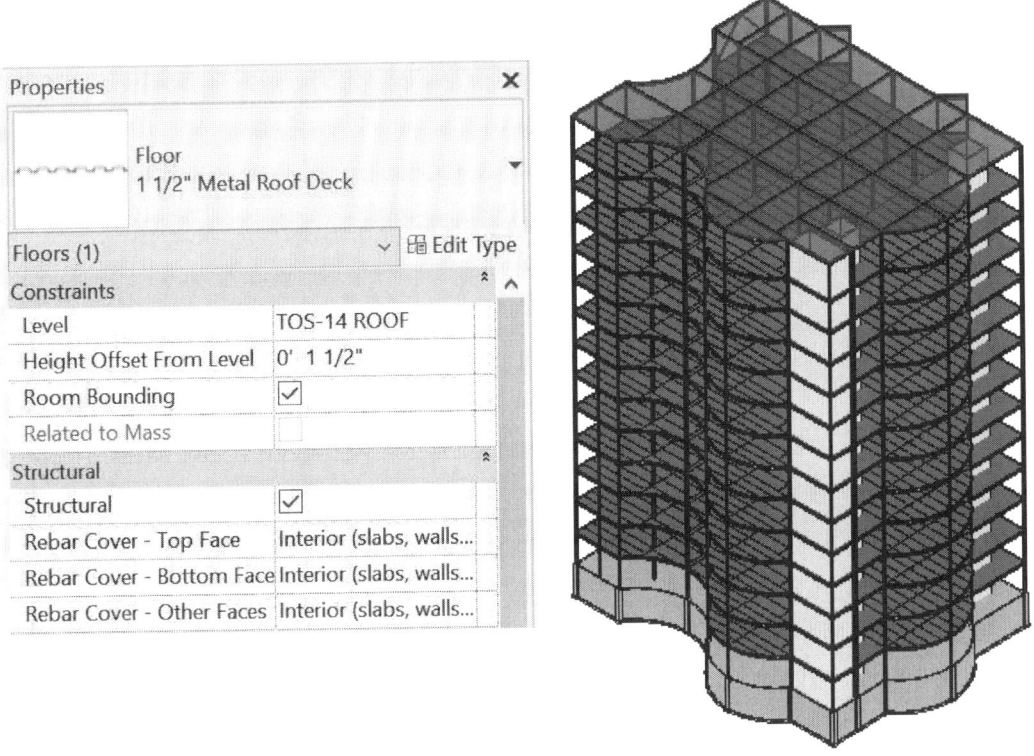

Figure 9–23

9. Click in an empty area in the view to clear the selection.
10. Save the project.

Task 5: Add a slab edge to the ground floor.

Slab edges are copied with the slab. Since a slab edge is not required on the upper floors, add the slab edge after copying the slab.

1. While remaining in a 3D view, zoom in on the ground floor slab and select it.
2. From the View Control Bar, expand 👓 (Temporary Hide/Isolate) and select **Isolate Element** to only see the slab floor.
3. Use the ViewCube to rotate the model so you are viewing the bottom of the slab, as shown in Figure 9–24.
4. In the *Structure* tab>Foundation panel, expand 🟦 (Slab) and click 🟦 (Floor: Slab Edges).

5. Hover over the bottom edge of the ground floor slab and press <Tab> to select the entire chain of lines.
6. Click to place the slab edge. It is placed around the entire edge of the slab, as shown in Figure 9–24.

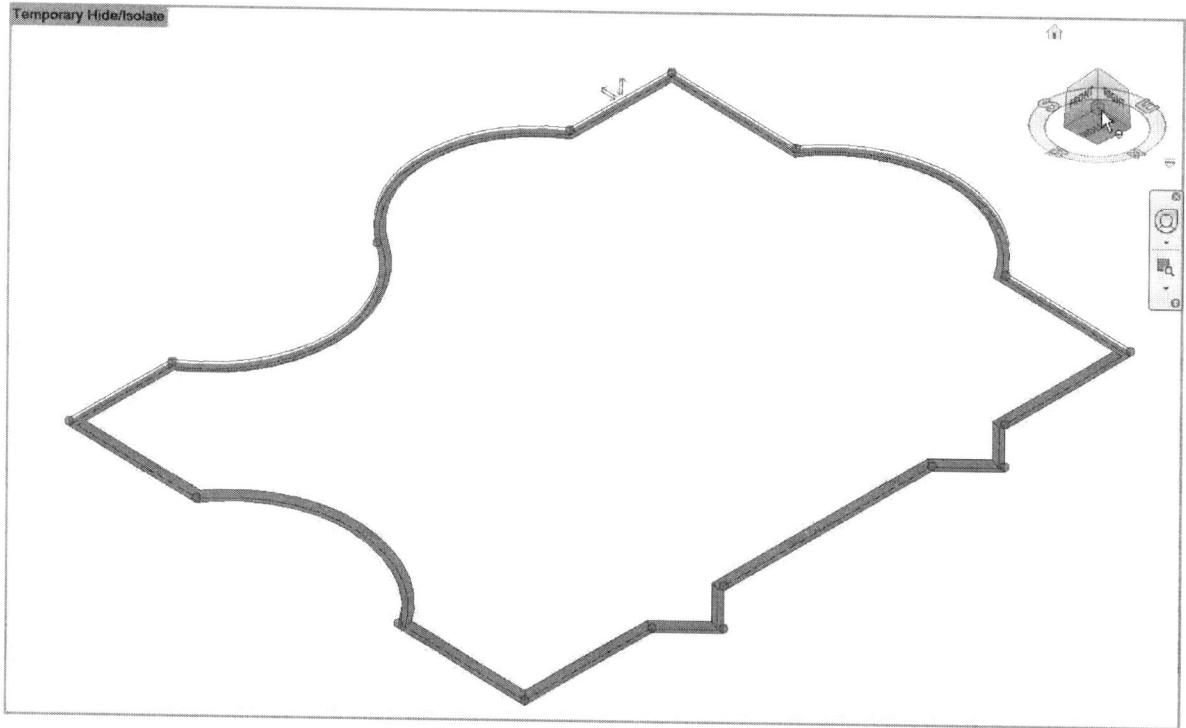

Figure 9–24

7. Reorient the view and select **Reset Temporary Hide/Isolate**.
8. Click (Modify).
9. Select all the walls by pressing <Tab>. With the walls selected, hover your cursor over the edge of the floor and press <Tab> until the Status Bar displays **Slab Edge**. Press <Ctrl> to select the slab edge.
10. From the View Control Bar, expand (Temporary Hide/Isolate) and select **Isolate Element** to only see the slab edge and the walls.
11. In the *Modify* tab>Geometry panel, click (Join).
12. On the Options Bar, check the check box next to **Multiple Join**.
13. Select the slab edge as the first pick and then select each wall. Use the viewcube to rotate the model around to ensure that each wall gets selected.
14. Reorient the view and select **Reset Temporary Hide/Isolate**.
15. Save and close the project.

End of practice

9.2 Creating Shaft Openings

Shaft openings are designed to create a void through multiple levels in the structure, cutting through only floors/slabs, roofs, and ceilings. Structural components like beams, walls, and framing can pass through the opening, as shown in Figure 9–25. If the geometry of the shaft opening changes or moves on one level, it automatically updates on all levels.

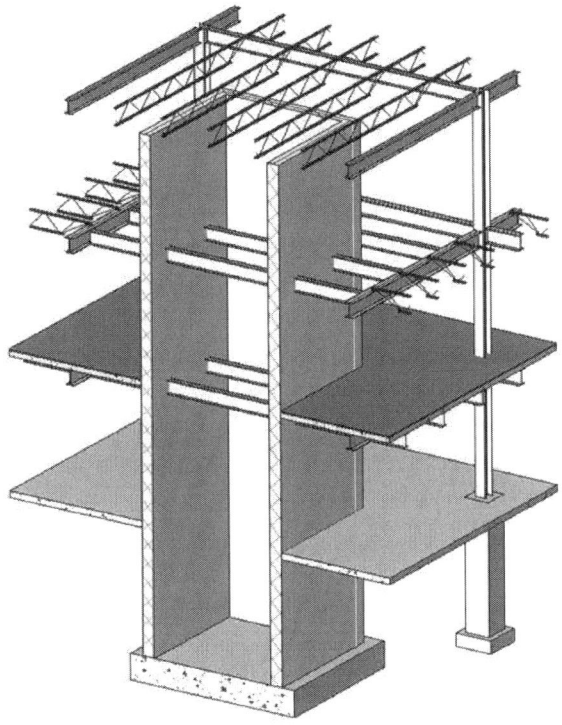

Figure 9–25

How To: Create a Shaft Opening

1. In the *Structure* tab>Opening panel, click (Shaft Opening).
2. In the *Modify | Create Shaft Opening Sketch* tab>Draw panel, click (Boundary Line) and draw a line to deflne the opening.
3. In the Draw panel, click (Symbolic Line) and add lines that show the opening symbol in plan view.
4. In Properties, set the following:
   - *Base and Top Constraint*
   - *Base and Top Offset* or *Unconnected Height*
5. In the Options Bar, set the *Offset* and select **Chain**, if needed.

6. Click ✓ (Finish Edit Mode) to create the opening.

   - When using ▦ (Pick Walls) or other drawing tools to define the perimeter of the opening, you can select the Flip control to flip the lines to the outside, as shown in Figure 9–26.

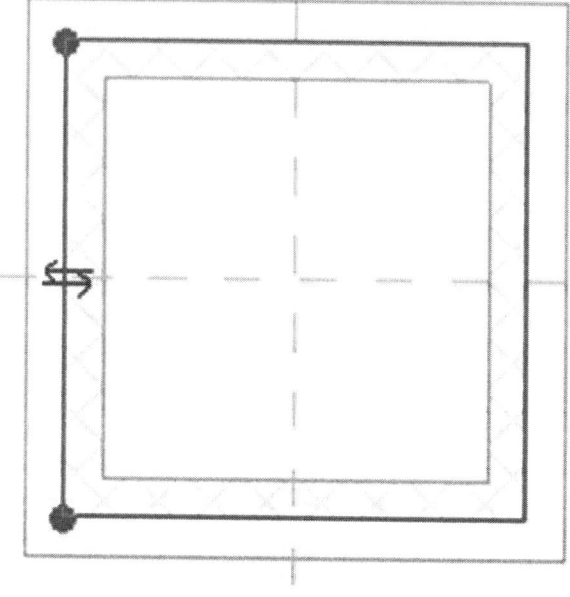

Figure 9–26

   - A shaft opening element can include symbolic lines that repeat on each level, displaying the shaft in a plan view.

7. A shaft is a separate element from the floor, roof, ceiling, or wall, and can be deleted without selecting a host element.

Practice 9b
Create Shaft Openings

Practice Objective

- Create shaft openings.

In this practice, you will add shaft openings in the two elevator shafts and the stairwell, as shown in Figure 9–27.

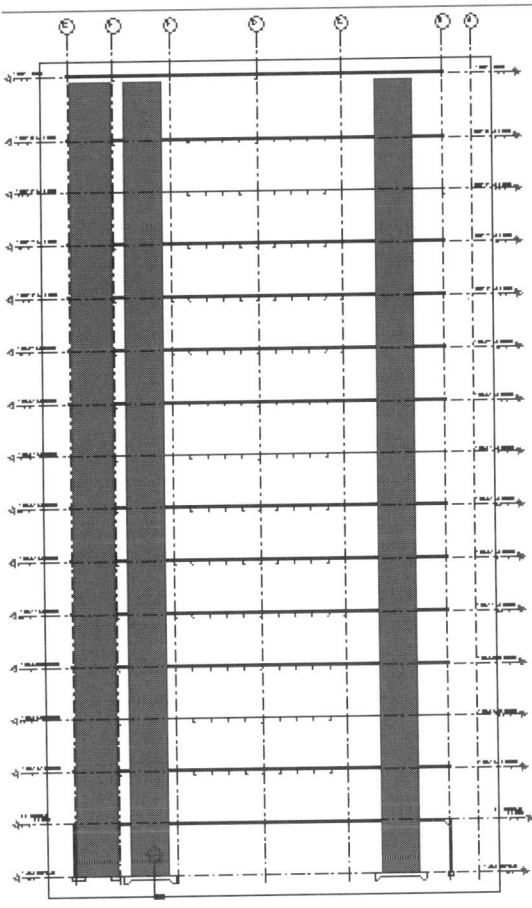

Figure 9–27

Task 1: Add shaft openings.

1. Open **Structural-Shafts.rvt** from the practice files folder.
2. Open the **Structural Plans: 00 T.O. FOOTING** view. Zoom in on the stairwell between grid intersections **F9.1** and **G10**, in the lower-right corner.

3. In the *Structure* tab>Opening panel, click (Shaft).
4. In the *Modify | Create Shaft Opening Sketch* tab>Draw panel, ensure that (Boundary Line) is highlighted and click (Pick Walls).
5. Verify that in the Options Bar, the *Offset* is **0'-0"** and **Extend into wall (to core)** is unchecked.
6. Select the exterior face of the masonry walls around the stairwell (select one wall and press <Tab> to select the chain of walls). If needed, select the Flip control to flip the lines to the exterior side of the walls, as shown in Figure 9–28.

Figure 9–28

7. In the *Draw* panel, click (Symbolic Line).
8. Using (Line), draw an **X** in the opening, as shown in Figure 9–29.

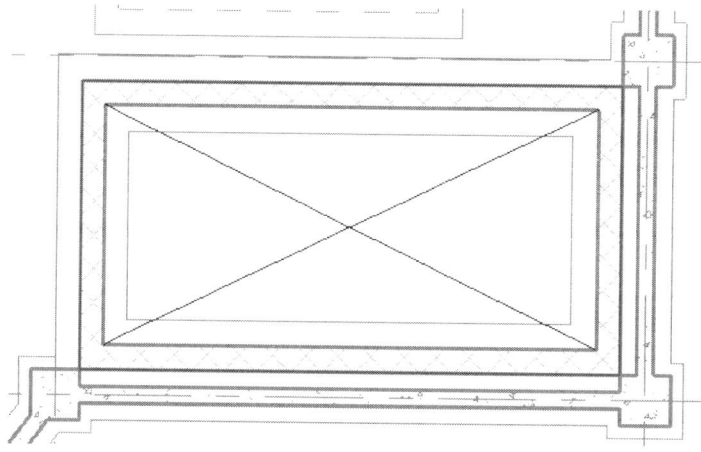

Figure 9–29

9. In the Mode panel, click (Finish Edit Mode).
10. Repeat the procedure for the two elevator shafts. Ensure that the shaft openings are aligned with the outside faces of the shaft walls.
11. Zoom to fit the view and save the project.

Task 2: Modify the shaft properties.

1. Create a building section through the three shafts, limiting the width of the section so that it does not display the entire building.
2. Open the section view. The shafts do not display, but you can hover over one of them near the base of the footing and select it. The shaft only extends through one set of floors, as shown in Figure 9–30.

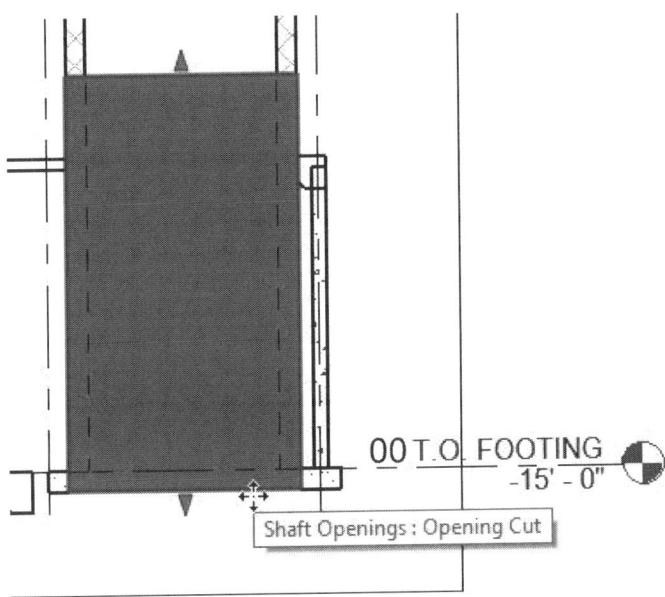

Figure 9–30

3. Hold <Ctrl> and select the other two shafts.
4. In Properties, set the following parameters:
    - *Base Constraint:* **00 T.O. FOOTING**
    - *Base Offset:* **1"**
    - *Top Constraint:* **Up to level: TOS-14TH ROOF**
    - *Top Offset:* (negative) **-1'-3"**
5. Zoom out to see that the shafts now expand from the top of the footing to just below the roof.
    - Note: Setting the base and top offset prevents the void from cutting the foundation and roof.
6. Click in an empty space in the view to clear the selection.
7. Save and close the project.

End of practice

Chapter Review Questions

1. When creating a slab, which of the following Draw tools used to create a boundary automatically updates the slab boundary if the other elements are changed? (Select all that apply.)

    a. ╱ (Line)

    b. ⚆ (Pick Lines)

    c. ▥ (Pick Walls)

    d. ▥ (Pick Supports)

2. Foundation slabs often have slab edges, as shown in a section in Figure 9–31. Which of the following is true of slab edges?

    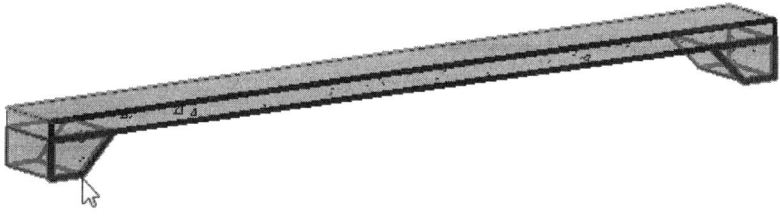

    Figure 9–31

    a. They come in automatically when you draw the slab.
    b. You can add them by selecting **Slab Edge** in the Options Bar.
    c. You need to add them with the separate **Slab Edge** command.
    d. You can add them by modifying the Type Properties of the slab.

3. Which of the following elements cannot be cut by a shaft opening, such as those shown in Figure 9-32?

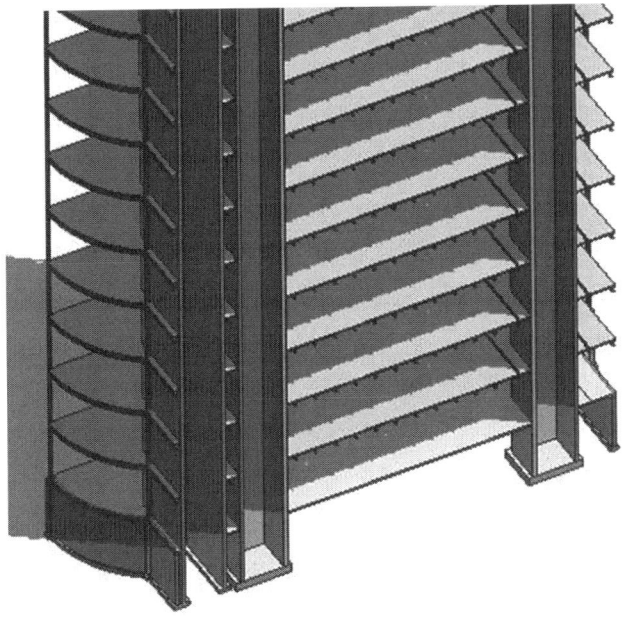

Figure 9-32

   a. Roofs
   b. Floors
   c. Ceilings
   d. Beams

4. Which tool would you use to set or modify the direction of metal decking in a structural floor?

   a. Boundary Line
   b. Slope Arrow
   c. Span Direction
   d. Pick Supports

Command Summary

Button	Command	Location
	Align Perpendicular	• **Ribbon:** *Modify	Foundation Span Direction Symbol* tab
	Floor: Slab Edge	• **Ribbon:** *Structure* tab>Foundation panel, expand Slab
	Floor: Structural	• **Ribbon:** *Structure* tab>Structure panel, expand Floor • **Shortcut:** SB
	Roof by Footprint	• **Ribbon:** *Architecture* tab>Build panel, expand Roof
	Shaft	• **Ribbon:** *Structure* tab>Opening panel
	Structural Foundation: Slab	• **Ribbon:** *Structure* tab>Foundation panel, expand Slab

Chapter 10

Structural Reinforcement

Adding reinforcement is an important part of the process when designing concrete structures. One of the primary methods of adding reinforcement is rebar, which comes in many possible sizes and shapes. You can add rebar types individually, in an area, along a path, and using fabric reinforcement sheets.

Learning Objectives

- Examine the types of elements that can have reinforcement added to them.
- Set the reinforcement settings.
- Place existing rebar shapes and sketch custom shapes for single or multi-planar rebar.
- Modify rebar by using controls, properties, and other modification tools.
- Add a rebar coupler and modify coupler ends.
- Place area and path reinforcement in walls or floors.
- Add fabric reinforcement.

10.1 Structural Reinforcement

Revit provides tools for modeling reinforcement in concrete and structural elements, as shown in Figure 10–1. Rebar components are attached to host elements, such as concrete or precast concrete beams, columns, or foundations.

> **Note:** Walls, structural floors, and slab edges can also be valid hosts as long as they have a structural usage and contain a concrete layer.

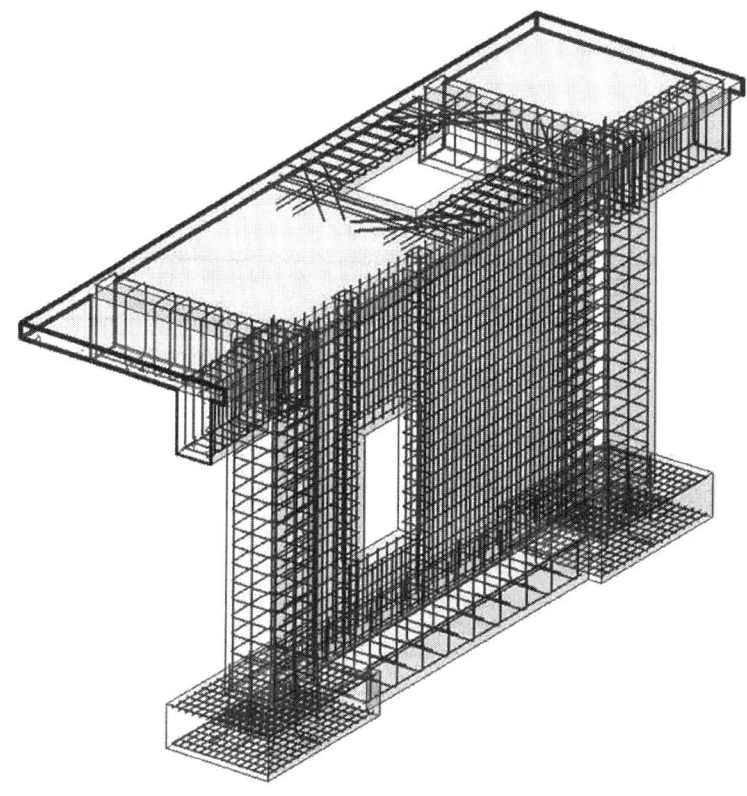

Figure 10–1

You can place reinforcements using the following element types:

- Structural Framing
- Structural Foundations
- Structural Floors
- Foundation Slabs
- Slab Edges
- Structural Columns
- Walls
- Structural Connections
- Wall Foundations
- Imported concrete elements from SAT files or InfraWorks

• Rebar can be placed in free-form concrete elements, such as curved columns and slabs.

Before you add rebar to a project, there are two groups of settings you can establish.

- *Rebar Cover Settings* control the acceptable distance from the element's face, so that when you add rebar to a host you are limited to that setting.
- *Reinforcement Settings* indicate the reinforcement elements display and how to annotate the reinforcement using custom symbols and tags.

Setting the Rebar Cover Depth

Rebar cover settings can differ depending on the project's soil or regional conditions and other issues. Although the software has default settings, they can be changed or additional cover settings can be created when required. As you place reinforcement, the cover depth displays with dashed lines as shown in Figure 10–2.

Figure 10–2

- Each structural element has preset cover settings. You can customize the settings by element or by the individual faces in an element.

How To: Add a Rebar Cover Setting

1. In the *Structure* tab, expand the Reinforcement panel title and click (Rebar Cover Settings).
2. In the Rebar Cover Settings dialog box, click **Add** to create a new cover setting, or select an existing setting and click **Duplicate**.

3. A new setting is added as shown in Figure 10–3. Rename the *Description* for the purpose of the setting and set the *Setting* clearance.

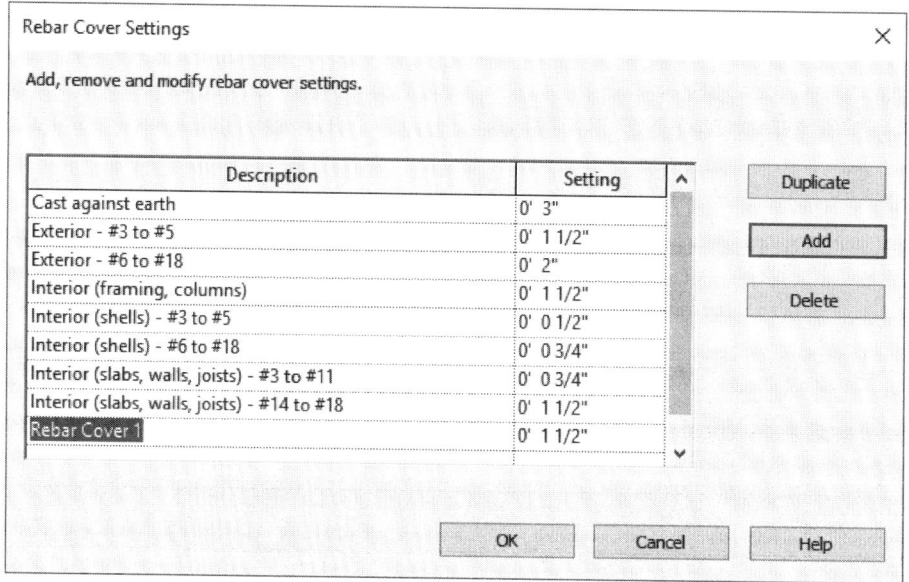

Figure 10–3

4. Click **OK**.

How To: Edit the Rebar Cover

1. In the *Structure* tab>Reinforcement panel, click (Cover).
2. In the Options Bar, select (Pick Elements) or (Pick Faces).
3. Select an element or the face of an element.
4. In the Options Bar, select the cover settings for this specific object, as shown in Figure 10–4.

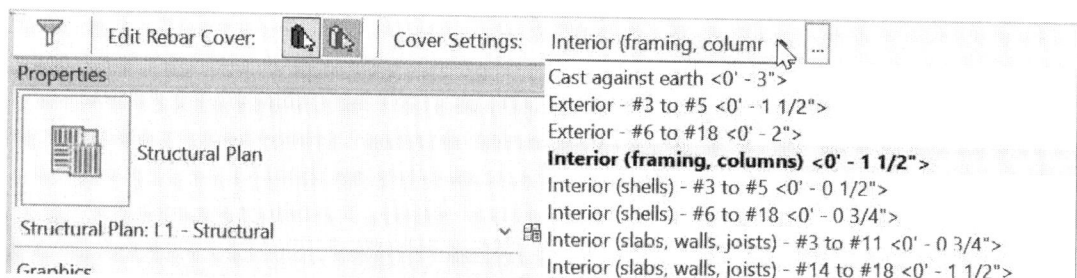

Figure 10–4

- For more options, click (Browse) to open the Rebar Cover Settings dialog box in which you can add a new cover restraint.

- Cover settings can also be modified in Properties when a rebar host element is selected, as shown in Figure 10–5. This only modifies the selected element.

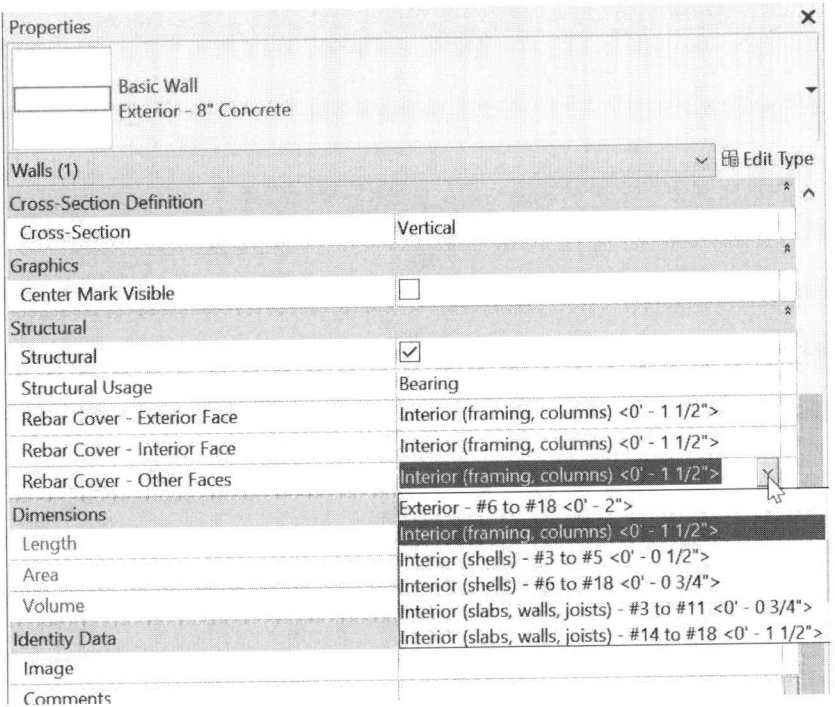

Figure 10–5

Reinforcement Settings

Using Reinforcement Settings, you can specify the structural rebar hosting of area/path reinforcement and annotate the area/path reinforcement region using custom symbols and tags.

- In the *Structure* tab>Reinforcement panel, expand the panel title and click

    (Reinforcement Settings).

General Pane

In the *General* pane, as shown in Figure 10–6, you can determine how area and path reinforcements work in their host elements of floors and walls as well as if hooks are included in rebar shapes. Both of these are on by default in new projects. If you are using couplers to define end treatments then select **Include end treatments in Rebar Shape definition**. This option is off by default.

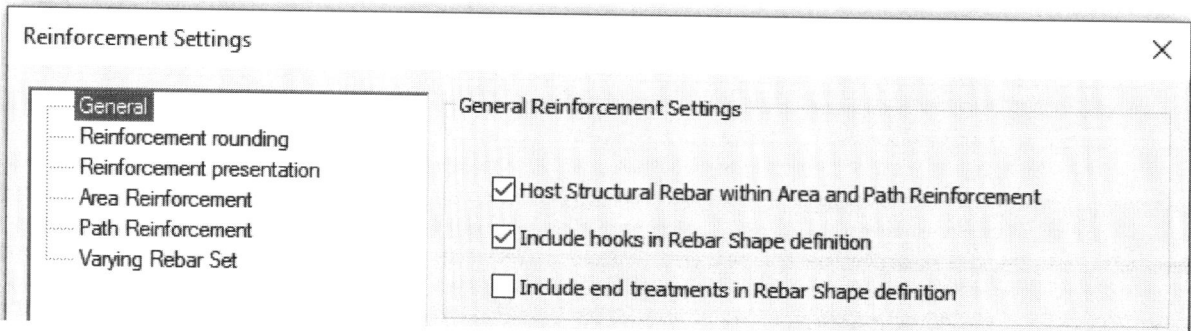

Figure 10–6

- These options must be set before you place any rebar in a project.

- The first time you place rebar, an alert box displays noting which settings are selected, as shown in Figure 10–7.

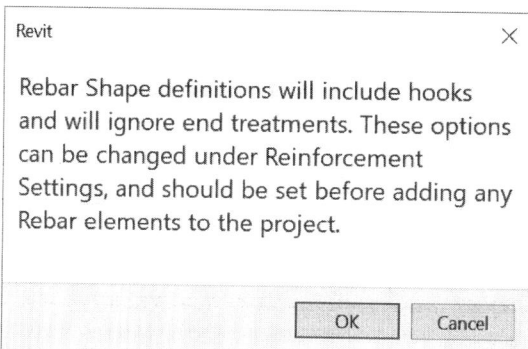

Figure 10–7

Structural Reinforcement

When **Host Structural Rebar with Area and Path Reinforcement** is selected, the structural rebar elements display in the floor or wall, as shown on the left in Figure 10–8. When this option is cleared, the structural rebar elements do not display in the floor or wall, as shown on the right in Figure 10–8, but you can annotate the area/path reinforcement region using custom symbols and tags.

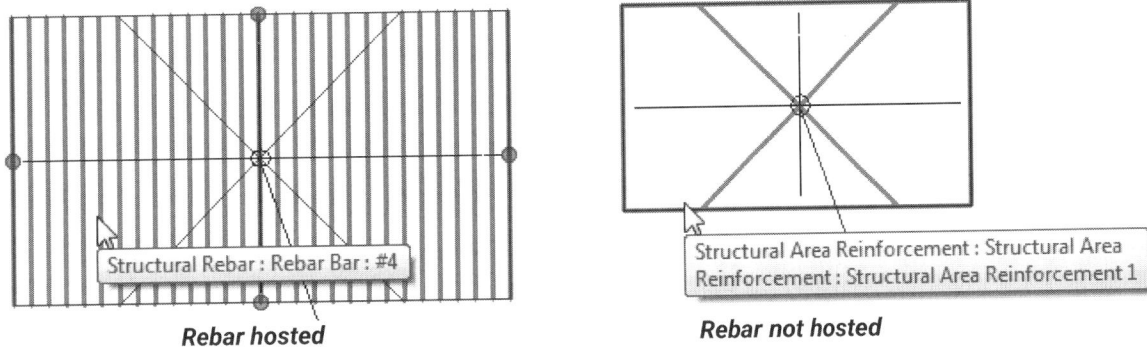

Figure 10–8

When **Include hooks in Rebar Shape definition** is selected, any added hooks are included in standard rebar shapes. This minimizes the number of custom shapes in a project. When this option is cleared, adding hooks to a shape creates additional shapes.

Reinforcement Rounding Pane

In the *Reinforcement rounding* pane (shown in Figure 10–9), you can specify and set up the rounding method (Nearest, Up, or Down) and the amount of rounding for Structural Rebar and Structural Fabric Reinforcement. This overrides Project Units rounding for these elements.

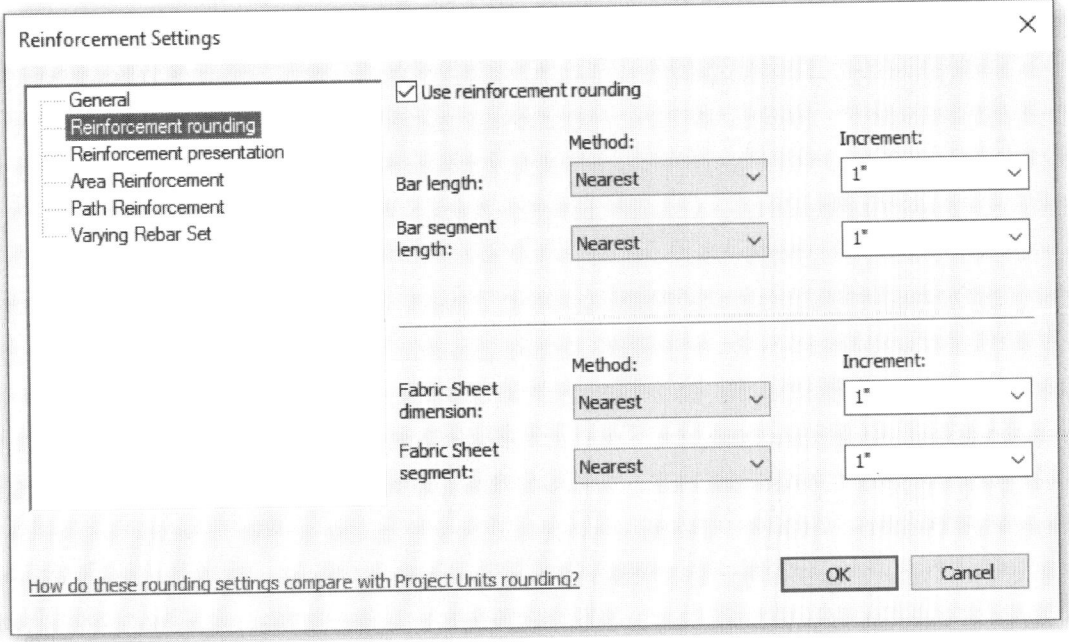

Figure 10–9

Reinforcement Presentation Pane

In the *Reinforcement presentation* pane you can specify how Rebar Sets display in views and sections, as shown in Figure 10–10.

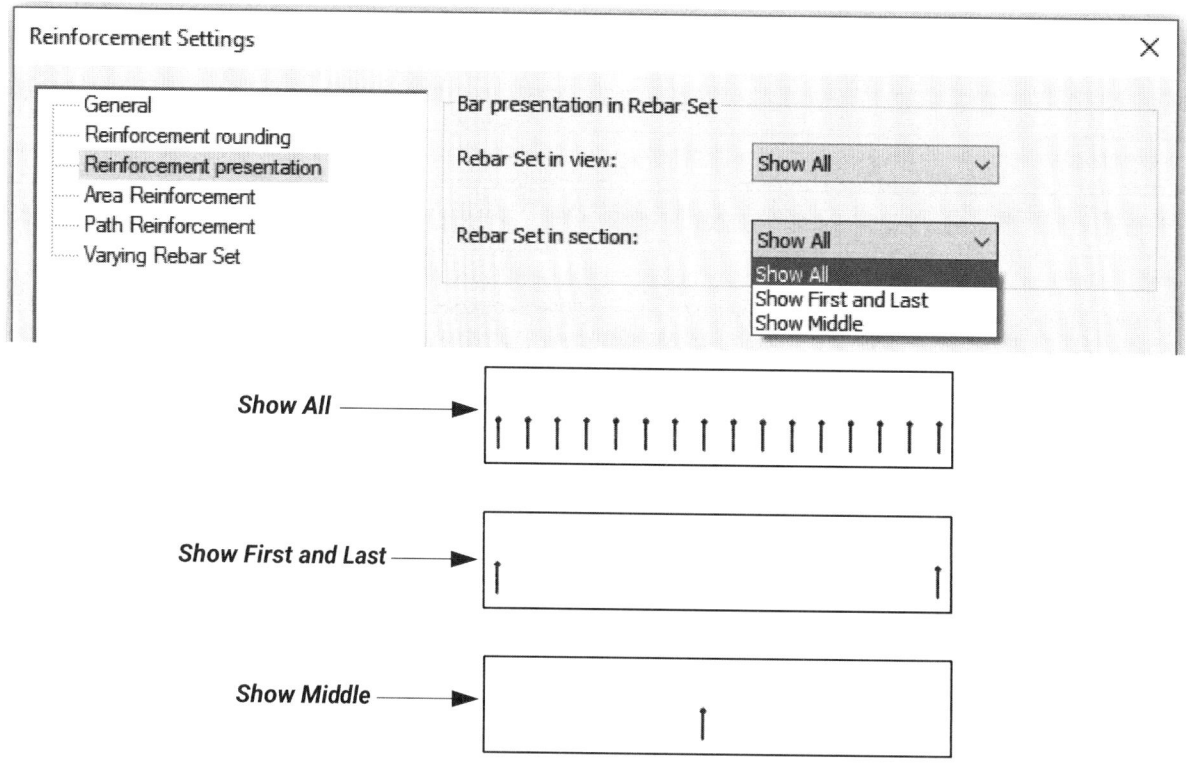

Figure 10–10

Area and Path Reinforcement Panes

In the *Area Reinforcement* or *Path Reinforcement* panes, specify the values (abbreviations) used in tags. For example, for **Area Reinforcements**, you might want to change the *Value* for Slab Top - Major Direction and Slab Top - Minor Direction to **Slab Top**, as shown in Figure 10–11.

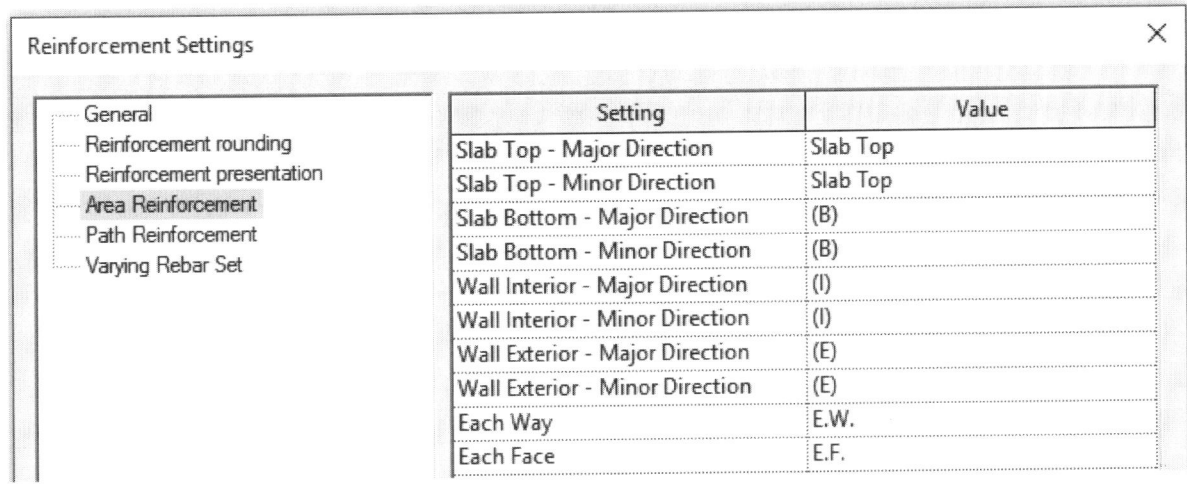

Figure 10–11

Varying Rebar Set

In the Varying Rebar Set pane (shown in Figure 10–12), you can specify the numbering method for the rebar set of different lengths.

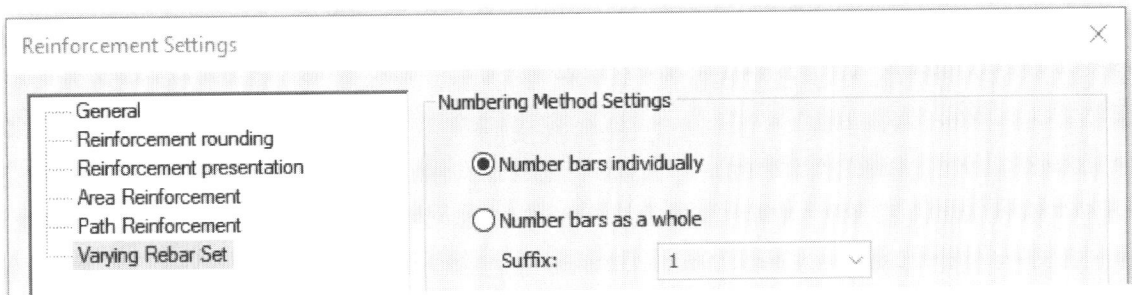

Figure 10–12

- **Number bars Individually:** Each rebar in the set is assigned a different number, though similar rebar will be matched throughout the project.

- **Number bars as a whole:** Each rebar in the set is assigned the same number with additional suffix numbers.

Rebar Visibility

By default, rebar automatically displays in section views, but not in other views. If you want to display rebar in other views, such as the 3D view shown in Figure 10–13, set the **View Visibility States** of the rebar.

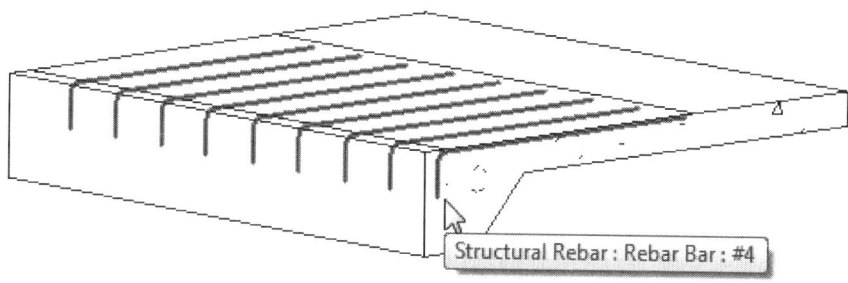

Figure 10–13

How To: Set the Rebar Visibility

1. In a section view, select the rebar in a structural element.
2. In Properties, in the *Graphics* area, beside *View Visibility States*, click **Edit…**.
3. In the Rebar Element View Visibility States dialog box, as shown in Figure 10–14, you can set the views in which you want to display your model's reinforcement.
4. In the View Control Bar, set the *Detail Level* to **Fine** to view the rebar as solid.

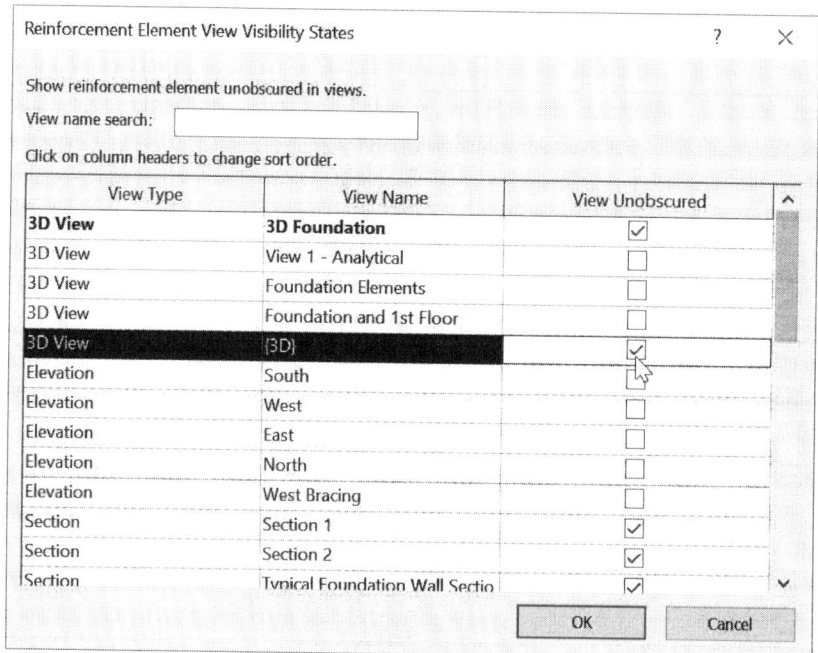

Figure 10–14

> **Hint: Structural Precast Tab**
>
> To take your Autodesk Revit model to the next level, you can use the Autodesk Structural *Precast* tab. The tools in the tab (shown in Figure 10–15) enable you to create complex assemblies required for construction, and they automatically create shop drawings and generate CAM files.

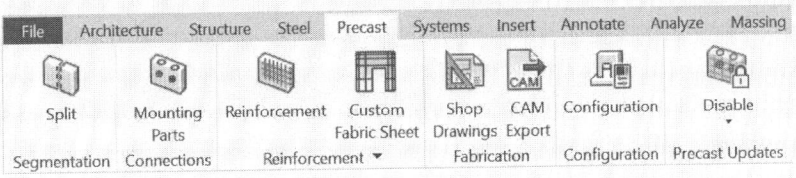

Figure 10–15

10.2 Adding Rebar

As you start reinforcing structural walls, columns, slabs, and framing, you can add rebar shapes directly into the host elements individually or as a rebar set. You can place existing rebar shapes either parallel to the work plane (or cover) or perpendicular to the cover. You can also draw a custom sketch (as shown in Figure 10–16) and model freeform rebar.

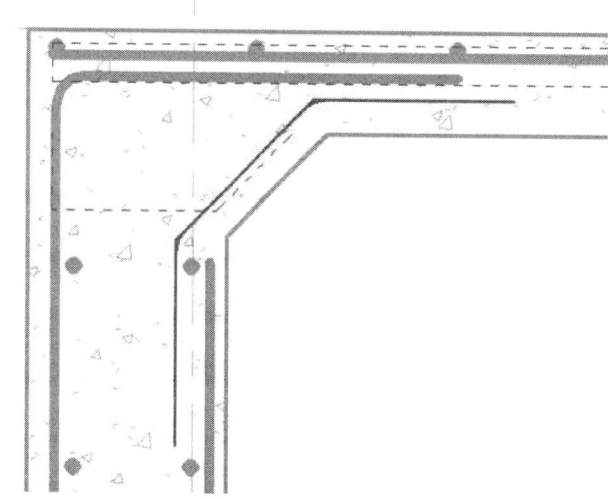

Figure 10–16

You typically work in a wall section as you place the rebar, but rebar can be added in any 2D view. You can sketch rebar and add free-form rebar in 3D views.

- The Rebar tools are available in the *Structure* tab>Reinforcement panel.

  - When a structural host element is selected first, you can start the rebar tool from the *Modify | Structural* contextual tab>Reinforcement panel, as shown in Figure 10–17.

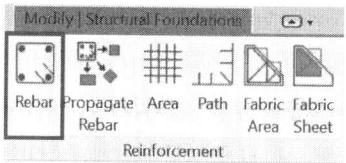

Figure 10–17

Structural Reinforcement

When working with rebar sizes, you can set the *Model Bar Diameter* in the rebar's Type Properties so it includes the ribbing of the rebar, as shown in Figure 10–18.

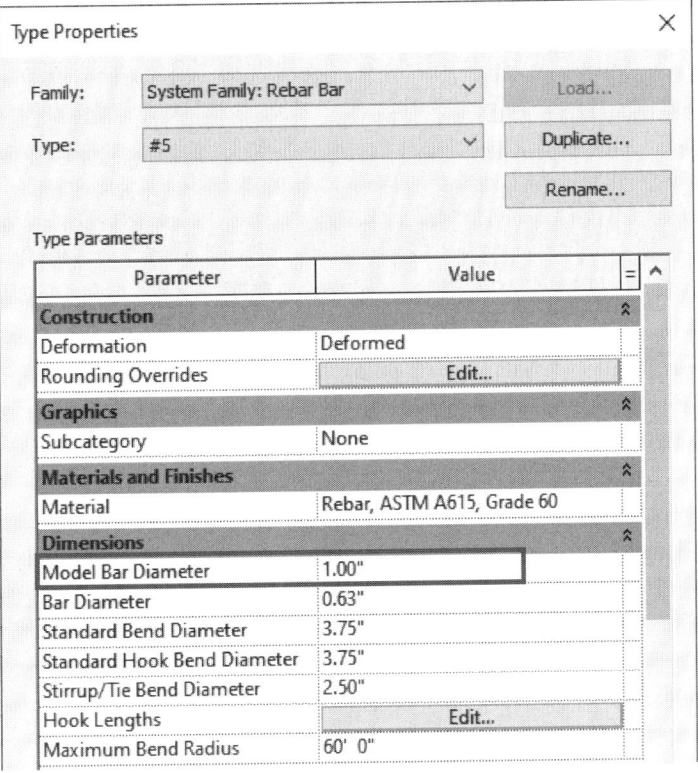

Figure 10–18

- The view you are in (e.g., 3D, section, plan, or elevation) will determine which options you see on the ribbon. When you start the **Rebar** command in a section, elevation, or plan view, the contextual *Modify | Place Rebar* tab displays, as shown on the top in Figure 10–19. If in a 3D view, the *Modify | Place Free Form Rebar* contextual tab displays, as shown on the bottom in Figure 10–19.

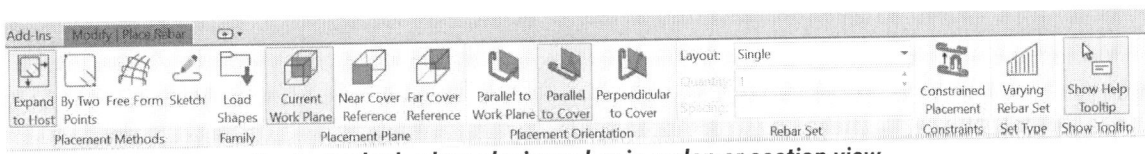

Contextual tab when placing rebar in a plan or section view

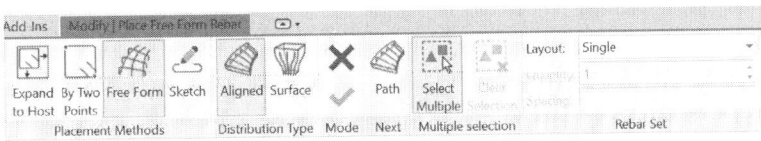

Contextual tab when placing rebar in a 3D view

Figure 10–19

Placement Methods

To reinforce your structural model elements, you can add rebar either by placing predefined rebar shapes or sketching custom rebar.

	Expand to Host	Allows you to place an instance of a rebar shape to fill and expand to the space allowed by the concrete host.
	By Two Points	Place an instance of rebar using two pick points to define the size and rebar shape.
	Free Form	Place free-form rebar on irregularly shaped concrete hosts and specify the distribution type and rebar set.
	Sketch	Using the draw tools, draw a free-form rebar shape within a concrete surface in 2D or 3D views.

- If you select **Expand to Host** or **By Two Points**, you can toggle (Show Help Tooltip) on or off. When on, this option adds a tooltip to the end of the cursor, as shown in Figure 10–20, indicating what can be done to the rebar while it is being placed. For instance, pressing <Spacebar> will rotate or flip the rebar.

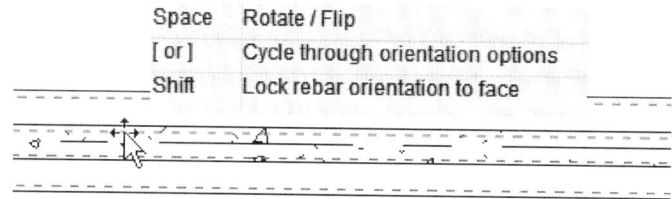

Figure 10–20

Placement Plane

The placement plane that is selected defines the plane the rebar will be placed at in the host. This can either be a work plane or a plane in relationship to the cover.

	Current Work Plane	Places rebar on the active work plane in the view.
	Near Cover Reference	Places rebar on the closest cover reference parallel to the view.
	Far Cover Reference	Places rebar on the farthest cover reference parallel to the view.

Structural Reinforcement

> **Hint: Rebar Ribbon Options**
>
> Depending on the size and shape of your screen you may not see the information in the panels. Click on the arrow at the bottom of the panel to display the full panel, as shown in Figure 10–21.

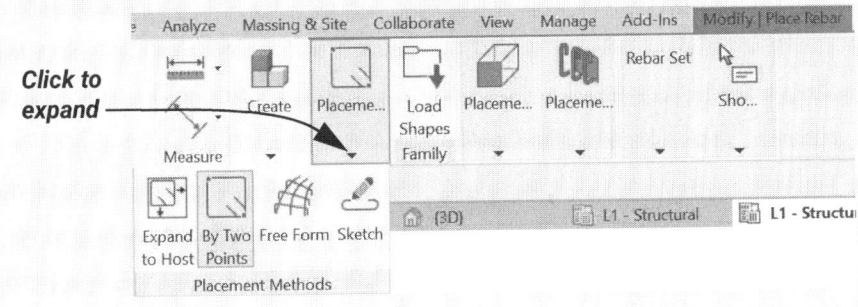

Figure 10–21

Placement Orientation

When placing rebar using either the **Expand to Host** or **By Two Points** method, the placement orientation options will display differently on the contextual tab. Setting the orientation defines how the rebar will align based off of the current work plane and the host that the rebar will be placed on. The placement orientation options are described in the table below.

	Parallel to Work Plane	Places rebar parallel to the established work plane and in the cover references.
	Parallel to Cover	Places rebar parallel to the nearest cover reference and perpendicular to the work plane.
	Perpendicular to Cover	Places rebar perpendicular to the work plane and perpendicular to the nearest cover reference.
	Perpendicular Segment	Places a single rebar segment perpendicular to the work plane.
	Horizontal	Places rebar perpendicular and horizontally to the current view's work plane.
	Vertical	Places rebar perpendicular and vertically to the current view's work plane.

How To: Place Rebar

1. Verify the reinforcement settings are set up. In the *Structure* tab>Reinforcement panel, expand the panel title and click ✦ (Reinforcement Settings).

2. In the *Structure* tab>Reinforcement panel, click ▭ (Rebar).

3. In the *Modify | Place Rebar* tab>Placement Methods panel, select a placement method.
   - Alternatively you can select a rebar host element, and from the contextual tab>Reinforcement panel, click ⬚ (Rebar).

4. In the Options Bar or Rebar Shape Browser, select a rebar shape, as shown in Figure 10–22. You can also select the rebar type from the Type Selector.
   - If the Rebar Shape Browser does not display, in the Options Bar, click the ⬚ (Browse) button.

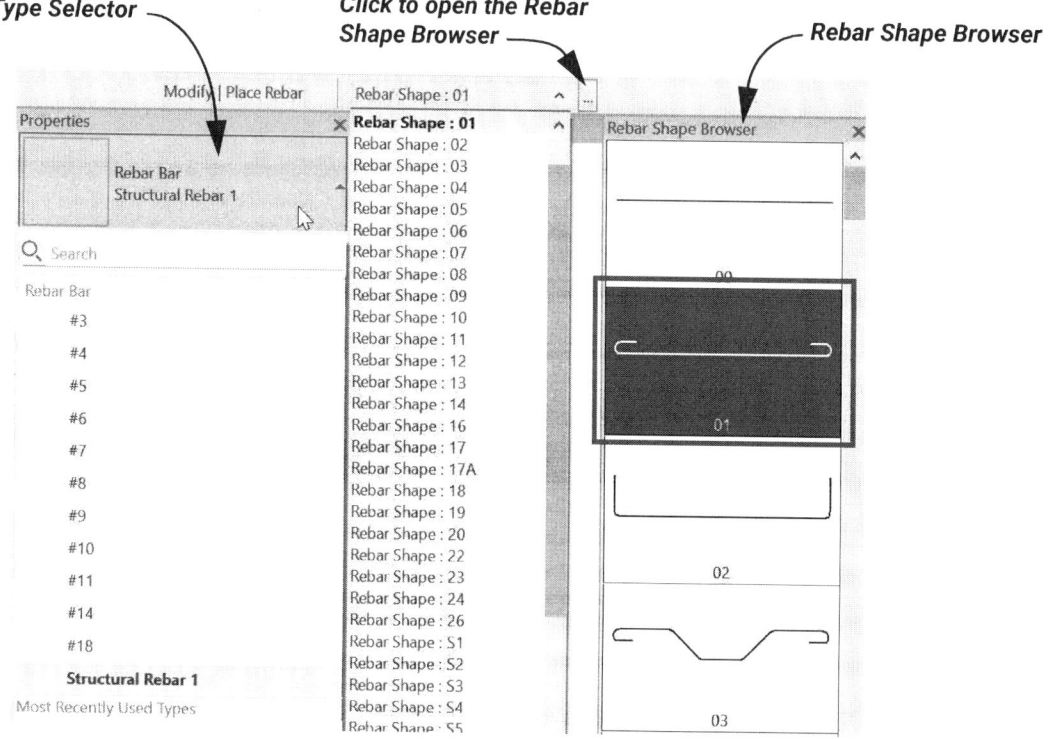

Figure 10–22

- In the *Modify | Place Rebar* tab>Family panel, click ⬚ (Load Shapes) to load additional rebar family types.

5. In the *Modify | Place Rebar* tab>Placement Plane panel select the placement location.
6. In the *Modify | Place Rebar* tab>Placement Orientation panel, select the parallel or perpendicular placement orientation.

7. In the *Modify | Place Rebar* tab>Rebar Set panel (shown in Figure 10-23), or in the *Rebar Set* area of Properties (shown in Figure 10-24), specify the *Layout Rule* and then set up the corresponding *Quantity* and *Spacing* as required. The *Layout Rule* options are:

   - **Single**
   - **Fixed Number**
   - **Maximum Space**
   - **Number with Spacing**
   - **Minimum Clear Spacing**

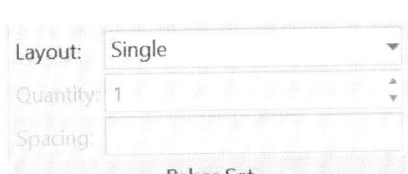

Figure 10-23

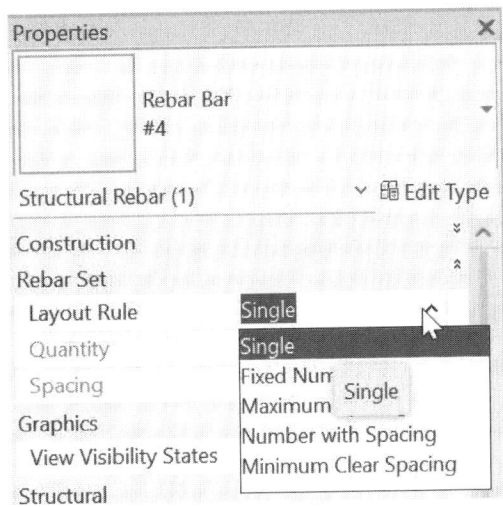

Figure 10-24

8. Hover the cursor over the element that you want to reinforce as shown in Figure 10-25. Click to place it when it is in the required position.

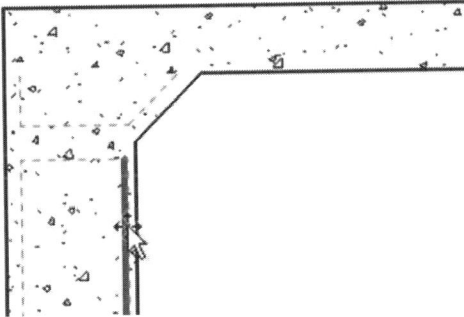

Figure 10-25

- The green dashed lines indicate the maximum cover settings of the host element.
- Press <Spacebar> to flip or rotate the rebar element before or after it is placed.
- Press <Shift> to place the rebar parallel to any host face.
- For the single session of Revit, your rebar selections on the *Modify | Place Rebar* tab are remembered the next time the Rebar command is started.

    Note: For more information on rebar types, see A.5 Creating Rebar Types.

Constraining Rebar to Other Rebar

To help you place rebar more precisely, you can constrain rebar to nearby shapes. When you move the original rebar, all the constrained elements move as well, as shown in Figure 10–26.

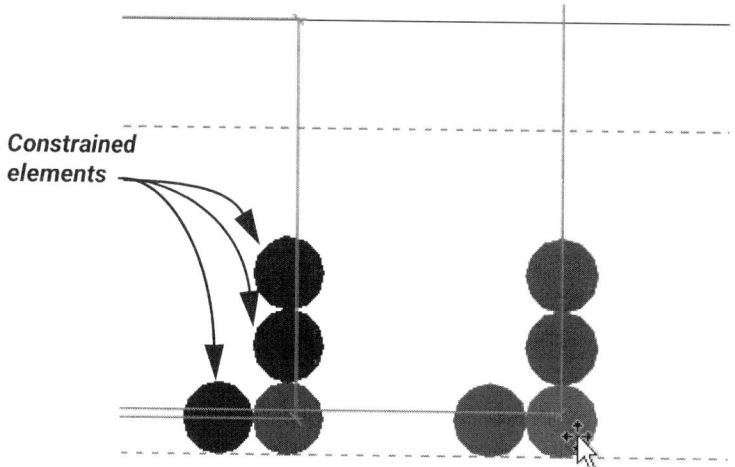

Figure 10–26

- In the *Modify | Place Rebar* tab> Rebar Constraints panel, click (Constrained Placement). Then, move the cursor close to the other rebar and click when you see it snap to the preferred constraint.
- Once the rebar is placed, you can select it and use the temporary dimensions to change the location. This breaks the constraint.
    - This tool only works when placing single rebar.

Sketching Rebar Shapes

At times, the standard rebar shapes are not exactly what is required. In these cases, you can sketch a new shape as shown in Figure 10–27.

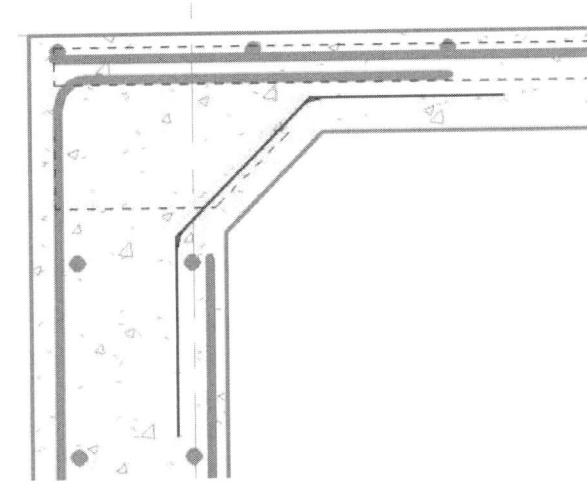

Figure 10–27

- When sketching rebar, you are not restricted to the rebar cover settings.

How To: Place a Rebar Shape by Sketch

1. In the *Structure* tab>Reinforcement panel, click (Rebar).
2. In the *Modify | Place Rebar* tab>Placement Methods panel, click (Sketch).
3. Select the host for the rebar (unless it is already selected).
4. To draw the sketch, use the tools in the *Modify | Create Rebar Sketch* tab>Draw panel, as shown in Figure 10–28.

Figure 10–28

5. Click (Finish Edit Mode).

- The new Rebar Shape displays in the Shape Browser. To change the shape name, in the Project Browser, expand the *Families>Structural Rebar>Rebar Shape* node, right-click on the shape name and select **Rename**.

Multi-planar Rebar

When you are sketching rebar you can also create multi-planar reinforcement. The rebar shape is sketched in 2D and then duplicated and connected by a segment, as shown in Figure 10–29.

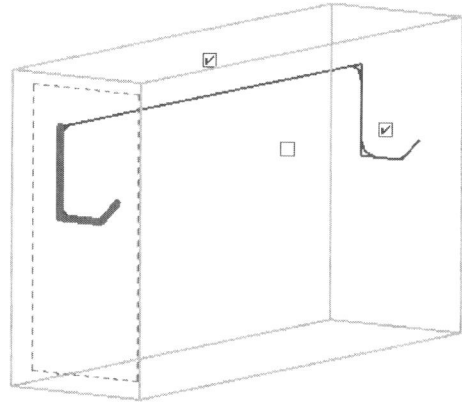

Figure 10–29

How To: Sketch Multi-planar Rebar

1. Start the **Rebar** command with the **Sketch** option.
2. Select the host if not already selected.
3. In the *Modify | Create Rebar Sketch* tab>Reinforcement panel, click (Multi-planar).
4. Draw the rebar sketch in the 2D view. It automatically displays in any open 3D views, as shown in Figure 10–30.
5. Select the appropriate checkboxes on the sketch.

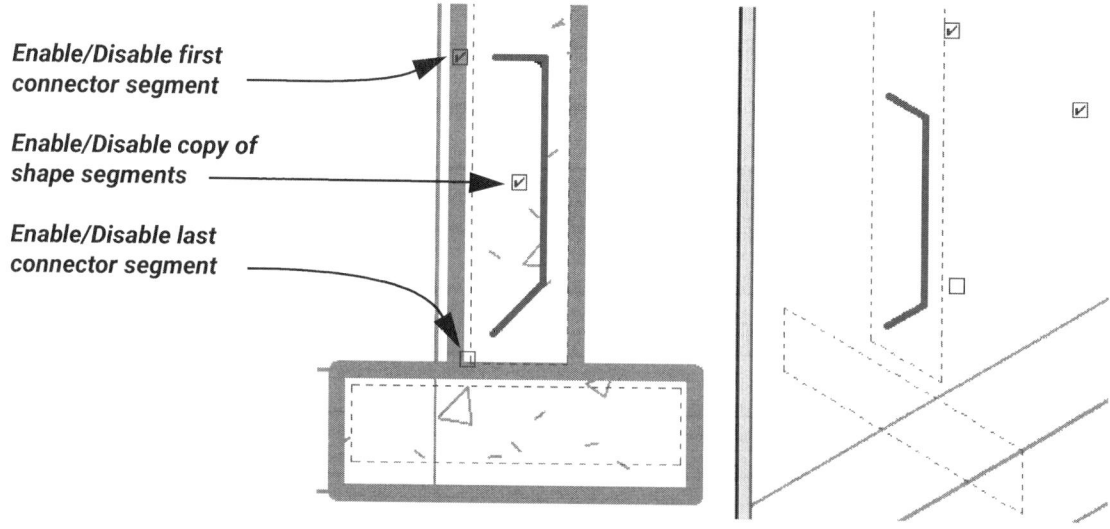

Figure 10–30

6. In the Type Selector, select the Rebar bar size, then set other parameters in Properties, as needed.
7. Click ✓ (Finish Edit Mode). The rebar is added to the length of the element as shown in Figure 10-31.

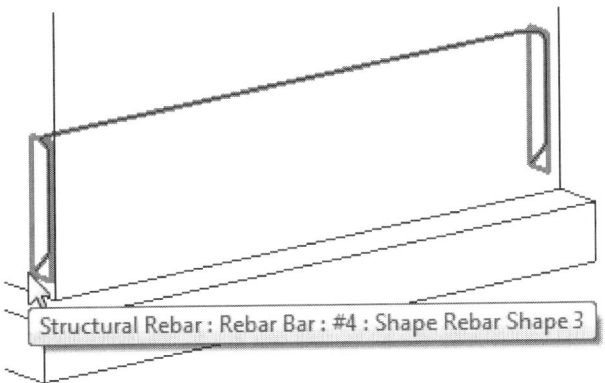

Figure 10-31

- You can modify the multi-planar rebar shape using the drag controls, as shown in Figure 10-32. Alternatively, in the *Modify | Structural Rebar* tab>Mode panel, click ✎ (Edit Sketch).

    Note: *For information about modifying detail views, see B.6 Creating a Repeating Detail.*

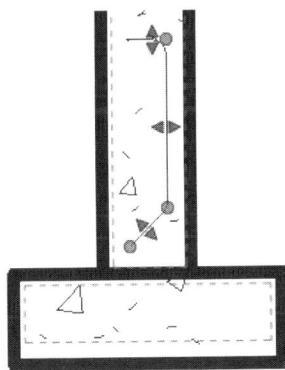

Figure 10-32

Free-Form Rebar

You can add free-form rebar when you need rebar to follow complex concrete structures, as shown in Figure 10–33. These elements are frequently created using model in place or family tools.

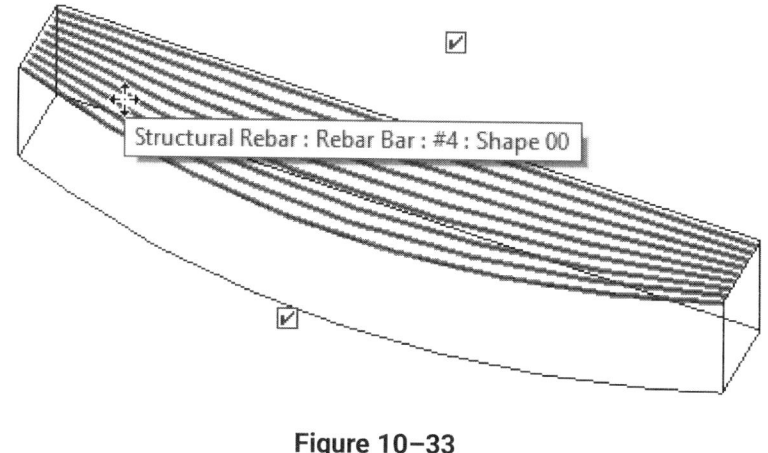

Figure 10–33

How To: Place Free-Form Rebar

1. In the *Structure* tab>Reinforcement panel, click (Rebar).

    Note: *If you are in a 3D view, the Free Form rebar tool is automatically selected.*

2. In the *Modify | Place Rebar* tab>Placement Methods panel, click (Free Form).

    - The *Modify | Place Free Form Rebar* tab displays with (Surface Distribution) selected.

3. In the Type Selector, select the rebar type.
4. In the Rebar Set panel, specify the *Layout*, *Number*, and *Spacing*, as needed.
5. Toggle (Select Multiple) off for simple surfaces or on for more complex surfaces, as needed.

6. Select the host surface(s), start surface(s), and end surface(s), as shown for a simple surface in Figure 10–34.

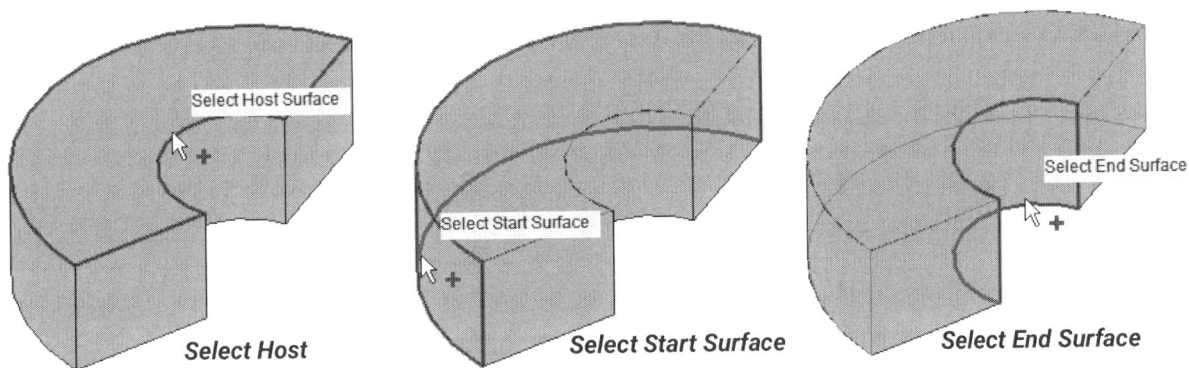

Figure 10–34

Note: Applying a rebar set is covered in 10.3 Modifying Rebar.

7. Press <Esc> to finish the selections. The rebar displays as shown in Figure 10–35 with a Rebar Set specified.

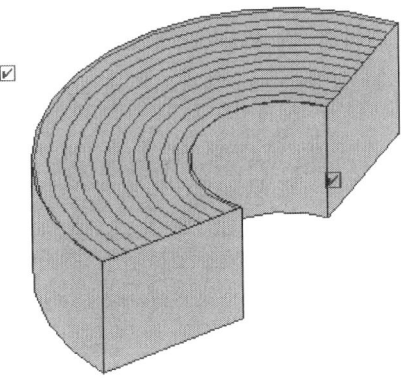

Figure 10–35

- If you are selecting multiple faces you can press <Spacebar> between sets of selections and press <Enter> to finish.
- You can add rebar to model-in-place stairs and ramps which frequently need free-form rebar.

10.3 Modifying Rebar

You can make additional changes to the rebar once it is placed. For example, select the rebar and use the shape handles to move it into place, as shown in Figure 10–36. Rebar that is perpendicular to the work plane also has temporary dimensions.

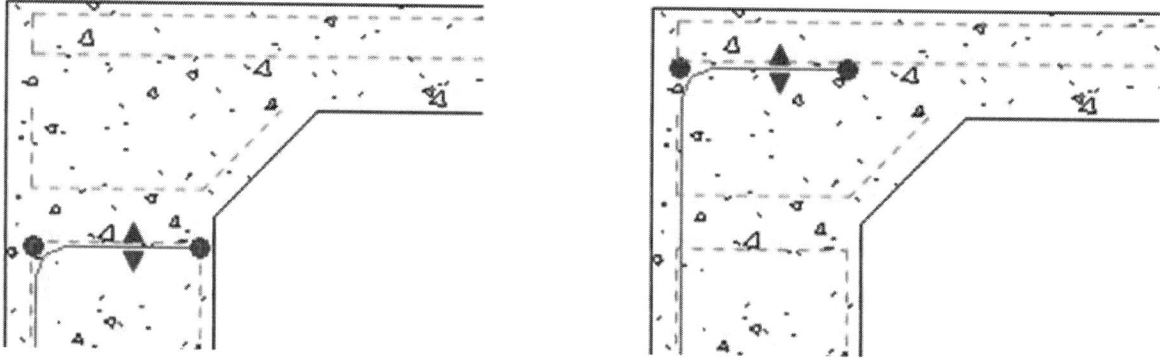

Figure 10–36

- To quickly select multiple instances of related rebar, select one, right-click, and select **Select All Rebar in Host**.

- You can use other modify tools to place rebar, such as **Move**, **Copy**, and **Mirror**.

When you select existing rebar in a model a number of tools display in the *Modify | Structural Rebar* tab, as shown in Figure 10–37. You can create or modify rebar sets, pick a new host for the rebar, edit the constraints of the rebar, edit or remove individual bars within a set, apply rebar couplers, and specify a variable length rebar set type.

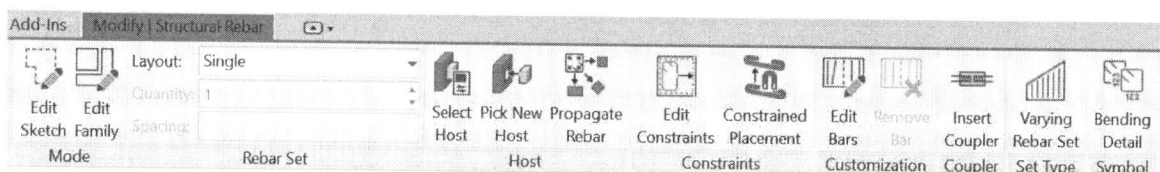

Figure 10–37

- When the rebar that is placed in a view is interfering with another element, you can edit the rebar set and either modify or remove rebar from a set.

	Modify Bars	Modify the selected rebar by using the **Move**, **Rotate**, or **Align** tools. You can also select to remove the selected rebar.
	Show Removed	Shows any rebar that was removed from the selected rebar set.
	Remove Bar	Remove selected rebar from the rebar set.

	Reset Position	Reset a rebar's position if it was moved, rotated, or aligned out of its original place.
	Reset All	Reset moved or removed rebar.

- Rebar couplers can be added to the end or between lengths of rebar. When couplers are added, the rebar dimensions are altered.

Rebar Set Visibility

In a view, when you select a rebar set, you can specify how that set displays. The default presentation style is set in the Reinforcement Settings dialog box, but you can change each rebar set individually.

Select a rebar set and in the *Modify | Structural Rebar* tab>Presentation panel, choose the presentation style, as shown in Figure 10–38.

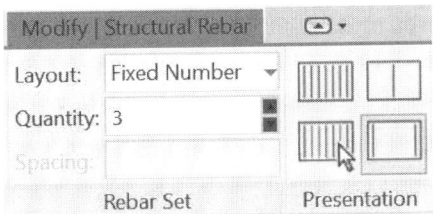

Figure 10–38

- You can also choose to display each end of a rebar set using checkboxes, as shown in Figure 10–39.

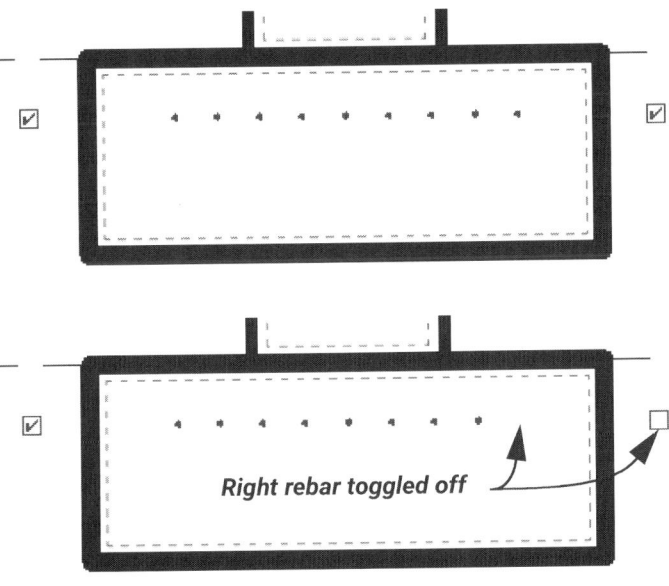

Figure 10–39

How To: Pick a New Host

1. To change the element that supports rebar. Select the rebar and, in the *Modify | Structural Rebar* tab>Host panel, click (Pick New Host).
2. Select the new host element.

For example, in Figure 10–40, the rebar is hosted by the wall on the left and by the slab on the right. You can see the difference in the constraints.

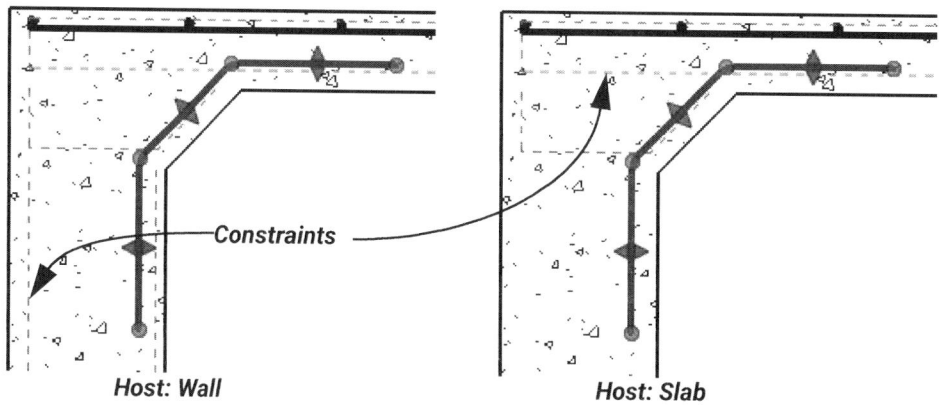

Figure 10–40

How To: Edit Rebar Constraints

1. To graphically override the nearby constraints, select the rebar you want to modify.
2. In the *Modify | Structural Rebar* tab>Rebar Constraints panel, click (Edit Constraints). The element and reference are highlighted in orange.

3. Using the temporary dimension, type in a new distance, as shown in Figure 10–41.

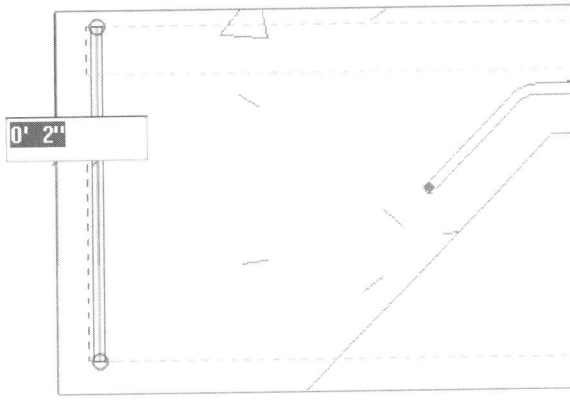

Figure 10–41

4. Click ✓ (Finish).

- If additional constraint references are available, they are highlighted in blue. Click on the blue reference to switch to that dimension.
- You can edit rebar constraints in 3D views.

How To: Edit or Remove Bars

1. In a view, select a rebar or rebar set.
2. In the *Modify | Structural Rebar* tab>Customization panel, select (Edit Bars).
3. In the *Modify | Modify* tab>Mode panel, select (Modify Bars).
4. Select one or more rebar that you want to modify and do one of the following to modify the selected rebar:
    - In the *Modify | Structural Rebar* tab>Modify panel, select the **Move**, **Rotate** or **Align** tool to modify the selected rebar.
    - Select (Remove Bar) to remove the selected bar(s).
    - If you have accidentally repositioned or removed rebar, select (Reset Position) or (Reset All).
5. Click ✓ (Finish).
    - Select (Show Removed) to temporarily see the removed rebar.

How To: Add Varying Rebar Sets

1. To have rebar follow the angle of a host element, set up the rebar following standard processes as shown for a wall in Figure 10–42. Varying rebar sets can be placed in curved and free-form elements.

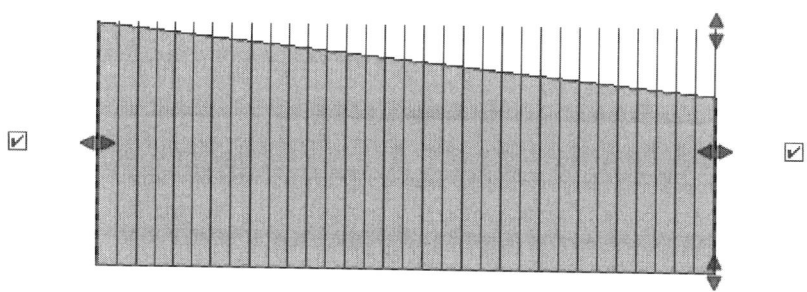

Figure 10–42

2. In the *Modify | Structural Rebar* tab>Rebar Set Type panel, click (Varying Rebar Set). The rebar now follows the edge as shown in Figure 10–43. This tool is an on/off toggle.

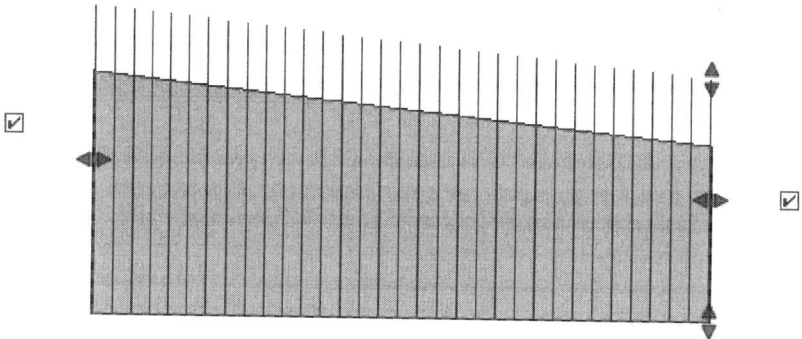

Figure 10–43

3. Use the arrow-like shape handles to resize the rebar to fit the element if needed, as shown in Figure 10–44.

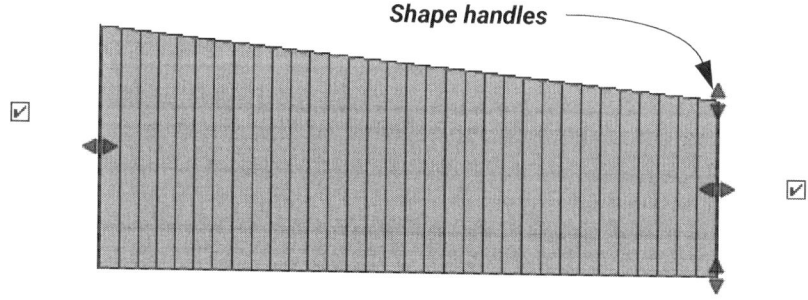

Figure 10–44

Propagate Rebar

The propagate rebar tool allows you to quickly layout rebar in elements such as columns, walls, or stairs, and copy or propagate the rebar design to other host elements. If the host elements are of different sizes, the rebar keeps its association based on the host elements needs. You can align the rebar using the by host or by face methods and you are able to switch between the two methods while propagating rebar in the model.

- You can propagate free form rebar (as shown in Figure 10–45) using align by face and align by host options with the constraints of the host being a consideration when copying the rebar.

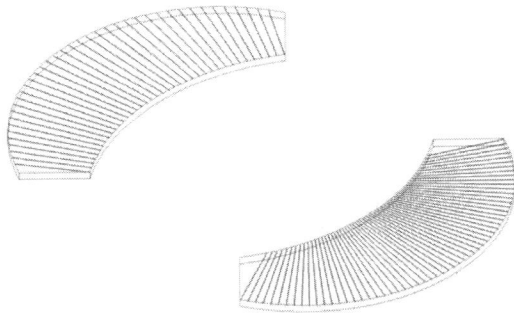

Figure 10–45

- (Align By Face) is used when propagating rebar to another face of the same host element. For example, when adding rebar to the top face of a ramp and then propagating the rebar to the bottom face of the ramp.

- (Align By Host) is used when propagating rebar from one host element to a similar host element. For example, when adding rebar to a building's foundation bearing footing perimeter.

How To: Add Propagate Rebar

1. Select the rebar you want to propagate to another host.

2. In the *Modify | Structural Rebar* tab>Host panel, click (Propagate Rebar).

3. In the *Modify | Structural Rebar* tab>Propagate Rebar panel, click either (Align By Host) or (Align By Face).

4. When you are done, click (Finish).

3D Rebar Shapes

For standees reinforcing rebar in footings or slabs, you can model 3D rebar shapes by placing rebar, then rotating the hook's start and/or end and, if needed, adjusting the hook length by instance with the rebar properties. The hook rotation and length can also be modified with existing rebar in the model, as shown in Figure 10–46.

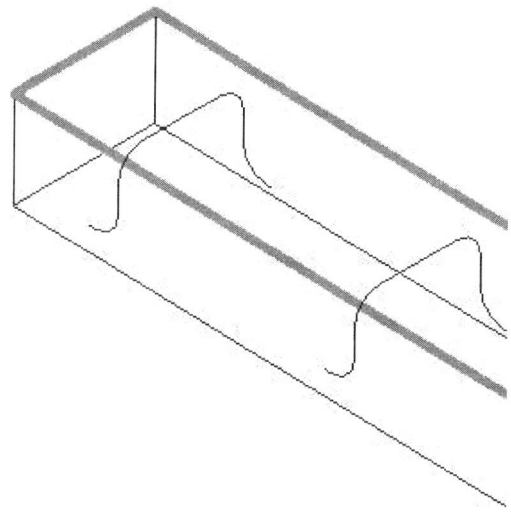

Figure 10–46

- For existing rebar, select it and adjust the *Hook At Start/Hook At End* and *Hook Rotation At Start/Hook Rotation At End* settings within Properties, as shown in Figure 10–47. These settings are available to modify before adding free-form and sketched rebar in a 2D or 3D view.

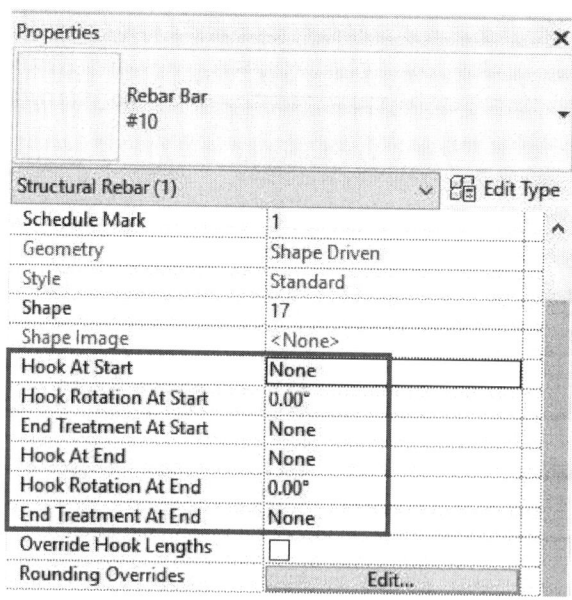

Figure 10–47

Structural Reinforcement

How To: Override Rebar Rounding

1. In the *Structure* tab> expand the Reinforcement panel and click 🔧 (Reinforcement Settings).
2. In the Reinforcement Settings dialog box, select Reinforcement rounding and then click the checkbox for the **Use reinforcement rounding option** (as shown in Figure 10–48), and set the bar and bar segment length.

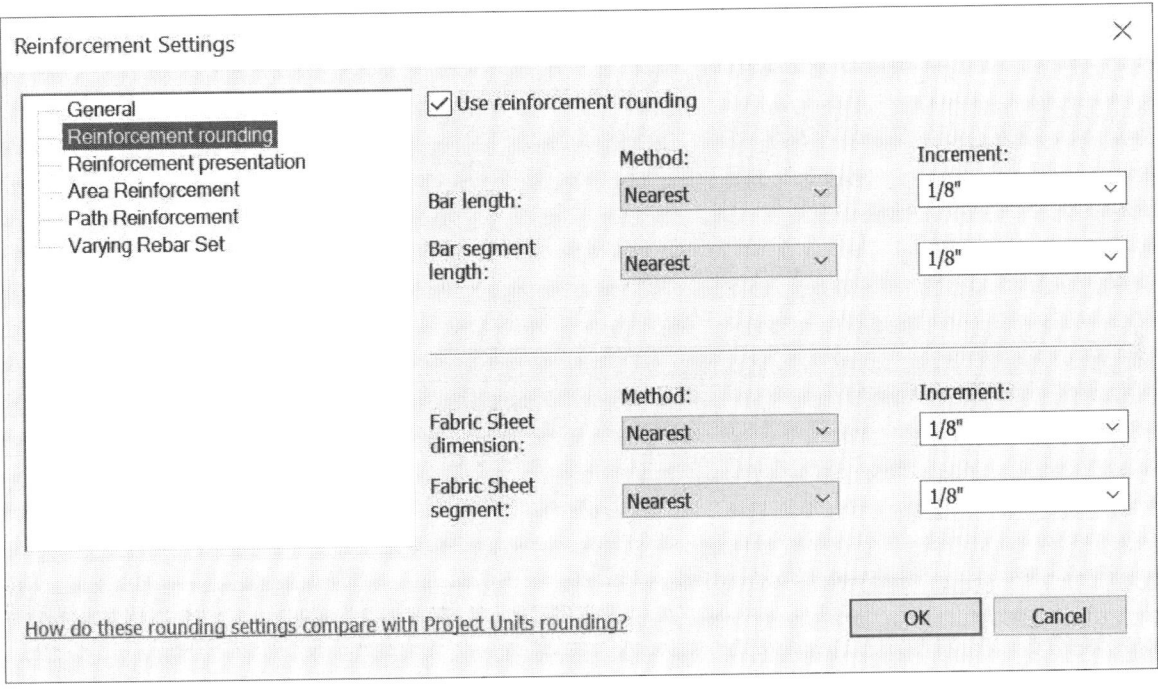

Figure 10–48

3. Click **OK**.

- Upon placing rebar, you can modify the hook lengths by checking the box to **Override Hook Lengths** and then changing them within the *Dimensions* area within Properties, as shown in Figure 10–49.

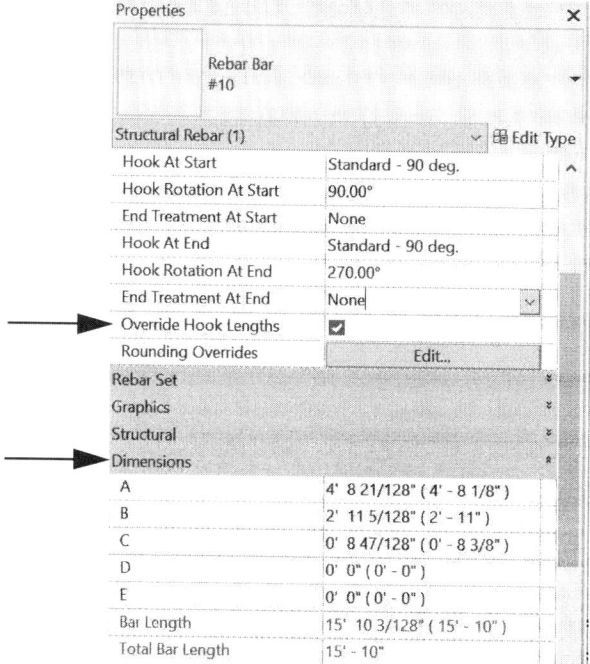

Figure 10–49

- You can press <Spacebar> to rotate the rebar before or after placing it.

How To: Rotate Hooks and Adjust Hook Length

1. Select an existing rebar or rebar set.
2. In Properties, specify the *Hook At Start*, *Hook At End*, *Hook Rotation At Start*, and *Hook Rotation At End*.
3. To adjust the hook's length, check the box next to **Override Hook Lengths** and adjust the length values in the *Dimensions* area in Properties.

- If you are adding rebar in 2D or 3D using the Free Form or Sketch placement methods, you can specify the rotation before you place the rebar.

Rebar Coupler

A rebar coupler joins adjacent or spliced rebar together so they behave as one continuous length of reinforcement, as shown on the top in Figure 10–50. Rebar couplers will populate across a rebar set or can be placed on individual bars. You can also add headed anchors or cap the end of rebar instances or sets, as shown on the bottom in Figure 10–50. For curved walls, concrete tanks, or tunnels, you can connect tangent arc rebar with couplers.

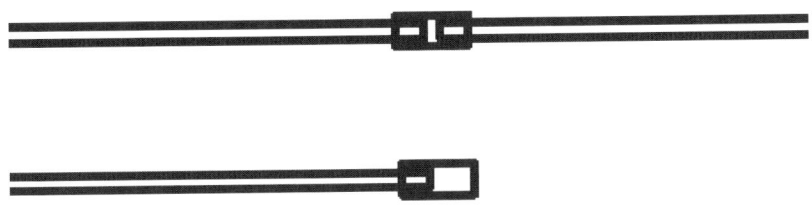

Figure 10–50

- When couplers are added to rebar, the end treatment of the rebar adjusts within its properties to threaded.
- Couplers can be moved along the length of the rebar and the bars will adjust.
- Couplers can be added to groups and assemblies and be tagged and scheduled.
- You can add an end treatment to rebar without using a coupler.

Coupler Tolerance

- Rebar ends need to have a tolerance of 10 bar diameters or an offset no more than 3 bar diameters from each other to be connected by a coupler.
- If you need to join to arc bars, the centers need to be in the same position.

How To: Add a Rebar Coupler to Join Two Rebar

1. In the *Structure* tab>Reinforcement panel, click (Rebar Coupler). Alternatively, you can select a rebar and in the *Modify |Structural Rebar* tab, click (Insert Coupler).
2. If no couplers are loaded, you are prompted to load one. If you need to load a different coupler, you can stay in the command and switch to the *Insert* tab>Load from Library panel and click (Load Family).
3. In the Type Selector, select the coupler type needed.
4. In the *Modify | Insert Rebar Coupler* tab>Placement Options panel, select (Place between Two Bars).
5. Select the first rebar and then the second rebar to place the coupler.

How To: Add a Coupler to the End of a Bar

1. In the *Structure* tab>Reinforcement panel, click (Rebar Coupler). Alternatively, you can select a rebar and in the *Modify |Structural Rebar* tab, click (Insert Coupler).
2. If no couplers are loaded, you are prompted to load one. If you need to load a different coupler, you can stay in the command and switch to the *Insert* tab>Load from Library panel and click (Load Family).
3. In the Type Selector, select the coupler type needed.
4. In the *Modify | Insert Rebar Coupler* tab>Placement Options panel, select (Place on Bar End).
5. Select the end of the bar that you want to add the coupler end to.

Practice 10a
Add Rebar

Practice Objectives

- Add individual rebar elements.
- Create a repeating layout of rebar.
- Sketch a rebar design.

In this practice, you will add individual rebar to a wall in a foundation section using premade shapes, and then modify the exact location and size using controls. You will then change the layout to create rebar sets. You will also sketch a new rebar shape, as shown in Figure 10-51.

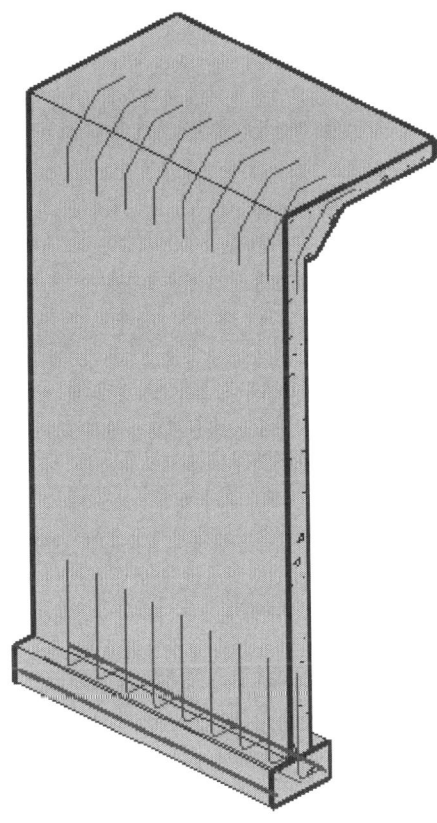

Figure 10-51

Task 1: Add rebar.

1. Open **Structural-Rebar.rvt** from the practice files folder.
2. Open the **Sections (Wall Section): Typical Foundation Wall Section** view.
3. Zoom in on the footing.
4. In the *Structure* tab>Reinforcement panel, click (Rebar). read the message about rebar shapes and click **OK**.
5. In Properties, in the Type Selector, select **Rebar Bar: #4**.
6. In the *Modify | Place Rebar* tab, verify that the following are selected:

    - Placement Methods panel - (Expand to Host)
    - Placement Plane panel - (Current Work Plane)
    - Placement Orientation panel - (Parallel to Work Plane)

7. In the Rebar Shape Browser, select **Rebar Shape: 17A**.
8. Add the rebar shape to the footing, as shown in Figure 10–52.

    Note: The rebar shape fits exactly within the preset constraints.

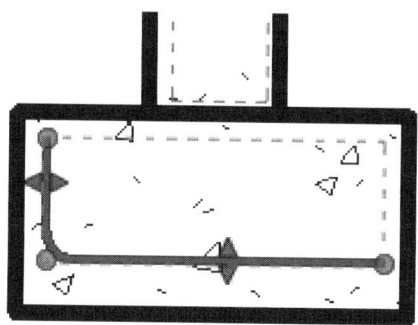

Figure 10–52

9. Click (Modify) after the rebar is placed and then select the rebar.
10. Use the handles and controls to modify the shape so that it can extend into the wall, as shown in Figure 10–53.

    - You can also modify the *B* and *C* rebar dimensions in Properties in the *Dimensions* section.

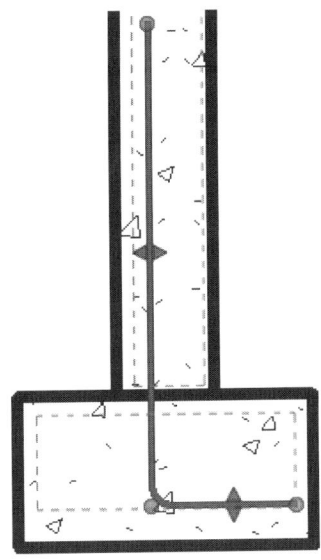

Figure 10–53

11. Click (Modify).

12. In the *Structure* tab>Reinforcement panel, click (Rebar).

13. In Properties, in the Type Selector, verify that **Rebar Bar: #4** is selected.

14. In the *Modify | Place Rebar* tab, verify that the following are selected:

    - Placement Methods panel - (Expand to Host)
    - Placement Plane panel - (Current Work Plane)
    - Placement Orientation panel - (Perpendicular to Cover)

15. In the Rebar Set panel, change the *Layout* to **Fixed Number** and the *Quantity* to **3**.

16. Add **Rebar Shape: 00** to the bottom left face of the footing. Three rebar are placed, as shown in Figure 10–54.

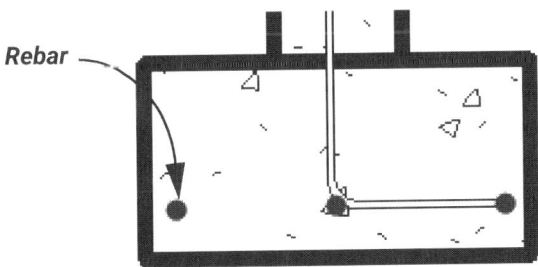

Figure 10–54

17. Click (Modify). Select and move the L-shaped rebar above the three Rebar Shape: 00 of the continuous footing, as shown in Figure 10–55.

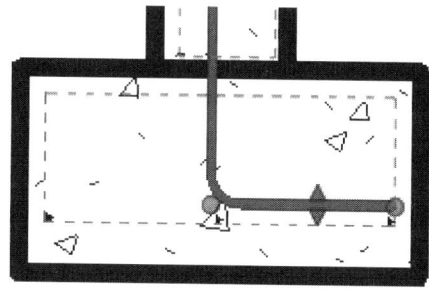

Figure 10–55

18. With the L-shaped rebar still selected, in the *Modify | Structural Rebar* tab>Rebar Set panel, change the *Layout* to **Maximum Spacing** and the *Spacing* to **1'-0"**, as shown in Figure 10–56.

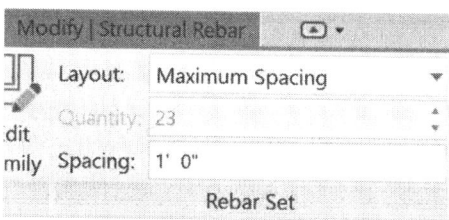

Figure 10–56

19. Click (Modify).

20. In the *Structure* tab>Reinforcement panel, click (Rebar).

21. In Properties, in the Type Selector, verify that **Rebar Bar: #4** is selected.

22. In the *Modify | Place Rebar* tab verify that the following are selected:

    - Placement Methods panel: (By Two Points)

    - Placement Plane panel: (Current Work Plane)

    - Placement Orientation panel: (Parallel to Work Plane)

23. In the Rebar Shape Browser, select **Rebar Shape: 17**.

24. Select the bottom left corner as the first pick point, as shown in Figure 10–57. Click above the far right rebar, as shown in Figure 10–58. Add the rebar shape to the footing below the three straight rebar.

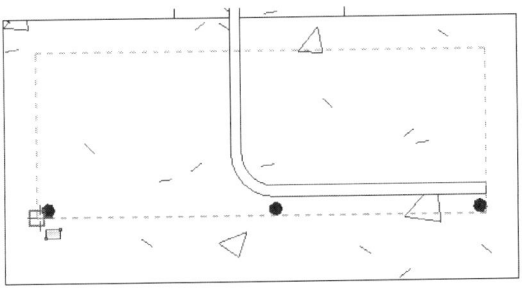

Figure 10–57   Figure 10–58

25. Click (Modify) after the rebar is placed and then select the rebar.
26. Use the handles and controls to modify the shape so that it extends into the wall foundation, as shown in Figure 10–59.

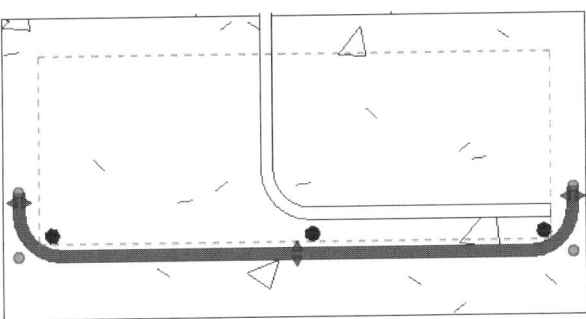

Figure 10–59

27. Click (Modify).
28. Select the new rebar and set the following in the *Modify | Structural Rebar* tab>Rebar Set panel:
    - *Layout:* **Maximum Spacing**
    - *Spacing:* **0'-10"**
29. Click in an empty area in the view to clear the selection.
30. Save the project.

Task 2: Sketch individual rebar.

1. Pan up to the slab and slab edge.
2. In the *Structure* tab>Reinforcement panel, click (Rebar).

3. In the *Modify | Place Rebar* tab>Placement Methods panel, click (Sketch).
4. In the Status Bar, the software prompts you to pick a host for the rebar. Select the wall.
   - Although most of this rebar is outside the wall (i.e. slab and slab edge), selecting the wall ensures that the rebar is only along this specific wall. If you had selected the slab, the rebar would have spaced themselves along the entire span of the slab or even on the other side of the building, regardless of the wall underneath them.
5. Use the **Draw** tools to sketch a rebar similar to the one shown in Figure 10–60.

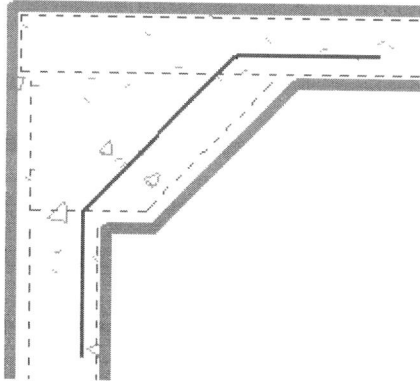

Figure 10–60

6. In the *Modify | Create Rebar Sketch* tab>Mode panel, click (Finish Edit Mode). A rebar is created with the new Rebar Shape in the Rebar Browser, as shown in Figure 10–61.

   Note: *The picture might vary depending on how you drew the shape.*

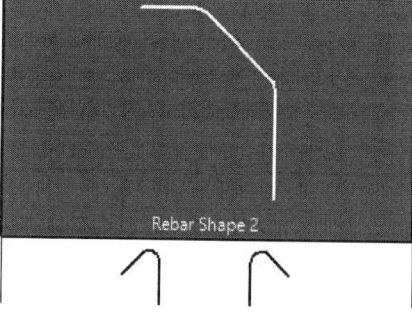

Figure 10–61

7. Click (Modify) and select the new rebar. Use the controls on the ends and the shape handles on the midpoint of the bar to make small adjustments.
8. In the Rebar Set panel, set *Layout* to **Maximum Spacing** and *Spacing* to **1'-0"**.
9. Save the project.

Task 3: Create a 3D section view.

1. In the Quick Access Toolbar, click ⌂ (Default 3D View).
2. Right-click on the ViewCube and select **Orient to View> Sections>Section: Typical Foundation Wall Section**.
3. Rotate the view and hide the section box, as shown in Figure 10–62.

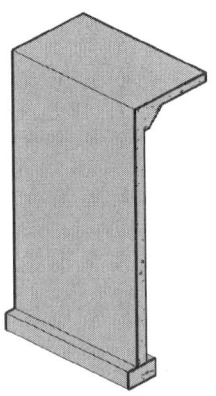

Figure 10–62

4. In the Project Browser, in the 3D Views node, rename the view to **3D Foundation**.
5. Window around everything and select it. You can see the rebar. Using ▽ (Filter), select only the Structural Rebar.
6. In Properties, next to *View Visibility States,* click **Edit...**.
7. In the Rebar Element View Visibility States dialog box, beside the *3D Foundation* view name, select **View unobscured** and click **OK**.
8. The rebar sets now display in the view.
9. In the View Control Bar, set the *Detail Level* to ▦ (Fine).
10. Save the project.

Task 4: Add 3D hooks.

1. Open the **Sections (Wall Section) Typical Foundation Wall Section** view and select **Rebar Shape: 17A**.

2. In Properties (as shown on the left in Figure 10–63), set the value for *Hook At Start* to **Standard - 90 deg.**, select **Override Hook Lengths**, and set the *Dimensions A* value to **0'-4"**. The rebar should now look like the image on the right in Figure 10–63.

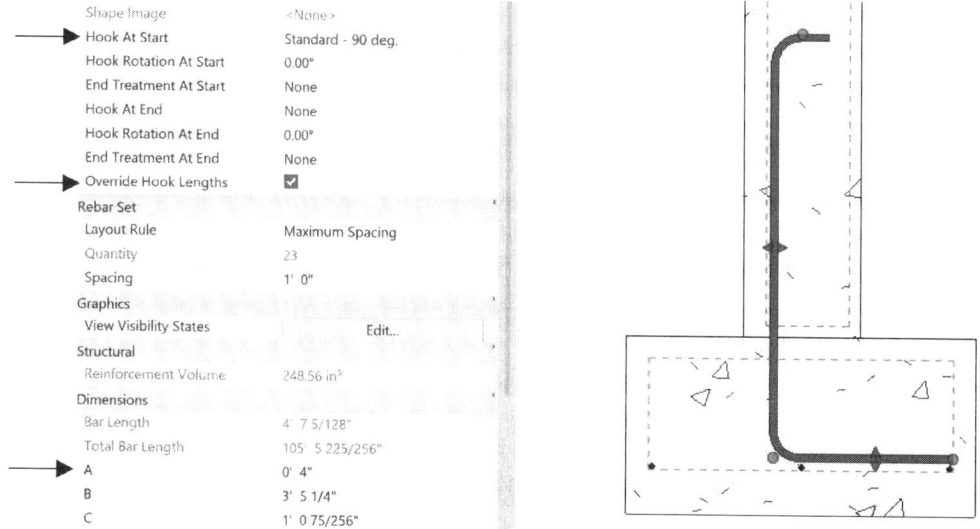

Figure 10–63

3. Save and close the project.

End of practice

10.4 Reinforcing Walls, Floors, and Slabs

Instead of adding individual rebar to large surfaces, there are three types of reinforcement that can be used with walls, floors, and slabs.

- Area Reinforcement places evenly spaced rebar in structural walls and floors according to a boundary you specify, as shown on the wall in Figure 10–64.
- Path Reinforcement enables you to specify reinforcing that bends from the slab into the bearing wall, as shown on the floor in Figure 10–64.
- Fabric Reinforcement places sheets of reinforcing wires within a boundary you specify.

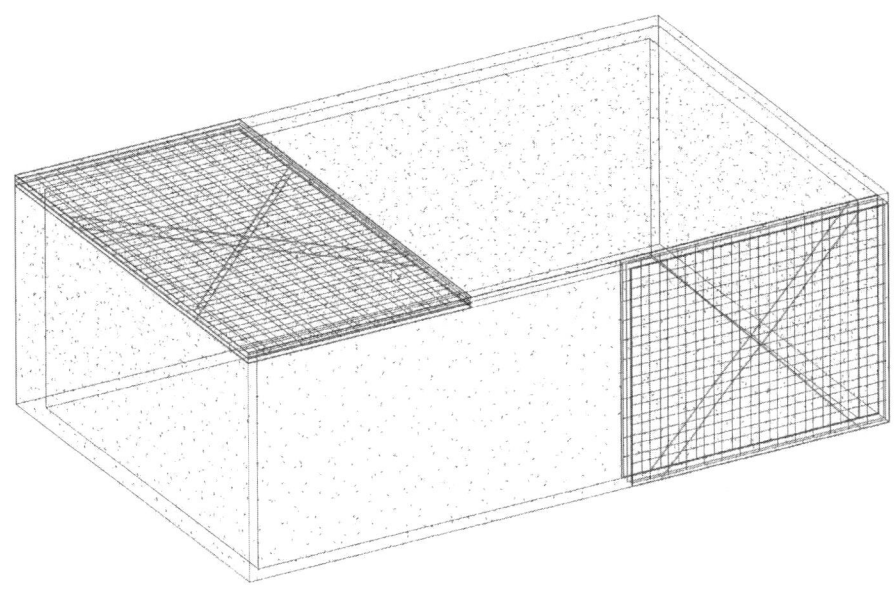

Figure 10–64

> **Hint: Structural Precast for Revit**
>
> You can create complex precast assemblies using additional reinforcement tools found on the *Precast* tab (shown in Figure 10–65).
>
>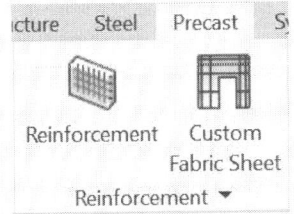
>
> Figure 10–65

Area Reinforcement

When creating an **Area Reinforcement**, you sketch a boundary, as shown in Figure 10–66, and then set up the spacing and layers in Properties. Using area reinforcement, you can place up to four layers of reinforcement in a large area like foundation slabs, floors, walls, and other structural concrete hosts. Area reinforcement can be placed in 3D, plan, elevation, or section views depending on the element you are reinforcing.

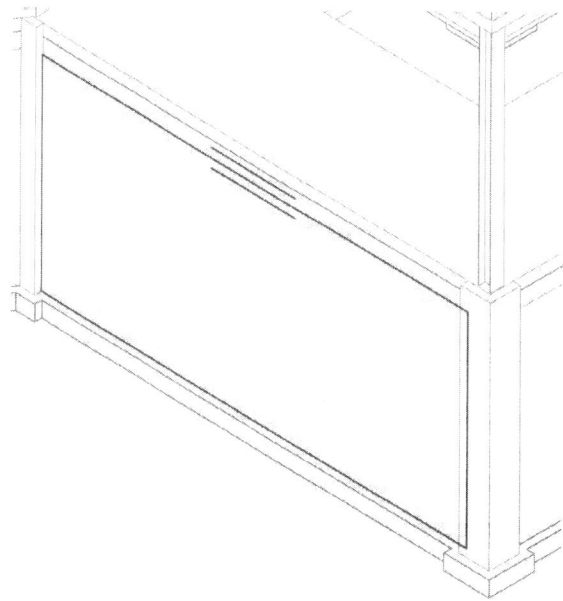

Figure 10–66

- To avoid conflict with other elements in the model, individual rebar within an area reinforcement can be modified or removed.

How To: Add Area Reinforcement

1. In the *Structure* tab>Reinforcement panel, click ▦ (Area) and select a structural floor or a wall.
2. If an element is already selected, in the *Modify* contextual tab>Reinforcement panel, click ▦ (Area).
    - Area reinforcement can be added to architectural walls and floors.
3. In Properties, modify the parameters as needed for the exterior and interior major and minor direction and spacing.
4. Click **Apply**.
5. In the *Modify | Create Reinforcement Boundary* tab>Draw panel, click (Pick Lines) or one of the other draw tools.

- If you are using **Pick Lines**, you can lock the lines to the elements you pick. When you select an edge a padlock symbol displays. Select it to lock the area reinforcement boundary to the wall or slab edge perimeter so that any changes made to the wall or slab automatically update the area reinforcement as well.
- If you select **Lock** in the Options Bar, each sketch line is locked to the selected edge. This only works with **Pick Lines**.
- The boundary must be a closed loop without any overlapping lines. Use the **Modify** tools if needed.

Note: Locking sketches to elements increases the size of the model. You should only do this if it is more efficient in the long run.

6. Click ✓ (Finish Edit Mode). The reinforcement displays either as just the symbol, as shown in Figure 10–67, or displays the rebar depending on how the view is set.

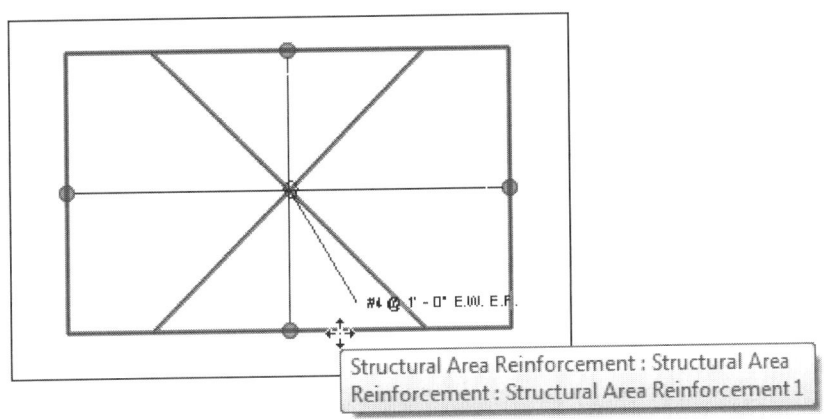

Figure 10–67

- When drawing the boundary, the first line you select displays a set of double lines indicating the major direction, as shown in Figure 10–68. To change it, in the *Modify | Structural Area Reinforcement>Edit Boundary* tab>Draw panel, click ⦀ (Major Direction) and select or draw the edge that defines the direction for the major bars.

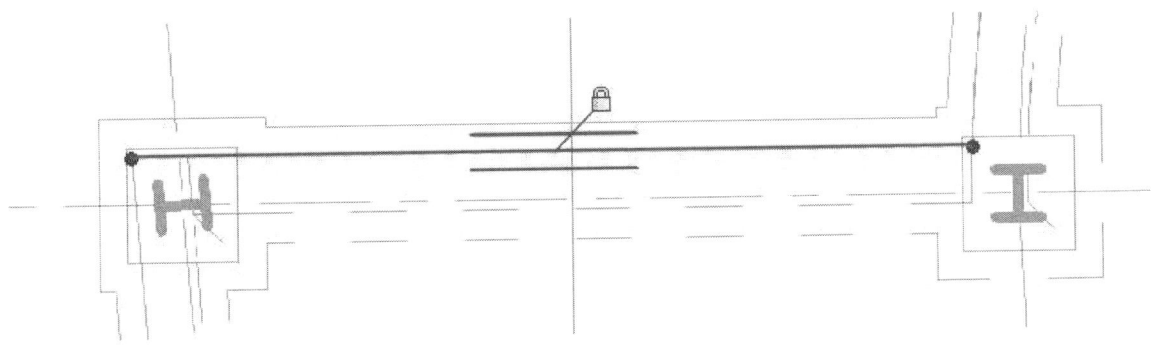

Figure 10–68

> **Hint: Displaying Area and Path Reinforcement**
>
> When you first place area or path reinforcement, a box displays at the boundary of the elements. By default, the rebar does not display, but it can be displayed when the Visual Style is set to (Wireframe) or if you modify the View Visibility State of the rebar element in Properties, as shown in Figure 10–69.

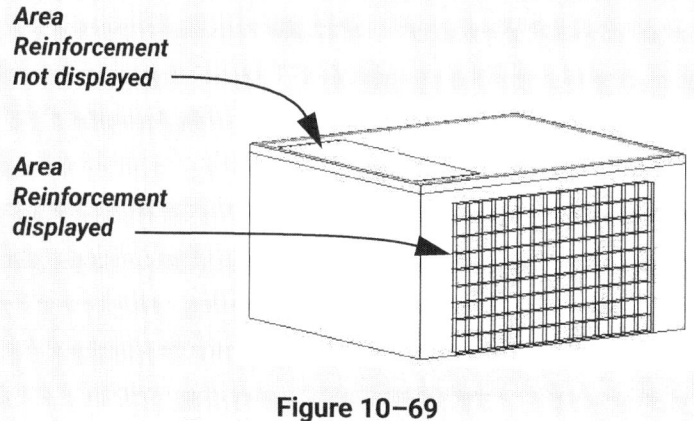

Figure 10–69

How To: Edit or Remove Rebar in Area Reinforcements

1. In a view, select an area reinforcement.
2. In the *Modify | Structural Rebar* tab>Customization panel, select (Edit Bars).
3. In the *Modify | Modify* tab>Mode panel, select (Modify Bars).
4. Select one or more rebar that you want to modify and do one of the following to modify the selected rebar:

   - In the *Modify | Structural Rebar* tab>Modify panel, select the **Move**, **Rotate** or **Align** tools to modify the selected rebar.

   - Select (Remove Bar) to remove the selected bar(s).

   - If you have accidentally repositioned or removed rebar, select (Reset Position) or (Reset All).

5. Click (Finish).

   - Select (Show Removed) to temporarily see the removed rebar.

Path Reinforcement

In some cases, additional reinforcement is required along the length of some edges to prevent curling and other issues. Path Reinforcement creates reinforcing that bends from the slab into the bearing wall, but is only extended into the slab at a specified distance, as shown in Figure 10–70. This is also handy for the foundation design of pre-engineered metal structures, where the pilasters and other elements need to be pinned back to the slab.

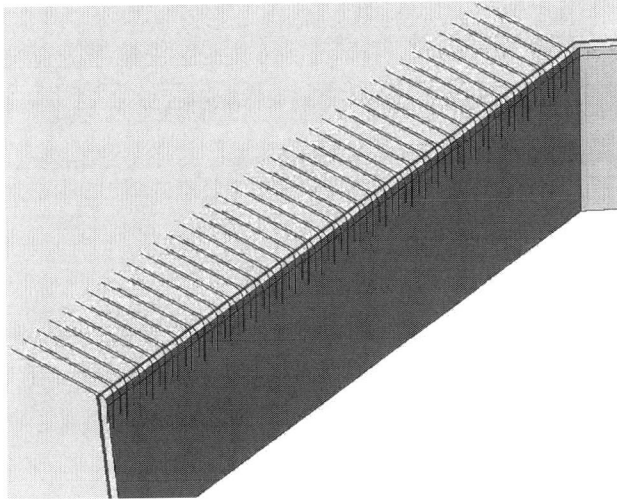

Figure 10–70

- To avoid conflict with other elements in the model, individual rebar within a path reinforcement can be modified or removed.

How To: Add Path Reinforcement

1. In the *Structure* tab>Reinforcement panel, click (Path Reinforcement).
2. Select the structural floor or wall.
3. In the *Modify | Create Reinforcement Path* tab>Draw panel, use the Draw tools to place a single line specifying an open path, as shown in Figure 10–71.

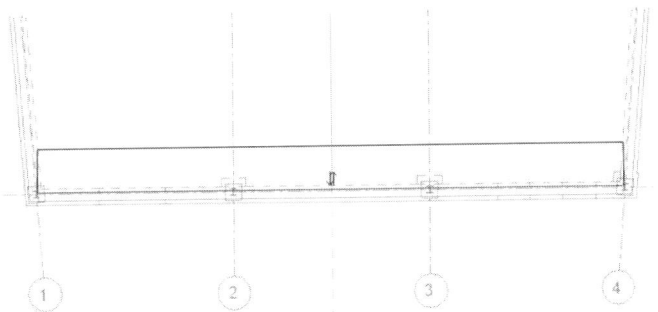

Figure 10–71

4. Click ⇆ (Flip) as required, to set the placement of the path.
5. In Properties, as shown in Figure 10–72, modify the parameters as needed.

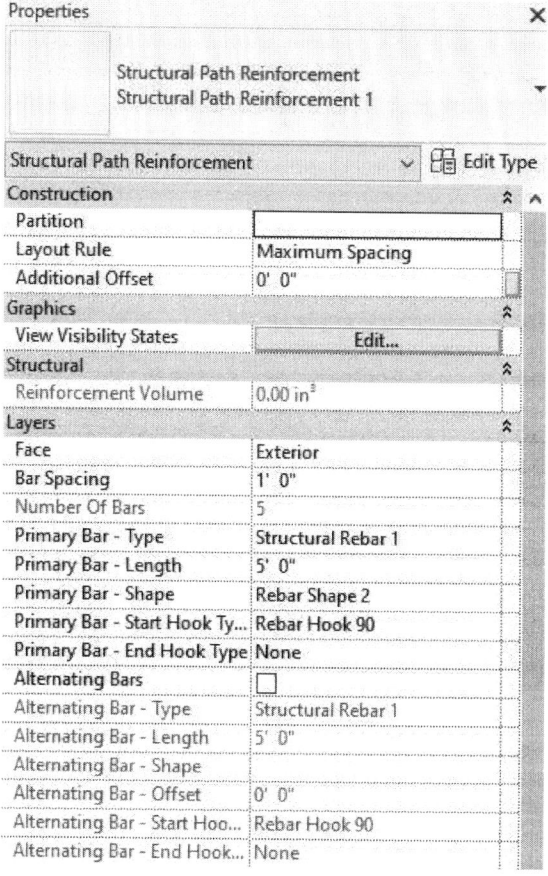

Figure 10–72

6. In the Mode panel, click ✓ (Finish Edit Mode). The Reinforcement is added as shown in Figure 10–73.

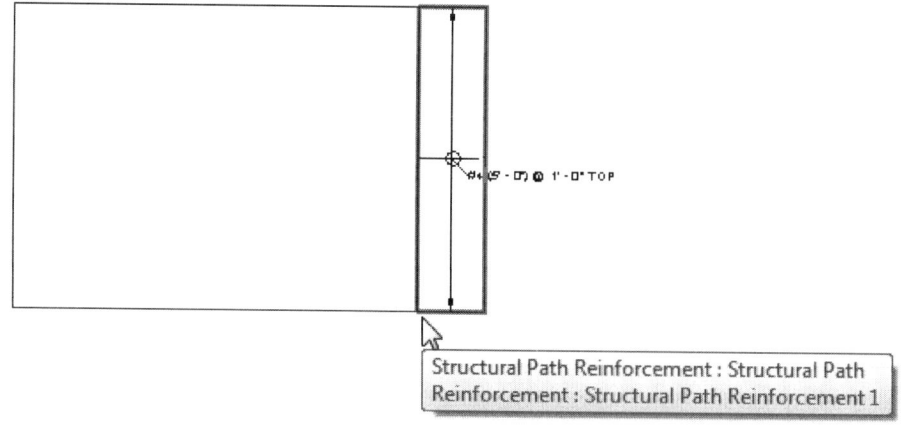

Figure 10–73

How To: Edit or Remove Rebar in Path Reinforcements

1. In a view, select a path reinforcement.
2. In the *Modify | Structural Rebar* tab>Customization panel, select (Edit Bars).
3. In the *Modify | Modify* tab>Mode panel, select (Modify Bars).
4. Select one or more rebar that you want to modify and do one of the following to modify the selected rebar:
   - In the *Modify | Structural Rebar* tab>Modify panel, select the **Move**, **Rotate** or **Align** tools to modify the selected rebar.
   - Select (Remove Bar) to remove the selected bar(s).
   - If you have accidentally repositioned or removed rebar, select (Reset Position) or (Reset All).
5. Click (Finish).
   - Select (Show Removed) to temporarily see the removed rebar.

Fabric Reinforcement

The Structural Fabric Area tool sketches the boundary of a fabric area to populate with fabric sheets, as shown in Figure 10–74. Fabric reinforcement is made up of two element types, Fabric Wire and Fabric Sheets. The Fabric Wire is used to define the reinforcing wire which is used to create the Fabric Sheets. You can also add individual fabric sheets.

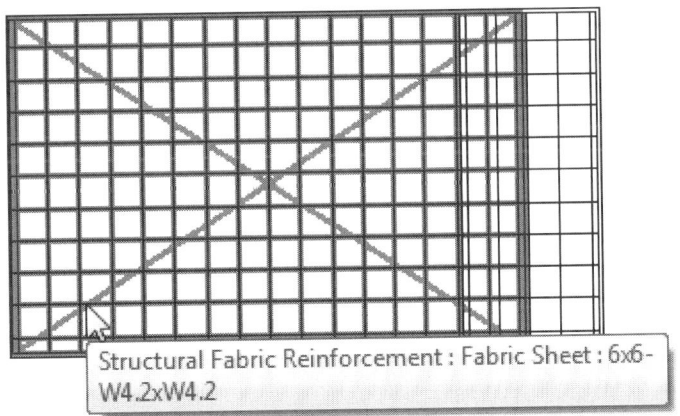

Figure 10–74

- Fabric reinforcement can be hosted in structural floors, foundation slabs, and structural walls.
- If there are no fabric reinforcement symbols or tags loaded, you are prompted with the opportunity to load one, as shown in Figure 10–75.

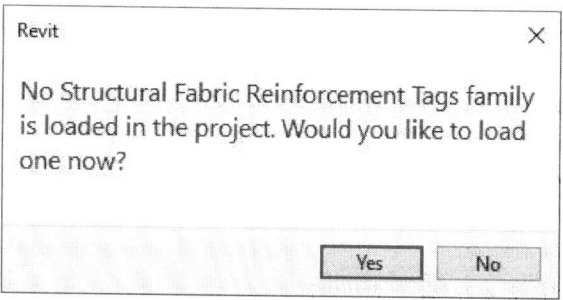 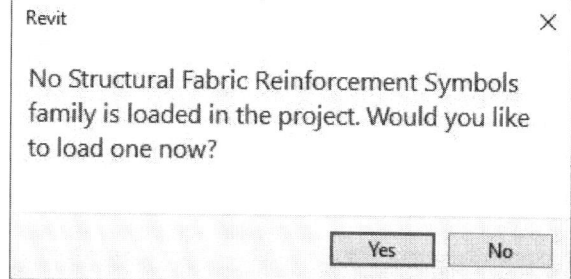

Figure 10–75

How To: Add a Single Fabric Sheet

1. In the *Structure* tab>Reinforcement panel (or if you have already selected an element, in the *Modify* contextual tab), click (Fabric Sheet).
2. In the Type Selector specify the type of sheet you want to use.
3. In Properties specify the *Location* (**Top** or **Bottom**), and other settings.
4. Click to place the sheet where you want it. (It must be in a concrete host, such as a wall, floor, or foundation slab.)
5. The command remains active and you can place additional sheets, as shown in Figure 10–76.

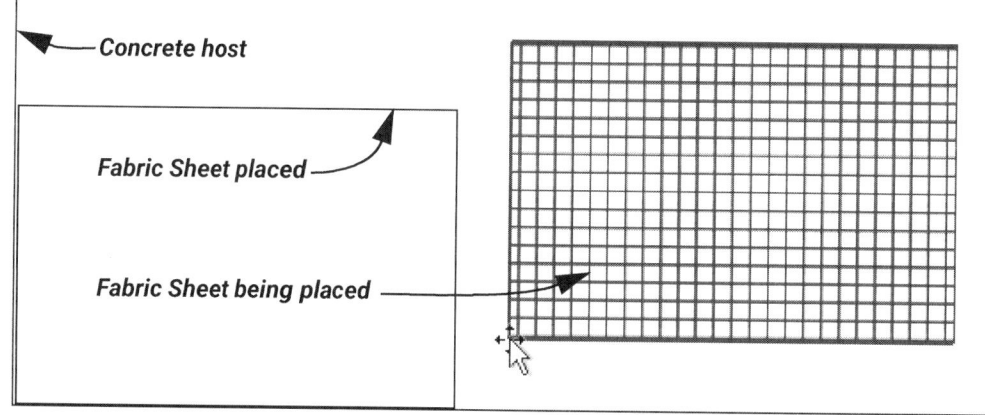

Figure 10–76

6. Click (Modify) to end the command.

How To: Add a Bent Fabric Sheet

1. Open a view perpendicular to the work plane, such as a section.
2. Start the (Fabric Sheet) command.
3. In the *Modify | Place Fabric Sheet* tab> Mode panel, click (Bend Sketch)
4. Select the host for the bent fabric sheet.
5. Using the tools in the *Modify | Create Bend Profile* tab, sketch a profile such as the one shown in Figure 10–77.

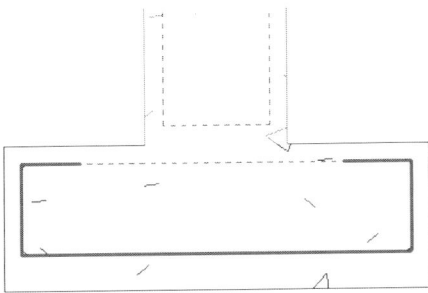

Figure 10–77

6. Click (Finish). The fabric sheet is bent following the sketch, as shown in Figure 10–78.

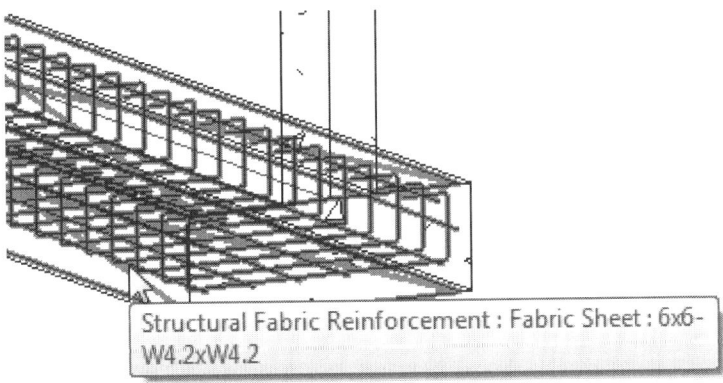

Figure 10–78

How To: Add Fabric Area Reinforcement

1. In the *Structure* tab>Reinforcement panel (or in the *Modify* contextual tab if you have already selected an element), click (Fabric Area).

2. Select the structural wall, floor, or slab if you did not select it already.

3. In the *Modify | Create Fabric Boundary* tab>Draw panel, use the Draw tools to define the closed boundary.

   - Use (Pick lines) and lock the boundary to the host element so that it automatically updates if the host is changed.
   - The set of double lines indicates the major direction. To change it, in the *Modify | Create Fabric Boundary* tab> Draw panel, click (Major Direction) and select one of the other lines to set the direction of the reinforcement.

4. The preview graphics displays the full size of the sheets as delivered to the construction site, as shown in Figure 10–79. Use the checkboxes and Properties to obtain the needed fabric sheet layout.

- The checkboxes at each edge determine the start point of the Fabric sheet layout and its direction. The start point is defined by at least two selected checkboxes on the rectangular edges, as shown in Figure 10–79. Select additional checkboxes to determine the fabric sheet alignment.

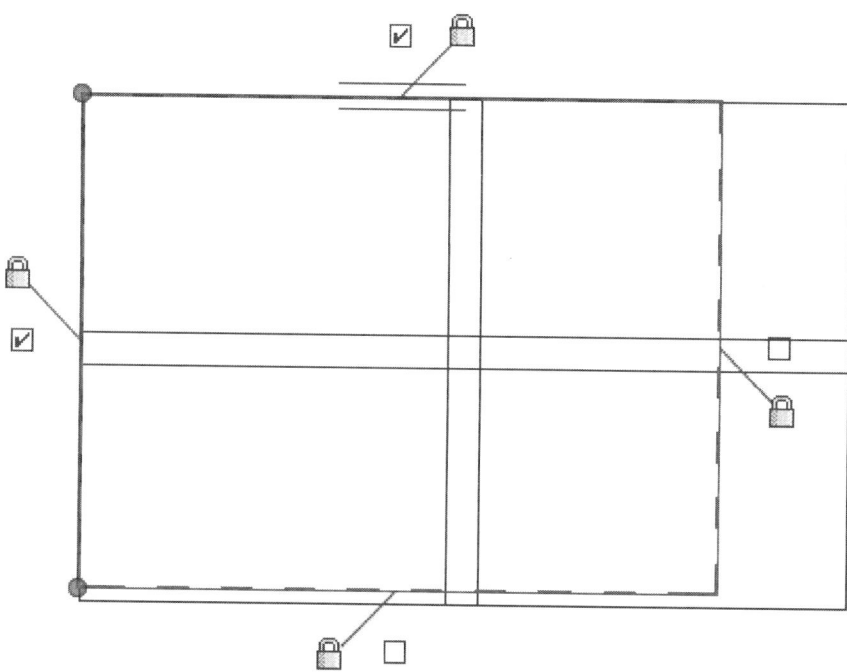

Figure 10–79

Structural Reinforcement

5. In Properties, as shown in Figure 10–80, modify the parameters as required for the *Fabric Sheet*, *Location*, *Lap Splice Position*, *Major* and *Minor lap Splice Length*, etc.

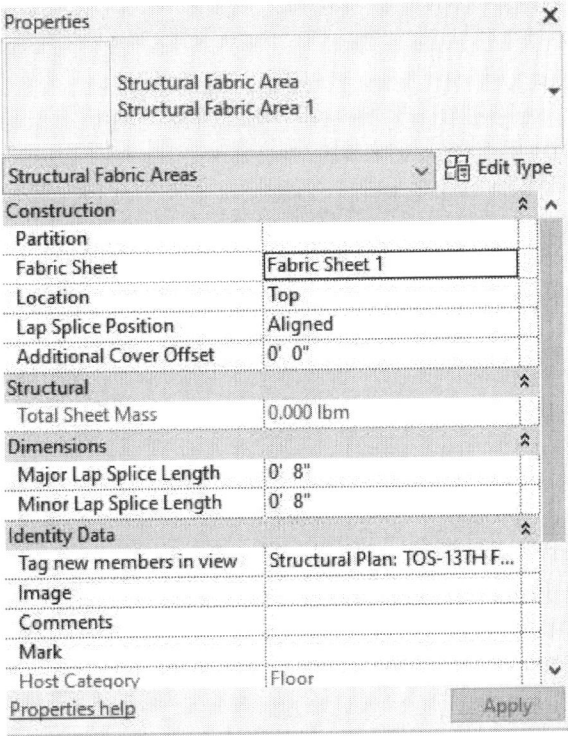

Figure 10–80

6. Click ✓ (Finish Edit Mode) and the fabric reinforcement is added to the element with the specified overlaps, as shown in Figure 10–81.

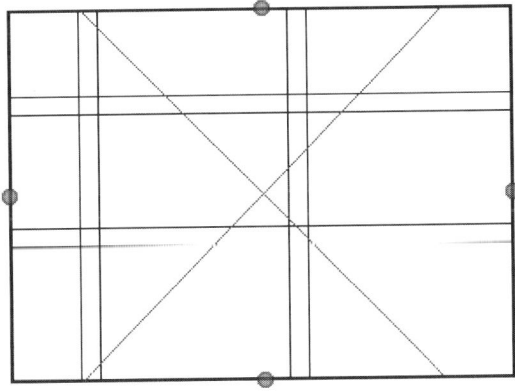

Figure 10–81

- If you want to change the way the fabric sheets overlap, modify the *Lap Splice Position* in Properties. For example, the sheets shown in Figure 10–82 are set to **Major Half-way Stagger**. The *Major* and *Minor Lap Splice Lengths* can also be modified.

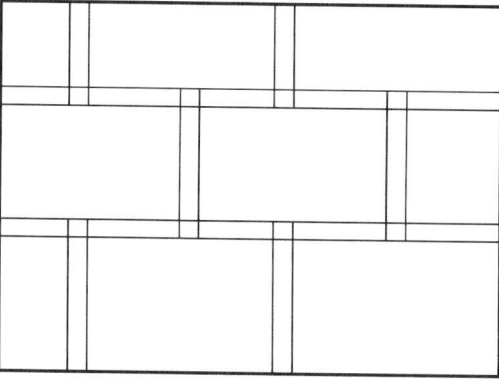

Figure 10–82

- To place symbols and tags automatically, in Properties, under *Identity Data*, select a view from the *Tag new members in view* drop-down list, as shown in Figure 10–83.

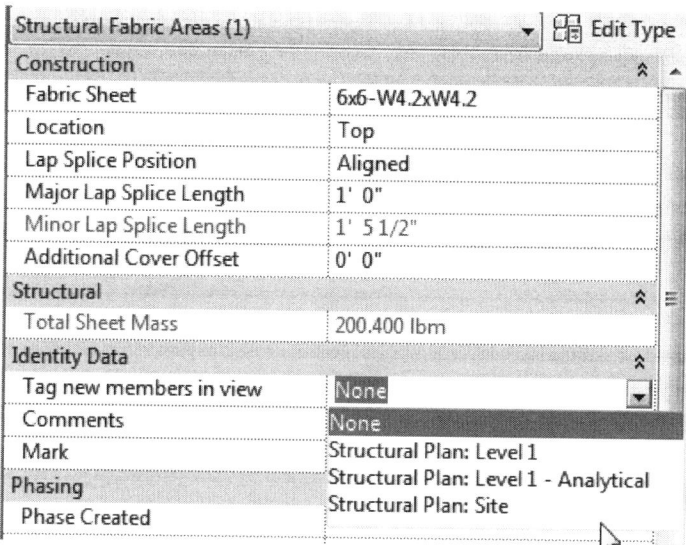

Figure 10–83

- Only views that are parallel to the placement plane are listed in the drop-down list. Using this parameter also defines the view to place new symbols and tags if the fabric area changes size during regeneration.

Modifying Area, Path, and Fabric Reinforcement

As with most elements in Autodesk Revit software, there are a variety of ways to modify area, path, and fabric reinforcement, including editing the boundary or path, using shape handles, and changing the properties, as shown in Figure 10–84. You can also delete entire systems or break the systems down into individual rebar elements or sheets.

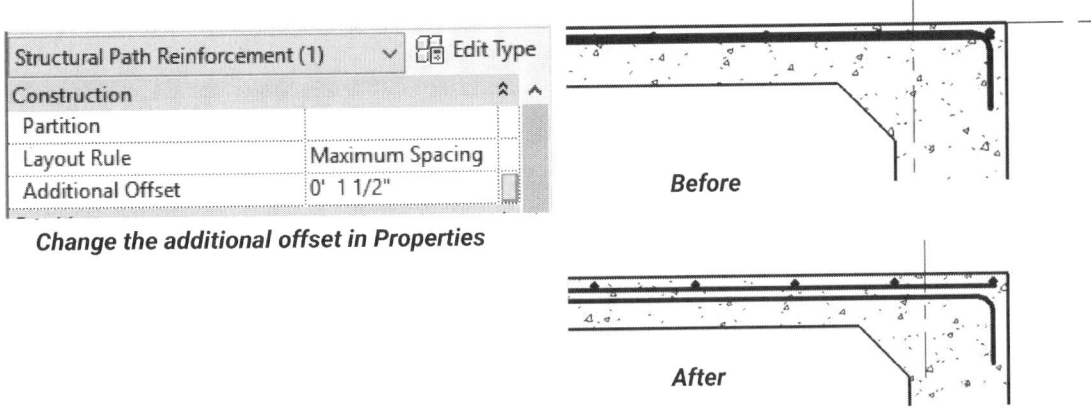

Figure 10–84

- To quickly select multiple instances of related rebar or fabric, select one, right-click and select **Select All Rebar in Host** or **Select All Fabric in Host**.

- When you select the area, path, or fabric area reinforcement you can adjust the boundary by stretching the shape handles, as shown in Figure 10–85.

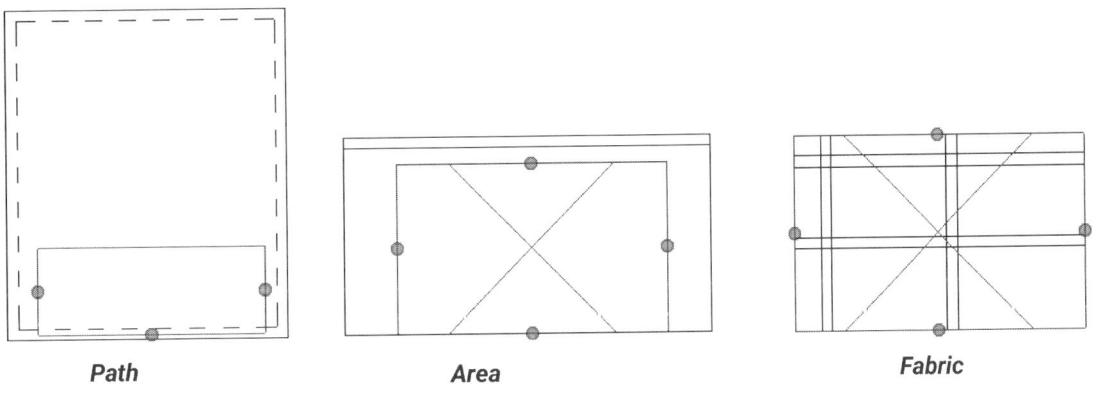

Figure 10–85

- When you have the reinforcement selected you can use the related (Edit Boundary) tool found in the Mode panel. This opens the sketch mode where you can use the draw tools to change the boundary or path.

- If you want to remove the reinforcement completely, ensure that you select the boundary of the system and then delete it.

- If you want to keep the individual rebar elements but remove the system, click ![icon] (Remove Area System), ![icon] (Remove Path System), or ![icon] (Remove Fabric System) in the respective *Modify* tabs.

- When you remove a fabric system it deletes the boundary and leaves the full size of all of the sheets, as shown on the right in Figure 10–86.

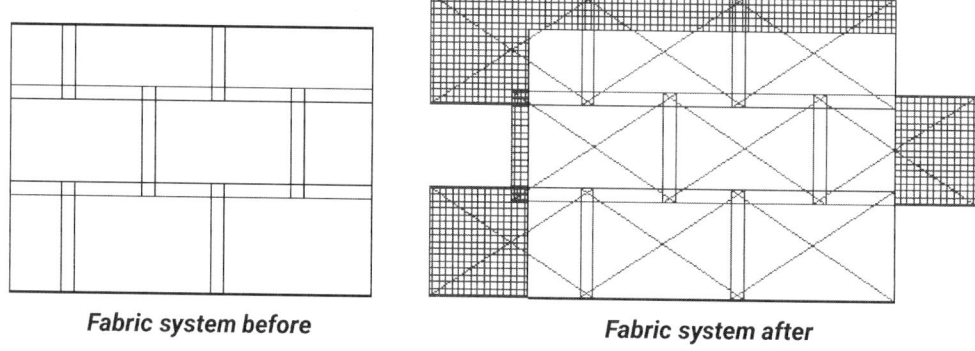

Fabric system before   Fabric system after

Figure 10–86

- When the area or path system is removed, the individual bars create standard joins to the hosting elements. In some cases this can cause these bars to shift slightly. This is much more evident if Stirrup/Tie bars are in close proximity to the hosted bars.

- When the system is removed, the associated tags, symbols, and dimensions are also removed.

- It can help to view reinforcement in a section view. For example, in path reinforcement you can check the hook direction and modify it with the **Toggle Hook Orientation** control, as shown in Figure 10–87.

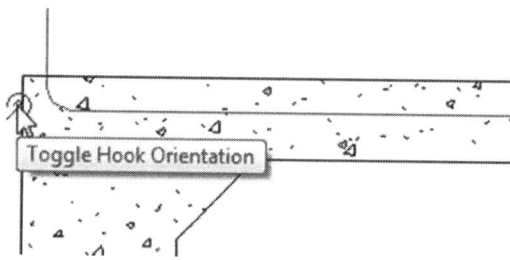

Figure 10–87

- You can also modify the other hook information in Properties. For example, you can change the **Primary Bar-Start Hook Type** as shown in Figure 10–88.

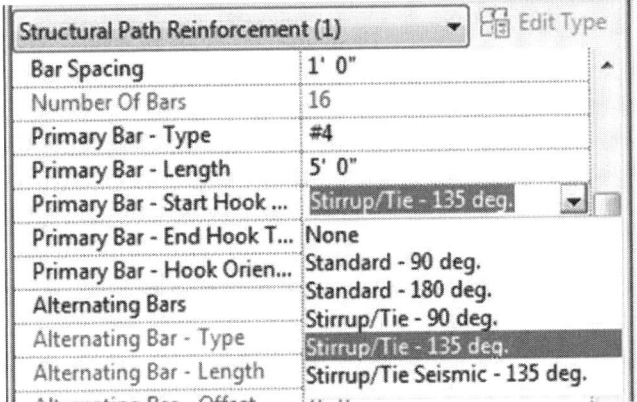 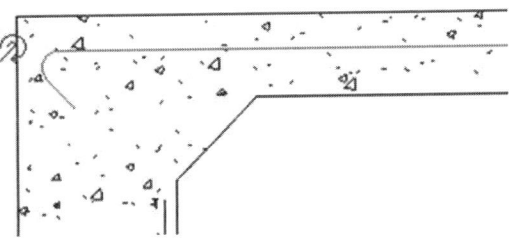

Figure 10–88

Practice 10b
Reinforce Structural Elements

Practice Objective

- Add area, path, and fabric reinforcement.

In this practice, you will apply area and path reinforcement to a slab. You will also add area reinforcement to a wall and fabric reinforcement, as shown in Figure 10-89.

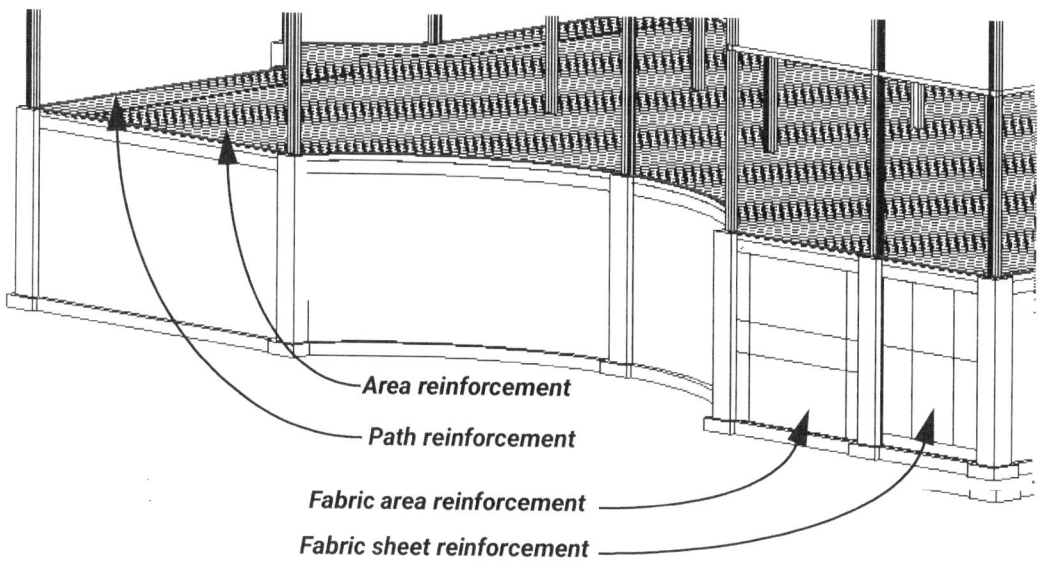

Figure 10-89

Task 1: Apply area reinforcement.

1. Open **Structural-Reinforcing.rvt** from the practice files folder.

2. In the **Structural Plans: 00 GROUND FLOOR** view, change the *Visual Style* to (Hidden Line).

3. Select the structural floor by clicking on an edge. You can use <Tab> to cycle through elements.

4. In the View Control Bar, expand (Temporary Hide/ Isolate) and select **Isolate Element**. This makes it easier for you to work specifically with the slab outline only.

5. In the *Modify | Floors* tab>Reinforcement panel, click (Area Reinforcement) and select the floor.

6. In Properties, under *Layers,* clear the **Bottom Major Direction** and **Bottom Minor Direction** parameters.
7. In the *Modify | Create Reinforcement Boundary* tab>Draw panel, click (Pick Lines).
8. In the Options Bar, select **Lock**. This ensures that, if the floor slab is modified, the boundary of the area reinforcement will update to match.
9. Select the outside edges of the slab and the outlines of the elevator and stairwell. To quickly select the outlines, hover over one line and press <Tab> so that all the connected lines highlight.
    - Verify that the magenta sketch lines do not overlap, do not have any gaps, and form a closed loop on the outside and around each opening.
10. In the *Modify | Create Reinforcement Boundary* tab>Draw panel, click (Major Direction) and select a horizontal line.
11. In the Mode panel, click (Finish Edit Mode). The area reinforcement symbol and tag display as shown in Figure 10-90.

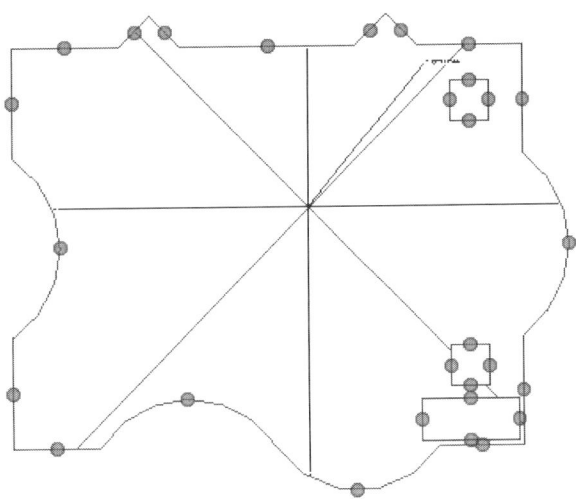

Figure 10-90

12. In the View Control Bar, expand (Temporary Hide/Isolate) and select **Reset Temporary Hide/Isolate**.
13. Select the area reinforcement, and in Properties, next to *View Visibility States*, click **Edit...**.

14. In the Rebar Element View Visibility States dialog box, for *Structural Plan: 00 GROUND FLOOR*, select **View unobscured,** as shown in Figure 10–91. Click **OK**.

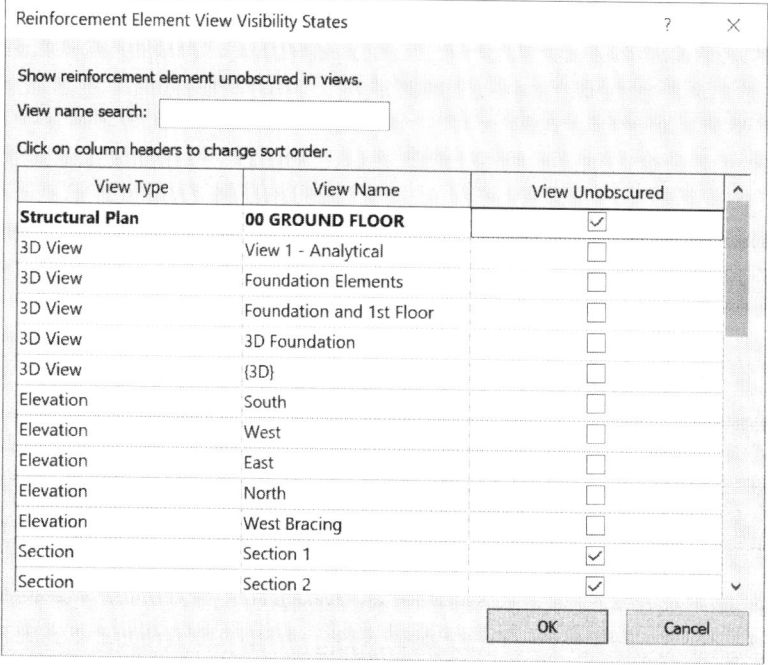

Figure 10–91

15. Press <Esc> so that the area reinforcement is not selected. Then highlight the elements. Each rebar displays individually, as shown in Figure 10–92.

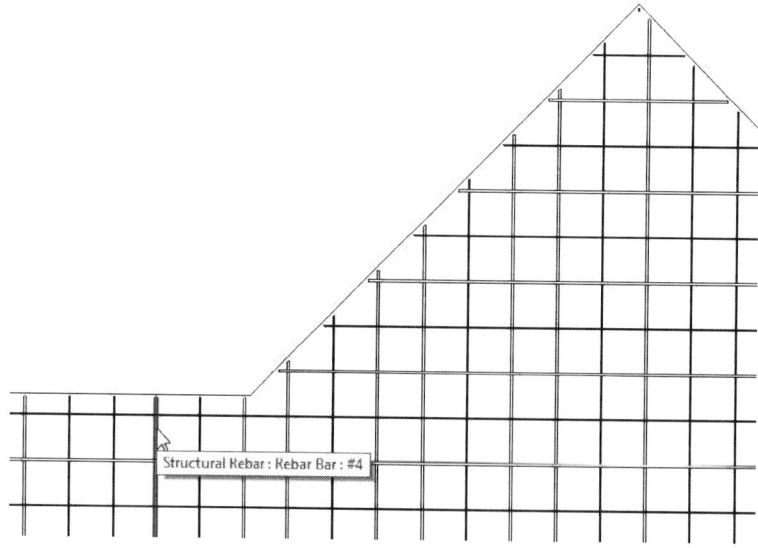

Figure 10–92

16. Select one of the rebar elements and review its properties. Most of the parameters are automatically assigned by the area reinforcement element but you can change the *Schedule Mark* and *View Visibility States*.
17. Select the entire area reinforcement element. Edit *View Visibility States* and clear the **View unobscured** for the *Structural Plan: 00 GROUND FLOOR* view and click **OK**. The view displays just the outline.
18. Open the **Sections (Wall Section): Typical Foundation Wall Section** view. The area reinforcement displays in the section as shown in Figure 10–93. The rebar and area reinforcement elements can be selected separately.

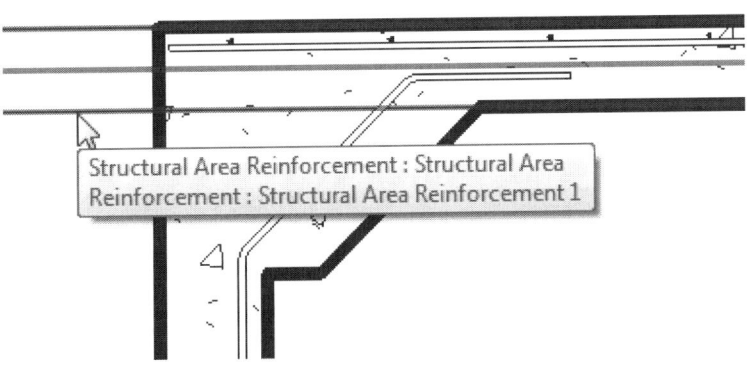

Figure 10–93

19. Save the project.

Task 2: Apply path reinforcement.

1. Switch back to the **Structural Plans: 00 GROUND FLOOR** view with only the floor displaying.
2. In the View Control Bar, expand (Temporary Hide/Isolate) and select **Isolate Element**. This makes it easier for you to work specifically with the slab outline only.
3. In the *Structure* tab>Reinforcement panel, click (Path) and select the floor.

4. In Properties, set the *Additional Offset* to **1 1/2"** and the *Primary Bar - Shape* to **Rebar Shape 1**, as shown in Figure 10–94. Ensure that the *Alternating Bars* is toggled off.

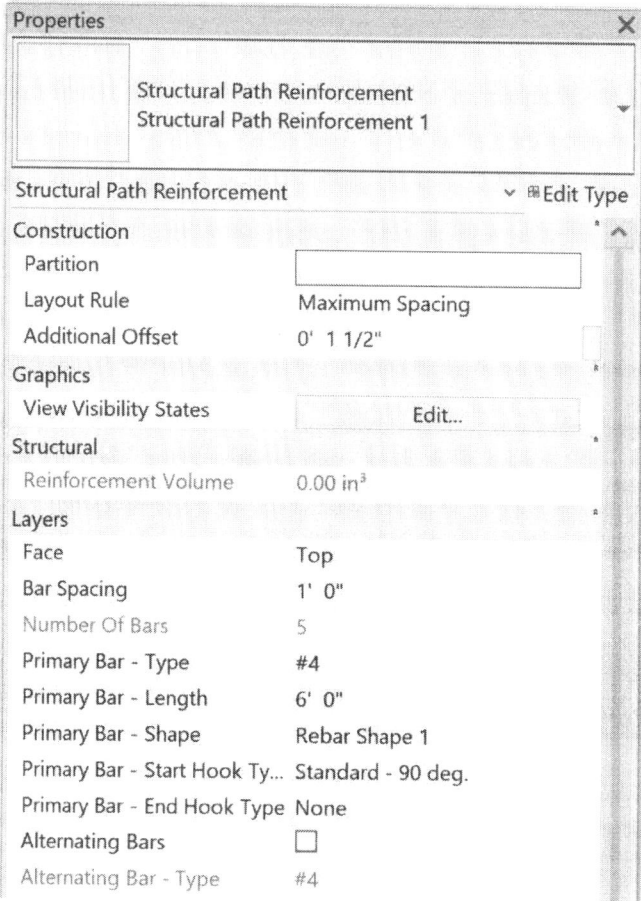

Figure 10–94

5. Using the tools in the Draw panel, draw a single line path along the north wall. Flip the path reinforcement, if needed, so that it is set to the inside, as shown in Figure 10–95.

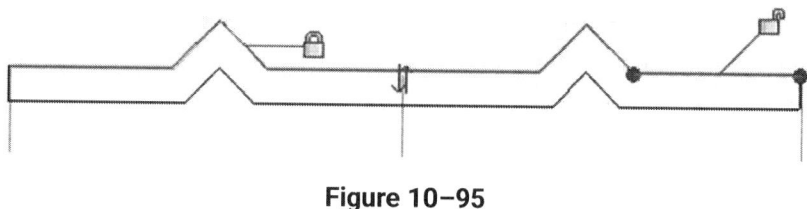

Figure 10–95

6. In the Mode panel, click ✔ (Finish Edit Mode).

7. In the View Control Bar, click ◈ (Temporary Hide/Isolate) and select **Reset Temporary Hide Isolate**.

Structural Reinforcement

8. Open the **Sections (Wall Section): Typical Foundation Wall Section** view. The path reinforcement displays in the section as shown in Figure 10–96.

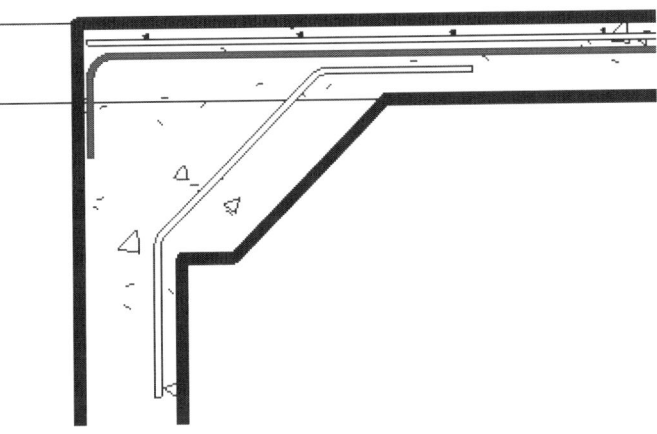

Figure 10–96

9. Save the project.

Task 3: Reinforce walls.

1. In the **Typical Foundation Wall Section** view, select the wall.
2. Open the **Elevations (Building Elevation): North** view and zoom in on the selected foundation wall. Do not isolate the element because you need to see the other elements to draw the correct boundary.
3. In the *Modify | Walls* tab>Reinforcement panel, click ▦ (Area).
4. Draw the boundary between the piers excluding the slab and set the *Major Direction* to the vertical sketch line to the left, as shown in Figure 10–97. Use the **Trim** command to clean up the corners. Remember that there cannot be any gaps or overlapping lines.

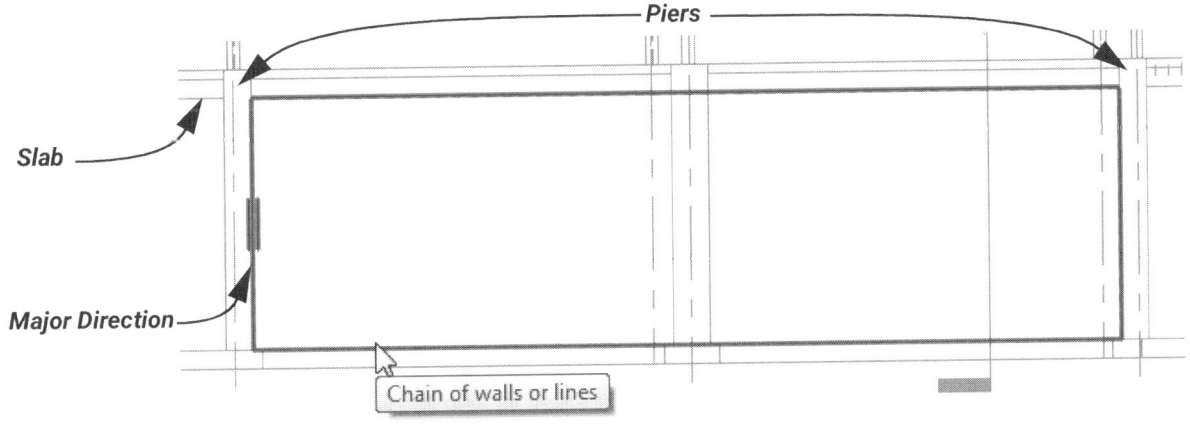

Figure 10–97

5. In Properties, ensure that both the *Interior* and *Exterior Major* and *Minor* spacing is set to **1'-0"**.

6. In the Mode panel, click ✓ (Finish Edit Mode).

7. The new area reinforcement is added, as shown in Figure 10–98.

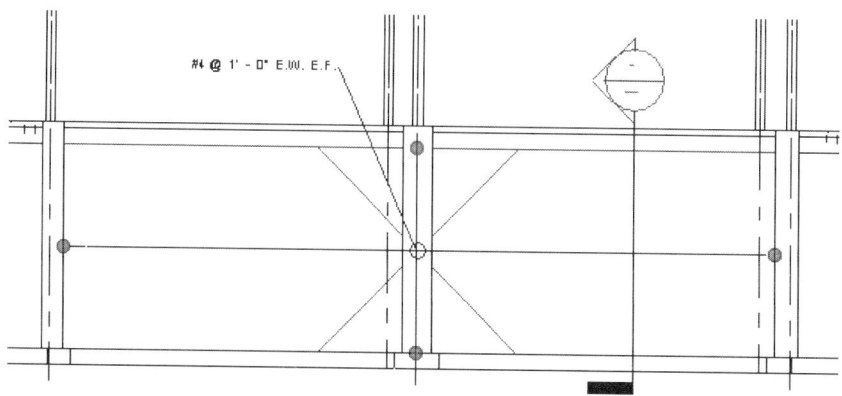

Figure 10–98

8. Save the project.

Task 4: Add fabric area and sheet reinforcement.

1. Open **Elevations (Building Elevation): West** view.
2. Zoom in to the lower right corner of the building and select the wall as shown in Figure 10–99.

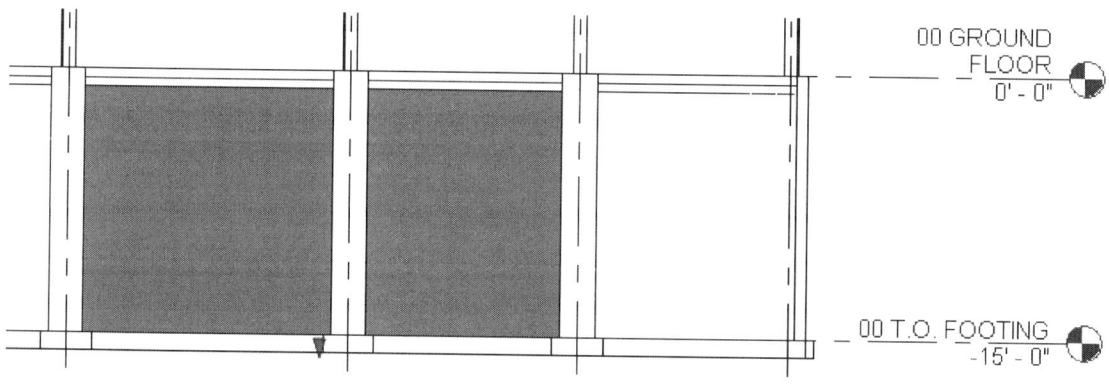

Figure 10–99

3. In the *Modify | Walls* tab>Reinforcement panel, click (Fabric Area).
4. If prompted, do not load the Structural Fabric Reinforcement Symbols or Tags by clicking **No**.

5. Use the ⬜ (Rectangle) Draw tool and draw the boundary shown in Figure 10–100. The sheets extend beyond the boundary.

   Note: The boundary is highlighted for clarity.

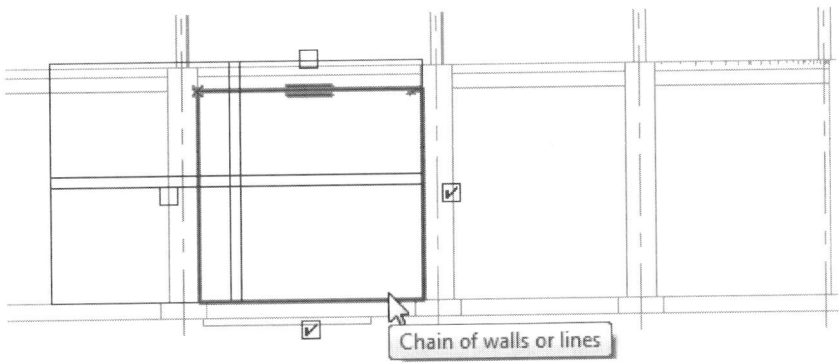

Figure 10–100

6. Select all of the checkboxes so that the ending edges are set up, as shown in Figure 10–101.

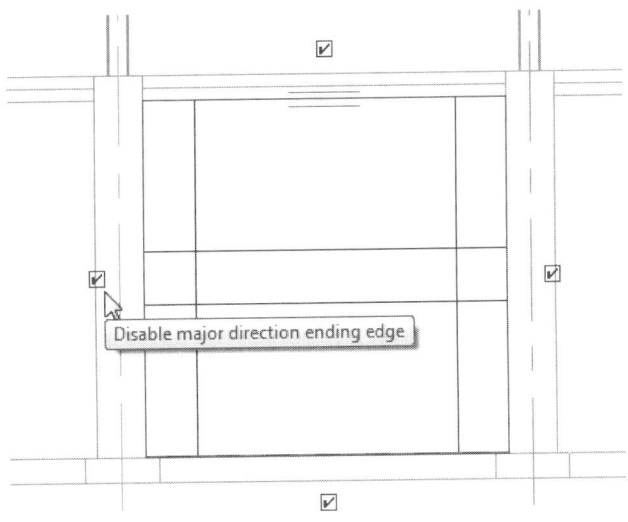

Figure 10–101

7. Click ✓ (Finish Edit Mode).
8. The fabric sheets display. You can modify the fabric sheet origins to change the fit, if needed.
9. Select the same wall and in the *Modify | Walls* tab>Reinforcement panel, click (Fabric Sheet).
10. When prompted, do not load the Structural Fabric Reinforcement Tags by clicking **No**.

11. Add individual fabric sheets to the wall area to the right of the previous fabric area reinforcement, as shown in Figure 10–102. You can press <Spacebar> to rotate the sheets as you place them.

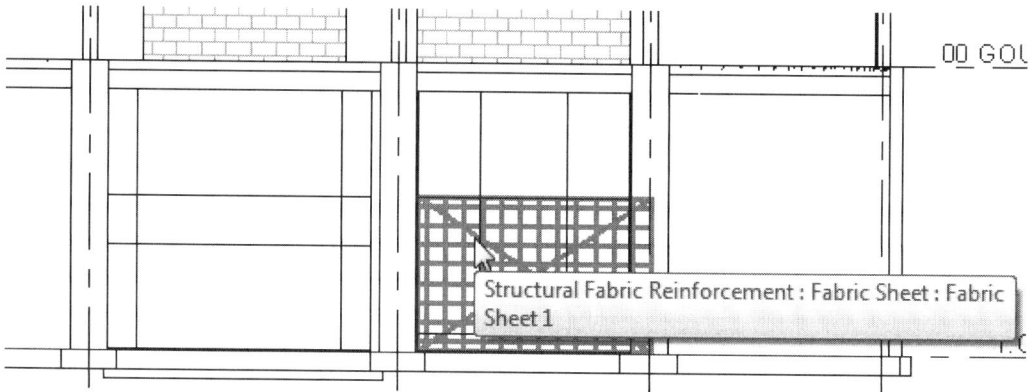

Figure 10–102

12. Open a 3D view and rotate it to display the area where the fabric reinforcement is added, as shown in Figure 10–103.

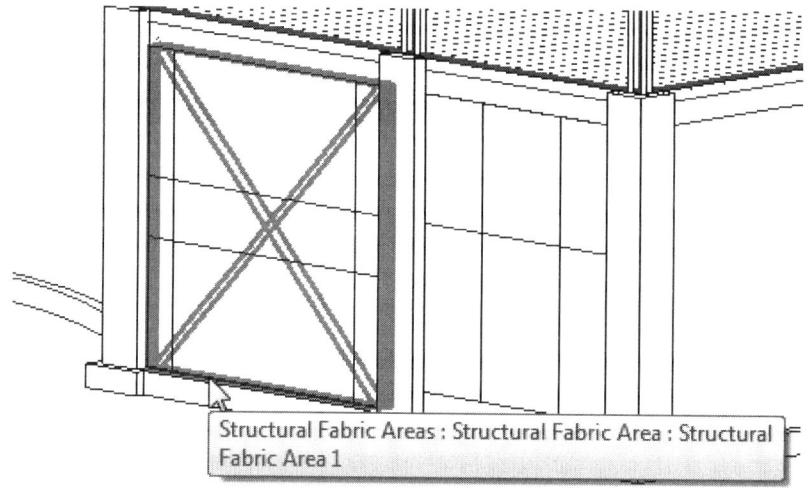

Figure 10–103

13. Select the fabric sheet and area and, in Properties, click **Edit** next to *View Visibility States*. Select **View unobscured** for the 3D view you are currently in, as shown in Figure 10-104.

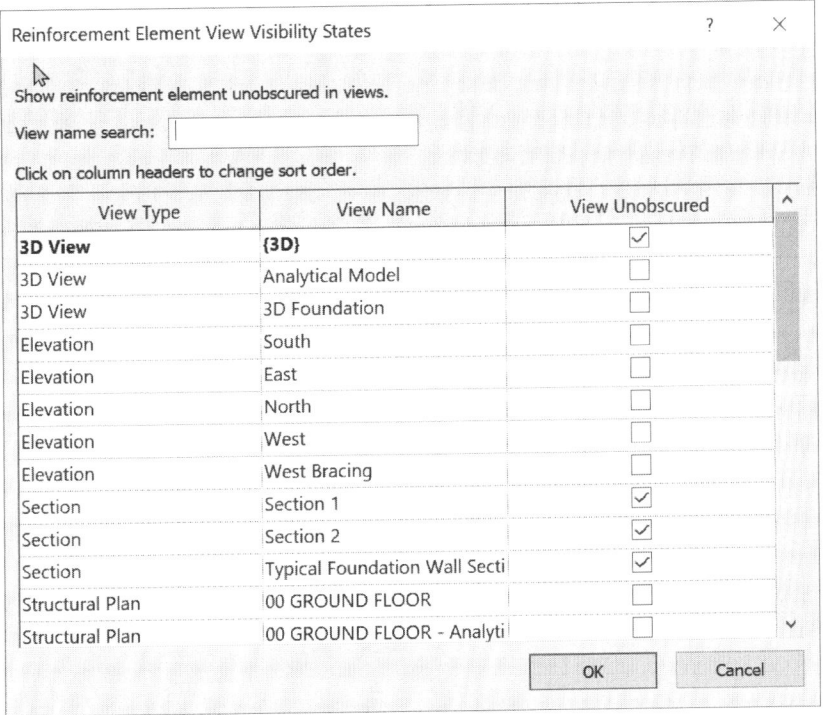

Figure 10-104

14. Change the level of detail to **fine** in the View control bar.
15. Save and close the project.

End of practice

Chapter Review Questions

1. Which of the following elements can have reinforcement added to it? (Select all that apply.)

    a. Structural walls

    b. Non-structural walls

    c. Foundation walls

    d. Partition walls

2. The settings in the Rebar Cover Settings dialog box, as shown in Figure 10–105, are contained in the host that is being reinforced.

    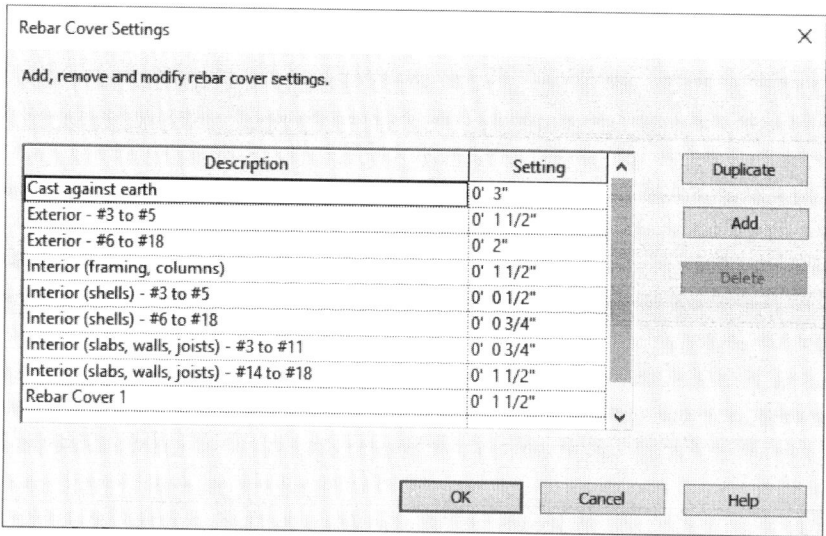

    Figure 10–105

    a. True

    b. False

3. How do you load additional reinforcement into your model if it is not already available? (Select all that apply.)

    a. In the Rebar Shape Browser, right-click and select **Load**.

    b. In the *Modify | Place Rebar* tab>Family panel, select **Load Shapes**.

    c. In the *Insert* tab>Load from Library panel, select **Load Family**.

    d. In the Project Browser, in the Families>Structural Rebar section, right-click and select **Load Shapes**.

4. How do you add multiple evenly spaced instances of rebar such as that shown in Figure 10–106?

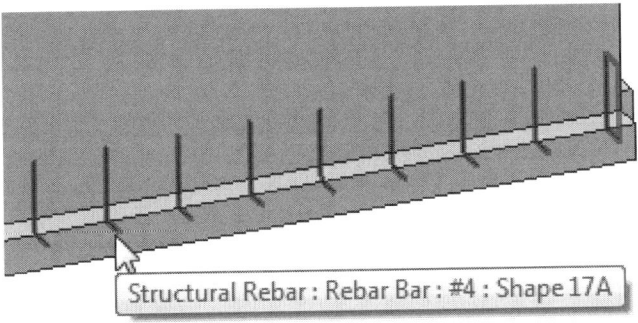

Figure 10–106

   a. Modify the Layout Rule.
   b. Use the **Array** command.
   c. Edit the Constraints.
   d. Change the **Quantity** option.

5. After sketching a custom rebar shape, as shown in Figure 10–107, where do you assign the name?

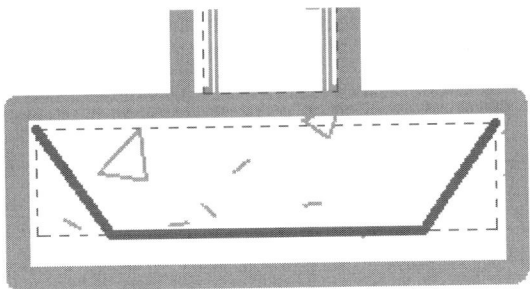

Figure 10–107

   a. Right-click on the rebar and select **Rename**.
   b. After finishing the sketch type it in the Name dialog box that comes up.
   c. In Properties, beside the Shape parameter.
   d. In the Project Browser, under Structural Rebar>Rebar Shape.

6. In which type of elements can you add structural area reinforcement as shown in Figure 10–108? (Select all that apply.)

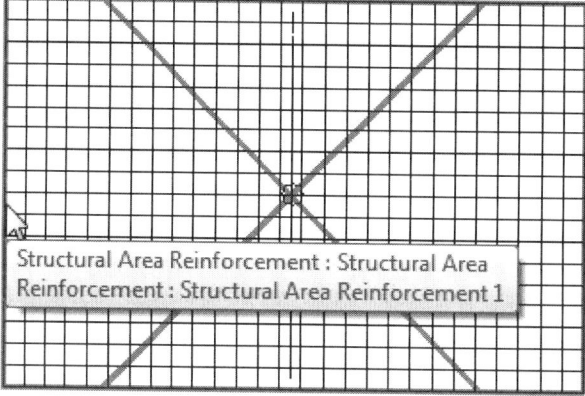

Figure 10–108

   a. Foundation slabs
   b. Structural floors
   c. Structural walls
   d. Wall foundations

7. To display reinforcement in a 3D view, as shown in Figure 10–109, where do you make the modification?

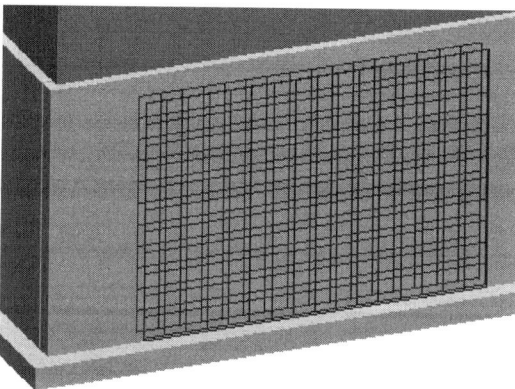

Figure 10–109

   a. The Visibility/Graphic Overrides dialog box.
   b. The View Visibility State in the rebar properties.
   c. The 3D View Properties in the view properties.
   d. The Visual Style of the view.

Command Summary

Button	Command	Location
Rebar Set Presentation Tools		
	Select	• **Ribbon:** In a plan view with a rebar set selected, *Modify	Structural Rebar* tab>Presentation panel
	Show All	• **Ribbon:** In a plan view with a rebar set selected, *Modify	Structural Rebar* tab>Presentation panel
	Show First and Last	• **Ribbon:** In a plan view with a rebar set selected, *Modify	Structural Rebar* tab>Presentation panel
	Show Middle	• **Ribbon:** In a plan view with a rebar set selected, *Modify	Structural Rebar* tab>Presentation panel
Reinforcement Elements		
	Area	• **Ribbon:** *Structure* tab>Reinforcement panel or with a concrete structural member selected *Modify	contextual* tab>Reinforcement panel
	Fabric Area	• **Ribbon:** *Structure* tab>Reinforcement panel or with a concrete structural member selected *Modify	contextual* tab>Reinforcement panel
	Fabric Sheet	• **Ribbon:** *Structure* tab>Reinforcement panel or with a concrete structural member selected *Modify	contextual* tab>Reinforcement panel
	Free Form Rebar	• **Ribbon:** *Modify	Place Rebar* tab>Placement Methods panel
	Path	• **Ribbon:** *Structure* tab>Reinforcement panel or with a concrete structural member selected *Modify	contextual* tab>Reinforcement panel
	Rebar	• **Ribbon:** *Structure* tab>Reinforcement panel or with a concrete structural member selected *Modify	contextual* tab>Reinforcement panel
Reinforcement Tools		
	Cover	• **Ribbon:** *Structure* tab>Reinforcement panel
	Edit Constraints	• **Ribbon:** *Modify	Structural Rebar* tab>Rebar Constraints panel

Button	Command	Location
	Constrained Placement	• **Ribbon:** *Modify	Structural Rebar* tab>Rebar Constraints panel
	Multi-planar	• **Ribbon:** *Modify	Create Rebar Sketch* tab>Reinforcement panel
	Parallel to Work Plane	• **Ribbon:** *Modify	Place Rebar* tab>Placement Orientation panel
	Parallel to Cover	• **Ribbon:** *Modify	Place Rebar* tab>Placement Orientation panel
	Perpendicular to Cover	• **Ribbon:** *Modify	Place Rebar* tab>Placement Orientation panel
	Pick New Host	• **Ribbon:** *Modify	Structural Rebar* tab>Host panel
	Rebar Cover Settings	• **Ribbon:** *Structure* tab>Reinforcement panel
	Reinforcement Settings	• **Ribbon:** *Structure* tab>Reinforcement panel
	Remove Fabric System	• **Ribbon:** with a structural fabric area selected *Modify	contextual* tab>Reinforcement panel
	Sketch Rebar	• **Ribbon:** *Modify	Place Rebar* tab>Placement Methods panel

Construction Documentation

The third section of this guide continues to teach the Autodesk® Revit® tools, focusing on tools that help you to create accurate construction documents for a design.

This section includes the following chapters:

- Chapter 11: Creating Construction Documents
- Chapter 12: Working with Annotations
- Chapter 13: Adding Tags and Schedules
- Chapter 14: Creating Details

Chapter 11

Creating Construction Documents

The accurate creation of construction documents in Revit® ensures that the design is correctly communicated to downstream users. Construction documents are created primarily in special views call sheets. Knowing how to select title blocks, assign title block information, place views, and print the sheets are essential steps in the construction documentation process.

Learning Objectives

- Add sheets with title blocks and views of a project.
- Enter the title block information for individual sheets and for an entire project.
- Place and organize views on sheets.
- Print sheets using the default Print dialog box.

11.1 Setting Up Sheets

While you are modeling a project, the foundations of the working drawings are already in progress. Any view (such as a floor plan, section, callout, or schedule) can be placed on a sheet, as shown in Figure 11–1.

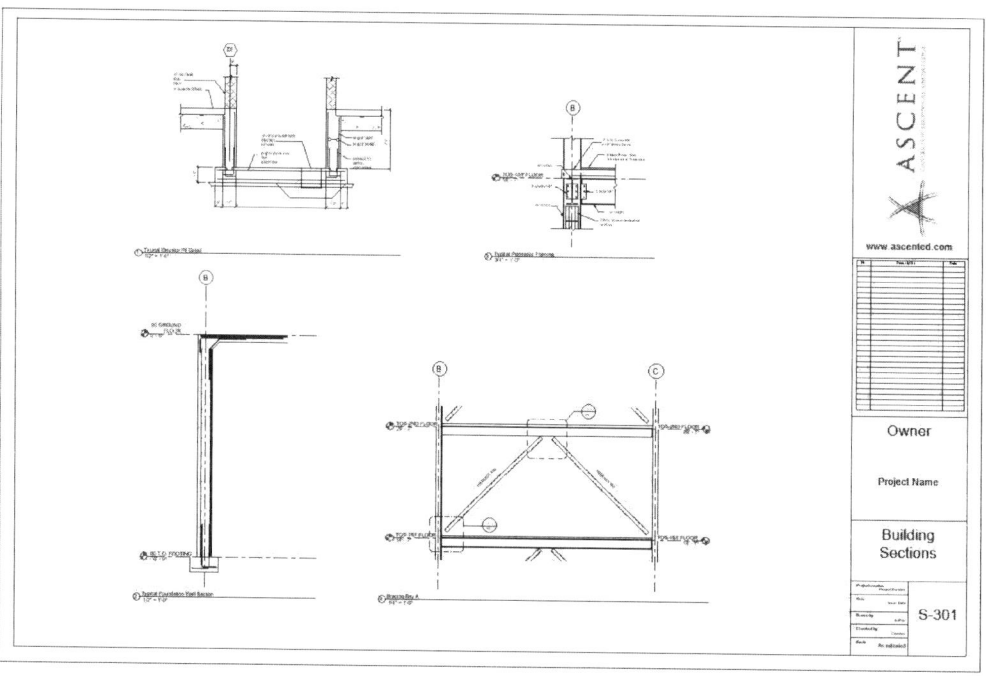

Figure 11–1

- Company templates can be created with standard sheets using the company (or project) title block and related views already placed on the sheet.
- The sheet size is based on the selected title block family.
- Sheets are listed in the *Sheets* area in the Project Browser.
- Most information on sheets is included in the views. You can add general notes and other non-model elements directly to the sheet, though it is better to add them using drafting views or legends, as these can be placed on multiple sheets.

How To: Set Up Sheets

1. In the Project Browser, right-click on the *Sheets* area header and select **New Sheet...**, or in the *View* tab>Sheet Composition panel, click (Sheet).

    - Alternatively, in the Project Browser, right-click on **Sheets (all)** and select **New Sheet...**.

2. In the New Sheet dialog box, select a title block from the list, as shown in Figure 11–2.

   Note: Click **Load...** to load a sheet from the Revit Library or your company's custom sheet.

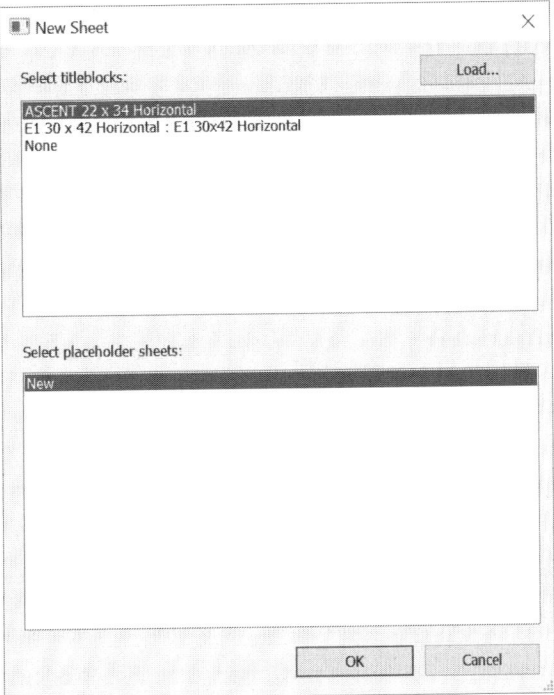

Figure 11–2

3. Click **OK**. A new sheet is created using the selected title block.
4. Fill out the information in the title block as needed.
5. Add views to the sheet.

- When you create sheets, the next sheet is incremented numerically.
- Double-click on the sheet name to change the name and number in the Sheet Title dialog box.
- When you change the *Sheet Name* and/or *Number* in the title block, it automatically changes the name and number of the sheet in the Project Browser.
- The plot stamp on the side of the sheet automatically updates according to the current date and time. The format of the display uses the regional settings of your computer.
- The Scale is automatically entered when a view is inserted onto a sheet. If a sheet has multiple views with different scales, the scale displays **As Indicated**.

Sheet (Title Block) Properties

Each new sheet includes a title block. You can change the title block information in Properties, as shown on the left in Figure 11–3, or by selecting any blue label you want to edit (Sheet Name, Sheet Number, Drawn by, etc.), as shown on the right.

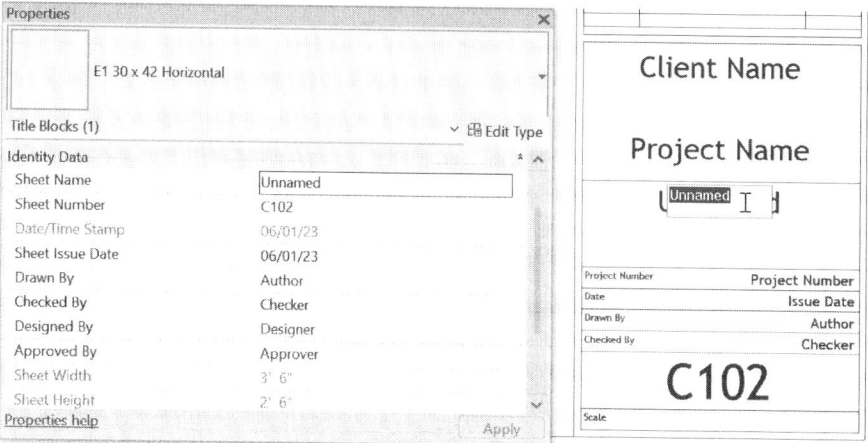

Figure 11–3

Properties that apply to all sheets can be entered in the Project Information dialog box (shown in Figure 11–4). In the *Manage* tab>Settings panel, click (Project Information).

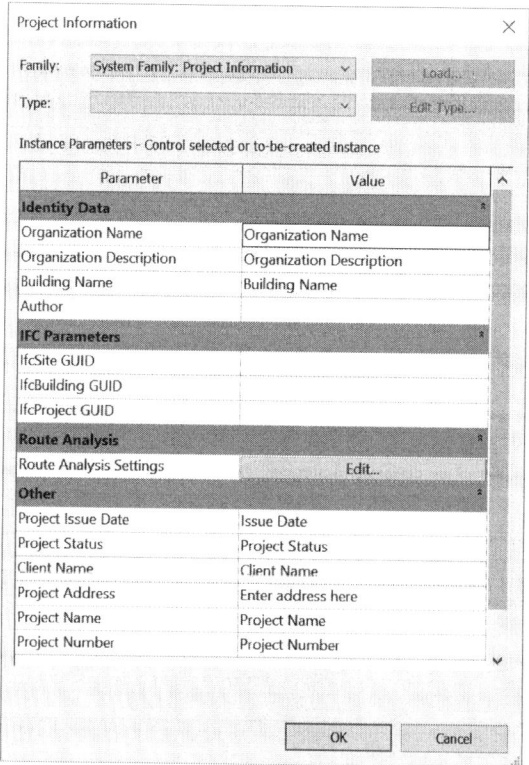

Figure 11–4

11.2 Placing and Modifying Views on Sheets

The process of adding views to a sheet is simple. Drag and drop a view from the Project Browser onto the sheet, as shown in Figure 11–5. The new view on the sheet is displayed at the scale specified in the original view. The view title displays the name, number, and scale of the view. Once the view has been placed on a sheet, the icon next to the view name in the Project Browser is filled in.

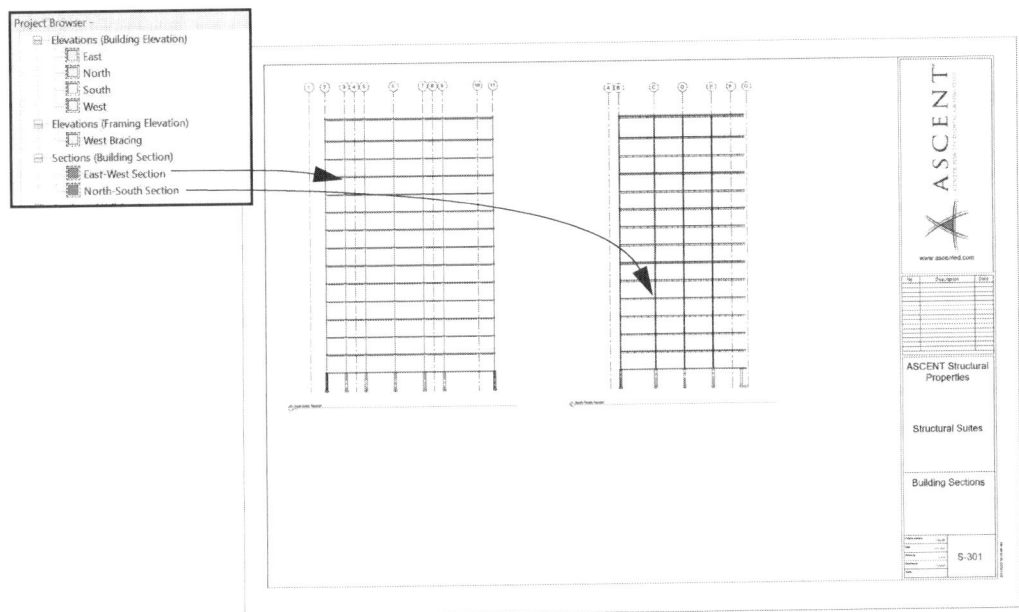

Figure 11–5

How To: Place Views on Sheets

1. Set up the view as you want it to display on the sheet, including the scale and visibility of elements.
2. Create or open the sheet where you want to place the view.
3. Select the view in the Project Browser, and drag and drop it onto the sheet.

   Note: Alignment lines from existing views display to help you place additional views.

4. The center of the view is attached to the cursor. Click to place it on the sheet.

- Views can only be placed on a sheet once. However, you can duplicate the view and place that copy on a sheet.
- Views on a sheet are associative. They automatically update to reflect changes to the project.

- Each view on a sheet is listed under the sheet name in the Project Browser, as shown in Figure 11–6.

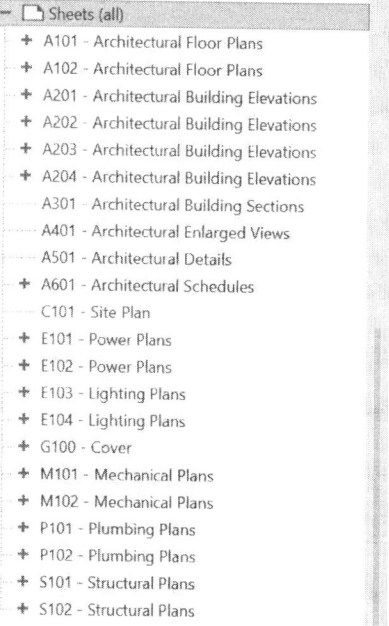

Figure 11–6

How To: Add Multiple Views and Schedules to a Sheet

1. Open a sheet that you want to place views on.

   - In the *View* tab>Sheet Composition panel, click (Place View). Alternatively, in the Project Browser, right-click on the sheet name and select **Add View...**.

2. In the Select View dialog box (shown in Figure 11–7), you can use the search at the top of the dialog box to narrow down the views in the list, then use <Shift> or <Ctrl> to select multiple views you want to use and click **OK**.

   Note: This method lists only those views which have not yet been placed on a sheet.

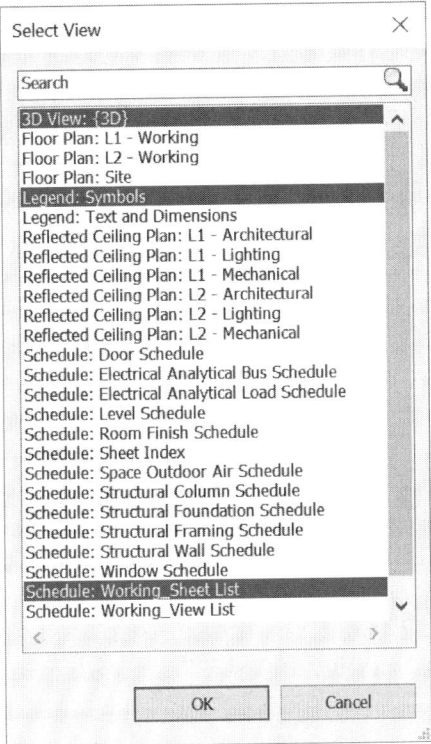

Figure 11–7

3. The views will be attached to your cursor, as shown in Figure 11–8. Click to place the views on the sheet.

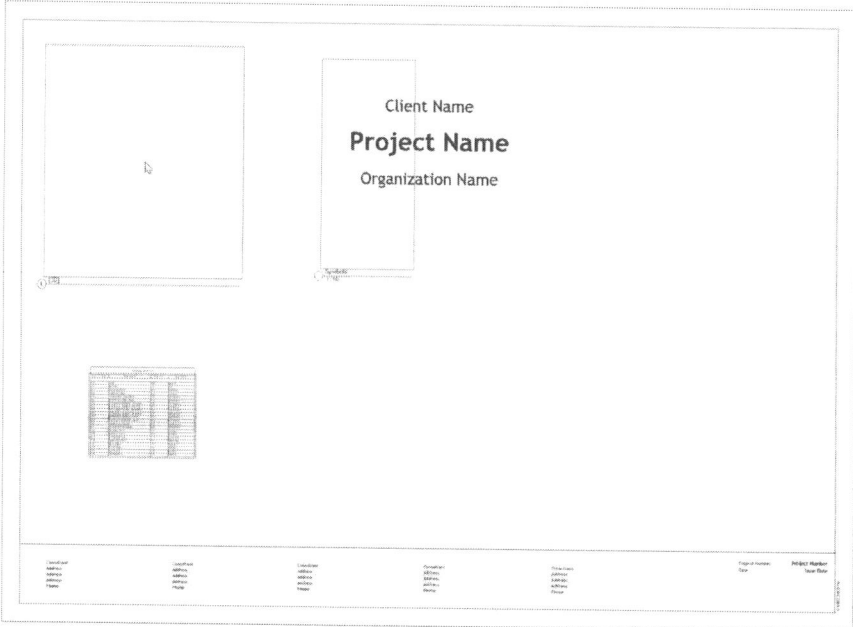

Figure 11–8

- Alternatively, you can open a sheet that you want to place views on. From the Project Browser, use <Shift> or <Ctrl> to select multiple views, then drag them to the sheet.

- To remove a view from a sheet, select it and press <Delete>. Alternatively, in the Project Browser, expand the individual sheet information to show the views, right-click on the view name, and select **Remove From Sheet**.

Open Sheet

To open sheets from the Project Browser, you can double-click on a sheet from the *Sheets (all)* section. As the project gets larger, you can easily open multiple views, schedules, legends, and 3D views directly from the drawing area or from the Project Browser.

- In an open view with nothing selected, right-click and select **Open Sheet**, as shown in Figure 11–9.

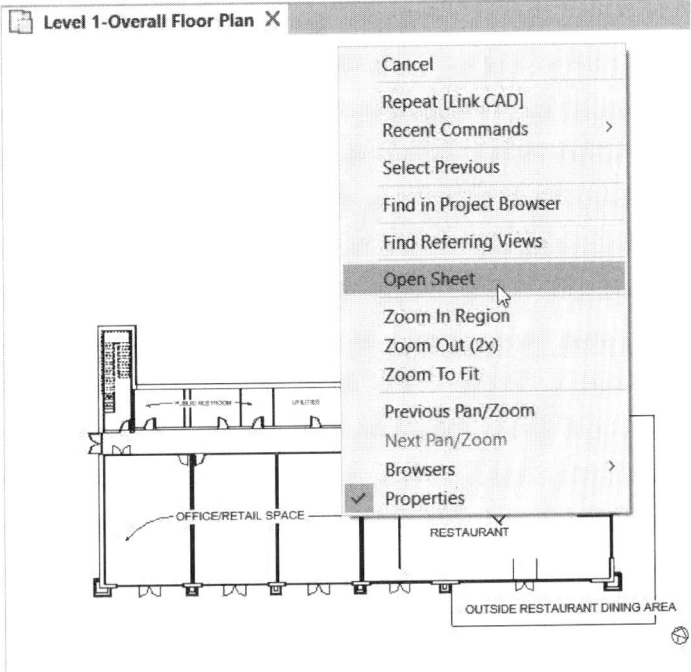

Figure 11–9

- Select multiple views (e.g., plan views, 3D views, schedules, and legends) that have the placed on sheet indicator next to them, as shown in Figure 11–10. Right-click and select **Open Sheet**. Click **OK** in the Open View dialog box to open all the sheets.

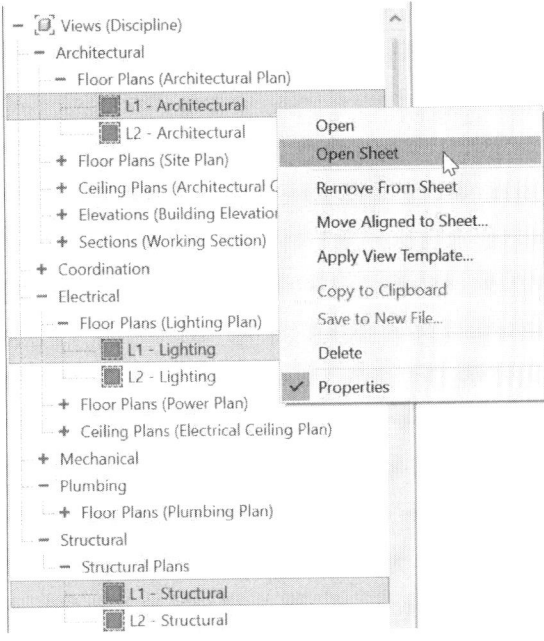

Figure 11–10

11.3 Swapping Views on a Sheet

You can reduce the time it takes to modify the views that are placed on a sheet by quickly swapping out a view with another view from the ribbon or Properties.

- You can swap a view on a sheet with a view that is already on another sheet.
- When swapping views, you can specify if you want to retain the view title's position from a viewport's Type Properties, as shown in Figure 11–11. When **Preserve Title Position** is checked, the view title will resize to the viewport when a different size view is swapped.

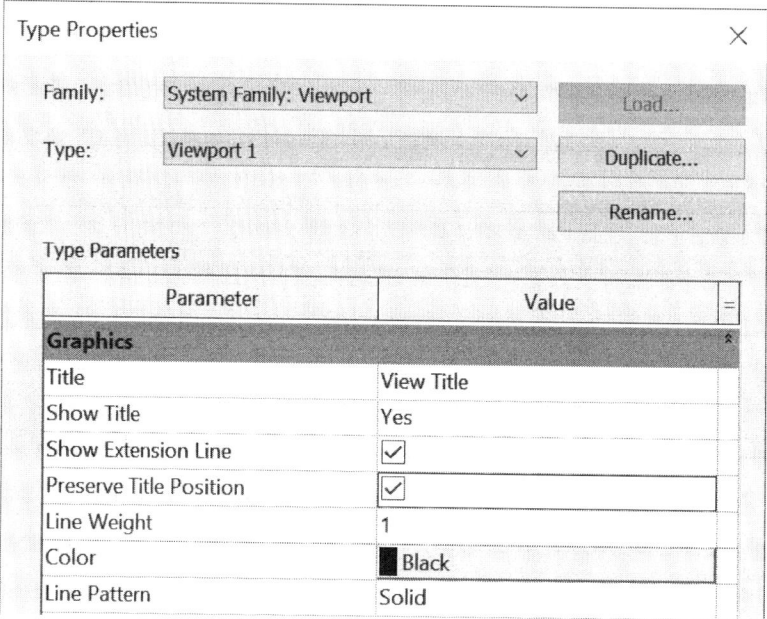

Figure 11–11

How To: Swap a View on a Sheet

1. From the Project Browser>*Sheets* node, open the sheet view.
2. Select the view that is on the sheet.

Creating Construction Documents

3. In the *Modify | Viewports* tab>Positioning & View panel, expand the views, as shown in Figure 11–12, and select one from the list. You can use the search bar to filter the list.

   - Views already on sheets will have suffixes at the end of their names with the sheet number.

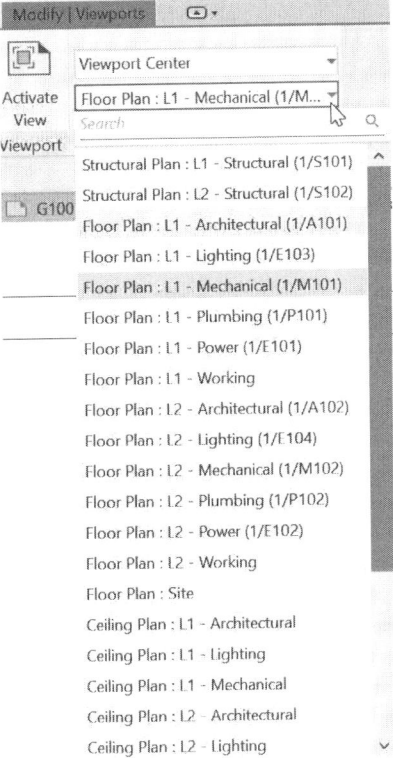

Figure 11–12

4. If you select a view that is already on a sheet, the View Already Placed dialog box will display, as shown in Figure 11–13.

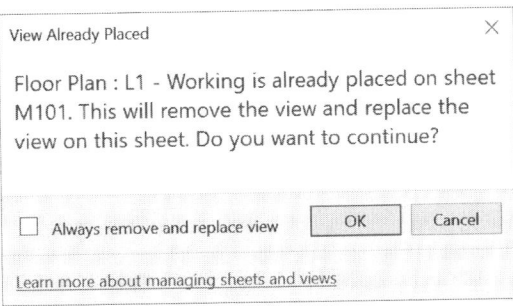

Figure 11–13

5. Select **OK** to swap the view.

   - Alternatively, with the viewport selected, in Properties, in the *Identity Data* section, change the *View* on the sheet by expanding the parameter's drop-down list and selecting a different view, as shown in Figure 11–14. If you select a view that is already on another sheet, the View Already Placed dialog box will display.

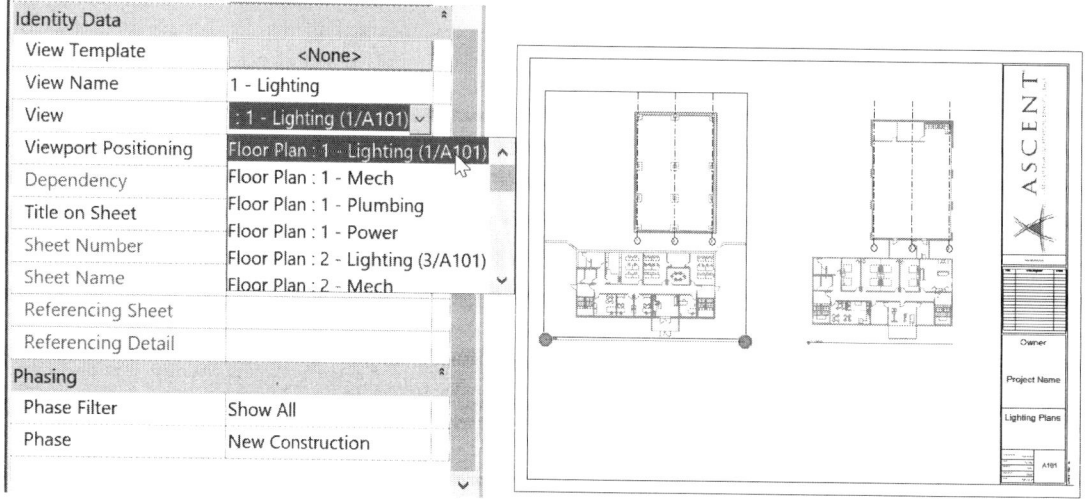

Figure 11–14

How To: Drag a View Aligned to Another Sheet

1. In the Project Browser, *Sheet* section, expand a sheet and select one or multiple views, right-click, and select **Move View Aligned to Sheet...**, as shown in Figure 11–15.

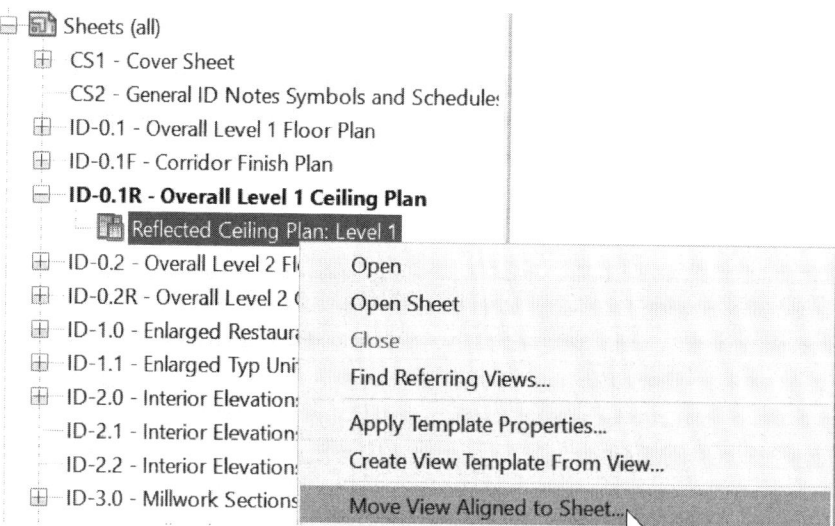

Figure 11–15

2. In the Select Sheet dialog box, select a sheet and click **OK**, as shown in Figure 11–16. The view moves to the sheet, keeping its original alignment.

   - To quickly find a sheet from the list, use the search bar at the top of the dialog box.

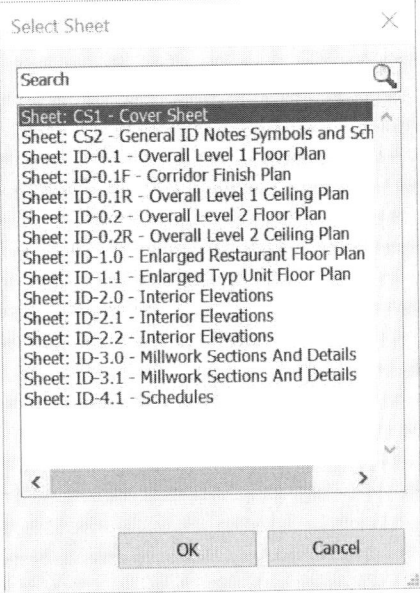

Figure 11–16

- Alternatively, under the *Sheet* section, expand a sheet and manually drag a view to another sheet. The view is moved and keeps its original alignment.

Removing Views from a Sheets

There are three ways to remove a view from a sheet:

- In the Project Browser, select one or multiple views, right-click, and select **Remove From Sheet**, as shown in Figure 11–17.

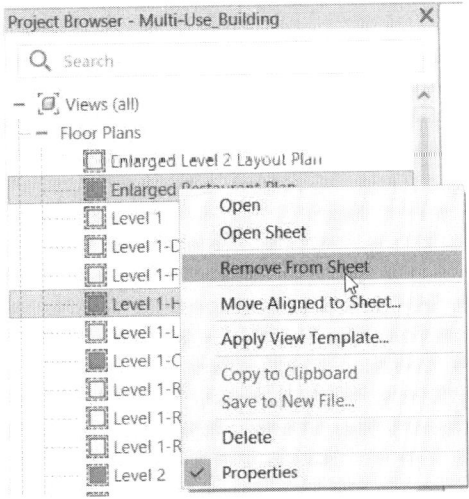

Figure 11–17

- If multiple views are selected, click **OK** in the Remove From Sheet dialog box, as shown in Figure 11–18.

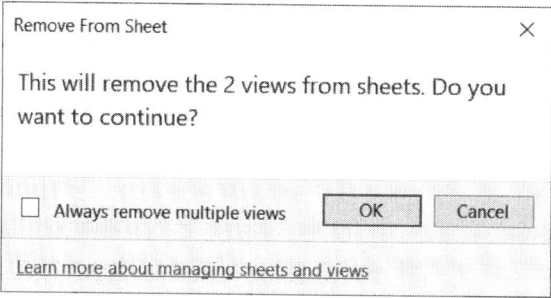

Figure 11–18

- In the Project Browser under the *Sheets* node, you can expand the sheet, select the views, right-click, and select **Remove From Sheet**, as shown in Figure 11–19. If multiple views are selected, click **OK** in the Remove From Sheet dialog box.

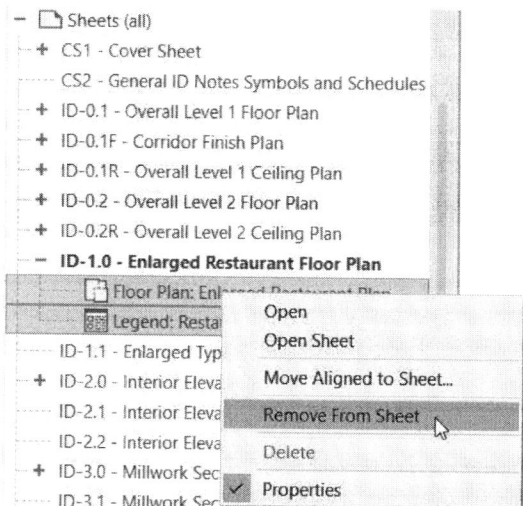

Figure 11–19

- You can remove a view directly from a sheet by selecting the view and pressing <Delete>.

Duplicating Sheets

Duplicating a sheet will add a suffix of *Copy 1* after the sheet name, as shown in Figure 11–20. It will also automatically generate with the next available sheet title number, like G101 shown in Figure 11–20.

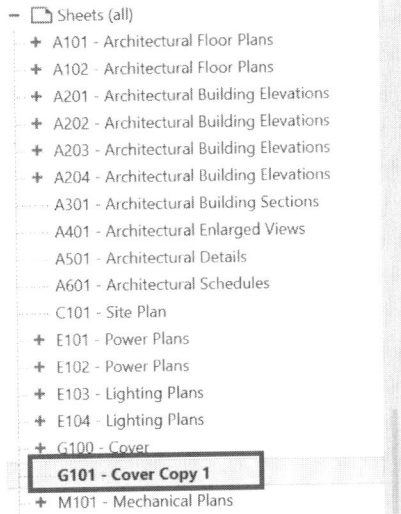

Figure 11–20

How To: Duplicate Sheets

1. In the Project Browser>*Sheets* node, right-click on a sheet and select **Duplicate Sheet**.
2. Select one of the following options:
   - **Duplicate Empty Sheet:** Creates a new sheet with the same titleblock and project information.
     - No model or annotation elements on the sheet are duplicated.
   - **Duplicate with Sheet Detailing:** Creates a new sheet with the same titleblock, project information, and any legends, keynotes, schedules, and annotations.

- **Duplicate with Views:** Before a sheet gets created, you are prompted to specify how you would like the views on the sheet to be duplicated, as shown in Figure 11–21.

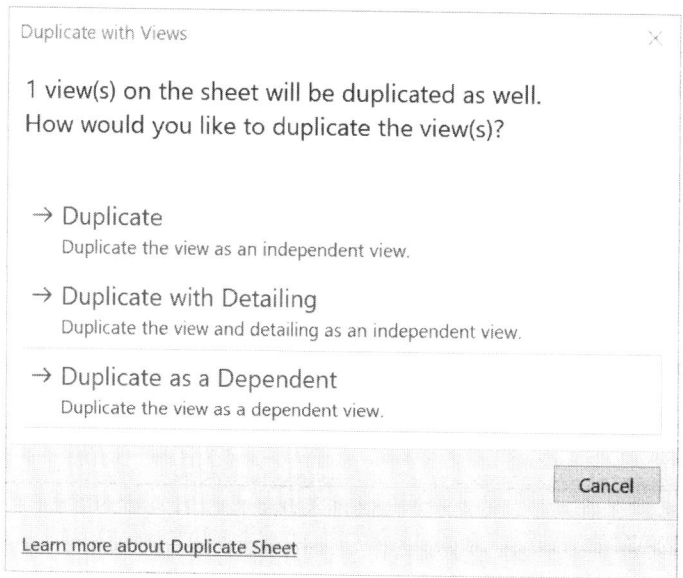

Figure 11–21

Note: *To review duplicating view types, refer to Working with Views.*

- In the Duplicate with Views dialog box, select **Duplicate**, **Duplicate with Detailing**, or **Duplicate as a Dependent**.
- If you are duplicating a sheet that has drafting views and want to duplicate the view with the model and annotation elements, you need to use the **Duplicate with Detailing** option.

11.4 Modifying Views and View Titles

After you have the desired views on a sheet, you can modify their locations and titles. You can use some of the modify tools, like **Move** and **Rotate**, as well as the arrow keys.

- You cannot use any tools that utilize the copy feature, like **Copy**, **Mirror**, and **Offset**.

How To: Move a View on a Sheet

1. Open a sheet view.
2. Select and drag a view to another location on the sheet. When selecting the view, the view title moves with the view.

How To: Modify the Viewport's View Title

1. Open a sheet view.
2. Select only the view title and drag it to the new location.

- To modify the length of the line under the title name, select the viewport and drag the controls, as shown in Figure 11–22.

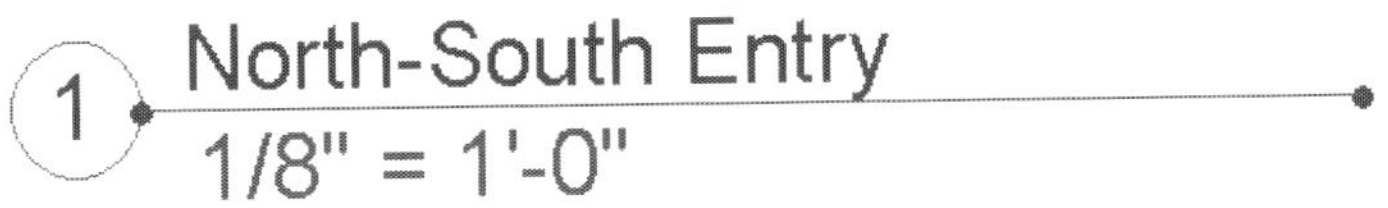

North-South Entry
1/8" = 1'-0"

Figure 11–22

- To change the title of a view on a sheet without changing its name in the Project Browser, select either the viewport or the view title, then in Properties, in the *Identity Data* section, type a new title for the *Title on Sheet* parameter, as shown in Figure 11–23.

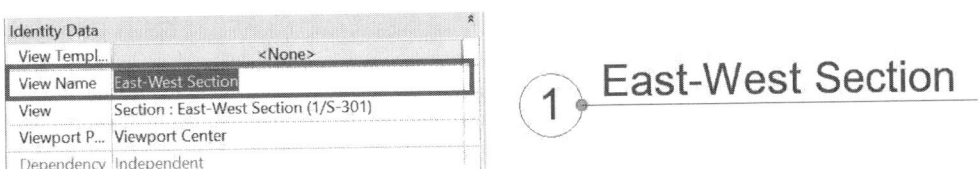

Figure 11–23

Rotating Views

When creating a vertical sheet, you can rotate the view on the sheet by 90°. Select the view on the sheet and set the direction of rotation in the **Rotation on Sheet** drop-down list in the Options Bar, as shown in Figure 11–24.

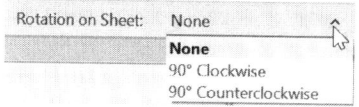

Figure 11–24

Note: For more information about rotating the project or individual views to angles other than 90°, refer to the ASCENT guide Autodesk Revit: Site Planning and Design.

Working Inside Views

To make small changes to a view while working on a sheet:

- Double-click *inside* the view to activate it.
- Double-click *outside* the view to deactivate it.

Only elements in the viewport are available for modification. The rest of the sheet is grayed out, as shown in Figure 11–25.

- Use this method only for small changes. Significant changes should be made directly in the view.

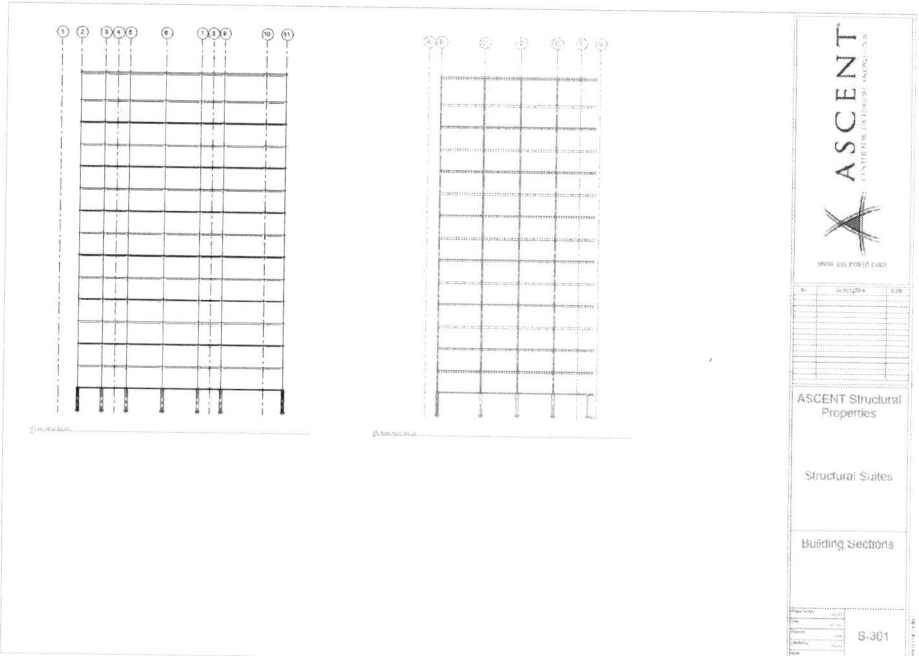

Figure 11–25

- You can activate and deactivate views by selecting the viewport, right-clicking, and selecting from the menu, or by using the tools found in the *Modify | Viewports* or *Views* tab>Sheet Composition panel.
- Changes you make to elements when a view is activated also display in the original view.
- If you are unsure which sheet a view is on, right-click on the view in the Project Browser and select **Open Sheet**. This is not available for schedules and legends, which can be placed on more than one sheet.

Resizing Views on Sheets

Each view displays the extents of the model or the elements contained in the crop region. If the view does not fit on a sheet (as shown in Figure 11–26), you might need to crop the view or move the elevation markers closer to the building.

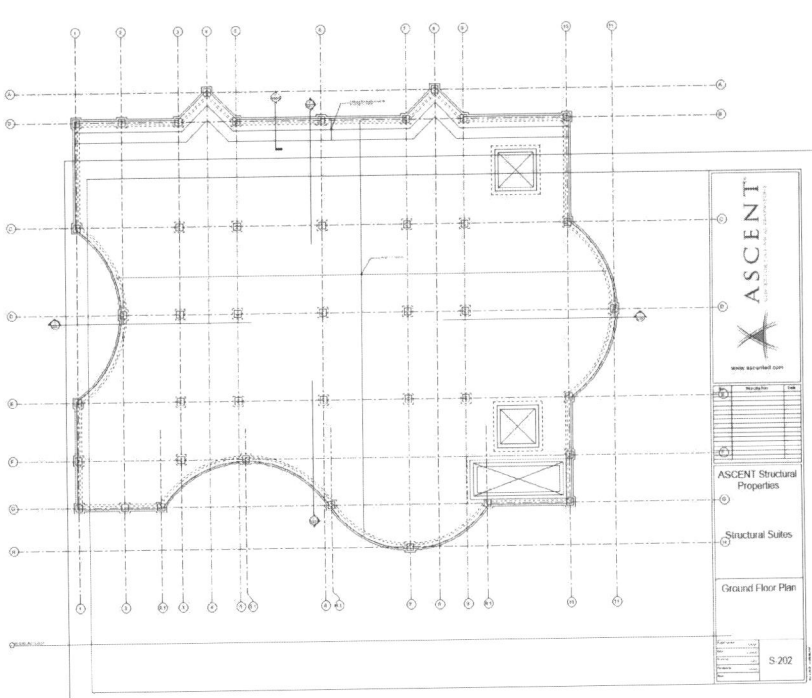

Figure 11–26

Note: If the extents of the view change dramatically based on a scale change or a crop region, it is easier to delete the view on the sheet and drag it over again.

- For information about laying out views on sheets using guide grids, see *B.1 Working with Guide Grids on Sheets*.
- For information about working with revisions in views and on sheets, see *B.2 Revision Tracking*.

How To: Add an Image to a Sheet

Company logos and renderings saved to image files (such as .JPG and .PNG) can be added directly on a sheet or in a view.

1. In the *Insert* tab>Import panel, click 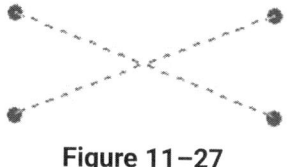 (Image).
2. In the Import Image dialog box, select and open the image file. The extents of the image display, as shown in Figure 11–27.

Figure 11–27

3. Place the image where you want it.
4. The image is displayed. Pick one of the grips and extend it to modify the size of the image.

- In Properties, you can adjust the height and width and also set the *Draw Layer* to either **Background** or **Foreground**, as shown in Figure 11–28.

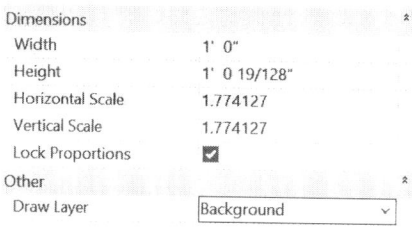

Figure 11–28

- You can select more than one image at a time and move them as a group to the background or foreground.

- In the *Modify | Raster Images* tab (shown in Figure 11–29), you can access the Arrange options and the **Manage Images** command.

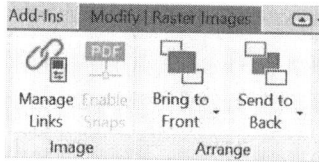

Figure 11–29

Practice 11a
Set Up Sheets

Practice Objectives

- Set up project properties.
- Create sheets individually.
- Place views on sheets.

In this practice, you will complete the project information, create new sheets and then add views to the sheets, such as the **00 T.O. FOOTING** shown in Figure 11–30. You will also fill in title block information and import an image for the cover sheet. Complete as many sheets as you have time for.

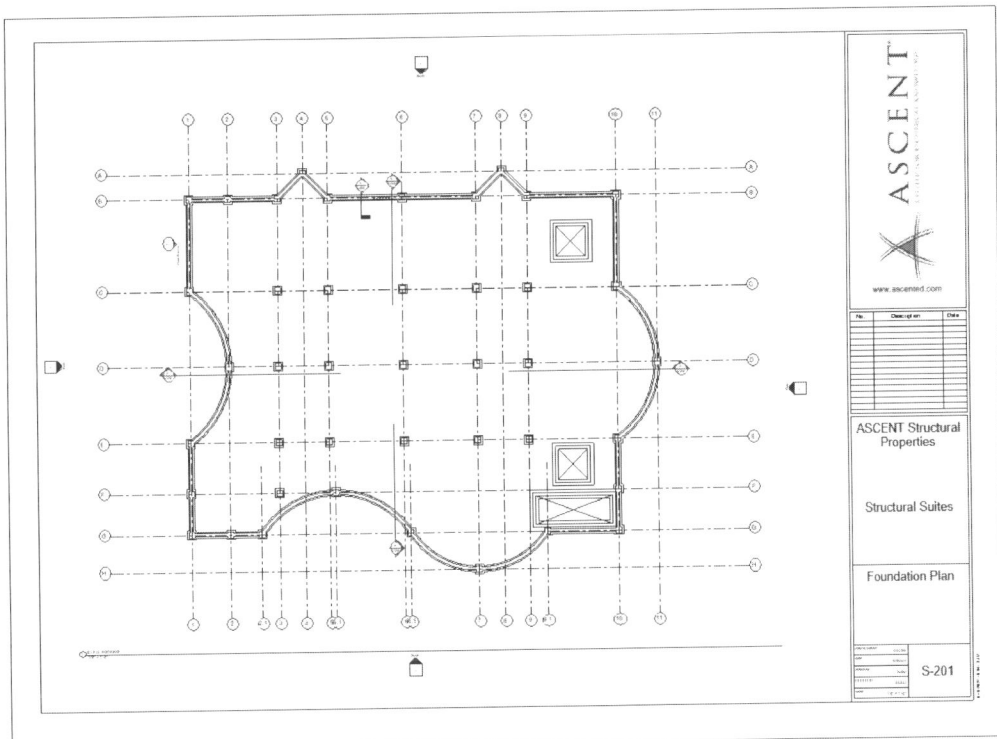

Figure 11–30

Task 1: Complete the project information.

1. Open the project **Structural-Sheets.rvt** from the practice files folder.

2. In the *Manage* tab>Settings panel, click (Project Information).

3. In the Project Information dialog box, in the *Other* section, set the following parameters:

   Note: These properties are used across the entire sheet set and do not need to be entered on each sheet.

   - *Project Issue Date:* Enter a date
   - *Project Status:* **Design Development**
   - *Client Name:* **ASCENT Structural Properties**
   - *Project Address:* Click **Edit...** and enter your address
   - *Project Name:* **Structural Suites**
   - *Project Number:* **1234-567**

4. Click **OK**.
5. Save the project.

Task 2: Create a cover sheet and floor plan sheets.

1. In the *View* tab>Sheet Composition panel, click (Sheet).
2. In the New Sheet dialog box, select the **ASCENT_Cover Sheet: 30x42 Horizontal** title block.
3. Click **OK**.
4. In the Project Browser, in the *Sheets* area, right-click on the new sheet and select **Rename**.
5. In the Sheet Title dialog box, set *Number* to **S-000** and *Name* to **Cover Sheet**, as shown in Figure 11–31. Click **OK**.

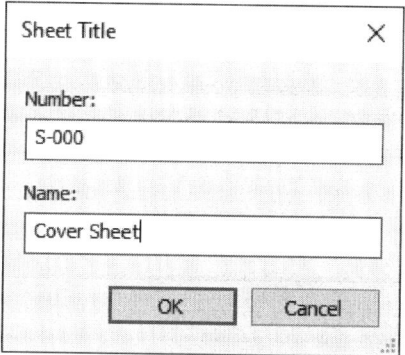

Figure 11–31

*Note: If you know the image will be updated or changed, use **Link Image** instead.*

6. In the *Insert* tab>Import panel, click (Import Image).
7. In the Import Image dialog box, navigate to the practice files *Images* folder and select **Structural Suite Perspective.png**.

8. Click **Open**.
9. Your cursor will have an X shape (indicating the size of your image), as shown in Figure 11–32. Click to place the image on the sheet.

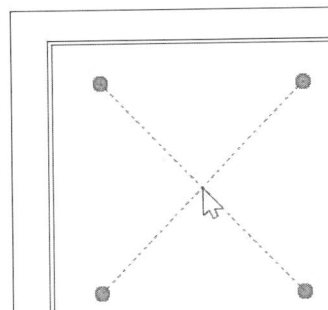

Figure 11–32

10. Use the grips to adjust the size of the image to make room for notes and other views.

11. Click (Modify).

12. From the Project Browser>3D Views section, drag and drop the **Perspective View** on to the sheet, as shown in Figure 11–33.

Figure 11–33

13. Select the viewport, expand the Type Selector and select **Viewport: No Title**.

14. Click (Modify).

15. Create a new sheet. In the Project Browser, right-click on the **Sheets (All)** node and select **New Sheet...**.

16. In the New Sheet dialog box, select the **ASCENT_22 x 34 Horizontal** title block.
17. Zoom in on the lower-right corner of the title block.
    - Notice the project properties filled out earlier are automatically added to the sheet (e.g., Project Number, Project Status, etc.).
18. Continue filling out the title block by changing the sheet name and number. Click on the default *sheet number* and rename it to **S-201**, then click on *Unnamed* and rename it to **Foundation Plan**, as shown in Figure 11–34.

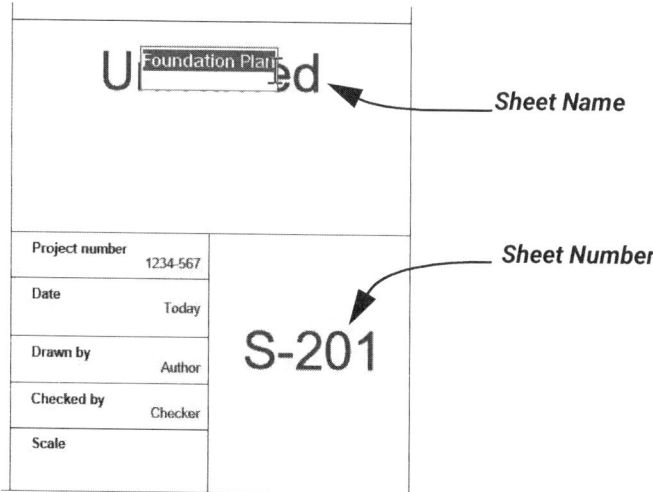

Figure 11–34

19. Zoom back out to display the whole sheet.
20. In the Project Browser, note that the two items you manually changed on the sheet's title block are shown as your sheet name and sheet number.
21. In the Project Browser, find the **00 T.O. FOOTING** structural plan view and drag it onto the sheet, centering it in the view, as shown in Figure 11–35.

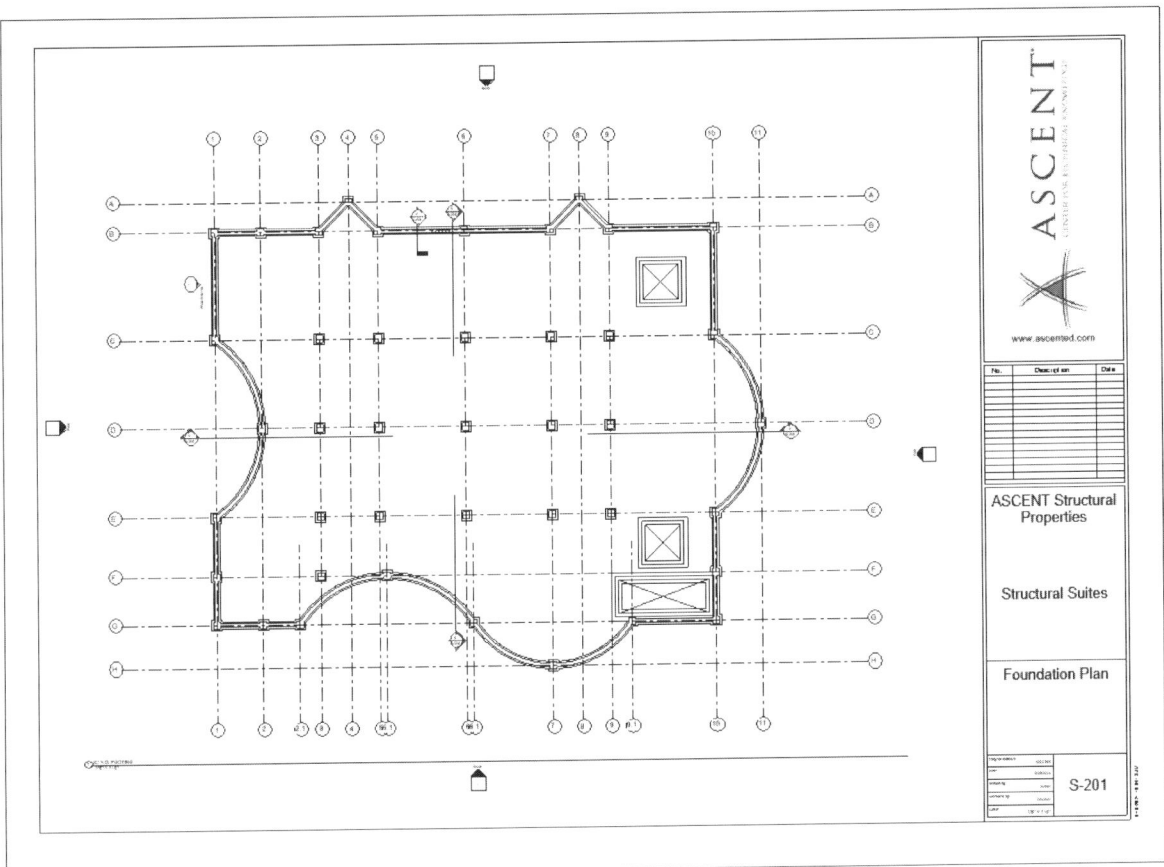

Figure 11-35

22. There are sheets that already exist in the project. Place the **Structural Plans: 00 GROUND FLOOR** view on the sheet **S-202 - Ground Floor Plan.**

23. Zoom in to see the title of the view. It displays as **00 GROUND FLOOR**, as shown in Figure 11-36.

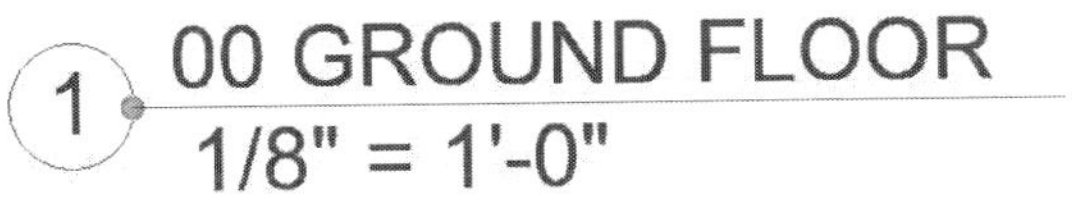

Figure 11-36

24. In the Project Browser, select the view. In Properties, scroll down to the *Identity Data* section and change the *Title on Sheet* to **GROUND FLOOR - STRUCTURAL PLAN**, as shown in Figure 11–37.

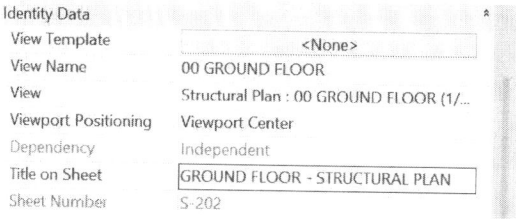

Figure 11–37

25. Click **Apply**. The title changes on the sheet, as shown in Figure 11–38.

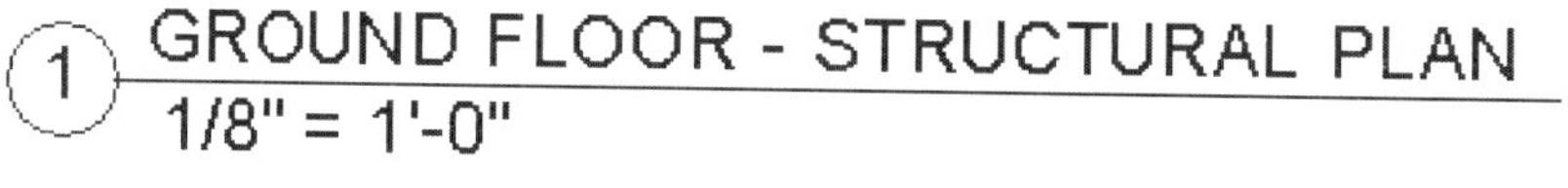

Figure 11–38

Note: The crop region defines the extent of the view on the sheet.

26. Double-click inside the viewport; the title block grays out and you can modify the actual view.

27. In Properties, in the *Extents* section, clear the check from **Crop Region Visible**. (This could also be done in the View Control Bar.)

28. Double-click outside the viewport to return to the sheet.

29. Save the project.

Task 3: Duplicate sheets and add views.

1. In the Project Browser, right-click on a sheet (but not on the cover sheet) and select **Duplicate Sheet>Duplicate Empty Sheet.**
2. Rename the sheet **S-302 - Building Elevation**.
3. In the Project Browser, right-click on that sheet and select **Add View....**

Creating Construction Documents

4. In the Select View dialog box, scroll down and select **Elevation: North**, as shown in Figure 11–39. Click **OK** and place the view on the sheet.

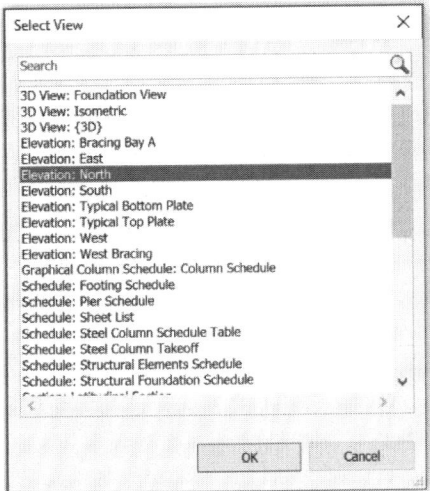

Figure 11–39

- Note that on the *Modify | Viewports* tab>Positioning & View panel (shown in Figure 11–40), the Elevation: North shows **(1/S-302)** meaning that it is the first view on sheet S-302.

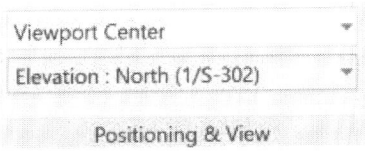

Figure 11–40

5. From the Project Browser, drag and drop the Elevation South view on to the sheet and note that this view shows **(2/S-302)** in the Positioning & View panel.

6. From the Project Browser, open **00 T.O. FOOTING** and zoom and pan to the north elevation marker. Note that the marker now displays the sheet number, as shown in Figure 11–41. Zoom and pan down to the south elevation marker to see that it also has the sheet number displayed in the marker.

Figure 11–41

© 2023, ASCENT - Center for Technical Knowledge®

7. In the Project Browser, right click on the **S-302 - Building Elevations** sheet and select **Duplicate Sheet>Duplicate with Views**, as shown in Figure 11–42.

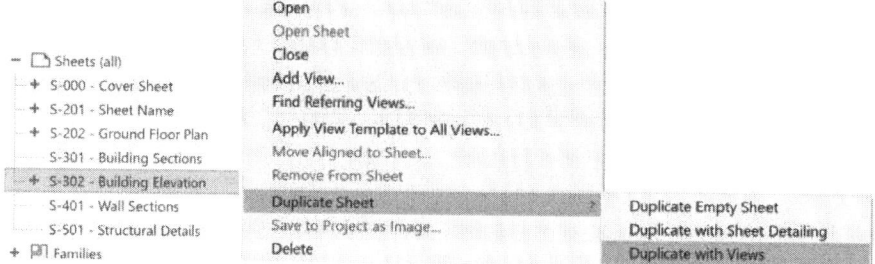

Figure 11–42

8. In the Duplicate with Views dialog box, select **Duplicate**, as shown in Figure 11–43.

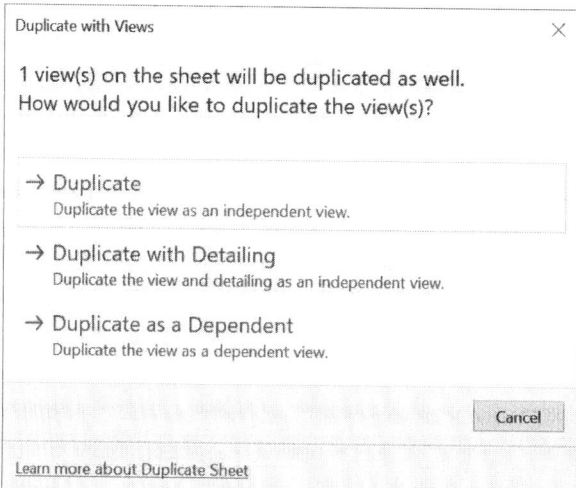

Figure 11–43

Note: This is useful if you need to modify the view to accommodate the sheet but do not want to modify the original view.

9. The new sheets opens. Notice in the Elevations (Building Elevation) section of the Project Browser there is now a new **North Copy 1** and **South Copy 1** view.

10. Select the view on the sheet and from the *Modify | Viewports* tab>Postioning & View panel, expand *View* and select the **Elevation: West** view and again by changing the south copy 1 to the **Elevation: East**. The view on the sheet updates with the new view.

11. Delete the **North Copy 1** and **South Copy 1** view.

12. Save and close the project.

End of practice

11.5 Printing Sheets

With the **Print** command, you can print individual sheets or a list of selected sheets. You can also print an individual view or a portion of a view for check prints or presentations. To open the Print dialog box (shown in Figure 11–44), in the *File* tab, click 🖶 (Print), or press <Ctrl>+<P>.

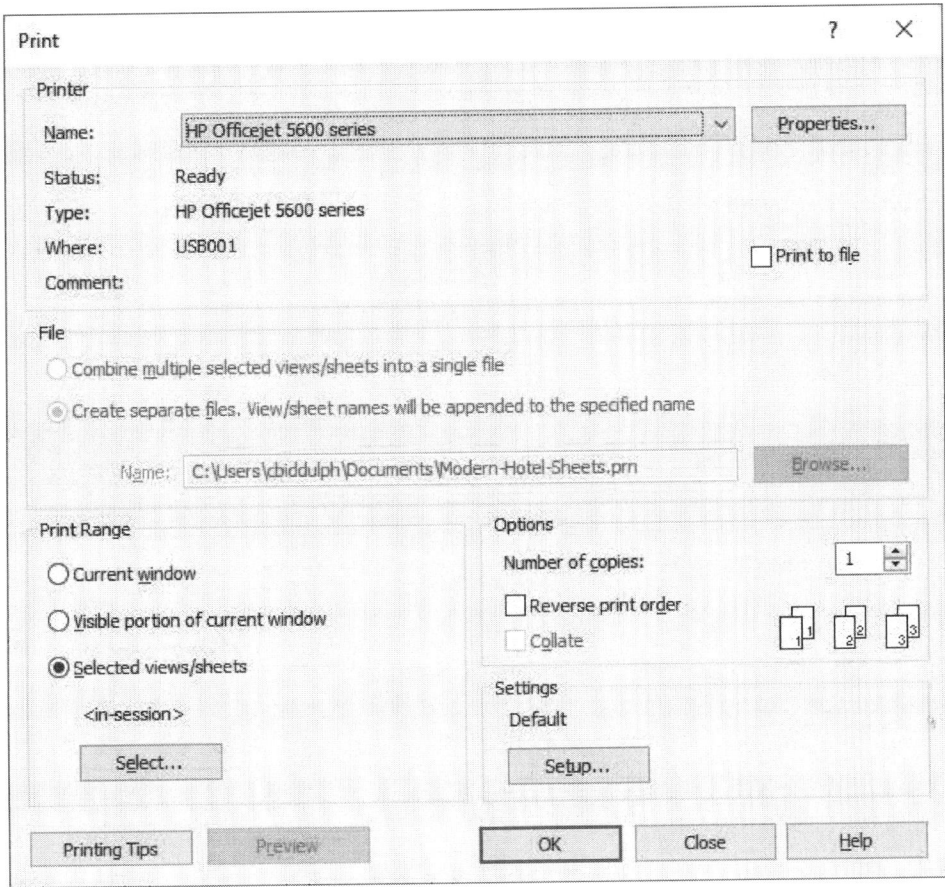

Figure 11–44

Printing Options

The Print dialog box is divided into the following areas: *Printer*, *File*, *Print Range*, *Options*, and *Settings*. Modify them as needed to produce the plot you want.

- **Printing Tips**: Opens Autodesk WikiHelp online, in which you can find help with troubleshooting printing issues.

- **Preview**: Opens a preview of the print output so that you can see what is going to be printed.

Printer

Select from the list of available printers, as shown in Figure 11–45. Click **Properties...** to adjust the properties of the selected printer. The options vary according to the printer. Select the **Print to file** option to print to a file rather than directly to a printer. You can create .PLT or .PRN files.

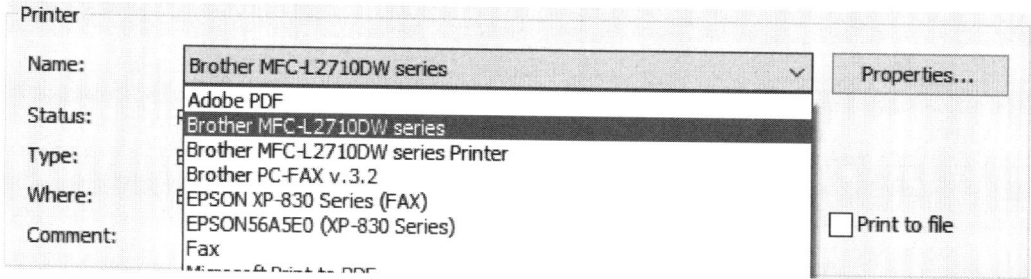

Figure 11–45

- You must have a PDF print driver installed on your system to print to PDF, or you can export views and sheets to PDF.

File

The *File* area is only available if the **Print to file** option has been selected in the *Printer* area or if you are printing to an electronic-only type of printer. You can create one file or multiple files depending on the type of printer you are using, as shown in Figure 11–46. Click **Browse...** to select the file location and name.

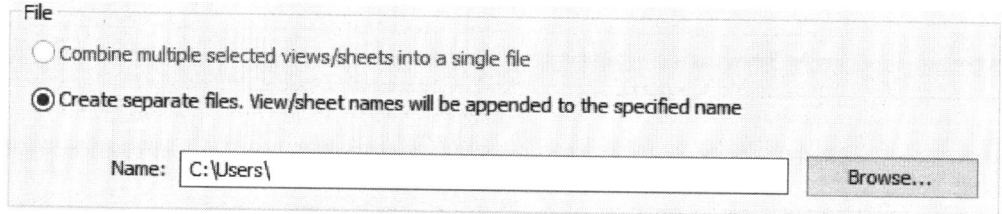

Figure 11–46

Print Range

The *Print Range* area enables you to print individual views/sheets or sets of views/sheets, as shown in Figure 11–47.

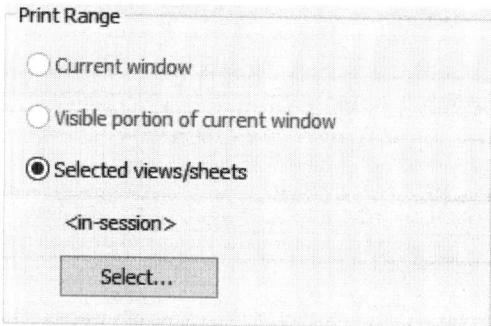

Figure 11–47

- **Current window:** Prints the entire current sheet or view you have open.
- **Visible portion of current window:** Prints only what is displayed in the current sheet or view.
- **Selected views/sheets:** Prints multiple views or sheets. Click **Select...** to open the Select Views/Sheets dialog box (shown in Figure 11–48) to choose what to include in the print set. You can save these sets by name so that you can more easily print the same group again.

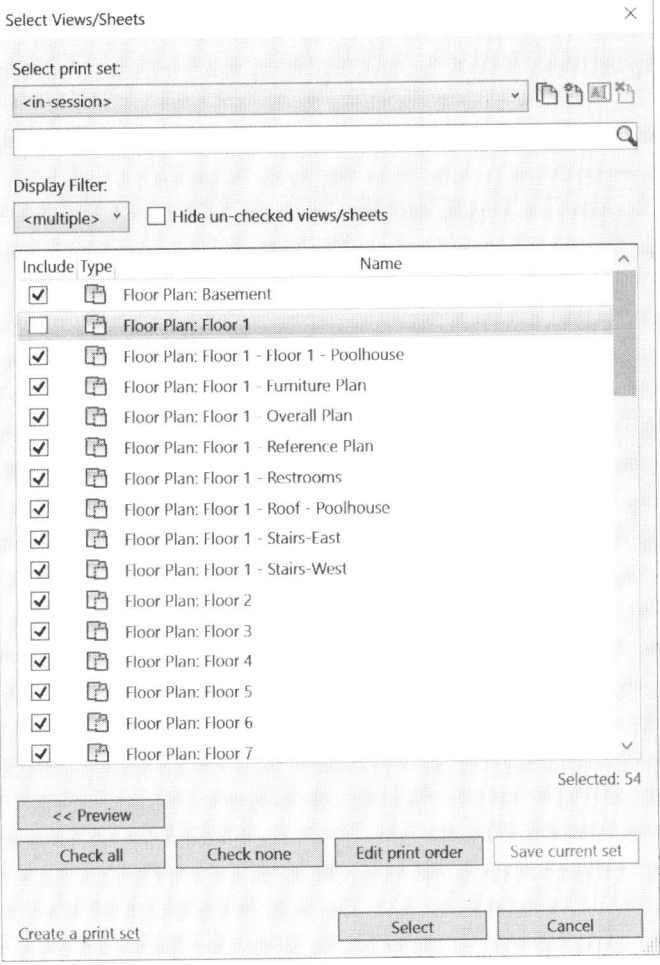

Figure 11–48

- You can edit the selected views and sheets by **Browser organization**, **Sheet Number (Ascending)**, or **Manual order**. If you select **Manual order**, you can drag the views and sheets to put them in a custom order, as shown in Figure 11–49.

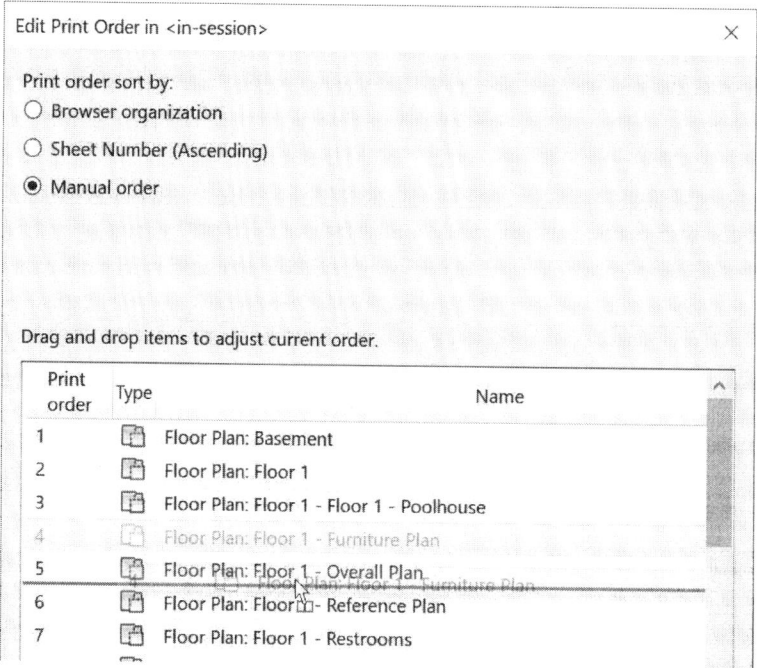

Figure 11–49

Options

If your printer supports multiple copies, you can specify the number in the *Options* area, as shown in Figure 11–50. You can also reverse the print order or collate your prints. These options are also available in the printer properties.

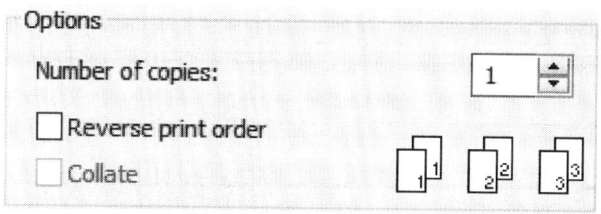

Figure 11–50

Settings

Click **Setup...** to open the Print Setup dialog box, as shown in Figure 11–51. Here, you can specify the *Orientation* and *Zoom* settings, among others. You can also save these settings by name.

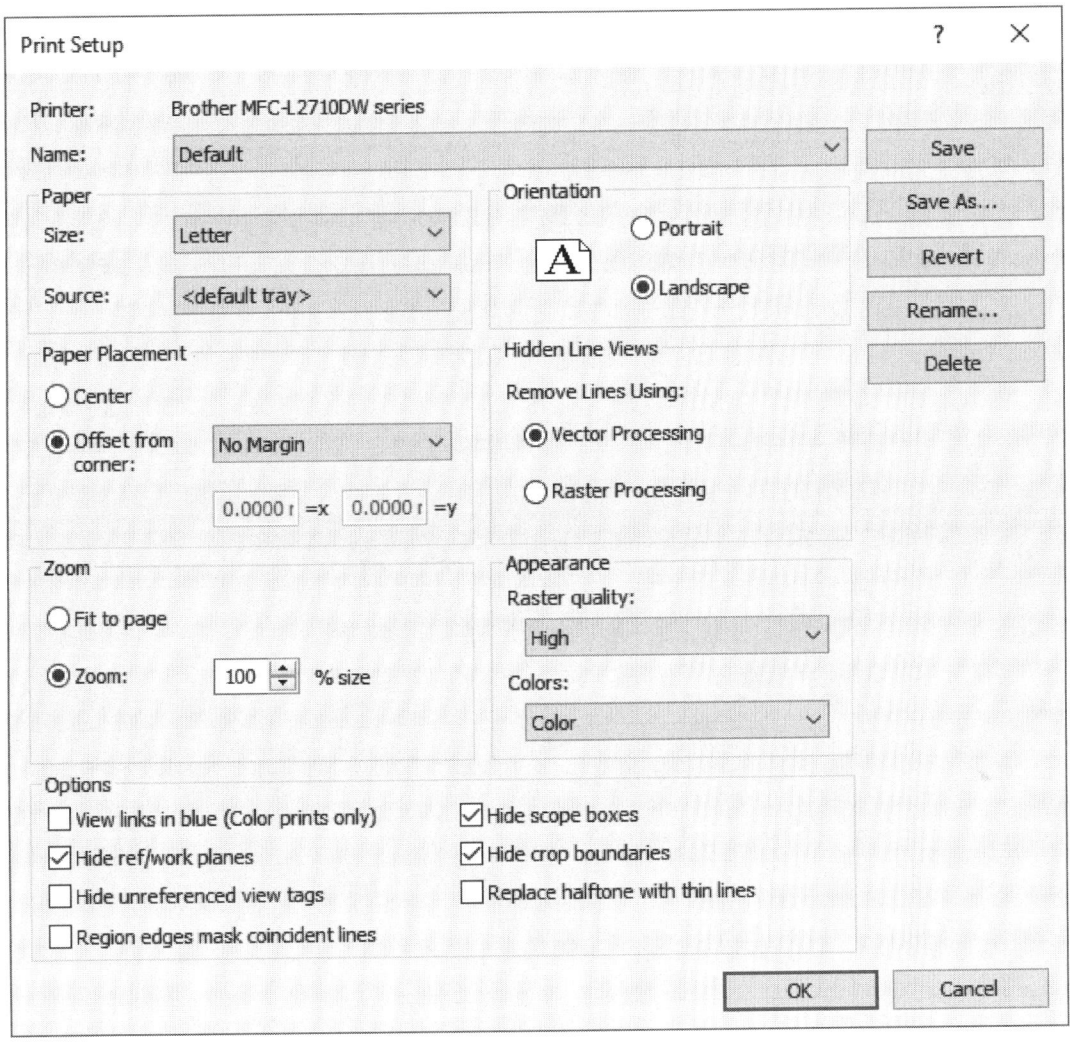

Figure 11–51

- In the *Options* area, specify the types of elements you want to print or not print. Unless specified, all of the elements in a view or sheet print.

- Sheets should always be printed at **Zoom** set to **100%** size unless you are creating a quick markup set that does not need to be exact.

Export Views and Sheets to PDF

If you do not have a PDF driver to utilize in the Print dialog box, you can export your views or sheets to PDF. If you set the *Export Range* to **Selected views/sheets**, you have the ability to edit the print order of the views/sheets by **Browser organization**, **Sheet Number (Ascending)**, or **Manual order**.

How To: Export Views and Sheets to PDF

1. In the File menu, select (Export)> (PDF).
2. In the PDF Export dialog box (shown in Figure 11–52), enter a *File Name* and the *Location* you would like the PDF to be exported to, and select the other settings, as needed.
    - The PDF Export settings are similar to those found in the Revit Print dialog box.

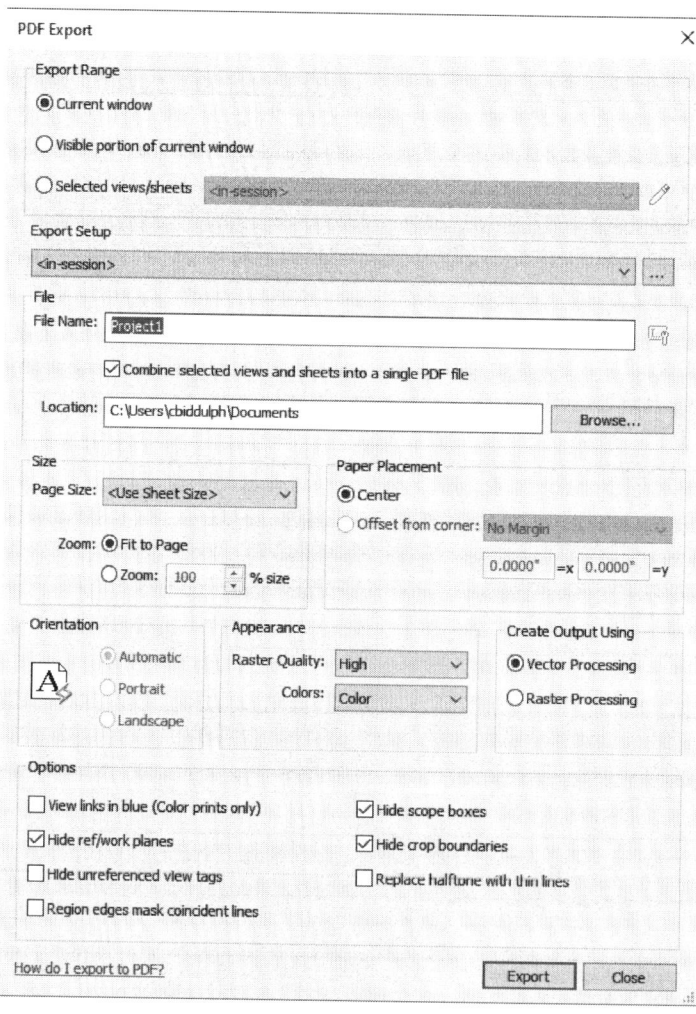

Figure 11–52

3. Click **Export**.

Chapter Review Questions

1. How do you specify the size of a sheet?

    a. In the Sheet Properties, specify the **Sheet Size**.

    b. In the Options Bar, specify the **Sheet Size**.

    c. In the New Sheet dialog box, select a title block to control the Sheet Size.

    d. In the Sheet view, right-click and select **Sheet Size**.

2. How is the title block information filled in, as shown in Figure 11–53? (Select all that apply.)

    Figure 11–53

    a. Select the title block and select the label that you want to change.

    b. Select the title block and modify it in Properties.

    c. Right-click on the sheet in the Project Browser and select **Information**.

    d. Some of the information is filled in automatically from the Project Information.

3. On how many sheets can a floor plan view be placed?

    a. 1

    b. 2-5

    c. 6+

    d. As many as you want

4. Which of the following is the best method to use if the size of a view is too large for a sheet, as shown in Figure 11–54?

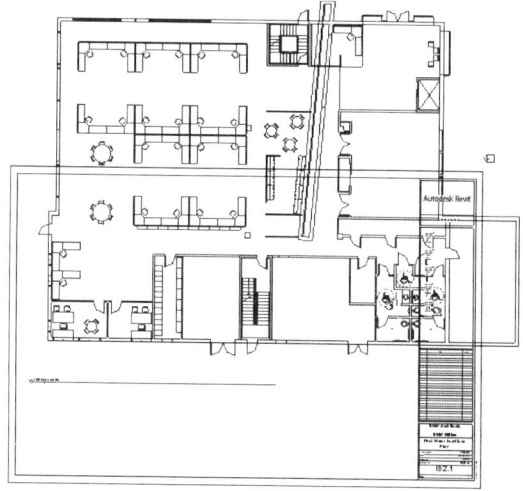

Figure 11–54

   a. Delete the view, change the scale, and place the view back on the sheet.
   b. Change the scale of the sheet.

5. How do you set up a view on a sheet that only displays part of a floor plan?
   a. Drag and drop the view to the sheet and use the crop region to modify it.
   b. Activate the view and rescale it.
   c. Create a callout view displaying the part that you want to use and place the callout view on the sheet.
   d. Open the view in the Project Browser and change the View Scale.

6. You can only export sheets to PDF.
   a. True
   b. False

Command Summary

Button	Command	Location
	Activate View	- **Ribbon:** (*select the view*) *Modify	Viewports* tab> Viewport panel - **Double-click:** *(in viewport)* - **Right-click:** (*on view*) Activate View
	Deactivate View	- **Ribbon:** *View* tab>Sheet Composition panel, expand Viewports - **Double-click:** *(on sheet)* - **Right-click:** (*on view*) Deactivate View
	PDF	- *File* **tab**>Export
	Place View	- **Ribbon:** *View* tab>Sheet Composition panel
	Print	- *File* **tab**
	Sheet	- **Ribbon:** *View* tab>Sheet Composition panel

Chapter 12

Working with Annotations

When you create construction documents, annotations are essential for showing the design intent. Annotations such as dimensions and text can be added to views at any time during the creation of a project. Detail lines and symbols can also be added to views as you create the working drawing, while legends can be created to provide a place to document any symbols that are used in a project.

Learning Objectives

- Add dimensions to the model as a part of the working drawings.
- Add text to a view and use leaders to create notes pointing to a specific part of the model.
- Create text types using different fonts and sizes to suit your company standards.
- Draw detail lines to further enhance the documentation view.
- Add view-specific annotation symbols for added clarity.
- Create legend views and populate them with symbols of elements in the project.

12.1 Working with Dimensions

You can create permanent dimensions using aligned, linear, angular, radial, diameter, and arc length dimensions. These can be individual or a string of dimensions, as shown in Figure 12-1. With aligned dimensions, you can also dimension entire walls with openings, grid lines, and/or intersecting walls. With structural plates and webbing, you can dimension to the center of a plate or webbing for a more detailed communication.

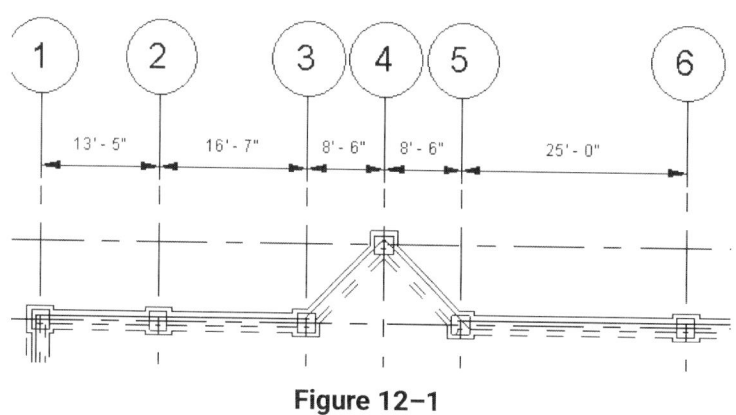

Figure 12-1

- Dimensions referencing model elements must be added to the model in a view. You can dimension on sheets, but only to items added directly on the sheets.

- Dimensions are available in the *Annotate* tab>Dimension panel (shown in Figure 12-2) and in the *Modify* tab>Measure panel.

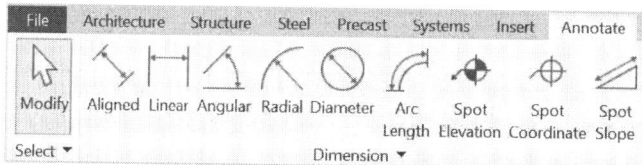

Figure 12-2

Note: (Aligned) is also located in the Quick Access Toolbar.

- Dimensions can be added to isometric 3D views whether they are locked or not. Proceed with caution when selecting the items to dimension. You can set the work plane or use <Tab> to cycle through elements.

- Ensure that the witness lines and text orientation is snapping to and extending in the correct direction as intended.

How To: Add Aligned Dimensions with Options

1. Start the (Aligned) command or type **DI**.

2. In the Type Selector, select a dimension style.
3. In the Options Bar, select the location line of the wall to dimension from, as shown in Figure 12–3.
    - This option can be changed as you add dimensions.

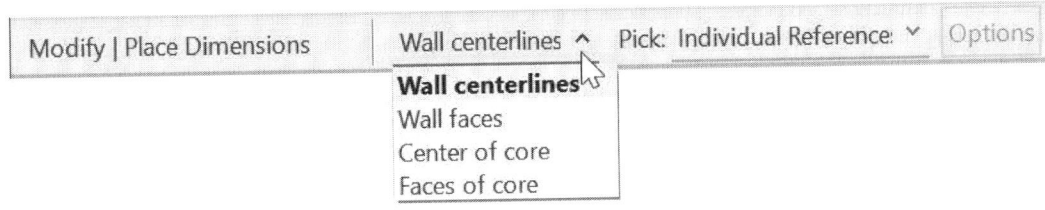

Figure 12–3

4. In the Options Bar, select your preference from the Pick drop-down list:
    - **Individual References:** Select the elements in order (as shown in Figure 12–4) and then click in an empty space in the view to position the dimension string.

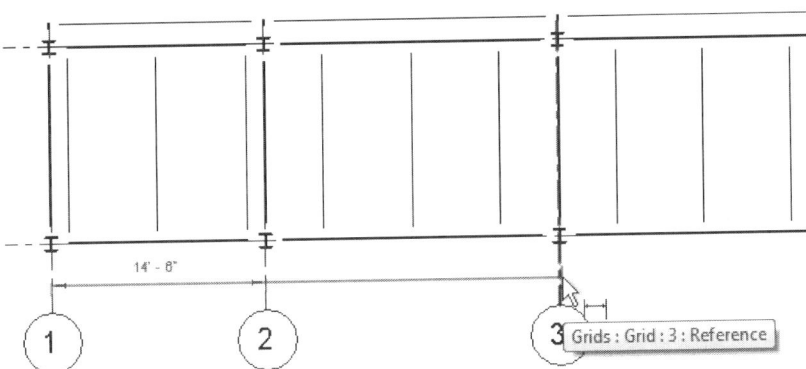

Figure 12–4

- **Entire Walls:** Select the wall you want to dimension and then click the cursor to position the dimension string, as shown in Figure 12–5.

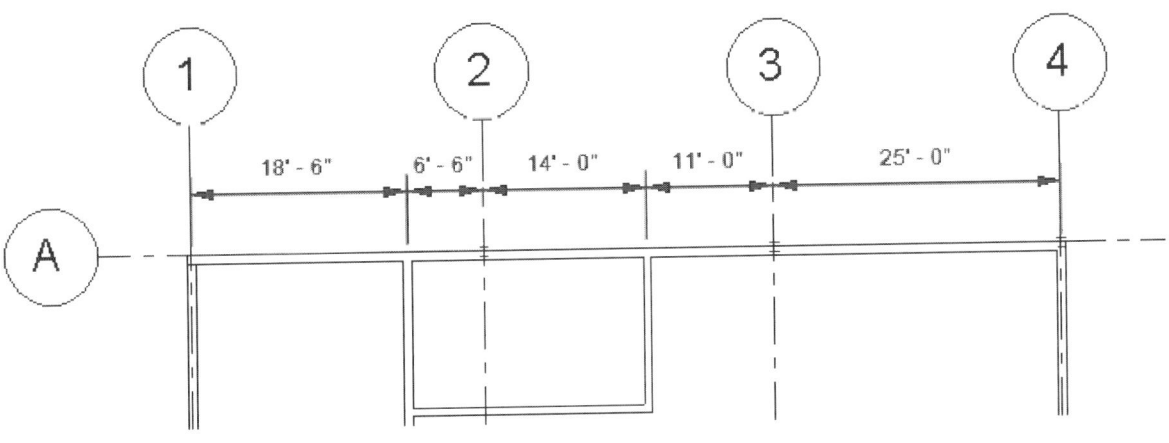

Figure 12–5

- When dimensioning entire walls, you can specify how you want *Openings*, *Intersecting Walls*, and *Intersecting Grids* to be treated by the dimension string. In the Options Bar, click **Options**. In the Auto Dimension Options dialog box (shown in Figure 12–6), select the references you want to have automatically dimensioned.

  Note: *If the* **Entire Wall** *option is selected without additional options, it places an overall wall dimension.*

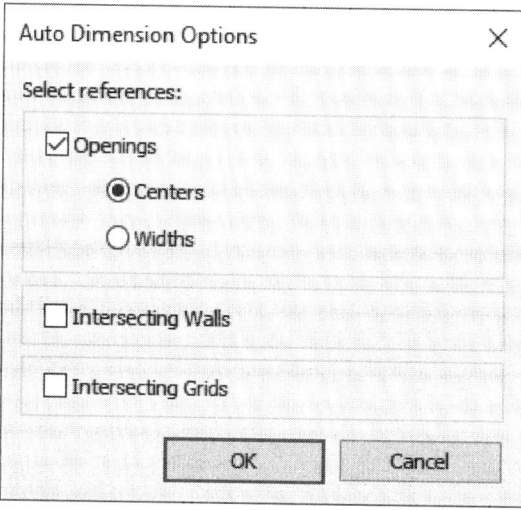

Figure 12–6

How To: Add Other Types of Dimensions

1. In the *Annotate* tab>Dimension panel, select a dimension method.

	Aligned	Most commonly used dimension type. Select individual elements or entire walls to dimension.
	Linear	Used when you need to specify certain points on elements.
	Angular	Used to dimension the angle between two elements.
	Radial	Used to dimension the radius of circular elements.
	Diameter	Used to dimension the diameter of circular elements.
	Arc Length	Used to dimension the length of the arc of circular elements.

Note: *The dimension methods are also accessible in the Modify | Place Dimensions tab> Dimension panel when any of the dimension commands are active.*

2. In the Type Selector, select the dimension type.
3. Follow the prompts for the selected method.

Spot Slope on Ramps

You can add a spot slope to a straight or curved ramp. They can be added in a plan (as shown in Figure 12–7), section, elevation, or 3D view.

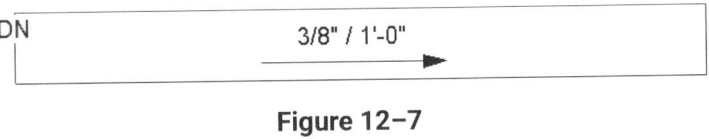

Figure 12–7

How To: Add a Spot Slope

1. Zoom in to a ramp in the model.
2. In the *Annotate* tab>Dimensions panel, click (Spot Slope).
3. Click on the ramp surface to place the spot slope.

Modifying Dimensions

When you move elements that are dimensioned (e.g., a wall), the dimensions automatically update. You can also modify dimensions by selecting a dimension or dimension string and making changes. Figure 12–8 shows the various parts of dimensions that aid in modifying.

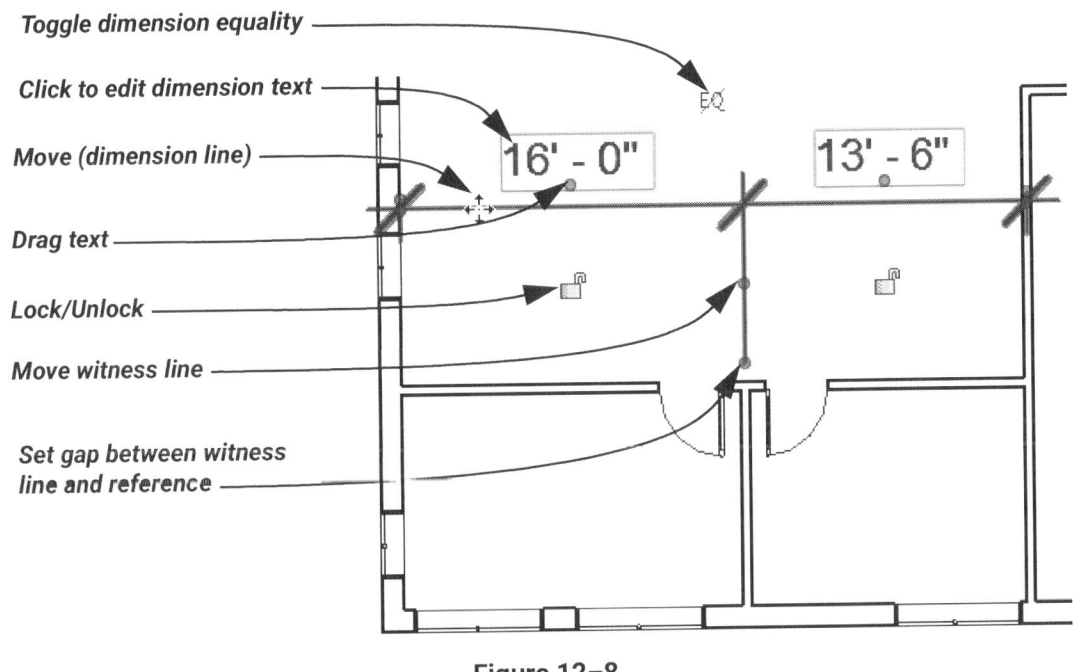

Figure 12–8

- To move the dimension text, select the **Drag text** control under the text and drag it to a new location. It automatically creates a leader from the dimension line if you drag it away. The style of the leader (arc or line) depends on the dimension style.

- To move the dimension line (the line parallel to the element being dimensioned), simply drag the line to a new location, or select the dimension and drag the ✥ (Drag to new position) control.

- To change the gap between the witness line and the element being dimensioned, drag the control at the end of the witness line.

- To move the witness line (the line perpendicular to the element being dimensioned) to a different element or face of a wall, use the **Move Witness Line** control in the middle of the witness line. While moving the witness line, you can hover your cursor over a element or component and press <Tab> repeatedly to cycle through the various options. You can also drag this control to move the witness line to a different element, or right-click on the control and select **Move Witness Line**.

Adding and Deleting Dimensions in a String

- To add a witness line to a string of dimensions, select the dimension and, in the *Modify | Dimensions* tab>Witness Lines panel, click ⊢⊣ (Edit Witness Lines). Select the element(s) you want to add to the dimension. Click in an empty space in the view to finish.

- To delete a witness line, drag the **Move Witness Line** control to a nearby witness line's element. Alternatively, you can hover the cursor over the control, right-click, and select **Delete Witness Line**.

- To delete one dimension in a string and break the string into two separate dimensions, select the string, hover your cursor over the dimension that you want to delete, and press <Tab>. When it highlights (as shown on the top in Figure 12–9), pick it and press <Delete>. The selected dimension is deleted and the dimension string is separated into two elements, as shown on the bottom in Figure 12–9.

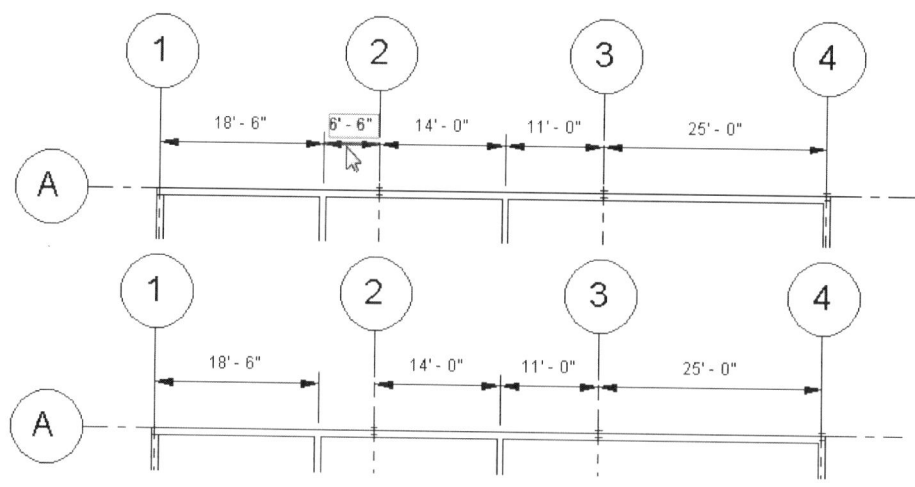

Figure 12–9

Modifying the Dimension Text

Because Revit is parametric, changing the dimension text without changing the elements dimensioned would cause problems throughout the project. These issues could cause problems beyond the model if you use the project model to estimate materials or work with other disciplines.

You can append the existing dimension text with prefixes and suffixes (as shown in Figure 12–10), or create a dimension style that has a prefix or suffix preset in the Type Properties. This can help you in renovation projects.

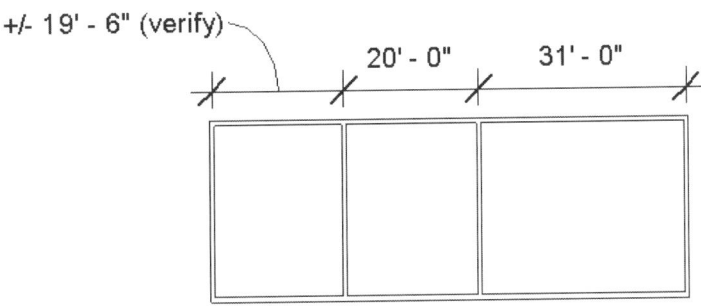

Figure 12–10

Double-click on the dimension text to open the Dimension Text dialog box, as shown in Figure 12–11, and make modifications as needed.

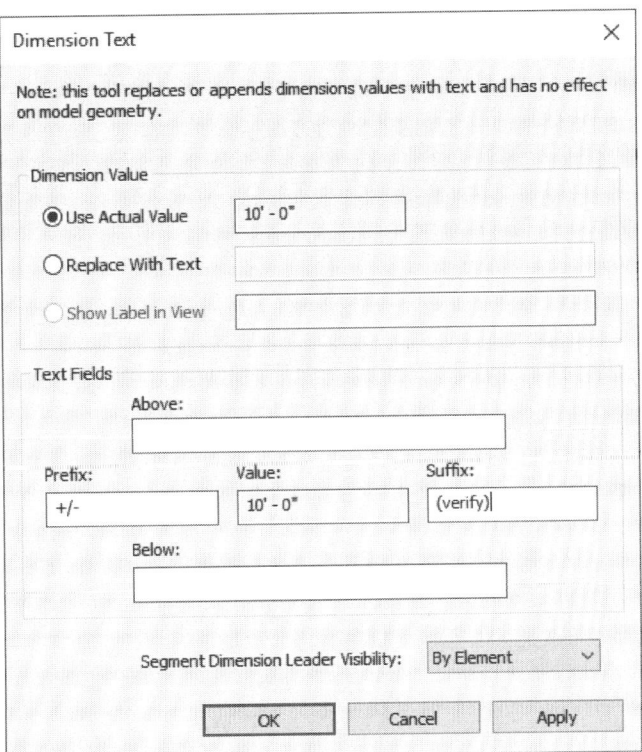

Figure 12–11

Hint: Multiple Dimension Options

If you are creating details that show one element with multiple dimension values, as shown in Figure 12–12, you can easily modify the dimension text.

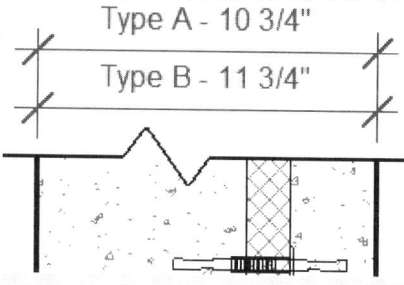

Figure 12–12

Select the dimension and then the dimension text. The Dimension Text dialog box opens. You can replace the text, as shown in Figure 12–13, or add text fields above or below, as well as a prefix or suffix.

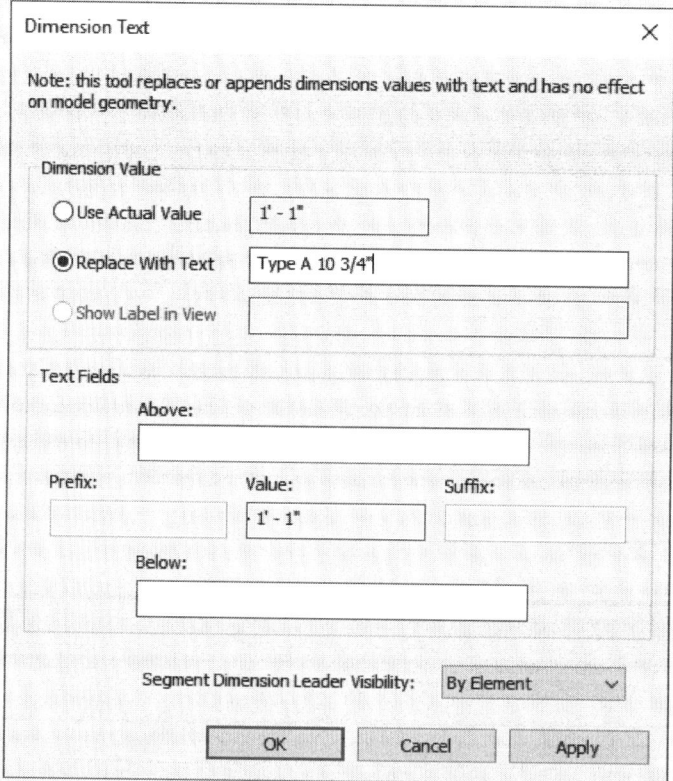

Figure 12–13

- This also works with Equality Text Labels.

If you find that you are always modifying dimensions manually, you can create a type-driven dimension style by duplicating the dimension style and specifying a set prefix and suffix within the type parameters, as shown in Figure 12–14.

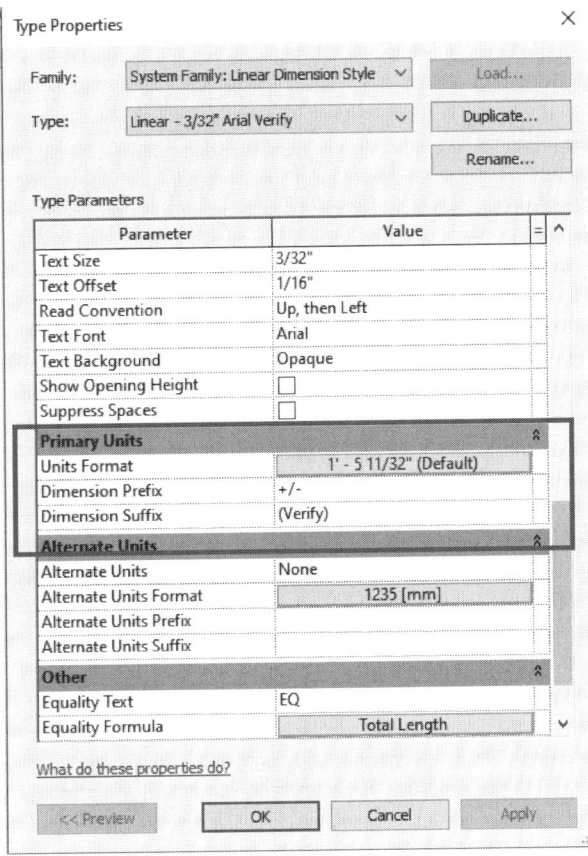

Figure 12–14

This eliminates the need to manually modify the dimension every time you need to add a prefix or suffix.

Setting Constraints

The three types of constraints that work with dimensions are locks and equal settings, as shown in Figure 12–15, as well as labels.

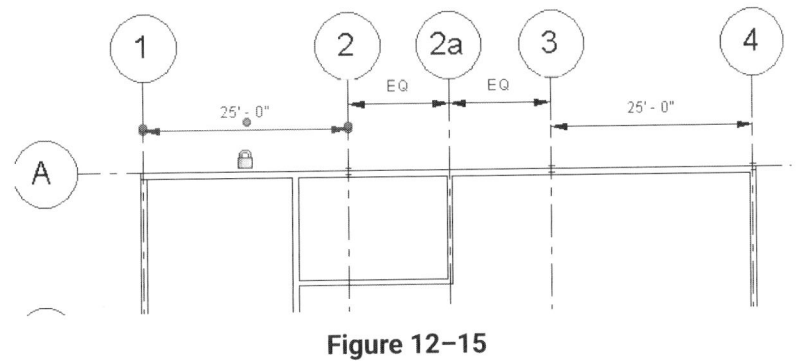

Figure 12–15

Locking Dimensions

When you lock a dimension, the value is set and you cannot make a change between it and the referenced elements. If it is unlocked, you can move it and change its value.

Note that when you use this and move an element, any elements that are locked to the dimension also move.

Setting Dimensions Equal

For a string of dimensions, select the **EQ** symbol to constrain the elements to be at an equal distance apart. This actually moves the elements that are dimensioned.

- The equality text display can be changed in Properties, as shown in Figure 12–16. The style for each of the display types is set in the dimension type.

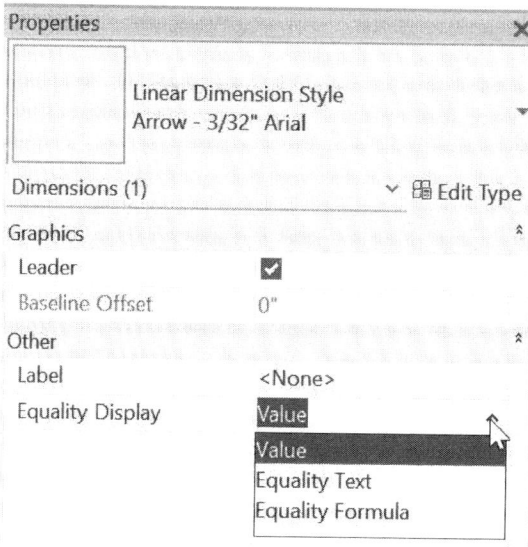

Figure 12–16

Labeling Dimensions

If you have a distance that needs to be repeated multiple times, such as the *Wall to Window* label shown in Figure 12–17, or one where you want to use a formula based on another dimension, you can create and apply a global parameter, also called a label, to the dimension.

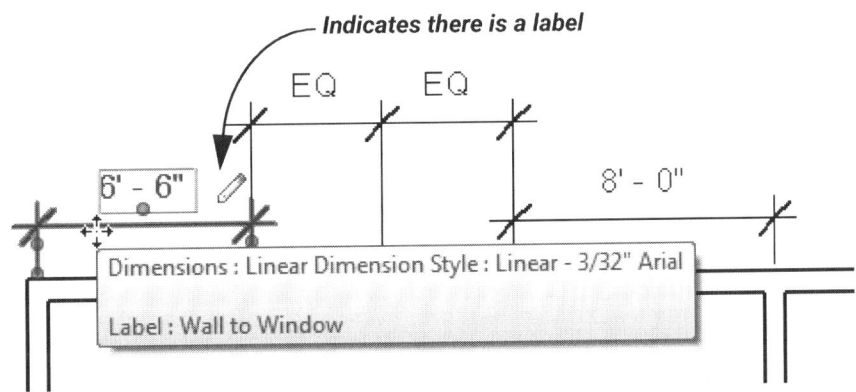

Figure 12–17

- To apply an existing label to a dimension, select the dimension and in the *Modify | Dimensions* tab>Label Dimension panel, select the label in the drop-down list, as shown in Figure 12–18.

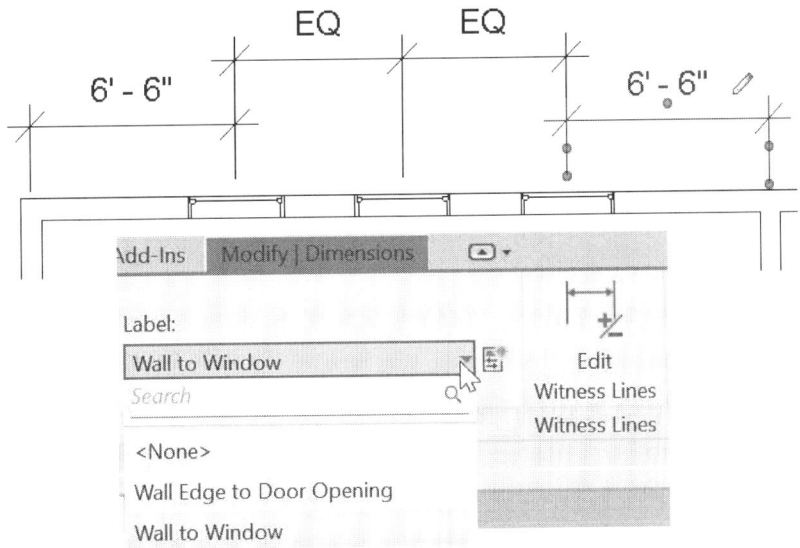

Figure 12–18

How To: Create a Label

1. Select a dimension.
2. In the *Modify | Dimensions* tab>Label Dimension panel, click (Create Parameter).

3. In the Global Parameter Properties dialog box, type in a *Name*, as shown in Figure 12-19, and click **OK**.

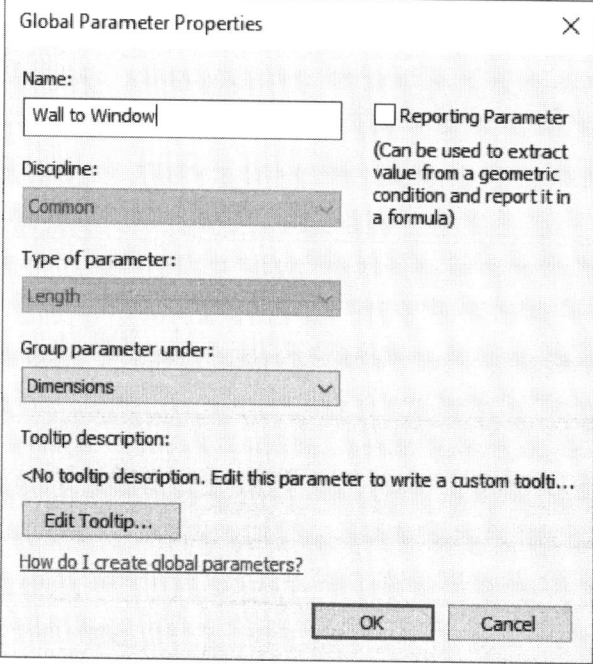

Figure 12-19

4. The label is applied to the dimension.

How To: Edit the Label Information

1. Select a labeled dimension.

2. Click (Global Parameters), as shown in Figure 12-20.

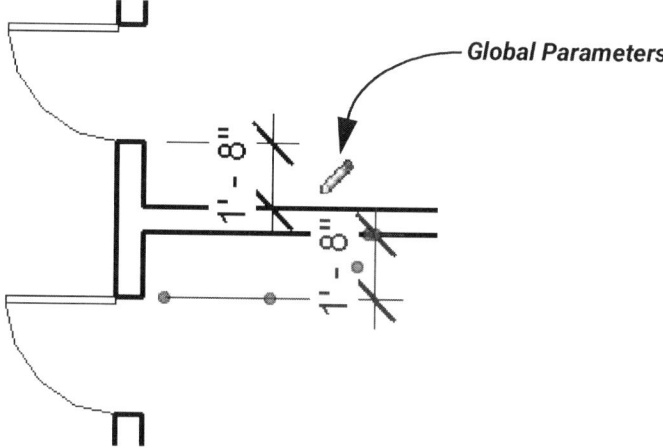

Figure 12-20

3. In the Global Parameters dialog box, in the *Value* column, type the new distance, as shown in Figure 12–21.

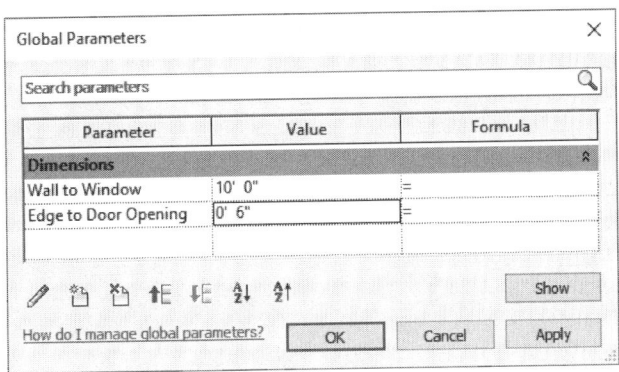

Figure 12–21

4. Click **OK**. The selected dimension and any other dimensions using the same label are updated.

- You can also edit, create, and delete global parameters in this dialog box.

Working with Constraints

To find out which elements have constraints applied to them, in the View Control Bar, click (Reveal Constraints). Constraints display as shown in Figure 12–22.

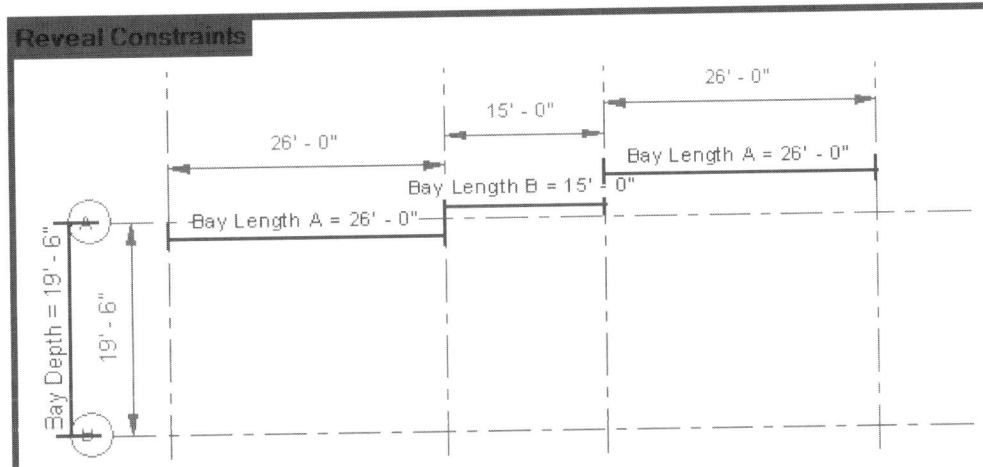

Figure 12–22

- If you try to move the element beyond the appropriate constraints, a warning dialog box displays, as shown in Figure 12–23.

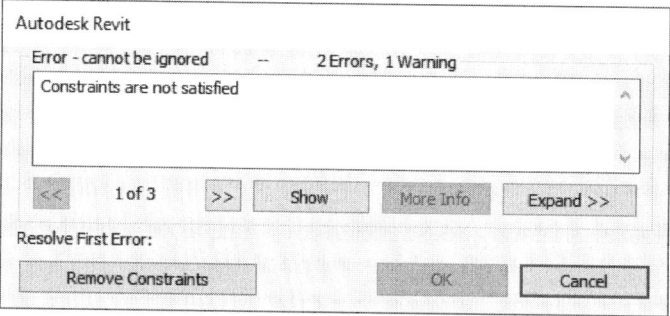

Figure 12–23

- If you delete dimensions that are constrained, a warning dialog box displays, as shown in Figure 12–24. Click **OK** to retain the constraint or click **Unconstrain** to remove the constraint.

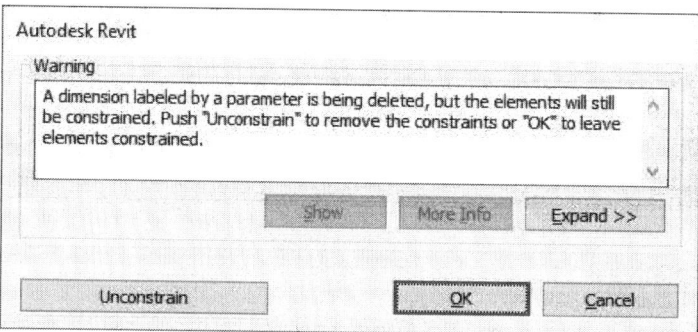

Figure 12–24

Multi-Rebar Annotation

The dimension-like Multi-Rebar Annotation tool dimensions and tags multiple rebar elements based on the parameters from the referenced elements, as shown in Figure 12–25.

Note: These annotations only work with rebar created using the multi-rebar layout. This does not work with structural area, path, or fabric reinforcement.

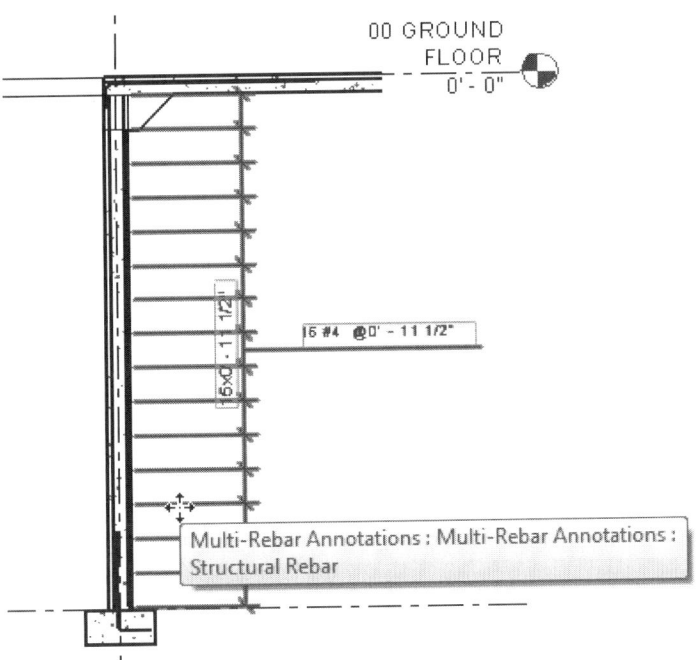

Figure 12–25

- There are two different types: aligned (annotations display parallel to the tagged rebar) and linear (annotations are aligned to the horizontal or vertical axis of the view).
- There must be at least two rebar elements in a set for the multiple-rebar dimensions to work.
- Multi-Rebar Annotation can be used with curved and angled rebar sets.

How To: Add Multi-Rebar Annotation

1. In the *Annotate* tab>Tag panel, expand (Multi-Rebar Annotation) and select (Aligned Multi-Rebar Annotation) or (Linear Multi-Rebar Annotation).
2. In the Type Selector, select the annotation type you want to use.
3. Select the element to tag.
4. Select the edge of the concrete, as required.
5. Click to place the dimension string.
6. Click to place the line off the dimension string
7. Click to place the tag (text).

- The dimensions and tags can be modified separately. After you select one of the elements, in the *Modify | Multi-Rebar Annotations* tab>Edit panel, click (Select Tag) or (Select Dimension), then modify the elements using controls, as shown for a tag in Figure 12–26.

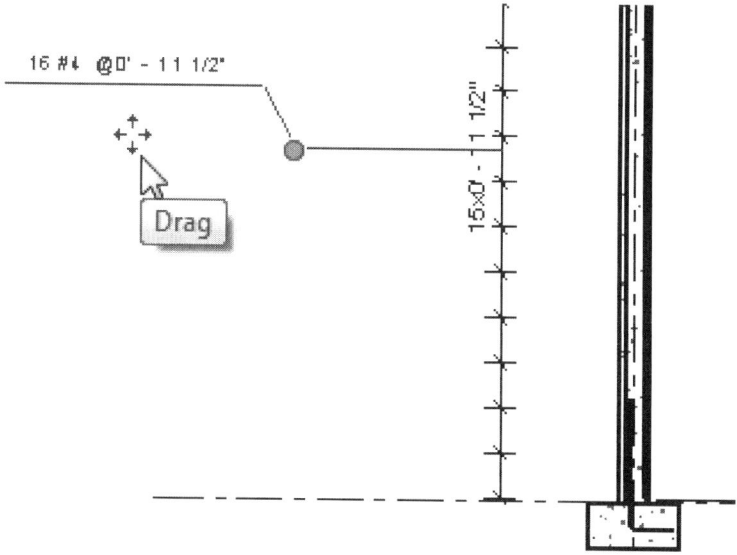

Figure 12–26

- Editing the dimension uses the same controls as other dimension strings.
- The dimensions of the Multi-Rebar Annotation change automatically in relation to the Rebar Presentation style. For example, in Figure 12–27, (Show First and Last) is shown on the left and (Show All) on the right. This graphic uses the **Structural Rebar Section** Multi-Rebar Annotations type.

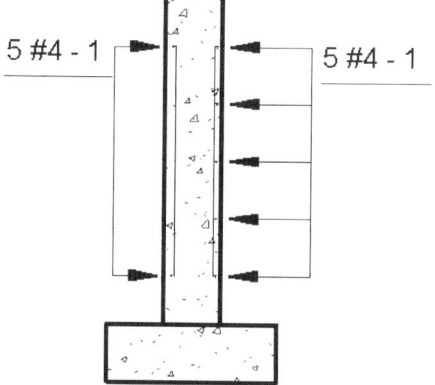

Figure 12–27

Practice 12a
Work with Dimensions

Practice Objectives

- Add a string of dimensions.
- Dimension using the **Entire Walls** option.
- Edit the witness lines of dimensions.

In this practice, you will annotate a structural plan by adding Aligned dimensions for grid line locations and Radial dimensions for curved beams, as shown in Figure 12–28. You will also add text notes to a plan and detail view, and multi-rebar annotation to an elevation callout.

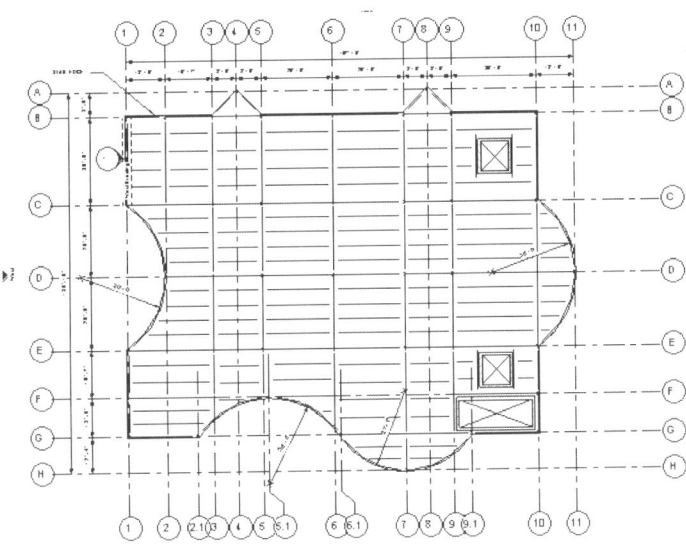

Figure 12–28

Task 1: Duplicate a view and create a typical dimension type.

1. Open **Structural-Dimensions.rvt** from the practice files folder.
2. In the Project Browser, right-click on the **Structural Plans: TOS-1ST FLOOR** view and select **Duplicate View>Duplicate**.
3. Rename the new view to **TOS-1ST FLOOR - Dimensioned**.
4. In the View Control Bar, change the *Scale* to **1/16" = 1'-0"**.
5. In the *Annotate* tab>Dimension panel or Quick Access Toolbar, click (Aligned Dimensions).

6. In Type Properties, duplicate the **Arrow - 3/32" Arial** dimension style and call it **3/32" Arial (TYP)**.
7. In the *Primary Units* section, enter **(TYP)** next to *Dimensions Suffix* and click **OK**.
8. Click (Modify).
9. Save the project.

Task 2: Place dimensions.

1. While remaining in the **TOS-1ST FLOOR - Dimensioned** plan, start the **Aligned Dimension** command.
2. In the Type Selector, select **3/32" Arial (TYP)**.
3. Dimension the elevator walls on the north side of the building, as shown in Figure 12–29.

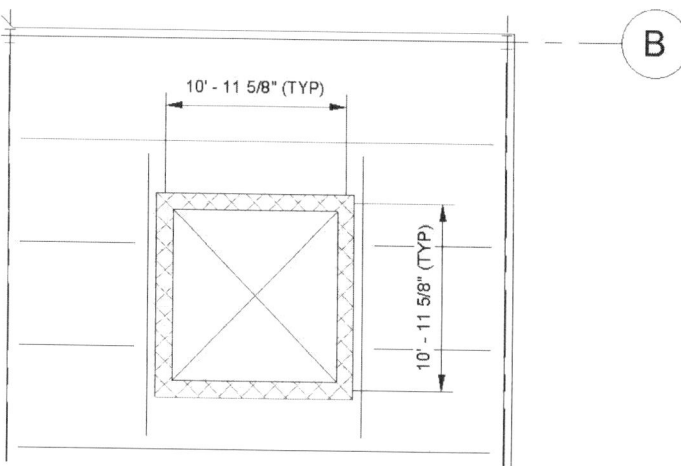

Figure 12–29

4. Stay in the Dimension command. In the Type Selector, change the dimension style to **Arrow - 3/32" Arial**.
5. Zoom out or pan so you can see grid lines **1** and **11**.

6. Dimension from grid line **1** to grid line **11** and then click out to the right of grid line **11** to create one overall dimension, as shown across the top in Figure 12–30.

7. You are still in the Dimension command. Select grid line **1** and continue selecting the other grid lines in sequence without stopping until you select grid line **11**. When you get to the end, click to the right of the string to place the dimensions, as shown below the overall dimension in Figure 12–30.

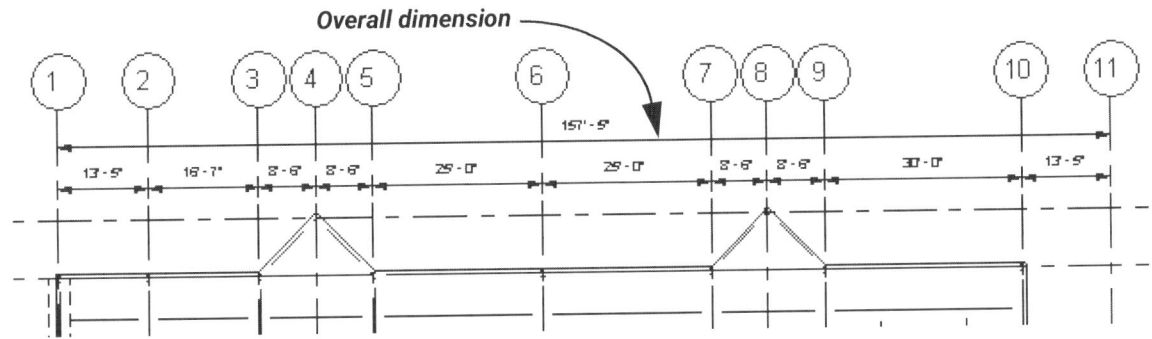

Figure 12–30

8. Add an overall dimension vertically from grid line **A** to grid line **H** and sequential dimensions from grid line **A** to grid line **H**. Modify the location of the grid markers as needed.

9. In the *Modify | Place Dimension* tab>Dimension panel, click (Radial) and add radial dimensions to the four circular bays, as shown for one of them in Figure 12–31. First click the arc beam, then click away from the arc beam to place the dimension.

   Note: *If there is overlapping text, select the text and move it to an open area where it can be read.*

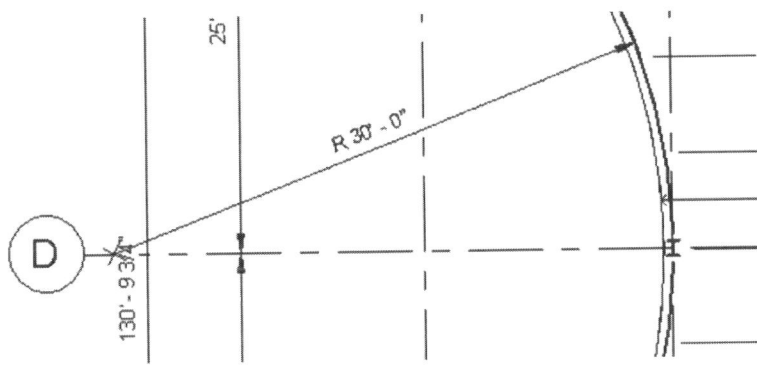

Figure 12–31

10. Save the project.

Task 3: Add multi-rebar annotation.

1. Open the **Elevations (Building Elevation): North** view.

2. Zoom in on the foundation wall between grid lines **5** and **7** where you see the area reinforcement tag, as shown in Figure 12–32.

3. In the *View* tab>Create panel, click (Callout). In the Type Selector, select **Detail**. Draw the callout as shown in Figure 12–32.

    - When you use the **Detail** callout type, it automatically displays the rebar. If you use the **Elevation** type, you need to modify the **View Visibility State** of the rebar for that view.

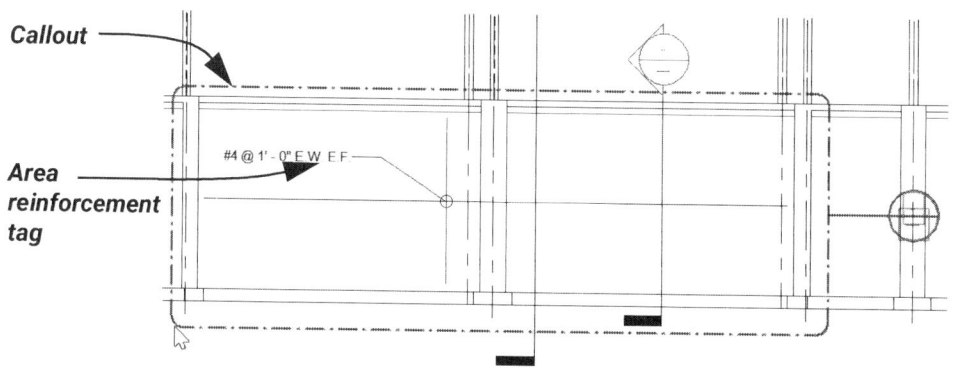

Figure 12–32

4. In the Project Browser, in the **Detail Views (Detail)** node, rename the new view to **Foundation Rebar Elevation** and open it.

5. Drag the level head away from the crop region for clarity.

6. In the *Annotate* tab>Tag panel, expand (Multi-Rebar) and select (Aligned Multi-Rebar Annotation).

7. Select the top rebar set and then move the cursor outside of the cropped region and click to place the annotation above it. Every instance in the rebar set is automatically dimensioned with an overall dimension added, as shown in Figure 12–33.

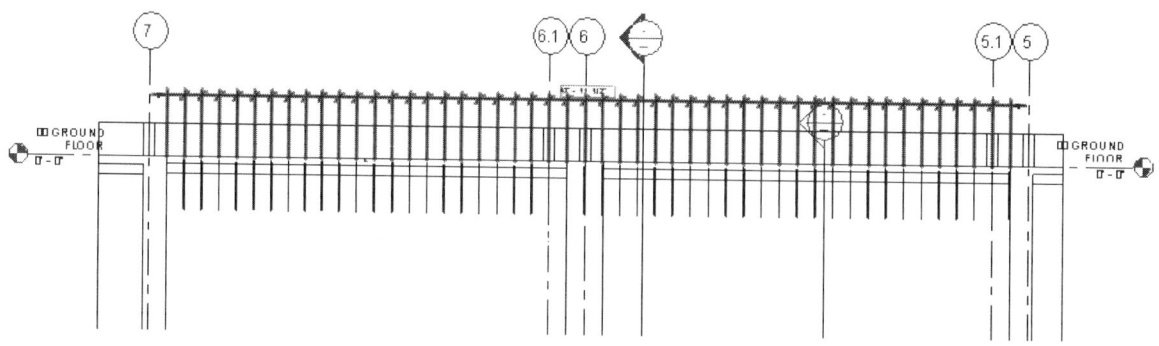

Figure 12–33

8. Click ▶ (Modify) and select the rebar set.
9. In the *Modify | Structural Rebar* tab>Presentation panel, click ▢ (Show First and Last).
10. The dimensions are modified to fit the presentation style, as shown in Figure 12–34.

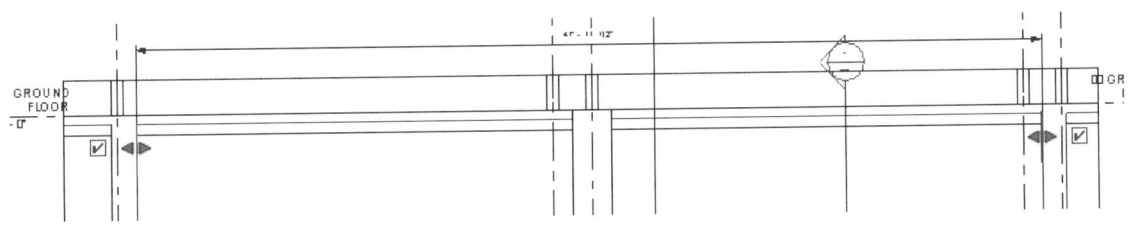

Figure 12–34

11. Save and close the project.

End of practice

12.2 Working with Text

The **Text** command enables you to add notes to views or sheets, such as the detail shown in Figure 12–35. The same command is used to create text with or without leaders.

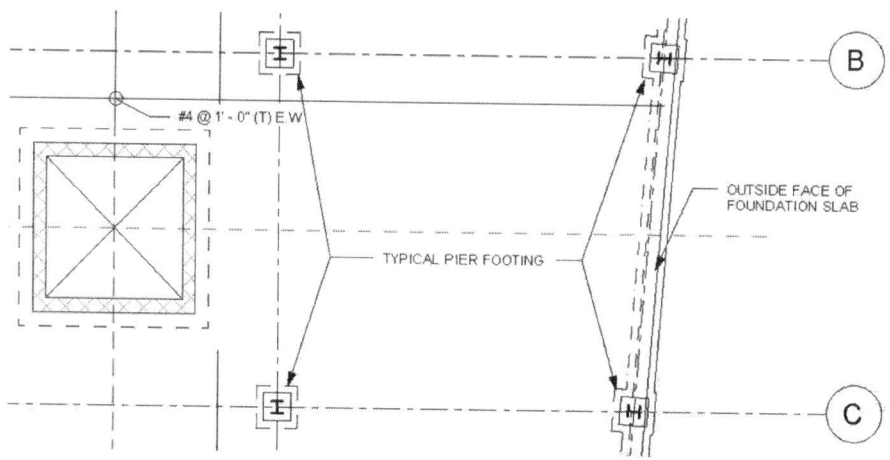

Figure 12–35

The text height is automatically set by the text type in conjunction with the scale of the view (as shown in Figure 12–36, using the same size text type at two different scales). Text types display at the specified height, both in the views and on the sheet.

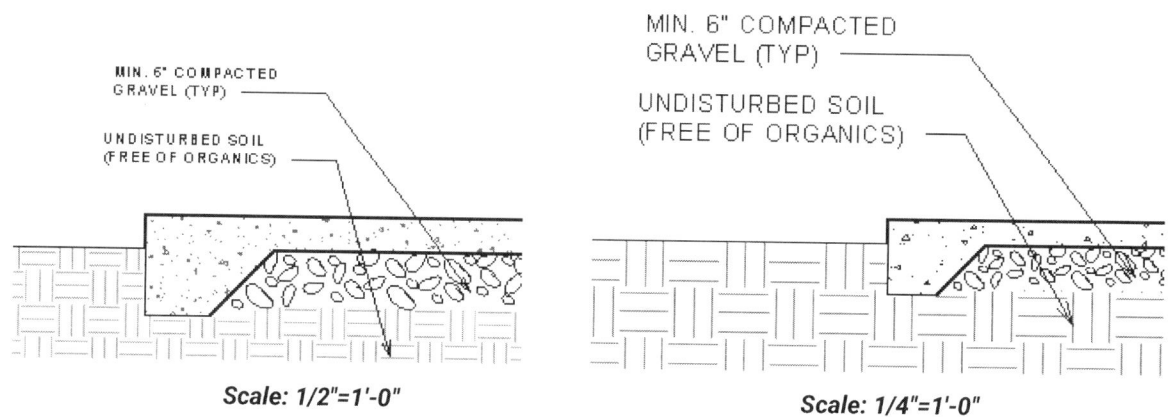

Figure 12–36

How To: Add Text

1. In the Quick Access Toolbar or *Annotate* tab>Text panel, click **A** (Text).
2. In the Type Selector, set the text type.

   Note: The text type sets the font and height of the text.

3. In the *Modify | Place Text* tab>Leader panel, select the method you want to use: **A** (No Leader), **←A** (One Segment), **⌐A** (Two Segments), or **⌒A** (Curved).
4. In the Alignment panel, set the overall justification for the text and leader, as shown in Figure 12–37.

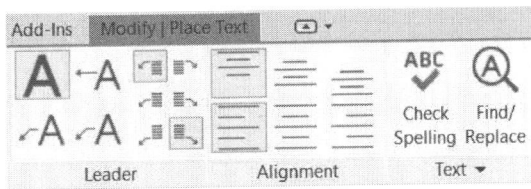

Figure 12–37

5. Select the location for the leader and text.
   - Use alignment lines to help you align the text with other text elements.
   - If **No leader** is selected, select the start point for the text and begin typing.
   - If using a leader, the first point places the arrow and you then select points for the leader. The text starts at the last leader point.
   - To set a word wrapping distance, click and drag the circle grip controls to set the start and end points of the text.
6. Type the needed text. In the *Edit Text* tab, specify additional options for the font and paragraph, as shown in Figure 12–38.

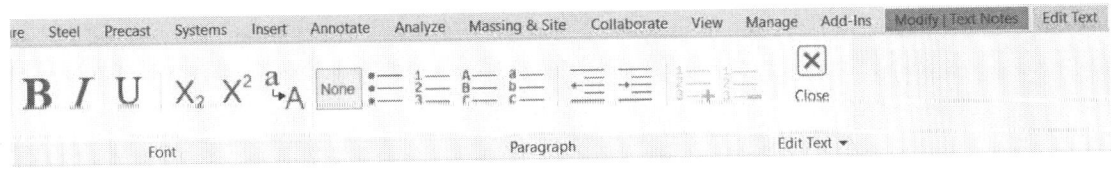

Figure 12–38

7. In the *Edit Text* tab>Edit Text panel, click ☒ (Close) or click outside the text box to complete the text element.
   - Pressing <Enter> after a line of text starts a new line of text in the same text window.

How To: Add Text Symbols

1. Start the **Text** command and click to place the text.
2. As you are typing text and need to insert a symbol, right-click and select **Symbols** from the shortcut menu. Select from the list of commonly used symbols, as shown in Figure 12–39.

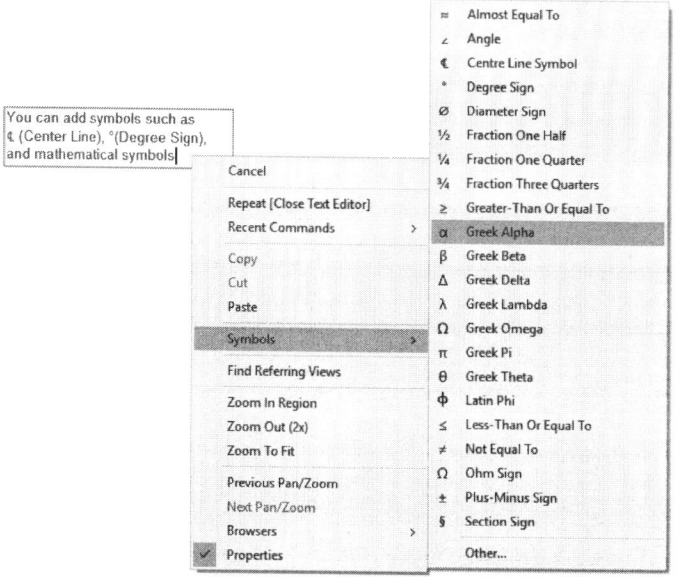

Figure 12–39

3. If the symbol you need is not listed, click **Other...**.
4. In the Character Map dialog box, click on a symbol and click **Select**, as shown in Figure 12–40.

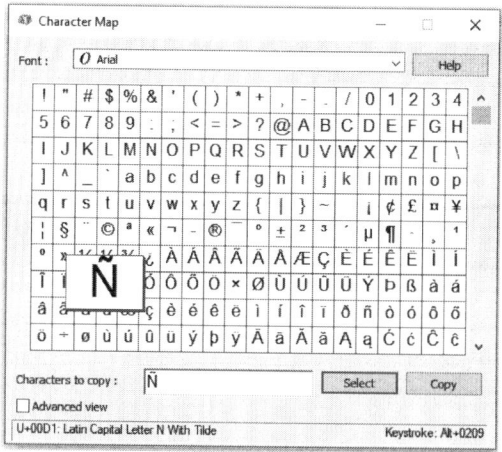

Figure 12–40

5. Click **Copy** to copy the character to the clipboard and paste it into the text box.
- The font in the Character Map should match the font used by the text type. You do not want to use a different font for symbols.

Editing Text

Editing text notes takes place at two levels:

- Modifying the text note, which includes the **Leader** and **Paragraph** styles.
- Editing the text, which includes changes to individual letters, words, and paragraphs in the text note.

Modifying the Text Note

Click once on the text note to modify the text box and leaders using controls, as shown in Figure 12–41, or using the tools in the *Modify | Text Notes* tab.

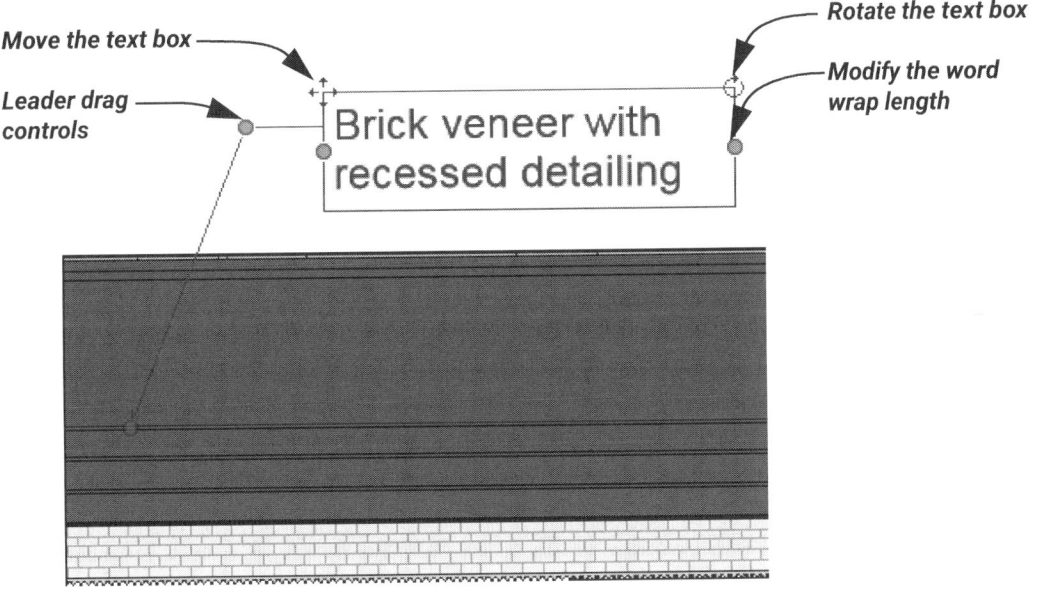

Figure 12–41

How To: Add a Leader to Text Notes

1. Select the text note.
2. In the *Modify | Text Notes* tab>Leader panel, select the direction and justification for the new leader, as shown in Figure 12–42.

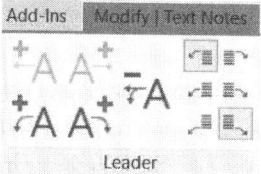

Figure 12–42

3. The leader is applied, as shown in Figure 12–43. Use the drag controls to place the arrow as needed.

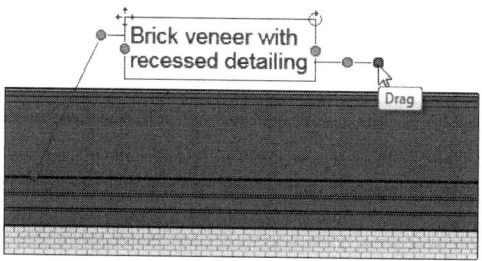

Figure 12–43

- You can remove leaders by clicking ⲘA (Remove Last Leader).

Editing the Text

The *Edit Text* tab enables you to make various customizations. These include modifying the font of selected words as well as creating bulleted and numbered lists, as shown in Figure 12–44.

General Notes
1. Notify designer of intention to start construction at least 10 days prior to start of site work.
2. Installer shall provide the following:
   - 24-hour notice of start of construction
   - Inspection of bottom of bed or covering required by state inspector
   - All environmental management inspection sheets must be emailed to designer's office within 24 hours of inspection.

Figure 12–44

Working with Annotations

- You can **Cut**, **Copy**, and **Paste** text using the clipboard. For example, you can copy text from a document and then paste it into the text editor in Revit.
- To help you see the text better as you are modifying it, in the *Edit Text* tab, expand the Edit Text panel and select one or both of the options, as shown in Figure 12–45.

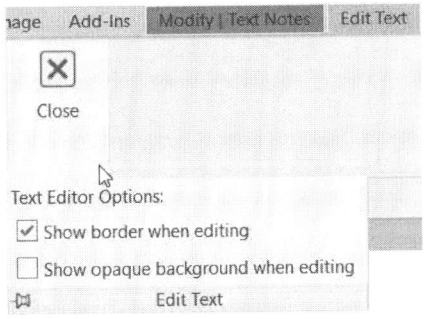

Figure 12–45

How To: Modify the Font

1. Select individual letters or words.
2. Click on the font modification you want to include:

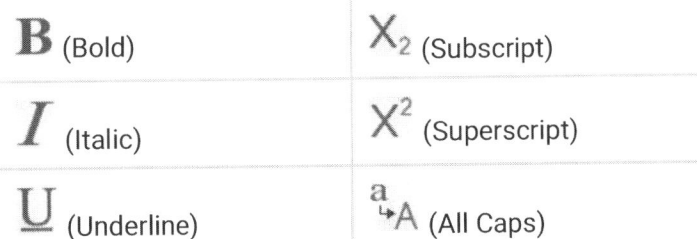

- When pasting text from a document outside of Revit, font modifications (e.g, Bold, Italic, etc.) are retained.

How To: Create Lists

1. In Edit Text mode, place the cursor in the line where you want to add to a list.
2. In the *Edit Text* tab>Paragraph panel, click the type of list you want to create:

3. As you type, press <Enter> and the next line in the list is incremented.

   Note: *If you do not want a line to be a part of the list, select the line and click* None *(None) on the Paragraph panel.*

4. To include sub-lists, at the beginning of the next line, click ≡ (Increase Indent) or press <Tab>. This indents the line and applies the next level of lists, as shown in Figure 12–46.

```
4. The applicant shall be responsible:
   A. First Indent
      a. Second Indent
         • Third Indent
```

Figure 12–46

Note: The indent distance is set up by the text type Tab Size.

- You can change the type of list after you have applied the first increment. For example, you might want to use a list of bullets instead of letters, as shown in Figure 12–47.

5. Click ≡ (Decrease Indent) or press <Shift>+<Tab> to return to the previous list style.

- Press <Shift>+<Enter> to create a blank line in a numbered list.
- To create columns or other separate text boxes that build on a numbering system (as shown in Figure 12–47), create the second text box and list, then place the cursor on one of the lines and in the Paragraph panel, click ≡₊ (Increment List Value) until the list matches the next number in the sequence.

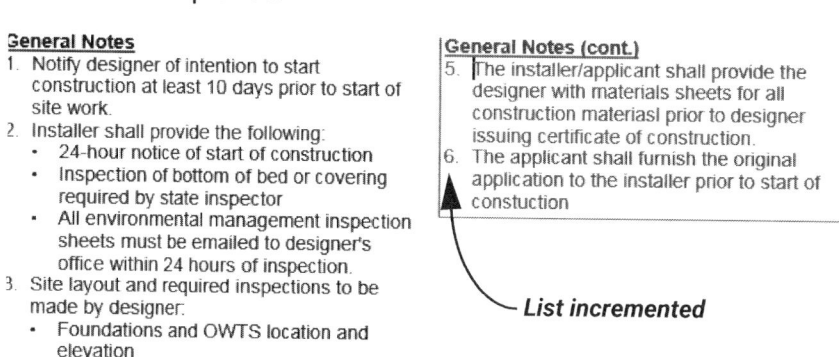

Figure 12–47

6. Click ≡ (Decrement List Value) to move back a number.

Working with Annotations

> **Hint: Model Text**
>
> Model text is different from annotation text. It is designed to create full-size text on the model itself. For example, you would use model text to create a sign on a door, as shown in Figure 12–48. One model text type is included with the default template. You can create other types as needed.

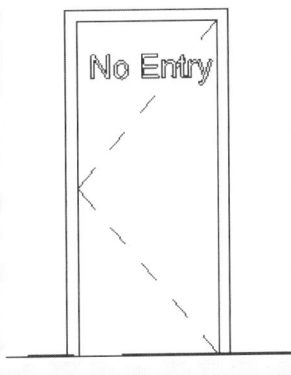

Figure 12–48

- Model text can be viewed in all views.
- Model text is added from the *Architecture* tab>Model panel by clicking (Model Text).

Spell Checking

The Check Spelling dialog box displays any misspelled words in context and provides several options for changing them, as shown in Figure 12–49.

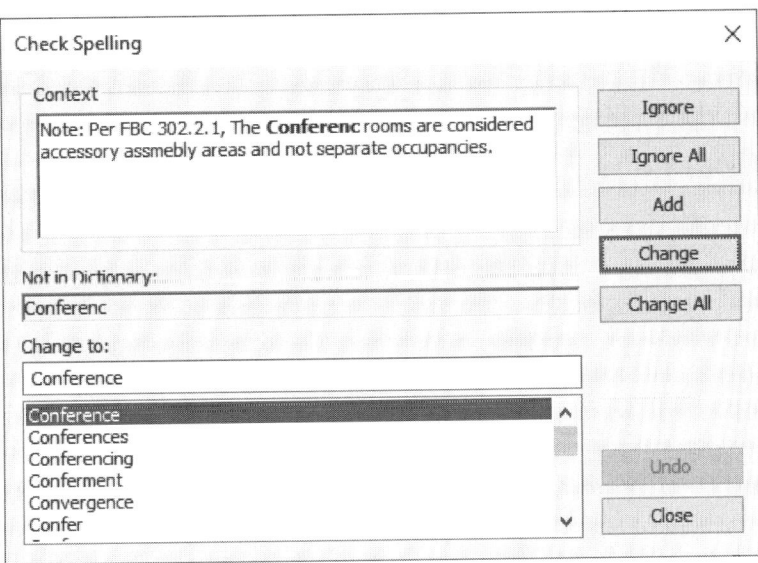

Figure 12–49

- Revit does not have active spell checking. It will only spell check when the command is activated.

- To spell check all text in a view, in the *Annotate* tab>Text panel, click ABC✓ (Spelling), or press <F7>. As with other spell checkers, you can **Ignore**, **Add**, or **Change** the word.

- You can also check the spelling in selected text. With text selected, in the *Modify | Text Notes* tab>Tools panel, click ABC✓ (Check Spelling).

Creating Text Types

If you need new text types with a different text size or font (such as for a title or hand-lettering), you can create new ones, as shown in Figure 12–50. It is recommended that you create these in a project template so they are available in future projects.

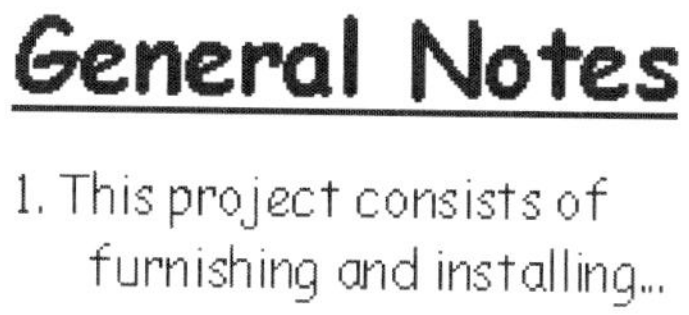

General Notes

1. This project consists of furnishing and installing...

Figure 12–50

- You can copy and paste text types from one project to another or use **Transfer Project Standards**.

How To: Create Text Types

1. In the *Annotate* tab>Text panel, click ⁕ (Text Types).
   - Alternatively, start the **Text** command.
2. In Properties, click **Edit Type**.
3. In the Type Properties dialog box, click **Duplicate**.
4. In the Name dialog box, type a new name and click **OK**.

5. Modify the text parameters, as needed. The parameters are shown in Figure 12–51.

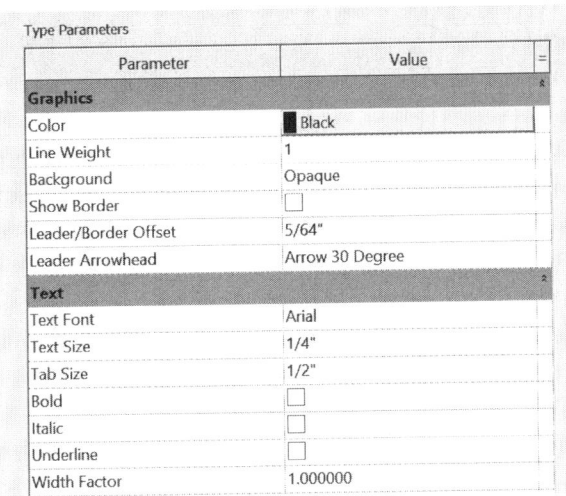

Figure 12–51

- The *Background* parameter can be set to **Opaque** or **Transparent**. An opaque background includes a masking region that hides lines or elements behind the text.

- In the *Text* area, the *Width Factor* parameter controls the width of the lettering, but does not affect the height. A width factor greater than **1** spreads the text out and a width factor less than **1** compresses it.

- The *Show Border* parameter, when selected, includes a rectangle around the text.

6. Click **OK** to close the Type Properties dialog box.

Practice 12b
Work with Text

Practice Objectives

- Add text notes.
- Modify text with lists.

In this practice, you will add text into a structural plan view and a framing elevation, as shown in Figure 12–52. You will then copy in a text note and create a numbered list.

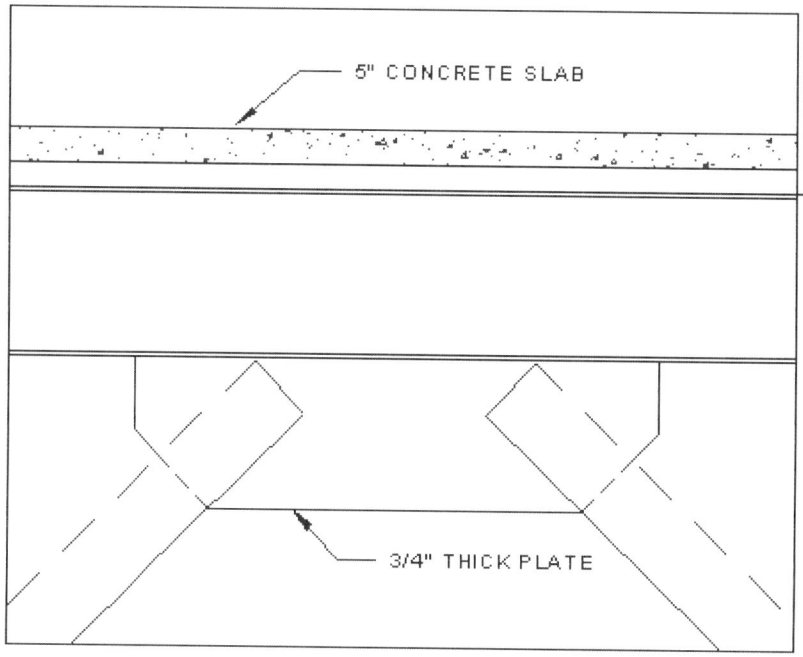

Figure 12–52

Task 1: Create text types.

1. Open the project **Structural-Text.rvt** from the practice files folder.

2. In the *Annotate* tab>Text panel, click A (Text).

3. In Properties, click 🔳 (Edit Type).

4. In the Type Properties dialog box, duplicate an existing text type and create new text types using the properties outlined below.

	1/8" Arial Narrow	1/8" Arial Narrow Italic
Text Font	Arial Narrow	Arial Narrow
Text Size	1/8"	1/8"
Tab Size	1/4"	1/4"
Width Factor	0.9	.09
Italic	No	Yes

5. Click **OK** to save the settings and close the dialog box.
6. Save the project.

Task 2: Add text to a structural plan view.

1. Open the **Structural Plans: TOS-1ST FLOOR - Dimensioned** view.
2. Zoom in on the upper-left corner of the plan.
3. In the *Annotate* tab>Text panel, click **A** (Text).
4. In the Type Selector, select **Text: 3/32" Arial**.
5. In the *Modify | Place text* tab>Leader panel, click ⌐A (Two Segments).
6. Select the first point so that the text points to the slab edge. This is what you are going to label. Select the second point any distance away from the first point.
7. Type **Slab Edge** and click ⬚ (Modify).
8. Position the text as needed.
9. Double click on the text so that the *Edit Text* tab opens.
10. Highlight all of the letters and in the *Edit Text* tab>Font panel, click ᵃA (All Caps). The text updates as shown in Figure 12-53. Click **Close** to close the *Edit Text* tab.

    Note: Do you use uppercase letters for your notes? It is not important anymore because of the clarity of typed in text. Check your office standards.

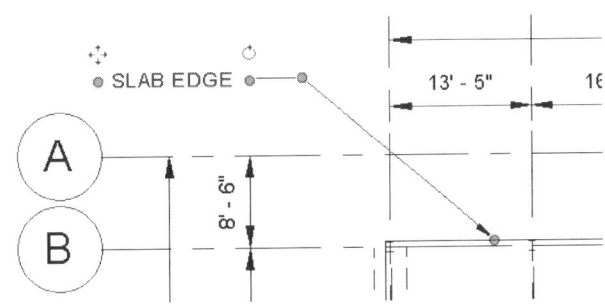

Figure 12-53

11. Click in an empty space in the view to clear the selection.
12. Zoom out to fit the view.
13. Save the project.

Task 3: Add text to a framing elevation.

1. Open the **Elevations (Framing Elevation): Typical Top Plate** view.
2. Modify the location of the level markers so that they do not overlap the view.
3. Add the text **3/4" THICK PLATE** and **5" CONCRETE SLAB** with leaders, as shown in Figure 12–54.

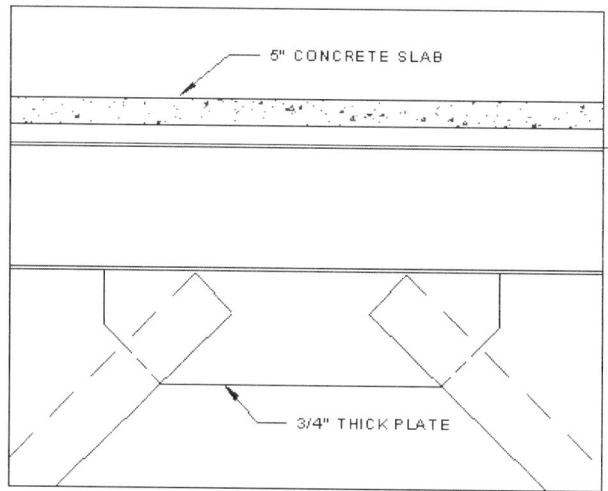

Figure 12–54

4. Save the project.

Task 4: Add general notes and create lists.

1. Open the **S-000 - Cover Sheet** view.
2. Zoom in on the area below the project name.
3. Start the **Text** command and in the *Modify | Place Text* tab>Leader panel, click **A** (No Leader).
4. In the Type Selector, select **Text: 1/4" Arial**.

5. Click and drag to place a box similar to Figure 12–55. The size of the box does not need to be exactly what is shown below as you can modify it later.

Figure 12–55

6. From the practice files *Documents* folder, open **Structural Steel Notes.txt** in a text editor.

7. Select all of the text and copy it to the clipboard (press <Ctrl>+<C>).

8. Return to Revit and in the *Edit Text* tab>Clipboard panel, click (Paste). The text is added as shown in Figure 12–56. The text will differ depending on the width of the text box you created.

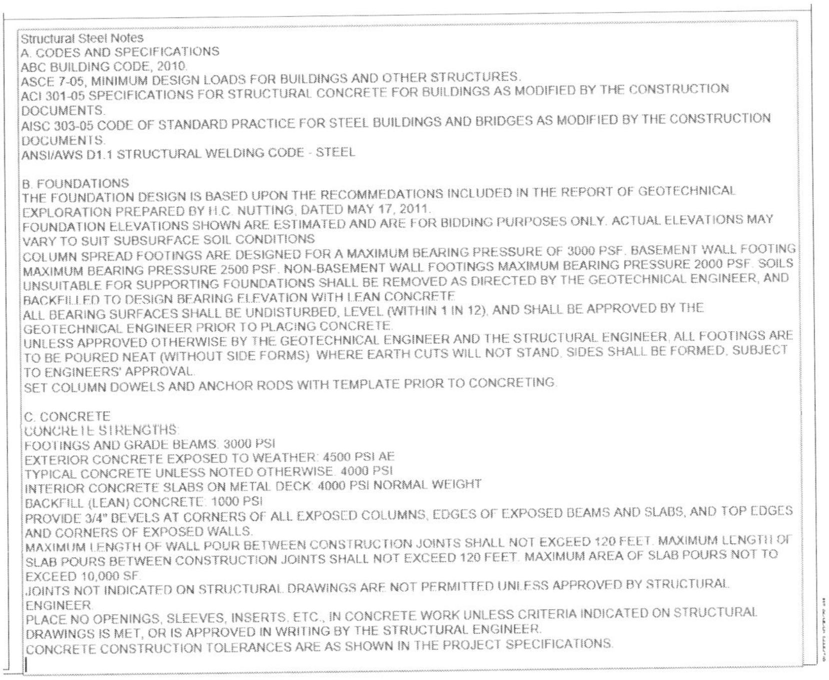

Figure 12–56

9. You should still be in edit text mode and see the *Edit Text* tab on the ribbon. Zoom in and modify the text so it resembles Figure 12–57.

   - Select the **Structural Steel Notes** heading and click (All Caps), **B** (Bold) (or press <Ctrl>+<B>), and U (Underline) (or press <Ctrl>+<U>). Press <Enter> to add a space between the note and the **A. CODES AND SPECIFICATIONS** heading.

   - Set the **A.**, **B.**, and **C.** headings to **B** (Bold).

   - Under each heading, select the group of text and click (List: Numbers) and (Increase Indent).

```
STRUCTURAL STEEL NOTES

A. CODES AND SPECIFICATIONS
   1. ABC BUILDING CODE, 2010.
   2. ASCE 7-05, MINIMUM DESIGN LOADS FOR BUILDINGS AND OTHER STRUCTURES.
   3. ACI 301-05 SPECIFICATIONS FOR STRUCTURAL CONCRETE FOR BUILDINGS AS MODIFIED BY THE CONSTRUCTION
      DOCUMENTS.
   4. AISC 303-05 CODE OF STANDARD PRACTICE FOR STEEL BUILDINGS AND BRIDGES AS MODIFIED BY THE
      CONSTRUCTION DOCUMENTS.
   5. ANSI/AWS D1.1 STRUCTURAL WELDING CODE - STEEL

B. FOUNDATIONS
   1. THE FOUNDATION DESIGN IS BASED UPON THE RECOMMEDATIONS INCLUDED IN THE REPORT OF GEOTECHNICAL
      EXPLORATION PREPARED BY H.C. NUTTING, DATED MAY 17, 2011.
   2. FOUNDATION ELEVATIONS SHOWN ARE ESTIMATED AND ARE FOR BIDDING PURPOSES ONLY. ACTUAL ELEVATIONS
      MAY VARY TO SUIT SUBSURFACE SOIL CONDITIONS
   3. COLUMN SPREAD FOOTINGS ARE DESIGNED FOR A MAXIMUM BEARING PRESSURE OF 3000 PSF. BASEMENT WALL
      FOOTING MAXIMUM BEARING PRESSURE 2500 PSF. NON-BASEMENT WALL FOOTINGS MAXIMUM BEARING PRESSURE
      2000 PSF. SOILS UNSUITABLE FOR SUPPORTING FOUNDATIONS SHALL BE REMOVED AS DIRECTED BY THE
      GEOTECHNICAL ENGINEER, AND BACKFILLED TO DESIGN BEARING ELEVATION WITH LEAN CONCRETE.
   4. ALL BEARING SURFACES SHALL BE UNDISTURBED, LEVEL (WITHIN 1 IN 12), AND SHALL BE APPROVED BY THE
      GEOTECHNICAL ENGINEER PRIOR TO PLACING CONCRETE.
   5. UNLESS APPROVED OTHERWISE BY THE GEOTECHNICAL ENGINEER AND THE STRUCTURAL ENGINEER, ALL FOOTINGS
      ARE TO BE POURED NEAT (WITHOUT SIDE FORMS). WHERE EARTH CUTS WILL NOT STAND, SIDES SHALL BE FORMED,
      SUBJECT TO ENGINEERS' APPROVAL.
   6. SET COLUMN DOWELS AND ANCHOR RODS WITH TEMPLATE PRIOR TO CONCRETING.

C. CONCRETE
   1. CONCRETE STRENGTHS:
   2. FOOTINGS AND GRADE BEAMS: 3000 PSI
   3. EXTERIOR CONCRETE EXPOSED TO WEATHER: 4500 PSI AE
   4. TYPICAL CONCRETE UNLESS NOTED OTHERWISE: 4000 PSI
   5. INTERIOR CONCRETE SLABS ON METAL DECK: 4000 PSI NORMAL WEIGHT
   6. BACKFILL (LEAN) CONCRETE: 1000 PSI
   7. PROVIDE 3/4" BEVELS AT CORNERS OF ALL EXPOSED COLUMNS, EDGES OF EXPOSED BEAMS AND SLABS, AND TOP
      EDGES AND CORNERS OF EXPOSED WALLS.
   8. MAXIMUM LENGTH OF WALL POUR BETWEEN CONSTRUCTION JOINTS SHALL NOT EXCEED 120 FEET. MAXIMUM
      LENGTH OF SLAB POURS BETWEEN CONSTRUCTION JOINTS SHALL NOT EXCEED 120 FEET. MAXIMUM AREA OF SLAB
      POURS NOT TO EXCEED 10,000 SF.
   9. JOINTS NOT INDICATED ON STRUCTURAL DRAWINGS ARE NOT PERMITTED UNLESS APPROVED BY STRUCTURAL
      ENGINEER.
   10. PLACE NO OPENINGS, SLEEVES, INSERTS, ETC., IN CONCRETE WORK UNLESS CRITERIA INDICATED ON STRUCTURAL
       DRAWINGS IS MET, OR IS APPROVED IN WRITING BY THE STRUCTURAL ENGINEER.
   11. CONCRETE CONSTRUCTION TOLERANCES ARE AS SHOWN IN THE PROJECT SPECIFICATIONS.
```

Figure 12–57

10. In the **C. CONCRETE** section, select the five lines below **CONCRETE STRENGTHS:** and click (Increase Indent) twice so the lines are indented as shown in Figure 12–58.

Before Increase Indent

C. CONCRETE
   1. CONCRETE STRENGTHS:
   2. FOOTINGS AND GRADE BEAMS: 3000 PSI
   3. EXTERIOR CONCRETE EXPOSED TO WEATHER: 4500 PSI AE
   4. TYPICAL CONCRETE UNLESS NOTED OTHERWISE: 4000 PSI
   5. INTERIOR CONCRETE SLABS ON METAL DECK: 4000 PSI NORMAL WEIGHT
   6. BACKFILL (LEAN) CONCRETE: 1000 PSI
   7. PROVIDE 3/4" BEVELS AT CORNERS OF ALL EXPOSED COLUMNS, EDGES OF

After Increase Indent

C. CONCRETE
   1. CONCRETE STRENGTHS:
      A. FOOTINGS AND GRADE BEAMS: 3000 PSI
      B. EXTERIOR CONCRETE EXPOSED TO WEATHER: 4500 PSI AE
      C. TYPICAL CONCRETE UNLESS NOTED OTHERWISE: 4000 PSI
      D. INTERIOR CONCRETE SLABS ON METAL DECK: 4000 PSI NORMAL WEIGHT
      E. BACKFILL (LEAN) CONCRETE: 1000 PSI
   2. PROVIDE 3/4" BEVELS AT CORNERS OF ALL EXPOSED COLUMNS, EDGES OF EXP

Figure 12–58

11. From the *Edit Text* tab>Edit Text panel, click **Close**.

12. Zoom out to see the full sheet.

13. Save and close the project.

End of practice

12.3 Adding Detail Lines and Symbols

While annotating views for construction documents, you might need to add detail lines and symbols to clarify the design intent or show information, such as the span direction symbol shown in Figure 12–59.

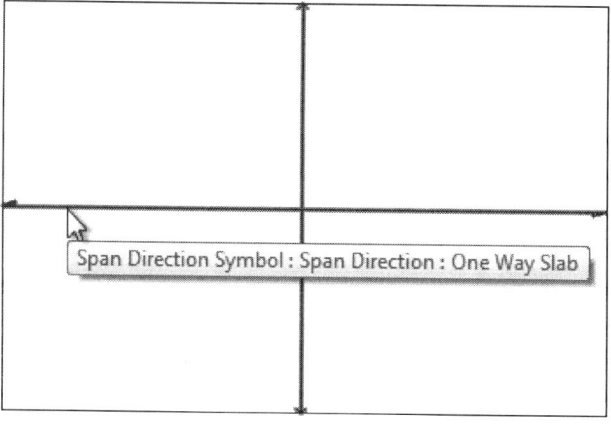

Figure 12–59

- Detail lines and symbols are view-specific, which means that they only display in the view in which they were created.

How To: Draw a Detail Line

1. In the *Annotation* tab>Detail panel, click (Detail Line).
2. In the *Modify | Place Detail Lines* tab>Line Style panel, select the type of line you want to use, as shown in Figure 12–60.

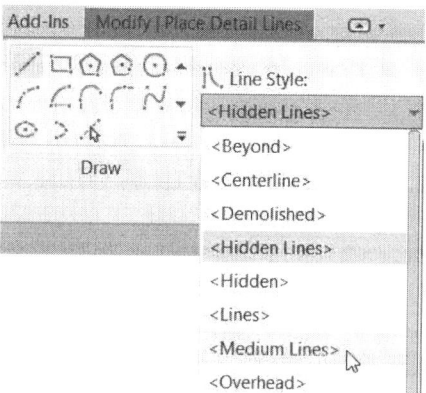

Figure 12–60

3. Use the tools in the Draw panel to create the detail line.

Using Symbols

Many of the annotations used in working drawings are frequently repeated. Several of them have been saved as symbols in Revit, such as the North Arrow, Center Line, and Graphic Scale annotations shown in Figure 12–61.

Note: Symbols are 2D elements that only display in one view, while components can be in 3D and display in many views.

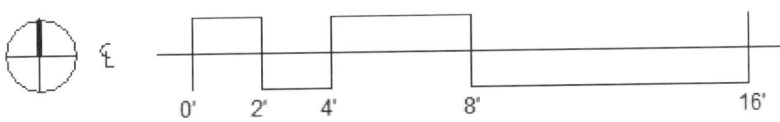

Figure 12–61

- You can also create or load custom annotation symbols.

How To: Place a Symbol

1. In the *Annotate* tab>Symbol panel, click (Symbol).
2. In the Type Selector, select the symbol you want to use.
3. In the Options Bar (shown in Figure 12–62), set the *Number of Leaders* and select **Rotate after placement** if you want to rotate the symbol as you insert it.

Figure 12–62

4. Place the symbol in the view. Rotate it if you selected the **Rotate after placement** option. If you specified leaders, use the controls to move them into place.

Structural Specific Symbols

Several types of structural elements use symbols or symbols and tags together. If the associated symbols are not applied when you create the element, you can add them later. They are found in the *Annotate* tab>Symbol panel, as shown in Figure 12–63.

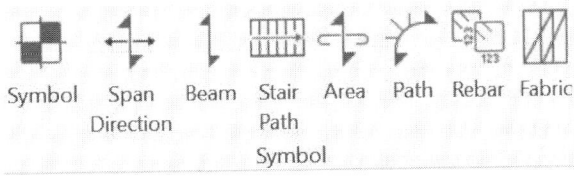

Figure 12–63

- You can also use the **Tag All Not Tagged** command to add symbols to a view.

How To: Add Reinforcement Symbols

1. In the *Annotate* tab>Symbol panel, click the type of symbol you want to use:

   - (Beam System Symbol)
   - (Span Direction Symbol)
   - (Area Reinforcement Symbol)
   - (Path Reinforcement Symbol)
   - (Rebar Bending Symbol)
   - (Fabric Reinforcement Symbol)

2. Select the related reinforcement element (not the individual rebar).
3. Select a location for the symbol. The symbol expands to fit the extents of the beam system, as shown for **Path Reinforcement** in Figure 12–64.

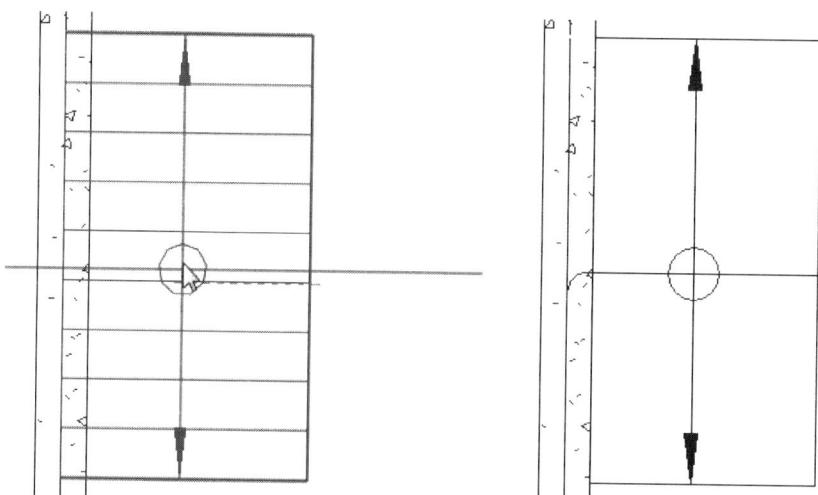

Figure 12–64

4. You can continue selecting similar elements and placing the symbol.

5. When you are finished, click (Modify) or press <Esc> to end the command.

- To add a tag to the reinforcement elements, use the (Tag by Category) command.

Changing the Span Direction of Floors and Slabs

By default, span direction symbols are added when you create a structural floor or foundation slab. They can be used to change the span direction of the floor or slab without having to edit the sketch. You can modify the floor span direction symbol once it is in the view through the Type Selector, as shown in Figure 12-65. (Note that Foundation Span Direction Symbols do not have these choices.)

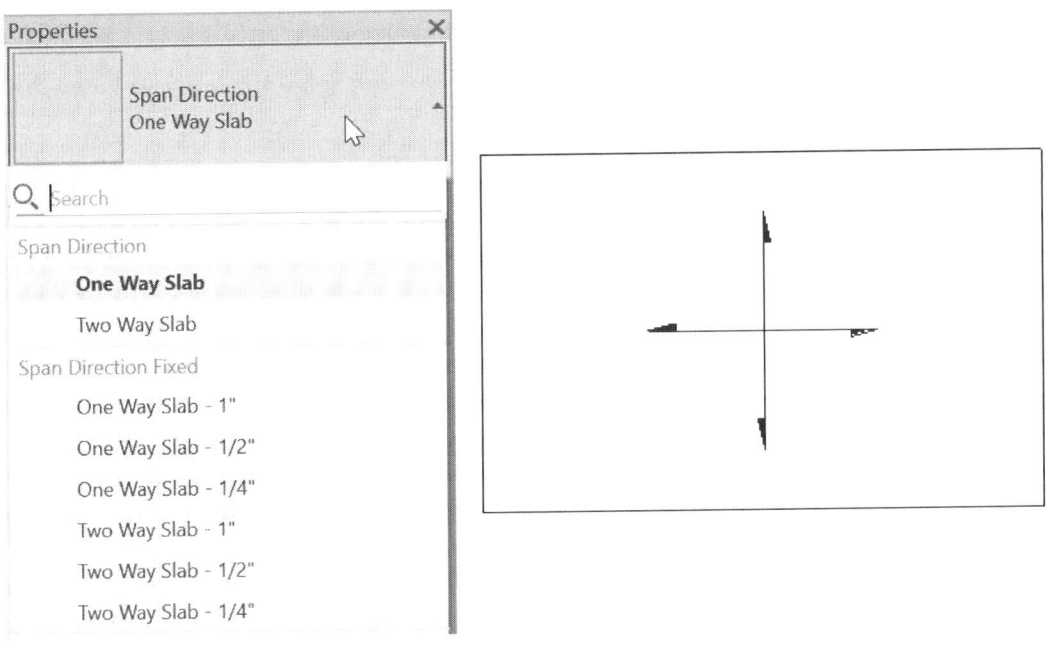

Figure 12-65

How To: Change the Span Direction

1. Select the Span Direction symbol.
2. In the *Modify | Span Direction Symbol* tab>Align Symbol panel, click (Align Perpendicular).
3. Select the side of the slab that you want the span to be perpendicular to.
4. The Span Direction Symbol changes direction, as shown in Figure 12-66.

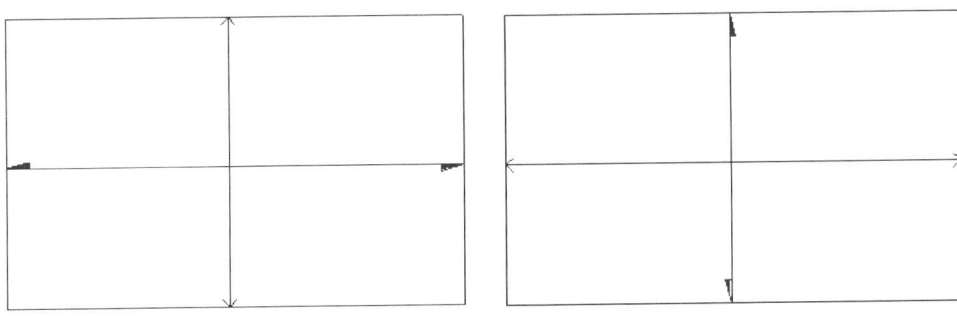

Figure 12-66

12.4 Creating Legends

A legend is a separate view that can be placed on multiple sheets. Legends can be used to hold installation notes that need to be placed on a sheet with each floor plan, key plans, or any 2D items that need to be repeated. You can also create and list the annotations, line styles, and symbols that are used in your project, and provide explanatory notes next to the symbol, as shown in Figure 12-67. Additionally, legends can provide a list of materials or elevations of beam types used in the project.

> *Note: The elements in this figure are inserted using the **Symbol** command rather that the **Legend Component** or **Detail Component** commands.*

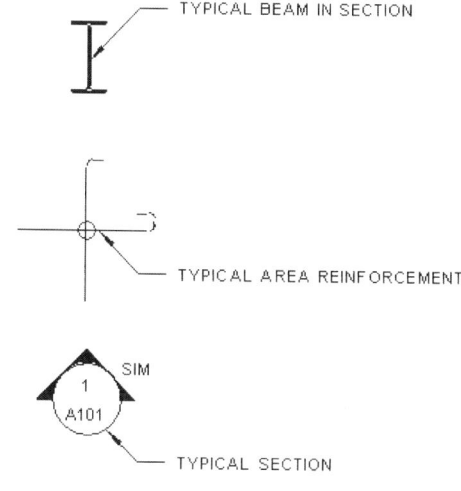

Figure 12-67

- You use (Detail Line) and (Text) to create the table and explanatory notes. Once you have a legend view, you can use commands, such as (Legend Component), (Detail Component), and (Symbol), to place elements in the view.
- Unlike other views, legend views can be attached to more than one sheet.
- You can set a legend's scale in the View Control Bar.
- Elements in legends can be dimensioned.

Working with Annotations

How To: Create a Legend

1. In the *View* tab>Create panel, expand (Legends) and click (Legend), or in the Project Browser, right-click on the *Legends* area title and select **Legend**.
2. In the New Legend View dialog box, enter a name and select a scale for the legend, as shown in Figure 12–68, then click **OK**.

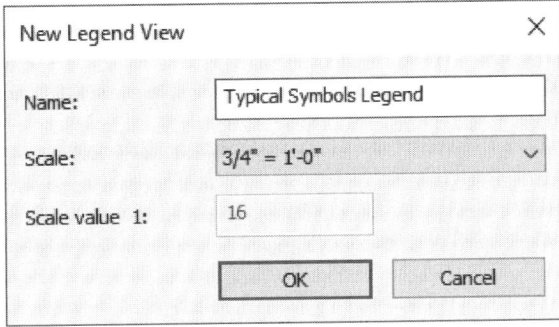

Figure 12–68

3. Place the components in the view first, and then sketch the outline of the table when you know the sizes. Use the **Reference Plane** command to line up the components.

How To: Use Legend Components

1. In a legend view, in the *Annotate* tab>Detail panel, expand (Detail Component) and click (Legend Component).
2. In the Options Bar, select the *Family* type that you want to use, as shown in Figure 12–69.
   - This list contains all of the elements in the project that can be used in a legend. For example, you might want to display the elevation of all door types used in the project.

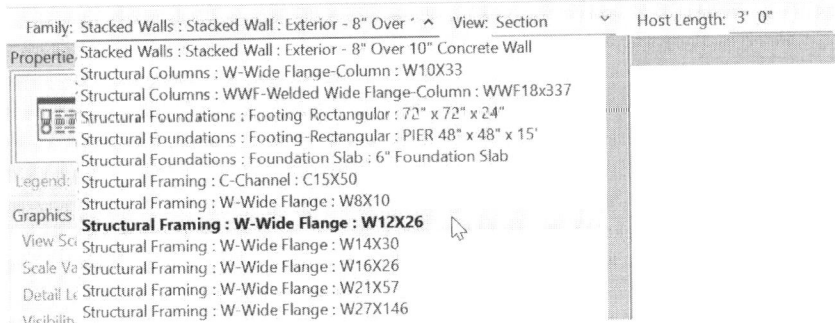

Figure 12–69

3. Select the *View* of the element that you want to place. For example, you might want to display the section or elevation of the structural slabs (as shown in Figure 12–70).

Figure 12–70

4. For section elements (such as walls, floors, and roofs), type a distance for the *Host Length*.

- Elements that are full size, such as planting components or doors, come in at their full size.
- Legends are views that can be placed on multiple sheets. You can use **Copy to the Clipboard** and **Paste** to copy legends from sheet to sheet.

Practice 12c
Create Legends

Practice Objective

- Create legends using legend components and text.

In this practice, you will add a legend and populate it with legend components, symbols, associated text, and detail lines (as shown in Figure 12–71), as well as create a key plan for use on multiple sheets.

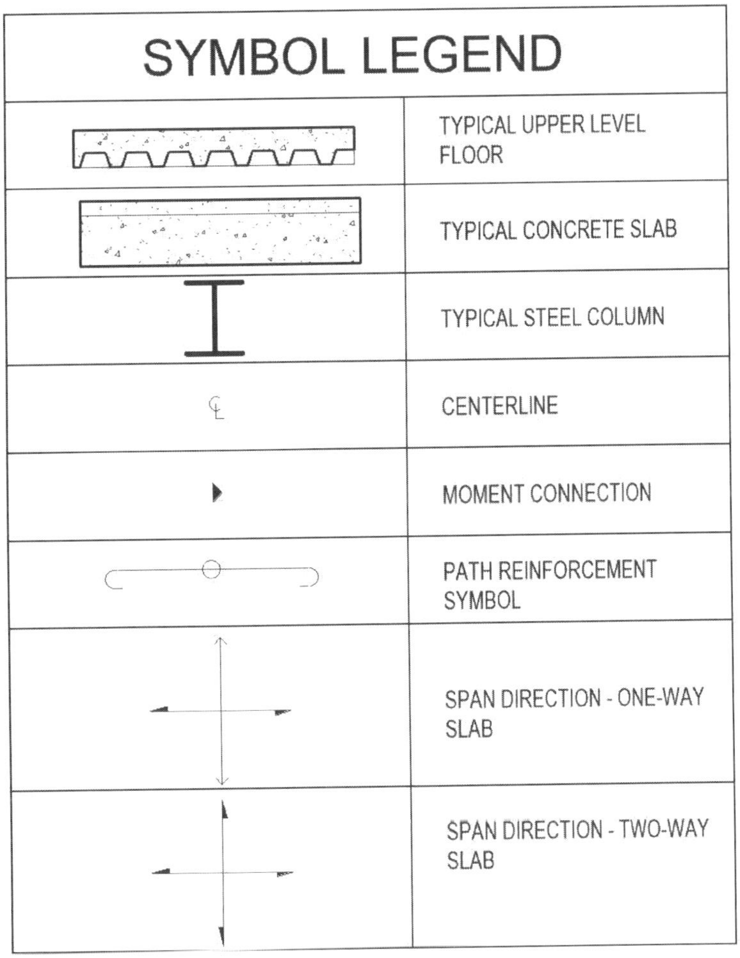

Figure 12–71

Task 1: Add a symbol legend.

1. Open **Structural-Legends.rvt** from the practice files folder.

2. In the *View* tab>Create panel, expand ▦ (Legends) and click ▦ (Legend).
3. In the New Legend View dialog box, set the *Name* to **Typical Symbols Legend** and set the *Scale* to **3/4" = 1'-0"**, as shown in Figure 12–72.

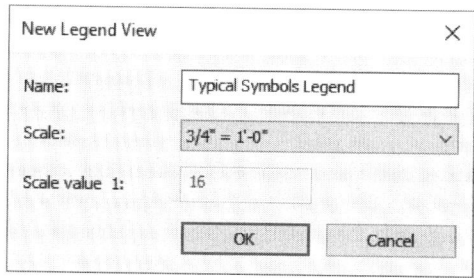

Figure 12–72

4. Click **OK**.

5. In the *Annotate* tab>Detail panel, expand ▦ (Component) and click ▦ (Legend Component).

6. In the Options Bar, set the following, as shown in Figure 12–73:
   - *Family*: **Floors: Floor: 3" LW Concrete on 2" Composite Metal Deck**
   - *View*: **Section**
   - *Host Length*: **4'-0"**

Figure 12–73

7. Click to place the floor legend component in the view.
8. Add the text **TYPICAL UPPER LEVEL FLOOR** close to legend, as shown in Figure 12–74. Adjust the text size from the Type Selector as needed.

Figure 12–74

9. Add several other legend components such as a wall in plan view, a column in section view, and add titles beside them.

10. In the *Annotate* tab>Symbol panel, click ✥ (Symbol).
11. In the Type Selector, select **Centerline**. Place it below at the bottom of the symbol legend and add the text **CENTER OF LINE DESIGNATION** next to it.
12. Add another symbol, **Connection - Moment - Filled**, and label it **MOMENT CONNECTION**.

13. Add several more elements and label them, as shown in Figure 12–75.

14. In the *Annotate* tab>Detail panel, click (Detail Line). Select a Line Style and use (Rectangle) and/or (Line) in the Draw panel to draw a frame around the symbols and text as shown in Figure 12–75, and then at the top of the legend, add the text note **SYMBOL LEGEND** as a title.

    Note: Your legend will vary according to the symbols you selected to add.

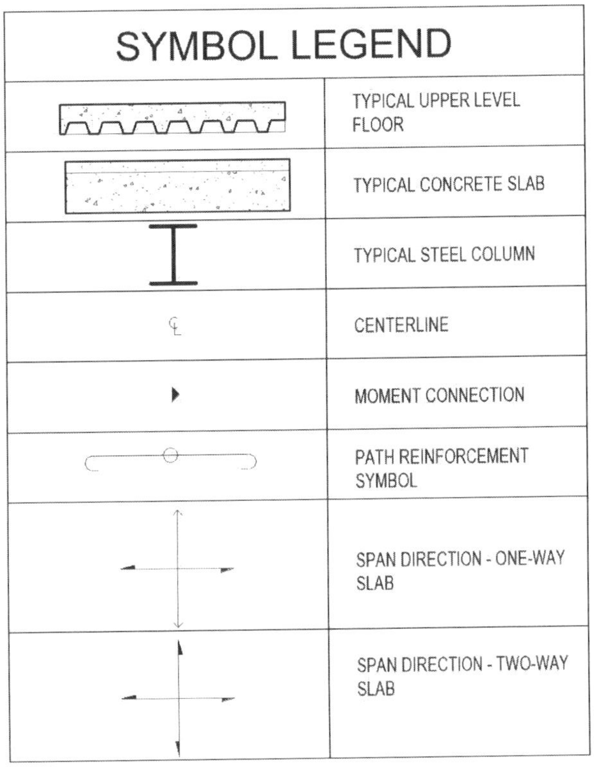

SYMBOL LEGEND	
	TYPICAL UPPER LEVEL FLOOR
	TYPICAL CONCRETE SLAB
	TYPICAL STEEL COLUMN
₵	CENTERLINE
▶	MOMENT CONNECTION
	PATH REINFORCEMENT SYMBOL
	SPAN DIRECTION - ONE-WAY SLAB
	SPAN DIRECTION - TWO-WAY SLAB

Figure 12–75

15. Save the project.

Task 2: Create a key plan legend.

1. Open the **Structural Plans: 00 GROUND FLOOR** view.
2. Select everything in the view. Open Filter and uncheck Structural Foundations and leave everything else checked.
3. Temporarily hide elements in view.

4. We do not need the footings, select everything in the view again this time press <Shift> and select the foundation slab, as shown in Figure 12–76.

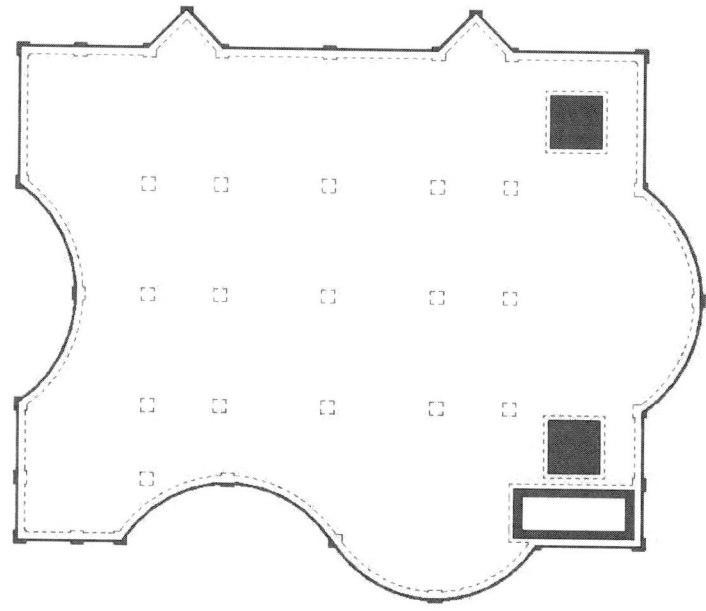

Figure 12–76

5. Temporarily hide the selected elements in view.
6. Only the **Foundation Slab 6" Foundation Slab** should display.
7. In the *Annotate* tab>Detail panel, click (Detail Line).
8. In the *Modify | Place Detail Lines* tab>Line Styles panel, select the *Line Style*: **Wide Lines**.
9. In the Draw panel, click (Pick Lines).
10. Select the lines of the slab all of the way around to establish the key plan outline.
11. Click (Modify) to clear the selection of the lines.
12. Select all of the detail lines. (Hint: Use Filter.)
13. In the *Modify Lines* tab>Clipboard panel, click (Cut to Clipboard). You can also press <Ctrl>+<X>.
14. In the *View* tab>Create panel, expand (Legends) and click (Legend).

15. Give the legend a *Name* and *Scale* as shown in Figure 12–77.

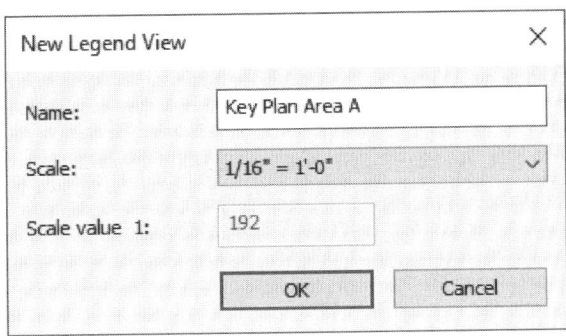

Figure 12–77

16. Click **OK**.
17. Press <Ctrl>+<V> and then click to place the elements.
18. In the *Modify | Detail Groups* tab>Edit Pasted panel, click ✔ (Finish).
19. If you are satisfied with the lines, go back to the **00 GROUND FLOOR** view and reset temporary hide/isolate elements in the view.
20. Modify the outline as required to create a useful key plan, as shown in Figure 12–78.
    - Use **Detail Lines** to divide the outline.
    - Use **Text** to add information. Create a new text size so it is large enough to see.

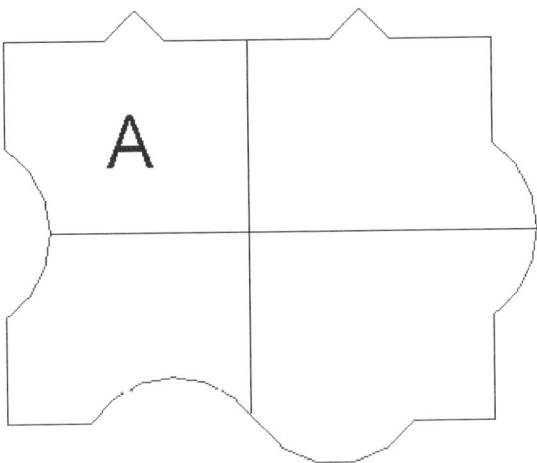

Figure 12–78

*Note: It is important to use the **Duplicate with Detailing** option as **Detail Lines** and **Text** are detail elements.*

21. In the Project Browser, in the *Legends* area, select the **Key Plan Area A** legend view. Right-click and select **Duplicate>Duplicate with Detailing**. This creates a copy of the key plan that you can modify as shown in Figure 12–79.

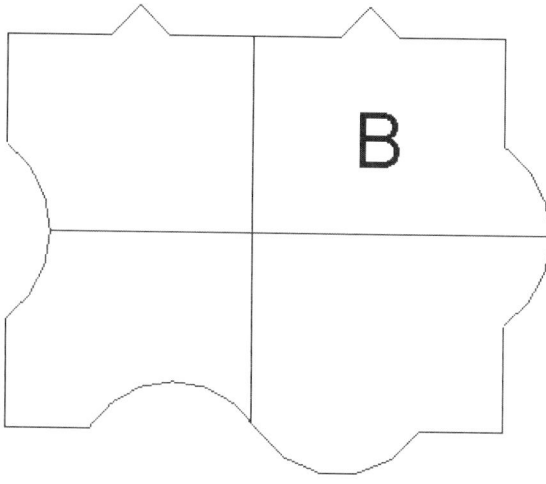

Figure 12–79

22. Save and close the project.

End of practice

Chapter Review Questions

1. When a wall is moved (as shown in Figure 12–80), how do you update the dimension?

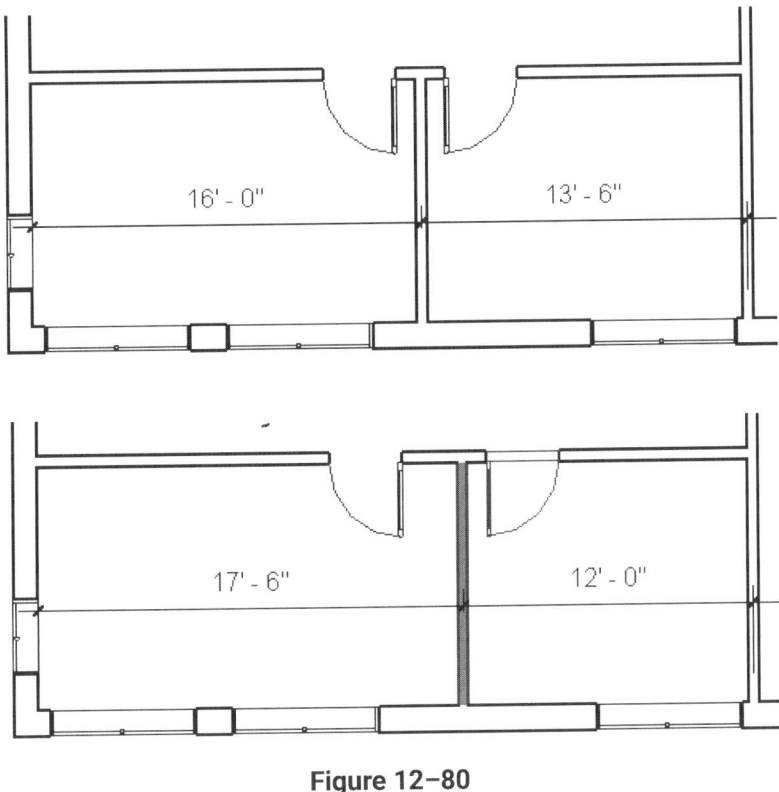

Figure 12–80

    a. Edit the dimension and move it over.

    b. Select the dimension and then click **Update** in the Options Bar.

    c. The dimension automatically updates.

    d. Delete the existing dimension and add a new one.

2. How do you create new text styles?

    a. Using the **Text Styles** command.

    b. Duplicate an existing type.

    c. They must be included in a template.

    d. Using the **Format Styles** command.

3. When you edit text, how many leaders can be added using the leader tools shown in Figure 12–81?

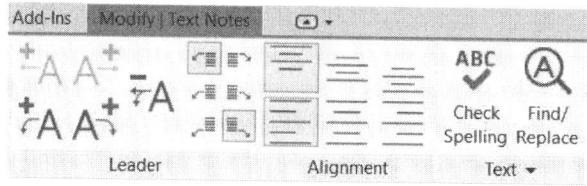

Figure 12–81

   a. One
   b. One on each end of the text
   c. As many as you want at each end of the text

4. Detail lines created in one view also display in the related view.
   a. True
   b. False

5. Which of the following describes the difference between a symbol and a component?
   a. Symbols are 3D and only display in one view. Components are 2D and display in many views.
   b. Symbols are 2D and only display in one view. Components are 3D and display in many views.
   c. Symbols are 2D and display in many views. Components are 3D and only display in one view.
   d. Symbols are 3D and display in many views. Components are 2D and only display in one view.

6. When creating a legend, which of the following elements cannot be added?
   a. Legend components
   b. Tags
   c. Rooms
   d. Symbols

Command Summary

Button	Command	Location
Dimensions and Text		
	Aligned (Dimension)	• **Ribbon:** *Annotate* tab>Dimension panel or *Modify* tab>Measure panel, expanded drop-down list • **Quick Access Toolbar** • **Shortcut:** DI
	Angular (Dimension)	• **Ribbon:** *Annotate* tab>Dimension panel or *Modify* tab>Measure panel, expanded drop-down list
	Arc Length (Dimension)	• **Ribbon:** *Annotate* tab>Dimension panel or *Modify* tab>Measure panel, expanded drop-down list
	Diameter (Dimension)	• **Ribbon:** *Annotate* tab>Dimension panel or *Modify* tab>Measure panel, expanded drop-down list
	Linear (Dimension)	• **Ribbon:** *Annotate* tab>Dimension panel or *Modify* tab>Measure panel, expanded drop-down list
	Radial (Dimension)	• **Ribbon:** *Annotate* tab>Dimension panel or *Modify* tab>Measure panel, expanded drop-down list
	Text	• **Ribbon:** *Annotate* tab>Text panel • **Shortcut:** TX
Detail Lines and Symbols		
	Detail Line	• **Ribbon:** *Annotate* tab>Detail panel • **Shortcut:** DL
	Symbol	• **Ribbon:** *Annotate* tab>Symbol panel
Legends		
	Legend (View)	• **Ribbon:** *View* tab>Create panel, expand Legends
	Legend Component	• **Ribbon:** *Annotate* tab>Detail panel, expand Component

Chapter 13

Adding Tags and Schedules

Adding tags to your views helps you to identify elements such as doors, windows, or walls in the model. Tags are 2D annotation families with labels that extract information about the elements being tagged from their properties. Tags are typically added when you insert an element, but can also be added at any point in the design process.

Schedules are used to gather information stored in the various elements in the project and present them in a table format. In Revit®, you can create schedules specifically for structural projects, such as building component schedules, material takeoff schedules, and graphical column schedules. These schedules can then be added to sheets to create construction documentation.

Learning Objectives

- Add tags to elements in 2D and 3D views to prepare the views to be placed on sheets.
- Load tags that are required for projects.
- Understand schedules and their use in a project.
- Create and modify graphical column schedules that show the number, location, and height of columns.
- Modify schedule content, including the instance and type properties of related elements.
- Add schedules to sheets as part of the construction documents.

13.1 Adding Tags

Tags are used to identify elements in a project. When placing certain elements, such as beams and columns, you can select **Tag on Placement** from the ribbon and a tag will be placed along with the element. Revit supplies tags for every category in the family library, which can then be placed on elements in the drawing anytime during the design process. Figure 13–1 shows elements that have been tagged.

> **Note:** Additional tags are stored in the Revit Library in the Annotations folder.

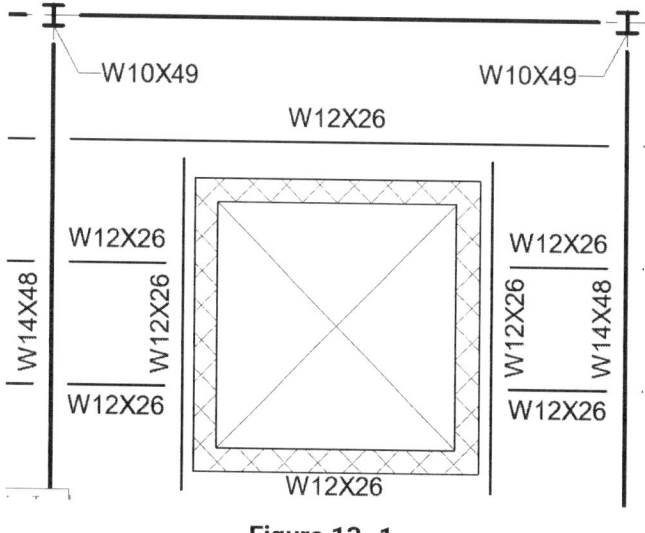

Figure 13–1

- The **Tag by Category** command works for most elements, except for a few that have separate commands.

- Tags can be letters, numbers, or a combination of the two.

You can place three types of tags, as follows:

- (Tag by Category): Tags according to the category of the element. It places door tags on doors and wall tags on walls.

- (Multi-Category Tag): Tags elements belonging to multiple categories. The tags display information from parameters that they have in common.

- (Material Tag): Tags that display the type of material. They are typically used in detailing.

How To: Add Tags

1. In the *Annotate* tab>Tag panel, click (Tag by Category), (Multi-Category Tag), or (Material Tag) depending on the type of tag you want to place.
2. In the Options Bar, set the options as needed, as shown in Figure 13–2.

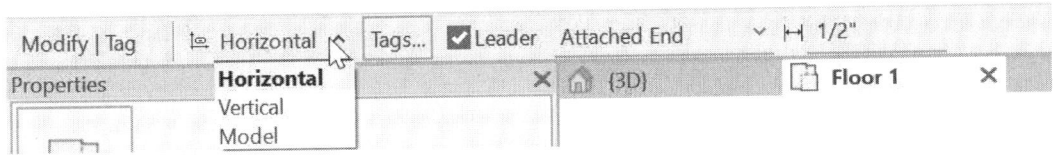

Figure 13–2

3. Select the element you want to tag. If a tag for the selected element is not loaded, you are prompted to load it from the Revit Library.

Tag Options

- In the Options Bar, you can set tag options for leaders and tag orientation, as shown in Figure 13–3. You can also press <Spacebar> to toggle the rotation while placing or modifying the tag.

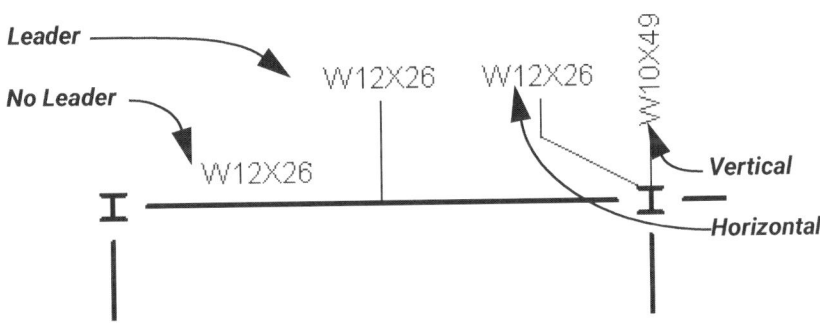

Figure 13–3

- Tag orientation can be set to the following:
    - **Horizontal:** Tag stays horizontal (0°) to the element it is tagging.
    - **Vertical:** Forces the tag to stay vertical (90°) to the element it is tagging no matter what.
    - **Model:** Tag rotates freely from the element, similar to room tags.

- Leaders can have an **Attached End** or a **Free End**, as shown in Figure 13–4. The attached end must be connected to the element being tagged. A free end has an additional drag control where the leader touches the element.

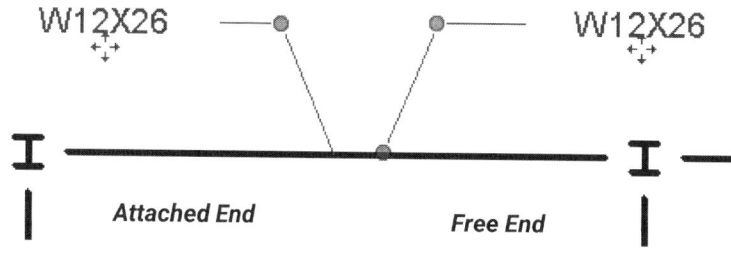

Figure 13–4

- If you change between **Attached End** and **Free End**, the tag does not move and the leader does not change location.

- The **Length** option specifies the length of the leader in plotting units. It is grayed out if **Leader** is not selected or if a **Free End** leader is defined.

- If a tag is not loaded, a No Tag Loaded dialog box opens, as shown in Figure 13–5. Click **Yes** to open the Load Family dialog box in which you can select the appropriate tag.

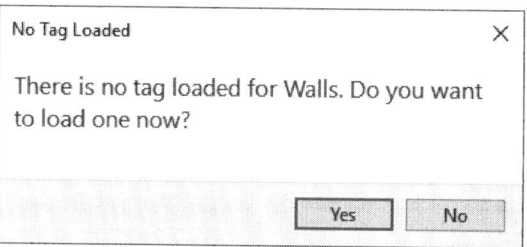

Figure 13–5

- Tags can be pinned so they stay in place if you move the element that is tagged. This is primarily used when tags have leaders, as shown in Figure 13–6.

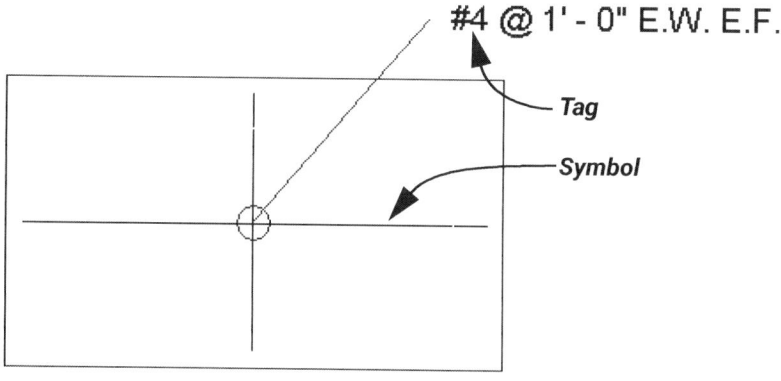

Figure 13–6

Multi-Leader Tags

If you have elements that need to be tagged that are in close proximity to one another, you can tag one element and then select other similar elements. This adds more leader lines from the elements to the tag, as shown with the beams in Figure 13–7. When selecting the tag, you can see how many host elements it is tagging in Properties (as shown on the left in Figure 13–7).

You cannot select elements that are of different categories, like a beam and a column. You can only select similar elements to share a tag, like all beams or all columns.

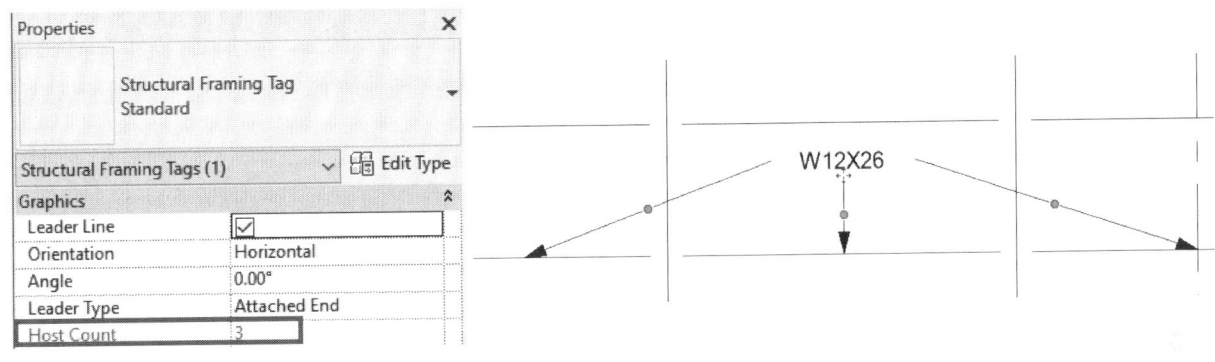

Figure 13–7

If you select, for instance, both structural framing joists and girders that are different sizes, you will get a <varies> tag, as shown in Figure 13–8, because they are not the same size.

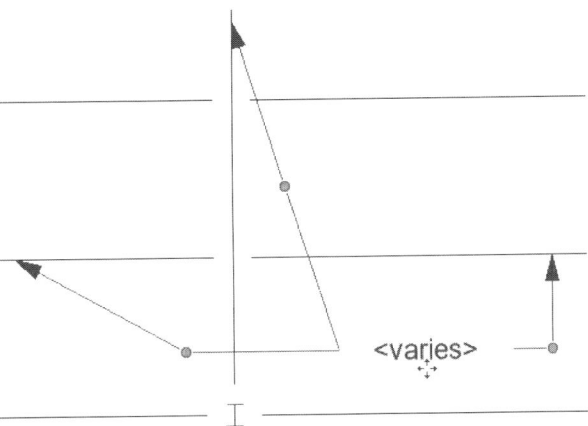

Figure 13–8

You can modify how the leaders are displayed when using the multi-leader tags. You can adjust how they will display in the view by showing all leaders, hiding select leaders, or hiding all leaders.

(Show All Leaders)	This turns on all leaders of any tag that is selected that used Multi-Leader tagging.
(Hide All Leaders)	This turns off all leaders of any tag that is selected that used Multi-Leader tagging.

(Show One Leader)	This turns off all leaders except for one leader of any tag that is selected that used Multi-Leader tagging.
(Select Leaders to Show)	This puts you into edit mode and enables you to select specific leaders to show or hide. When finished, you need to click ✔ (Finish).
(Merge Leaders)	Select to turn this feature on. This will merge all the leader line elbows to one location on the main leader line. You will not have the ability to adjust the leader lines individually. To get the leader line elbows back, select the **Merge Leaders** icon.

How To: Add a Multi-Leader Tag

1. Start the **Tag by Category** command.
2. Set the Options Bar settings.
3. Tag one element in the model.
4. Verify **Add/Remove Host** is on, as shown in Figure 13–9.

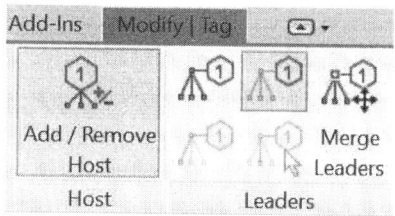

Figure 13–9

5. Select the other similar elements to add to the tag.
- Alternatively, if you have a tag already placed in the model and you want to add elements to the tag, select the tag, and in the contextual tab, click (Add/Remove Host), then select the other elements.
6. Set the leaders options as needed.
7. A leader line will be added for each element you select.

How To: Remove Elements from a Multi-Leader Tag

1. To remove an element from the tag, select the tag and in the ribbon, select (Add/Remove Host).
2. Select the element in the model. The leader line is removed.

How To: Add Multiple Tags

1. In the *Annotate* tab>Tag panel, click (Tag All).
2. In the Tag All Not Tagged dialog box (shown in Figure 13–10), select the checkbox beside one or more categories to tag. Selecting the checkbox beside the *Category* title selects all of the tags.

   Note: *To tag only some elements, select them before starting this command. In the Tag All Not Tagged dialog box, select* **Only selected objects in current view**.

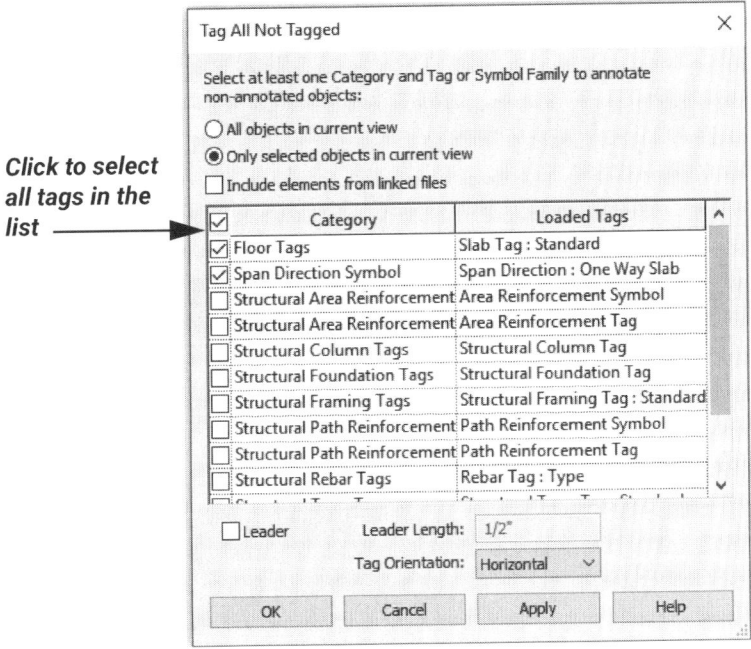

Figure 13–10

3. Set the *Leader* and *Tag Orientation* as needed.
4. Click **Apply** to apply the tags and stay in the dialog box. Click **OK** to apply the tags and close the dialog box.

- When you select a tag, the properties of that tag display. To display the properties of the tagged element, in the *Modify* contextual tab>Host panel, click (Select Host).

How To: Load Tags

1. In the *Annotate* tab, expand the Tag panel and click (Loaded Tags And Symbols) or, when a Tag command is active, in the Options Bar, click **Tags...**.
2. In the Loaded Tags And Symbols dialog box (shown in Figure 13–11), click **Load Family...**.

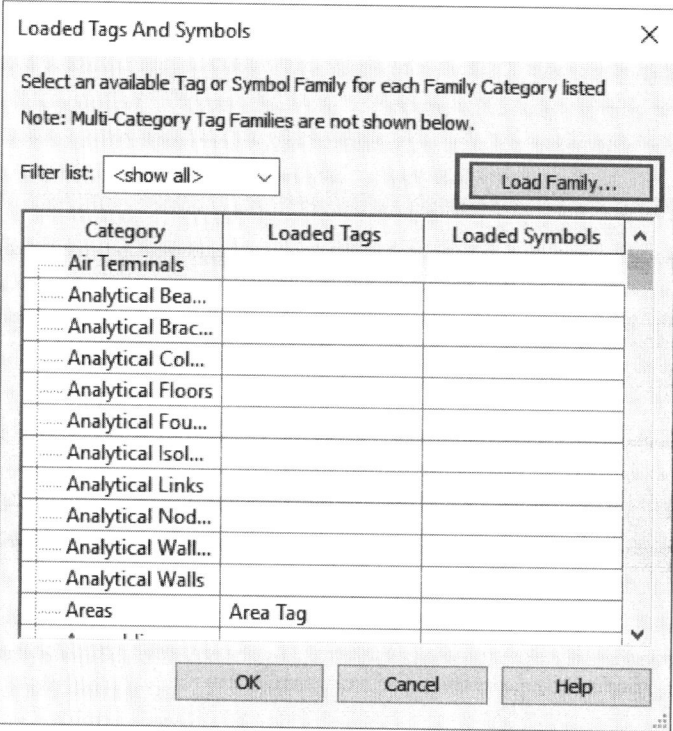

Figure 13–11

3. In the Load Family dialog box, navigate to the appropriate *Annotations* folder in the Revit Library, select the tag(s) needed, and click **Open**.
4. The tag is added to the category in the dialog box. Click **OK**.

Instance vs. Type Based Tags

Many elements (such as doors) are tagged in a numbered sequence, with each instance of the element having a separate tag number. Other elements (such as trusses and walls) are tagged by type. Changing the information in one tag changes all instances of that element.

- To modify the number of an instance tag (such as a door), slowly click twice directly on the number in the tag and modify it, or you can modify the *Mark* property. Only that one instance updates.

- To modify the number of a type tag, you can slowly click twice directly on the number or letter in the tag and modify it. Alternatively, you can select the element and in Properties, click ▦ (Edit Type). In the Type Properties dialog box, in the *Identity Data* section, modify the *Type Mark*, as shown in Figure 13–12. All instances of this element then update.

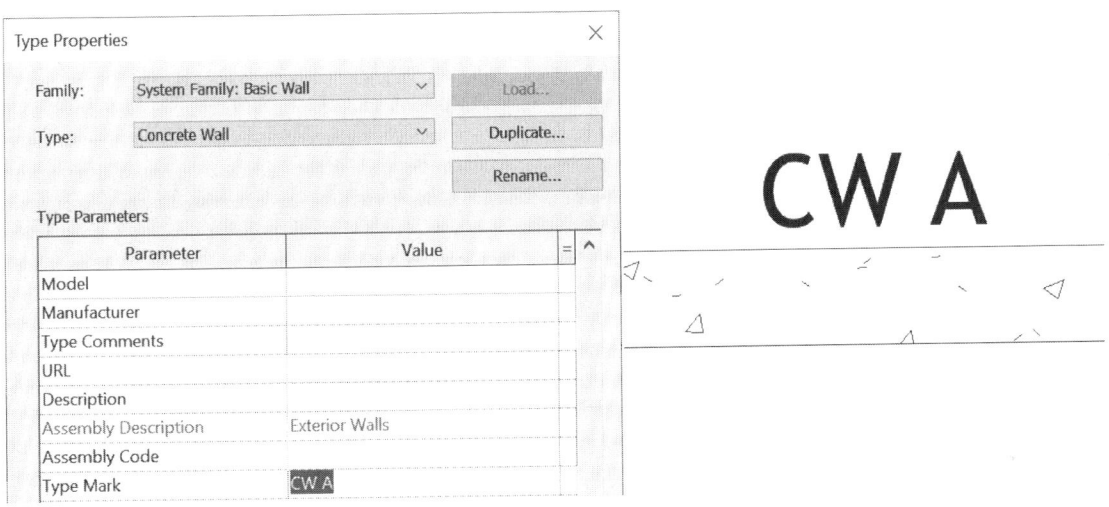

Figure 13–12

- When you change a type tag, an alert box opens to warn you that changing a type parameter affects other elements, as shown in Figure 13–13. If you want this tag to modify all other elements of this type, click **Yes**.

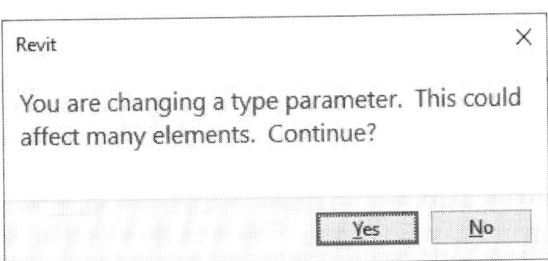

Figure 13–13

- If a tag displays with a question mark, it means that no information has been assigned to that element's parameter yet.

Tagging in 3D Views

You can add tags to isometric 3D views, as shown in Figure 13–14, as long as the views are locked first. Locking a 3D view enables you to create the view as you want it and then save it from being modified.

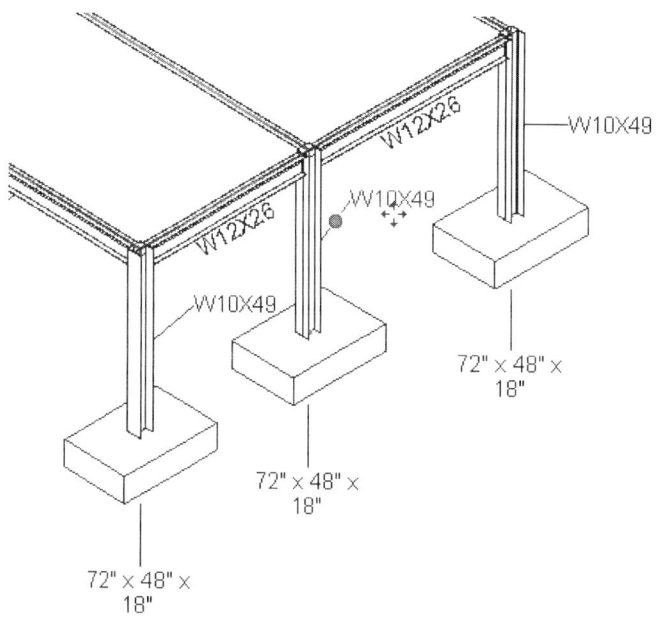

Figure 13–14

- You must lock an isometric 3D view in order to place tags. Dimensions can be added to isometric 3D views whether they are locked or not. Proceed with caution when selecting the items to dimension to ensure that the witness lines and text orient is snapping to and extending in the correct direction as intended. Locked views can be used with perspective views. This enables you to create the view as you want it and then save it from being modified. You cannot tag or add dimensions in a perspective view, as these are views created with the camera tool.

How To: Lock a 3D View

1. Open a 3D view and set it up as you want it to display.

   Note: When adding text in a 3D view, you do not have to lock the view. When tagging in a 3D view, you have to lock the view.

2. In the View Control Bar, click (Unlocked 3D View), then click (Save Orientation and Lock View).

- If you are using the default 3D view and it has not been saved, you are prompted to name and save the view first.

Adding Tags and Schedules

- You can modify the orientation of the view by clicking (Locked 3D View), then clicking (Unlock View). This also removes any tags you have applied.

- To return to the previous locked view, click (Unlocked 3D View), then click (Restore Orientation and Lock View).

Beam Annotations

The Beam Annotation tools enable you to place beam tags, annotations, and spot elevations to all elements in a view, as shown in Figure 13–15.

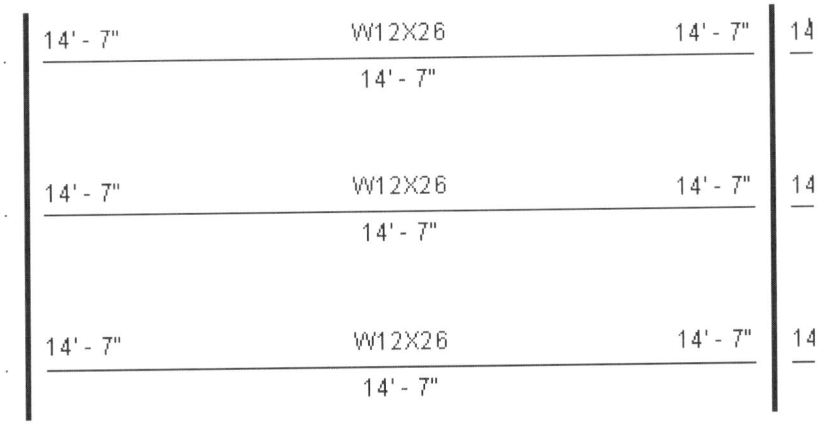

Figure 13–15

- Beam annotations can be put at the end points and midpoints on either side of beams. You can also specify different annotations for level beams and sloped beams.
- To limit the number of beams that are annotated, select them first and then start the command. Otherwise, all of the beams in a view are annotated.
- Beams in linked files can be included.
- You can replace existing annotations or leave them in place without duplicating them.
- You can define values for steel connection parameters, including releases and member forces. These values can be used by the designer, fabricator, and analysis applications. They are available for use in schedules and annotations.

How To: Place Beam Annotations

1. In the *Annotate* tab>Tag panel, click (Beam Annotations).
2. In the Beam Annotations dialog box (shown in Figure 13–16), specify the locations of the annotation at which you want them to display on each beam.

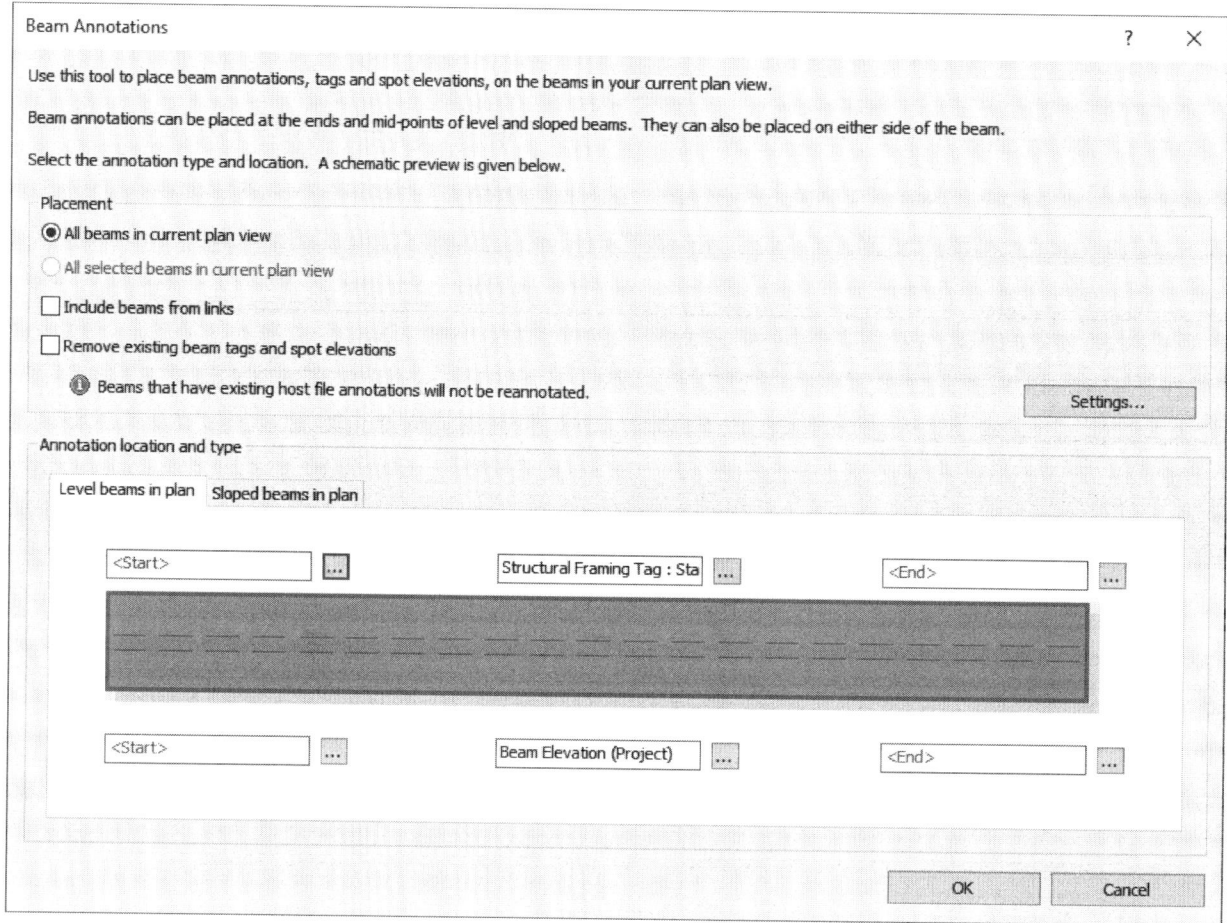

Figure 13–16

3. To change the type of annotation at various locations, click ▭ (Browse) next to the edit box to open the Select Annotation Type dialog box. In the *Select Element to Place* area, specify an option, such as the **Spot Elevation** shown in Figure 13–17. The option you select modifies the information you can specify.

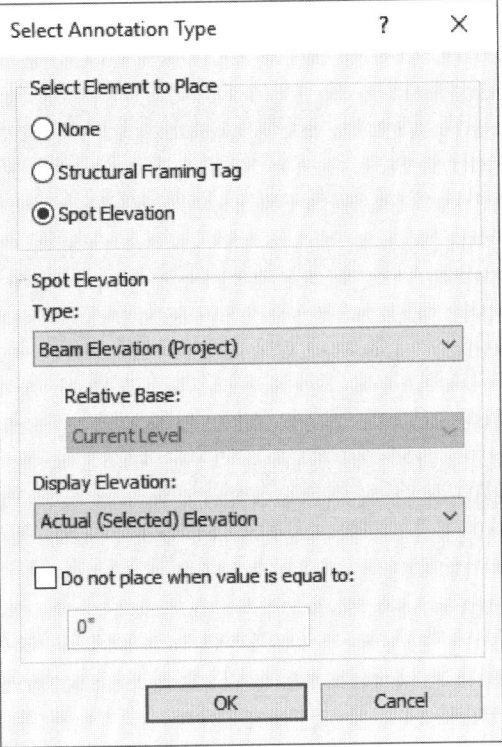

Figure 13–17

4. Specify the options in the dialog box and click **OK**.
5. Click **OK** to place the beam annotations.

Beam System Symbols vs. Framing Tags

Beam systems can be annotated by either tagging each individual beam, or by using a beam system symbol, as shown in Figure 13-18. When placing a beam system, you can select (Tag on Placement), and in the Options Bar, set the *Tag Style* to either **Framing** or **System**. The *Framing* option tags each beam in the system, while the *System* option applies a beam system symbol.

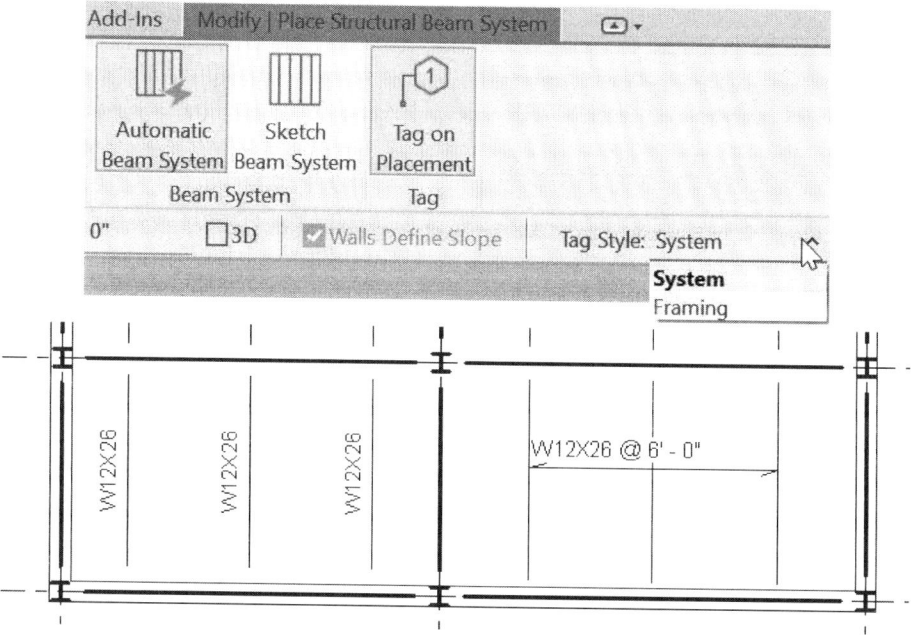

Figure 13-18

- To add the individual framing tags later, use the (Tag by Category) command. To add a beam system symbol, use the (Beam System Symbol) command.

Practice 13a
Add Tags and Symbols

Practice Objectives

- Add tags.
- Place beam system symbols.

In this practice, you will tag some framing elements using the **Tag by Category** command and the **Beam System Symbol.** You will then use **Tag All Not Tagged** to tag the rest of the framing elements. You will then add the rest of the beam system symbols, as shown in Figure 13–19.

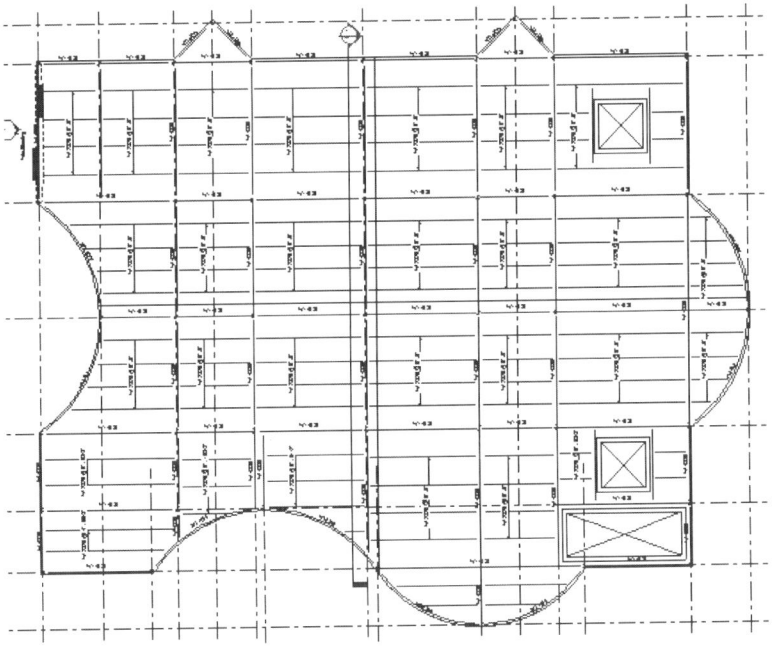

Figure 13–19

Task 1: Tag framing elements using Tag by Category and Beam System Symbol.

1. Open **Structural-Tags.rvt** from the practice files folder.
2. Create a duplicate of the **Structural Plans: TOS-1ST FLOOR** view and name it **TOS-1ST FLOOR - Framing**.
3. In the *Annotate* tab>Tag panel, click (Tag by Category).
4. In the Options Bar, ensure that **Leader** is not selected.

5. Tag several of the outside beams, as shown in Figure 13-20.

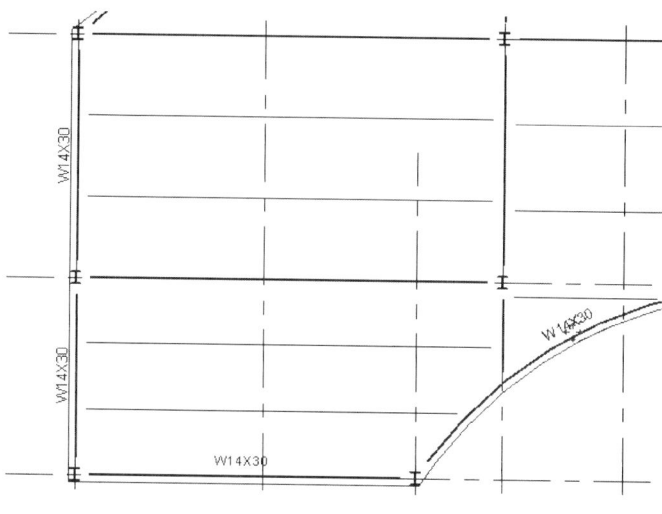

Figure 13-20

6. While remaining in the command, hover the cursor over the inside beams. Note that you can tag each beam separately.

7. Click ⬚ (Modify).

8. In the *Annotate* tab>Symbol panel, click ↑ (Beam).

9. Click on a beam system and then click to place the location of the symbol. It automatically fits to the correct size of the beam system, as shown in Figure 13-21.

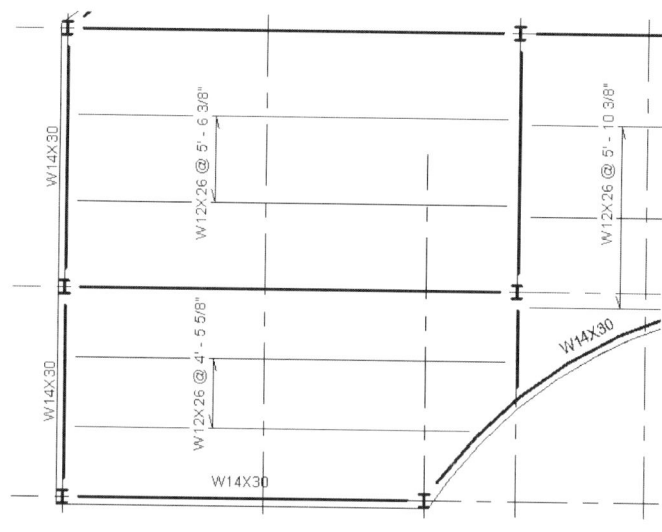

Figure 13-21

10. Save the project.

Adding Tags and Schedules

Task 2: Tag framing elements that are not tagged.

1. Continue working in the **TOS-1ST FLOOR - Framing** view.
2. In the *Annotate* tab>Tag panel, click (Tag All).
3. In the Tagged All Not Tagged dialog box, ensure that **All objects in current view** is selected.
4. Browse to the *Structural Framing* category and select **Structural Framing Tag: Standard**, as shown in Figure 13–22. Click **OK**.

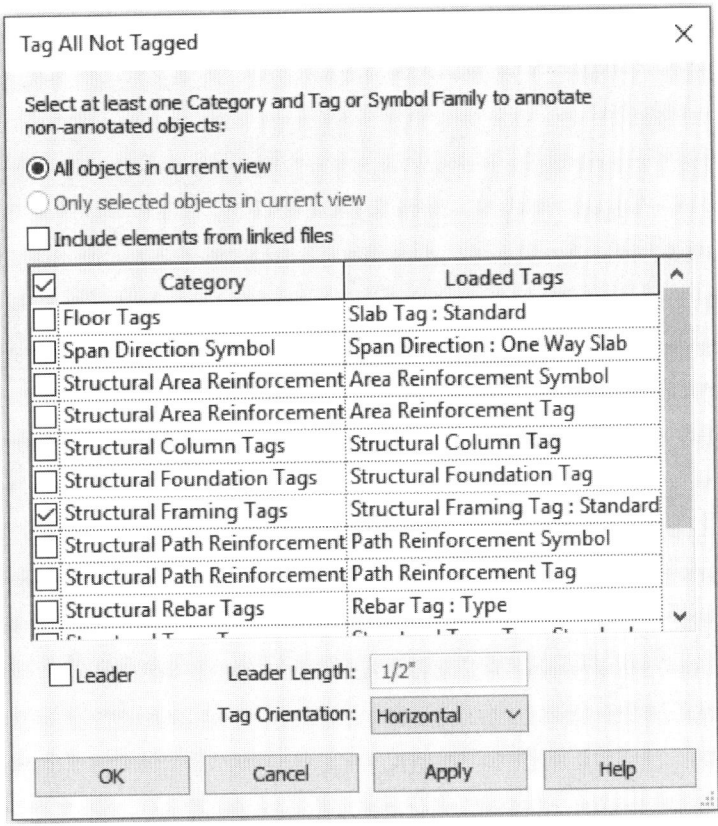

Figure 13–22

5. This tags all of the structural framing elements, including each one of the beams in the beam systems.
6. Undo the tagging.
7. Select one of the beam system joist beams in the framing system.

8. Right-click and select **Select All Instances>Visible in View**. All of the joists that are the same are selected, as shown in Figure 13–23.

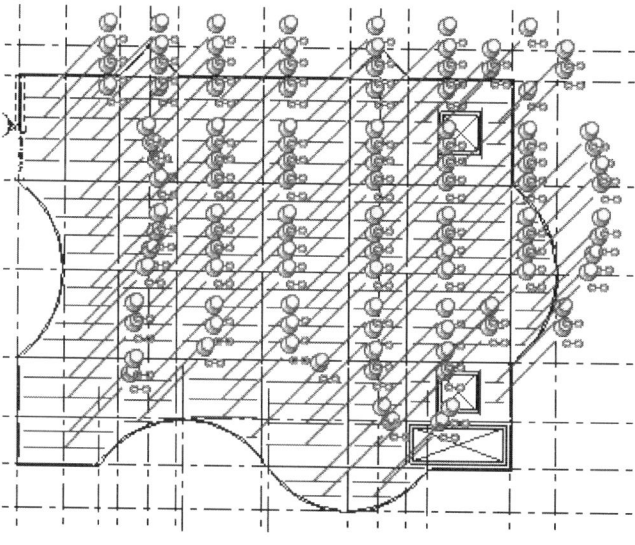

Figure 13–23

9. In the View Control Bar, select (Temporary Hide/Isolate) and then select **Hide Element**. (Do not hide the category as you still want to be able to tag the rest of the beams.

10. Run the (Tag All) command again, selecting the same structural framing tag.

11. This time only the non-joist beams are tagged.

12. In the View Control Bar, select (Temporary Hide/Isolate) and then select **Reset Temporary Hide/Isolate**. The beam system joists display once again.

13. The Beam System Symbol is not available in **Tag All Not Tagged**, therefore you need to use the (Beam System Symbol) command to tag the rest of these. Use the alignment lines to help you place the symbols relative to other nearby symbols.

14. Zoom to fit the view.

15. If you have time, you can apply the various reinforcement symbols to other views as applicable.

16. Save and close the project.

End of practice

13.2 Working with Schedules

- Revit enables you to quickly create accurate schedules that can otherwise be time-consuming and difficult to maintain accurately throughout the lifecycle of a project. When you add model elements to a project, the schedule automatically updates to include the elements. Some of the default Revit templates have schedules included in them. For example the **Imperial Multi-discipline.rte** template file includes useful schedules. If there are no schedules in a project, you can create one of the following types of schedules:

  - (Schedule/Quantities) allows you to create building component schedules of elements in your project.

  - (Graphical Column Schedule) allows you to create a schedule for specific columns or all columns in the project including off-grid columns.

- Schedules can be created in templates so that they can be reused in multiple projects.
- You are not required to have actual elements in the model when you are creating schedules. You can schedule information that model elements contain.
- All properties that are stored in the model elements, as well as those specified by the user, can be added to schedules.

Building Component Schedules

A building component schedule is a table view of the type and instance parameters of a specific element. You can specify the parameters (fields) you want to include in the schedule. All of the parameters found in the type of element you are scheduling are available for use.

- Schedules are automatically filled out with the information stored in the instance and type parameters of related elements that are added to the model. Fill out additional information either in the schedule or in Properties.
- When selecting on a schedule's row, it will highlight in blue.
- You can drag and drop the schedule onto a sheet.
- You can zoom in to read small text in schedule views. Hold down <Ctrl> and scroll using the mouse wheel or press <Ctrl>+<+> to zoom in or <Ctrl>+<-> to zoom out.

For example, a concrete column schedule (as shown in Figure 13–24) can include instance parameters that are automatically filled in (such as the **Height** and **Width**) and type parameters that may need to be filled in manually in the schedule or element type (such as the **Fire Rating** and **Frame**), as shown in Figure 13–24.

<Concrete Column Material Takeoff>

A	B	C		D	E	F
		Dimensions				
Type Mark	Count	Type		Length	Base Level	Material
A	6	12 x 18		10' - 0"	Level 1	Concrete, Cast-in-Place gray
B	6	18 x 24		12' - 0"	T.O. Footing	Concrete, Cast-in-Place gray
C	14	24 x 30		12' - 0"	T.O. Footing	Concrete, Cast-in-Place gray
Grand total: 26						

Figure 13–24

How To: Create a Schedule

1. In the *View* tab>Create panel, expand (Schedules) and click (Schedule/Quantities), or in the Project Browser, right-click on the **Schedules/Quantities** node and select **New Schedule/Quantities**.

2. In the New Schedule dialog box, select the type of schedule you want to create (e.g., Structural Beam Systems) from the *Category* list, as shown in Figure 13–25.

   Note: *In the Filter list drop-down list, you can specify the discipline(s) to show only the categories that you want to display.*

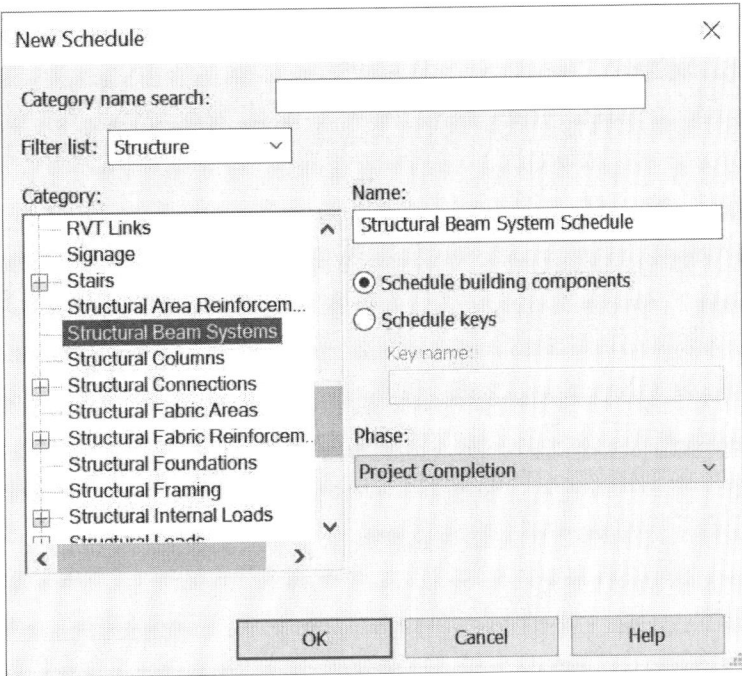

Figure 13-25

3. Revit assigns a name for the schedule. You can also type a new *Name* if the default does not suit.
4. Select **Schedule building components**.
5. Specify the *Phase*, as needed.
6. Click **OK**.
7. Fill out the information in the Schedule Properties dialog box. This includes the information in the *Fields, Filter, Sorting/Grouping, Formatting,* and *Appearance* tabs.
8. Once you have entered the schedule properties, click **OK**. A schedule view is created, displaying a report of the information configured in the schedule.

- Other elements that can be scheduled include model groups and Revit links.
- If a schedule is long, in the *Modify Schedule/Quantities* tab>Appearance panel, you can select (Freeze Header) to keep the header row visible while you scroll through the schedule.

Schedule Properties – Fields Tab

In the *Fields* tab, you can select from a list of available fields and organize them in the order in which you want them to display in the schedule, as shown in Figure 13–26. You can also sort the available fields by *Parameter Type* (such as Project Parameters), *Discipline*, or *Value Type*.

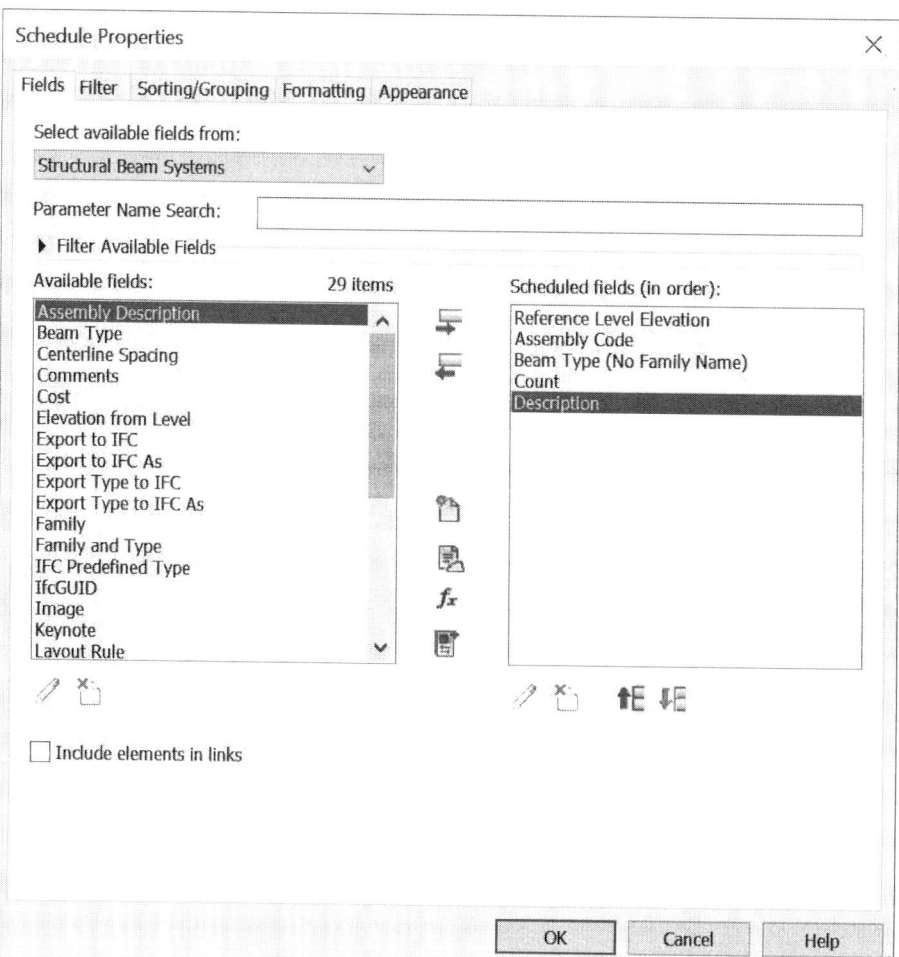

Figure 13–26

Adding Tags and Schedules

How To: Fill Out the Fields Tab

1. In the *Available fields* area, select one or more fields you want to add to the schedule and click ⬇ (Add parameter(s)). The field(s) are placed in the *Scheduled fields (in order)* area.
2. Continue adding fields, as required.

   - Click ⬆ (Remove parameter(s)) to move a field from the *Scheduled fields* area back to the *Available fields* area.

   Note: You can also double-click on a field to move it from the Available fields area to the Scheduled fields area, and double-click on a field to remove it from the Scheduled fields area.

   - Use ↑E (Move parameter up) and ↓E (Move parameter down) to change the order of the scheduled fields.

Other Fields Tab Options

Select available fields from	Enables you to select additional category fields for the specified schedule. The available list of fields depends on the original category of the schedule. Typically, they include room information.
Include elements in links	Includes elements that are in files linked to the current project, so that their elements can be included in the schedule.
(New parameter)	Adds a new field according to your specification. New fields can be placed by instance or by type.
f_x **(Add Calculated parameter)**	Enables you to create a field that uses a formula based on other fields.
(Combine parameters)	Enables you to combine two or more parameters in one column. You can put any fields together even if they are used in another column.
(Edit parameter)	Enables you to edit custom fields. This is grayed out if you select a standard field.
(Delete parameter)	Deletes the selected custom fields. This is grayed out if you select a standard field.

Schedule Properties – Filter Tab

In the *Filter* tab, you can set up filters so that only elements meeting specific criteria are included in the schedule. For example, you might only want to show information for one level, as shown in Figure 13–27. You can create filters for up to eight values. All values must be satisfied for the elements to display.

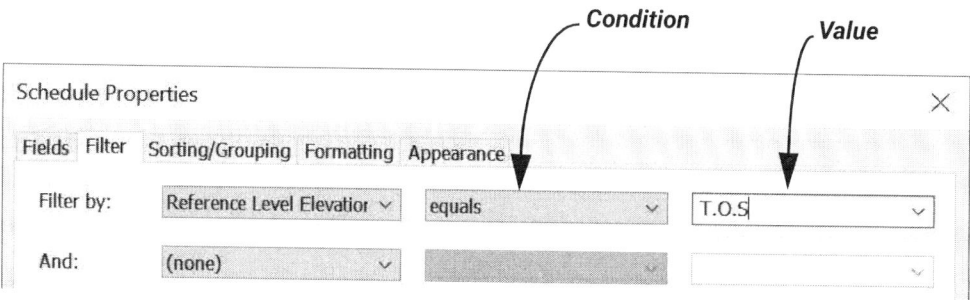

Figure 13–27

- The parameter you want to use as a filter must be included in the schedule. You can hide the parameter once you have completed the schedule, if needed.

Filter by	
Field/Parameter	Specifies the field/parameter to filter. Not all fields/parameters are available to be used to filter.
Condition	Specifies the condition that must be met. This includes options such as **equal**, **not equal**, **greater than**, and **less than**.
Value	Specifies the value of the element to be filtered. You can select from a drop-down list of appropriate values. For example, if you set *Filter by* to **Level**, it displays the list of levels in the project.

Schedule Properties – Sorting/Grouping Tab

In the *Sorting/Grouping* tab, you can set how you want the information to be sorted, as shown in Figure 13–28. For example, you can sort by **Mark** (number) and then **Type**.

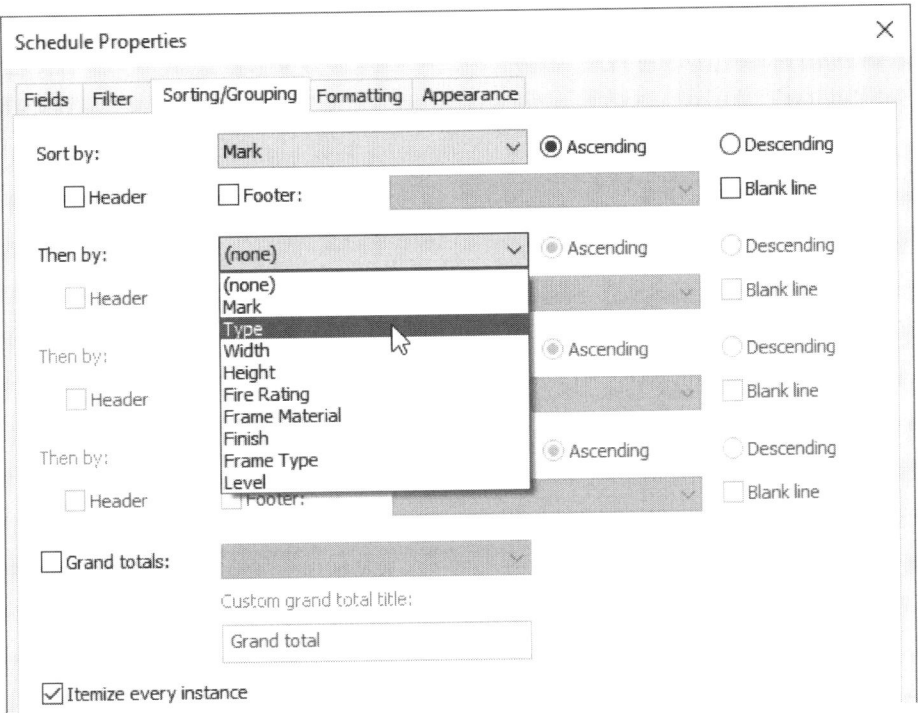

Figure 13–28

Sort by	Enables you to select the field(s) you want to sort by. You can select up to four levels of sorting.
Ascending/ Descending	Sorts fields in **Ascending** or **Descending** order based on an alphanumeric system.
Header/Footer	Enables you to group similar information and separate it by a **Header** with a title and/or a **Footer** with quantity information.
Blank line	Adds a blank line between groups.
Grand totals	Selects which totals to display for the entire schedule. You can specify a name to display in the schedule for the grand total.
Itemize every instance	If selected, displays each instance of the element in the schedule. If not selected, displays only one instance of each type based on the sorting/grouping categories.

Schedule Properties – Formatting Tab

In the *Formatting* tab, you can control how the headers of each field display, as shown in Figure 13–29. The *Multiple values indication* options enable you to control how fields with multiple values display.

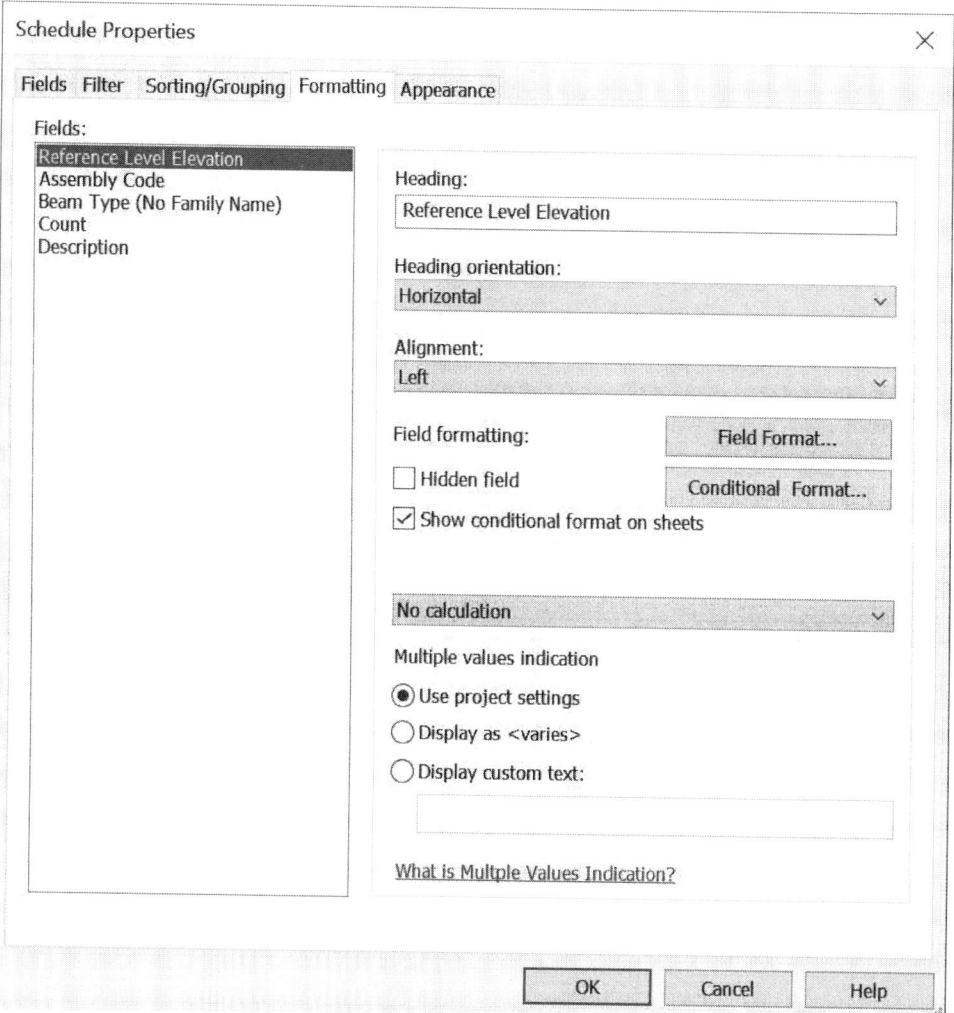

Figure 13–29

Adding Tags and Schedules

Fields	Enables you to select the field for which you want to modify the formatting.
Heading	Enables you to change the heading of the field if you want it to be different from the field name. For example, you might want to replace **Mark** (a generic name) with the more specific **Door Number** in a door schedule.
Heading orientation	Enables you to set the heading on sheets to **Horizontal** or **Vertical**. This does not impact the schedule view.
Alignment	Aligns the text in rows under the heading to be **Left**, **Right**, or **Center** justified.
Field Format...	Sets the units format for numerical fields, e.g., length, area, HVAC air flow, pipe flow, etc. By default, this is set to use the project settings.
Conditional Format...	Sets up the schedule to display visual feedback based on the conditions listed.
Hidden field	Enables you to hide a field. For example, you might want to use a field for sorting purposes, but not have it display in the schedule. You can also modify this option in the schedule view later.
Show conditional format on sheets	Select if you want the color code set up in the Conditional Format dialog box to display on sheets.
Calculation options	Select the type of calculation you want to use. • **No Calculation:** All values in a field are calculated separately. • **Calculate totals:** All values in a field are added together. This enables a field to calculate and display in the Grand Totals or Footers. • **Calculate minimum:** Only the smallest amount displays. • **Calculate maximum:** Only the largest amount displays. • **Calculate minimum and maximum:** Both the smallest and largest amounts display. Minimum and maximum calculations only show when **Itemize every instance** is unchecked in the *Sorting/Grouping* tab.
Multiple values indication	When a schedule is not set to itemize every instance, select how the value will display.

> 💡 **Hint: Hiding Columns**
>
> If you want to use the field to filter or sort, but do not want it to display in the schedule, select **Hidden field**. Alternatively, once the schedule is completed, select the column header, right-click on it, and select **Hide Columns**.

Schedule Properties – Appearance Tab

In the *Appearance* tab, you can set the text style and grid options for a schedule, as shown in Figure 13–30.

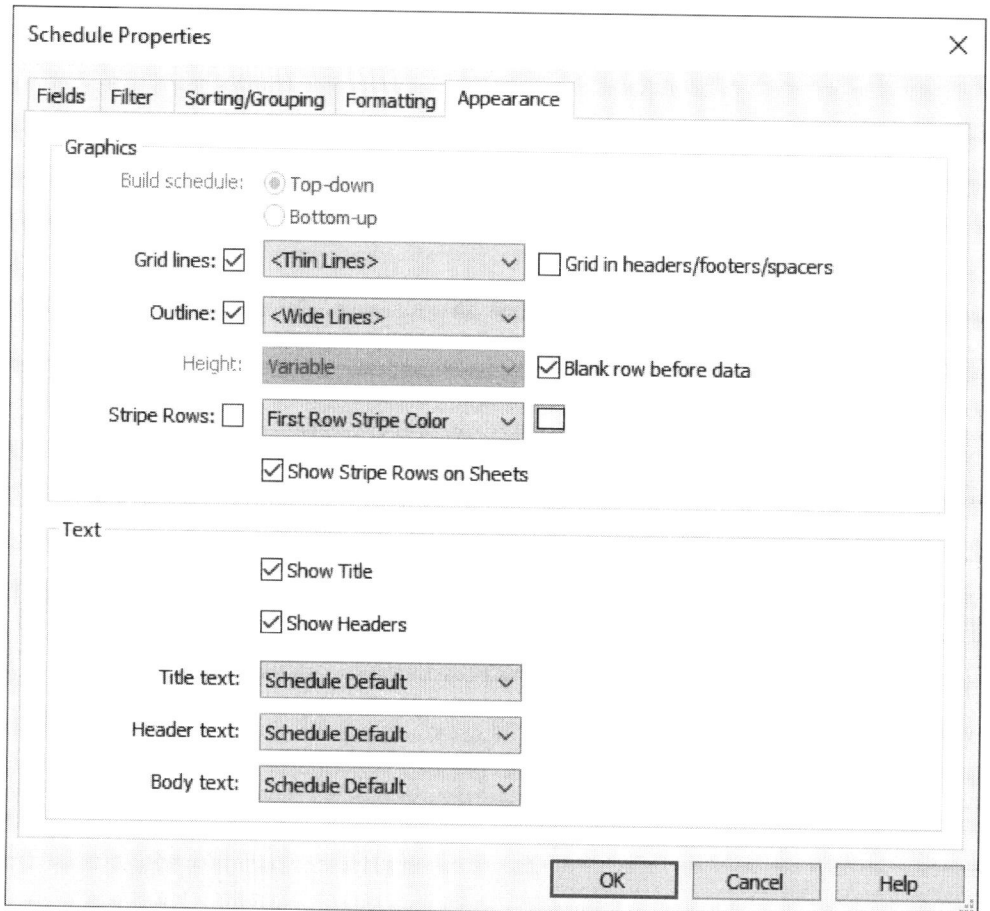

Figure 13–30

Grid lines	Displays lines between each instance listed and around the outside of the schedule. Select the style of lines from the drop-down list; this controls all lines for the schedule, unless modified.
Grid in headers/footers/ spacers	Extends the vertical grid lines between the columns.
Outline	Specify a different line type for the outline of the schedule.
Blank row before data	Select this option if you want a blank row to be displayed before the data begins in the schedule.
Stripe Rows	Select this option if you want to highlight alternating rows within the schedule to help differentiate the rows in large schedules.

Show Title/Show Headers	Select these options to include the text in the schedule.
Title text/Header text/ Body text	Select the text style for the title, header, and body text.

Schedule View Properties

Schedule views have properties, including the *View Template, View Name, Phases*, and methods of returning to the Schedule Properties dialog box (as shown in Figure 13–31). In the *Other* section, click the button next to the tab name that you want to open in the Schedule Properties dialog box. In the dialog box, you can switch from tab to tab and make any required changes to the overall schedule.

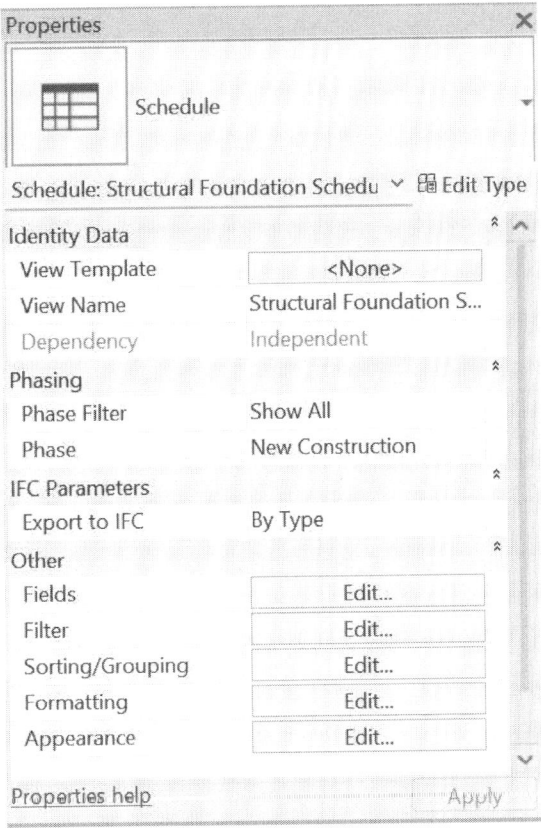

Figure 13–31

Just like other views, schedules can have view templates applied. When you specify a view template directly in the view, none of the schedule properties can be modified, as shown in Figure 13–32.

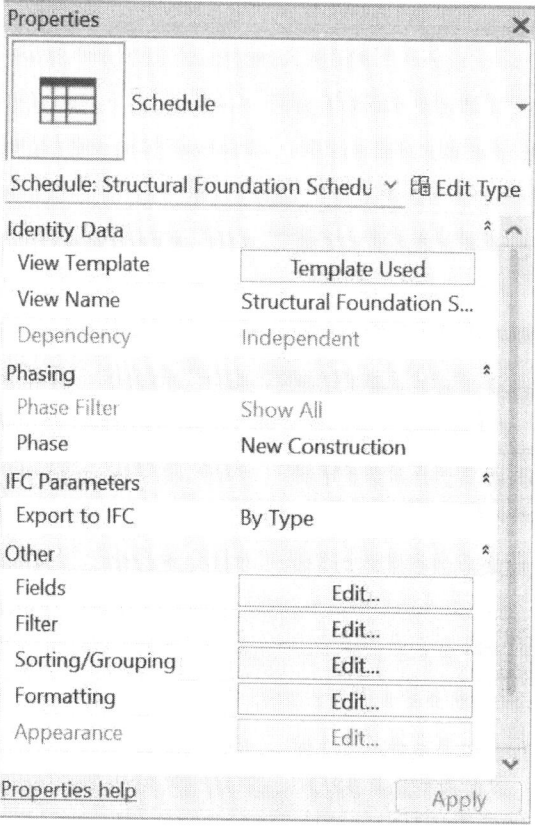

Figure 13–32

- Schedule view templates are type-specific. If you apply one to a different type of element, only the *Appearance* information is applied.

- If you apply a schedule view template to a schedule of the same type, it overrides everything in the existing schedule, including the fields.

- If you have a complicated schedule, you might want to create a view template for it to avoid losing that organization.

- To create schedule view templates, you need to create at least one from an existing view, then you can modify it and duplicate it in the View Templates dialog box.

Filtering Elements from Schedules

When you create schedules based on a category, you might need to filter out some of the element types in that category. For example, in Revit, doors (and windows) in curtain walls are automatically added to a door schedule, as shown at the top in Figure 13–33, but are typically estimated as part of the curtain wall rather than as a separate door. To remove them from the schedule, as shown at the bottom in Figure 13–33, assign a parameter that identifies them and then use that parameter to filter them out of the schedule.

All structural foundations displayed

\<Structural Foundation Schedule\>				
A	B	C	D	E
Family and Type	Level	Width	Foundation Thickness	Count
Wall Foundation: Bearing Footing - 42" x		3' - 6"	2' - 0"	17
Footing-Rectangular: PIER 48" x 48" x 15'	00 GROUND FLOOR	4' - 0"		42
Foundation Slab: 6" Foundation Slab	00 GROUND FLOOR	155' - 3 15/32"	0' - 6"	1
Footing-Rectangular: 72" x 72" x 24"	00 T.O. FOOTING	6' - 0"		42

Footings filtered out

\<Structural Foundation Schedule\>				
A	B	C	D	E
Family and Type	Level	Width	Foundation Thickness	Count
Wall Foundation: Bearing Footing - 42" x		3' - 6"	2' - 0"	17
Foundation Slab: 6" Foundation Slab	00 GROUND FLOOR	155' - 3 15/32"	0' - 6"	1

Figure 13–33

- This type of filtering can be used for any schedule in any discipline.

How To: Filter Elements in a Schedule

1. Select an element (such as a column) and modify the Type Parameters. Add a value to one of the parameters that you are not otherwise using in your schedule. For example, you could set *Type Mark* to **WSC**, as shown Figure 13–34.

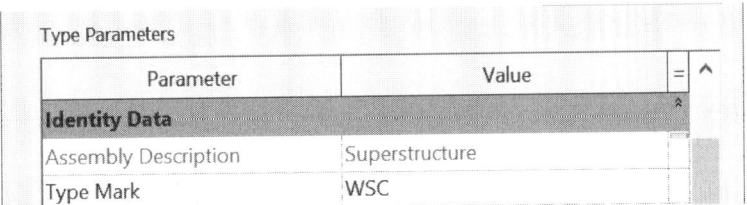

Figure 13–34

2. Create a schedule and include the field for the parameter you used (such as *Type Mark* in the above example).

3. Modify the *Filter* of the schedule so that the parameter does not equal the specified value. In the example shown in Figure 13–35, the filter is set so **Type Mark** > **does not equal** > **WSC**. Any types that match this filter are excluded from the schedule.

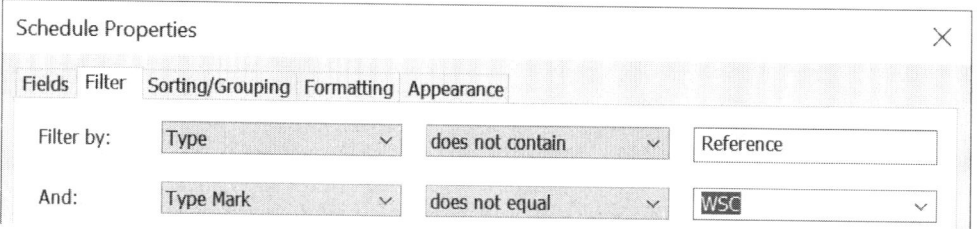

Figure 13–35

4. In the final schedule, the elements display with the specified value. Right-click on the column header for the parameter you used to filter the schedule and select **Hide Columns**. It is just used as a filter and does not need to be part of the final schedule.

***Note:** Hiding a parameter/field in a schedule enables you to use it as a filter, but not have it visible in the schedule.*

Modifying Schedules

Information in schedules is bi-directional:

- Make changes to elements and the schedule automatically updates.
- Make changes to information in the schedule cells and the elements automatically update.

How To: Modify Schedule Cells

1. Open the schedule view.
2. Select the cell you want to change. Some cells have drop-down lists, as shown in Figure 13–36. Others have edit fields.

A	B	C	D	E
Family and Type	Major Direction Wir	Major Spacing	Minor Direction Wir	Minor Spacing
Fabric Sheet: 6	W4.2	0' - 6"	W4.2	0' - 6"
Fabric Sheet: 6	W4.0	0' - 6"	W4.2	0' - 6"
Fabric Sheet: 6	W4.2	0' - 6"	W4.2	0' - 6"
Fabric Sheet: 6	W4.4	0' - 6"	W4.2	0' - 6"
Fabric Sheet: 6	W4.7	0' - 6"	W4.2	0' - 6"
Fabric Sheet: 6	W7.5	0' - 6"	W4.2	0' - 6"
Fabric Sheet: 6	W8.1	0' - 6"	W4.2	0' - 6"
Fabric Sheet: 6	W8.3	0' - 6"	W4.2	0' - 6"
Fabric Sheet: 6	W4.2	0' - 6"	W4.2	0' - 6"
Fabric Sheet: 6	W4.2	0' - 6"	W4.2	0' - 6"

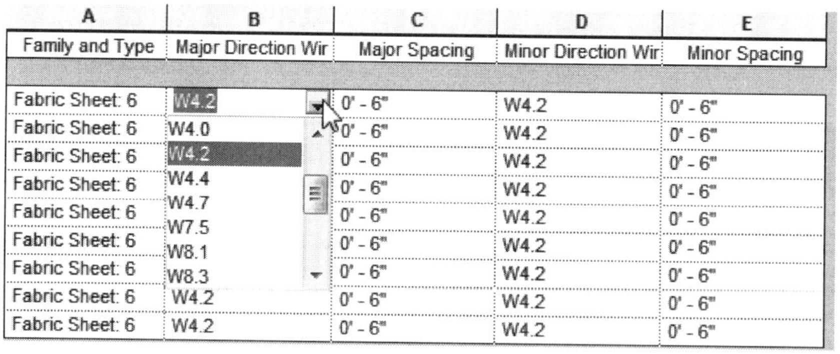

Figure 13–36

3. Add the new information. The change is reflected in the schedule, on the sheet, and in the elements of the project.

- If you change a type property, an alert box opens, as shown in Figure 13–37.

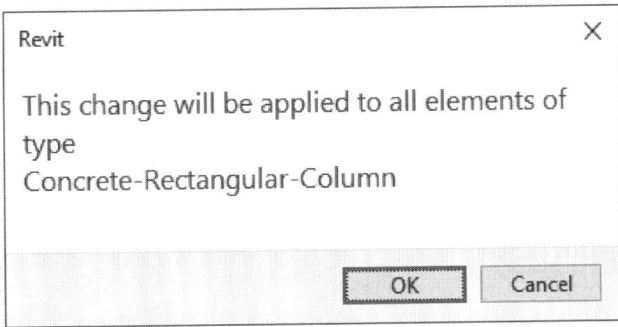

Figure 13–37

Note: If you change a type property in the schedule, it applies to all elements of that type. If you change an instance property, it only applies to that one element.

- When you select an element in a schedule, in the *Modify Schedule/Quantities* tab>Element panel, you can click (Highlight in Model). This opens a close-up view of the element with the Show Element(s) in View dialog box, as shown in Figure 13–38. Click **Show** to display more views of the element. Click **Close** to finish the command.

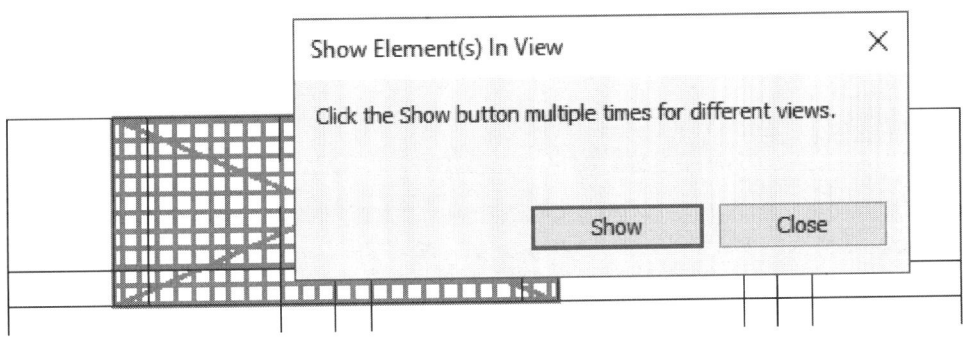

Figure 13–38

Hint: Customizing Schedules

Schedules are typically included in project templates, which are set up by the BIM manager or other advanced users. They can be complex to create as there are many options.

- For information about creating material takeoff schedules, see *B.4 Material Takeoff Schedules*.
- For information on using schedule data outside of Revit, see *B.5 Importing and Exporting Schedules*.
- For more information about creating schedules, refer to the ASCENT guide *Autodesk Revit: BIM Management: Template and Family Creation*.

Modifying a Schedule on a Sheet

Once you have placed a schedule on a sheet, you can manipulate it to fit the information into the available space. Select the schedule to display the controls that enable you to modify it, as shown in Figure 13–39.

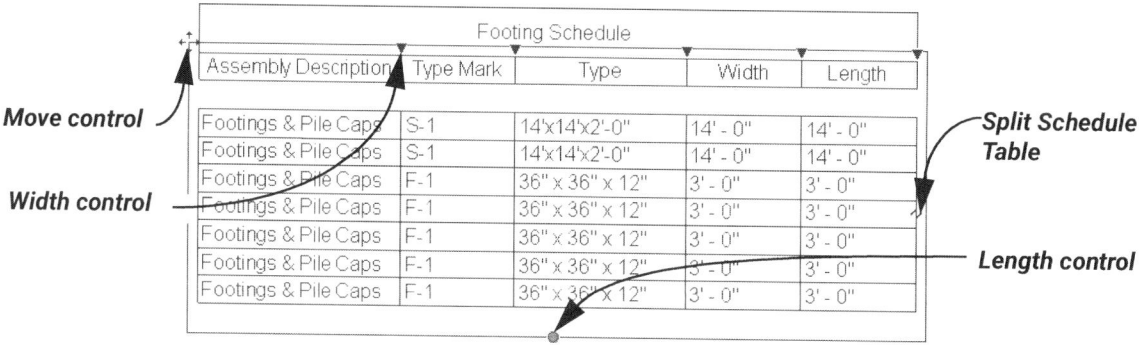

Figure 13–39

- The blue triangles modify the width of each column.
- The break mark splits the schedule into two parts.
- In a split schedule, you can use the arrows in the upper-left corner to move that portion of the schedule table. The control at the bottom of the first table changes the length of the table and impacts any connected splits.
- To unsplit a schedule, drag the Move control from the side of the schedule that you want to unsplit back to the original column.

Split a Schedule Across Multiple Sheets

When a schedule becomes too long, you need to be able to split it and place it on multiple sheets. You can split a schedule evenly or by setting a custom height. When a schedule has been split, you can expand **Schedules/Quantities (all)** in the Project Browser to see the segments of the schedule, as shown in Figure 13–40.

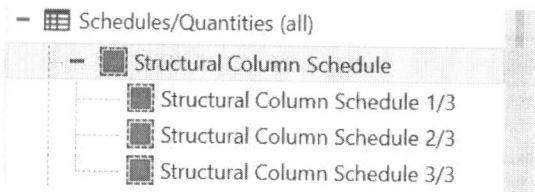

Figure 13–40

If the split is not what you wanted, you can delete the segmented schedules from the Project Browser. Do not delete the main schedule.

How To: Split a Schedule and Place It on Multiple Sheets

1. Make additional sheets, if needed. In a schedule view, in the *Modify Schedule/Quantities* tab>Split panel, click (Split & Place).
2. In the Split Schedule and Place on Sheets dialog box, select the sheets that you want to distribute the split schedule to, as shown in Figure 13–41.

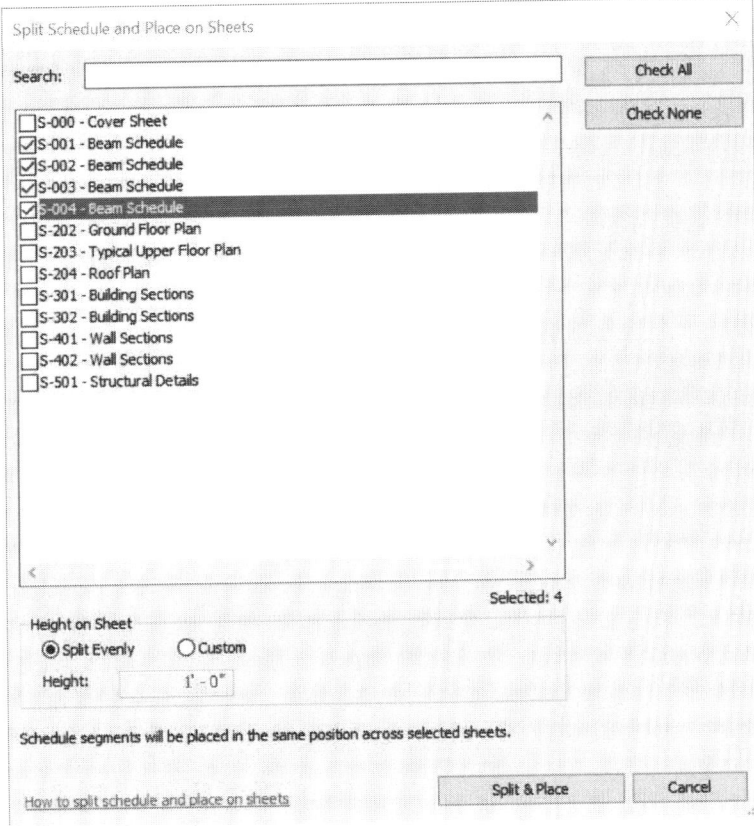

Figure 13–41

3. In the *Height on Sheet* section, select **Split Evenly** or **Custom**. If custom is selected, specify a *Height*.
4. Click **Split & Place**.
5. The first sheet selected in the list opens and the first segment of the split schedule is attached to your cursor. Place it on the sheet.
6. If you had selected multiple sheets in the Split Schedule and Place on Sheets dialog box, the rest of the segment schedule will automatically be placed exactly where you had initially placed the first segment of the schedule.
7. Open each sheet and use the control grips to adjust the columns and stretch the schedule to fit the sheet, as needed.

How To: Remove Split Schedules

1. In the Project Browser, expand the schedule.
2. Select the segmented schedules and press <Delete>, or right-click and select **Delete**.

Filter by Sheet

If you place your schedule on a sheet that has a view on it, you can filter the schedule to only display the elements that are in that viewport. In Figure 13–42, the door schedule is only showing Floor 1 doors because the sheet contains the Floor 1 - Plan view and the **Filter by sheet** option has been selected.

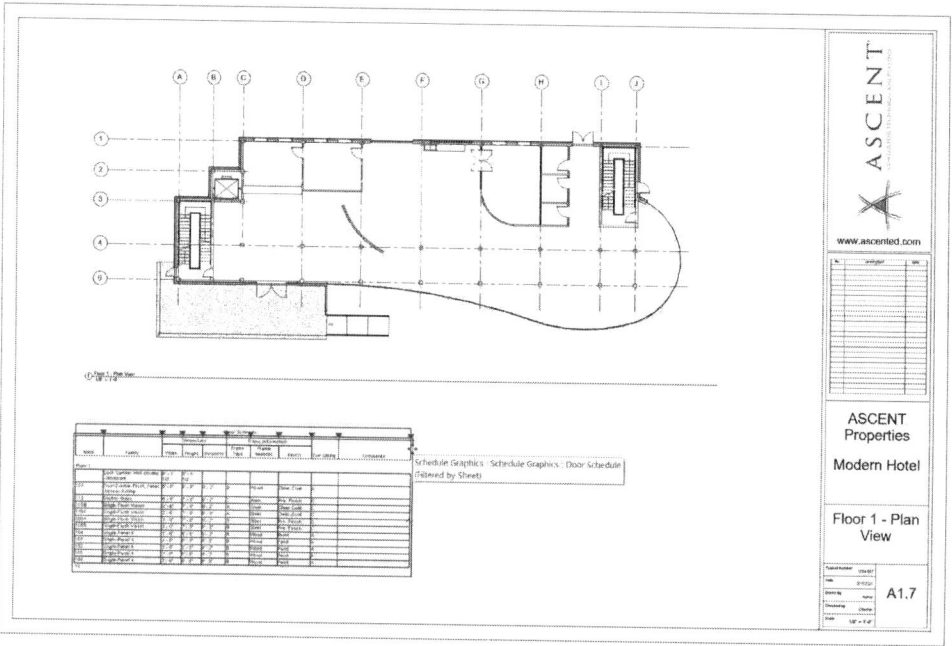

Figure 13–42

- If a view is changed or modified, the schedule and the same sheet will update accordingly.
- Schedules that are split across multiple sheets cannot use the **Filter by sheet** option.
- Panel and revision schedules cannot use the **Filter by sheet** option.

How To: Filter a Schedule by Sheets

1. Open a schedule view.
2. In Properties, click **Edit...** next to *Filter*.
3. In the Schedule Properties dialog box, check the checkbox for **Filter by sheet**, as shown in Figure 13–43.

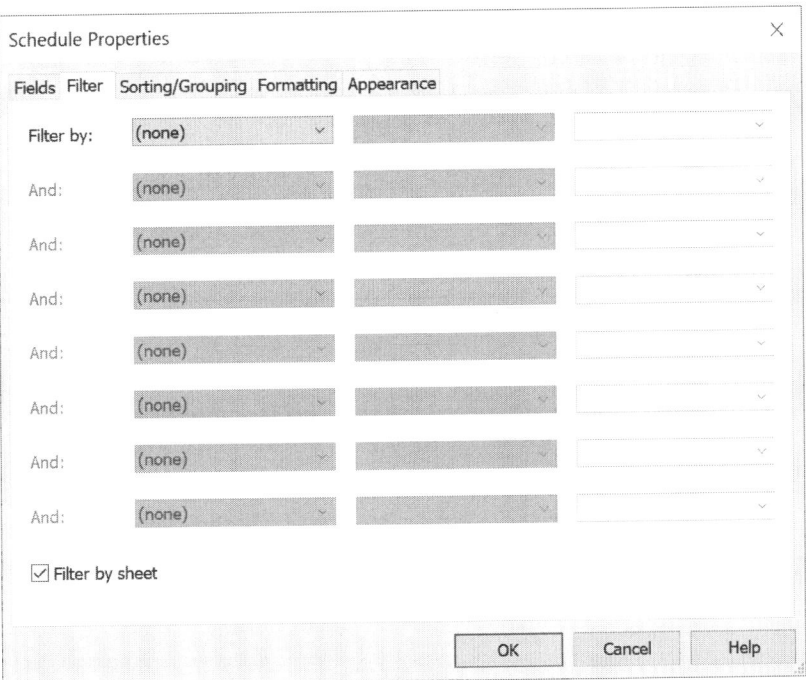

Figure 13–43

4. Click **OK**.
    - You cannot use this feature if you have split the schedule.

Practice 13b
Work with Schedules

Practice Objectives

- Update schedule information.
- Add a schedule to a sheet.

In this practice, you will add *Type Mark* information to a structural elements schedule and the elements that are connected to that schedule. You will then place the schedule on a sheet and add elements in the project. The final information displays as in Figure 13–44.

Structural Elements Schedule		
Type Mark	Family and Type	Count
Structural Columns		
P-1	Concrete-Rectangular-Column: 24 x 24	43
	W-Wide Flange-Column: W8X10	2
	W-Wide Flange-Column: W10X33	41
Structural Foundations		
	Footing-Rectangular: 14'x14'x2'-0"	2
	Footing-Rectangular: 36" x 36" x 12"	43
	Foundation Slab: 6" Foundation Slab	1
W-1	Wall Foundation: Bearing Footing - 24" x 12"	17
W-2	Wall Foundation: Bearing Footing - 36" x 12"	4
Structural Framing		
	HSS-Hollow Structural Section: HSS6X6X.500	28
	K-Series Bar Joist-Rod Web: 14K6	16
	K-Series Bar Joist-Rod Web: 16K7	100
	W-Wide Flange: W12X26	1558
	W-Wide Flange: W14X30	1023

Figure 13–44

Task 1: Review a schedule.

1. Open **Structural-Schedules.rvt** from the practice files folder.
2. In the Project Browser, expand the **Schedules/Quantities (all)** node. Note that four schedules have been added to this project.
3. Double-click on the **Footing Schedule** to open it.
4. Note that the Bearing Footing lengths are shown as **<varies>**, as shown in Figure 13–45, indicating that there is more than one length.

<Footing Schedule>			
A	B	C	D
Type Mark	Type	Width	Length
	6" Foundation Slab	180' - 11 3/4"	180' - 11 3/4"
F-2	14'x14'x2'-0"	14' - 0"	14' - 0"
F-1	36" x 36" x 12"	3' - 0"	3' - 0"
	Bearing Footing - 24" x 12"	2' - 0"	<varies>
	Bearing Footing - 36" x 12"	3' - 0"	<varies>
Grand total: 66			

Figure 13–45

5. In Properties, click **Edit...** next to *Sorting/Grouping*. In the Schedule Properties dialog box, select **Itemize every instance**.

6. Click **OK**.

7. The schedule now lists all the footing types and their lengths.

8. Save the project.

Task 2: Fill in schedules.

1. Open the **3D Views: Foundation View**. This view only displays the foundation elements, including concrete piers, footings, walls, and wall footings.

2. Rotate the view so you can see the stair and elevator shaft openings, as shown in Figure 13–46.

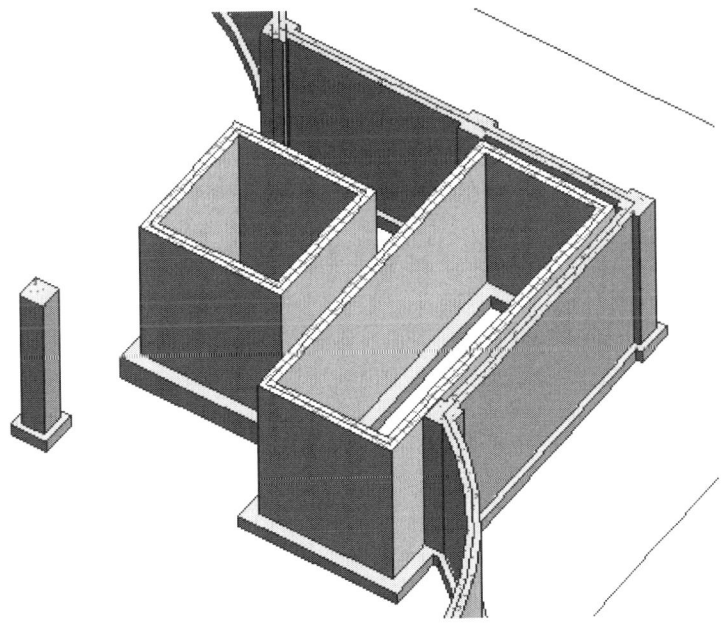

Figure 13–46

3. Close any other open view tabs and projects.

4. Open the **Structural Elements Schedule**. The existing structural elements in the project populate the schedule, as shown in Figure 13–47. Expand the width of the columns, as needed, to read the content.

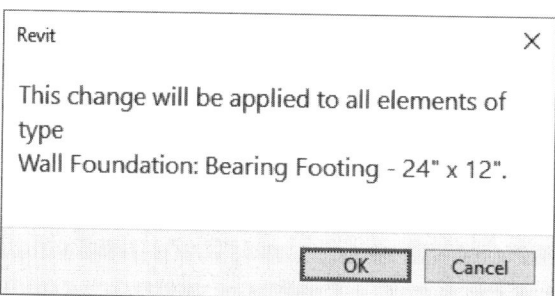

<Structural Elements Schedule>		
A	B	C
Type Mark	Family and Type	Count
Structural Columns		
P-1	Concrete-Rectangular-Column: 24 x 24	42
	W-Wide Flange-Column: W8X10	2
	W-Wide Flange-Column: W10X33	41
Structural Foundations		
	Footing-Rectangular: 14"x14"x2'-0"	2
	Footing-Rectangular: 36" x 36" x 12"	42
	Foundation Slab: 6" Foundation Slab	1
	Wall Foundation: Bearing Footing - 24" x 12"	17
	Wall Foundation: Bearing Footing - 36" x 12"	4
Structural Framing		
	HSS-Hollow Structural Section: HSS6X6X.500	28
	K-Series Bar Joist-Rod Web: 14K6	16
	K-Series Bar Joist-Rod Web: 16K7	100
	W-Wide Flange: W12X26	1558
	W-Wide Flange: W14X30	1023

Figure 13–47

5. Note that only the *Concrete* columns have a **Type Mark**.
6. In the *Type Mark* column beside **Wall Foundation: Bearing Footing - 24" x 12"**, type **W-1**.
7. The warning dialog box shown in Figure 13–48 displays because the element is a type parameter; therefore, you are alerted before you make any changes. Click **OK**.

Figure 13–48

8. Select **Wall Foundation: Bearing Footing - 36" x 12"**.
9. In the *Modify | Schedule/Quantities* tab>Element panel, click (Highlight in Model).
10. In the Show Element(s) in View dialog box, click **Show** until you see a foundation element displayed in the **3D Foundations** view, as shown in Figure 13–49. Click **Close**.

Adding Tags and Schedules

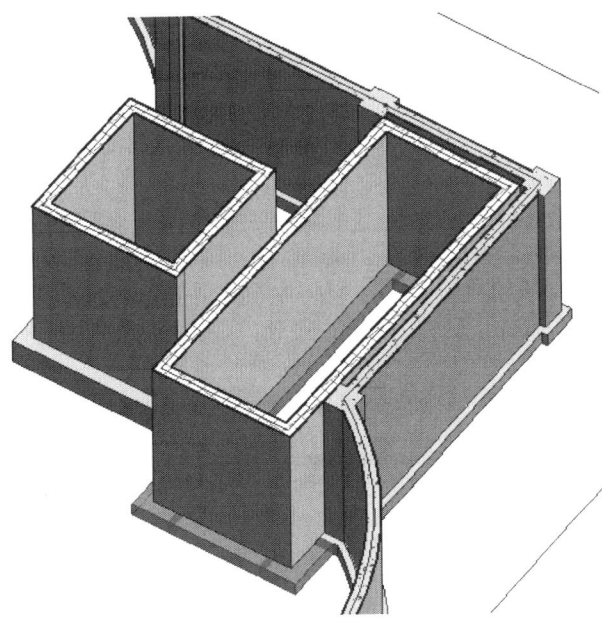

Figure 13–49

11. With the elements highlighted, in Properties, click ▦ (Edit Type).
12. In the Type Properties dialog box, in the *Identity Data* section, set the *Type Mark* to **W-2**.
13. Click **OK** to finish.
14. Return to the **Structural Elements Schedule** view, as shown in Figure 13–50. The *Type Mark* is now applied.

A	B	C
Type Mark	Family and Type	Count
Structural Columns		
P-1	Concrete-Rectangular-Column: 24 x 24	42
	W-Wide Flange-Column: W8X10	2
	W-Wide Flange-Column: W10X33	41
Structural Foundations		
	Footing-Rectangular: 14"x14"x2'-0"	2
	Footing-Rectangular: 36" x 36" x 12"	42
	Foundation Slab: 6" Foundation Slab	1
W-1	Wall Foundation: Bearing Footing - 24" x 12"	17
W-2	Wall Foundation: Bearing Footing - 36" x 12"	4
Structural Framing		
	HSS-Hollow Structural Section: HSS6X6X.500	28
	K-Series Bar Joist-Rod Web: 14K6	16
	K-Series Bar Joist-Rod Web: 16K7	100
	W-Wide Flange: W12X26	1558
	W-Wide Flange: W14X30	1023

Figure 13–50

15. Open the other schedules and review the information.
16. Save the project.

Task 3: Add schedules to a sheet.

1. In the Project Browser, Create a new sheet called **S-801 - Schedules**.
2. Drag and drop the **Structural Elements Schedule** view onto the sheet, as shown in Figure 13–51. Your schedule may look different then the one shown.

Type Mark	Family and Type	Count
Structural Columns		
P-1	Concrete-Rectangular-Column: 24 x 24	42
	W-Wide Flange-Column: W8X10	2
	W-Wide Flange-Column: W10X33	41
Structural Foundations		
	Footing-Rectangular: 14'x14'x2'-0"	2
	Footing-Rectangular: 36" x 36" x 12"	42
	Foundation Slab: 6" Foundation Slab	1
W-1	Wall Foundation: Bearing Footing - 24" x 12"	17
W-2	Wall Foundation: Bearing Footing - 36" x 12"	4
Structural Framing		
	HSS-Hollow Structural Section: HSS6X6X.500	28
	K-Series Bar Joist-Rod Web: 14K6	16
	K-Series Bar Joist-Rod Web: 16K7	100
	W-Wide Flange: W12X26	1558
	W-Wide Flange: W14X30	1024

Figure 13–51

3. Zoom in and use the arrows at the top of the schedule to modify the width of the columns to ensure that the titles display correctly.
4. In the schedule, note the number of concrete columns and their related footings.
5. Open the **Structural Plans: 00 T.O. Footing** view.

6. Zoom in and copy a concrete column and its footing to a nearby grid line location that does not have an existing column, similar to that shown in Figure 13–52.

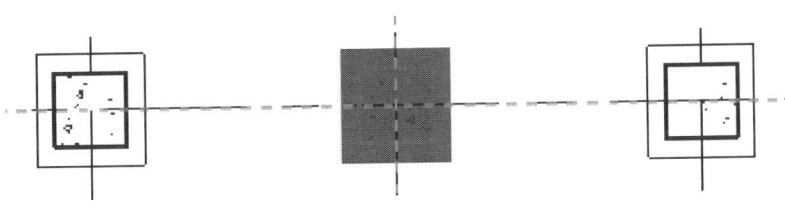

Figure 13–52

7. Switch back to the sheet view. Note that the numbers in the schedule have automatically updated to include the new column.

8. Switch to the **Structural Elements Schedule** view. Note that these column numbers have also been updated.

9. Save and close the project.

End of practice

13.3 Graphical Column Schedules

Graphical column schedules are commonly displayed at the end of a set of construction documents. The schedule identifies the type of column, the floors to which the column extends, column locations, and the group to which similar columns belong, as shown in a closeup view in Figure 13–53.

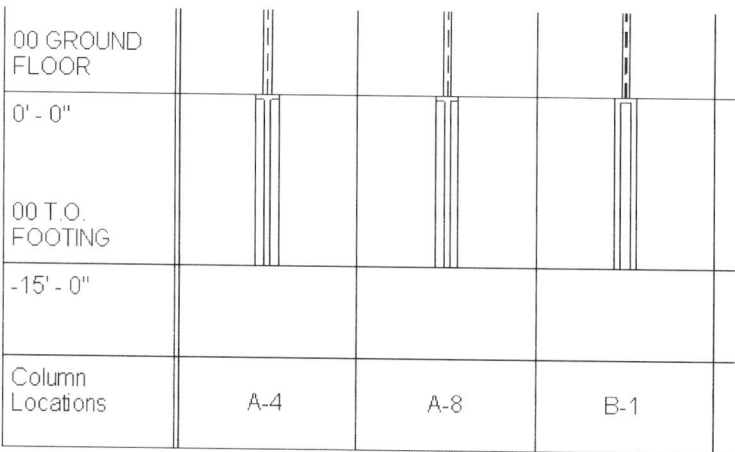

Figure 13–53

How To: Create a Graphical Column Schedule

1. In the *View* tab>Create panel, expand (Schedules) and click (Graphical Column Schedule), or in the Project Browser, right-click on the Schedule/Quantities node and select **New Graphical Column Schedule...**.

   - A warning dialog box might open stating *Some columns in Graphical Column Schedule exceed the segment's upper/lower bounds. You can add levels or adjust the view parameters.*, which you can ignore. This can be fixed later.

2. A column schedule is created using the columns already placed in the project, as shown in Figure 13–54.

   Note: Graphical column schedules are located in the Project Browser under Graphical Column Schedules (not under Schedule/Quantities like most other schedules).

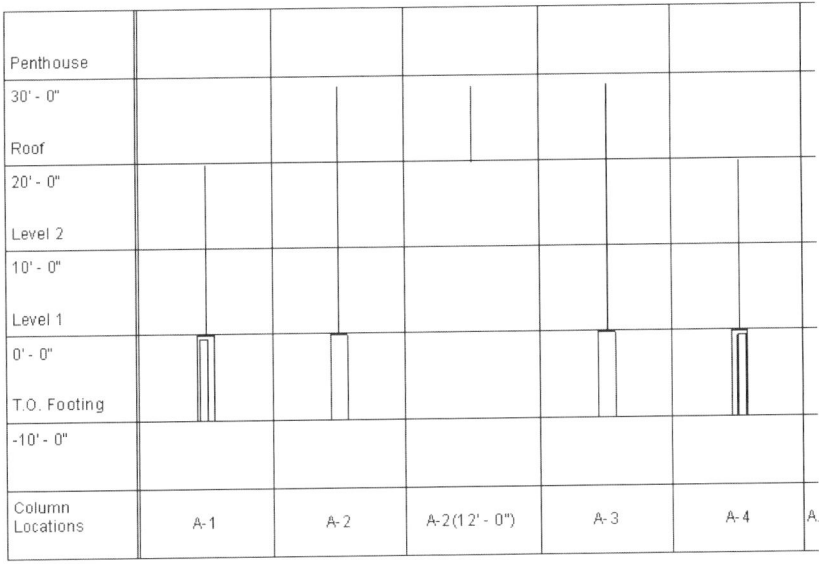

Figure 13-54

Modifying Graphical Column Schedules

Once you have a graphical column schedule in your project, you can adjust the properties, as shown in Figure 13-55. You can format the schedule and display the information to suit your particular requirements.

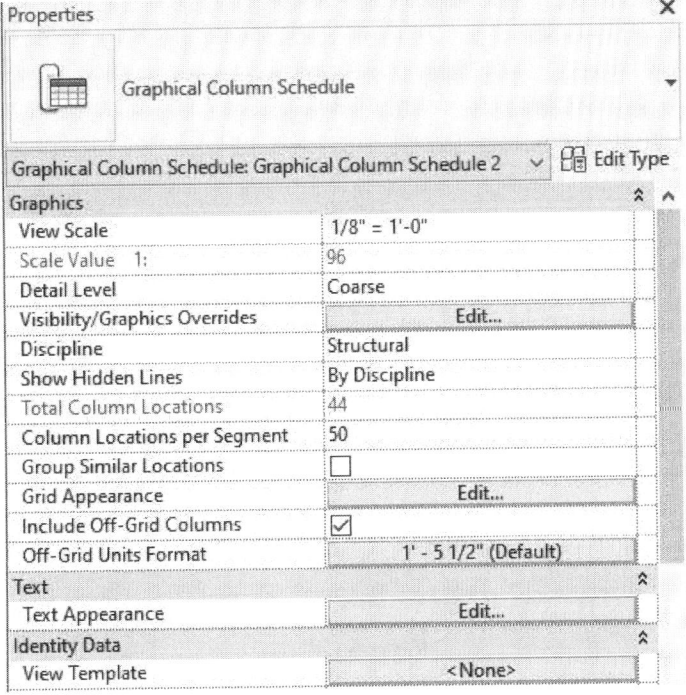

Figure 13-55

- **Group Similar Locations:** Modifies the column layout to only display one type of each column and then lists the applicable column locations for each type.
- **Grid Appearance:** Opens the Graphical Column Schedule Properties dialog box with the *Grid Appearance* tab selected, as shown in Figure 13–56, with options on how to display the grid lines.

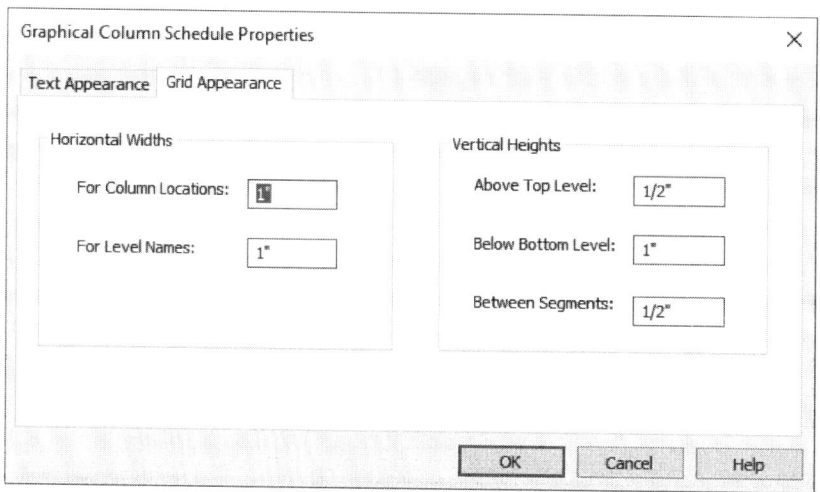

Figure 13–56

- **Include Off-Grid Columns** and **Off-Grid Units Format:** Groups the column with the column designation and adds the offset dimension in the box below the column.
- **Text Appearance:** Opens the Graphical Column Schedule Properties dialog box with the *Text Appearance* tab selected, as shown in Figure 13–57. This is where you set up the font style, size, and options for the text in the schedule.

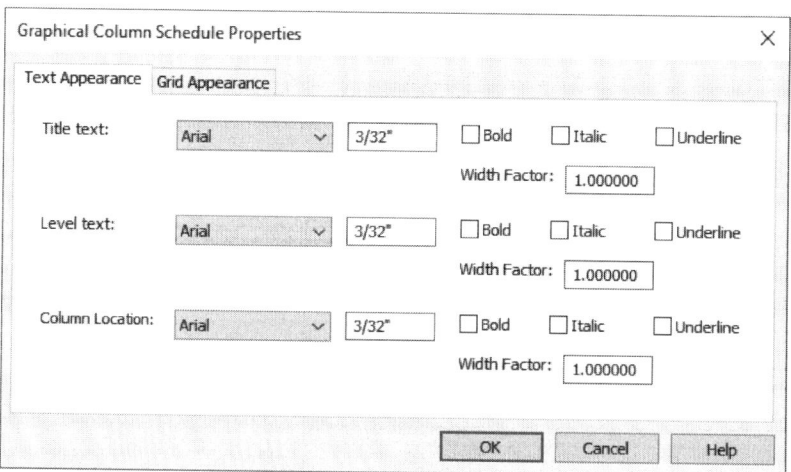

Figure 13–57

In the *Other* section, as shown in Figure 13–58, you can specify the columns, levels, and materials that are displayed.

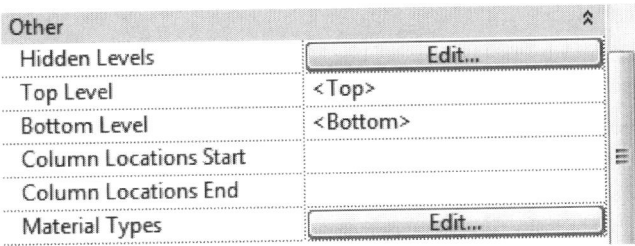

Figure 13–58

- **Hidden Levels:** Enables you to remove any arbitrary levels using the Levels Hidden in Graphical Column Schedules dialog box, as shown in Figure 13–59.

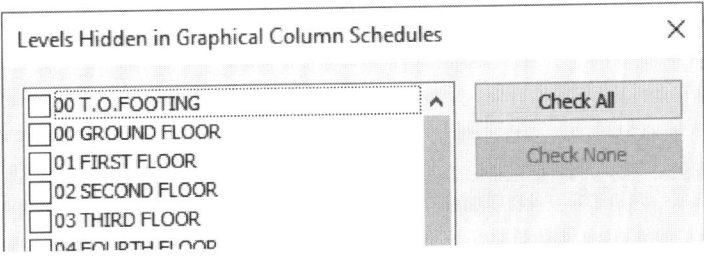

Figure 13–59

- **Top Level** and **Bottom Level:** Sets where the schedule displays the top and bottom levels. The default is normally used.

- **Column Locations Start** and **Column Locations End:** Enables you to specify the locations that are used to start and end the schedule. Sometimes the start is not logically going to be A1.

- **Material Type:** Enables you to create a filter of columns by materials. For example, if you only want the schedule to display steel columns, select that material in the Structural Material dialog box, as shown in Figure 13–60.

Figure 13–60

Practice 13c
Create a Graphical Column Schedule

Practice Objective

- Create a graphical column schedule.

In this practice, you will create a graphical column schedule that shows only steel columns, as shown in part in Figure 13-61.

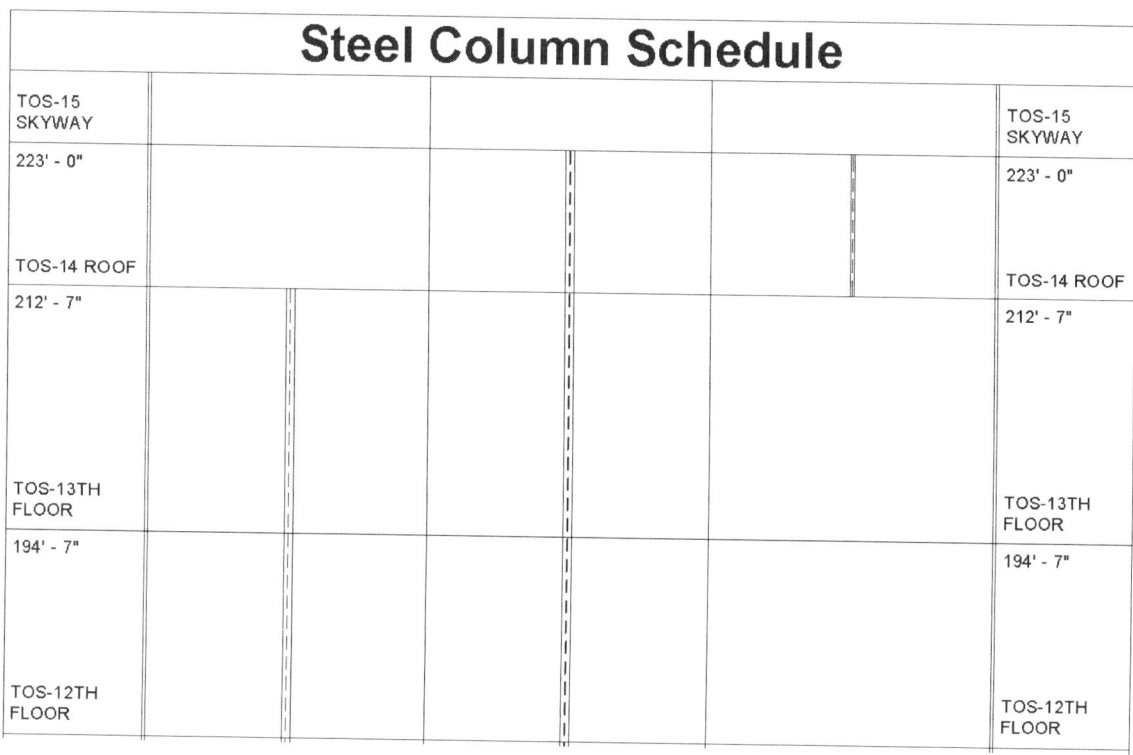

Figure 13-61

1. Open **Structural-Schedules.rvt** from the practice files folder.

2. In the *View* tab>Create panel, expand ▦ (Schedules) and click ▦ (Graphical Column Schedule). A graphical column schedule view displays.

3. In the Project Browser, expand the *Graphical Column Schedule* category and rename the new schedule to **Steel Column Schedule**.

4. In the View Control Bar, change the *Scale* to **3/32" = 1'-0"** and set the *Detail Level* to **Fine**.

5. In Properties, select the *Group Similar Locations* option. The schedule changes to display only one of each type of column.

6. Next to *Grid Appearance*, click **Edit....**

7. In the Graphical Column Schedule Properties dialog box, in the *Grid Appearance* tab, set the following, as shown in Figure 13–62:

    - *Horizontal Widths>For Column Locations:* **2"**
    - *Vertical Heights>Below Bottom Level:* **2"**

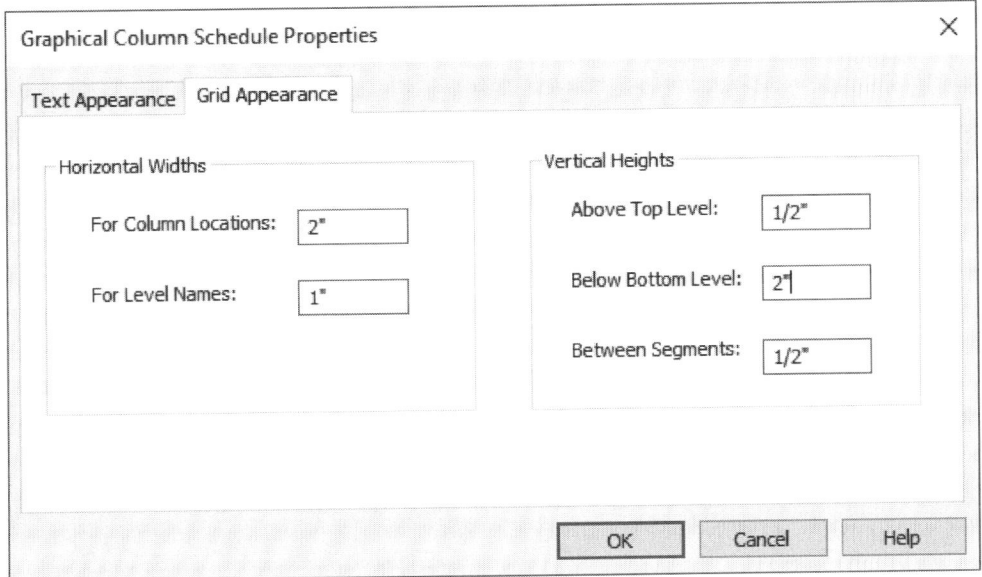

Figure 13–62

8. Switch to the *Text Appearance* tab.
9. Ensure that the *Title text* font is **Arial**, increase the size to **1/4"**, and make the text **Bold**, as shown in Figure 13–63.

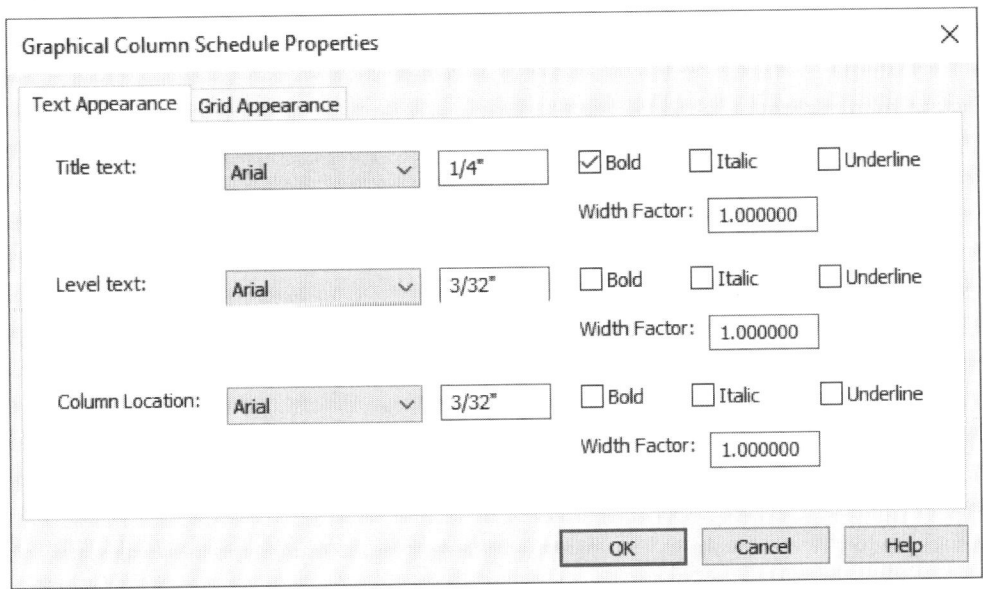

Figure 13–63

10. Click **OK**.
11. In the *Other* section, beside *Material Types,* click **Edit...**.
12. In the Structural Material dialog box, click **Check None** and then select only the **Steel** option, as shown in Figure 13–64.

Figure 13–64

13. Click **OK**. The schedule is now limited to steel columns.
14. Change Bottom Level to **00 Ground Floor**, as shown in Figure 13–65.

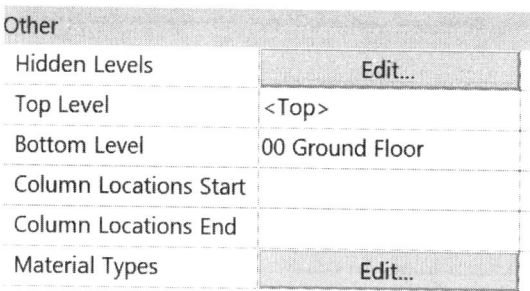

Figure 13–65

15. In Properties, in the *Identity Data* section, type **Steel Column Schedule** next to *Title*.
16. Save and close the project.

End of practice

Chapter Review Questions

1. You can tag in a 3D view, but you first have to do what to the view?
   a. You cannot tag in a 3D view.
   b. Rename the view.
   c. Lock the view.
   d. Unlock the view.

2. Which of the following elements cannot be tagged using **Tag by Category**?
   a. Rooms
   b. Floors
   c. Walls
   d. Doors

3. What happens when you delete a door in a Revit model?
   a. You must delete the door on the sheet.
   b. You must delete the door from the schedule.
   c. The door is removed from the model, but not from the schedule.
   d. The door is removed from the model and the schedule.

4. In a schedule, if you change type information (such as a Type Mark), all instances of that type update with the new information.
   a. True
   b. False

Command Summary

Button	Command	Location
	Freeze Header	• **Ribbon:** *Modify Schedule/Quantities* tab>Titles & Header panel
	Graphical Column Schedule	• **Ribbon:** *View* tab>Create panel, expand Schedules
	Highlight in Model	• **Ribbon:** *Modify Schedule/Quantities* tab>Element panel
	Material Tag	• **Ribbon:** *Annotate* tab>Tag panel
	Multi-Category	• **Ribbon:** *Annotate* tab>Tag panel
	Schedule/Quantities	• **Ribbon:** *View* tab>Create panel, expand Schedules
	Stair Tread/Riser Number	• **Ribbon:** *Annotate* tab>Tag panel
	Tag All Not Tagged	• **Ribbon:** *Annotate* tab>Tag panel
	Tag by Category	• **Ribbon:** *Annotate* tab>Tag panel • **Shortcut: TG**
	Tag Room (Room Tag)	• **Ribbon:** *Architecture* tab>Room & Area panel • **Ribbon:** *Annotate* tab>Tag panel • **Shortcut: RT**

Chapter 14

Creating Details

Creating details is a critical part of the design process, as it is the step where you specify the exact information that is required to build a construction project. The elements that you can add to a model include detail components, detail lines, text, tags, symbols, and filled regions. Details can be created from views in the model, but you can also add 2D details in separate views.

Learning Objectives

- Create drafting views where you can add 2D details.
- Add detail components that show the typical elements in a detail.
- Annotate details using detail lines, text, tags, symbols, and patterns that define materials.

14.1 Setting Up Detail Views

Most of the work you do in Revit is exclusively with *smart* elements that interconnect and work together in the model. However, the software does not automatically display how elements should be built to fit together. For this, you need to create detail drawings, as shown in Figure 14–1.

> **Note:** Details are created either in 2D drafting views or in callouts from plan, elevation, or section views.

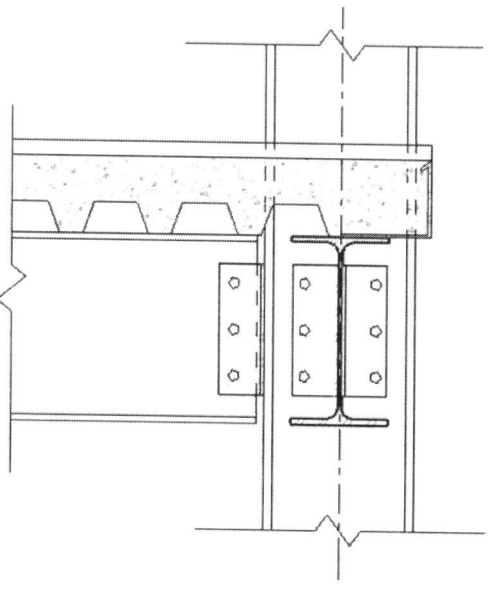

Figure 14–1

How To: Create a Drafting View

1. In the *View* tab>Create panel, click ⬜ (Drafting View).
2. In the New Drafting View dialog box, enter a *Name* and set a *Scale*, as shown in Figure 14–2.

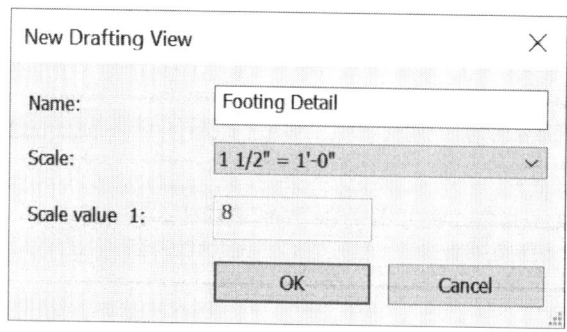

Figure 14–2

3. Click **OK**. A blank view is created with space in which you can sketch the detail.

   Note: Drafting views are listed in their own section in the Project Browser.

How To: Create a Detail View from Model Elements

1. Start the **Section** or **Callout** command.
2. In the Type Selector, select the **Detail View: Detail** type.
   - The marker indicates that it is a detail, as shown for a section in Figure 14–3.

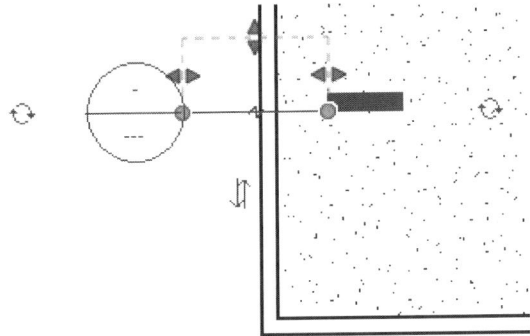

Figure 14–3

3. Place the section or a callout of the area you want to use for the detail.

   Note: Callouts also have a Detail View type that can be used in the same way.

4. Open the new detail.
- Change the detail level to see more or less of the element materials.
- Use the **Detail Line** tool to sketch on top of or add to the building elements.

- Because you are working with smart elements, a detail of the model is a true representation. When the building elements change, the detail changes as well, as shown in Figure 14-4.

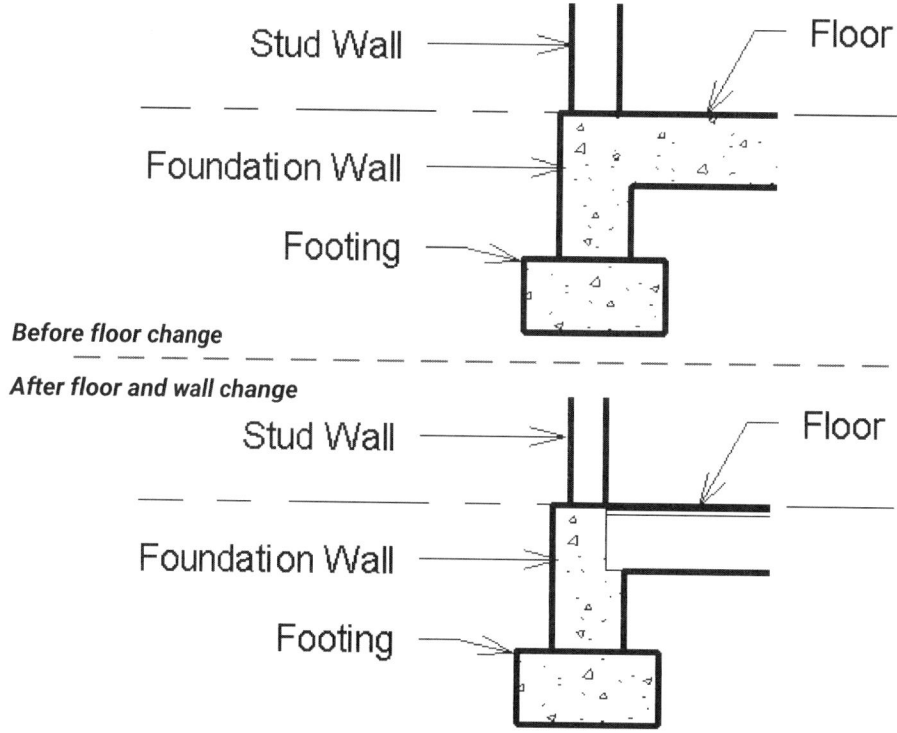

Figure 14-4

- You can create detail elements on top of the model and then toggle the model off so that it does not show in the detail view. In Properties, in the *Graphics* section, change *Display Model* to **Do not display**. You can also set the model to **Halftone**, as shown in Figure 14-5.

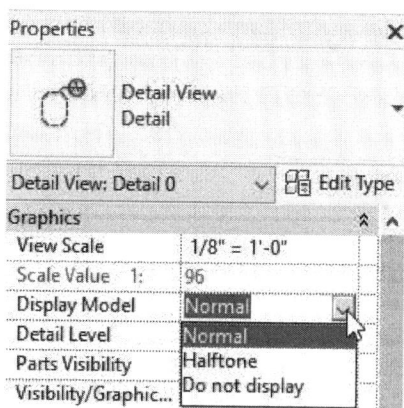

Figure 14-5

Referencing a Drafting View

Once you have created a drafting view, you can reference it in another view (such as a callout, elevation, or section view), as shown in Figure 14–6. For example, in a section view, you might want to reference an existing roof detail. You can reference drafting views, sections, elevations, and callouts.

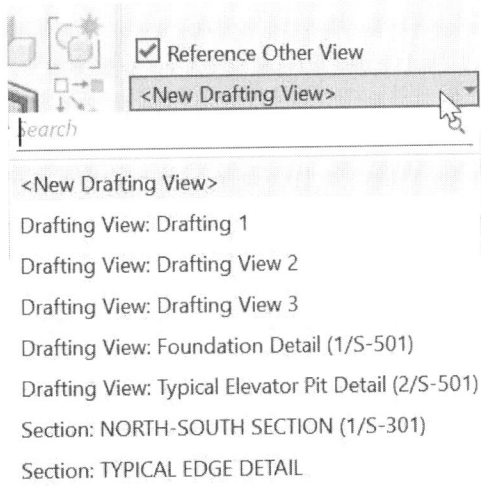

Figure 14–6

- You can use the search feature to limit the information displayed.

How To: Reference a Drafting View

1. Open the view in which you want to place the reference.
2. Start the **Section**, **Callout**, or **Elevation** command.
3. In the *Modify* contextual tab>Reference panel, select **Reference Other View**.
4. In the drop-down list, select **<New Drafting View>** or an existing drafting view.
5. Place the view marker.
6. When you place the associated drafting view on a sheet, the marker in this view updates with the appropriate information.

- If you select **<New Drafting View>** from the drop-down list, a new view is created in the *Drafting Views (Detail)* area in the Project Browser. You can rename it as needed. The new view does not include any model elements.
- When you create a detail based on a section, elevation, or callout, you do not need to link it to a drafting view.
- You can change a referenced view to a different view. Select the view marker and in the ribbon, select the new view from the list.

Saving Drafting Views

To create a library of standard details, save the non-model specific drafting views to your server. They can then be imported into a project and modified to suit. They are saved as .RVT files.

Drafting views can be saved in two ways:

- Save an individual drafting view to a new file.
- Save all of the drafting views as a group in one new file.

How To: Save One Drafting View to a File

1. In the Project Browser, right-click on the drafting view you want to save and select **Save to New File...**, as shown in Figure 14–7.

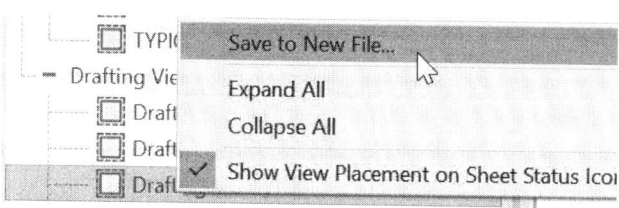

Figure 14–7

2. In the Save As dialog box, specify a name and location for the file and click **Save**.

How To: Save a Group of Drafting Views to a File

Note: You can save sheets, drafting views, model views (floor plans), schedules, and reports.

1. In the *File* tab, expand (Save As), expand (Library), and then click (View).
2. In the Save Views dialog box, in the *Views:* area, expand the list and select **Show drafting views only**.
3. Select the drafting views that you want to save, as shown in Figure 14–8.

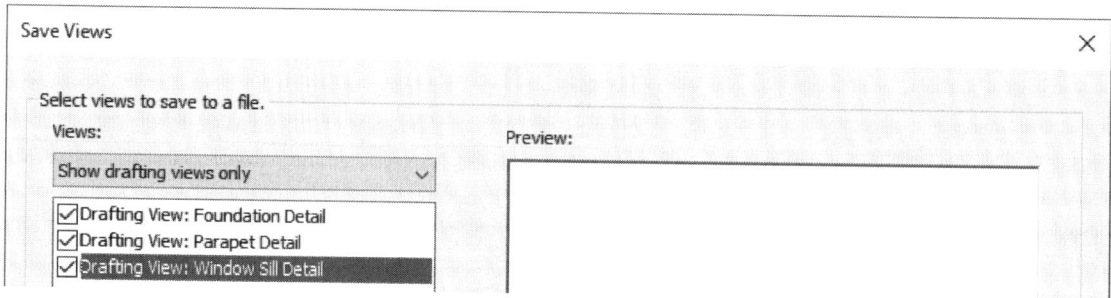

Figure 14–8

4. Click **OK**.
5. In the Save As dialog box, specify a name and location for the file and click **Save**.

How To: Use a Saved Drafting View in Another Project

1. Open the project to which you want to add the drafting view.
2. In the *Insert* tab>Load from Library panel, expand (Insert from File) and click (Insert Views from File).
3. In the Open dialog box, select the project in which you saved the detail and click **Open**.
4. In the Insert Views dialog box, limit the types of views to **Show drafting views only**, as shown in Figure 14–9.

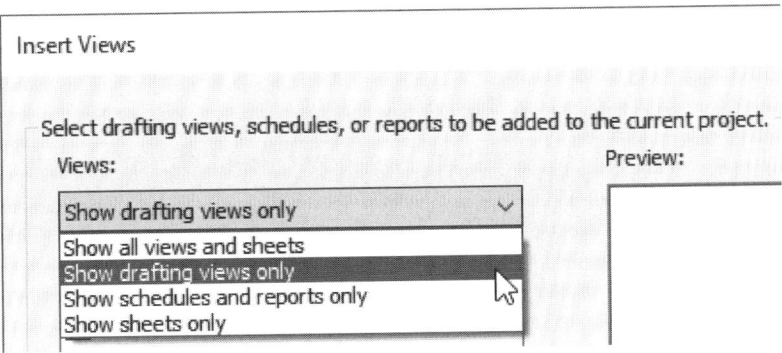

Figure 14–9

5. Select the view(s) that you want to insert and click **OK**.

Hint: Importing Details from Other CAD Software

You might already have a set of standard details created in a different CAD program, such as the AutoCAD® software. You can reuse the details in Revit by importing them into a temporary project. Once you have imported the detail, it helps to clean it up and save it as a view before bringing it into your active project.

1. In a new project, create a drafting view and make it active.
2. In the *Insert* tab>Import panel, click (Import CAD).
3. In the Import CAD dialog box, select the file to import. Most of the default values are what you need. You might want to change the *Layer/Level colors* to **Black and White**.
4. Click **Open**.
5. Use Revit detail lines and other tools to trace over the imported file.
6. Once finished, unpin the imported file and press <Delete>.

- If necessary, you can explode the imported file to modify it. This method is not recommended because it increases the file size and, depending on the importing objects, it could potentially take a long time to clean up and convert the objects and Revit-Specific elements and styles.

  - Select the imported data. In the *Modify | [filename]* tab>Import Instance panel, expand (Explode) and click (Partial Explode) or (Full Explode). Click (Delete Layers) before you explode the detail. A full explode greatly increases the file size.
  - Modify the detail using tools in the Modify panel. Change all the text and line styles to Revit-specific elements.

14.2 Adding Detail Components

Revit elements, such as the section shown in Figure 14–10, typically require additional information to ensure that they are constructed correctly. To create details such as the one shown in Figure 14–11, you add detail components, detail lines, and various annotation elements.

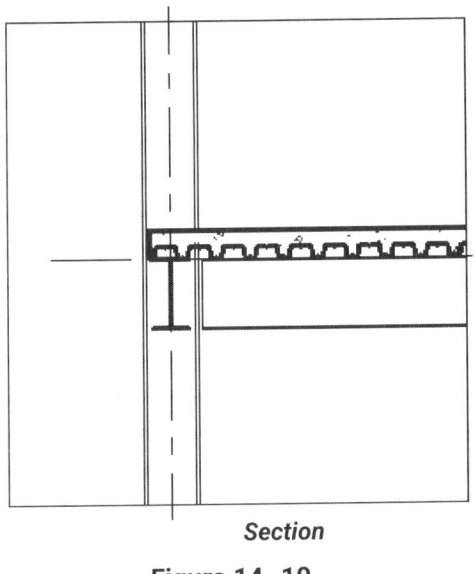

Section

Figure 14–10

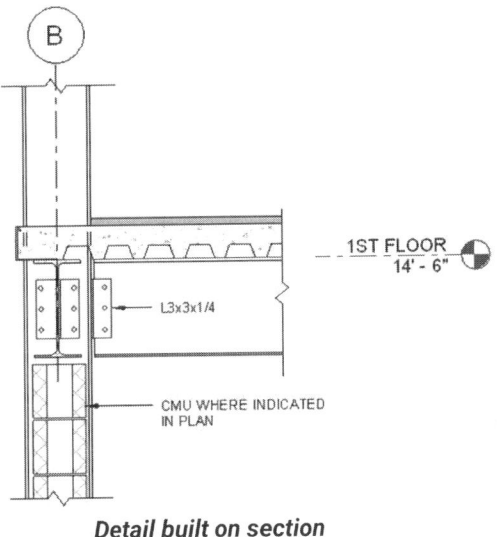

Detail built on section

Figure 14–11

- Detail elements are not directly connected to the model, even if model elements display in the view.
- If you want to draw detail lines in 3D, use the **Model Line** tool. Detail Line is grayed out when you are in a 3D view or perspective view.

Detail Components

Detail components are families made of 2D and annotation elements. Over 500 detail components organized by CSI format are found in the *Detail Items* folder of the Revit Library.

> **Note:** For more information on how to load detail items using the Load Autodesk Family dialog box, see 4.2 Loading Components.

How To: Add a Detail Component

1. In the *Annotate* tab>Detail panel, expand **Component** and click (Detail Component).
2. In the Type Selector, select the detail component type. You can load additional types from the Revit Library.

3. Many detail components can be rotated as you insert them by pressing <Spacebar>. Alternatively, select **Rotate after placement** in the Options Bar.
4. Place the component in the view.

Adding Break Lines

The break line is a detail component found in the Revit Library's *Detail Items\Div 01-General* folder. It consists of a rectangular area (shown highlighted in Figure 14–12) that is used to block out elements behind it. You can modify the size of the area that is covered and change the size of the cut line using the controls.

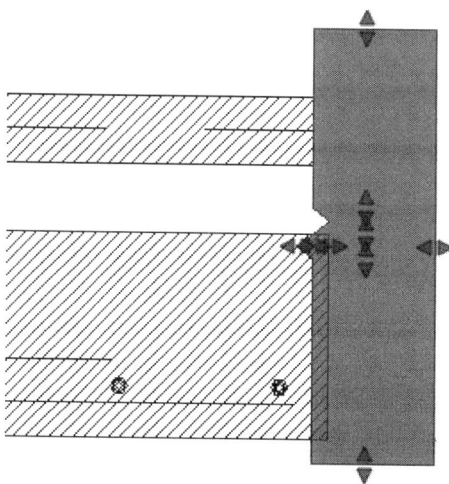

Figure 14–12

Creating Details

> **Hint: Working with the Draw Order of Details**
>
> When you select detail elements in a view, you can change the draw order of the elements in the *Modify | Detail Items* tab>Arrange panel. You can bring elements in front of other elements or place them behind elements, as shown in Figure 14–13.

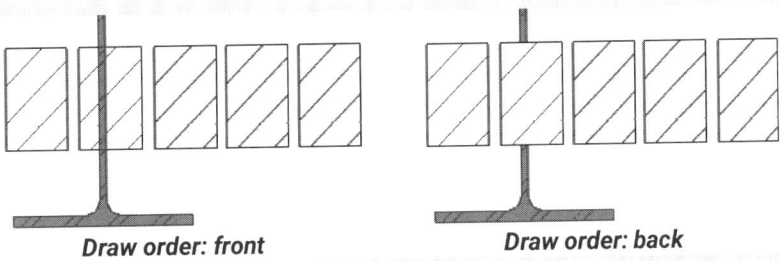

Figure 14–13

- **(Bring to Front):** Places element in front of all other elements.
- **(Send to Back):** Places element behind all other elements.
- **(Bring Forward):** Moves element one step to the front.
- **(Send Backward):** Moves element one step to the back.

You can select multiple detail elements and change the draw order of all of them in one step. They keep the relative order of the original selection.

Repeating Details

Instead of having to insert a component multiple times (such as brick or concrete block), you can use (Repeating Detail Component) and create a string of components, as shown in Figure 14–14.

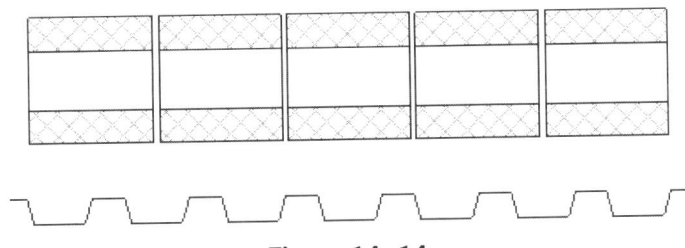

Figure 14–14

How To: Insert a Repeating Detail Component

1. In the *Annotate* tab>Detail panel, expand **Component** and click (Repeating Detail Component).
2. In the Type Selector, select the detail you want to use.
3. In the Draw panel, click (Line) or (Pick Lines).
4. In the Options Bar, type a value for the *Offset,* if needed.
5. The components repeat, as required, to fit the length of the sketched or selected line, as shown in Figure 14–15. You can lock the components to the line.

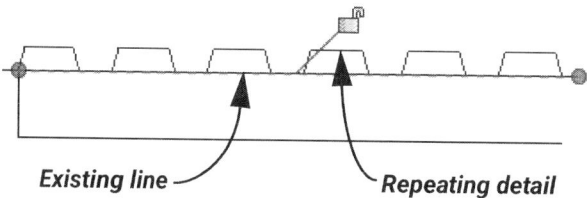

Figure 14–15

- For information on customizing repeating details, see *B.6 Creating a Repeating Detail*.

14.3 Annotating Details

After you have added components and sketched detail lines, you need to add annotations to the detail view. You can place text notes and dimensions, as shown in Figure 14–16, as well as symbols and tags. Filled regions are used to add hatching.

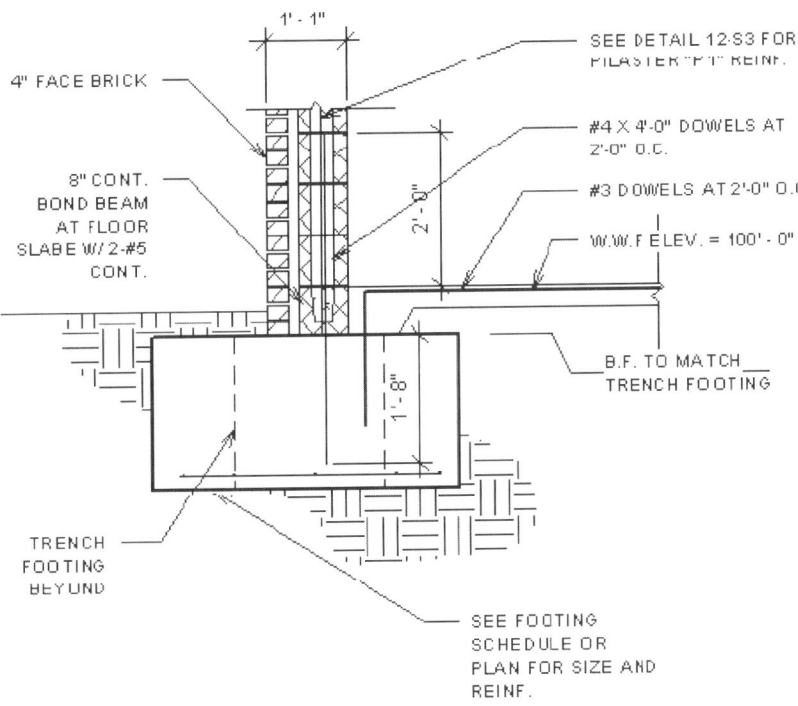

Figure 14–16

Creating Filled Regions

Many elements include material information that displays in plan and section views, while other elements need more details to be added. For example, the concrete wall shown in Figure 14–17 includes material information, while the earth to the left of the wall needs to be added using the **Filled Region** command.

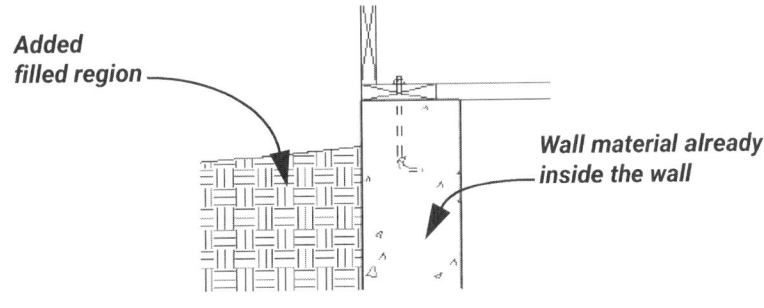

Figure 14–17

The patterns used in details are *drafting patterns*. They are scaled to the view scale and update if you modify it. You can also add full-size *model patterns*, such as a Flemish Bond brick pattern, to the surface of some elements.

How To: Add a Filled Region

1. In the *Annotate* tab>Detail panel, expand ▦ (Region) and click ▦ (Filled Region).
2. Create a closed boundary using the Draw tools.
3. In the Line Style panel, select the line style for the outside edge of the boundary. If you do not want the boundary to display, select the **<Invisible lines>** style.
4. In the Type Selector, select the fill type, as shown in Figure 14–18.

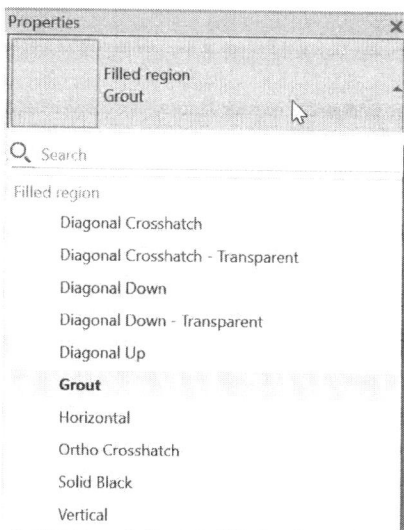

Figure 14–18

5. Click ✔ (Finish Edit Mode).

- You can modify a region by changing the fill type in the Type Selector or by editing the sketch.

- Double-click on the edge of the filled region to edit the sketch. If you have the Selection option set to ▸ (Select elements by face), you can select the pattern.

Creating Details

> **Hint: Creating a Filled Region Pattern Type**

You can create a custom pattern by duplicating and editing an existing pattern type.

1. Select an existing region or create a boundary.
2. In Properties, click ▣ (Edit Type).
3. In the Type Properties dialog box, click **Duplicate** and name the new pattern.
4. Select the *Foreground/Background Fill Pattern* and *Color* and specify the *Line Weight* and *Masking*, as shown in Figure 14–19.

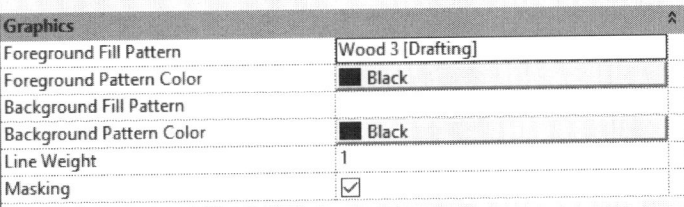

Figure 14–19

5. Click **OK**.

- You can select from two types of fill patterns: **Drafting** (as shown in Figure 14–20) and **Model**. Drafting fill patterns scale to the view scale factor. Model fill patterns display full scale on the model.

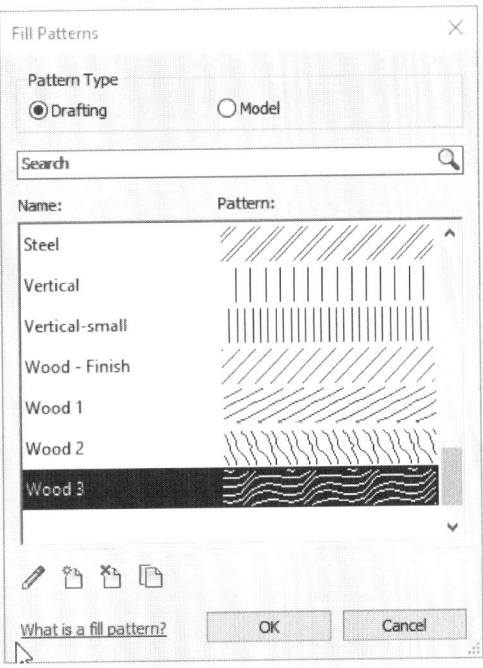

Figure 14–20

Adding Detail Tags

Besides adding text to a detail, you can tag detail components using 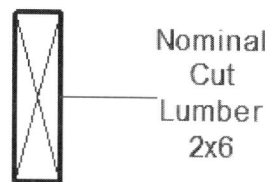 (Tag By Category). The tag name is set in the Type Parameters for that component, as shown in Figure 14-21. This means that if you have more than one copy of the component in your project, you do not have to rename it each time you place its tag.

Note: The **Detail Item Tag.rfa** tag is located in the Annotations folder in the Revit Library.

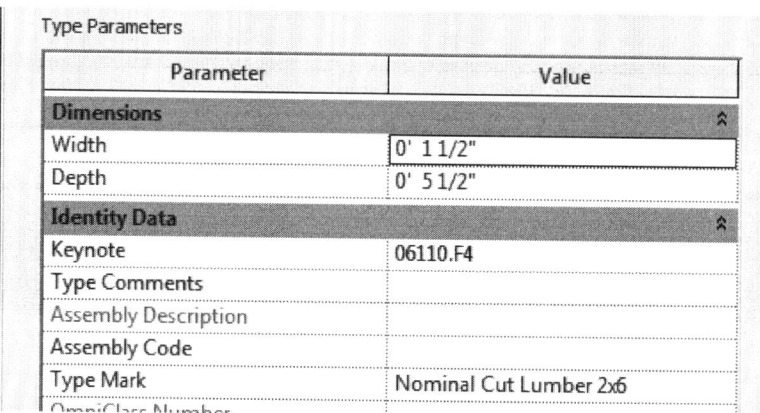

Figure 14-21

- For more information on annotating using keynotes see *B.7 Keynoting and Keynote Legends*.

When you tag elements in a cropped view, the tag is placed at the default location of the element and might not display in the callout. In the View Control Bar, click (Do not Crop). Tag the elements, and then move the new tags in the crop window, as shown in Figure 14-22. Click (Crop View) to return to the area of the callout view.

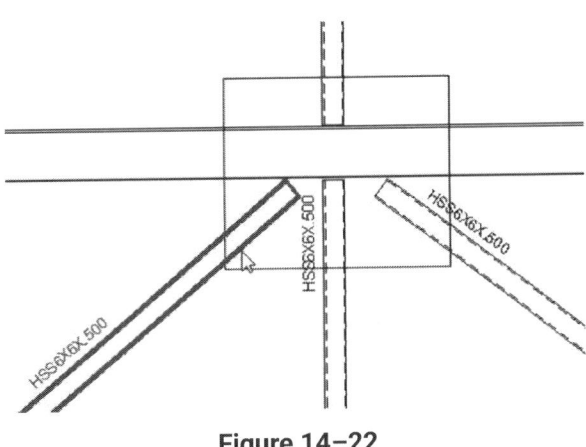

Figure 14–22

Linework

To emphasize a particular line or change the look of a line in elevations and other views, modify the lines with the **Linework** command. Changes made to lines with the **Linework** command are view-specific, applying only to the view in which you make them.

- The **Linework** command can be used on project edges of model elements, cut edges of model elements, edges in imported CAD files, and edges in linked Revit models.
- You cannot use the **Linework** command to change the line style of annotation lines like a dimension line or leader line.

How To: Adjust Linework

1. In the *Modify* tab>View panel, click (Linework), or type the shortcut **LW**.
2. In the *Modify | Linework* tab>Line Style panel, select the line style you want to use from the list.
3. Move the cursor and highlight the line you want to change. You can use <Tab> to toggle through the lines as needed.
4. Click on the line to change it to the new line style.
5. Click on other lines as needed or click (Modify) to end the command

- If the line is too long or short, you can modify the length using the controls at the end of the line.

Practice 14a
Create a Detail Based on a Section Callout

Practice Objectives

- Create a detail based on a section.
- Add filled regions, detail components, and annotations.

In this practice, you will create an enlarged detail based on a section, modify line weights, create filled regions, and add detail components and annotations, as shown in Figure 14-23.

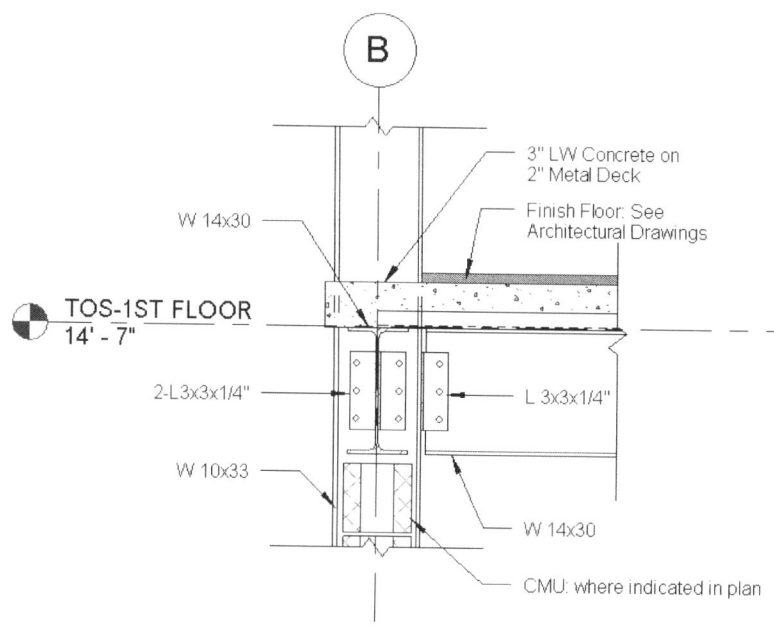

Figure 14-23

Task 1: Create an enlarged detail.

1. Open **Structural-Detailing.rvt** from the practice files folder.
2. Open the **Sections (Building Section): North-South Section** view.
3. Zoom in on the intersection of the **TOS-1ST FLOOR** level and grid line **B** (on the left). Adjust the crop region.
4. In the *View* tab>Create panel, click (Callout).

Creating Details

5. Create a callout as shown in Figure 14–24, then double-click on the callout head to open it.

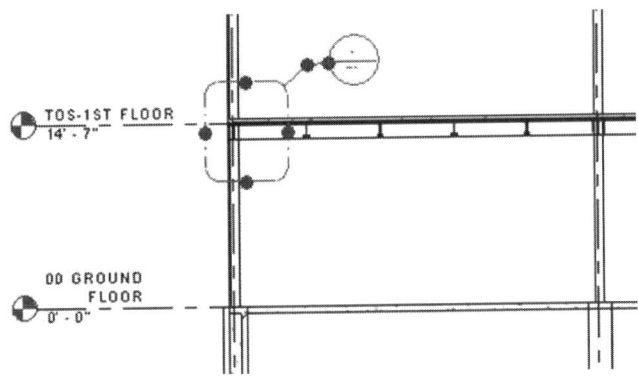

Figure 14–24

Note: *Set the Detail Level to* ▦ *(Fine), if needed.*

6. In the View Control Bar, set the *Scale* to **3/4"=1'-0"**.
7. Select the **TOS-1ST FLOOR** level datum and use the **Hide Bubble** control to hide the bubble on the right.
8. Zoom in close to the intersection to display the line thicknesses. The slab and beam section cut lines are too heavy.
9. Select the slab. Right-click and select **Override Graphics in View>By Element...**.
10. In the View-Specific Element Graphics dialog box, change the *Cut Lines Weight* to **2**, as shown in Figure 14–25.

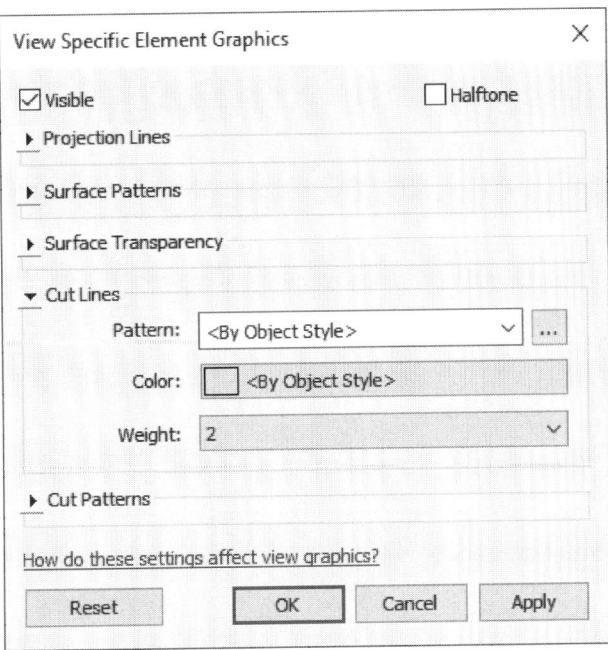

Figure 14–25

© 2023, ASCENT - Center for Technical Knowledge®

14–19

11. Click **OK**.
12. Select the beam that is cut in section and change the *Cut Lines Weight* to **3**.
13. Save the project.

Task 2: Create filled regions to display an architectural floor.

1. In the *Annotate* tab>Detail panel, expand ▨ (Region) and click ▨ (Filled Region).
2. In the Type Selector, select **Filled Region: Solid Black**.
3. Click ▦ (Edit Type).
4. In the Type Properties dialog box, click **Duplicate...** and create a new type named **Solid Gray**.
5. In the Type Parameters, change the *Color* to a light gray.
6. Click **OK** to return to the sketch.
7. In the *Modify | Create Filled Region Boundary* tab>Draw panel, use the drawing tools to create a **1"** thick boundary above the floor slab, as shown in Figure 14–26.

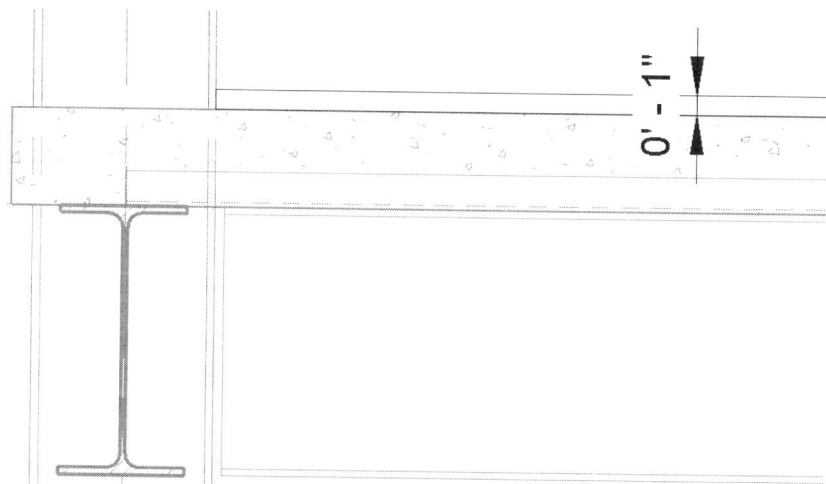

Figure 14–26

8. Click ✔ (Finish Edit Mode) in the Mode panel. The region representing an architectural floor displays, as shown in Figure 14–27.

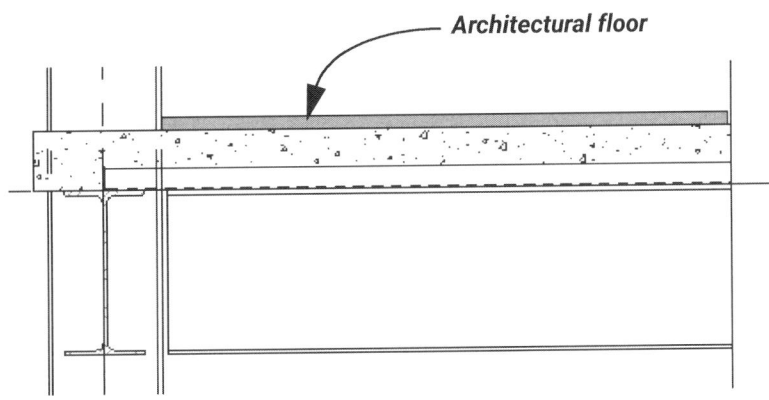

Figure 14–27

Task 3: Add detail components.

1. In the *Annotate* tab>Detail panel, expand **Component** and click (Detail Component).
2. In the *Modify | Place Detail Component* tab>Mode panel, click (Load Family).
3. Browse to the practice files *Families* folder. Press <Ctrl> to select both **L-Angle-Bolted Connection-Elevation.rfa** and **L-Angle-Bolted Connection-Section.rfa**, then click **Open**.
4. In the Type Selector, select **L-Angle-Bolted Connection-Elevation: L3x3x1/4"**.
5. Click (Edit Type).
6. In the Type Properties dialog box, change the *Number Of Bolts* to **3**. Click **OK**.
7. Place the component at the intersection of the midpoint on the beam in elevation and the column it frames into, as shown in Figure 14–28.

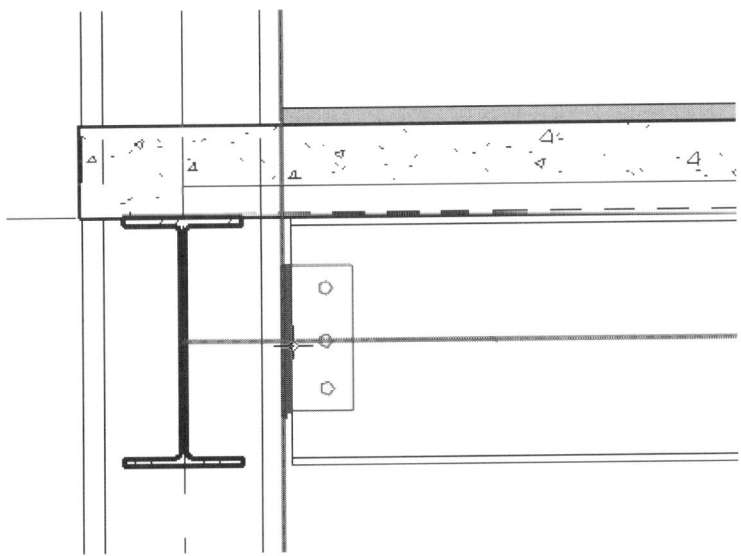

Figure 14–28

8. Repeat the procedure. This time place the **L-Angle-Bolted Connection-Section** on the sectioned beam. After it is placed, select it and stretch the ◄ ► grips to be tight around the member, as shown in Figure 14–29.

   Note: To make it easier to see, toggle on ≣ (Thin Lines) in the Quick Access Toolbar.

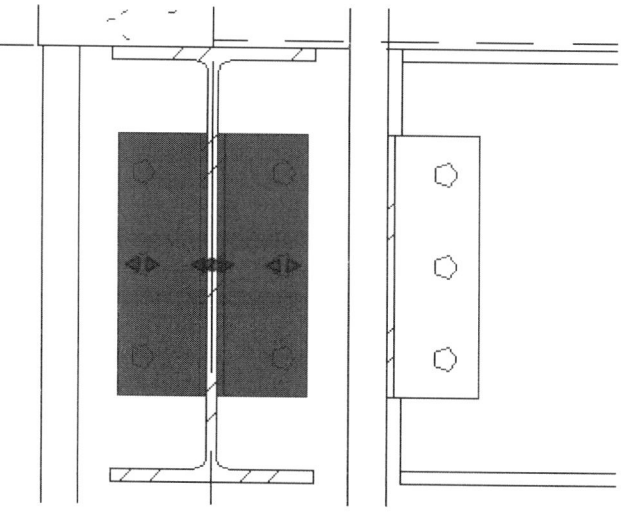

Figure 14–29

9. Click (Modify).
10. Save the project.

Task 4: Add repeating detail components.

1. In the *Annotate* tab>Detail panel, expand **Component** and click (Repeating Detail Component).
2. In the Type Selector, select **Repeating Detail: CMU**.
3. In the Options Bar, set the *Offset* to **0'-3-13/16"** (or **=7-5/8" / 2**). (Hint: You can type formulas wherever a number can be added.)

Creating Details

4. Select the bottom midpoint of the **W14x30** section and draw a line down to display at least 2 CMU blocks, as shown in Figure 14–30.

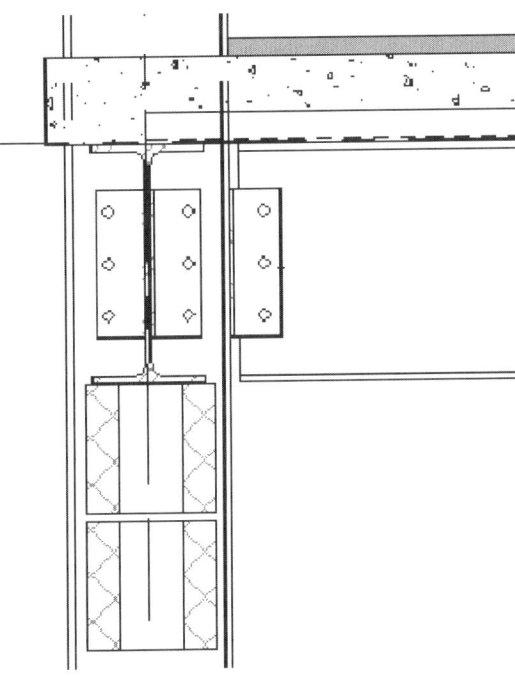

Figure 14–30

5. Select the new CMU wall, and in the *Modify | Detail Items* tab>Arrange panel, click (Send to Back).

6. Click (Move) to move the entire CMU wall down **1"** to create space for a bearing plate for the beam.

7. Click (Modify).

8. Save the project.

Task 5: Annotate the detail.

Note: For more information on loading families, see 4.2 Loading Components.

1. In the *Annotate* tab>Detail panel, expand **Component** and click (Detail Component). In the Type selector select, **Break Line.rfa**.

2. Add break lines to the top, bottom, and right side of the detail, as shown in Figure 14–31. Press <Spacebar> to rotate the break line, as needed.

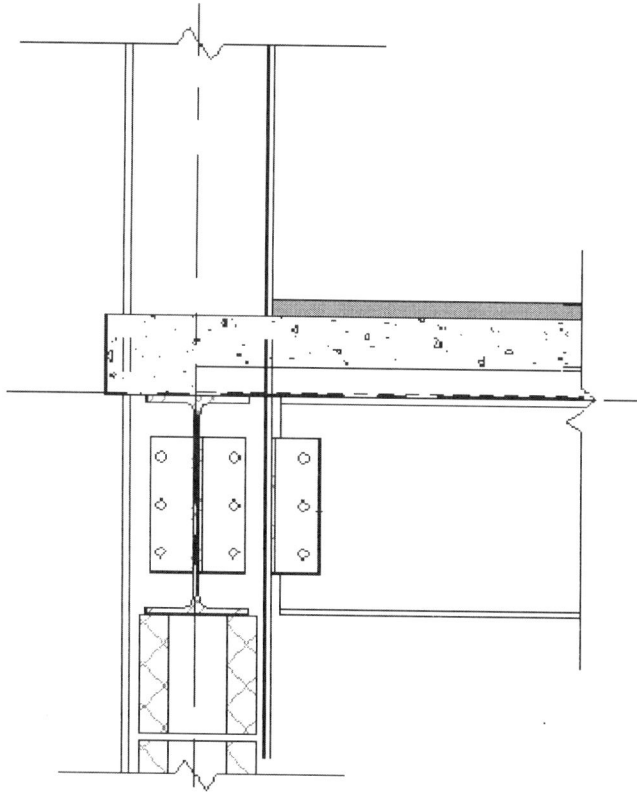

Figure 14–31

Note: Modify the crop region so that excess elements do not display on the outside of the break lines.

3. Leave plenty of room for annotations by making the annotation crop region larger.

4. In the *Annotate* tab>Text panel, click **A** (Text).

5. Add notes to complete the detail, as shown in Figure 14-32.

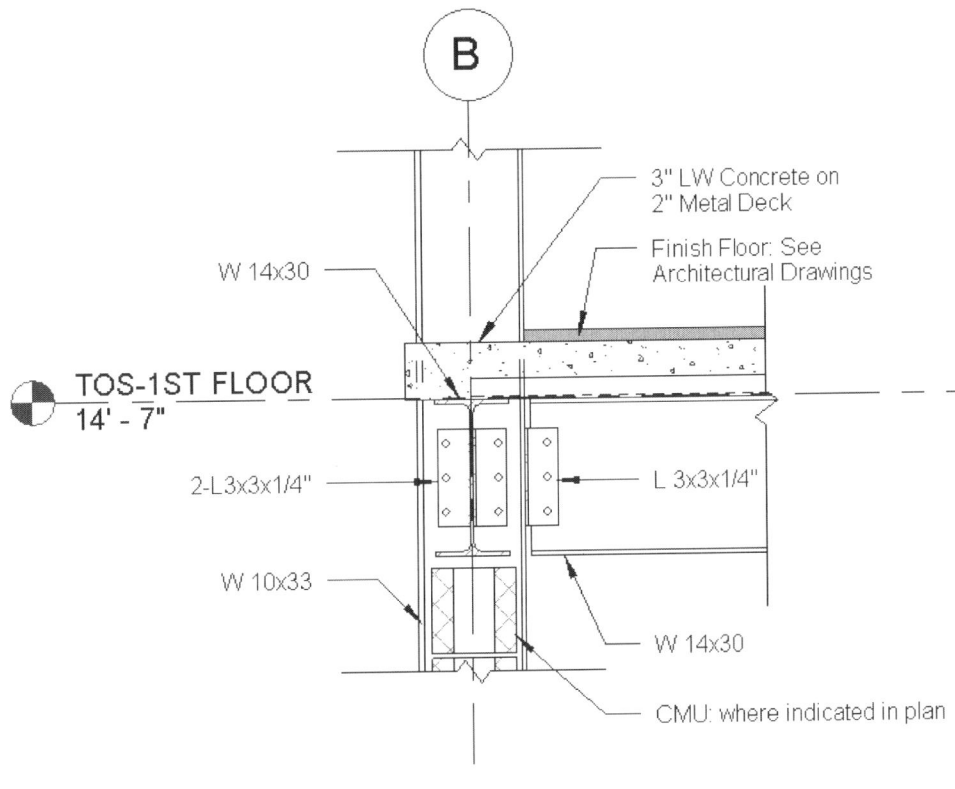

Figure 14-32

6. In the View Control Bar, click (Hide Crop Region).
7. Save and close the project.

End of practice

Practice 14b
Create a Bracing Detail

Practice Objective

- Create callouts and add tags and details lines.

In this practice, you will create a callout of a framing elevation and add tags and a detail of a top plate, as shown in Figure 14–33.

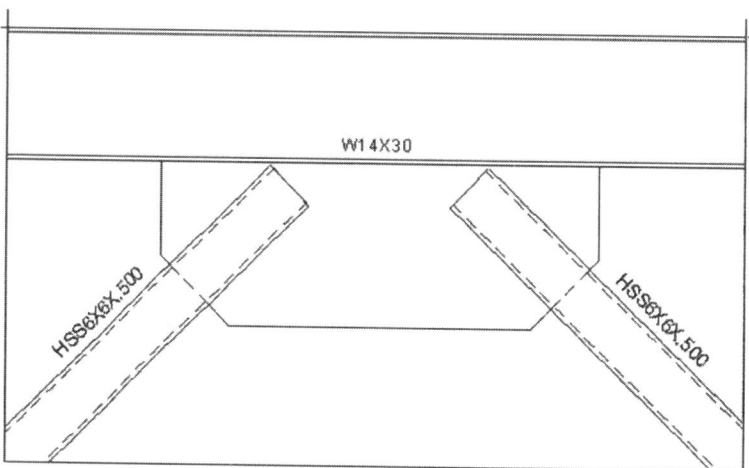

Figure 14–33

Task 1: Create a bracing detail.

1. Open **Structural-Detailing.rvt** from the practice files folder.
2. Open the **Elevations (Framing Elevation): West Bracing** view.
3. In the *View* tab>Create panel, click (Callout).
4. In the Type Selector, select **Elevation: Framing Elevation**.

5. Draw the callout around the entire bay between the 1st and 2nd floors, as shown in Figure 14–34.

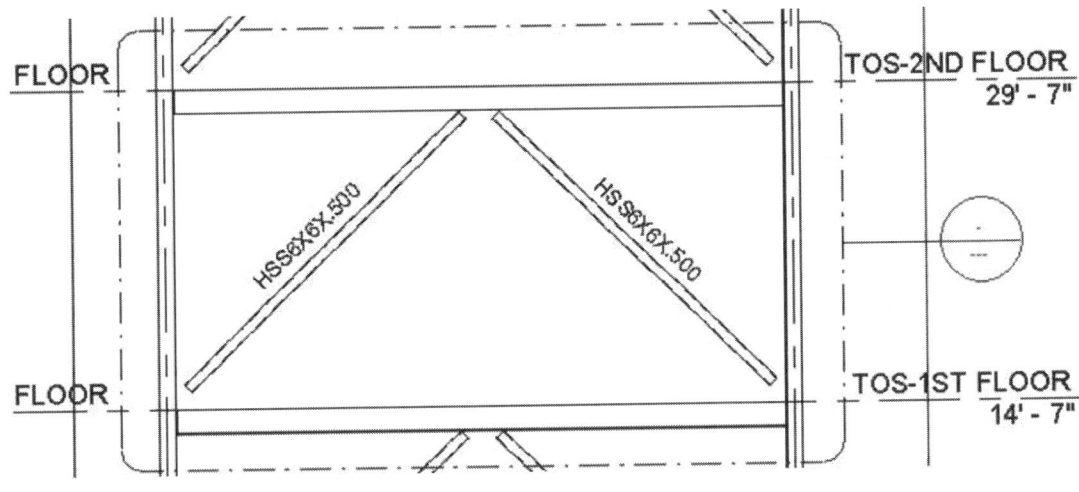

Figure 14–34

6. In the Project Browser, in the *Elevations (Framing Elevation)* area, rename the callout as **Bracing Bay A**.
7. Open the callout.
8. Set the *Scale* to **1/4"=1'-0"**, if it is not already set.
9. Add tags to the braces.
10. Save the project.

Task 2: Create a detail of a callout.

1. Create another callout of the area where the top plate should be added.
2. Open it and set the *Scale* to **3/4"=1'-0"**.
3. In the Type Selector, set the type to **Elevation: Framing Elevation**.
4. In the Project Browser, rename the callout **Typical Top Plate**.
5. In the View Control Bar, click (Do Not Crop View).

6. Use ⌐⌐ (Tag by Category) without a leader and tag the bracing. It shows outside of the cropped area, so you need to move the tags into the crop area, as shown in Figure 14–35.

7. In the View Control Bar, click ▭ (Crop View) to reapply the cropping.

8. In the *Annotate* tab>Detail panel, click ⌐⌐ (Detail Line).

9. In the *Modify | Place Detail Lines* tab>Line Styles panel, select **Thin Lines**. Use the **Line** command to draw and represent a gusset plate, as shown in Figure 14–35.

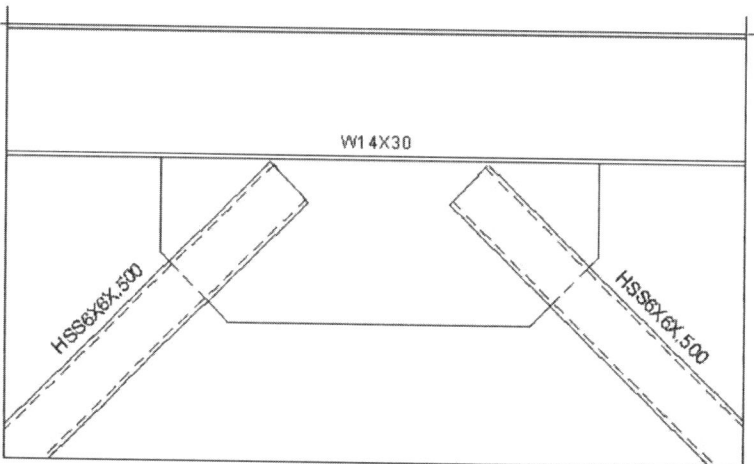

Figure 14–35

10. If time permits create, annotate, and detail a typical bottom plate.

11. Save and close the project.

End of practice

Practice 14c
Create Additional Details

Practice Objective

- Create and annotate details.

In this practice, you will create two structural details. Use the project **Structural-Detailing.rvt** from the practice files folder for these details.

Task 1: Create a foundation detail.

1. Create a new drafting view and draw the detail shown in Figure 14–36 using the various sketching tools and structural detail components.

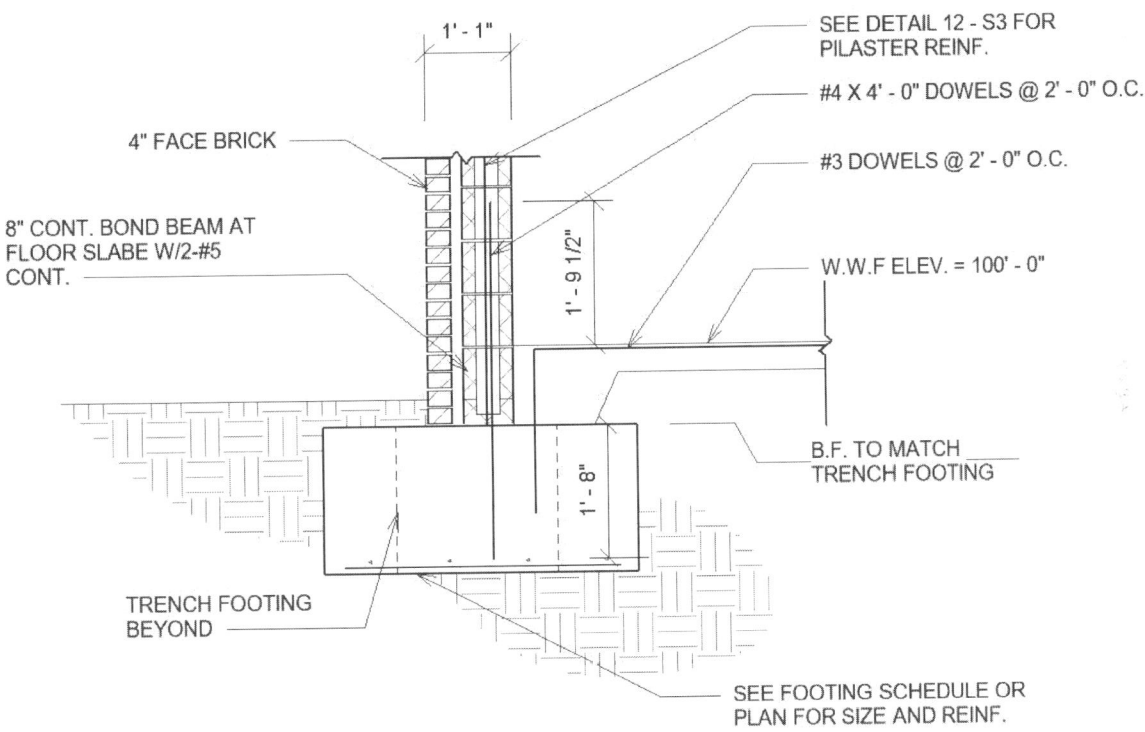

Figure 14–36

- Use the **Invisible lines** line type when you draw the lines for the fill boundary. The curved lines are made with splines.
- Create the Earth pattern type by duplicating an existing type and assigning a new drafting pattern to it.

Task 2: Create a typical elevator pit detail.

1. Create a new drafting view and draw the detail shown in Figure 14-37 using the various sketching tools, annotation elements, and filled regions.

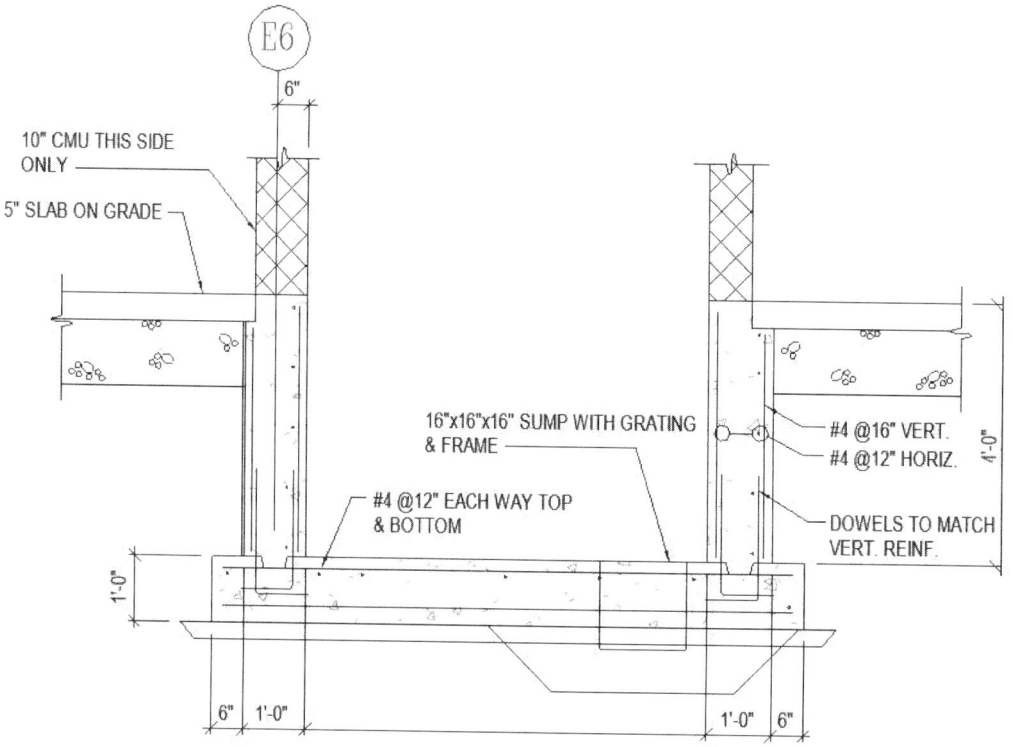

Figure 14-37

2. Add concrete filled regions as shown in Figure 14-38.

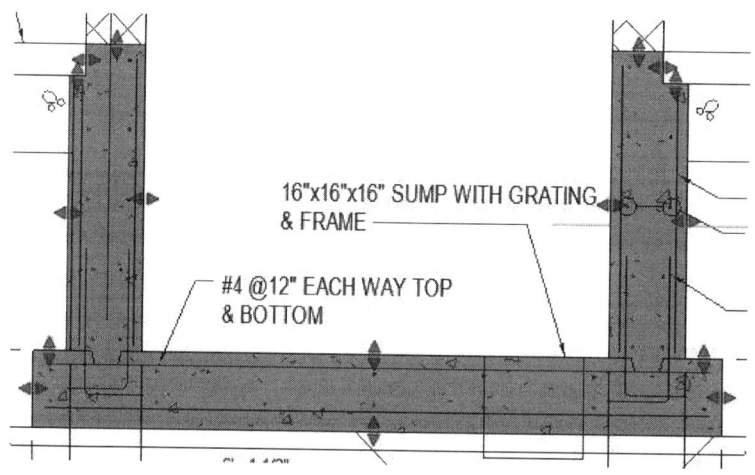

Figure 14-38

End of practice

Chapter Review Questions

1. Which of the following are ways in which you can create a detail? (Select all that apply.)

   a. Make a callout of a section and sketch over it.

   b. Draw all of the elements from scratch.

   c. Import a CAD detail and modify or sketch over it.

   d. Insert an existing drafting view from another file.

2. In which type of view (access shown in Figure 14–39) can you NOT add detail lines?

   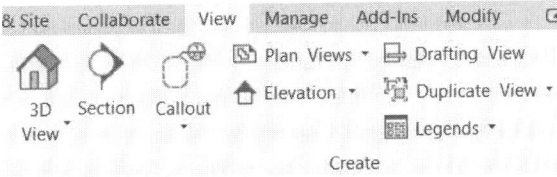

   Figure 14–39

   a. Plans

   b. Elevations

   c. 3D views

   d. Legends

3. How are detail components different from building components?

   a. There is no difference.

   b. Detail components are made of 2D lines and annotations only.

   c. Detail components are made of building elements, but only display in detail views.

   d. Detail components are made of 2D and 3D elements.

4. Which of the following statements is true when you sketch detail lines?

   a. Always the same width.

   b. Vary in width according to the view.

   c. Display in all views associated with the detail.

   d. Display only in the view in which they were created.

5. Which command do you use to add a pattern (such as concrete or earth, as shown in Figure 14–40) to part of a detail?

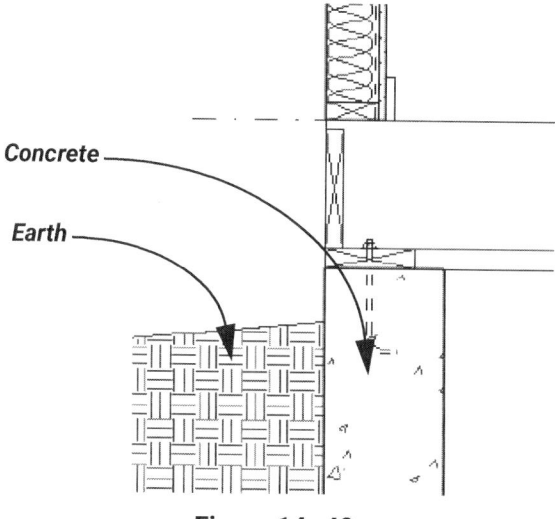

Figure 14–40

   a. Region
   b. Filled Region
   c. Masking Region
   d. Pattern Region

Command Summary

Button	Command	Location
CAD Import Tools		
	Delete Layers	• **Ribbon:** *Modify	<imported filename>* tab>Import Instance panel
	Full Explode	• **Ribbon:** *Modify	<imported filename>* tab>Import Instance panel, expand Explode
	Import CAD	• **Ribbon:** *Insert* tab>Import panel
	Partial Explode	• **Ribbon:** *Modify	<imported filename>* tab>Import Instance panel, expand Explode
Detail Tools		
	Detail Component	• **Ribbon:** *Annotate* tab>Detail panel, expand Component
	Detail Line	• **Ribbon:** *Annotate* tab>Detail panel
	Insulation	• **Ribbon:** *Annotate* tab>Detail panel
	Filled Region	• **Ribbon:** *Annotate* tab>Detail panel
	Repeating Detail Component	• **Ribbon:** *Annotate* tab>Detail panel, expand Component
View Tools		
	Bring Forward	• **Ribbon:** *Modify	Detail Items* tab>Arrange panel
	Bring to Front	• **Ribbon:** *Modify	Detail Items* tab>Arrange panel
	Drafting View	• **Ribbon:** *View* tab>Create panel
	Insert from File: Insert Views from File	• **Ribbon:** *Insert* tab>Load from Library panel, expand Insert from File
	Send Backward	• **Ribbon:** *Modify	Detail Items* tab>Arrange panel
	Send to Back	• **Ribbon:** *Modify	Detail Items* tab>Arrange panel

Appendix A

Additional Tools for Design Development

There are many other tools available in Revit® that you can use when creating and working in models. This appendix provides details about several tools and commands that are related to those covered in the Design Development section of this guide.

Learning Objectives

- Save and use selection sets of multiple building elements.
- Purge unused component elements to increase the processing speed of the model.
- Edit wall joins.
- Create structural slab types for foundation slabs.
- Create rebar types.
- Understand worksharing and working with workset-related files.

A.1 Selection Sets

When multiple elements types are selected, you can save the selection set so that it can be reused. For example, a structural column and an architectural column need to move together. Instead of picking each element, create a selection set that you can quickly access, as shown in Figure A–1. You can also edit selection sets to add or remove elements from the set.

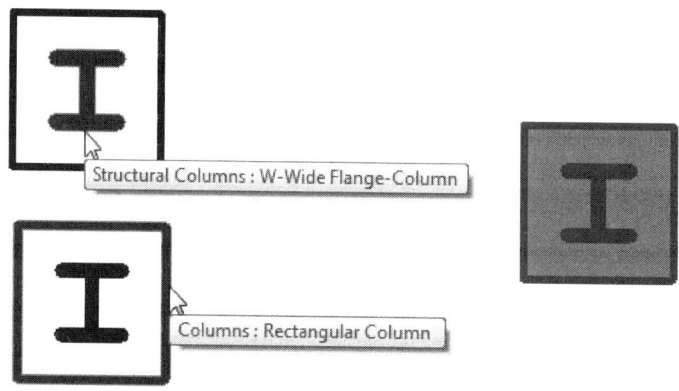

Figure A–1

- Selection sets are a filter of specific elements rather than types of elements.

How To: Save Selection Sets

1. Select the elements that you want to include in the selection set.
2. In the *Modify | Multi-Select* tab>Selection panel, click (Save).
3. In the Save Selection dialog box, type a name for the set, as shown in Figure A–2, and click **OK**.

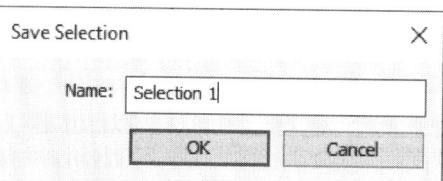

Figure A–2

How To: Retrieve Selection Sets

1. Select any other elements you might want to use. In the *Modify | Multi-Select* tab>Selection panel, click (Load). Alternatively, without any other selection, in the *Manage* tab>Selection panel, click (Load).

2. In the Retrieve Filters dialog box (shown in Figure A–3), select the set that you want to use and click **OK**.

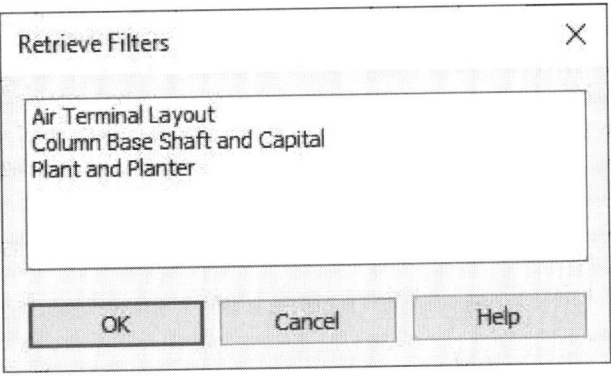

Figure A–3

3. The elements are selected, and you can continue to select other elements or use the selection.

How To: Edit Selection Sets

1. If elements are selected, in the *Modify | Multi-Select* tab>Selection panel, click (Edit).

   Alternatively, without any selection, in the *Manage* tab>Selection panel, click (Edit).

2. In the Edit Filters dialog box (shown in Figure A–4), in the **Selection Filters** node, select the set that you want to edit and click **Edit...**.

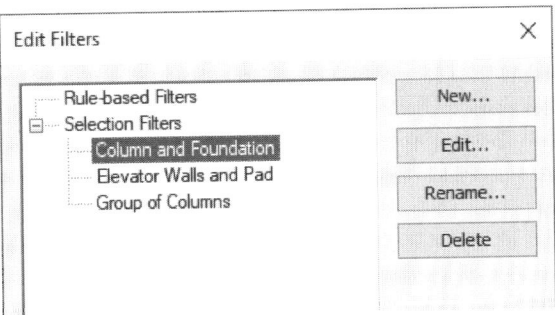

Figure A–4

- If you want to modify the name of the filter, click **Rename...**.

3. The selection set elements remain black while the rest of the elements are grayed out. The *Edit Selection Set* contextual tab displays as well, as shown in Figure A–5.

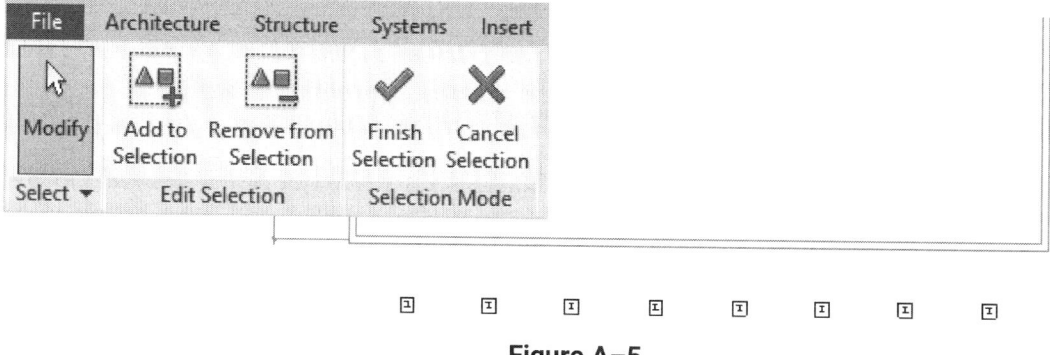

Figure A–5

4. Use (Add to Selection) to select additional elements for the set and (Remove from Selection) to delete elements from the set.

5. When you have finished editing, click (Finish Selection).

6. In the Filters dialog box, click **OK** to finish.

A.2 Purging Unused Elements

To reduce file size and remove unused elements from a project, including individual component types, you can purge the project, as shown in Figure A–6.

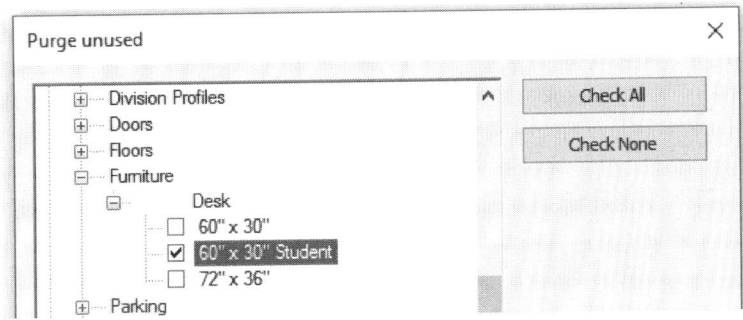

Figure A–6

- Some elements are nested in other elements and it might require several rounds of purging the project to remove them.

How To: Purge Unused Elements

1. In the *Manage* tab>Settings panel, click (Purge Unused).
2. In the Purge unused dialog box, click **Check None** and select the elements you want to purge.
3. Click **OK**.

- Purging unused components helps simplify the list of families loaded in a project.

A.3 Editing Wall Joins

Use **Edit Wall Joins** to modify the configuration of the intersections, as shown in Figure A–7. Do not use this command if you have complex wall joins; instead, modify the length of the wall in relation to the adjoining walls.

Figure A–7

How To: Modify the Configuration of a Wall Join

1. In the *Modify* tab>Geometry panel, click (Wall Joins).
2. Click on the wall join that you want to edit. There is a square box around the join. Hold <Ctrl> to select multiple joins.
3. In the Options Bar, the configuration options display, as shown in Figure A–8. Select the required option.

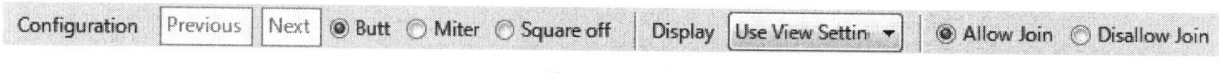

Figure A–8

- Select from three configurations: **Butt**, **Miter**, and **Square off**, as shown in Figure A–9.

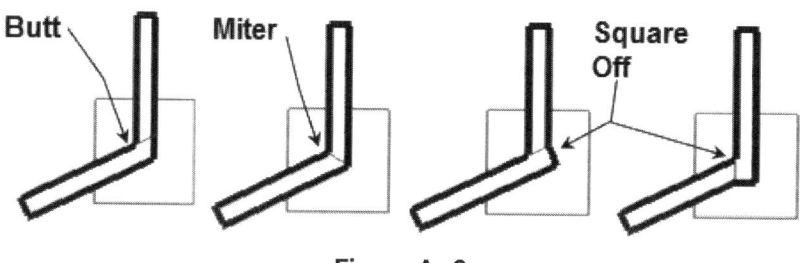

Figure A–9

- Click **Previous** and **Next** to toggle the butt or squared-off corner configurations through the various intersection options.
- **Allow Join** automatically cleans up the join while **Disallow Join** breaks the connection.

4. The **Wall Joins** command remains active until you select another command.

Additional Tools for Design Development

How To: Modify Display Options of Wall Joins

1. In the *Modify* tab>Geometry panel, click (Wall Joins).
2. Click on the wall join that you want to edit.
   - To modify multiple joins at the same time, draw a window around several wall intersections (as shown in Figure A-10), or hold <Ctrl> and pick additional intersections. A square box displays around each join.

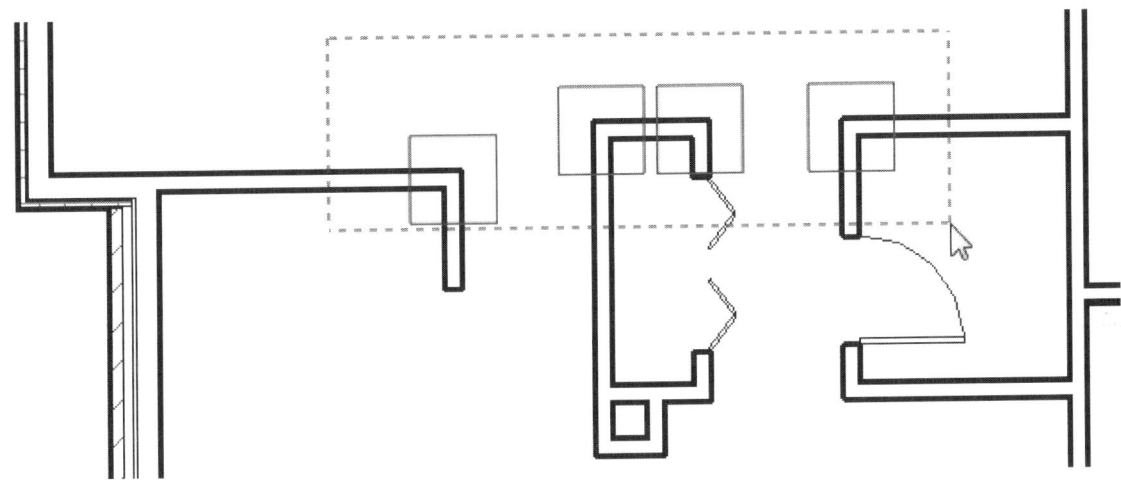

Figure A-10

- The *Display* controls whether or not wall joins are displayed. The options are **Use View Settings** (set up in View Properties), **Clean Join**, and **Don't Clean Join**, as shown in Figure A-11.

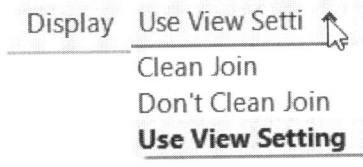

Figure A-11

3. If you select the end of a wall that is not joined to another wall, you can change the option to **Allow Join** in the Options Bar, as shown in Figure A-12. Reselect the wall join to make the configurations available.

Figure A-12

A.4 Creating Slab Types

Several slab types are available in the template files that are included with the software, as shown in Figure A–13. You can also create additional slab types based on the provided types, as needed.

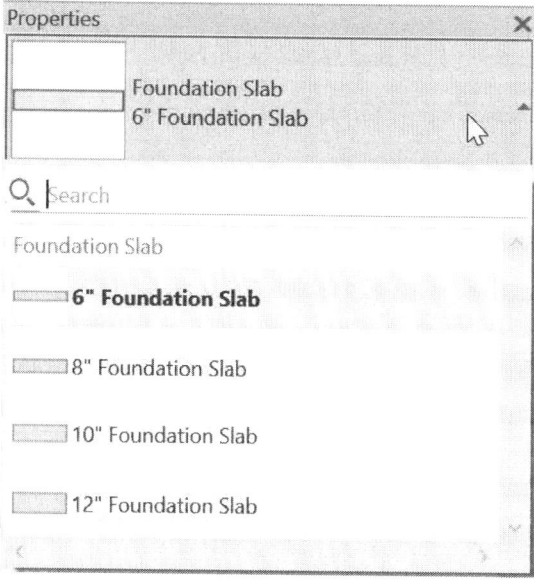

Figure A–13

- Reinforcement is placed in a slab in a separate function. Therefore, you are not required to add it to the slab type.
- The process of creating a structural floor or roof slab type is similar.

How To: Create a Slab Type

1. Start the **Structural Foundation: Slab** command or select an existing slab.
2. In the Type Selector, select a type similar to the one you want to create. In Properties, click ▦ (Edit Type).
3. In the Type Properties dialog box, click **Duplicate...** and enter a name for the new type.
4. Next to the *Structure* parameter, click **Edit...**, as shown in Figure A–14.

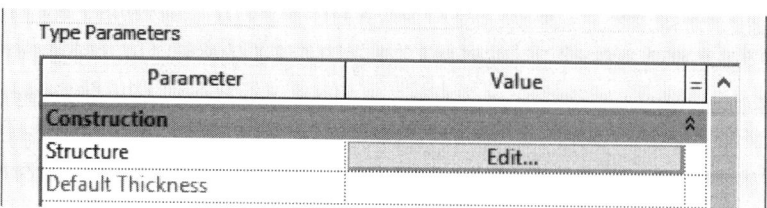

Figure A–14

- You can also set up *Graphics*, *Identity Data*, and some *Analytical Properties* in the Type Properties dialog box.

5. In the Edit Assembly dialog box, as shown with the Preview pane open in Figure A–15, you can change the composition of the slab. When you are finished, click **OK** to close the Edit Assembly dialog box and to close Type Properties.

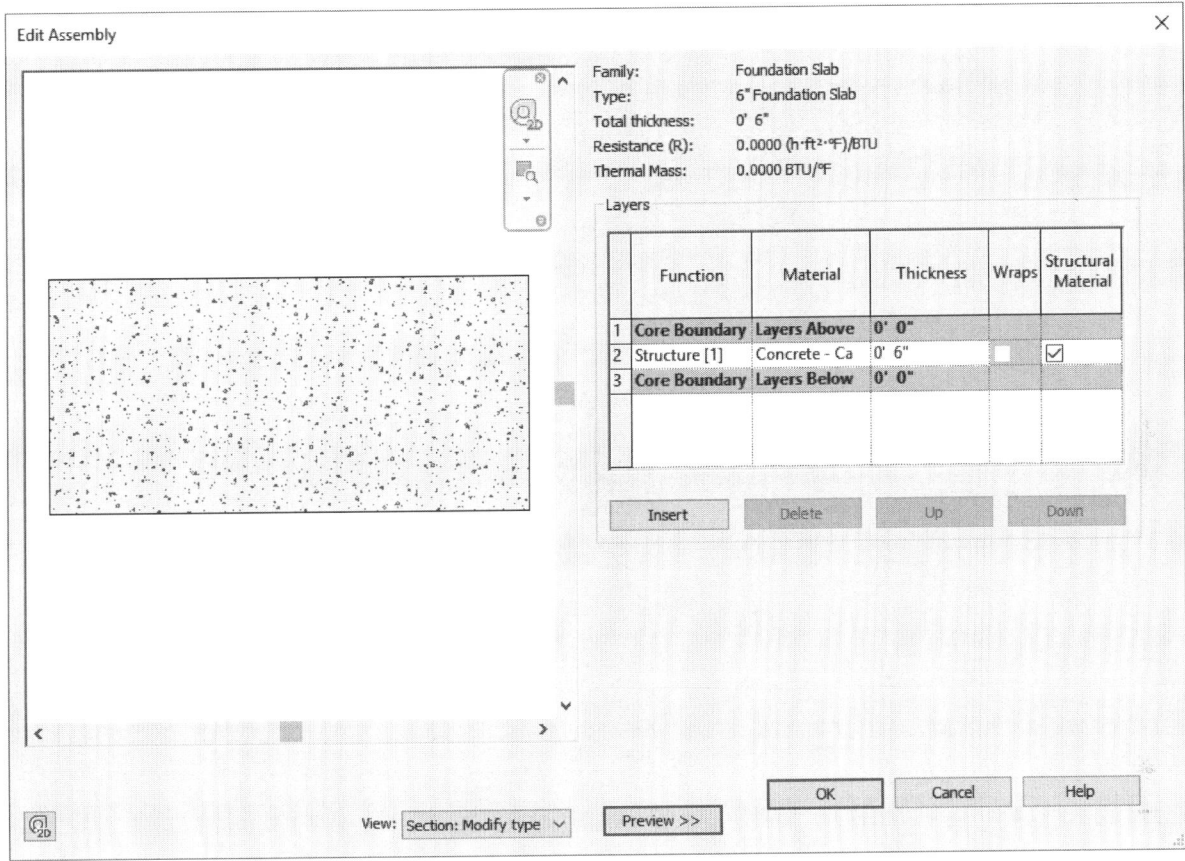

Figure A–15

- When you specify the layers for the compound element, you assign them a *Function*, *Material*, and *Thickness*.

- Use the buttons to insert additional layers and to rearrange them in the layer list. You can also delete layers from the list.

- Core boundaries separate the structural core of the slab assembly from non-structural layers above and below.

- Click **<<Preview** to display the layers of the slab in section. This tool is most useful when the slab is more complex.

A.5 Creating Rebar Types

You can create new rebar types. When a rebar element is selected, click ⊞ (Edit Type) in Properties. In the Type Properties dialog box, duplicate an existing type and fill out the rest of the parameters, as shown in Figure A–16. Any changes made here impact all other instances of the Rebar Bar type.

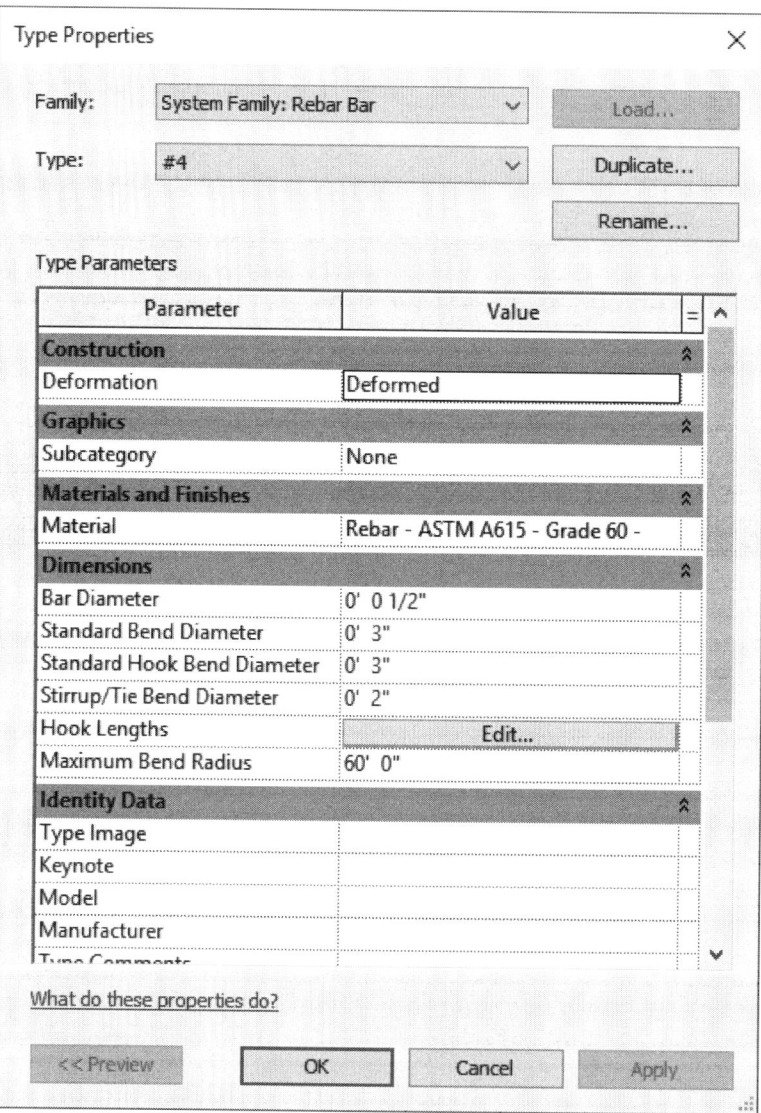

Figure A–16

Additional Tools for Design Development

- You can change the *Hook Lengths* parameter by clicking **Edit...** and using the Rebar Hook Lengths dialog box, as shown in Figure A–17. Options include *Hook Length*, *Tangent Length*, and *Offset Length*.

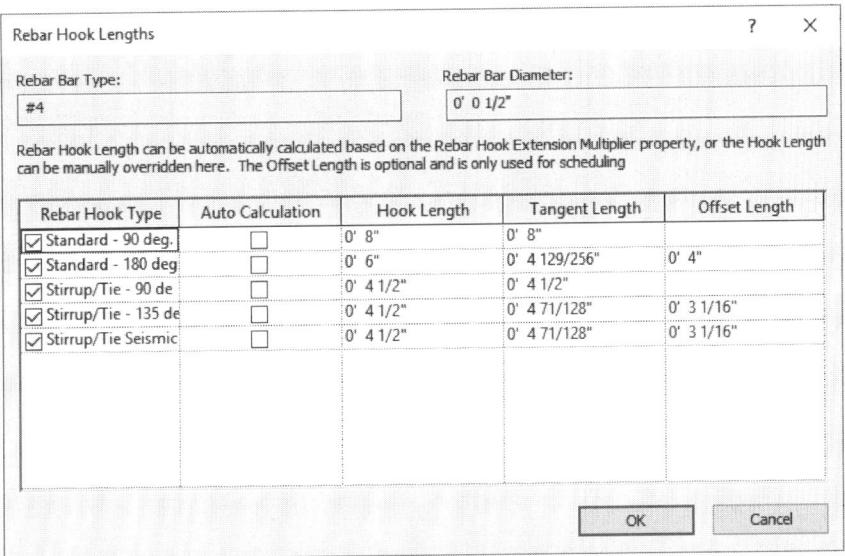

Figure A–17

> **Hint: Creating Rebar Hook Types**
>
> If you need to add rebar hook types, you can duplicate an existing type in the Project Browser, in the *Families>Structural Rebar* category.
>
> Double-click on the new hook type. This opens the Type Properties in which you can modify the *Style*, *Hook Angle*, and *Extension Multiplier,* as shown in Figure A–18.

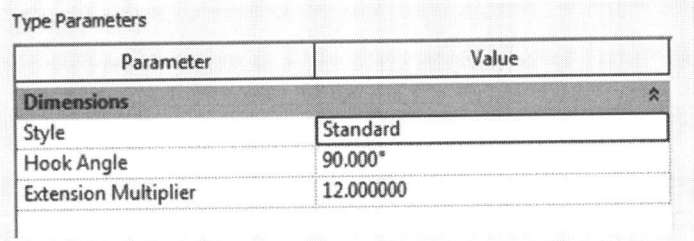

Figure A–18

The *Extension Multiplier* value is multiplied by the diameter of the bar and then adds the bend radius to the equation. Therefore, if the bar *Diameter* is **0.5"** and the *Multiplier* is **24**, the actual hook *Length* is **1'-0"**.

A.6 Introduction to Revit Worksharing

When a project becomes too big for one person, it needs to be subdivided so that a team of people working on the same network can work on it. Since Revit projects include the entire building model in one file, the file needs to be separated into logical components, as shown in Figure A–19, without losing the connection to the whole. This process is called *worksharing* and the main components are worksets.

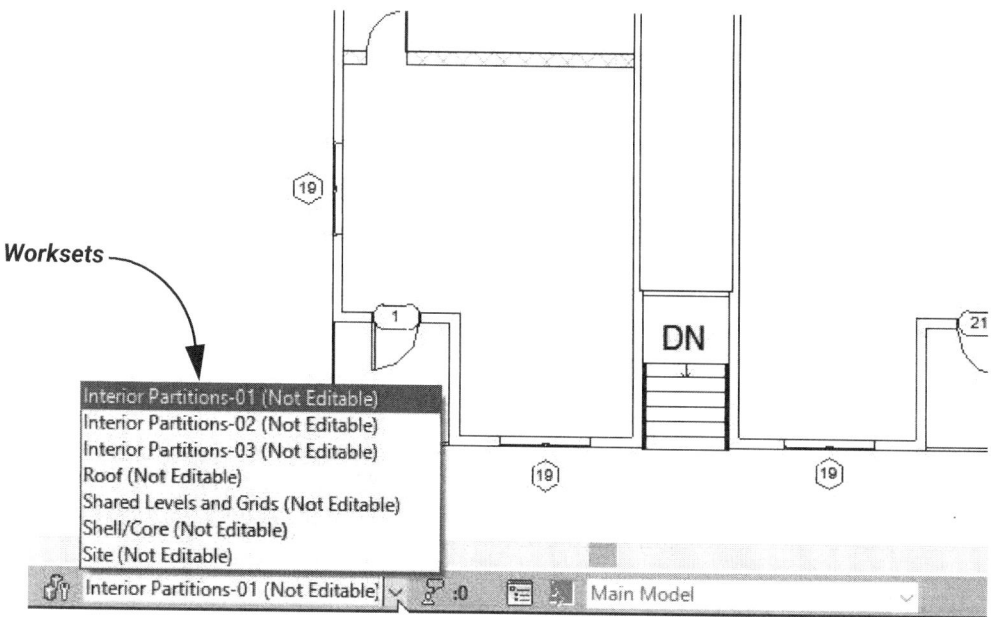

Figure A–19

Revit worksharing gives multiple team members connected on the same network the ability to co-author a single project model (one .RVT file). The appropriate team member creates a central model with multiple worksets (such as element interiors, building shell, and site) that are used by the project team members. Team members open and work in a local copy of the model that is linked back to the central model through saving and synchronizing. For more information about establishing and using worksets, refer to the ASCENT guide *Autodesk Revit: Collaboration Tools*.

A workshared project consists of one central model (also known as a central file) and individual models for each user known as local files, as shown in Figure A–20. Each team member will work in their local file and use a function called *synchronizing with central* to send and receive updates with the central model.

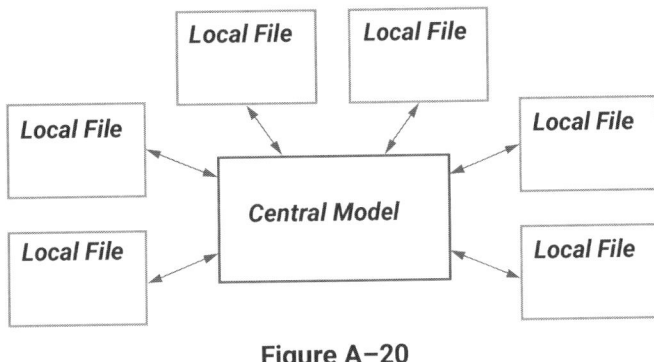

Figure A–20

- The **central model** is created by the BIM manager, project manager, or project lead and is stored on a server or in the cloud, enabling multiple users to access it.
- A **local file** is a copy of the central model that is stored on your computer.
- All local files are saved back to the central model, and updates to the central model are sent out to the local files. This way, all changes remain in one file, while the project, model, views, and sheets are automatically updated.

Worksharing Definitions

Worksharing: This is a functionality that, when enabled, allows multiple members of the team to access a project stored in one centralized location, which gives multiple users the ability to work on the same project simultaneously.

Workshared file: This is a project that has worksets enabled. If the project has no worksets enabled, it is called a *non-workshared file*.

Workset: This is a collection of elements that are related geometrically, parametrically, or by location within an overall project that are subdivided so they can be worked on while isolated from the rest of the model. When worksharing is enabled, worksets are automatically activated and the *Workset1* and *Shared Grids and Levels* worksets are added to the project by default.

Central model: Also called the central file, this is the main project file that is stored on a local network that all users can access. Using a central model is called *file-based worksharing*. The central model stores workset and element information in the project and is the file to which everyone saves and synchronizes their changes. The central model updates all the local files with the latest model information. This file should not be edited directly.

Local file: This is a copy of the central model that is saved to your local computer. This is the file that you modify and work in. As you work, you save the file locally and synchronize it with the central model.

Element borrowing: This refers to the process of modifying items in the project that are not part of the workset you have checked out. This either happens automatically (if no one else has checked out a workset) or specifically, when you request to have control of the elements (if someone else has a workset checked out).

Active workset: The workset that displays in the Status Bar is the active workset. Any new elements that are added will be placed on this workset. As you work, you will change the active workset accordingly.

Relinquish: This releases or returns a checked-out workset so that others can work on the elements within that workset. If you do not release or relinquish your checked-out worksets, other users will get a warning that they cannot edit the workset until you relinquish it, and they are given the option to request to borrow the workset. **Relinquish All Mine** allows you to relinquish worksets without synchronizing to the central model.

Reload Latest: This updates your local file without you needing to synchronize with the central model.

General Process of Using Worksets

1. Wait for the appropriate team member to enable worksharing, set up worksets, and create the central model.
2. Create a local file from the central model.
3. Work in your local file and select the worksets that you need to work on by verifying the active workset.
   - Work in your local model by adding, deleting, and modifying elements.
   - You may need to request to borrow elements in worksets that are currently checked out by other team members.
4. Save the local file as frequently as you would save any other project.
5. Synchronize the local file with the central model several times a day or as required by company policy or project status.
   - This reloads any changes from the central model to your local file and vice versa.
   - If the option to **Save Local File before and after synchronizing with central** is checked, your local file will be saved, but it is always recommended to save the local file yourself every time you synchronize to the central model.

Opening Workset-Related Files

When you open a workset-related file, it creates a new local file on your computer. Do not work in the main central model.

How To: Create a Local File

1. In the *File* tab or Quick Access Toolbar, click 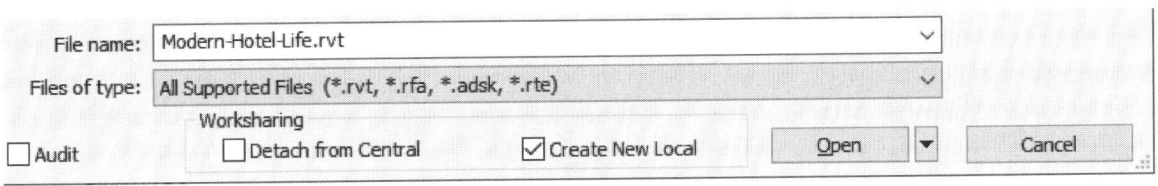 (Open).
2. In the Open dialog box, navigate to the central model server location and select the central model. Do not work in this file. Select **Create New Local**, as shown in Figure A–21, and click **Open**.

Figure A–21

3. A copy of the project is created. It will have the same name as the central model with your Autodesk Revit username added to the end.

- If you are working with a recently used central model, it may display on the Home screen with the icon shown in Figure A–22. Clicking this file automatically creates a local copy of the model. The first time you use this option, a warning displays, as shown in Figure A–23.

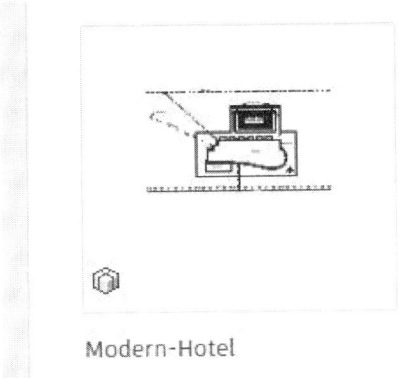

Figure A–22

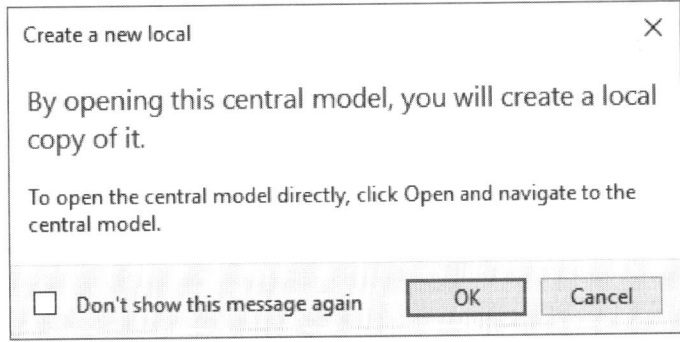

Figure A–23

4. You can save the file using the default name, or use  (Save As) and name the file according to your office's standard. It should include *Local* in the name to indicate that it is saved on your local computer, or that you are the only one working with that version of the file.

- Delete any old local files to ensure that you are working on the latest version.

How To: Work in a Workshared Project

1. Open your local file.
2. In the Status Bar, expand the *Active Workset* drop-down list and select a workset, as shown in Figure A–24. By setting the active workset, other people can work in the project but cannot edit elements that you add to the workset.

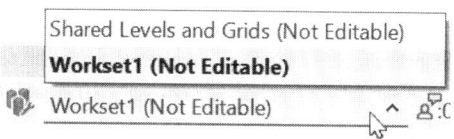

Figure A–24

3. Work on the project as needed.

Saving a Workshared Project

When you are working on a workshared project, you need to save the project locally and centrally.

- Save the local file frequently (every 15-30 minutes). In the Quick Access Toolbar, click ▣ (Save) to save the local file just as you would any other project.

- Synchronize the local file with the central model periodically (every hour or two) or after you have made major changes to the project.

> **Hint: Set Up Notifications to Save and Synchronize**
>
> You can set up reminders to save and synchronize files to the central model in the Options dialog box, on the *General* tab, as shown in Figure A–25.

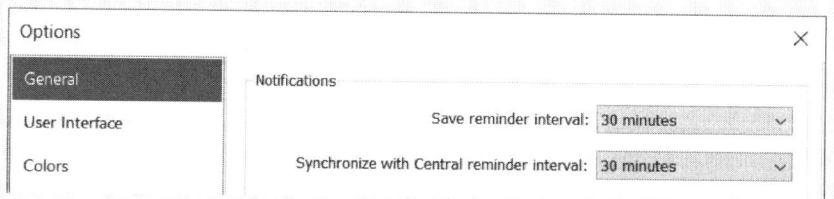

Figure A–25

Synchronizing to the Central Model

There are two methods for synchronizing to the central model. In the *Quick Access Toolbar* or *Collaborate* tab>Synchronize panel, expand (Synchronize with Central) and click (Synchronize Now) or (Synchronize and Modify Settings). The last-used command is active if you click the top-level icon.

- **Synchronize Now:** Updates the central model and then the local file with any changes to the central model since the last synchronization without prompting you for any settings. It automatically relinquishes elements borrowed from any workset but retains worksets used by the current user.
- **Synchronize and Modify Settings:** Opens the Synchronize with Central dialog box, shown in Figure A–26, so you can set the options for relinquishing worksets and elements, add comments, and specify to save the file locally before and after synchronization.

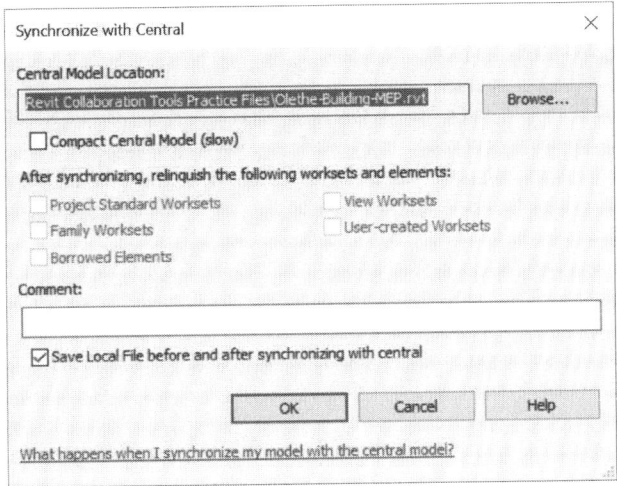

Figure A–26

- Always keep **Save Local File before and after synchronizing with central** checked to ensure your local copy is up to date with the latest changes from the central model.

- When you close a local file without saving to the central model, you are prompted to do so, as shown in Figure A–27.

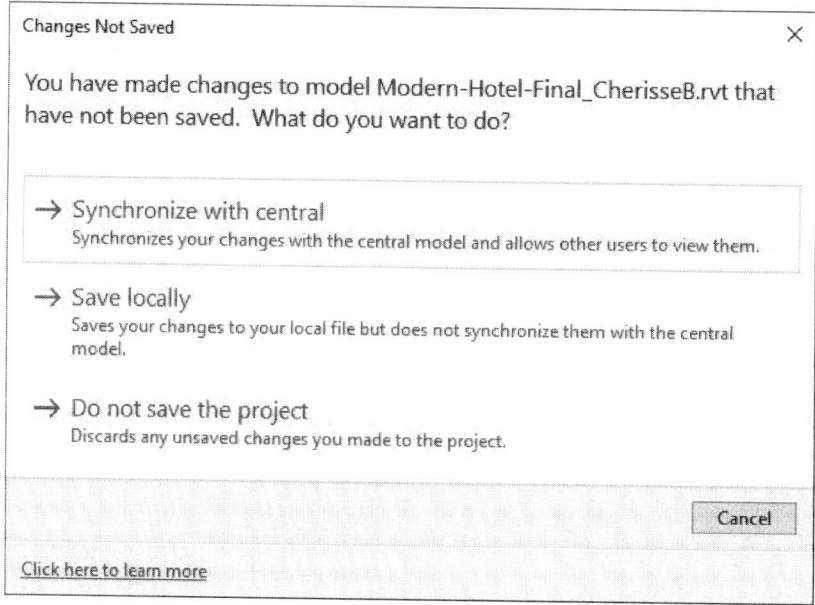

Figure A–27

- The maximum number of backups for workset-enabled files is set to 20 by default.
- Note: Workshared files do not have the same backup files as non-workshared files.

Command Summary

Button	Command	Location
Purge Elements		
	Purge Unused	• **Ribbon:** *Manage* tab>Settings panel
Selection Sets		
	Edit Selection	• **Ribbon:** *Modify	Multi-Select* tab>Selection panel
	Load Selection	• **Ribbon:** *Modify	Multi-Select* tab>Selection panel
	Save Selection	• **Ribbon:** *Modify	Multi-Select* tab>Selection panel
	Add to Selection	• **Ribbon:** *Edit Selection Set* tab>Edit Selection panel
	Remove from Selection	• **Ribbon:** *Edit Selection Set* tab>Edit Selection panel
Worksharing		
	Save	• **Quick Access Toolbar** • *File* **tab:** Save • **Shortcut:** <Ctrl>+<S>
	Synchronize and Modify Settings	• **Quick Access Toolbar** • **Ribbon:** *Collaborate* tab>Synchronize panel, expand Synchronize with Central
	Synchronize Now	• **Quick Access Toolbar** • **Ribbon:** *Collaborate* tab>Synchronize panel, expand Synchronize with Central

# Appendix B

Additional Tools for Construction Documents

There are many other tools available in Revit® that you can use when creating construction documents. This appendix provides details about several tools and commands that are related to those covered in the Construction Documentation section of this guide.

Learning Objectives

- Use guide grids to help place views on sheets.
- Add revision clouds, tags, and information.
- Annotate dependent views with matchlines and view references.
- Create material takeoff schedules.
- Import and export schedules.
- Create repeating detail types.
- Place keynotes in a detail and add keynote legends that describe the full content of the keynotes

B.1 Working with Guide Grids on Sheets

You can use a guide grid to help you place views on a sheet, as shown in Figure B–1. Guide grids can be set up per sheet. You can also create different types with various grid spacings.

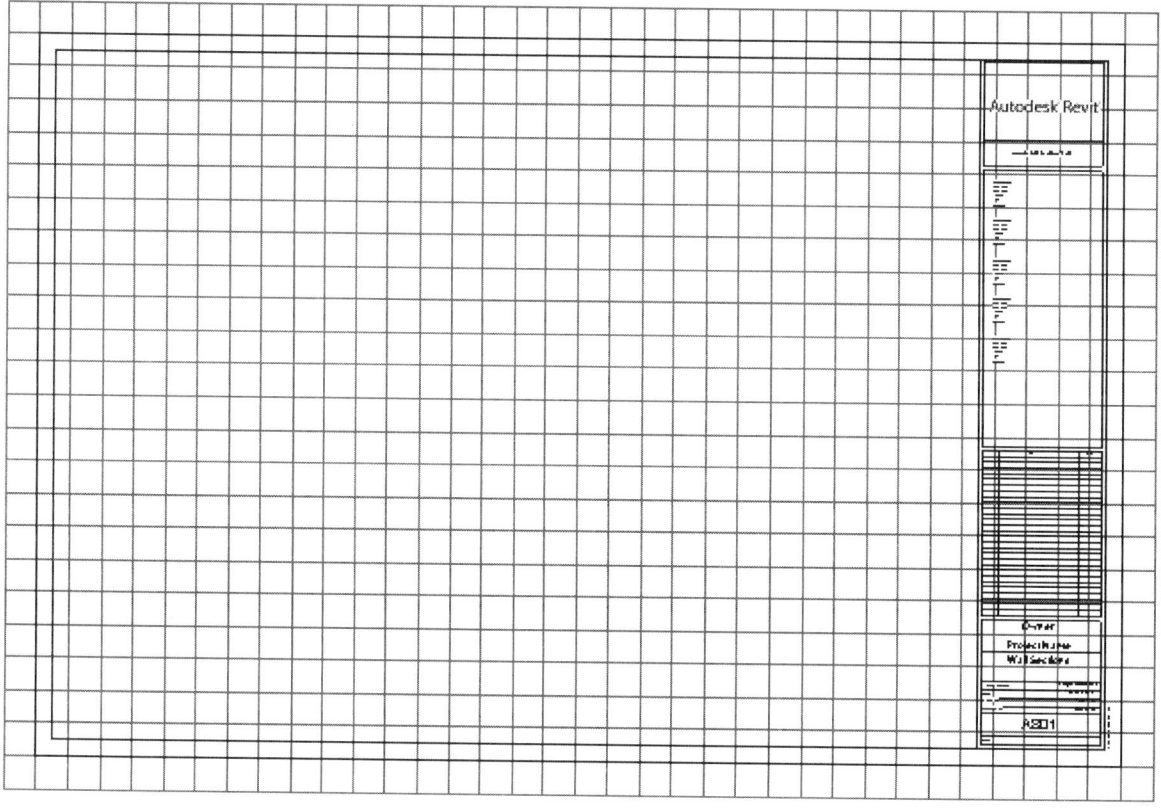

Figure B–1

- You can move guide grids and resize them using controls.

    Note: When moving a view to a guide grid, only orthogonal datum elements (levels and grids) and reference planes snap to the guide grid.

How To: Add a Guide Grid

1. When a sheet is open, in the *View* tab>Sheet Composition panel, click ▦ (Guide Grid).
2. In the Assign Guide Grid dialog box, select from existing guide grids (as shown in Figure B–2), or create a new one and give it a name.

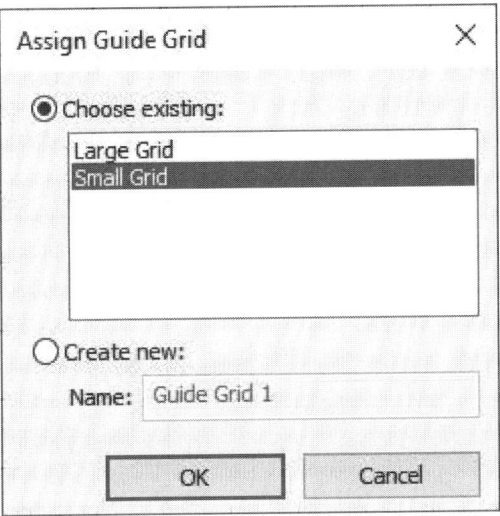

Figure B–2

3. The guide grid displays using the specified sizing.

How To: Modify Guide Grid Sizing

1. If you create a new guide grid you need to update it to the correct size in Properties. Select the edge of the guide grid.
2. In Properties, set the *Guide Spacing*, as shown in Figure B–3.

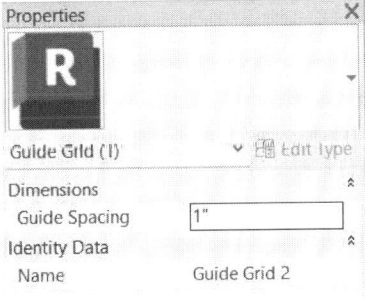

Figure B–3

B.2 Revision Tracking

When a set of working drawings has been put into production, you need to show where changes are made. Typically, these are shown on sheets using revision clouds and tags along with a revision schedule in the title block, as shown in Figure B–4. The revision information is set up in the Sheet Issues/Revisions dialog box.

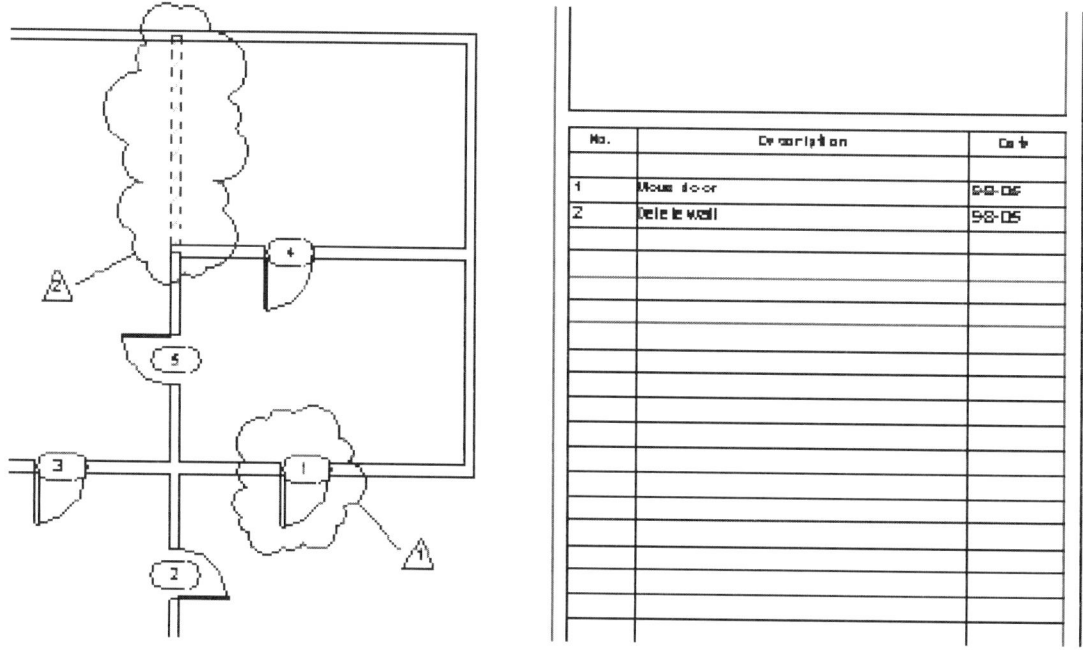

Figure B–4

- More than one revision cloud can be associated with a revision number.

- The title blocks that come with Revit already have a revision schedule inserted into the title area. It is recommended that you also add a revision schedule to your company title block.

- You have the ability to create multiple revision numbering sequences and you can use **Transfer Project Standards** to transfer these custom revision settings and revision numbering sequences to other projects.

- You can create a revision cloud schedule that can include multiple revisions. In a sheet view, from Properties, you can click **Edit...** and specify which revision you want to display on the sheet even if the revision is not on the sheet.

How To: Add Revision Information to the Project

1. In the *View* tab>Sheet Composition panel, click (Sheet Issues/Revisions).
2. In the Sheet Issues/Revisions dialog box, set the type of *Numbering* you want to use.
3. Click **Add** to add a new revision.
4. Specify the *Date* and *Description* for the revision, as shown in Figure B–5.

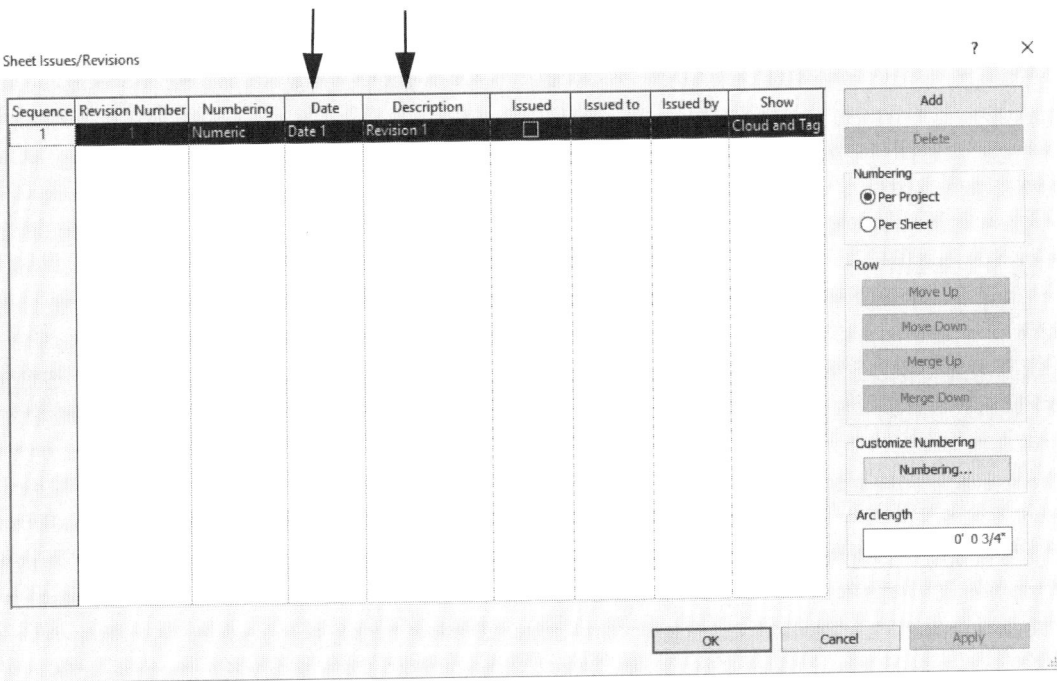

Figure B–5

- Do not modify the *Issued*, *Issued by*, or *Issued to* columns. You should wait to issue revisions until you are ready to print the sheets.

5. Click **OK** when you have finished adding revisions.

- To remove a revision, select its *Sequence* number and click **Delete**.

Revision Options

- *Numbering*: Specify **Per Project** (the numbering sequence is used throughout the project) or **Per Sheet** (the number sequence is per sheet).
- *Row*: To reorganize the revisions, select a row and click **Move Up** and **Move Down**, or use **Merge Up** and **Merge Down** to combine the revisions into one.

- *Customize Numbering:* Click **Numbering...** to bring up the Numbering dialog box (shown in Figure B–6). You can edit the Alphanumeric or Numeric sequences or create custom sequences.

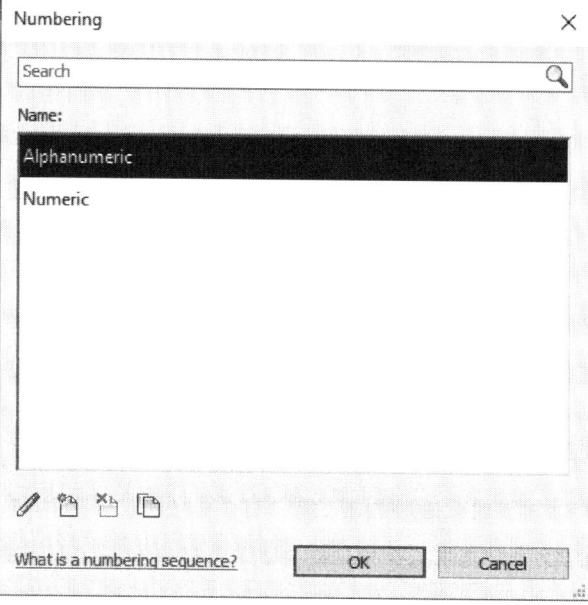

Figure B–6

- You can specify whether to create a new numbering sequence based off of **Numeric** or **Alphanumeric** as well as any prefix or suffix, as shown for the New Numbering Sequence dialog box in Figure B–7.

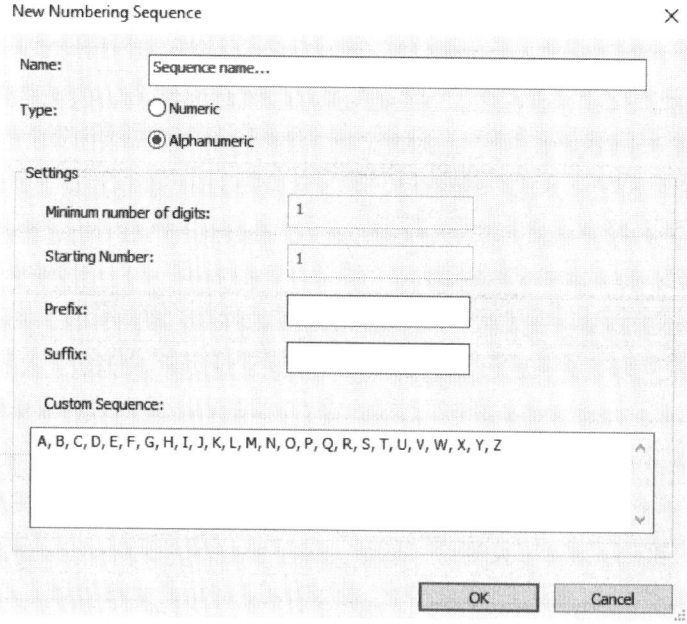

Figure B–7

- *Arc length:* Specify the length of the arcs that form the revision cloud. It is an annotation element and is scaled according to the view scale.

How To: Add Revision Clouds and Tags

1. In the *Annotate* tab>Detail panel, click (Revision Cloud).
2. In the *Modify | Create Revision Cloud Sketch* tab>Draw panel, use the draw tools to create the cloud.
3. In Properties, select which *Revision* type to use, as shown in Figure B–8.

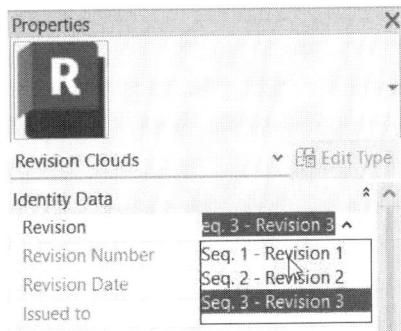

Figure B–8

4. Click (Finish Edit Mode).

- To modify a revision cloud, select a revision cloud, then in the Options Bar or Properties, expand the Revision drop-down list and select the revision, as shown in Figure B–9.

   Note: If the revision table has not be set up, you can do this at a later date.

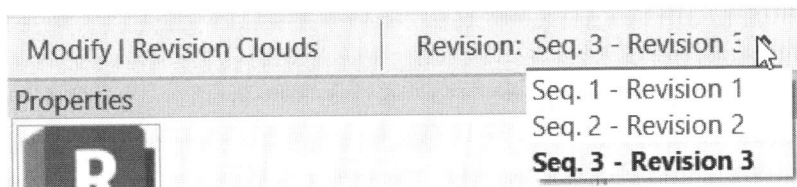

Figure B–9

5. In the *Annotate* tab>Tag panel, click (Tag By Category).

6. Select the revision cloud to tag. A tooltip containing the revision number and revision from the cloud properties displays when you hover the cursor over the revision cloud, as shown in Figure B–10.

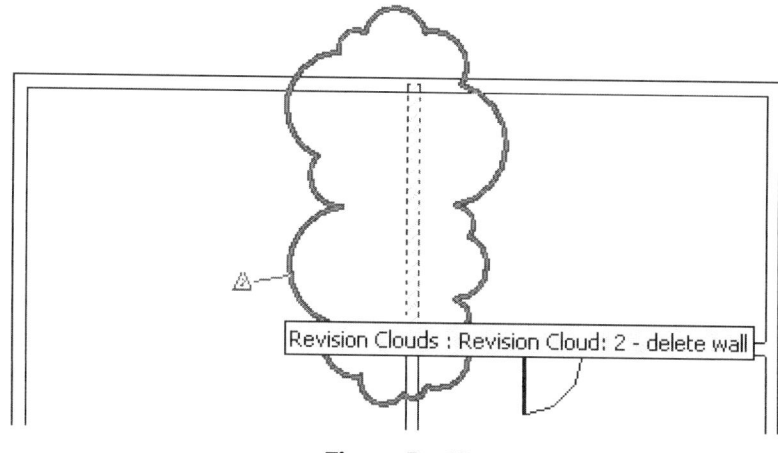

Figure B–10

- If the revision cloud tag is not loaded, load **Revision Tag.rfa** from the *Annotations* folder in the Revit Library.

- The *Revision Number* and *Date* are automatically assigned according to the specifications in the revision table.

- Double-click on the edge of revision cloud to switch to Edit Sketch mode and modify the size or location of the revision cloud arcs.

- You can create an open cloud (e.g., as a tree line), as shown in Figure B–11.

Figure B–11

Issuing Revisions

When you have completed the revisions and are ready to submit new documents to the field, you should first lock the revision for the record. This is called issuing the revision. An issued revision is noted in the tooltip of a revision cloud, as shown in Figure B–12.

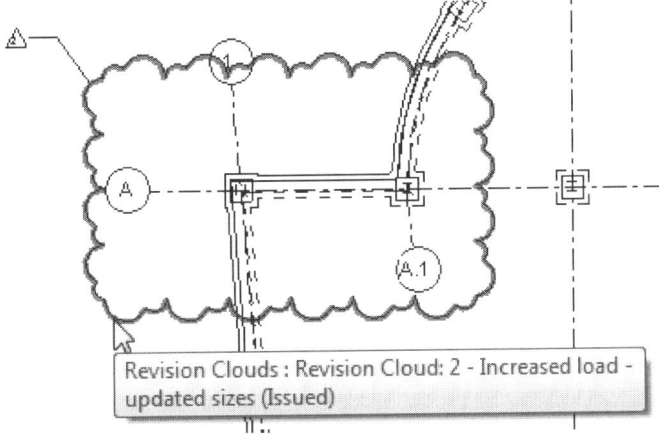

Figure B–12

How To: Issue Revisions

1. In the *View* tab>Sheet Composition panel, click (Sheet Issues/Revisions).
2. In the Sheet Issues/Revisions dialog box, in the row for the revision that you are issuing, type a name in the *Issued to* and *Issued by* fields, as needed.
3. In the same row, select **Issued**.
4. Continue issuing any other revisions, as needed.
5. Click **OK** to finish.

- Once **Issued** is selected, you cannot modify that revision in the Revisions dialog box or by moving the revision cloud(s). The tooltip on the cloud(s) note that it is **Issued**.
- You can unlock the revision by clearing the **Issued** option. Unlocking enables you to modify the revision after it has been locked.

B.3 Annotating Dependent Views

The **Duplicate as a Dependent** command creates a copy of the view and links it to the selected view. Changes made to the original view are also made in the dependent view and vice-versa. Use dependent views when the building model is so large you need to split the building up on separate sheets, as shown in Figure B–13.

Figure B–13

- Using one overall view with several dependent views makes it easier to see changes, such as to the scale or detail level.

- Dependent views display in the Project Browser under the top-level view, as shown in Figure B–14.

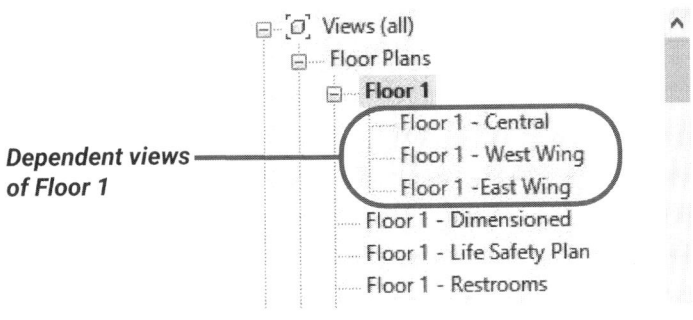

Figure B–14

How To: Duplicate Dependent Views

1. Select the view you want to use as the top-level view.
2. Right-click and select **Duplicate View>Duplicate as a Dependent**.
3. Rename the dependent views as needed.
4. Modify the crop region of the dependent view to show the specified portion of the model.

- If you want to separate a dependent view from the original view, right-click on the dependent view and select **Convert to independent view**.

Annotating Views

To clarify and annotate dependent views, use **Matchlines** and **View References**, as shown in Figure B–15.

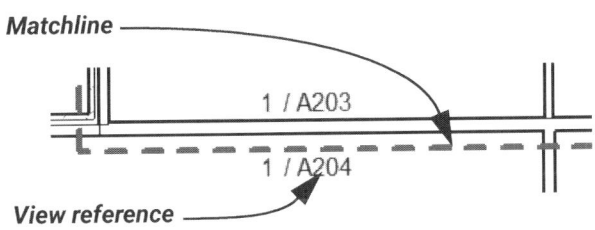

Figure B–15

- Sketch matchlines in the primary view to specify where dependent views separate. They display in all related views and extend through all levels of the project by default.
- View references are special tags that display the sheet location of the dependent views.

How To: Add Matchlines

1. In the *View* tab>Sheet Composition panel, click (Matchline).

2. In the Draw panel, click (Line) and sketch the location of the matchline.

3. In the Matchline panel, click (Finish Edit Mode) when you are finished.

- To modify an existing matchline, select it and click (Edit Sketch) in the *Modify | Matchline* tab>Mode panel.

- To modify the color and line type of Matchlines, in the *Manage* tab>Settings panel, click (Object Styles). In the Object Styles dialog box that opens, in the *Annotation Objects* tab, you can make changes to Matchline properties.

How To: Add View References

1. In the *View* tab>Sheet Composition panel or *Annotate* tab>Tag panel, click (View Reference).

2. In the *Modify | View Reference* tab>View Reference panel, search for or specify the *View Type* and *Target View*, as shown in Figure B–16.

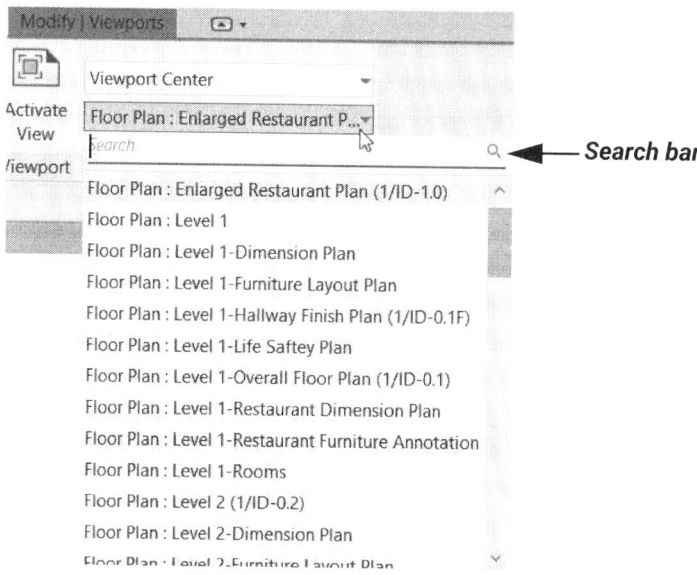

Figure B–16

3. Place the tag on the side of the matchline that corresponds to the target view.

4. Click (Modify) to clear the selection.

5. Repeat the process and place the tag on the other side of the matchline.

6. The tags display as empty dashes until the views are placed onto sheets. They then update to include the detail and sheet number, as shown in Figure B–17.

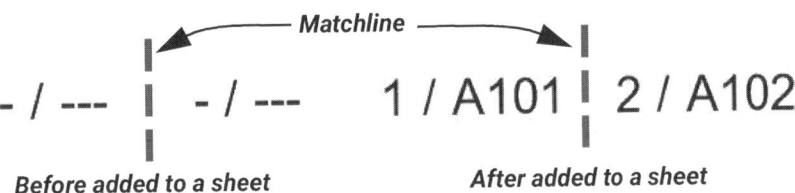

Figure B–17

- Double-click on the view reference to open the associated view.

- If only a label named **REF** displays when you place a view reference, it means you need to load and update the tag. The **View Reference.rfa** tag is located in the *Annotations* folder in the Revit Library. Once you have the tag loaded, in the Type Selector, select one of the view references and, in Properties, click (Edit Type). Select **View Reference** in the drop-down list, as shown in Figure B–18, and click **OK** to close the dialog box. The new tag displays.

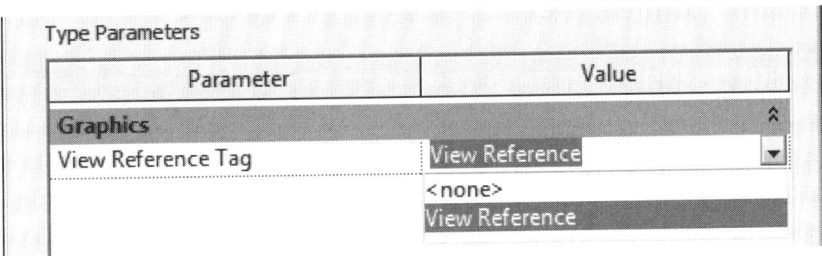

Figure B–18

B.4 Material Takeoff Schedules

Material takeoff or count schedules (shown in Figure B–19) are used for material estimates and organization. This type of schedule can be added to a drawing sheet, but is typically intended for project quantities.

A	B	C	D	E	F
		Diimensions			
Type Mark	Count	Type	Length	Base Level	Material
A	6	12 x 18	10' - 0"	Level 1	Concrete, Cast-in-Place gray
B	6	18 x 24	12' - 0"	T.O. Footing	Concrete, Cast-in-Place gray
C	14	24 x 30	12' - 0"	T.O. Footing	Concrete, Cast-in-Place gray
Grand total: 26					

<Concrete Column Material Takeoff>

Figure B–19

- The procedure for creating material takeoff schedules is the same as building component schedules, except that it uses a different command. In the *View* tab>Create panel, expand (Schedules) and click (Material Takeoff). Alternatively, in the Project Browser, right-click on the *Schedule/Quantities* node and select **New Material Takeoff**.

- The available fields include all of the material parameters, as shown in Figure B–20.

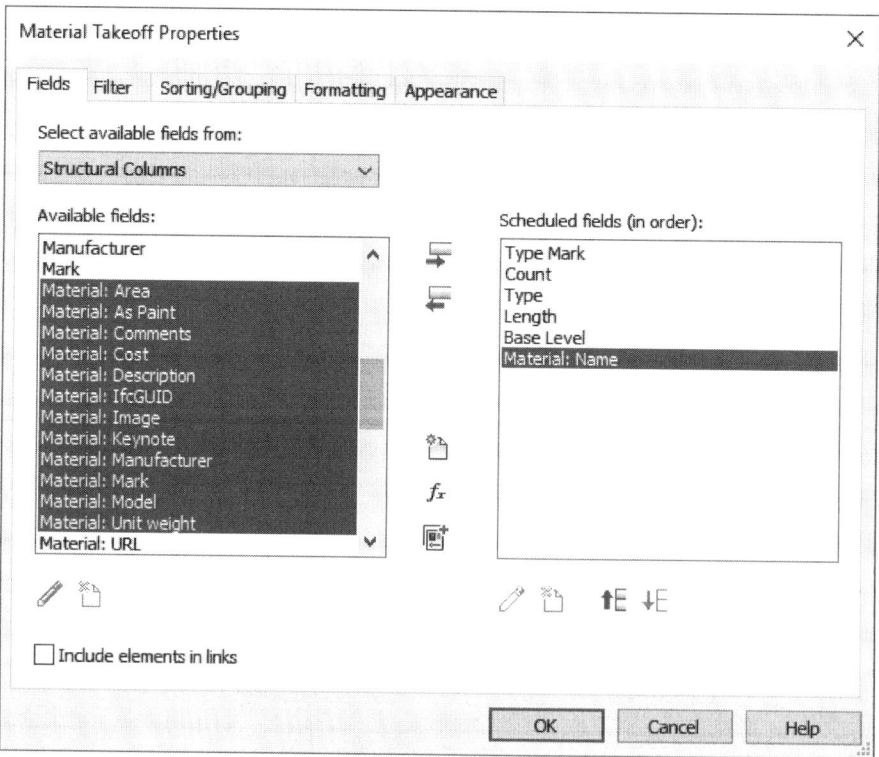

Figure B–20

B.5 Importing and Exporting Schedules

Schedules are views and can be copied into your project from other projects. Only the formatting information is copied; the information about individually scheduled items is not included. That information is automatically added by the project the schedule is copied into. You can also export the schedule information to be used in spreadsheets.

How To: Import Schedules

1. In the *Insert* tab>Load from Library panel, expand ▫ (Insert from File) and click ▫ (Insert Views from File).
2. In the Open dialog box, locate the project file containing the schedule you want to use.
3. Select the schedules you want to import, as shown in Figure B–21.

    *Note: If the referenced project contains many types of views, change Views: to **Show schedules and reports only**.*

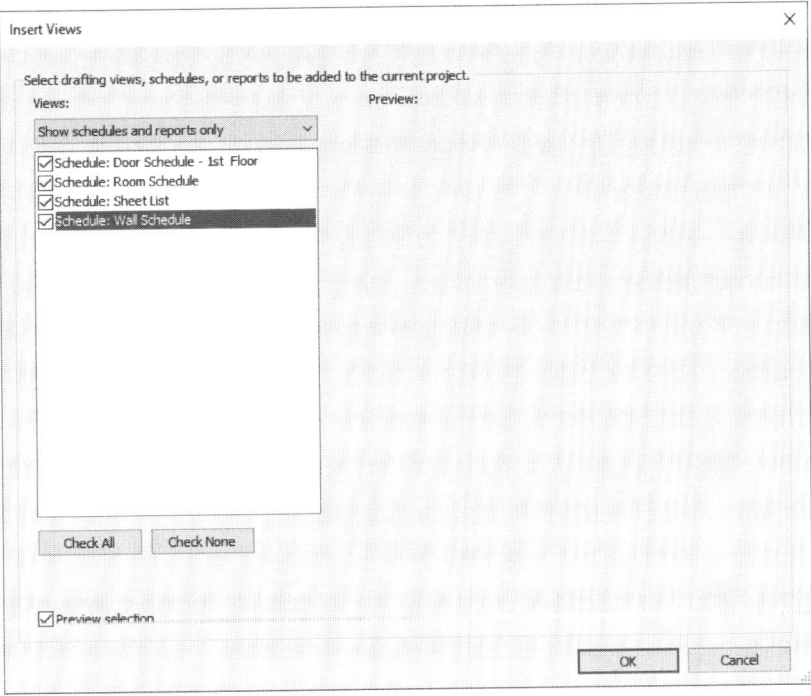

Figure B–21

4. Click **OK**.

How To: Export Schedule Information

1. Switch to the schedule view that you want to export.
2. In the *File* tab, click (Export)> (Reports)> (Schedule).
3. Select a location and name for the text file in the Export Schedule dialog box and click **Save**.
4. In the Export Schedule dialog box, set the options in the *Schedule appearance* and *Output options* areas that best suit your spreadsheet software, as shown in Figure B–22.

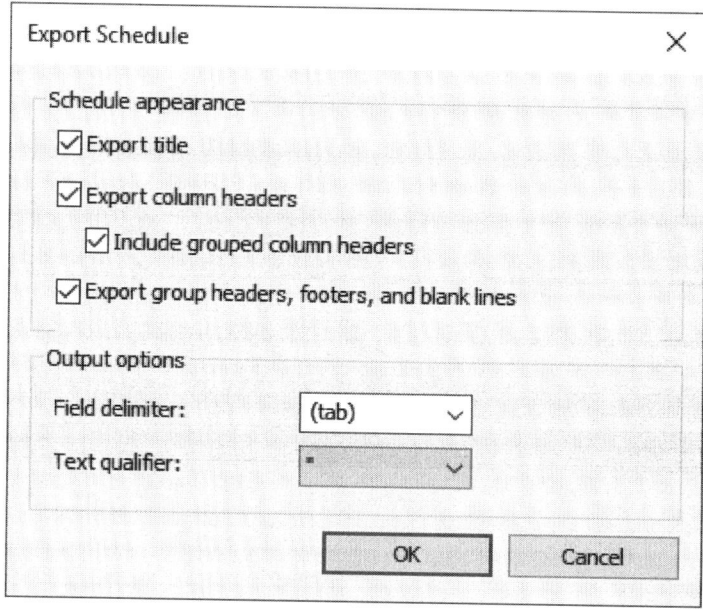

Figure B–22

5. Click **OK**. A new text file is created that you can open in a spreadsheet, as shown in Figure B–23.

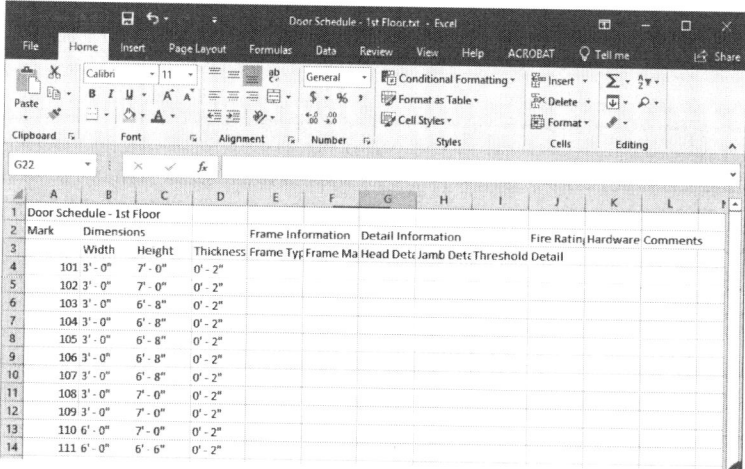

Figure B–23

B.6 Creating a Repeating Detail

Repeating detail components are very useful when working on complex details, such as those that include a brick wall. You can also create a repeating detail using any detail component, such as the glass block shown in Figure B–24.

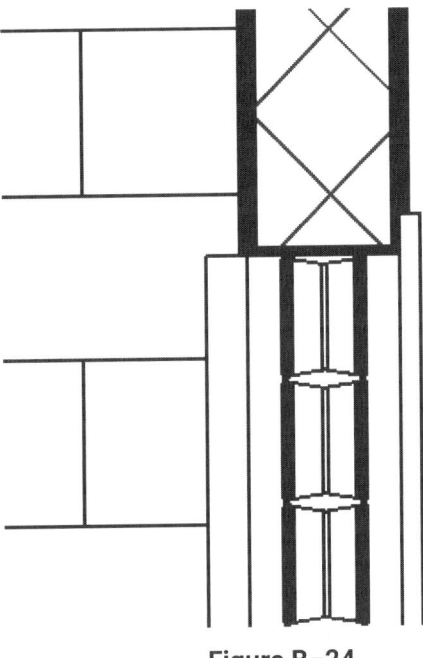

Figure B–24

How To: Create a Repeating Detail

1. Load the detail component you want to use.
2. In the *Annotate* tab>Detail panel, expand (Component) and click (Repeating Detail Component).
3. In Properties, click (Edit Type).
4. In the Type Properties dialog box, click **Duplicate...**. Enter a name.
5. Set the *Detail* parameter. This is the component name.

6. Fill out the rest of the parameters, as shown in Figure B–25.

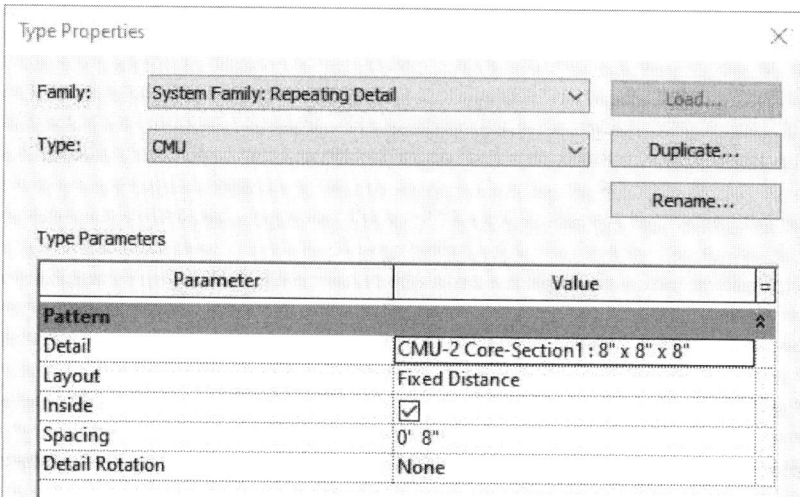

Figure B–25

7. Set the *Layout* to **Fill Available Space**, **Fixed Distance**, **Fixed Number**, or **Maximum Spacing**. Select **Inside** if you want all components to be within the specified distance or line. Leaving this option clear causes the first component to start before the first point.

8. Set the *Spacing* between components if you are using **Fixed Distance** or **Maximum Spacing**.

9. Set the *Detail Rotation* as needed, and close the dialog box.

B.7 Keynoting and Keynote Legends

A keynote is a special kind of tag that applies specific numbers to various elements in a detail. Keynotes can be used on all model and detail elements, as well as materials. Using keynotes requires less room on a view than standard text notes, as shown in Figure B–26. The full explanation of the note is shown in a corresponding *keynote legend* placed elsewhere in the sheet or sheet set.

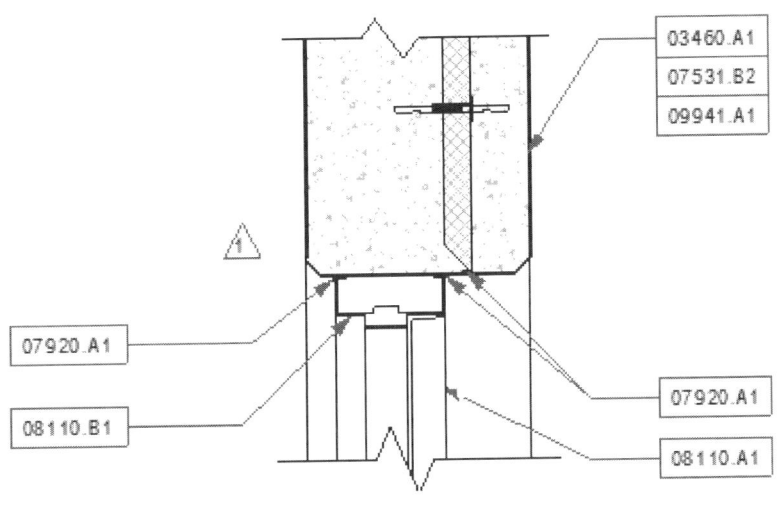

Figure B–26

- Keynote tags are found in the Revit Library in the *Annotations* folder and should be loaded into a project before you can apply them.

    Note: By default, Revit uses the CSI master format system of keynote designations.

There are three types of keynote tags:

- **Element:** Used to tag elements, such as a door, wall, or detail components.
- **Material:** Used for the material assigned to a component or applied onto a surface.
- **User:** A keynote that must first be developed in a keynote table.

How To: Place a Keynote

1. In the *Annotate* tab>Tag panel, expand (Keynote) and click (Element Keynote), (Material Keynote), or (User Keynote).
2. Move the cursor over the element you want to keynote and select it.

3. If an element has keynote information assigned to it, the keynote is automatically applied. If it is not assigned, the Keynotes dialog box opens, as shown in Figure B–27.

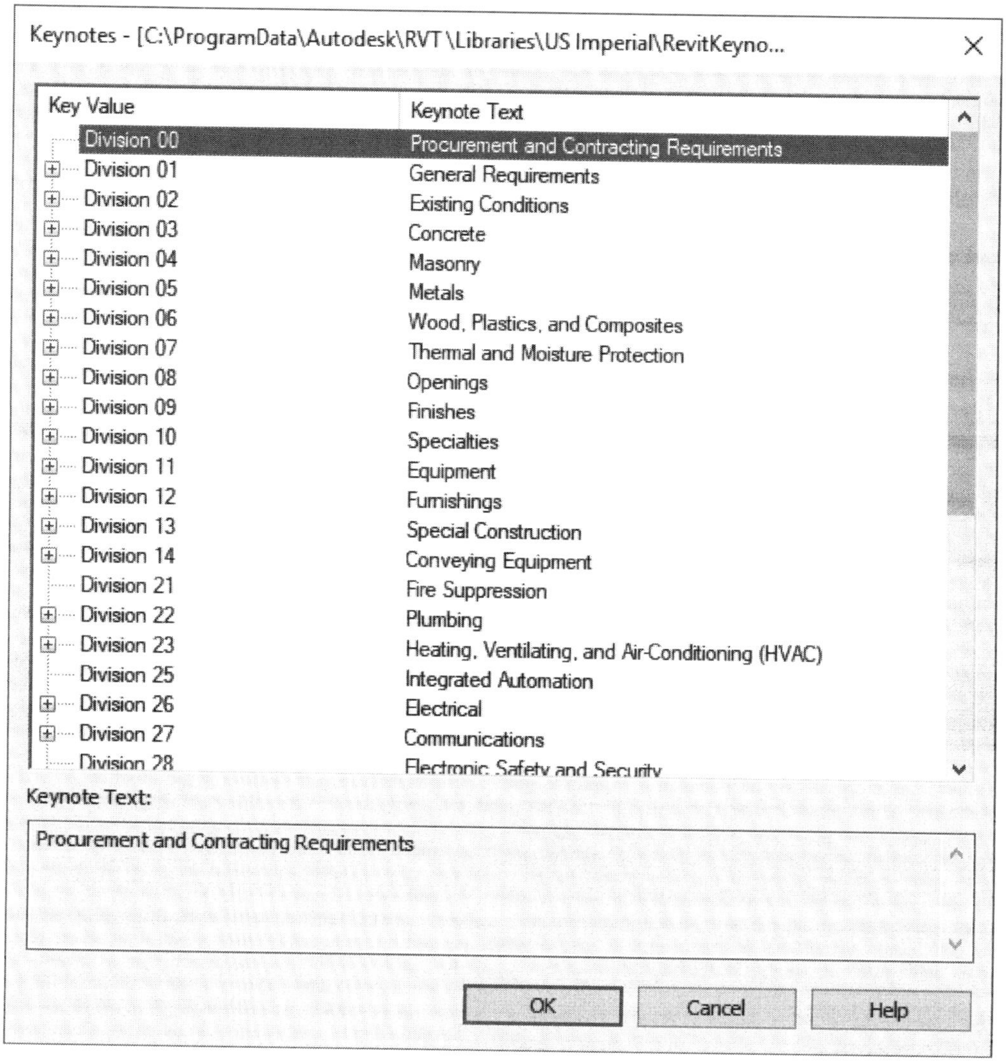

Figure B–27

4. Select the keynote you need from the list of divisions and click **OK**.

- The options for keynotes are the same as for other tags, including orientation and leaders, as shown in Figure B–28.

Note: *The keynote remembers the leader settings from the last time it was used.*

Figure B–28

💡 Hint: Setting the Keynote Numbering Method

Keynotes can be listed by the full keynote number or by sheet, as shown in Figure B–29. Only one method can be used at a time in a project, but you can change between the two methods at any time in the project.

1. In the *Annotate* tab>Tag panel, expand (Keynote) and click (Keynoting Settings).

Figure B–29

2. In the Keynoting Settings dialog box, specify the *Keynote Table* information and the *Numbering Method*, as shown in Figure B–30.

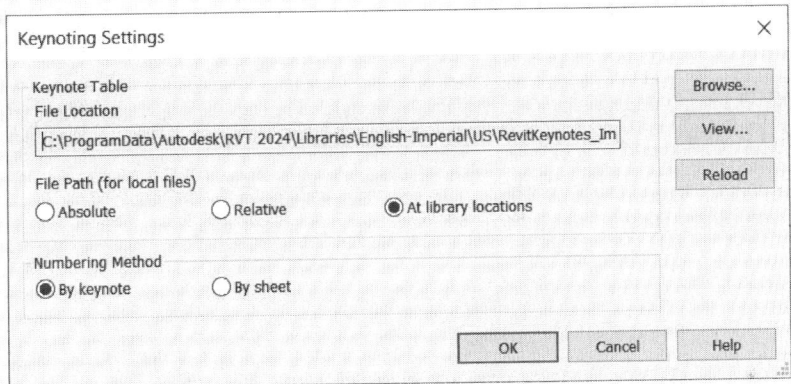

Figure B–30

- If you are using keynoting by sheet, create the Keynote Legend, and in the Keynote Legend Properties in the *Filter* tab, select **Filter by Sheet.**

- Keynotes are stored in a keynote table (a text file), as shown in Figure B–31. Any updates made to the keynote table are reflected in the project after it is closed and then re-opened.

Figure B–31

Keynote Legends

A keynote legend is a table containing the information stored in the keynote that is placed on a sheet, as shown in Figure B–32. In Revit, it is created in a similar way to schedules.

Note: A keynote legend is different from a standard legend.

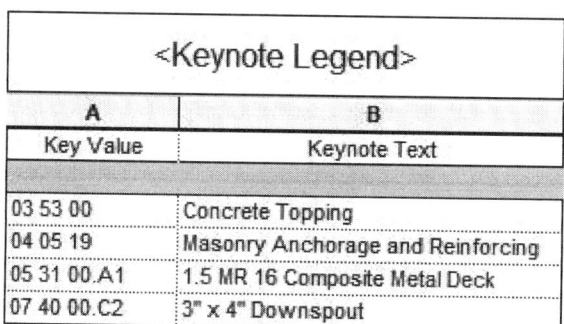

Figure B–32

How To: Create a Keynote Legend

1. In the *View* tab>Create panel, expand (Legends) and click (Keynote Legend).
2. Type a name in the New Keynote Legend dialog box and click **OK**.

3. The Keynote Legend Properties dialog box typically only displays two scheduled fields, which are already set up for you, as shown in Figure B–33.

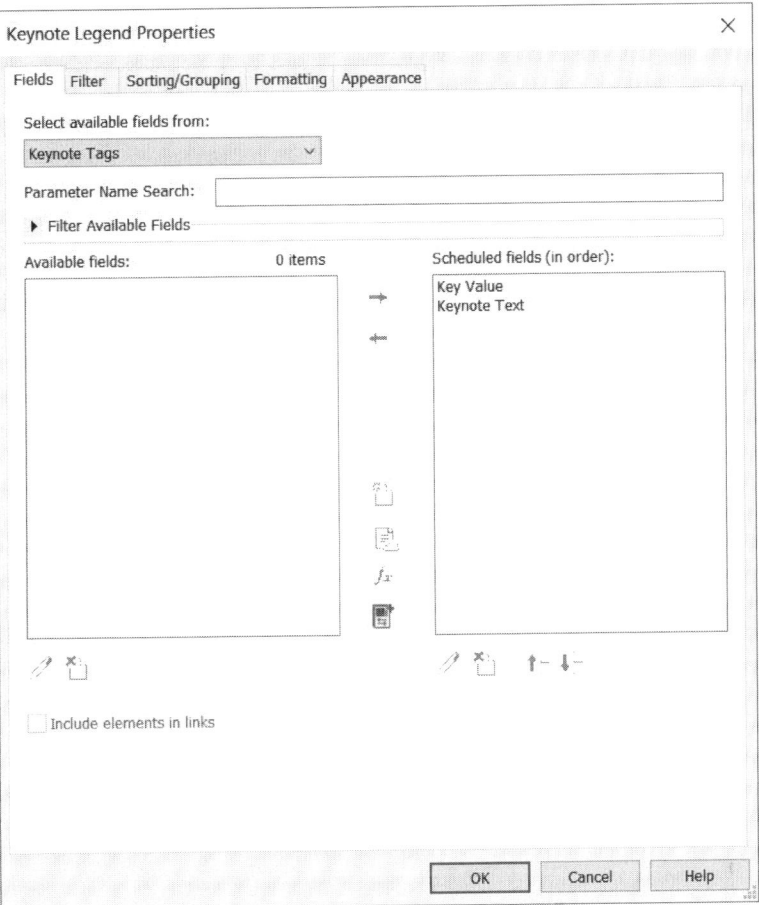

Figure B–33

4. In the other tabs, set up the format of the table as needed.
5. Click **OK** to create the keynote legend.
6. When you are ready to place a keynote legend, drag it from the Project Browser onto the sheet. You can manipulate it in the same way, similar to modifying other schedules.

- As you add keynotes to the project, they are added to the keynote legend.

Command Summary

Button	Command	Location
Annotations		
	Element Keynote	• **Ribbon:** *Annotate* tab>Tag panel, expand Keynote
	Material Keynote	• **Ribbon:** *Annotate* tab>Tag panel, expand Keynote
	User Keynote	• **Ribbon:** *Annotate* tab>Tag panel, expand Keynote
	Matchline	• **Ribbon:** *View* tab>Sheet Composition panel
	View Reference	• **Ribbon:** *View* tab>Sheet Composition panel or *Annotate* tab>Tag panel
Details		
	Edit Type	• **Properties** (with a Repeating Detail element selected)
Revisions		
	Revision Cloud	• **Ribbon:** *Annotate* tab>Detail panel
	Sheet Issues/Revisions	• **Ribbon:** *Manage* tab>Settings panel, expand Additional Settings
Schedules		
	Insert Views from File	• **Ribbon:** *Insert* tab, expand Insert from File
	Material Takeoff	• **Ribbon:** *View* tab>Create panel, expand Schedules • **Project Browser:** right-click on Schedule/Quantities node>New Material Takeoff
n/a	Schedule (Export)	• *File* **tab:** expand Export>Reports>Schedule
	Schedule/Quantities	• **Ribbon:** *View* tab>Create panel, expand Schedules • **Project Browser:** right-click on Schedule/Quantities node>New Schedule/Quantities...

Appendix C

Project - Concrete Structure

This appendix contains a practice project that can be used to gain additional hands-on experience with the topics and commands covered in this learning guide. This project is intended to be self-guided and does not include step-by-step information.

Learning Objectives

- Start a new project and add datum elements (levels and grid lines) and concrete columns that establish the base of the concrete structure.
- Create the foundation elements of the building, including walls, wall foundations, and footings under the columns.
- Add beams and beam systems to complete the structural framework, and add floors.

Practice C1
Start a Structural Project

Practice Objectives

- Start a new project based on a template.
- Add levels and grid lines.
- Add structural columns.

In this practice, you will start a new project and add levels, grid lines, and concrete columns, as shown in Figure C–1.

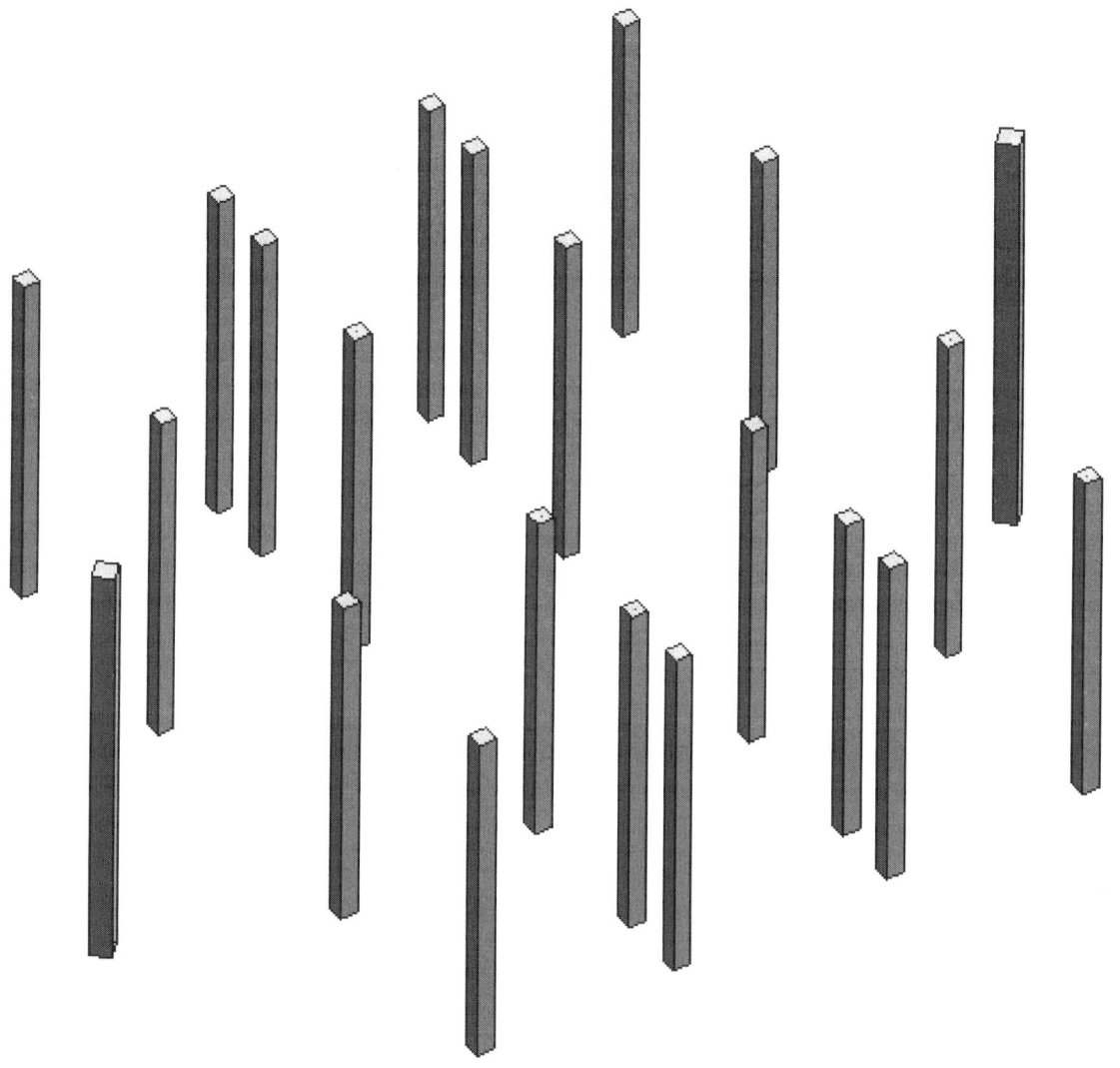

Figure C–1

Project - Concrete Structure

Task 1: Start a new project and add datum elements.

1. Start a new project based on the default **Structural Template**. Save the new project to your practice files folder as **Concrete Structure.rvt**.

2. Open the **Elevations (Building Elevation): South** view.

3. Add the levels shown in Figure C-2.

    Note: Ensure that you create plan views for each level. If you copy them, you need to add the plan views after finishing the levels.

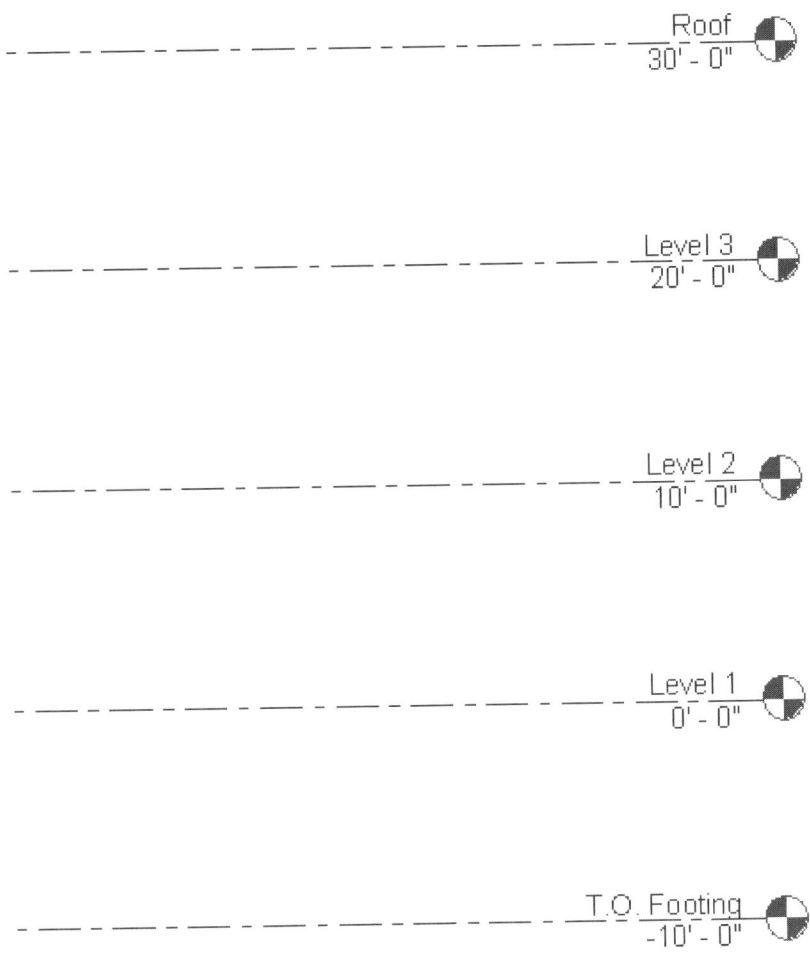

Figure C-2

4. Open the **Structural Plans: Level 1** view.

5. Add the grid lines that are shown in Figure C–3. The dimensions are for information only.

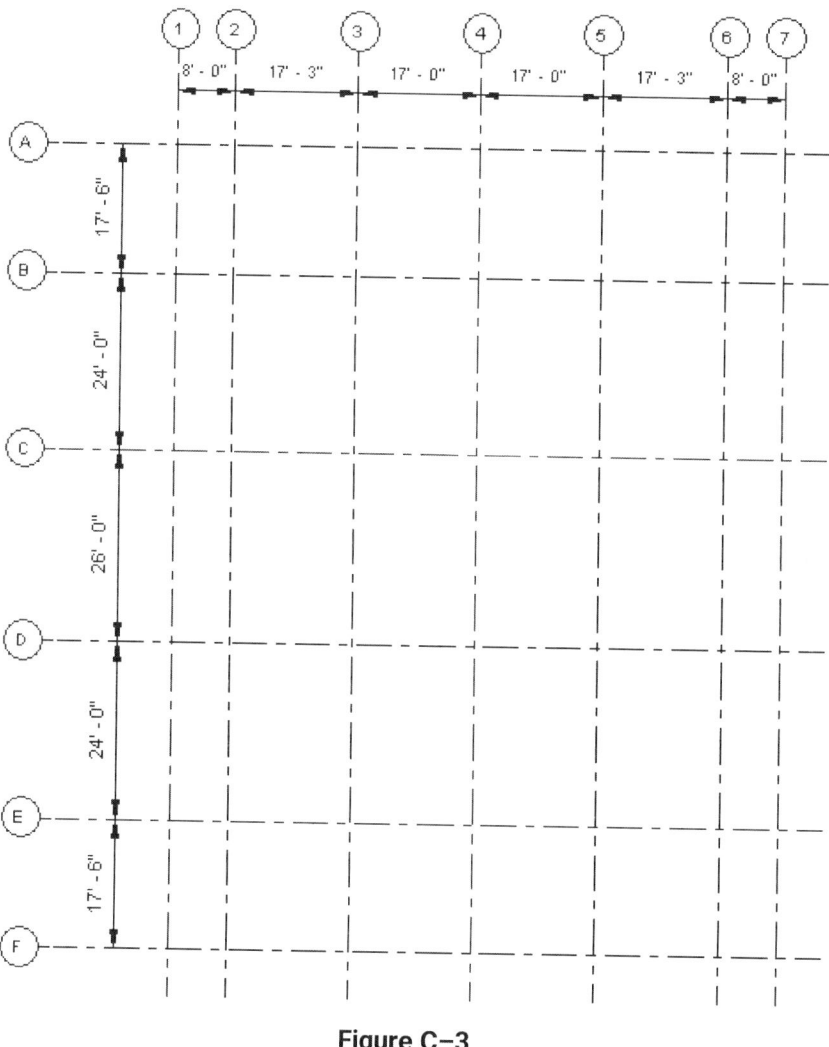

Figure C–3

6. Save the project.

Task 2: Add columns.

1. Open the **Structural Plans: Level 1** view.

2. Start the (Structural Column) command. Duplicate one of the **Concrete-Rectangular Columns** types and create a new 24 x 24 column type.

3. Add columns that go from the **T.O. Footing** level to the **Roof** level, as shown in Figure C–4.

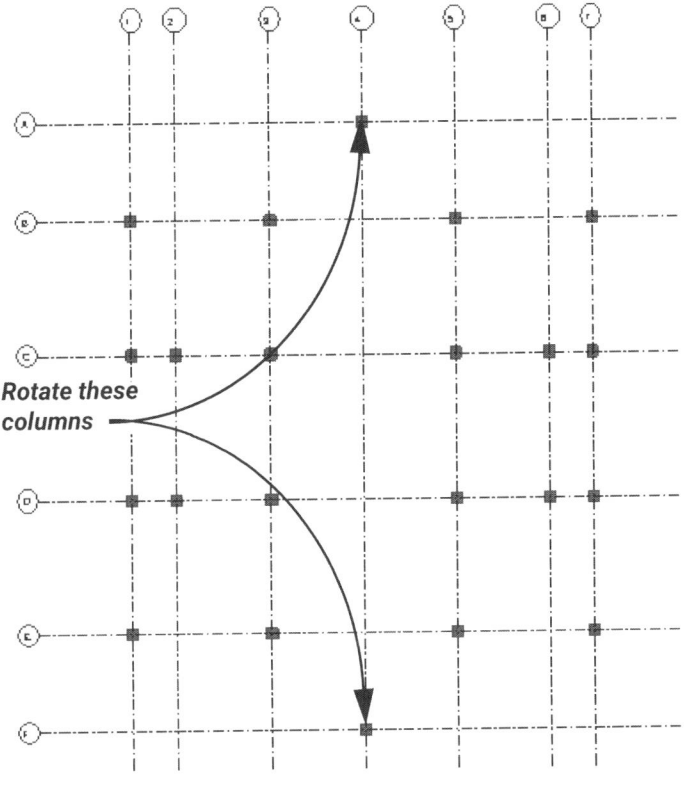

Figure C–4

4. Rotate the top and bottom columns 45°.
5. Open a 3D view to view the columns.
6. Save and close the project.

End of practice

Practice C2
Create Foundation Elements

Practice Objectives

- Add structural foundation walls.
- Add wall footings and isolated footings.

In this practice, you will add walls, foundation walls, and isolated foundations, as shown in Figure C-5.

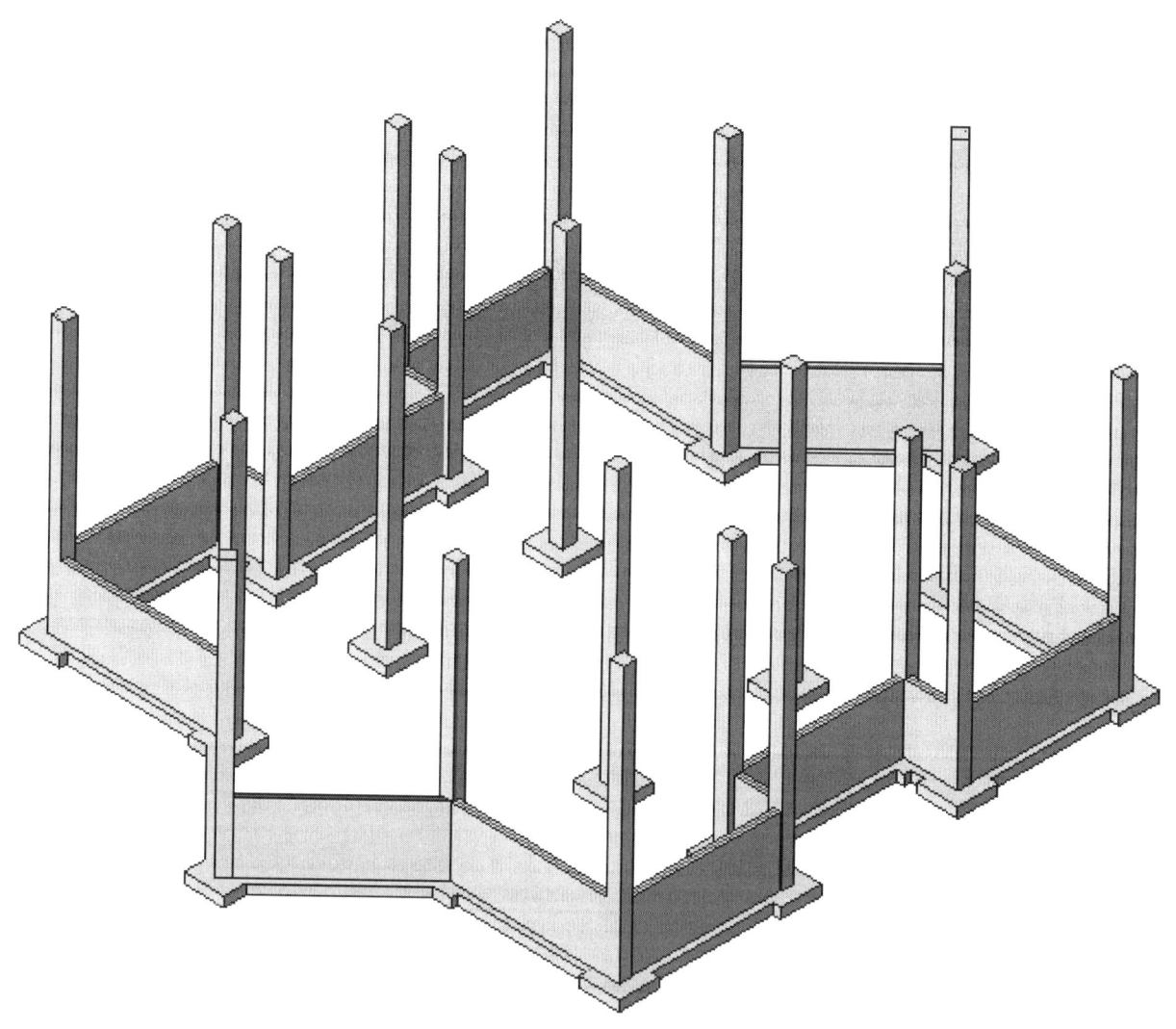

Figure C-5

Task 1: Add walls.

1. Open **Xtra-Appx-1.rvt** from the practice files folder.
2. Open the **Structural Plans: Level 1** view.
3. Draw the walls shown in Figure C–6 using the following information:
   - *Type:* **Basic Wall: Foundation** - 12" **Concrete**
   - *Base Constraint:* **Level 1**
   - *Base Offset:* (negative) **-10'-0"**
   - *Top Constraint:* **Up to level: Level 1**
   - *Top Offset:* **0'-0"**

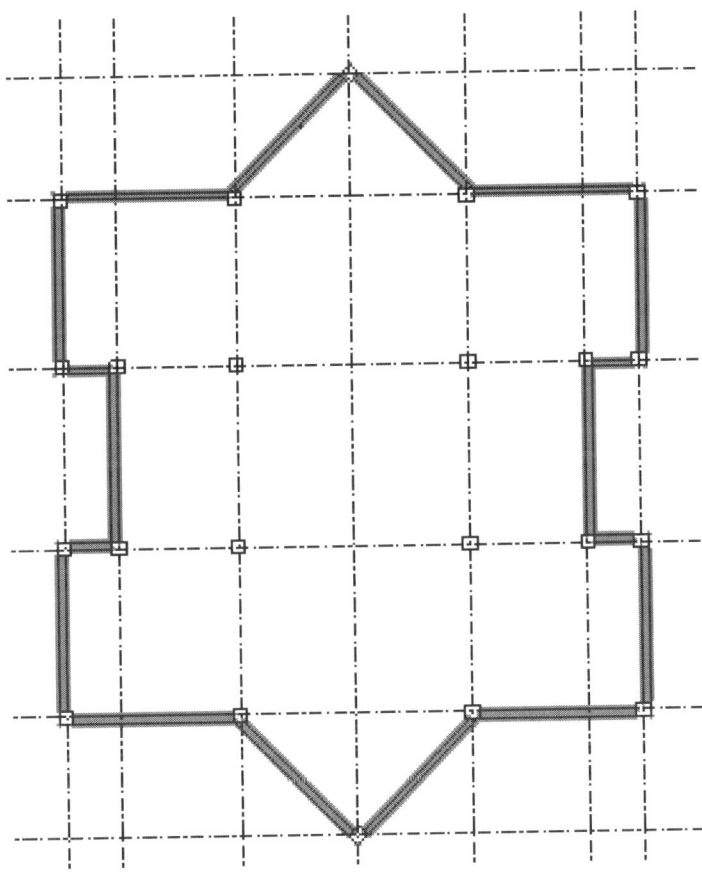

Figure C–6

- The outside edge of the walls are aligned to the outside of the columns.

4. Save the project.

Task 2: Add foundations.

1. Open the **Structural Plans: T.O. Footing** view.
2. Add isolated footings under all of the columns. Create a new **Footing-Rectangular: 72" x 72" x 18"** in size.
3. Add wall footings under all of the walls. Create a new **Wall Foundation: Bearing Footing - 36" x 18"** in size. When you are finished, the plan should look like Figure C–7.

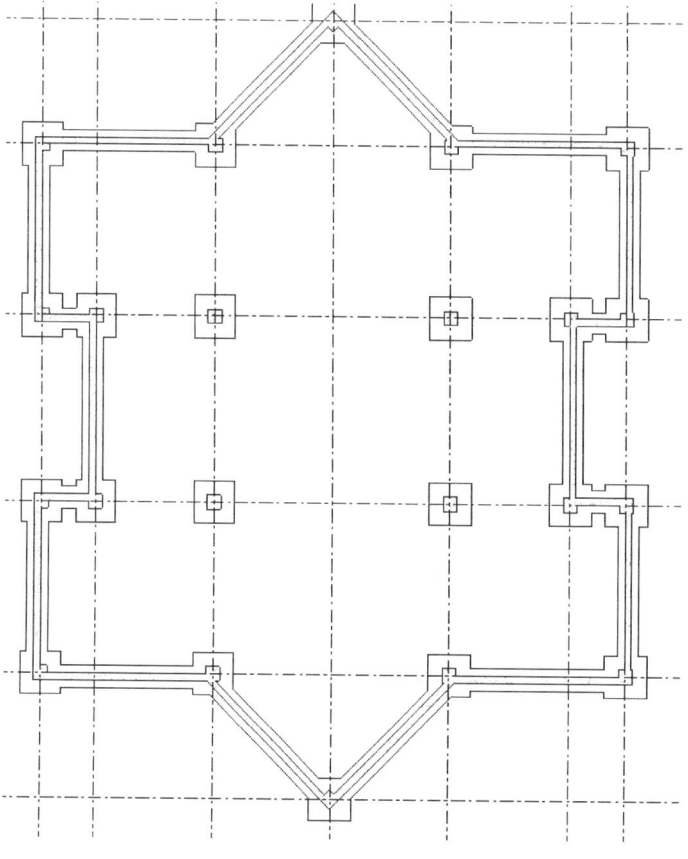

Figure C–7

4. Save and close the project.

End of practice

Practice C3
Frame a Concrete Structure

Practice Objectives

- Add beams and beam systems.
- Add structural floors.

In this practice, you will frame the concrete structure shown in Figure C–8. You will add girders using individual beams and joists using beam systems. You will then copy and paste the structural elements to additional floors. Finally, you will add a floor and then copy it to the other levels.

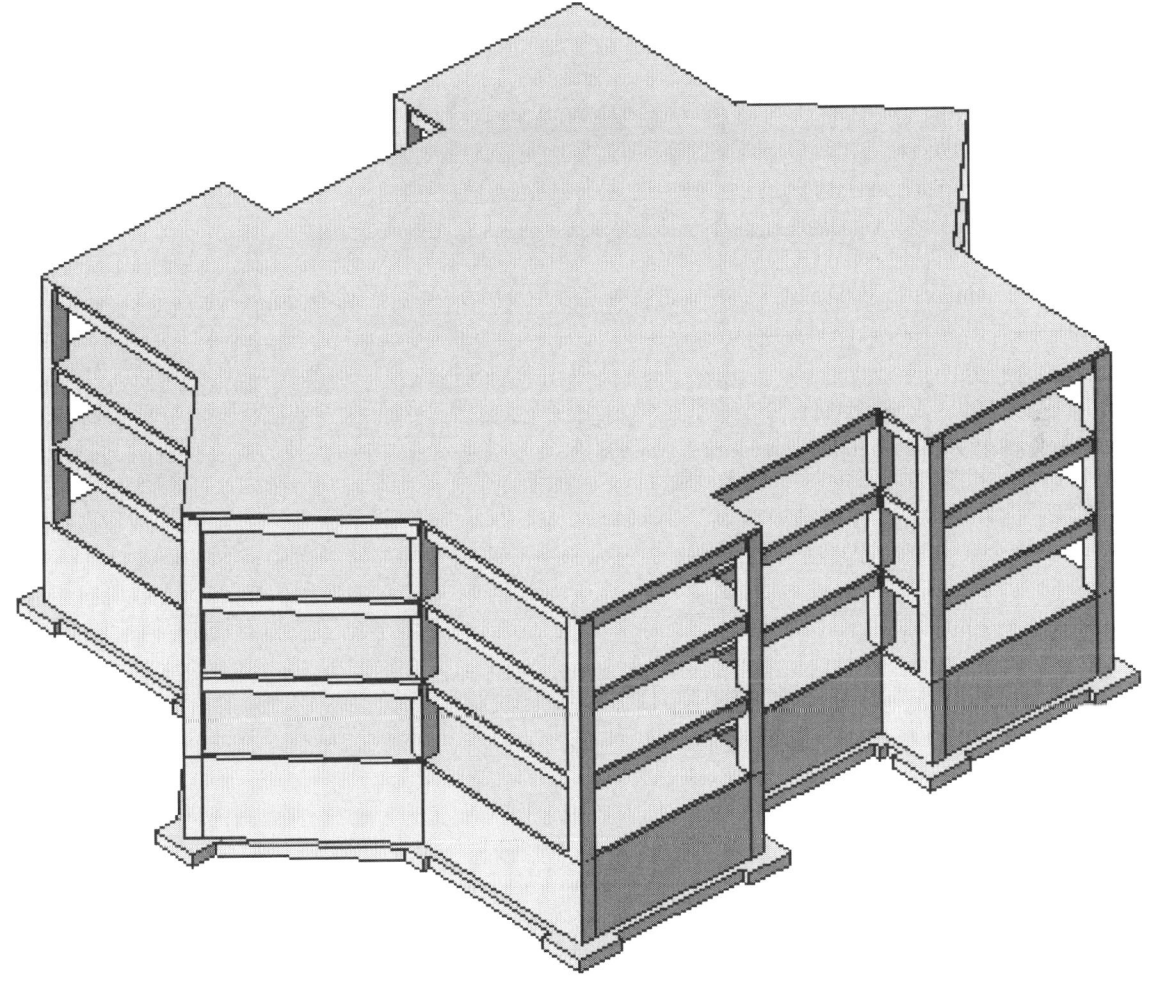

Figure C–8

Task 1: Add girders.

1. Open **Xtra-Appx-2.rvt** from the practice files folder.
2. On Level 1, add beams using the type **Concrete Rectangular Beam: 12x24,** as shown in Figure C–9.

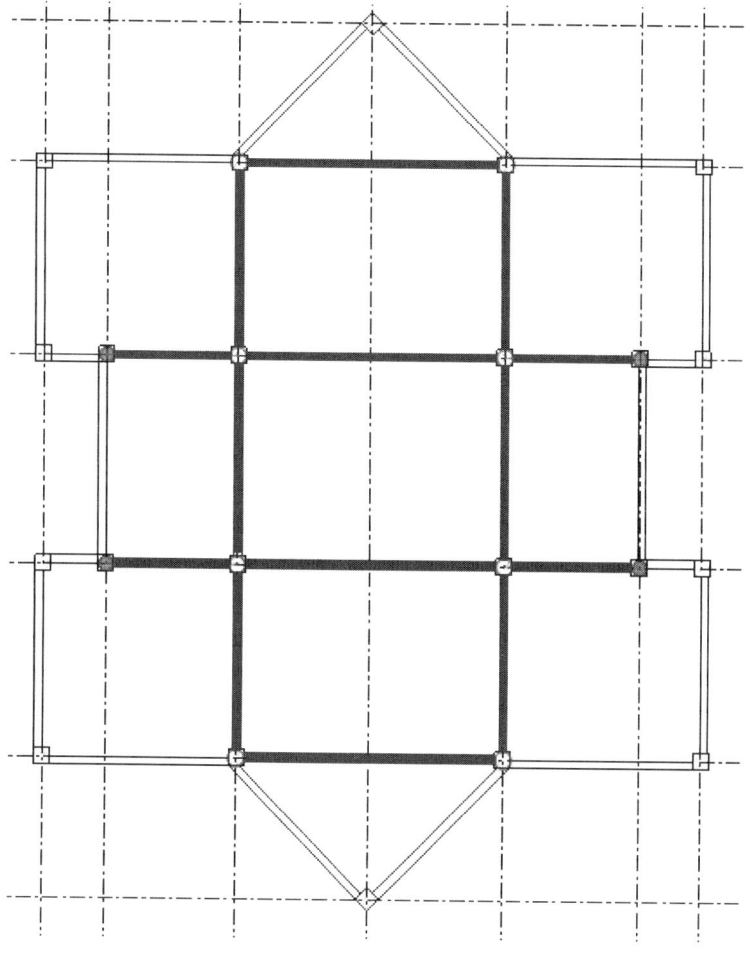

Figure C–9

3. Save the project.

Task 2: Add joists using beam systems.

1. Load the **Pan Joist.rfa** family from the practice files *Families* folder.

2. Using the (Beam System) command and the following parameters, add the joists as shown in Figure C–10. Where you cannot use **Automatic Beam System**, sketch the beam system.

    - *Elevation:* **4-1/2"**
    - *Layout Rule:* **Maximum Spacing**
    - *Maximum Spacing:* **5'-0"**
    - *Beam Type:* **Pan Joist: 8 x 24**
    - *Tag on Placement:* off
    - *Tag new Members in view:* **None** (for Sketched)

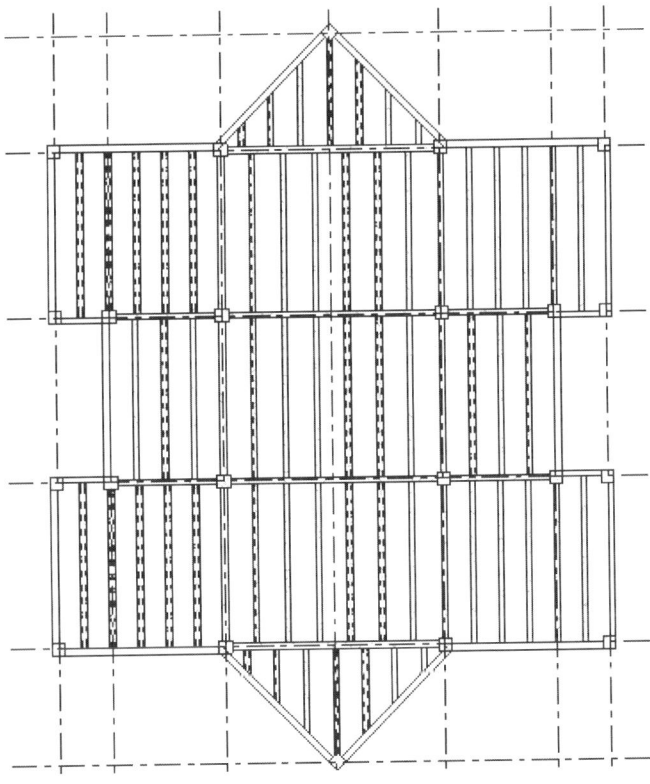

Figure C–10

3. Save the project.

Task 3: Add beams and beam systems to the other floors.

1. Repeat the process of creating beams and beam systems on Level 2. All girders should be on center (as shown in Figure C–11) and, therefore, all of the beam systems can be placed automatically.

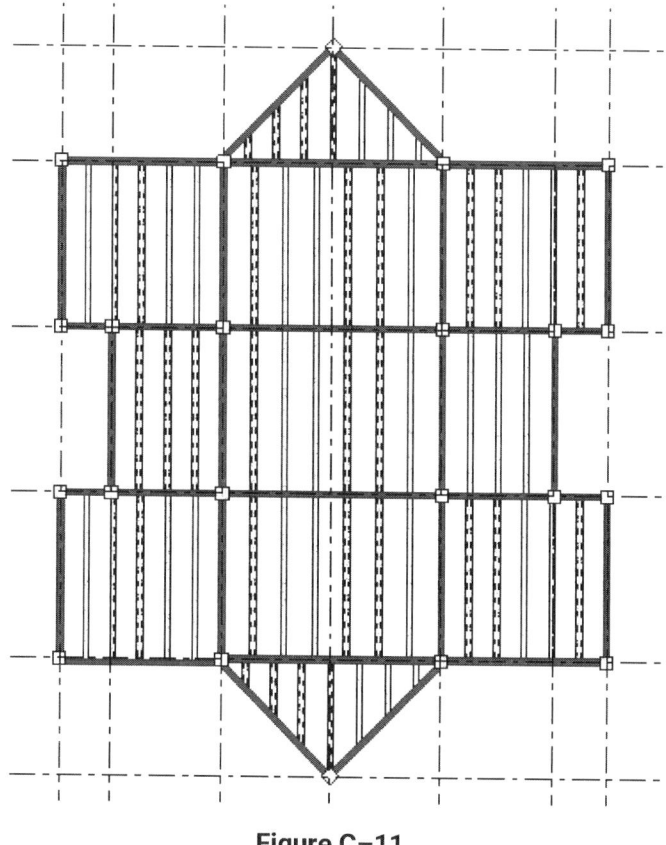

Figure C–11

- For the angled bays, it is easiest to add the beam system using one of the default directions, and then edit the boundary to change the beam direction.

2. Copy (using **Copy to the Clipboard** and **Paste Aligned**) all of the beams and beam systems from Level 2 to Level 3 and the Roof level.

    - Select only the **Structural Framing (Girder)** and **Structural Beam Systems**, not **Structural Framing (Joist)** as they are part of the beam system.

3. Open a 3D view. The copied beams and beam systems display as shown in Figure C–12.

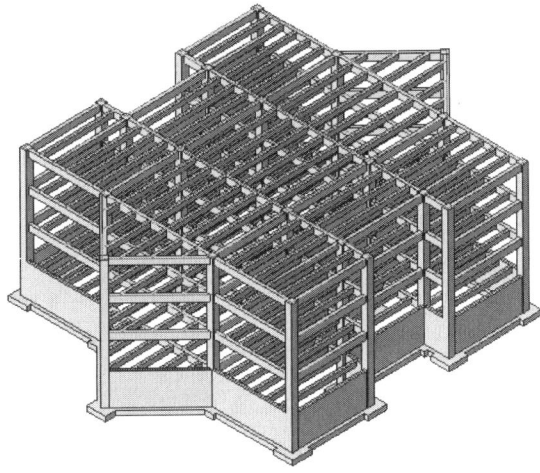

Figure C–12

4. Save the project.

Task 4: Add floors.

1. In the **Level 1** view, add a structural floor using the **Floor: 6" Concrete** type with the *Height Offset From Level* set to **6"**. Select the outside face of the wall for the boundary and attach the walls to the floors.
2. Copy the floor to the other levels above the first floor.
3. The new floors display as shown in Figure C–13.

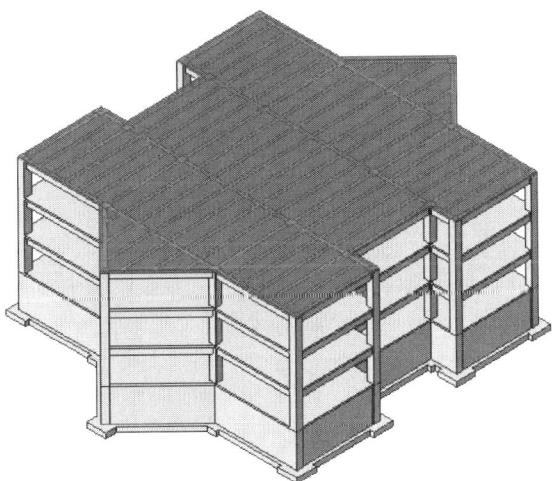

Figure C–13

4. Save and close the project.

End of practice

Index

#
2023.1 Enhancement
    Open multiple views from Project Browser **1-20, 3-3**
    Option to reserve view title position **11-10**
    Remove multiple views from a sheet **11-13**
    Select all instances in entire project including legends **5-14**
    Swap a view already placed on a sheet **11-11**
2023.2 Enhancement
    Specify the revisions to include in revision schedule **B-4**
2024 Enhancement
    Access My Insights from the home screen **1-7**
    Change drawing area to dark mode **1-26**
    Drag multiple views from Project Browser to sheet **11-8**
    Linked and imported CAD files in US Survey Feet **2-4**
    Open sheet from drawing area **11-9**
    Search bar added to Select View dialog box **11-7**
    Search bar in the Modify Viewports drop-down list **11-11**
    Select multiple views in Select View dialog box **11-7**
    Visual style that shows material textures **1-41**
3D Views
    Default **1-34**
    Isometric **1-34**
    Locking **13-10**

A
Align command **5-33**
Aligned Multi-Rebar Annotation **12-15**
Alignment Lines **5-6**
Area Reinforcement
    Adding **10-44**
    Displaying **10-46**
    Modifying **10-55**
Array
    Linear **5-30**
    Modifying Groups **5-32**
    Radial **5-31**
Automatic locking for Align **5-34**

B
Beam Systems **8-5**
    Automatic **8-5**
    Sketching **8-7**
Beams
    Adding **8-3**
    Adding Multiple **8-3**
    Annotations **13-12**
    Attaching a Column **8-31**
    Coping **8-32**
    Joins **8-33**
Bearing Footings **7-20**
BIM
    Building Information Modeling **1-2**
    Construction Documents **1-5**
    Workflow **1-3**
Bottom Chord **8-39**
Bracing
    Adding **8-8**
    Settings **8-9**
Break Lines **14-10**

C
Callout command **3-22**
Callout Views
    Modifying **3-24**
    Rectangular **3-22**
    Sketched **3-22**
Camera **1-35, 1-36**
Clipboard
    Copy to **4-15, 5-26**
    Cut to **4-15, 5-26**
Close Inactive Views **1-12**
Columns **6-2**
    At Columns **6-3**
    at Grids **6-3**
    Creating **6-2**
    Modifying **6-8**
    Move with Grids **6-9**
    Slanted **6-5**
Components
    Adding **4-5**
    Modifying **4-13**
Contextual Tabs **5-10**
Controls **5-10**
Copy **5-25**
    To Clipboard **4-15, 5-26**
Copy/Monitor **6-17**
Create
    Local Files **A-15**
    Multi-Segment Grid **2-40**
    Repeating Details **B-17**
    Text Types **12-30**
Cut to Clipboard **4-15, 5-26**

D

Datum Elements **1-5**
Default 3D View command **1-34**
Delete **5-10**
Dependent Views **B-11**
Detail Components **14-9**
    Repeating **14-12**
Detail Lines **12-38**
Details
    Annotating **14-13**
    Import **14-8**
    Tagging **14-16**
Dimensions
    Aligned **12-4**
    Angular **12-4**
    Arc Length **12-4**
    Constraints **12-9**
    Diameter **12-4**
    Feet and inches **5-6**
    Labeling **12-11**
    Linear **12-4**
    Modifying **12-5**
    Radial **12-4**
Doors
    Creating Sizes **4-16**
Drafting Views
    Creating **14-2**
    Referencing **14-5**
    Saving **14-6**
Drag Elements on Selection **1-24**
Draw Order **14-11**
Draw Tools **5-3**
Drawing Aids **5-6**
Duplicate
    As Dependent **3-8**
    Detailing **3-7**
Duplicate views **3-7**

E

Edit Crop **3-24**
Edit Type **4-16**
Edit Wall Joins command **A-6**
Elements
    Datum **1-5**
    Model **1-4**
    View-specific **1-5**
Elevations **3-32**
    Framing Elevations **3-32**
    Modifying **3-35**
Export Schedules **B-16**

F

Fabric Reinforcement
    Adding **10-49**
    Modifying **10-55**
Families
    Create Types **4-16**
    Files (.rfa) **1-27**
File Tab **1-16**
File Types **1-27**
Filled Regions **14-14**
Filter **5-16**
Floors
    Slab Edge **9-7**
    Structural **9-2**
Footings
    Bearing **7-20**
    Retaining **7-20**
Foundation Wall **7-20**
Framing Elevations **3-32**
Freeze Schedule Headers **13-21**

G

Global Parameters **12-12**
Graphical Column Schedule
    Creating **13-44**
Graphical Column Schedules
    Modifying **13-45**
Grids
    Modifying **2-42**
    Multi-Segment **2-40**

H

Hide
    Categories **3-14**
Hide Elements **3-14**
Hide in View **3-14**
Hook Lengths **A-11**

I

Images **11-20**
Import
    Details **14-8**
    Hide Layers **2-17**
    Image Files **2-7**
    Raster Images **2-8**
    Schedules **B-15**
Import CAD command **2-5**
Import Trimble SketchUp files **2-4**
Improved graphics in Realistic views **1-41**
InfoCenter **1-8**
Insert Views from File command **B-15**
Instance Properties **1-18**
Interface **1-6**
Isolated Footings
    Placing **6-11**, **7-27**
Isometric Views **1-34**

J

Join/Unjoin Geometry **9-8**

K

Key Plan Legend **12-47**
Keynotes **B-19**
    Legends **B-22**
    Placing **B-19**

L

Legend **12-42**
    Components **12-43**
    Create **12-43**
    Key Plan **12-47**
Levels
    Create **2-25**
    Modify **2-27**
Linear Multi-Rebar Annotation **12-15**
Linework **14-17**
Linework command **14-17**
Link
    Raster Images **2-8**
Link CAD command **2-5**
Link PDF and Raster images **2-3**
Link Revit command **2-12**
Load Family **7-30**
Loaded Tags And Symbols command **13-8**
Local Files
    Create **A-15**
Lock 3D Views **13-10**

M

Match Type **7-18**
Matchlines **B-12**
Mirror - Draw Axis **5-29**
Mirror - Pick Axis **5-29**
Model Elements **1-4**
Model Text **12-29**
Modify command **1-15**
Monitor **6-18**
Move **5-25**
Multi-planar Rebar **10-20**
Multi-Segment Grid **2-40**

N

Navigation Bar **1 15**
New Project **2 2**

O

Offset **5-45, 5-46**
Open **1-28**
Options Bar **1-12**
or **B-12**
Orient to a Direction **3-40**
Orient to a Plane **3-41**
Orient to View **3-39**
Overriding Graphics **3-15**

P

Paste
    Aligned to Current View **4-15**
    Aligned to Picked Level **4-15**
    Aligned to Same Place **4-15**
    Aligned to Selected Levels **4-15**
    Aligned to Selected Views **4-15**
    From Clipboard **4-15, 5-26**
Path Reinforcement
    Adding **10-47**
    Displaying **10-46**
    Modifying **10-55**
Perspective Views **1-35**
Pick a New Host **10-26**
Pick New Host command **4-14**
Pick Tools **5-5**
Pin **5-27**
Pinned Elements **5-27**
Place rebar using Expand to Host **10-14**
Place rebar using two pick points **10-14**
Plan Regions **3-26**
Plan Views **2-30**
Print command **11-29**
Project Browser **1-20**
Propagating Datum Extents **2-44**
Properties **5-10**
Purge Unused **A-5**

Q

Quick Access Toolbar **1-8**

R

Raster Images
    Import and Link **2-8**
Rebar
    Constrained Placement **10-18**
    Creating Types **A-10**
    Edit Constraints **10-26**
    Element Types **10-2**
    Hook Types **A-11**
    Modifying **10-24**
    Multi-planar Rebar **10-20**
    Pick New Host **10-26**
    Place **10-15**
    Place By Sketch **10-19**
    Rebar Set Visibility **10-25**
    Rebar Sets **10-17**
    Set Visibility **10-10**
    Varying Rebar Sets **10-28**
Rebar Cover Settings
    Adding **10-3**
    Editing **10-4**
Rebar Sets **10-17**
Rebar settings remembered for single session of Revit **10-18**

Reference Plane command **5-7**
Reflected Ceiling Plan Views **2-30**
Reinforcement Settings **10-5**
Rename Views **1-34**
Repeating Detail Component **14-12**
Repeating Details **B-17**
Reports **1-4**
Reset Crop **3-24**
Retaining footings **7-20**
Reveal Hidden Elements **3-18**
Review Warnings **6-28**
Revisions
    Issuing **B-9**
    Tracking **A-8**, **B-4**
Ribbon **1-13**
Roof by Footprint **9-5**
Rotate **5-27**

S
Saving **1-29**
Scale **5-30**
Schedule/Quantities Command **13-20**
Schedules
    Building Component Schedule **13-20**
    Export **B-16**
    Import **B-15**
    Material Takeoff **B-14**
    Modifying Cells **13-32**
    Sheets **13-34**
Sections **3-34**
    Add Jog **3-37**
    Modifying **3-35**
Select
    Drag elements **1-24**
    Elements **5-13**
    Links **1-24**
    Pinned elements **1-24**
    Select elements by face **1-24**
    Underlay elements **1-24**
Selection Box **3-39**
Selection Sets **A-2**
Shaft Opening **9-17**
Shape Handles **5-10**
Sheets
    Add **11-2**
    Guide Grids **B-2**
    Placing Views **11-5**
Shortcut Keys **1-14**
Shortcut Menus **1-10**, **1-11**, **1-25**
Show Related Warnings **6-28**
Size Crop **3-25**

Slab
    Creating Types **A-8**
    Edges **9-7**
    Floor **9-2**
    Foundation **9-2**
    Roof **9-5**
Slanted Columns **6-5**
Slanted Walls **7-3**
Snap mid-point between two points **4-11**
Snaps **5-7**
Spelling **12-29**
Split
    Split Element **5-42**
    Split with Gap command **5-43**
Status Bar **1-23**
Stop Monitoring command **6-24**, **6-25**
Structural Columns
    Attach Top/Base **6-10**
Structural Foundation
    Isolated **6-11**, **7-27**
    Wall **7-20**
Structural Settings **8-9**
Structural Slabs **9-2**
Switch Windows **1-11**
Symbols **12-39**

T
Tab Views **1-12**
Tags
    3D Views **13-10**
    Adding **13-3**
    Adding Multiple **13-7**
    By Category **13-2**
    Instance vs. Type **13-9**
    Loading **13-8**
    Material **13-2**
    Multi-Category **13-2**
    Tag All **13-7**
    Tag All Not Tagged **13-7**
Tapered Walls **7-3**
Template Files (.RTE) **1-27**
Temporary Dimensions **5-6**, **5-10**
    Editing **5-12**
Text
    Adding **12-23**
    Create Types **12-30**
    Model **12-29**
    Symbols **12-24**
Tile Views **1-12**
Tooltip when placing rebar **10-14**
Tooltips **1-14**
Top Chord **8-39**

Trim/Extend
    Multiple Elements **5-44**
    Single Element **5-44**
    To Corner **5-43**
Trusses
    Adding **8-39**
    Attach to Roofs **8-40**
    Bottom Chord **8-39**
    Top Chord **8-39**
    Type Properties **8-41**
    Web **8-39**
Type Properties **1-18**
    Doors and Windows **4-16**
Type Selector **1-19, 5-10**

U
Unhide
    Category **3-18**
    Element **3-18**

V
Varying Rebar Sets **10-28**
View Control Bar **1-22**
View Range **3-13**
View References **B-12**
View Visibility States (Rebar) **10-10**
ViewCube **1-38**
Views **1-4**
    Camera **1-33**
    Default 3D View **1-33**
    Dependant **B-11**
    Duplicate View **3-8**
    Duplication Types **3-7**
    Insert from File **B-15**
    Plan Region **3-26**
    Renaming **1-34**
    Underlay **3-12**
View-Specific Elements **1-5**
Visibility/Graphics Overrides **3-16**
    Halftone **2-14**
Visual Styles **1-40**

W
Walls **7-2**
    Edit Profile **7-16**
    Foundation **7-20**
    Modeling **7-7**
    Modifying **7-11**
    Opening **7-16**
Web **8-39**
Windows
    Creating Sizes **4-16**
Worksets
    Saving Files **A-16**